D1614153

SHADERX6:

ADVANCED RENDERING TECHNIQUES

Wolfgang Engel

Course Technology PTR

A part of Cengage Learning

Australia, Brazil, Japan, Korea, Mexico, Singapore, Spain, United Kingdom, United States

COURSE TECHNOLOGY
CENGAGE Learning™

ShaderX6: Advanced Rendering Techniques
Wolfgang Engel

Publisher and General Manager, Course Technology PTR and CRM: Stacy L. Hiquet

Associate Director of Marketing: Sarah Panella

Manager of Editorial Services: Heather Talbot

Marketing Manager: Jordan Casey

Senior Acquisitions Editor: Emi Smith

Project Editor: Kate Shoup

CRM Editorial Services Coordinator: Jen Blaney

Copy Editor: Heather Urschel

Interior Layout Tech: William Hartman

Cover Designer: Tyler Creative Services

DVD-ROM Producer: Brandon Penticuff

Indexer: Larry Sweazy

Proofreader: Kate Shoup

Library of Congress Control Number: 2007939367

ISBN-13: 978-1-58450-544-0

ISBN-10: 1-58450-544-3

Course Technology
25 Thomson Place
Boston, MA 02210
USA

Cengage Learning is a leading provider of customized learning solutions with office locations around the globe, including Singapore, the United Kingdom, Australia, Mexico, Brazil, and Japan. Locate your local office at: **international. cengage.com/region**

Cengage Learning products are represented in Canada by Nelson Education, Ltd.

For your lifelong learning solutions, visit **courseptr.com**

Visit our corporate website at **cengage.com**

Printed in the United States of America
2 3 4 5 6 7 11 10 09 08

This book is dedicated to Anna Sergeevna Fomicheva
who passed away during the editing of this book.

—Natalya Tatarchuk

Acknowledgments

The talented editors and contributors of this book spent eight months writing, selecting, editing, and finalizing the articles for this newest volume of the *ShaderX* series. We hope you find these state-of-the-art graphics-programming articles useful in your own work. As with all of the other *ShaderX* books, all of the topics cover ready-to-use ideas and procedures that can solve many of your daily graphics-programming challenges.

I would like to thank the section editors for the fantastic job they did. The work of Kenneth Hurley, Wessam Bahnassi, Sebastien St. Laurent, Natalya Tatarchuk, Tom Forsyth, Carsten Dachsbacher, Matthias Wloka, and Willem H. de Boer ensures that the quality of the series stands up to the expectations of our readers.

The great cover screenshots were taken from Crysis. I want to thank Cevat Yerli and Carsten Wenzel for providing these shots (the last book that had Crytek shots on the cover was *ShaderX³*).

The team at Charles River Media made the whole project happen. Emi Smith, Jennifer Blaney, and the whole production team, who took the articles and made them into a book.

Special thanks go out to our families and friends, who spent many evenings and weekends during the long book production cycle without us.

I hope you have as much fun reading this book as we had creating it.

—Wolfgang Engel

P.S. Plans for an upcoming *ShaderXⁿ* are already in progress. Any comments, proposals, and suggestions are highly welcome (wolf@shaderx.com).

About the Authors

Khashayar Arman

Khashayar Arman received his Master of Science degree with Honor in 2006 from the Budapest University of Technology and Economics, and he is currently employed as an IT Associate at Morgan Stanley UK. In his spare time, he enjoys working on computer graphics related algorithms and techniques. His favorite research interests are real-time rendering and shader programming.

Wessam Bahnassi

Wessam has been working in computer graphics and game development for more than eight years now, concentrating on 3D engine and pipeline tools development. At In|Framez, he led the development team for several games and real-time demos. He has many contributions and publications in graphics and programming in general, and has been a Microsoft Most Valuable Professional (MVP) for DirectX technologies for the past five years. Currently, he works at Electronics Arts Montreal doing console and PC graphics and game programming for some of EA's great titles.

Rui Bastos

Rui Bastos is a member of the GPU architecture group at NVIDIA, where he has contributed to the design of GeForce chips since 1999. He received a Ph.D. (1999) and an M.S. (1997) in computer science from the University of North Carolina at Chapel Hill, and an M.S. in computer science (1992) and a B.S. in physics (1988) from the Federal University of Rio Grande do Sul (Brazil).

Maxime Beaudoin

Maxime Beaudoin is a 3D graphics programmer at Ubisoft Quebec studio, Canada. He started to learn real-time 3D graphics on his own in 2001, and received his B.S. degree in computer science in 2003. Since 2005, he has been working for Ubisoft during the day and developing his own next-gen game engine with some friends during his free time.

Kristof Beets

Kristof is Business Development Manager for POWERVR Graphics in the Business Development Group at Imagination Technologies. Previously, he worked as a development engineer on SDKs and tools for both PC and mobile products as a member of the POWERVR Developer Relations Team. Kristof has a first degree in electrical engineering and a Master's degree in artificial intelligence, both from the University of Leuven, Belgium. Previous articles and tutorials have been published in *ShaderX²* and *ShaderX⁵*, *ARM IQ Magazine*, and online by the Khronos Group, Beyond3D, and 3Dfx Interactive.

Ken Catterall

Ken graduated from the University of Toronto in 2005 as a specialist in software engineering, where he developed an interest in computer graphics. Subsequently he has been working as a member of Imagination Technologies' Business Relations team as a Developer Engineer. Ken has worked on a wide range of 3D demos for Imagination's POWERVR Insider ecosystem program as well as supporting Imagination's network of developer partners.

João Luiz Dihl Comba

João Luiz Dihl Comba received a B.S. degree in computer science from the Federal University of Rio Grande do Sul, Brazil, an M.S. degree in computer science from the Federal University of Rio de Janeiro, Brazil, and a Ph.D. in computer science from Stanford University. He is an associate professor of computer science at the Federal University of Rio Grande do Sul, Brazil. His main research interests are in graphics, visualization, spatial data structures, and applied computational geometry. His current projects include the development of algorithms for large-scale scientific visualization, data structures for point-based modeling and rendering, and general-purpose computing using graphics hardware. He is a member of the ACM SIGGRAPH.

Keszegh Csaba

Csaba finished his studies at Eötvös Loránd University Faculty of Informatics. Now he works for Kishonti Informatics as senior programmer. His main work area includes 3D engine design and porting the native benchmarks to different mobile platforms. He also has experience in image compression and shader programming.

Jonathan Feldstein

Jonathan Feldstein is a graduate from the University of Waterloo. He has subsequently worked for a large Toronto studio on several computer animated television projects, the movie *Silent Hill*, and a variety of production tools. Jonathan has most recently made the transition over to mobile game development as a part of the AMD Imageon SDK team.

Markus Giegl

Markus holds a Master's degree in Theoretical Physics and recently earned a Ph.D. in Computer Graphics in parallel to his work as Community Manager in an EU project. He loves anything that challenges his creativity and has, among others, worked as game developer, database architect, cartoon book author, designer, and inventor. He lives in Austria in the world's third most livable city together with his wife and three-year-old son. If you live in New York, feel free to drop him a line.

Holger Gruen

Holger ventured into 3D real-time graphics writing fast software rasterizers. Since then he has held research and development positions in the games and the simulation industry. He got into developer relations pretty recently and now works for AMD's graphics products group. Holger, his wife, and his four kids live close to Munich near the Alps.

Tze-Yui Ho

Tze-Yui Ho received a Master's degree in electronic engineering from City University of Hong Kong in 2007. He is currently a Ph.D. student in the Department of Electronic Engineering, City University of Hong Kong. His research interests include global illumination algorithms and GPU programming. He has several years of GPU programming experience.

Szabolcs Horváth

Szabolcs is a member of the GLBenchmark group working for Kishonti Informatics. He implements graphics effects and his area of specialty is shader programming. During his graduation at Eötvös Loránd University Faculty of Informatics he researched digital image processing and gained experience in geographic information systems.

Laszlo Kishonti

Laszlo is founder and CEO of Kishonti Informatics, the leading mobile benchmarking company based in Budapest, Hungary. He is involved in performance analytics and optimizations of 3D benchmarks and data compression for mobile devices. Before launching his company, Laszlo worked for several years in the securities industry, pricing, investing, and benchmarking fixed income and derivative instruments.

Jerome Ko

Jerome Ko completed his undergraduate studies at the University of California, San Diego in 2007 with a degree in Mathematics-Computer Science. He is now currently working as a software engineer at Bunkspeed, focusing mostly on computer graphics. His current interests include realistic and real-time rendering.

Manny Ko

Manny Ko received his undergraduate and graduate education at Stanford University. He is currently at Naughty Dog doing mostly global illumination related work for the PS3. Previously he worked for Adobe, Multigen, and Pixar.

Jesse Laeuchli

Jesse is a software developer at ESRI in Redlands, California, working on 3D GIS software. His articles have appeared in *Game Programming Gems 2*, *Graphics Programming Methods*, *ShaderX2*, *ShaderX3*, and *More OpenGL Game Programming*. He graduated from the University of Notre Dame, and has lived overseas for much of his life in countries such as the Central African Republic, Hungary, China, Saudi Arabia, and Taiwan.

Sylvain Lefebvre

Sylvain completed his Ph.D. in 2004 at INRIA Rhône-Alpes (France) under the supervision of Fabrice Neyret. He then joined Microsoft Research as a postdoc and worked with Hugues Hoppe on real-time texture synthesis and texturing. In 2006 he joined INRIA Sophia-Antipolis (France) as a full-time researcher. His main interests are in automated content creation and compact data structures for interactive applications. In his spare time, Sylvain enjoys developing small pointless games (http://www.aracknea.net).

Chi-Sing Leung

Chi Sing Leung is currently an Associate Professor in the Department of Electronic Engineering, City University of Hong Kong. His research interests include neural computing, global illumination algorithms, and GPU programming. He has published more than 60 international journal papers. In 2005, he received the 2005 IEEE Transactions on Multimedia Prize Paper Award for his paper titled "The Plenoptic Illumination Function" published in 2002. His research interests include global illumination algorithms and GPU programming.

Jörn Loviscach

Jörn Loviscach is a professor of computer graphics, animation, and simulation at Hochschule Bremen, a University of Applied Sciences. He has authored and co-authored numerous academic and not-so-academic publications on computer graphics and on techniques for human-computer interaction.

Jonathan Maïm

Jonathan Maïm is a Ph.D. student at VRlab at the Swiss Federal Institute of Technology in Lausanne (EPFL). In April 2005, he received a Master's degree in Computer Science from EPFL after achieving his Master Project at the University of Montreal. His research efforts are concentrated on real-time crowd rendering, animation, and system architecture.

Morgan McGuire

Morgan McGuire is an Assistant Professor of Computer Science at Williams College and games industry consultant on titles including *Titan Quest* (2006), *ROBLOX* (2005), and *Zen of Sudoku* (2006). His research interests are game design and techniques that merge real-time computer vision and 3D rendering.

Frank Nielsen

Frank Nielsen is a researcher at Sony Computer Science Laboratories and Professor at Ecole Polytechnique (LIX). He prepared and received his Ph.D. in computational geometry at INRIA/University of Nice (France) in 1996. His research interests include computational information geometry, vision, graphics, optimization, and learning. Frank has written numerous scientific journal and conference papers, and blogs at http://blog.informationgeometry.org.

Anders Nivfors

Anders Nivfors received a B.S. degree in computer science from Kalmar University, Sweden, and an M.S. in computer science from Uppsala University, Sweden. He works now at EA DICE as a tools programmer.

Christopher Oat

Christopher Oat is a member of AMD's Game Computing Applications Group, where he is the technical lead for the group's demo team. In this role, he focuses on the development of cutting-edge rendering techniques for the latest graphics platforms. Christopher has published several articles in the *ShaderX* and *Game Programming Gems* series and has presented his work at graphics and game developer conferences around the world.

Damyan Pepper

Damyan Pepper has worked at Black Rock Studio since 2000 as a programmer on the *MotoGP* series. He's been involved in developing Black Rock's proprietary modeling and texturing package, Tomcat. He's currently the lead engine programmer on Black Rock's first release since becoming part of Disney Interactive Studios.

Emil Persson

Emil is a game developer working for Avalanche Studios. Previously Emil spent three years at ATI working as an ISV Engineer assisting the world's top game developers with optimizations and taking advantage of the latest hardware features. Emil also had a pivotal role in providing sample applications and technical papers for the ATI Radeon SDK. As a side project, Emil writes demo applications for his site www.humus.ca, showing interesting techniques, tricks, or just plain eye-candy.

Maurice Ribble

Maurice Ribble is a software engineer on the handheld 3D group at AMD, where he works on OpenGL ES 2.0 drivers for handheld GPUs. Over the past six years Maurice has worked on the desktop OpenGL driver team and the applications research group at AMD. He received a B.S. in Computer Engineering at Milwaukee School of Engineering in 2001.

Paweł Rohleder

Paweł has been interested in computer graphics and game programming since he was born :). He started programming games professionally in 2002, received a Master's degree in computer science at Wroclaw University of Technology in 2004, and has worked since 2006 as a 3D graphics programmer at Techland. He is a Ph.D. student in computer graphics (at Wroclaw University of Technology, since 2004).

Vlad Stamate

Vlad Stamate works in the R&D department of SCEA, leading the GPU performance analysis software team for the PlayStation 3 console. Previous to that he worked as an engineer for Imagination Technologies, taking part in developing OpenGL Linux drivers. He graduated Summa Cum Laude from the Richmond University London in 2001. He spends most of his time researching graphics algorithms that apply to modern graphics and central processing hardware ranging from PCs to next generation consoles. He is also known to spend thinking cycles on game search algorithms like Chess. Vlad has published articles in the *ShaderX* series of books (specifically in *ShaderX3* and *ShaderX4*) and presented at Game Developers Conference in 2007 (as part of a full-day tutorial).

László Szécsi

László Szécsi is an assistant professor at the Budapest University of Technology and Economics, where he lectures on computer graphics, game development, GPU programming, and object-oriented programming. His research interests include interactive global illumination rendering and procedural geometry modeling.

László Szirmay-Kalos

László Szirmay-Kalos is the head of Department of Control Engineering and Information Technology at the Budapest University of Technology and Economics in Hungary. His research interests include Monte Carlo global illumination algorithms and GPU-based photorealistic image synthesis. He is the author of several books and more than a hundred papers in this field. He has been responsible for illumination methods in the GameTools project and leads distributed GPU based visualization research in cooperation with HP.

Daniel Thalmann

Daniel Thalmann is Professor and Director of The Virtual Reality Lab (VRlab) at EPFL, Switzerland. He is a pioneer in research on virtual humans. He is coeditor-in-chief of the Journal of Computer Animation and Virtual Worlds, and is a member of the editorial board of five other journals. Daniel Thalmann has published numerous scientific papers. He is coauthor of several books including *Crowd Simulation*, published by Springer in October, 2007. He received an Honorary Doctorate from University Paul-Sabatier in Toulouse, France, in 2003.

Nicolas Thibieroz

Nicolas Thibieroz is part of the European Developer Relations team at ATI Technologies. As a kid he started programming on a Commodore 64 and Amstrad CPC before moving on to the PC world, where he realized the potential of real-time 3D graphics while playing *Ultima Underworld*. After obtaining a BEng of Electronic Engineering in 1996, he joined PowerVR Technologies where he occupied the role of Developer Relations Manager, supporting game developers on a variety of platforms and contributing to SDK content. His current position at ATI involves helping developers optimize the performance of their games and educating them about the advanced features found in cutting-edge graphics hardware.

Rafael P. Torchelsen

Rafael P. Torchelsen is a Ph.D. student at the Federal University of Rio Grande do Sul (UFRGS), Brazil, has a B.S in computer science from Catholic University of Pelotas, and an M.S. in computer graphics from University of Vale do Rio dos Sinos (UNISINOS). He worked in game engine development in several games in the Southlogic Company. Research interests include geometric algorithms, GPUs, and game programming.

Michal Valient

Michal Valient works as a senior technology programmer at Guerrilla, where he works on many aspects of the Killzone 2 rendering engine. Prior to joining the team in Amsterdam he worked as a senior programmer and leader and developed shader-based real-time rendering engines for Caligari trueSpace7. His interests include almost any aspect of light transfer, shadows, and parallel processing, and he wrote several graphics papers published in *ShaderX* books and conference journals during his Ph.D. studies in Slovakia.

Liang Wan

Liang Wan received her Ph.D. in computer science from the Chinese University of Hong Kong. She is currently a Research Fellow at the City University of Hong Kong. Liang created the example programs for all her research projects, including graphics and computer vision-related topics. She spoke at GDC2007 and wrote the article "Real-Time Environment Mapping with Equal Solid-Angle Spherical Quad-Map," published in *ShaderX⁴*.

Mikey Wetzel

Mikey has a long history with graphics APIs and sample code, starting back 12 years ago. Originally hired by Microsoft to work on the Talisman project, he soon became the "samples" guy writing most of the old-school Direct3D samples, training polygonal dolphins to swim in endless circles on computer monitors everywhere. After shipping DXSDK versions 6, 7, and 8, Mikey moved on to the Xbox and Xbox 360 teams where he still wrote samples and became somewhat of a globe-trotting expert on graphics and shader performance optimization. In his latest role, he now works for AMD on the team, bringing a mobile derivative of the Xbox 360 graphics core to a cell phone near you.

Tien-Tsin Wong

Tien-Tsin Wong is a professor in the Department of Computer Science and Engineering in the Chinese University of Hong Kong (CUHK). He has been programming for the last 19 years, including writing publicly available codes, libraries, demos, and toolkits (check his home page), and codes for all his graphics research. He works on GPU techniques, rendering, image-based relighting, natural phenomenon modeling, computerized manga, and multimedia data compression. He is a SIGGRAPH author. He received the IEEE Transaction on Multimedia Prize Paper Award 2005 and CUHK Young Researcher Award 2004.

Jonathan Zarge

Jonathan is a member of AMD's 3D Graphics Products Group and is currently leading the developer performance tools effort. Jonathan's extensive background ranges from computer vision to graphics research to 3D data visualization; his work on polygon decimation has been published in the proceedings of ACM SIGGRAPH and he has presented at Game Developers Conferences all around the world. He has an engineering degree from the University of Pennsylvania and a Masters of Engineering degree from Rensselaer Polytechnic Institute.

Jason Zink

Jason Zink is an electrical engineer currently working in the automotive industry. He is working toward a M.S. in Computer Science, and has a received a B.S. in Electrical Engineering. He has been writing software for about eight years in various fields such as industrial controls, embedded computing, business applications, automotive communication systems, and most recently game development with a great interest in graphics programming. He spends his spare time improving his multimedia engine and looking for ways to use it to make other applications more useful and interesting.

Matthias Zwicker

Matthias Zwicker is an Assistant Professor in Computer Science and Engineering at the University of California, San Diego. He earned his Ph.D. in computer science from the Federal Institute of Technology (ETH) in Zurich, Switzerland, in 2003. Prior to joining UCSD he was a post-doctoral associate at the Massachusetts Institute of Technology.

About the Section Editors

Wessam Bahnassi

Wessam has been working in computer graphics and game development for more than eight years now, concentrating on 3D engine and pipeline tools development. At In|Framez, he lead the development team for several games and real-time demos. He has many contributions and publications in graphics and programming in general, and has been a Microsoft Most Valuable Professional (MVP) for DirectX technologies for the past five years. Currently, he works at Electronics Arts Montreal doing console and PC graphics and game programming for some of EA's great titles.

Carsten Dachsbacher

Carsten Dachsbacher received his M.S. degree in computer science and his Ph.D. degree in computer graphics, both from the University of Erlangen-Nuremberg, Germany. He was post-doctoral fellow at REVES/INRIA Sophia Antipolis, France, within a Marie-Curie Fellowship. Since October 2007 he has been an assistant professor at VISUS (Institute for Visualization), University of Stuttgart, Germany. His research focuses on real-time, hardware-assisted computer graphics, interactive global illumination, perceptual rendering, and procedural models.

Willem de Boer

Willem is a computer graphics consultant and director at Botticelli Consulting Limited, and was previously a member of staff at Microsoft Research in Cambridge, England, where he worked on projects in computer vision and machine learning. Before that, Willem worked in the games industry as a programmer specializing in real-time graphics and audio. His home page can be found at http://www.whdeboer.com.

Wolfgang Engel

Wolfgang Engel is a senior graphics programmer in the core technology group of Rockstar. He is the editor of the *ShaderX* series and the author of *Programming Vertex and Pixel Shaders*. He speaks at conferences world-wide and teaches at several universities. Wolfgang has been a Microsoft Most Valuable Professional DirectX since July, 2006.

Tom Forsyth

Tom Forsyth has been obsessed by 3D graphics since seeing *Elite* on his ZX Spectrum. Since then he has always tried to make hardware beg for mercy. Tom has written triangle-drawing routines on the Spectrum, Sinclair QL, Atari ST, Sega 32X, Saturn, Dreamcast, PC, GamePark32, and XBox, and he's getting quite good at them now. Tom's coding past includes writing curved-surface stuff for Sega and graphics drivers for 3Dlabs. Currently he works in Guildford at Muckyfoot Productions, where past projects are *Urban Chaos*, *StarTopia*, and *Blade II*.

Kenneth Hurley

Kenneth has worked for such notable game and technology companies such as Electronic Arts and Intel, and most recently was a senior engineer at NVIDIA Corporation. While there, he participated in the development of the Xbox hardware and numerous video games including *Tiger Woods Golf*. Kenneth has been a consultant for several Silicon Valley companies and worked with the United States government on the latest military equipment, including the highly acclaimed Land Warrior. Kenneth's passion and experience for the gaming industry is what brings him to the helm of Signature Devices. With over 20 years of experience, this is Kenneth's second start-up as an independent developer, giving him perspective and a strong understanding of the demands of running an up-and-coming development company. He has contributed to best-selling computer books on 3D graphics and he is a requested speaker at conventions and workshops around the country. Kenneth received his Bachelor of Science degree in computer science from the University of Maryland.

Sebastien St. Laurent

Sebastien St. Laurent holds a degree in Computer Engineering from Sherbrooke University in Quebec (Canada), where he graduated at top of his class in 1999. Since then, he worked on many video game titles including the following: *Space Invaders*, *Dave Mira Freestyle BMX*, *Dave Mira Freestyle BMX2*, *Aggressive Inline*, and *BMX XXX*. Sebastien is now currently employed with the Microsoft Corporation, where he is a graphics developer for the Microsoft Game Studios. Sebastien St. Laurent is also a published author who has written *Shaders for Game Programmers and Artists* and *The COMPLETE Effect and HLSL Guide*.

Natalya Tatarchuk

Natalya Tatarchuk is a senior member of technical staff and a technical lead in the Game Computing Application Group under the Emerging Technologies and Applications group at AMD Graphics Products division. There she pushes GPU boundaries, investigating innovative graphics techniques and creating striking interactive renderings. In the past she led the creation of the state-of-the-art realistic rendering of city environments in the ATI demo *ToyShop* and has been the lead for the tools group at ATI Research. Natalya has been in the graphics industry for years, having previously worked on haptic 3D modeling software and scientific visualization libraries, among others. She has published multiple papers in various computer graphics conferences and articles in technical book series such as *ShaderX* and *Game Programming Gems*, and has presented talks at SIGGRAPH and at Game Developers Conferences worldwide, amongst others. Natalya holds B.A.s in Computer Science and Mathematics from Boston University.

Matthias Wloka

Matthias Wloka is a Senior Graphics Engineer in the Technology Group at Visual Concepts, where he contributes to the 2K Sports series of games. His primary responsibility is to enhance a game's look via advanced shading techniques, such as the unique players' sweat technology as featured in the national TV commercial "Sweat" for *NBA 2K6*. Prior to Visual Concepts, Matthias was a member of NVIDIA's Technical Developer Relations team, a Chief Technologist at GameFX/THQ, Inc., and a Computer Scientist at Fraunhofer CRCG. He received an M.S. in computer science from Brown University, and a B.S. from Christian Albrechts University in Kiel, Germany. Matthias has contributed to multiple conferences such as GDC, Microsoft's Meltdown events, and Eurographics, and is the author of multiple articles about real-time 3D graphics.

Contents

GEOMETRY
MANIPULATION

Introduction

Tom Forsyth

The "Geometry Manipulation" section of this book focuses on the ability of graphic processing units (GPUs) to process and generate geometry in exciting and interesting ways.

The first article, "Fast Evaluation of Subdivision Surfaces on Direct3D 10 Graphics Hardware" by György Antal and László Szirmay-Kalos, covers a subdivision algorithm that can provide coarser or smoother versions of a base mesh of arbitrary topology. The recursions of subdivisions are unfolded into one single geometry shader run, so this is a single pass algorithm. It operates without loops and without auxiliary texture memory writes, so the method is inherently fast.

The next article, "Improved Appearance Variety for Geometry Instancing" by Jonathan Maïm and Daniel Thalmann, introduces the concept of an *appearance set*, which allows the division of any object into several parts where specific colors, patterns, and illumination parameters can be applied. With this method, the designer has full control over the colors the parts can take and on the transitions between them, allowing for sharp variations as well as smooth color gradations.

The third article in the section, "Implementing Real-Time Mesh Simplification Using the GPU" by Christopher DeCoro and Natalya Tatarchuk, describes how the Lindstrom's vertex clustering method for mesh simplification can be directly adapted to the novel GPU computational pipeline, enabling real-time simplification of triangle meshes over an order of magnitude faster than an equivalent CPU implementation, but without any relative loss in quality.

Have fun,
TomF

1.1

Fast Evaluation of Subdivision Surfaces on Direct3D 10 Graphics Hardware

György Antal

László Szirmay-Kalos

Introduction

Subdivision surfaces are rapidly becoming popular in computer graphics because subdivision algorithms can easily provide coarser or smoother versions of a *base mesh* of arbitrary topology. Even though only a simple low-polygon base mesh needs to be stored in the model and passed to the graphics API, the rendered surface will still be smooth. However, GPU-based subdivision refinement has not appeared in games so far because of performance issues and the difficult integration of the subdivision tessellation into the existing polygon rendering pipeline.

Our proposed solution computes subdivisions in the *geometry shader* unit of Direct3D 10 compatible GPUs. The recursions of subdivisions are unfolded into one single geometry shader run, so this is a single pass algorithm. It operates without loops and without auxiliary texture memory writes, so the method is inherently fast. Each quad is sent down the pipeline as a point primitive and information on vertex locations and connected quads is read from prepared buffers by the geometry shader. The geometry shader subdivides each quad of the base mesh and directly generates an output vertex array encoding the triangle strips of the refined mesh. Since the current Direct3D 10 specification limits the number of vertices emitted per run, our algorithm cannot subdivide infinitely. In practice, two subdivision levels are easily achievable, which provides high enough quality for games.

Our program uses the Catmull-Clark subdivision scheme [Catmull78], but other schemes, such as Loop, Butterfly, and Kobbelt, can also be implemented similarly. The program also has features needed by games such as texture mapping and normal mapping. The method usually requires minimal pre-processing to produce buffers describing vertex locations, vertex indices of quads, and vertex indices of adjacent quads. These buffers can be prepared during the creation of the model.

Catmull-Clark Subdivision

Subdivision schemes take a mesh of large polygons, subdivide the polygons, and then modify the position of the vertices to give the resulting mesh a smoother appearance (Figure 1.1.1). The Catmull-Clark scheme is a particularly popular method that produces quads in each level of subdivision. The base mesh can have arbitrary topology that is converted to a quad mesh in the first step.

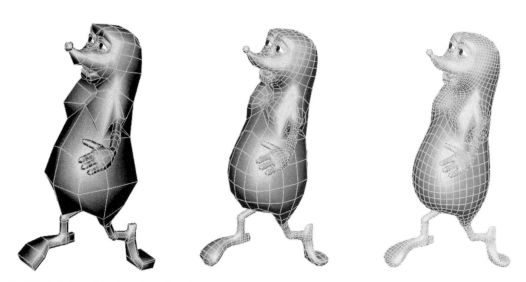

FIGURE 1.1.1 Original mesh and its level 1 and level 2 subdivisions applying the smoothing step once and twice, respectively.

In this article we assume that the base mesh is also built of quads. This is not a serious limitation. If the base mesh is not a quad mesh, the first subdivision step is performed as a preprocessing operation, and then the discussed algorithm can execute the additional refinement steps.

Let us consider a three-dimensional quadrilateral mesh (Figure 1.1.2). In the first step the Catmull-Clark scheme creates *face points* as the average of the vertices of each face polygon. Then *edge points* are computed in the vicinity of the middle of the original edges by averaging the vertices at the ends of the edge and the face points of polygons meeting at this edge. Finally, the original vertices are moved to the weighted average of the face points of those faces that share this vertex and of edge points of those edges that are connected to this vertex. Connecting the edge points with the face points, we create a refined surface that has four times more quadrilaterals.

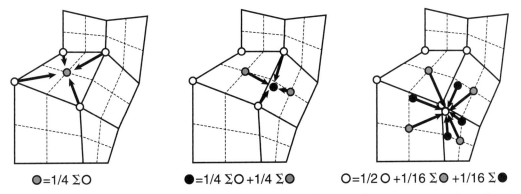

$\bigcirc$=1/4 ΣO   ●=1/4 ΣO +1/4 Σ●   O=1/2 O +1/16 Σ● +1/16 Σ●

FIGURE 1.1.2 One smoothing step of the Catmull-Clark subdivision scheme supposing valence four vertices. First the face points are found, then the edge midpoints are moved, and finally the original vertices are refined according to the weighted sum of its neighboring edge and face points.

The location of the new face points, edge points, and the modified original vertices can also be directly expressed from the vertices of the original polygon and its neighboring polygons. The weights used to compute these points are shown in Figure 1.1.3. Notice that the weights in the formula of the modified original vertices depend on how many edges meet in this particular vertex. The number of meeting edges is called the *valence*. Figure 1.1.3 shows the weights for valence values three, four, and five, respectively. Vertices of valence greater than five are very rare in models, and where they do exist it is possible to convert these models to have vertices of at most valence five. Thus we assume that valence five is the maximum and it is the modeler's responsibility to create the mesh accordingly.

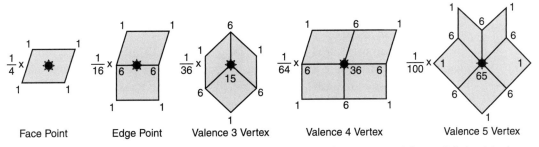

Face Point   Edge Point   Valence 3 Vertex   Valence 4 Vertex   Valence 5 Vertex

FIGURE 1.1.3 Weighting of the original vertices for face points, edge points, and for modified original vertices, respectively. The formula of the positions of the modified original vertices depends on the valence of the vertex.

Each subdivision step multiplies the number of quadrilaterals in the mesh by four. Thus, if the subdivision is executed on the CPU, then the size of the subdivided geometry uploaded to the GPU increases dramatically. To solve this problem, both the rendering and the subdivision operation should be executed on the GPU. In the following section such a solution is presented.

Subdivision on the GPU

Subdivision algorithms take the base mesh and replace each polygon with a series of polygons. Unfortunately, this operation does not fit into earlier GPU architectures (Direct3D 9 or Shader Model 3 and earlier) because they were not able to modify the topology of the uploaded geometry, nor could they introduce new primitives in the rendering pipeline. Although Direct3D 9 or earlier GPUs cannot render subdivision surfaces in a single pass, they can execute subdivision algorithms in multiple passes [Bunnel05]. These implementations store the vertices in textures and recognize that subdivision schemes are very similar to filtering these geometry images. They refine the geometry stored in textures with the fragment shader and transform the refined vertices in the next pass by the vertex shader. Every refinement level needs a new pass. These methods require a lot of texture fetches and cumbersome offline preparation of the input data before sending the geometry to the pipeline.

A straightforward single pass implementation of subdivision algorithms has become possible with the introduction of the geometry shader in Direct3D 10 GPUs.

The Geometry Shader Approach for Subdivision Surfaces

In Direct3D 10-compatible GPUs, the geometry goes through the vertex shader and then the geometry shader processes primitives one by one and outputs an array of triangles that are rasterized later in the pipeline [Blythe06]. When a triangle is processed by the geometry shader, the information on adjacent triangles is also available. However, the Catmull-Clark scheme works with quads rather than triangles, and subdivision rules need information about adjacent quads. Direct3D does not support quads, nor does it provide the geometry shader with their required adjacency. Our solution to this problem is to send quads encoded as points down the pipeline. The geometry shader assembles the subdivided mesh corresponding to a single base mesh quad and outputs the mesh as a triangle strip.

A single quad of vertices $v1$, $v2$, $v3$, $v4$ with adjacency information is shown in Figure 1.1.4. This figure corresponds to the case in which all vertices have valence five, i.e. the most complicated case that we consider. If a vertex had valence four or three, then connected quads and their vertices would be missing from Figure 1.1.4. To describe the topology, extra vertex indices of adjacent quads are also added to the quad information. The order of these extra vertex indices follows the order of quads connected only to $v1$, then to $v2$, and so on. If vertex $v1$ has valence five, then two adjacent quads are connected only to $v1$, which is surrounded by five extra vertices $v11$, $v12$, $v13$, $v14$, and $v15$. These extra vertices are called the *ear* of $v1$. If the vertex had valence four or three, then the ear would have three or one vertices, respectively.

The CPU sends the sequence of quad indices as a non-indexed vertex stream. The vertex shader simply passes these indices to the geometry shader. The geometry shader

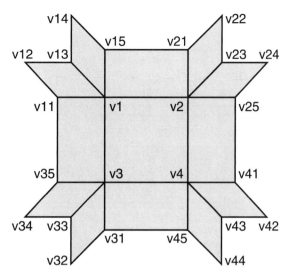

FIGURE 1.1.4 Topology of the processed quad and its neighboring quads of the base mesh assuming valence five at each vertex.

takes the quad index and reads all the other buffers to get the quad, vertex, and adjacency information. We use a `quadAndAjacencyBuffer` that specifies the four vertex indices of a given quad and then lists the vertex indices of the four ears of the given quad. The buffer always reserves enough space for the valence-five case, thus it allocates 24 items for each quad. This buffer holds indices into the `vertPosValence-Buffer`, which stores vertex coordinates in modeling space, and the valence of a vertex.

These buffers and their organization are shown in Figure 1.1.5. The CPU is responsible for creating these buffers and uploading them to the GPU's memory.

Using these buffers, the geometry shader collects the vertices of the processed and adjacent quads, applies the subdivision rules, and outputs a vertex array encoding the triangle strips of the refined mesh. The algorithm executes one or more subdivisions directly.

In the following sections we present the algorithms for zero and one subdivision steps. Theoretically, multi-level subdivisions could be realized by the multiple execution of the single-level subdivision step. However, this requires loops and the storage of the temporary meshes. Thus we also present a direct solution that immediately provides a level 2 subdivision of the base mesh.

vertPosValenceBuffer

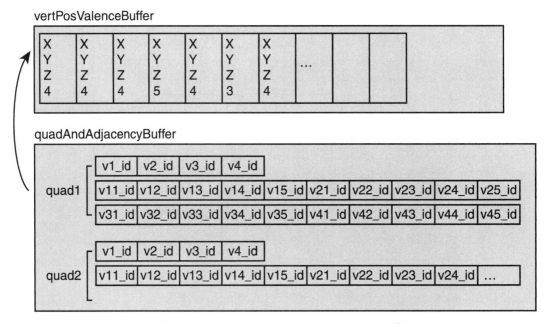

FIGURE 1.1.5 Organization of `quadAndAdjacency` and `vertPosValence` buffers

Level 0 Subdivision

Level 0 subdivision means no subdivision at all. The geometry shader just assembles a triangle strip of two triangles defining a single base mesh quad. We include this trivial case here to highlight the responsibilities of the geometry shader, such as fetching the indexed vertices from buffers, transforming them from model space to clip space, and outputting the quad in the form of a triangle strip. A simplified version of the geometry shader, which gets the index of the current quad in input variable `p_quadIndex`, is shown here:

```
void Subdiv0Function(uint p_quadIndex, /* index of the quad */
                     inout TriangleStream<PS_INPUT> p_stream)
{
  PS_INPUT output;
  // get vertex indices of the quad
  int quadBase = 6 * p_quadIndex;
  uint4 quadInd = quadAndAdjacencyBuffer.Load(quadBase);

  // get vertices
  float3 v1 = vertPosValenceBuffer.Load(quadInd.x).xyz;
  float3 v2 = vertPosValenceBuffer.Load(quadInd.y).xyz;
  float3 v3 = vertPosValenceBuffer.Load(quadInd.z).xyz;
  float3 v4 = vertPosValenceBuffer.Load(quadInd.w).xyz;
```

```
// transform vertices to clipping space and assemble a strip of two
triangles
  output.Pos = mul(float4(v1, 1), mWorldViewProj);
p_stream.Append(output);
  output.Pos = mul(float4(v3, 1), mWorldViewProj);
p_stream.Append(output);
  output.Pos = mul(float4(v2, 1), mWorldViewProj);
p_stream.Append(output);
  output.Pos = mul(float4(v4, 1), mWorldViewProj);
p_stream.Append(output);
  p_stream.RestartStrip();
}
```

It may seem strange that points are transformed to clip space by the geometry shader and not by the vertex shader. The reason is that we send quad indices down the pipeline and not vertices. Thus, the vertex shader cannot access vertex information directly.

Level 1 Subdivision

Level 1 subdivision takes the quad of Figure 1.1.4 and generates two triangle strips that encode four quads of vertices $a1$, $a2$, …, $a9$ as shown in Figure 1.1.6.

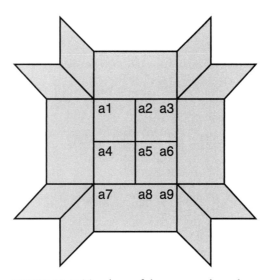

FIGURE 1.1.6 Topology of the processed quad and its level 1 subdivision.

In order to simplify the handling of different valence cases, the last vertex of the ear is also stored in variable v<i>Last, where <i> is the index of the vertex.

Assuming only valence four vertices, the geometry shader program of level 1 subdivision is as follows:

```
void Subdiv1Function(uint p_quadIndex, inout TriangleStream<PS_INPUT>
p_stream)
{
  PS_INPUT output;
  // the base index of the vertices of a quad in the quadAdjacency
buffer
  int quadBase = 6 * p_quadIndex;
  // get vertex indices of the quad
  uint4 quadInd = quadAndAdjacencyBuffer.Load(quadBase);
  // get the vertices
  float4 vpv1 = vertPosValenceBuffer.Load(quadInd.x);
  float4 vpv2 = vertPosValenceBuffer.Load(quadInd.y);
  float4 vpv3 = vertPosValenceBuffer.Load(quadInd.z);
  float4 vpv4 = vertPosValenceBuffer.Load(quadInd.w);
  float3 v1 = vpv1.xyz;
  float3 v2 = vpv2.xyz;
  float3 v3 = vpv2.xyz;
  float3 v4 = vpv2.xyz;
  // get valence values of the vertices
  uint val1 = vpv1.w;
  uint val2 = vpv2.w;
  uint val3 = vpv3.w;
  uint val4 = vpv4.w;
  // load 5 adjacencyData corresponding to 4 vertices
  int4 adjData1 = quadAndAdjacencyBuffer.Load(quadBase + 1);
  int4 adjData2 = quadAndAdjacencyBuffer.Load(quadBase + 2);
  int4 adjData3 = quadAndAdjacencyBuffer.Load(quadBase + 3);
  int4 adjData4 = quadAndAdjacencyBuffer.Load(quadBase + 4);
  int4 adjData5 = quadAndAdjacencyBuffer.Load(quadBase + 5);
  // retrieve ear for v1
  float3 v11 = vertPosValenceBuffer.Load(adjData1.x).xyz;
  float3 v12 = vertPosValenceBuffer.Load(adjData1.y).xyz;
  float3 v13 = vertPosValenceBuffer.Load(adjData1.z).xyz;
  float3 v14 = vertPosValenceBuffer.Load(adjData1.w).xyz;
  float3 v15 = vertPosValenceBuffer.Load(adjData2.x).xyz;
  float3 v1Last;
  if (val1 == 3)
        v1Last = v11;
  else if (val1 == 4)
        v1Last = v13;
  else
        v1Last = v15;
  // retrieve ear for v2 similarly
  ...
  // retrieve ear for v3 similarly
  ...
  // retrieve ear for v4 similarly
  ...
  // new vertices: 1 face point and 4 edge points
  float3 a5 = (v1 + v2 + v3 + v4) / 4;
  float3 a2 = (6 * (v1 + v2) + v1Last + v21 + v3 + v4) / 16;
  float3 a6 = (6 * (v2 + v4) + v2Last + v41 + v1 + v3) / 16;
```

```
    float3 a8 = (6 * (v4 + v3) + v4Last + v31 + v1 + v2) / 16;
    float3 a4 = (6 * (v3 + v1) + v3Last + v11 + v2 + v4) / 16;
    // modification of the original vertices if valence is 4
    a1 = (36 * v1 + 6 * (v11 + v13 + v2 + v3) + v3Last + v12 + v21 + v4)
/ 64;
    a3 = (36 * v2 + 6 * (v21 + v23 + v1 + v4) + v1Last + v22 + v41 + v3)
/ 64;
    a7 = (36 * v3 + 6 * (v31 + v33 + v1 + v4) + v4Last + v32 + v11 + v2)
/ 64;
    a9 = (36 * v4 + 6 * (v41 + v43 + v2 + v3) + v2Last + v42 + v31 + v1)
/ 64;
    // optionally caculate texture, normal, bi-normal data here . . .
    // transform vertices and emit 2 triangle strips
    output.Pos = mul(float4(a1, 1), mWorldViewProj);
p_stream.Append(output);
    output.Pos = mul(float4(a4, 1), mWorldViewProj);
p_stream.Append(output);
    output.Pos = mul(float4(a2, 1), mWorldViewProj);
p_stream.Append(output);
    output.Pos = mul(float4(a5, 1), mWorldViewProj);
p_stream.Append(output);
    output.Pos = mul(float4(a3, 1), mWorldViewProj);
p_stream.Append(output);
    output.Pos = mul(float4(a6, 1), mWorldViewProj);
p_stream.Append(output);
    p_stream.RestartStrip();
    output.Pos = mul(float4(a4, 1), mWorldViewProj);
p_stream.Append(output);
    output.Pos = mul(float4(a7, 1), mWorldViewProj);
p_stream.Append(output);
    output.Pos = mul(float4(a5, 1), mWorldViewProj);
p_stream.Append(output);
    output.Pos = mul(float4(a8, 1), mWorldViewProj);
p_stream.Append(output);
    output.Pos = mul(float4(a6, 1), mWorldViewProj);
p_stream.Append(output);
    output.Pos = mul(float4(a9, 1), mWorldViewProj);
p_stream.Append(output);
    p_stream.RestartStrip();
}
```

If the program needs to be prepared not only for valence four but also for other valence values, the part entitled "modification of the original vertices" should be changed to introduce several branches according to the actual valence. For example, the computation of vertex position $a1$ would look like this:

```
// modification of the original vertices
if (val1 == 3)
  a1 = (15*v1 + 6*(v11 + v2 + v3) + v3Last + v21 + v4) / 36;
else if (val1 == 4)
  a1 = (36*v1 + 6*(v11 + v13 + v2 + v3) + v3Last + v12 + v21 + v4) /
64;
else if (val1 == 5)
  a1 = (65*v1 + 6*(v11 + v13 + v15 + v2 + v3) + v3Last + v12 + v14 +
v21 + v4) / 100;
```

In addition to the position of each new vertex, its texture coordinate, normal vector, tangent, and bi-tangent should also be computed if we want to present a textured model with bump or displacement mapping. The linear interpolation of per-vertex data of the base mesh is the most efficient solution for generating this information for the new vertices.

Level 2 Subdivision

Level 2 subdivision generates four triangle strips that correspond to 16 quads and 25 vertices, $b1$, $b2$, ..., $b25$ (Figure 1.1.7). These vertices can be calculated from the original vertices $v1$,..., $v4$ and from the ears, similarly to the level 1 subdivision. However, the code is much longer; therefore we do not include it here. Our solution first calculates the vertices of level 1 subdivision ($a1$, $a2$, ..., $a9$), and these are then used to determine the vertices of level 2 subdivision.

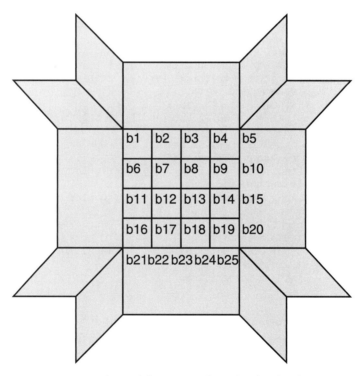

FIGURE 1.1.7 Topology of the processed quad and its level 2 subdivision

Level 3 and Greater Subdivisions

The strategy used for level 2 can be followed to deeper levels since higher order subdivisions can be unambiguously defined by the vertices of the neighboring quads that are available for the geometry shader. However, extending the subdivision level challenges the current output limit of the Direct3D 10 geometry shader. Currently a maximum of 1,024 float or `dword` values can be emitted in a geometry shader run. Level 3 subdivision generates 64 quads, that is, 144 triangle strip vertices, which permits a maximum of seven float values per vertex. However, a textured and normal mapped model requires a `float4` position, a `float2` texture coordinate pair, a `float3` normal, and a `float3` bi-tangent, i.e. 12 float values per vertex. So the practical limit of the subdivision is level 2, which provides enough quality for games. Additionally, a level 3 subdivision would produce 64 times more quads (triangles) than the original base mesh, which is likely to be prohibitively slow for real-time applications.

Implementation

The implementation is based on the August 2007 DirectX SDK using the latest NVIDIA driver 163.69. Texture mapping, normal mapping, and per-pixel lighting were used in the pixel shader to enhance the visual quality.

Figure 1.1.8 shows a lizard-like creature rendered by the algorithm. The original base mesh has 1,300 quads. Our measurements show that on an NVIDIA 8800GTX video card, the level 0, level 1, and level 2 subdivisions ran in 0.32, 0.93, and 25.32 milliseconds, respectively. For comparison, we also implemented a CPU version of

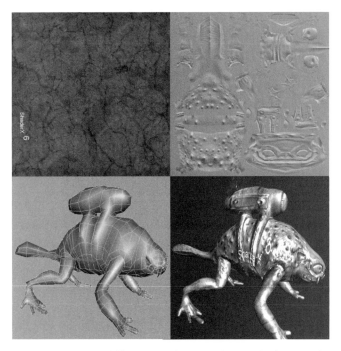

FIGURE 1.1.8 The diffuse map, the normal map, the base mesh in the 3D editor, and the subdivided mesh rendered by the discussed algorithm.

the same algorithm and ran it on an Intel Core2 Duo/2.66 GHz computer. When the CPU executed level 1 subdivision, it took 5.5 milliseconds, which means that the GPU implementation is more than five times faster.

Conclusion

This article presents a geometry shader program to render Catmull-Clark subdivision surfaces with valence three, four, and five vertices. To solve the problem of accessing the adjacency information of quads, only the quad indices are sent down the pipeline and the geometry shader builds up the subdivided meshes from buffers. The algorithm renders level 1 and level 2 subdivisions efficiently.

Acknowledgments

Lizard creature model courtesy of Bay Raitt.

References

[Blythe06] Blythe, David. "The Direct3D 10 System," in *SIGGRAPH 2006 Proceedings*, 2006, pp 724-734.

[Bunnel05] Bunnel, Michael. "Adaptive Tessellation of Subdivision Surfaces with Displacement Mapping," in *GPU Gems 2* (Edited by Matt Pharr). Addison Wesley, 2005, pp 109-122.

[Catmull78] Catmull, E. and Clark, J. "Recursively Generated B-Spline Surfaces on Arbitrary Topological Meshes," *Computer Aided Design*, Volume 10, 1978, pp. 350-355.

1.2

Improved Appearance Variety for Geometry Instancing

Jonathan Maïm (jonathan.maim@epfl.ch)

Virtual Reality Lab, Swiss Federal Institute of Technology (EPFL)

Daniel Thalmann (daniel.thalmann@epfl.ch)

Virtual Reality Lab, Swiss Federal Institute of Technology (EPFL)

Introduction

The richness of virtual worlds in video games or other interactive applications is paramount: a user feels immersed only when in an environment with many different aspects and details. To provide artistically rich content, skilled designers need to create thousands of different meshes and textures. This approach not only demands important human resources, but it is also difficult to achieve while retaining real-time performance because each new object increases the number of triangles and draw calls issued to the GPU. Thus, a trade-off between diversity and performance is necessary. Today, the common approach is to start with a limited number of meshes and then instantiate them multiple times in the environment at low cost [1]. The issue is then how to make instances of the same object look different. Diversity can be obtained by modifying the object's position, orientation, size, and color.

In this article, we present a novel and simple method to improve the appearance variety of instances of the same object, overcoming several drawbacks observed in previous approaches. We introduce the concept of an *appearance set*, which allows the division of any object into several parts where specific colors, patterns, and illumination parameters can be applied. With our method, the designer has full control over the colors the parts can take and on the transitions between them, allowing for sharp variations as well as smooth color gradations. Appearance sets are robust and versatile; they can be applied on any kind of object and in any number. Moreover, they are simple to implement; we show in this article how to use appearance sets with a fragment program. In the figures shown here and accompanying video on the DVD, we illustrate the use of appearance sets with several examples, including a large varied city generated from a small set of buildings and a crowd of virtual humans based on a single or a few human templates and the accessories they wear.

Overview

To locally apply color variety, pattern variations, and specific illumination parameters to an object instance, we need to identify its different parts. For example, the parts of a virtual human would be the hair, skin, shirt, pants, and so on. This segmentation can be achieved with traditional methods by splitting the object mesh into submeshes, but at a high cost. Instead, it is more efficient to divide the texture of the object into parts and store that information in another texture that we call a *segmentation map*. At most, each segmentation map can define four parts that correspond to each of the RGBA color channels. Each of these four parts is given a color for each instance. The four colors for every instance in the scene are stored in a single *CLUT* (*color look-up table*) texture.

In Figure 1.2.1, we describe the different data structures employed. At the creation of an object template, the designer also produces a series of appearance sets that are each composed of the following:

- One texture, which will be mapped onto the object instances.
- One or more segmentation maps to differentiate all parts of the object with this texture.

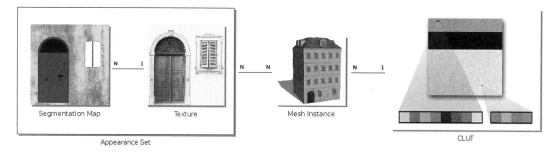

FIGURE 1.2.1 Relations between data structures. Each mesh instance possesses a set of colors in the CLUT. Applying colors smoothly to the texture parts is achieved through the use of segmentation maps.

Once the appearance sets are designed, they can be implemented at runtime to color the object instances:

- **Initialization process:** One color is associated with each part of each instance, and all the colors for all the instances are stored in a single CLUT.
- **Runtime process:** The CLUT is sent to the GPU as a texture and addressed in a fragment shader to apply the chosen color to the corresponding instance part.

Design

The first step in designing appearance sets is to create several textures that can be applied to the object's mesh. Indeed, it is possible to create many different textures for the same object with only one's imagination to limit you. For instance, the textures of a human mesh may vary the character's apparent age, skin color, clothes, and so on. For a building, textures can have different window positions, spacing, and size. Note that in order to later apply our color variation technique, the created textures are all desaturated.

For each texture of an object, we need to efficiently recognize its specific parts. We use a set of additional textures, called segmentation maps, that share the same UV parameterization as the texture. Each segmentation map is composed of four channels, R, G, B, and A, which are used to represent four parts. You can define more than four parts by using multiple segmentation maps. Figure 1.2.2 shows examples of appearance sets applied to the same building template.

For each texel of an object, we can specify whether it belongs to a specific part by changing the corresponding channel intensity in the segmentation map. For instance, imagine that the "window" part of a building is associated with the channel B (blue) in a segmentation map. For each texel of the object's texture, if it is inside a window, the corresponding texel in the segmentation map is set to blue. Thus, the resulting segmentation map has blue patterns everywhere a window is illustrated on the original texture. The same process is achieved for each part, i.e., for each channel of each segmentation map.

It is possible for an object's texel to belong to several parts at the same time. In a segmentation map, the intensity of a channel ranges between 0 and 255 and represents how fully each texel belongs to the associated part. If the channel is set to 0, the texel does not belong to the part, but with an intensity of 255, the texel completely lies in this part.

Thus, the final color of each texel of the object instance is computed as the sum of the colors chosen for the parts and is weighted by the intensity of the segmentation map channels. This weighting allows the creation of smooth transitions between two parts by slowly increasing the intensity of a channel over another in the segmentation map. This is very useful when you design transitions such as the one between the skin and hair of a virtual human.

In previous color variety techniques, no additional segmentation maps were used. Instead, parts were identified with the fourth (alpha) channel of the original texture, and each part was associated with a specific value between 0 and 255 in this channel. Although this approach is less costly in terms of memory [2, 3] because no additional textures are required, segmentation maps offer many advantages:

- Full control over the transitions between parts: smooth, sharp, and so on
- Allows a texel to belong to more than one part

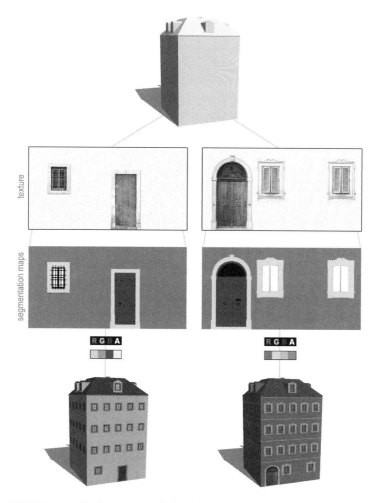

FIGURE 1.2.2 Each instance of a building template randomly chooses
an appearance set (a texture and a segmentation map).

- Tighter storage in the CLUT, which allows the storage of more colors for the
  same resolution (see the following section, "Implementation")
- Bilinear filtering and MIPmapping can be used on the texture, which was impossible in the previous approach, as filtering the part numbers is not a meaningful
  operation
- Allows the use of part-specific materials that each react differently to the light,
  e.g., specularity, reflectivity, and so on

Implementation

The color variety technique described in this article can be implemented mainly in a fragment shader. We detail how to do it here in GLSL using Shader Model 3.0 hardware. Note that for the sake of clarity and brevity, the following code shows how to apply color variety with an appearance set composed of a single segmentation map; that is, each fragment can at most belong to four different parts. However, once the concept is grasped, it is easily extended to multiple segmentation maps.

To facilitate the fragment shader comprehension, we begin by describing the basic code for applying color variation to every fragment of one instance. Then, in a second phase, we will add the necessary lines to include customized per-part illumination effects (specularity and reflection).

The uniforms needed for the basic color variation algorithm are the following:

```
uniform sampler2D texture;
uniform sampler2D segmentationMap;
uniform sampler2D clut;
uniform vec2             clutCoord;
```

The `texture` and `segmentationMap` `sampler2D` handles represent the components of the appearance set used for the current object instance.

Each instance possesses one set of four colors, one per part. The CLUT texture contains the color sets of all instances in the scene, ordered in a particular way. First, to simplify the CLUT addressing, colors belonging to a single instance are always placed contiguously on the same row of the CLUT texture. Second, we store a set of four RGB colors in only three texels to save space; because the CLUT is an RGBA texture, it is possible to store the first three colors in the RGB channels of three texels and use the vacant A channel to store the RGB components of the fourth color.

Finally, the uniform `clutCoord` contains the 2D coordinates that index the first color of the current instance. Note that since colors of the same set are always contiguous in the same row, we can efficiently iterate through the current set by only increasing the x coordinate of `clutCoord`.

The following code snippet shows how to color fragments:

```
01    vec3 colorAccum          = vec3( 0.0 );
02    vec3 clutFetchFourth     = vec3( 0.0 );
03    float whiteContribution  = 1.0;
04
05    const vec4 textureFetch  = texture2D( texture,
gl_TexCoord[ 0 ].st );
06    const vec4 segMapFetch = texture2D( segmentationMap, gl_TexCoord[
0 ].st );
07
08    // Iterate through the RGB channels of the segmentation map.
09    for ( int i = 0; i < 3; ++i )
10    {
11        const vec4 clutFetch =
```

```
12          texture2D( clut, vec2( clutCoord.x + INV_CLUT_RES*i,
clutCoord.y ) );
13
14      clutFetchFourth.r = clutFetch.a;
15
16      colorAccum += segMapFetch.r * clutFetch.rgb;
17
18      whiteContribution -= segMapFetch.r;
19
20      // Segmentation map  and color accum bonus texel swizzling.
21      segMapFetch = segMapFetch.gbar;
22      clutFetchFourth = clutFetchFourth.gbr;
23   }
24
25   // Get color accum bonus.
26   whiteContribution -= segMapFetch.r;
27   colorAccum          += segMapFetch.r * clutFetchFourth.rgb;
28
29   gl_FragColor.rgb =
30      textureFetch * ( max( colorAccum, vec3( 1.0 ) ) + vec3( max(
whiteContribution, 0.0 )  ) );
```

At lines 01 to 03 we declare three local variables. The variable `colorAccum` will accumulate the weighted contribution of each part's color.

At lines 05 and 06, the texture and segmentation map are both addressed by the same implicit built-in varying `gl_TexCoord[0].st` because they share the same UV parameterization. The corresponding fetched colors are saved in `textureFetch` and `segMapFetch`.

The core of the algorithm is a loop through the R, G, and B values of the segmentation map fetch.

First, at line 11, the color of the current part is retrieved from the CLUT. As previously explained, only the x coordinate of the CLUT needs to be incremented. Note that `INV_CLUT_RES` represents the reciprocal of the CLUT resolution and is used to normalize the computed coordinates between 0.0 and 1.0.

At line 14, the `clutFetchFourth` variable is used to save the fourth color in the CLUT. Recall that its RGB components are stored in the A channel of the CLUT's three texel set; this means that this color is only known at the end of the loop after the three CLUT texels have been read.

At line 16, the color contribution of the part currently being processed is added; the current segmentation map channel is used to weight the `clutFetch` color contribution. The fourth part's color contribution, saved in `clutFetchFourth`, is only added at line 27, after it is out of the loop. Note that in a shader, the intensity of a texture channel is no longer expressed between 0 and 255; it is normalized between 0.0 and 1.0. Thus, the RGB components of the resulting `colorAccum` are also in this range.

To iterate over the segmentation map's channels, a swizzling of the `segMapFetch` variable is achieved at line 21. Similarly, to save the fourth color's components, the `colorFetchFourth` variable is swizzled at line 22.

Sometimes, it happens that the sum of contributions for a texel does not reach precisely 1.0. This is the case when, in a segmentation map, the sum R+G+B+A does not equal 255 for a texel. It happens particularly often when designing smooth transitions between two parts. In the preceding code, care is taken to treat this particularity. If the sum exceeds 255 (1.0 in the shader), it is simply clamped (see line 29). If, however, the sum does not reach 255, the problem is trickier. From a design point of view, it means that a certain percentage of the texel belongs to no part at all. From a technical point of view, consider this example: imagine a transition texel in a segmentation map. Its R and G components both equal 100 (39%), the others equal 0. For simplicity, let us assume that the corresponding part colors in the CLUT are pure red and green. From the shader code above, the final color in `colorAccum` is 39% of red and 39% of green, which represents a dark yellow:

$$\frac{100}{255}\ \text{red}\ +\ \frac{100}{255}\ \text{green}\ \simeq\ 0.39\begin{pmatrix}1.0\\0.0\\0.0\end{pmatrix}+\ 0.39\begin{pmatrix}0.0\\1.0\\0.0\end{pmatrix}=\begin{pmatrix}0.39\\0.0\\0.39\end{pmatrix}$$

This seems to be the correct calculation. However, with this approach, when trying to achieve a gradient transitioning smoothly from red to green, the result is shades of yellow that are too dark. To compensate for this, we add in white to `colorAccum` to fill in the missing contribution. In our example, 22% of white is added, resulting in a `colorAccum` of (0.61, 0.22, 0.61). In the code at line 03, the variable `whiteContribution` is set to 1.0 (or 100%), and at lines 18 and 26, the percentage of other parts are deducted from it. The final color is computed at line 29, where the white contribution is added to `colorAccum`.

Multiple Materials

Now that the basic mechanism has been illustrated, we will show how to obtain per-part illumination effects. Here, we illustrate the case of specular and sphere map reflection parameters. First, we need three more uniforms:

```
uniform vec2         specularParams[ 4 ];
uniform sampler2D sphereMap;
uniform float        reflectivityParams[ 4 ];
```

To achieve specularity, two values are required from Phong's equation: intensity and exponent. Thus, `specularParams` is an array of four 2D vectors, one for each part of the segmentation map. For reflection effects, the sphere map (reflection texture) is sent in `sphereMap` and the reflectivity parameter in `reflectivityParams`. Once more, there are four parameters, one per part. Note that we only send one sphere map, thus all parts of this segmentation map potentially reflect the same environment.

The following code snippet is similar to the previous one except for a few additional lines, emphasized in bold.

```
01   vec3 colorAccum                 = vec3( 0.0 );
02   vec3 clutFetchFourth            = vec3( 0.0 );
03   float whiteContribution         = 1.0;
04   vec3 reflectionContribution = vec3( 0.0 );
05   float specularContribution;
06
07   const vec4 textureFetch         = texture2D( texture,
gl_TexCoord[ 0 ].st );
08   const vec4 segMapFetch          = texture2D( segmentationMap,
gl_TexCoord[ 0 ].st );
09   const vec3 sphereMapFetch = texture2D( sphereMap,
gl_TexCoord[ 1 ].st );
10
11   // Iterate through the RGB channels of the segmentation map.
12   for ( int i = 0; i < 3; ++i )
13   {
14     const vec4 clutFetch =
15        texture2D( clut, vec2( clutCoord.x + INV_CLUT_RES*i,
clutCoord.y ) );
16
17     clutFetchFourth.r = clutFetch.a;
18
19     colorAccum += segMapFetch.r * clutFetch.rgb;
20
21     specularContribution += segMapFetch.r * specularParams[ i ].x *
pow( rODotE, specularParams[ i ].y );
22     reflectionContribution += segMapFetch.r * reflectivity[ i ] *
sphereMapFetch;
23
24     whiteContribution -= segMapFetch.r;
25
26     // Segmentation map  and color accum bonus texel swizzling.
27     segMapFetch = segMapFetch.gbar;
28     colorAccumBonus = colorAccumBonus.gbr;
29   }
30
31   // Get color accum bonus.
32   whiteContribution            -= segMapFetch.r;
33   specularContribution     += segMapFetch.r * specularParams[ 3 ].x *
pow( rDotE, specularParams[ 3 ].y );
34   reflectionContribution += segMapFetch.r * reflectivity[ 3 ] *
sphereMapFetch;
35   colorAccum                   += segMapFetch.r *
clutFetchFourth.rgb;
36
37   gl_FragColor.rgb = textureFetch * ( max( colorAccum, vec3( 1.0 ) )
+ vec3( max( whiteContribution, 0.0 )  ) );
38   gl_FragColor.rgb += reflectionContribution + vec3(
specularContribution );
```

At line 09, the sphere map is addressed with the built-in varying gl_TexCo-ord[1].st, which was previously computed in the vertex shader (see vertex shader code on the DVD-ROM). The fetched color is saved in sphereMapFetch.

Then, in the loop at line 21, the variable `specularContribution` is computed as the weighted contribution of each part's specularity. The applied formula is the one commonly used in the Phong model.

Similarly for the reflection, the variable `reflectionContribution` accumulates all the parts' contributions as their reflectivity multiplied by the fetched sphere map color and weighted by the channel intensity in the segmentation map. At lines 33 and 34, the fourth part's contribution to specularity and reflection is accumulated. Note that it would be impossible to integrate the fourth part's contribution in the loop because we are constrained to three iterations corresponding to the CLUT's sets of three colors.

The presented code uses a loop, which is available only in Shader Model 3.0. However, by unrolling the loop, this technique can also be implemented on older GPUs, which is exactly what a good compiler should do, even on Shader Model 3.0 parts.

Case Study

To demonstrate the versatility and robustness of appearance sets, we show them in three different examples. First we have a handful of building templates; we instantiate them several times to create a city. Appearance sets composed of a single segmentation map allow the modification of their colors, patterns, and material properties. The buildings in Figure 1.2.3 take full advantage of appearance sets: Although a single

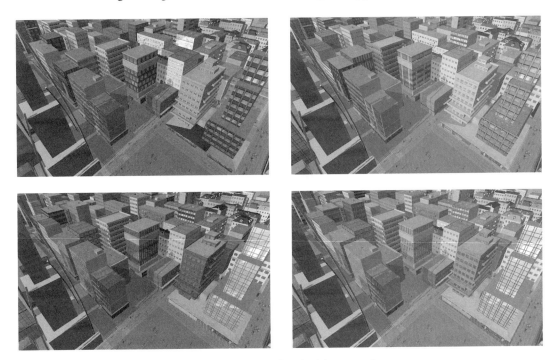

FIGURE 1.2.3 Appearance sets applied to instances of six building templates.

texture is applied to each of them, thanks to the segmentation maps it is possible to identify the windows and define particular specular and reflective parameters for them.

The second example is a crowd of virtual humans generated from a few human templates. Several appearance sets composed of two segmentation maps are defined for each human template, offering a large variety of effects as shown in Figure 1.2.4: cloth patterns, fabric shininess, make-up, and so on. In order to render crowds of characters in real time, it is common to use several levels of detail—that is, more or less costly representations depending on the distance of the character to the camera. We have been able to apply appearance sets to virtual humans represented with real-time skinned, animated skeletons, pre-computed rigid meshes, and impostors.

FIGURE 1.2.4 Appearance sets applied to instances of a single human template. Note the different specular effects on the body parts and the varying cloth patterns.

Finally, we have also used appearance sets to vary the accessories worn by the virtual humans. By accessories, we mean all kinds of small objects that can easily be attached to the character's mesh: hats, glasses, backpacks, wigs, etc. Each of them possesses at least one appearance set composed of a single segmentation map, thus allowing a large variety of colors and patterns. The result of a varied, accessorized crowd is illustrated in Figure 1.2.5, where only six human templates were instantiated.

FIGURE 1.2.5 Appearance sets composed of two segmentation maps (eight body parts) applied to instances of six human templates. Accessories are varied with appearance sets composed of one segmentation map (maximum four different parts).

In most cases, a random generation of CLUT colors provides unrealistic results. For instance, a virtual human could appear with bright red skin and green hair. Thus, we need to constrain the color space of each part to a range of believable values. There are multiple ways to do so, including the use of HSB maps [4]: for each part, we define minimum and maximum values for hue, saturation, and brightness. Colors randomly selected within theses ranges are thereby ensured to provide realistic colors.

Conclusion

In this article, we have introduced a new simple technique that obtains variety of appearance when instantiating objects multiple times. All the successive steps of this technique have been fully detailed, including a commented fragment shader implemented in GLSL. We have illustrated the use of appearance sets on several examples and demonstrated their versatility and scalability.

Acknowledgments

The authors would like to thank Barbara Yersin for technical support and reviews, Mireille Clavien for designing the characters and buildings along with their appearance sets, and Tom Forsyth for thorough proofreading.

References

Carucci, Francesco. "Inside Geometry Instancing," *GPU Gems 2*, Matt Pharr, Ed. Addison-Wesley Professional: pp. 47–67.

Gosselin, David R., Sander, Pedro V., and Mitchell, Jason L. *ShaderX3: Advanced Rendering Techniques in DirectX and OpenGL,* Wolfgang Engel, Ed. Charles River Media.

Dobbyn, Simon, Hamill, John, O'Connor, Keith, and O'Sullivan, Carol. "Geopostors: A Real-Time Geometry/Imposter Crowd Rendering System," *In proceedings of the 2005 Symposium on Interactive 3D Graphics and Games (I3D'05),* Washington, District of Columbia, April 8–11, 2005, ACM Press: pp. 95–102.

de Heras Ciechomski, Pablo, Schertenleib, Sébastien, Maïm, Jonathan, Maupu, Damien, and Thalmann, Daniel. "Real-Time Shader Rendering for Crowds in Virtual Heritage," *The Sixth International Symposium on Virtual Reality, Archaeology and Cultural Heritage (VAST'05),* Pisa, Italy, November 8–11, 2005, Eurographics Press: pp. 91–98.

1.3

Implementing Real-Time Mesh Simplification Using the GPU

Christopher DeCoro (cdecoro@cs.princeton.edu)

Game Computing Applications Group, AMD Graphics Products Group/Princeton University

Natalya Tatarchuk (natalya.tatarchuk@amd.com)

Game Computing Applications Group, AMD Graphics Products Group

Introduction

Advances in both modeling tools and data acquisition have resulted in the wide availability of massive polygonal datasets. The popularity of content authoring tools such as ZBrush® [Pixologic06] provide easy methods for creating extremely detailed art content with polygon counts in excess of several hundred million triangles. However, despite these tremendous leaps in GPU performance, interactive rendering of such massive geometry in computer games or other applications has performance implications due to the performance penalty for vertex throughput and the associated large memory storage requirements. In addition to increasing the complexity of their massive worlds, games have been employing a wider variety of lighting and shading techniques. Often, these interactive environments require multiple renderings of the same objects from different viewpoints in a single frame. The most common applications include rendering low-resolution versions of objects into a dynamic environment map for reflective or refractive effects, as well as shadow map rendering for multiple shadowing lights or cascading or omnidirectional shadow maps. Additionally, the introduction of streaming computational models such as [BFH04] enables physics computations for in-game objects directly on the GPU.

For nearly a decade, researchers and developers alike have employed mesh simplification algorithms, which, given a high-resolution target mesh, produce simplified levels of detail (LODs) that approximate the target, but with fewer triangles. Current methods for mesh simplification, such as the effective QSlim algorithm of Garland and Heckbert [GH97], are designed with the CPU architecture in mind, and to this date polygonal simplification has not been adapted for the GPU compute model.

Traditionally, mesh simplification has been a slow, CPU-limited operation performed as a pre-process on static meshes. With increasing programmability in modern graphics processors, especially with the introduction of the latest GPU pipeline with geometry shaders (such as DirectX®10), we can implement mesh simplification using the new GPU compute model. In this article, we describe how the Lindstrom's vertex clustering method for mesh simplification can be directly adapted to the novel GPU computational pipeline, enabling real-time simplification of triangle meshes over an order of magnitude faster than an equivalent CPU implementation, but without any relative loss in quality [Lindstrom00] (see Figure 1.3.1).

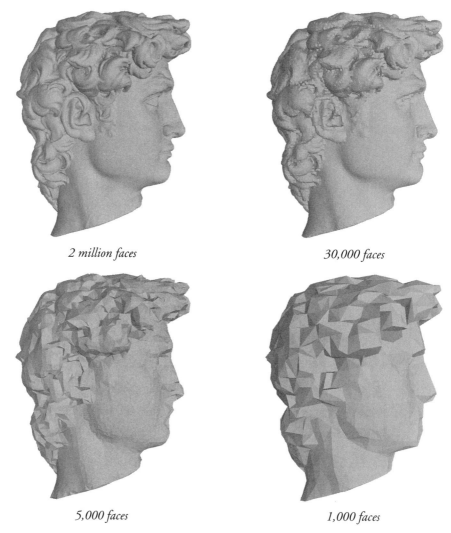

2 million faces   *30,000 faces*

5,000 faces   *1,000 faces*

FIGURE 1.3.1 Using our GPU-based mesh decimation algorithm, we are able to generate all of these levels of detail for this high-resolution model of David's head an order of magnitude faster than producing even a single simplified level of detail on the CPU.

Background: Mesh Simplification

A wide range of algorithms has been presented to decimate a triangle mesh—that is, given an input mesh containing some number of triangles, produce a mesh with fewer triangles that well-approximates the original. Some of the earliest algorithms fall under the classification of *vertex clustering*. In these, the bounding box of the mesh is divided into a grid (in the simplest case, a lattice of cubes), and all of the vertices in a given cell are replaced with a single representative vertex ("clustered"). Faces that become degenerate are removed from the resulting simplified mesh. Vertex clustering approaches can be used for a variety of other applications aside from mesh simplification.

Later work found that mesh quality could be improved with an iterative approach in which a series of primitive simplification operations are applied to an input mesh through intermediate simplification stages, usually chosen so as to minimize the incremental error incurred by the operation. Perhaps one of the most commonly applied iterative decimation techniques is the QSlim algorithm [GH97]. This algorithm iteratively applies the *pair collapse* operator, which replaces two vertices with one, causing neighboring faces to become degenerate. In order to select a collapsed pair of vertices from the potential candidates, QSlim defines the quadric error metric, which for a vertex v is defined as the point-plane distance from v to a set of associated planes (initially, the planes of the adjacent triangles):

$$f(v) = \sum_{p \in planes(v)} \left(p^T v\right)^2 \qquad = v^T \left(\sum_{p \in planes(v)} p^T p \right) v \qquad = v^T Q_v v$$

$$\qquad\quad 1 \qquad\qquad\qquad\qquad\qquad 2 \qquad\qquad\qquad\quad 3$$

Importantly, given this error formulation, it is possible to directly compute the vertex position that minimizes the error. The consequence is that with the same number of vertices, placing the vertices optimally we achieve a simplified result that better approximates the original. We accomplish this efficiently by solving the linear system given by the Q_v matrix.

Subsequent work by Lindstrom showed that many of the quality benefits of QSlim could be achieved in the context of vertex clustering [L00]. Notice that the vertex clustering operation is equivalent to performing the pair collapse operation of QSlim to each vertex in a cluster simultaneously. Thus, the quadric error metric can be used as a measure of mesh quality for such algorithms and, more importantly, can be used to directly compute the representative vertex of a cluster that minimizes the quadric error. This can be used to generate higher quality results than previously shown in a vertex clustering framework. The algorithm is as follows:

For each triangle F,

　　1. Compute the face quadric Q_F

2. For each vertex

$$v \in F$$

(a) Compute the cluster C containing v
(b) Add Q_F to the cluster quadric Q_C
3. If F will be non-degenerate, output F

The algorithm acts on each face independently and stores only the cluster grid as a representation of the intermediate mesh. Importantly, each vertex will access a single location in the grid. This locality and data-independence allows the algorithm to be efficient in the context of out-of-core simplification (for which it was originally presented). For the same reasons, such algorithms are also ideal for the stream computing architecture of the GPU, and our work implements this approach.

GPU Programmable Pipeline

The programmable vertex and pixel engines found in recent GPUs execute shader programs that contain arithmetic and texturing computations in parallel. The *vertex shader* is traditionally used to perform vertex transformations along with per-vertex computations. Once the rasterizer has converted the transformed primitives to pixels, the *pixel shader* can compute each fragment's color.

This pipeline was further extended in DirectX10 hardware such as the ATI Radeon HD 2000 generation, introducing an additional programmable *geometry shader* stage. This stage accepts vertices generated by the vertex shader as input and, unlike the previous stage, has access to the entire primitive information as well as its adjacency information. This enables the per-face computation of face quadrics required by the vertex clustering algorithm.

The geometry shader also has the ability to cull input triangles from the rendering stream and prevent their rasterization, clearly a necessary component for mesh decimation. Finally, the DirectX10 *stream-out* option allows reuse of the result of geometry processing by storing output triangles in a GPU buffer. This buffer may be reused arbitrarily in later rendering stages, or even read back to the host CPU. Our method implements the simplification algorithm taking advantage of the novel geometry shader stage functionality for computation of the quadric map for each face, and using the stream-out feature for storing and later rendering the simplified geometry.

Algorithm

We will first present the basic structure of our GPU simplification system. Our algorithm proceeds in three passes and requires the input mesh to be submitted twice through the rendering pipeline. We encode the mapping from cluster-cell index to cluster quadric in a render target (an off-screen buffer) used as a large two-dimensional array, which we will refer to as the *cluster-quadric map*. The quadric accumulation operation (Equation 2) can be mapped to the highly efficient additive blend.

Because the algorithm accesses each mesh triangle only once per pass, it is not necessary to store the entire input mesh in GPU-resident memory (the storage requirements are a function of the output mesh size only), which allows our algorithm to efficiently process meshes of arbitrary size. The passes are as follows, and are illustrated in Figure 1.3.2.

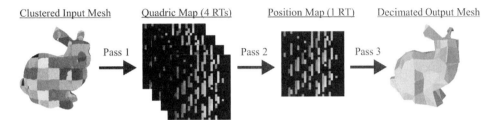

Clustered Input Mesh   Quadric Map (4 RTs)   Position Map (1 RT)   Decimated Output Mesh

Pass 1   Pass 2   Pass 3

FIGURE 1.3.2 GPU simplification pipeline. The original mesh (left) is subdivided into clusters according to a 9×9×9 grid. In Pass 1, we compute the cluster quadrics for each grid cell; the output (shown) is a set of render targets that contain the quadrics in the pixel values. Pass 2 minimizes the quadric error function to compute the optimal representative positions for each cluster. Finally, Pass 3 uses this to output the final, decimated mesh.

Pass 1: Cluster-Quadric Map Generation

Given the source mesh and its bounding box as input, as well as a user-specified number of subdivisions along each dimension, we render the input mesh as points. We then assign a unique ID to each cluster cell, and we treat the render target as a large array that is indexed by cluster ID. Each array location stores the current sum of the error quadric for that cell (10 floats for the 4×4 symmetric matrix), the average vertex position within that cell (three floats), and the vertex count.

The vertex shader computes the corresponding cluster for each vertex and its implied position in the render target (Listing 1.3.1). The geometry shader, which has access to all vertices in the triangle, uses the world positions to compute the face quadric for the triangle and assigns that value to each output vertex to be accumulated in the texture map by the pixel shader, which simply propagates the computed colors with additive blending enabled.

Listing 1.3.1 Cluster-quadric map generation shader

```
float3 Expand( float3 vX )
{
   return 2 * vX - 1;
}

//Map a point to its location (address) in the cluster map array
float2 WriteClusterMapAddress( float3 vPos )
```

```
{
  uint iX = clusterId(vPos) / iClusterMapSize.x;
  uint iY = clusterId(vPos) % iClusterMapSize.y;
  return Expand( float2(iX, iY)/float(iClusterMapSize.x) ) +
1.0/iClusterMapSize.x;
}

// Computes outer product of the arguments
float3x3 outer( float3 vA, float3 vB )
{
  float3x3 mOutput = { vA.x * vB.x, vA.x * vB.y, vA.x * vB.z,
                       vA.y * vB.x, vA.y * vB.y, vA.y * vB.z,
                       vA.z * vB.x, vA.z * vB.y, vA.z * vB.z };
  return mOutput;
}

// Given a quadric in (A,b,c) form, packs it into a FragmentData
structure
// suitable for output to the PS for rendering
void PackQuadric( float3x3 qA, float3 qb, float qc, inout FragmentData
output )
{
  // Output the components of the quadric to the fragment shader
  // A = [ 0  1  2  ]              11 elements for quadric, 1 for
count
  //     [    4  5  ]
  //     [       8  ]
  output.quadricA0 = float4( qA[0][0], qA[0][1], qA[0][2], qA[1][1]
);
  output.quadricA1 = float2( qA[1][2], qA[2][2] );
  output.quadricB = qb;
  output.quadricC = qc;
}

// Geometry shader code; vertex shaders and pixel shaders pass data
as-is
[maxvertexcount(3)]
void GSMain( triangle ClipVertex input[3], inout
PointStream<FragmentData> stream )
{
  //For the current triangle, compute the area and normal
  float3 vNormal = (cross( input[1].vWorldPos - input[0].vWorldPos,
                           input[2].vWorldPos - input[0].vWorldPos ));
  float fArea = length( vNormal ) / 6;
  vNormal = normalize( vNormal );

  //Then compute the distance of plane to the origin along the normal
  float fDist = -dot( vNormal, input[0].vWorldPos );

  // Compute the components of the face quadrics using the plane
coefficients
  float3x3 qA = fArea * outer( vNormal, vNormal);
  float3   qb = fArea * vNormal * fDist;
  float    qc = fArea * fDist * fDist;
```

```
            //Loop over each vertex in input triangle primitive
            for( int i = 0; i < 3; i++ )
            {
               //Assign the output position in the quadric map
               FragmentData output;
               output.vPos = float4( WriteClusterMapAddress( input[i].vPos ),
      0, 1 );

               //Write the quadric to be accumulated in the quadric map
               PackQuadric( qA, qb, qc, output );
               stream.Append( output );
            }
        }      // End of void main(..)
```

Pass 2: Computation of Optimal Representative Positions

Using the cluster-quadric map from Pass 1, we compute the optimal representative vertex position for each cluster. Note that we could do this on the next pass (generation of the decimated mesh) but we choose to do this in a separate pass so that the relatively expensive computation can be performed exactly once per cluster with higher parallelism. Note the improvement in mesh quality shown in the following example: Compared to the original on the left, when using the average of the vertices in a cluster as the representative vertex significant details are lost. By contrast, the optimally placed vertices preserve much of the detail, especially the shape of the front ear and the curvature of the leg. Examples like this demonstrate the utility and importance of optimal vertex placement (Figure 1.3.3).

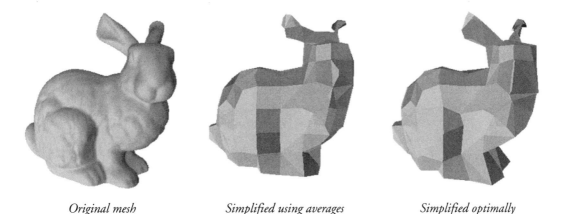

Original mesh   *Simplified using averages*   *Simplified optimally*

FIGURE 1.3.3 Simplification quality comparisons using average positions versus computing optimal positions.

We render a single full-screen quad the size of the cluster map render targets into another render target of equal size. In the pixel shader, we retrieve the values of the error quadric from the render target textures, and compute the optimal position by solving the quadric error equation with a matrix inversion [GH97]. If the matrix determinant is below a user-specified threshold (currently $1e^{-10}$), we assume that the quadric is singular and fall back to using the average vertex position. The position is saved into a render target and used in the next pass. Listing 1.3.2 demonstrates the code used to execute this pass.

Listing 1.3.2 A method to compute the optimal vertex position

```
// Computes the inverse of the symmetric matrix A
float3x3 SymInv( float3x3 A )
{
   float a11=A[0][0], a12=A[0][1], a13=A[0][2], a22=A[1][1],
a23=A[1][2], a33=A[2][2];

   float inv11 =  a22 * a33 - a23 * a23;
   float inv12 = -a12 * a33 + a13 * a23;
   float inv13 =  a12 * a23 - a13 * a22;
   float inv22 =  a11 * a33 - a13 * a13;
   float inv23 = -a11 * a23 + a12 * a13;
   float inv33 =  a11 * a22 - a12 * a12;

   float detA = a11*inv11 + a12*inv12 + a13*inv13;

   float3x3 Ainv = { inv11, inv12, inv13,
                     inv12, inv22, inv23,
                     inv13, inv23, inv33 };
   return Ainv / detA;
}

// Pixel shader: input from the application is a full screen quad with
[0,1] texcoords
float3 PSMain( float2 vTexcoord ) : COLOR0
{
   float3 vPos = float3( 0, 0, 0 );
   float4 mDataWorld, mDataA0, mDataB, mDataA1;

   // Read the vertex average from the cluster map:
   mDataWorld = tClusterMap0.SampleLevel( sClusterMap0, vTexcoord, 0
);
   int iCount = mDataWorld.w;

   // Only compute optimal position if there are vertices in this
cluster
   if ( iCount != 0 )
   {
      // Read all the data from the clustermap to reconstruct the
quadric
      mDataA0 = tClusterMap1.SampleLevel( sClusterMap1, vTexcoord, 0
);
      mDataA1 = tClusterMap2.SampleLevel( sClusterMap2, vTexcoord, 0
);
      mDataB  = tClusterMap3.SampleLevel( sClusterMap3, vTexcoord, 0 );
```

```
/ /Then re-assemble the quadric
float3x3 qA = { mDataA0.x, mDataA0.y, mDataA0.z,
                mDataA0.y, mDataA0.w, mDataA1.x,
                mDataA0.z, mDataA1.x, mDataA1.y   };
float3 qB = mDataB.xyz;
float  qC = mDataA1.z;

// Determine if inverting A is stable, if so, compute optimal
position
// If not, default to using the average position
const float SINGULAR_THRESHOLD = 1e-11;
if ( determinant( quadricA ) > SINGULAR_THRESHOLD )
   vPos = -mul( SymInv ( quadricA ), quadricB );
else
   vPos = mDataWorld.xyz / mDataWorld.w;
}

return vPos;
```

Pass 3: Decimated Mesh Generation

We send the original mesh through the pipeline a second time in order to remap vertices to their simplified positions and cull those triangles that become degenerate. The vertex shader again computes the corresponding cluster for each vertex, and the geometry shader determines if the three vertices are in different clusters, culling the triangle if they are not. Otherwise, the geometry shader retrieves the simplified positions from the output of Pass 2 and uses them as the target positions of the new triangle, which are streamed out to a GPU buffer for later use.

Multiple Levels of Detail

We can compute multiple levels of detail for the same mesh without repeating all three passes. When the resolution of the sampling grid is reduced by half, we can omit Pass 1 and instead create the quadric cluster map by appropriate downsampling of the higher-resolution quadric cluster map. Pass 2 operates as before; however, Pass 3 can use the previously simplified mesh as its input (rather than the full resolution input mesh) because the connectivity will be the same. This allows the construction of a sequence of LODs significantly faster than incurring the full simplification cost for each LOD independently.

Results and Applications

The most significant contribution of our system, as opposed to in-memory, CPU-based simplification, is the dramatic increase in speed. We show the timing results on a set of input meshes for both the CPU and GPU implementations of the algorithm in Table 1.3.1. Results are shown for a PC with dual Intel Pentium®4 CPUs (3.20GHz), 1 GB of RAM, and ATI Radeon HD 2600, collected on Windows Vista®. Note that the CPU implementation was implemented in an efficient manner for optimal performance. The results show that the GPU implementation is able to produce simplification rates of nearly 6 million triangles per second, as compared to a throughput of 300 K triangles per second on the CPU.

Table 1.3.1 Performance results for GPU real-time mesh simplification versus CPU mesh simplification.

Model	Faces	CPU	GPU	CPU:GPU
Bunny	70 K	0.2 s	0.013 s	15:1
Armadillo	345 K	1.2 s	0.055 s	22:1
Dragon	879 K	1.9 s	0.117 s	16:1
Buddha	1 M	2.5 s	0.146 s	17:1
David (head)	2 M	6.8 s	0.322 s	21:1
Atlas	4.5 M	14.8 s	0.741 s	20:1
St. Matthew	7.4 M	24.6 s	1.18 s	21:1

Note that all but the largest results on the GPU were rendered at highly interactive real-time rates, achieving a simplification throughput of nearly 6M faces/second.

We can achieve even faster speeds (per simplified mesh) when creating multiple LODs. We have also found that the most significant overhead in the simplification process is Pass 1, which tends to take 60% to 75% of the total simplification time. Once the cluster map has been created, we have observed that the generation of a new mesh skips this amount of time overhead by simply combining multiple quadrics in Pass 2.

Conclusion

We have presented a method for mesh simplification on the novel GPU programmable pipeline and demonstrated how mesh decimation becomes practical for real-time use through our approach by adapting the vertex clustering method to the GPU. Our approach can be used to simplify animated or dynamically (procedurally) generated geometry directly on the GPU or as a load-time algorithm, in which geometry is reduced to a level of detail suitable for display on the current user's hardware at the start of the program or change in scene. Simplified meshes can be used for collision detection and other purposes. Additionally, our technology allows an artist to rapidly create multiple levels of detail and quickly select those appropriate for the application. For interested readers, we refer them to [DT07] for further exploration of adaptive simplification for view-dependent simplification, user-directed decimation (artist-controlled regions are preserved), or for intrinsic adaptive simplification preserving the regions of models that inherently contain higher detail content. We also know that the vertex clustering set of techniques does not preserve parameterization, so future work is needed in that direction.

Acknowledgments

We would like to thank the Stanford Computer Graphics Lab for providing geometry data, including models from the Digital Michelangelo project.

References

[BFH04] Buck, I., Foley, T., Horn, D., Sugerman, J., Fatahalian, K., Houston, M., and Hanrahan, P. 2004. *Brook for GPUs: stream computing on graphics hardware.* ACM Trans. Graph. 23, 3, pages 777–786.

[DT07] DeCoro, C. and Tatarchuk, N. "Real-time Mesh Simplification on the GPU." *Proceedings of the ACM/SIGGRAPH Symposium on Interactive 3D Graphics and Games*, 2007.

[GH97] Garland, M., and Heckbert, P. S. 1997. "Surface simplification using quadric error metrics." *Proceedings of ACM SIGGRAPH 1997*, pp. 209–216.

[Lindstrom00] Lindstrom, P. 2000. "Out-of-core simplification of large polygonal models." *In SIGGRAPH 2000, Computer Graphics Proceedings*, ACM Press/ACM SIGGRAPH/Addison Wesley Longman, K. Akeley, Ed., pp. 259–262.

[Pixologic06] Pixologic, 2006. Zbrush™. Can be found online at http://www.pixologic.com/zbrush/home/home.php.

[SM05] Sander, P. V., and Mitchell, J. L. 2005. "Progressive Buffers: View-dependent geometry and texture for LOD rendering." *In Symposium on Geometry Processing*, pp. 129–138.

RENDERING TECHNIQUES

Introduction

Kenneth Hurley

It was a pleasure editing the "Rendering Techniques" section for the second time in the *ShaderX* series. There are two articles that are similar with respect to uniformly sampling cubemaps, but I thought the techniques were different enough to include the additional article in this section. Working with these authors has been fun and I'm looking forward to the next installment in the *ShaderX* series.

The nine articles are entitled "Care and Feeding of Normal Vectors," "Computing Per-Pixel Object Thickness in a Single Render Pass," "Filtered Tilemaps," "Parallax Occlusion Mapping Special Feature Rendering," "Isocube: A Cubemap with Uniformly Distributed and Equally Important Texels," "Uniform Cubemaps for Dynamic Environments," "Practical Geometry Clipmaps for Rendering Terrains in Computer Games," "Quantized Ring Clipping," and "Efficient and Practical Tile-Trees."

The article "Care and Feeding of Normal Vectors" delves into normal vector techniques and how to correctly combine them for the best visuals. The author, Jörn, shows you the math behind blending of normals and demonstrates how to do it correctly. He also discusses the pitfalls that some programmers face when dealing with dynamic normal maps.

The article entitled "Computing Per-Pixel Object Thickness in a Single Render Pass" was written in part by Christopher Oat, a long-time contributor to articles on vertex and pixel shader techniques. His technique can be used for many applications. One such application is self-shadowing of hair, and his screen shots presented here are impressive. This is definitely a must-read article.

"Filtered Tilemaps" outlines a great technique to improve the visual quality of tiled texture maps, and it is especially useful for terrains in which the textures are tiled to reduce the memory footprint of the terrain. This article goes into great depth about the technique and how to raise the quality of filtering of the tilemaps.

Parallax occlusion mapping is a technique that enables better looking depth cues from flat geometry. The article "Parallax Occlusion Mapping Special Feature Rendering" expands on this technique to allow constant coloring of silhouette edges.

Uniformly sampling cubemaps is a topic that is being widely discussed this year. We included two articles on the subject here as each article has its own merits with respect to the techniques presented. "Isocube: A Cubemap with Uniformly Distributed and Equally Important Texels" and "Uniform Cubemaps for Dynamic Environments" are both presented in this section so that you can choose the technique that is best suited for your applications.

"Practical Geometry Clipmaps for Rendering Terrains in Computer Games" is a fantastic technique that takes into consideration the real-time nature of games. There are several very good solutions provided here that allow the use of clipmaps for terrains in games at reasonable frame rates. I found this article especially useful because the author geared it toward video games.

"Quantized Ring Clipping" further helps clipmaps to get large terrains rendering in real-time with clipping techniques. It was based on the traditional geometry clipmap techniques, but reduces GPU bottlenecks and memory consumption with a revolutionary technique. It allows for unlimited terrain size and it is amazing what can be rendered with 1 MB of main memory and 29 MB of video memory.

"Efficient and Practical TileTrees" is brought to us by the people at INRIA. Carsten and Sylvain have some great techniques using what are called *TileTrees*. The application of this technique is especially suitable for 3D painting. The article also discusses another possible application in that the technique might also be a way to store a compact parameterization of a mesh for texture mapping.

One final note: Signature Devices, Inc. will be releasing a free open source engine on svn.phatyaffle.com that can be used for commercial and non-commercial purposes. The engine should be ready around the time this *ShaderX6* book is published and we encourage all *ShaderX* writers to use the engine for the next release of *ShaderX*. It is much more than just a 3D graphics engine, as it has all the components to write video games, 3D rendering, a Shader system, an animation system, A.I. through hierarchical state machines and LUA scripting, a 3D Sound System, an Ageia PhysX system, a WYSIWYG editor, and more. We hope that this will allow future books on shaders to show practical examples of working in a video game environment.

Care and Feeding of Normal Vectors

Jörn Loviscach (jlovisca@informatik.hs-bremen.de)

Hochschule Bremen

University of Applied Sciences

Introduction

Normal maps are omnipresent in today's games to provide surfaces with detailed bumps without increasing the polygon count. It would be nice to be able to modify normal maps on the GPU to allow more choices and more variations without sacrificing memory; the normal maps can even be altered in real time. This chapter introduces a range of efficient shader techniques to process and combine normal maps with geometrically correct results. In particular, it addresses how to scale, add, and blend normals, how to modulate normal maps, how to apply gradation curves to normal maps like those shown in Figure 2.1.1, and how to deform the *uv* coordinate space of normal maps.

For decades, photographs and other bitmap images have been routinely subjected to operations such as gradation curves and spatial distortion. However, it is not obvious how one can alter normal maps using similar image manipulation operations so

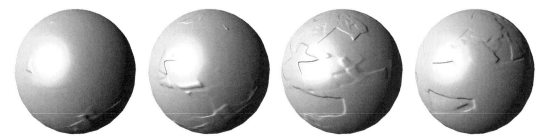

FIGURE 2.1.1 Image manipulation methods can be applied to normal maps. In this example, different height levels of a relief map are emphasized in real time.

that the normals still make sense in terms of geometry. If applied naively, most operations on a normal map contained in an RGB image will yield incorrect results. The "correct" approach is only slightly more costly in terms of computational power, but it requires us to go back to the source of a normal map, which is the height field from which it was generated.

Math of Normal Maps

Usually, a normal map is formed by computing a relief of a height field (bump map) over a flat surface. If $h(u,v)$ is the bump map's height at the texture coordinates (u,v), the standard definition of the normal map is

$$\mathbf{m}_h(u,v) = \text{normalize} \begin{bmatrix} -\partial h/\partial u \\ -\partial h/\partial v \\ 1 \end{bmatrix}.$$

1

Whereas the behavior of the normal map is not always easy to understand, operations on the corresponding height field are simple to understand, which leads to the basic idea of this article: to determine what happens to the normals when an image manipulation operation is applied to the height field. A major component for doing so is to recover the height field's partial derivatives from the normal map through

$$\begin{bmatrix} -\partial h/\partial u \\ -\partial h/\partial v \\ 1 \end{bmatrix} = \frac{\mathbf{m}_h(u,v)}{m_h(u,v)_z},$$

2

where $m(u,v)_z$ denotes the normal map's z component. Note that this value, which appears in the denominator, may in theory get arbitrarily close to zero, but this would signify an infinitely steep surface, which should be avoided with bump mapping.

Equations 1 and 2 represent an ideal view, even though, as the examples will show, this does not seriously limit their use in practice. First, the derivatives do not make sense since we are dealing with bitmaps. Thus, one may use the following computation:

$$\mathbf{m}_h(u,v) = \text{normalize} \begin{bmatrix} h(u-\Delta u,v) - h(u+\Delta u,v) \\ h(u,v-\Delta v) - h(u,v+\Delta v) \\ 2 \end{bmatrix}.$$

Second, typical normal maps are not stored as arrays of floating-point numbers but as 24-bit RGB images. Each of the three components falls into the floating-point range [–1,1], which is mapped onto the discrete set of numbers {0,1,2…,255} for storage. This mapping incurs a loss in accuracy and can only be approximately fixed in the shader.

The normal map's entry $\mathbf{m}(u,v)$ refers to a vector in a local coordinate frame that is tangent to the mesh at the point corresponding to the texture coordinates (u,v). However, the light direction and the view position are given in world space. To carry out correct lighting computations, $\mathbf{m}(u,v)$ needs to be converted to world space. The typical solution is to attach three perpendicular unit vectors $\mathbf{t}$ (tangent), $\mathbf{b}$ (binormal), and $\mathbf{n}$ to each vertex, where $\mathbf{n}$ is the standard, undistorted normal. These are interpolated on their way from the vertex to the pixel shader. Typically, the normal map of Equation 1 is used to compute a bumped normal vector in world space.

$$\mathbf{n}_h(u,v) = m_x(u,v)\,\mathbf{t} + m_y(u,v)\,\mathbf{b} + m_z(u,v)\,\mathbf{n}$$

3

This suffices for most cases, though it is only seldom geometrically correct, as will be discussed later in the section "Geometrically Precise Mapping."

Although the approach to compute a normal vector in a local frame is common, it is by no means the only viable solution. For instance, one may store precomputed lighting components of three spatial directions instead of the deformed normal vector's components. This can be used to encode radiosity-style effects for diffuse surface materials [Green07].

Operations on Normal Maps

We want to use a standard normal map, employ Equation 2 to partially uncover the derivatives of the height field, and then express the results of a range of standard image manipulation operations on the height field through the normal map. Examples are included on the DVD as projects for NVIDIA FX Composer 2.0.

Scaling, Adding, Blending

These seemingly simple operations provide a straightforward example of how the naive approach fails. The obvious method to scale a normal map by a factor α is through blending it with an undeformed, flat normal:

$$\mathbf{n}_{new} = \text{normalize}(\alpha\mathbf{n}_{map} + (1-\alpha)\mathbf{n}_{flat})$$

If you use $\alpha=-1$ hoping to create an inverted bump, you will turn an $\mathbf{n}_{map}$ that's nearly perpendicular to $\mathbf{n}_{flat}$ into an $\mathbf{n}_{new}$ that only forms an angle of about 30° with $\mathbf{n}_{flat}$, thus creating a substantially shallower bump. If you set $\alpha=2$ hoping to double the amount of bump, you may end up with a normal vector $\mathbf{n}_{new}$ that points to the inside of the surface, as you can see in Figure 2.1.2.

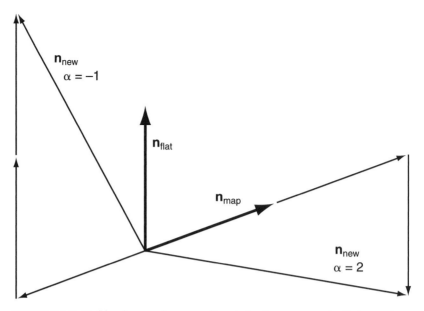

FIGURE 2.1.2 To blend normal vectors directly leads to geometrically inconsistent results.

Even though the normals as such should not be blended, the height field can be. To replace $h(u,v)$ with $\alpha h(u,v)$ makes perfect sense for all values of α, including $\alpha=-1$ and $\alpha=2$. Thus, the normal map should be equal to

$$\mathbf{m}_{\alpha h}(x, y) = \text{normalize}\begin{bmatrix} -\alpha \partial h / \partial u \\ -\alpha \partial h / \partial v \\ 1 \end{bmatrix}.$$

The derivatives of $h(u,v)$ can be determined from Equation 2, which leads to

$$\mathbf{m}_{\alpha h}(u, v) = \text{normalize}\begin{bmatrix} \alpha m_h(u,v)_x / m_h(u,v)_z \\ \alpha m_h(u,v)_y / m_h(u,v)_z \\ 1 \end{bmatrix} = \text{normalize}\begin{bmatrix} \alpha m_h(u,v)_x \\ \alpha m_h(u,v)_y \\ m_h(u,v)_z \end{bmatrix}.$$

This result for scaling a normal map can easily be generalized. If two normal maps are to be blended with respective weights α and β, a geometrically correct solution is to blend their height fields to form $\alpha h(u,v)+\beta g(u,v)$. The normal vector belonging to this blended height field is

$$\mathbf{m}_{\alpha h + \beta g}(u, v) = \text{normalize}\begin{bmatrix} \alpha m_h(u,v)_x / m_h(u,v)_z + \beta m_g(u,v)_x / m_g(u,v)_z \\ \alpha m_h(u,v)_y / m_h(u,v)_z + \beta m_g(u,v)_y / m_g(u,v)_z \\ 1 \end{bmatrix}.$$

Modulation

Modulation uses two normal maps. Again, this is easier to manage using the height fields. Where both height fields have peaks, the result should also have a peak. Where one of the height fields is zero, the result should also be zero, independent of the other height field (see Figure 2.1.3). Clearly the height fields are multiplied to form a combined height field $h(u,v)g(u,v)$.

FIGURE 2.1.3 To modulate two normal maps (left and middle columns), their corresponding height fields are multiplied (right column).

To determine the normal vector of this height field according to Equation 1, one needs the partial derivatives of $h(u,v)g(u,v)$. This is a simple application of the product rule:

$$\frac{\partial h(u,v)g(u,v)}{\partial u} = \frac{\partial h(u,v)}{\partial u}g(u,v) + h(u,v)\frac{\partial g(u,v)}{\partial u}$$

and similarly for the partial derivative with respect to v. Thus,

$$\mathbf{m}_{hg}(u,v) = \text{normalize}\begin{bmatrix} -\partial h/\partial u \ g - h \ \partial g/\partial u \\ -\partial h/\partial v \ g - h \ \partial g/\partial v \\ 1 \end{bmatrix}.$$

The partial derivatives of the single height fields can be found from Equation 2. In addition, however, we need the values of the height fields as is. The simple solution to this problem is to store the height field as an additional, fourth channel of the normal map. This way we are working with a combination of a normal map and a bump map. Software to create these textures is provided on the accompanying DVD, and you can refer to the section "Generating Bump and Normal Maps" later in this article.

Gradation Curves

In standard image manipulation software, a gradation curve is a function f that is applied to the color components of every pixel. A gradation curve can, for instance, steepen the response to dark tones in order to bring out color details in the shadows. In a similar fashion, a function may be applied to a height field to form $f(h(u,v))$ (see Figure 2.1.4).

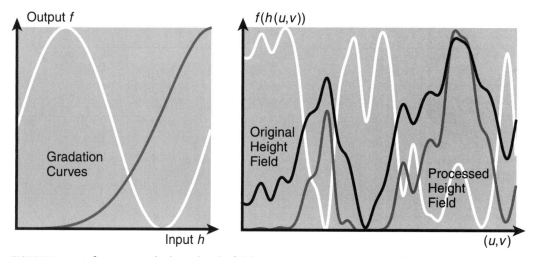

FIGURE 2.1.4 A function applied to a height field may emphasize certain levels (gray curve) or dramatically alter the shape (white curve).

This can be carried over to normal vectors with help of the Chain Rule:

$$\mathbf{m}_{foh}(u,v) = \text{normalize} \begin{bmatrix} -\partial f\left(h(u,v)\right)/\partial u \\ -\partial f\left(h(u,v)\right)/\partial v \\ 1 \end{bmatrix}$$

$$= \text{normalize} \begin{bmatrix} -f'\left(h(u,v)\right)\partial h(u,v)/\partial u \\ -f'\left(h(u,v)\right)\partial h(u,v)/\partial v \\ 1 \end{bmatrix} = \text{normalize} \begin{bmatrix} f'\left(h(u,v)\right)m_h(u,v)_x \\ f'\left(h(u,v)\right)m_h(u,v)_y \\ m_h(u,v)_z \end{bmatrix}.$$

This means that all we need of the gradation curve is its derivative f'. We do not have to bother with determining f itself. For the height values where the derivative f' is large, the bumps of the surface will be emphasized.

To boost the bumps around a fixed height level $H \in [0,1]$, for example, one can use

$$f'\big(h(u,v)\big) = \frac{1}{1 + P \cdot \big(h(u,v) - H\big)^2}$$

$$4$$

The factor P in the denominator controls the peaking of the filter—that is, how narrow the range of height values is that are boosted (see Figure 2.1.5).

FIGURE 2.1.5 The parameter P of Equation 4 allows boosting narrow or wide ranges of levels from a normal map (from left to right: $P = 0$, H = arbitrary; $P = 200$, $H = 0.2$; $P = 200$, $H = 0.6$; $P = 1,000$, $H = 0.5$).

Deformation

A standard color texture map $c(u,v)$ can easily be swirled or twisted around on an object by computing the texture coordinates from two other functions via $c(s(u,v), t(u,v))$. For instance, the texture pattern may be repeated three times along the first texture coordinate and may oscillate in the second by using $c(3u, \sin(10\pi v))$.

Normal maps, however, cannot simply be deformed using these deformation functions if the results are to look correct (see Figure 2.1.6). Care must be taken with respect to the movement of the normals that is caused by the point-to-point variation of the deformation. This boils down to yet another application of the Chain Rule:

$$\mathbf{m}_{h(s,t)}(u,v) = \text{normalize} \begin{bmatrix} -\partial h(s(u,u), t(u,v))/\partial u \\ -\partial h(s(u,v), t(u,v))/\partial v \\ 1 \end{bmatrix}$$

$$= \text{normalize} \begin{bmatrix} -\partial h(s,t)/\partial s \cdot \partial s/\partial u - \partial h(s,t)/\partial t \cdot \partial t/\partial u \\ -\partial h(s,t)/\partial s \cdot \partial s/\partial v - \partial h(s,t)/\partial t \cdot \partial t/\partial v \\ 1 \end{bmatrix}.$$

FIGURE 2.1.6 A normal map cannot be deformed by changing the texture coordinates alone (left); it requires an adjustment for the lateral changes introduced by the deformation (right).

As an example, consider $s(u,v)=u+C\sin(4\pi v)$ and $t(u,v)=v$. This deformation shifts the first texture coordinate forward or backward in an oscillatory pattern that depends on the second texture coordinate, as shown in Figure 2.1.6. The value of C controls the amount of oscillation (which is, by the way, fun to see animated). For this deformation we find

$$\mathbf{m}_{h(s,t)}(u,v) = \text{normalize}\begin{bmatrix} -\partial h(s,t)/\partial s \\ -\partial h(s,t)/\partial s \cdot 4\pi C\cos(4\pi v) - \partial h(s,t)/\partial t \\ 1 \end{bmatrix}$$

which with the help of Equation 2 becomes

$$\mathbf{m}_{h(s,t)}(u,v) = \text{normalize}\begin{bmatrix} m_h(s,t)_x \\ m_h(s,t)_x \cdot 4\pi C\cos(4\pi v) + m_h(s,t)_y \\ m_h(s,t)_z \end{bmatrix}$$

This expression can be computed from the original normal map alone with no direct reference to the height field.

Generating Bump and Normal Maps

On the DVD you will find a program to create corresponding four-channel DDS texture files. It takes as input a bitmap image containing a height field (bump map), computes the normal map by taking the pixel-wise differences, and creates a full set of MIP levels for both the bump map and the normal map. The software has been developed using Microsoft XNA Game Studio Express 1.0 Refresh and requires the corresponding XNA framework to run.

If the slopes of the height field are too gradual, the normals cluster along the z-axis. If the slopes are too steep, the normals end up almost in the xy plane. In both situations, resolution is lost. To overcome this limitation, the included software allows scaling the derivatives before the normalization of Equation 1 is applied. This allows us to more uniformly use eight-bit ranges for the normal map. To correctly combine different normals of the generated DDS files using modulation, both need to be generated with the same scaling factor.

Bundling the height data with the normal map comes at a price—an increase in memory consumption of 33 percent. In addition, texture compression schemes specialized on normal maps may not work with the fourth channel present. Another option would be to abandon the standard normal map and to store the three values $(\delta h/\delta x, \delta h/\delta y, h)$ per pixel. This also saves the division by the z component in Equation 2. However, the values of the partial derivatives soar as the surface gets steeper. This uneven distribution of the values is not easy to handle with a resolution of eight bits. Using a floating-point texture format is better suited in this case, but this incurs huge costs in memory and access times. On some hardware and with some floating-point texture formats, MIPmapping may not even be supported.

More Details in Dealing with Normals

Even though bump mapping is one of oldest techniques in computer graphics [Blinn78], many issues have been overlooked for a long time or have been discarded due to a lack of computing power. In this section, we address some of these issues.

Geometrically Precise Mapping

Usually we apply a normal map to the local frame through Equation 3. This computation rarely is geometrically precise. Following the derivation of bump mapping, let the texture coordinates (u,v) correspond to a point $\mathbf{p}(u,v)$ in space. Let $\mathbf{n}(u,v)$ be the unit normal vector of the surface at this point. We then can displace the surface by a height field by calculating a different position $\mathbf{d}(u,v) = \mathbf{p}(u,v) + h(u,v)\mathbf{n}(u,v)$. A geometrically correct normal map should return the normal to this deformed surface, which is

$$\mathbf{n}_h(u,v) = \text{normalize}\left(\frac{\partial \mathbf{p}(u,v) + h(u,v)\,\mathbf{n}(u,v)}{\partial u} \times \frac{\partial \mathbf{p}(u,v) + h(u,v)\,\mathbf{n}(u,v)}{\partial v}\right)$$

This requires that the u coordinate direction is always to the right from the v direction when one looks from the outside of the object. Otherwise, the resulting vector has to be flipped.

If one assumes that the height itself, in contrast to its derivatives, is negligible, the former expression reduces to [Blinn78]

$$\mathbf{n}_h(u,v) = \text{normalize}\left(\frac{\partial h}{\partial u}\mathbf{n}(u,v) \times \frac{\partial \mathbf{p}(u,v)}{\partial v} + \frac{\partial h}{\partial v}\frac{\partial \mathbf{p}(u,v)}{\partial u} \times \mathbf{n}(u,v) + \frac{\partial \mathbf{p}(u,v)}{\partial u} \times \frac{\partial \mathbf{p}(u,v)}{\partial v}\right)$$

This can be written

$$\mathbf{n}_h(u,v) = \text{normalize}\left(-\frac{\partial h}{\partial u}t(u,v) - \frac{\partial h}{\partial v}b(u,v) + n(u,v)\right)$$

if one defines

$$\mathbf{t}(u,v) = \left|\frac{\partial \mathbf{p}(u,v)}{\partial u} \times \frac{\partial \mathbf{p}(u,v)}{\partial v}\right|^{-1} \frac{\partial \mathbf{p}(u,v)}{\partial v} \times \mathbf{n}(u,v),$$
$$4$$

$$\mathbf{b}(u,v) = \left|\frac{\partial \mathbf{p}(u,v)}{\partial u} \times \frac{\partial \mathbf{p}(u,v)}{\partial v}\right|^{-1} \mathbf{n}(u,v) \times \frac{\partial \mathbf{p}(u,v)}{\partial u}.$$
$$5$$

This is not the usual definition of the local tangent frame. Even though these vectors are perpendicular to the normal of the original surface, they typically do not have unit length and are not perpendicular to each other. In addition, $t(u,v)$ does not necessarily point along the first texture coordinate. To that end, it would have to be a multiple of

$$\frac{\partial \mathbf{p}(u,v)}{\partial u}$$

If we are restricted to World transformations composed of translations, rotations, and scalings, we can use a preprocessor to compute $\mathbf{t}(u,v)$ and $\mathbf{b}(u,v)$ and insert them into the mesh data. Typical shader programs can be altered so that they do not normalize the vectors $\mathbf{t}(u,v)$ and $\mathbf{b}(u,v)$. If arbitrary World transformations are to be handled, one could compute

$$\frac{\partial \mathbf{p}(u,v)}{\partial u}$$

and

$$\frac{\partial \mathbf{p}(u,v)}{\partial v}$$

to insert them into the mesh data. The vertex shader can then transform these vectors with the current World matrix, as it transforms the normal vector with the World-InverseTranspose matrix. Equations 4 and 5 can then be applied to compute a tangent and a binormal vector that leads to geometrically correct results.

Note that in this framework the height field $h(u,v)$ defines the displacement in absolute terms (in inches or meters, so to speak), not relatively to the size of the object. This becomes obvious when the World matrix scales up the size of an object by a certain factor. Then

$$\frac{\partial \mathbf{p}(u,v)}{\partial u}$$

and

$$\frac{\partial \mathbf{p}(u,v)}{\partial v}$$

which also are transformed by the `World` matrix, are scaled up by the same factor. However, $\mathbf{t}(u,v)$ and $\mathbf{b}(u,v)$ as computed by Equations 4 and 5 are scaled *down*. On closer inspection, this is no surprise: As an object gets larger, bumps of constant height are diminished. To regain the scale-independent behavior of standard bump mapping, one can scale up $\mathbf{t}(u,v)$ and $\mathbf{b}(u,v)$ by $(\det(\texttt{World}))^{1/3}$.

Anti-aliasing

A normal map is not a regular color texture, especially with regard to anti-aliasing. If normal maps cannot be blended like color textures, MIPmapping of the normal maps probably doesn't work either. If we instead store $(\delta h/\delta x, \delta h/\delta y, h)$ in the map, MIPmapping does work correctly due to the linearity of the derivatives. If one works with a standard pseudo-RGB normal map, the best method is to not compute the higher MIP levels from a zero-level normal map, but to first resize the height field for a given MIP level and then compute the corresponding level of the normal map [Bjorke06]. However, such an approach has a major drawback: The height field should not be averaged, but the final colors on the screen should be. One very effective option is to look at how much the averaging of the normals caused by MIPmapping shortens the resulting vector. When widely differing directions are averaged, the result will be substantially shorter. Combining this with a statistical illumination model gives a very good estimate of the average color [Toksvig05]. A more precise approach is to collect the statistics of the normals in a Normal Distribution Function, which then is approximated through Spherical Harmonics or spherical Gaussian-like functions. This leads to coefficients that can be subjected to standard MIPmapping [Han07].

Conclusion

This article has shown better and more precise methods of operation on normal maps using real-time GPU-based functions. As it turns out, the seemingly close relationship between standard color textures and normal maps is only superficial. However, most of the computations to deal with normal maps accurately are fairly simple and can be done easily by current graphics processing units.

References

[Bjorke06] Bjorke, Kevin. "When Shaders and Textures Collide," *GDC* 2006 Presentation available online at http://developer.nvidia.com/object/texture-shaders-gdc-2006.html, 2006.

[Blinn78] Blinn, Jim. "Simulation of Wrinkled Surfaces," *Proceedings of SIGGRAPH '78*, 1978: pp. 286–292, 1978.

[Green07] Green, Chris. "Efficient Self-Shadowed Radiosity Normal Mapping," *SIGGRAPH Course Notes: Advanced Real-Time Rendering in 3D Graphics and Games*, 2007: pp. 1–8.

[Han07] Han, Charles, Sun, Bo, Ramamoorthi, Ravi, and Grinspun, Eitan. "Frequency Domain Normal Map Filtering," *ACM Transactions on Graphics*, Volume 26, Issue 3, 2007.

[Toksvig05] Toksvig, Michael. "Mipmapping Normal Maps," *Journal of Graphics Tools*, Volume 10, Issue 3, 2005: pp. 65–71.

2.2

Computing Per-Pixel Object Thickness in a Single Render Pass

Christopher Oat (chris.oat@amd.com)

AMD, Inc.

Thorsten Scheuermann (thorsten.scheuermann@amd.com)

AMD, Inc.

Introduction

A number of rendering techniques require knowledge of an object's per-pixel "thickness" from a camera's or a light's point of view. For example, a thickness value, along with an estimate of the object's density, allows a graphics programmer to estimate how opaque an object is and thus compute how that object attenuates light passing through it. These approximations are important when rendering materials such as volumetric fog or when computing volumetric self-shadowing for materials such as hair. A per-pixel object thickness estimation can also be used for making approximations for how a given light ray passes through a refractive material when using image-space refraction techniques [Wyman05][Oliveira06].

Single Pass Thickness

Previous techniques for computing per-pixel depth bounds required that the object be rendered twice: one pass to find the closest fragments and a second pass to find the most distant fragments [Baker02][James04]. This article will explain a straightforward technique for obtaining a "dual-depth" map containing the minimum and maximum distance of an object in a single rendering pass.

The approach is extremely simple. First, we render the object with depth testing and triangle culling disabled (both front- and back-facing triangles are rasterized). In the pixel shader, we output depth in NDC space to the red channel and one minus depth to the green channel. Alpha blending is enabled and the blending mode is set to MIN, which has the effect of building the desired two depth buffers in the red and green channels of our output render target. In our example, the red channel would contain the minimum depth value d_{min} (the distance to the closest fragment) and the green channel would contain one minus the maximum depth value d_{max} (the distance to the furthest fragment). By using a separate blend function for the alpha channel, we can use additive blending to accumulate another quantity, such as opacity or homogeneous volume density, in the same render pass. Using the dual-depth map, thickness is computed as $d_{max} - d_{min} = (1 - G) - R$.

Applications

This simple technique has many applications. Figures 2.2.1 and 2.2.2 demonstrate how our method for computing per-pixel thickness can be used to implement an efficient volumetric self-shadowing technique for particle systems and hair.

FIGURE 2.2.1 (a) Volumetric particle lighting and self-shadowing: Backlit particles exhibit rim-lighting (more light passes through the particle volume in areas where it is less dense). (b) Dual-depth buffer created using the single pass technique described in this chapter. (c) Cumulative density of the particle volume.

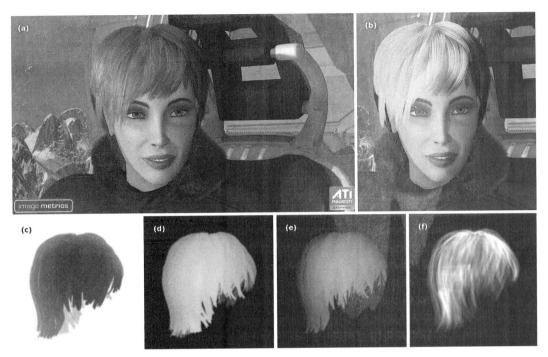

FIGURE 2.2.2 (a) Volumetric hair self-shadowing. (b) Visualization of the hair shadowing term. (c) Minimum depth extracted from dual-depth map (from light's point of view). (d) Maximum depth. (e) Thickness between the bounds specified by the dual-depth buffer. (f) Cumulative hair density.

Volumetric Self-Shadowing

We implement a simplified version of [Lokovic00] for volumetric self-shadowing in particle clouds and hair using an approximate volume lighting model that ignores internal scattering. Figure 2.2.3 illustrates how light rays enter the volume and are scattered toward the viewer. To compute the attenuation a of the incoming light at a point p inside the volume, we have to integrate the volume density along the light ray:

$$a = \exp(- \int_{ray} density(p)dp)$$

By making the assumption that volume density is uniform along each light ray, we can simplify the attenuation computation:

$$a = \exp(- d \cdot density_{avg} \cdot s)$$

Here d represents the distance between the ray's entry point to the volume and the point being shaded, while s is a density scale factor that allows for easy tweaking of the global volume density. Smaller values for s make the volume absorb less light.

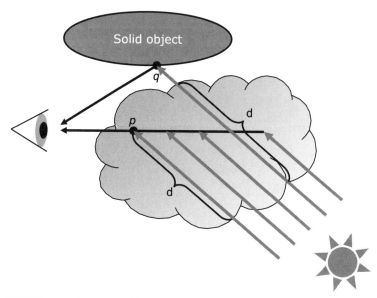

FIGURE 2.2.3 Intensity of light traveling through a volume is attenuated based on the distance *d* traveled through the volume.

For shadowing a point *q* outside the volume, we need to know the total distance the light ray traveled through the volume, which is just the volume's thickness from the light's point of view. To compute all the required distances, we render a dual-depth map of a polygonal object or view-aligned particle billboards that approximate the volume. The dual-depth map is rendered from the light's point of view, which is very similar to standard shadow mapping. To compute average density, we set the blend mode for the alpha channel to ADD and accumulate the particle volume alpha values into this channel. This yields the cumulative volume density for each ray in the alpha channel. Dividing this by the thickness provides us with the desired average density.

When rendering the thickness map for a particle system, rendering the flat camera-aligned particle billboards will cause severe discontinuities in the dual-depth map (see Figure 2.2.4a), which leads to objectionable shading artifacts (Figure 2.2.4b). In order to work around this problem, we add a depth offset texture map to both the min and max depth values rendered during the dual-depth map pass (Figure 2.2.4c). An additional blur pass over the dual-depth map can help smooth out remaining lighting discontinuities.

Other Uses

We have shown how dual-depth maps can be used for estimating thickness when rendering volumetric materials. However, there are various other applications for this technique. For example, a very similar dual-depth technique has been shown to be useful for generating irradiance slices, which are used for approximating global illumination for dynamic scenes [Evans06].

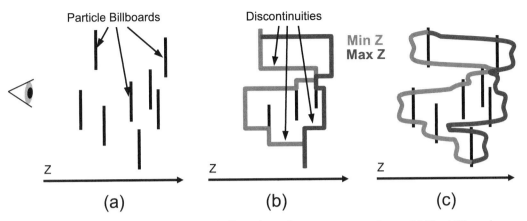

FIGURE 2.2.4 (a) Side view of the particle billboards used to represent a volume. (b) Flat billboards cause discontinuities in the dual-depth buffer. (c) Adding a depth offset texture to the billboards adds detail to the dual-depth buffer and smoothes out discontinuities.

Results and Conclusion

We have presented a simple technique for computing object thickness in a single pass using a dual-depth buffer. The advantage of the single-pass object thickness technique described in this article is its efficiency and the fact that it is applicable to arbitrary geometry. The techniques described in [Baker02] and [James04] only work on closed and watertight meshes and require multiple rendering passes. One drawback of our technique is that it does not provide exact thickness for non-convex objects, but tends to overestimate the cumulative distance a ray travels through an object (see Figure 2.2.5). In practice, we have not found this to be a problem for applications like volumetric self-shadowing or fog.

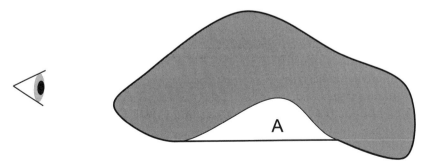

FIGURE 2.2.5 Dual-depth buffers cannot accurately represent non-convex shapes. In this example the area A is incorrectly assumed to be inside the volume.

Acknowledgments

The authors would like to thank their colleagues in AMD's Game Computing Applications Group for their fruitful discussion and thoughtful suggestions regarding this work. Many of the images used in this article come from *Ruby: Whiteout,* a real-time demo available for download [AMD07].

References

[AMD07] *Ruby: Whiteout* demo for AMD Radeon X2900, http://ati.amd.com/developer/demos/rhd2000.html.

[Baker02] Baker, Dan. VolumeFog Sample Application, Microsoft DirectX 9 SDK, http://msdn.microsoft.com/directx.

[Evans06] Evans, Alex. "Fast Approximations for Global Illumination on Dynamic Scenes," *Course 26 (Slides): Advanced Real-Time Rendering in 3D Graphics and Games. SIGGRAPH, Boston, MA,* August 2006.

[Gottlieb04] Gottlieb, Eli Z. "Rendering Volumes in a Vertex & Pixel Program by Ray Tracing," *ShaderX2: Shader Programming Tips & Tricks with DirectX 9,* Wolfgang Engel, Ed., Wordware Publishing, 2004: pp. 177–184.

[James04] James, Greg. "Rendering Objects as Thick Volumes," *ShaderX2: Shader Programming Tips & Tricks with DirectX 9,* Wolfgang Engel, Ed., Wordware Publishing, 2004: pp. 89–106.

[Laeuchli05] Laeuchli, Jesse. "Volumetric Clouds," *ShaderX3: Advanced Rendering with DirectX and OpenGL,* Wolfgang Engel, Ed., Charles River Media, 2005: pp. 611–616.

[Lokovic00] Lokovic, Tom and Veach, Eric. "Deep Shadow Maps," *ACM Transactions on Graphics,* Volume 19, Number 3, August 2000: pp. 385–392.

[Oliveira06] Oliveira, Manuel M. "Real-Time Refraction through Deformable Objects," *ACM SIGGRAPH Symposium on Interactive 3D Graphics and Games,* April 2006: pp. 89–96.

[Wyman05] Wyman, Chris. "An Approximate Image-Space Approach for Interactive Refraction," *ACM Transactions on Graphics,* Volume 24, Number 3, August 2005: pp. 1050–1053.

2.3

Filtered Tilemaps

Sylvain Lefebvre

Introduction

A simple texture map can dramatically enhance realism by adding fine details to an otherwise coarsely tessellated object. Unfortunately, texture mapping large surfaces such as terrains remains difficult. Large texture maps are extremely memory intensive and tedious to create, thus forcing most applications to simply repeat a small texture over surfaces. As a consequence, one of the major visual artifacts in games and simulators is repeating patterns due to direct tiling of a single texture.

A popular approach to reduce this issue is simply to rely on multiple square images—or *tiles*—and combine them in a regular grid—or *tilemap*—to cover the plane. Typically tiles are selected randomly [Lefebvre03], possibly enforcing edge constraints [Cohen03,Wei04]. This creates much more texture variety than a single tile and leads to a significant improvement in visual quality (such a tiling, referred to as a *random tiling,* is shown in Figure 2.3.1). A tilemap may also be used to progressively load very large high-resolution terrain texture maps: The large texture is divided into square tiles, which are dynamically loaded and unloaded at runtime as the user explores the scene. The tilemap is used to combine the tiles together into the visible sub-region of the texture. We refer to such tilings as *tiled-textures*.

Unfortunately, tiling presents difficulties when it comes to filtering (bilinear interpolation and MIPmapping). The discontinuities at tile boundaries hinder direct filtering by the graphics hardware. Often, proper filtering implies reimplementation of trilinear filtering in the fragment program, which results in long shaders and possibly rendering artifacts. Tiling also hinders the use of anisotropic filtering, which is crucial for terrain rendering.

In this article, we will start by explaining the difficulties associated with rendering a tiling. After a brief overview of existing methods, we will present a simple, generic approach to display a properly filtered tiling. Our approach exploits the recently introduced DirectX 10 texture arrays (or their OpenGL equivalent). It is as simple as summing four filtered lookups. In the far distance, where multiple entries of the tilemap project into a same pixel, a coarse texture is used to filter the tilemap itself. Our approach supports anisotropic filtering.

Tile set   Tiling, naïve approach   Same correctly filtered

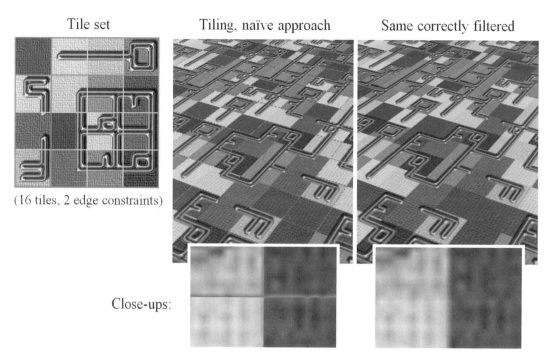

(16 tiles, 2 edge constraints)

Close-ups:

FIGURE 2.3.1 A *random tiling:* 16 square tiles are randomly combined together to form a larger texture. By enforcing some edge constraints a complex pattern is produced. The left image exhibits color bleeding at tile boundaries and aliasing in the distance, whereas the right image is properly filtered using the method described in this article.

Filtering Tilemaps

Before discussing filtering, we will start with a more detailed explanation about how a lookup is performed into a tilemap.

Lookup Through a Tilemap

In the following discussion, we will assume the square tiling is given as 1) a set of tiles packed into a single texture—the *packed tiles texture*—and 2) a tilemap encoded as a texture. Each entry of the tilemap is an index into the tile set. We note that T_{res}^2 is the resolution of the tiles, P^2 is the size of the tile set, and N^2 is the size of the tilemap, thus the perceived resolution of the resulting tiling is $(N \cdot T_{res})^2$. These notations are summarized in Figure 2.3.2. Note that packing the tiles into a same texture is mandatory for dynamic tile selection (this applies only to hardware prior to DX10).

The lookup is implemented within a fragment program; we have to determine the color at a given (u,v) coordinate in texture space. Recall that all texture coordinates are in the $[0,1]^2$ range, so the first step is to retrieve the index of the tile located under the (u,v) coordinates. This is done with a nearest-mode lookup into the tilemap. The retrieved tile index is the 2D coordinate (t_i, t_j) of the tile within the tile

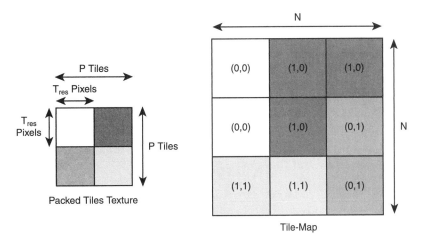

FIGURE 2.3.2 Tiling notations: Tiles have a resolution of T_{res}^2, the packed tiles texture holds P^2 tiles, and the tilemap has N^2 entries, each an index into the packed tile set.

set. The second step is to compute the relative coordinate (u_{tile}, v_{tile}) of the point at (u, v) *within* the tile. This is done with the following simple formula (in HLSL style):

$$float2(u_{tile}, v_{tile}) = frac(float2(u, v).N)$$

The third step is to compute final texture coordinates for the lookup into the packed tiles texture. The final coordinates (u_{packed}, v_{packed}) are obtained as follows:

$$float2(u_{packed}, v_{packed}) = float2(u_{tile}, v_{tile}) + \frac{float2(t_i, t_j)}{P}$$

The coordinates (u_{packed}, v_{packed}) are then directly used to access the tilemap. Here is the DirectX 10 naive lookup code:

```
Texture2D<uint  > TileMap;
Texture2D<float4> Tex2d;
static const uint P = 4;

PS_OUTPUT PackedTileMapPS( VS_OUTPUT In )
{
  PS_OUTPUT output;

  // -> get tile id
  // NOTE: In.TileMapUV ranges from (0,0) to (N,N).
  //       DX10 load instruction uses integer coordinates as input.
  uint   id       = TileMap.Load(int3(In.TileMapUV,0));

  // -> compute uv within packed tiles texture
  float2 uv_tile  = frac(In.TileMapUV);
  float2 uv_packed= (uv_tile + float2(id % P,id / P)) / float(P);
```

```
// -> compute correct derivatives
// This is mandatory to get proper MIPmap level selection.
// See section on MIP-mapping derivatives.
float2 duvdx    = ddx(In.TileMapUV / float(P));
float2 duvdy    = ddy(In.TileMapUV / float(P));
output.RGBColor = Tex2d.SampleGrad(Sampler,uv_packed,duvdx,duvdy);

// -> done!
return output;
}
```

The Problem

Graphics hardware natively supports trilinear interpolation for MIPmapping. Unfortunately, if we directly rely on the graphics hardware to interpolate through a tilemap, we will obtain something similar to what is shown in the image on the left in Figure 2.3.1: Some undesirable colors leak into the result around tile boundaries.

The main issue is that the graphics hardware knows nothing about the tiling. It performs trilinear interpolation in the packed tiles texture as if it were a standard texture. The consequence is that colors from the neighboring tiles in the packed tile textures bleed into the tiling. The interpolation completely ignores the fact that we shuffled the tiles inside the tilemap.

There is another consequence. During rendering, the graphics hardware computes texture coordinate derivatives to select the appropriate MIPmap level to be used. Because we shuffle the texture coordinates through the tilemap, these derivatives become unstable at tile boundaries. Hence, we have to compute the derivatives explicitly using the *ddx* and *ddy* instructions. The code given above includes correct computation of derivatives.

Finally, in the far distance, multiple tiles may project into a single screen pixel. The problem is that we are no longer looking into filtering the tiles, but the tilemap itself. The most convenient solution is to compute a color version of the tilemap, in which each tile index is replaced by the average color of the corresponding tile. This standard color texture is used for MIPmapping in the far distance.

Previous Approaches

Several interesting approaches have been proposed to reduce filtering issues, some in the context of random tilings, some in the context of tiled textures. Three of these approaches are briefly described here: explicit interpolation, border padding, and continuous packing. Table 2.3.1 summarizes the approaches and their properties, including ours.

- **Explicit interpolation.** Explicit interpolation consists of programming the filtered lookup in the fragment program instead of relying on the built-in hardware. To achieve trilinear interpolation (MIPmapping), four texture lookups must be performed into the tilemap and eight into the packed tiles texture. Seven lerps are then necessary to compute the final blending. While being very general, this method is inefficient as it requires a long shader. Also, anisotropic filtering cannot be used with this method.

- **Border padding.** The idea of border padding is to add a one-pixel border around the tiles so that a correct result is achieved when the hardware interpolates in the packed tiles texture [Kraus02]. The one-pixel border comes from neighboring tiles *in the tiling*. This is, of course, only possible with tiled-textures: Each tile appears once and always has the same neighbors, whereas in a random tiling each tile appears multiple times with different neighbors. Border padding is faster than explicit interpolation, but it requires duplicating samples, wasting memory, and adds some arithmetic computations on the texture coordinates to achieve proper MIPmapping [Purnomo04]. Anisotropic filtering is not supported unless the border is made much larger than one pixel.

- **Continuous packing.** The continuous packing approach only applies to random tilings [Wei04]. It exploits the fact that artifacts will not be visible if neighboring tiles in the tiling *and* neighboring tiles in the packed tiles texture have the same colors along their edges. The tile set is organized so that edge constraints are enforced *in the packed tiles texture* (refer to Figure 2.3.1). This approach is very fast, and filtering *appears* correct even using the naive lookup, including anisotropic filtering. However, the property of having the same colors along the edges must be true through *all* MIPmap levels, which imposes rather homogeneous texture content. Nevertheless, this approach offers a very good quality/speed compromise when the texture content is compatible. This is not the case in Figure 2.3.1 as each tile has a different color, thus producing artifacts.

Table 2.3.1 Summary of the different approaches and their properties

Random Tiling	Content Independent	Anisotropic Filtering	Arbitrary Tile Size
Explicit interpolation	Yes	No	No
Border padding	*Not applicable*	*Not applicable*	*Not applicable*
Continuous packing	No	Yes	No
Texture array (ours)	Yes	Yes	Yes
Tiled-Texture	**Content Independent**	**Anisotropic Filtering**	**Arbitrary Tile Size**
Explicit interpolation	Yes	No	No
Border padding	Yes	No	No
Continuous packing	*Not applicable*	*Not applicable*	*Not applicable*
Texture array (ours)	Yes	Yes	Yes

Toward a Generic Solution

None of the existing approaches are fully satisfactory. For random tilings, the best approach appears to be the continuous packing, but it depends on the tiles' content. For tiled textures, none of the approaches can handle anisotropic filtering, which is a severe drawback.

Fortunately, the introduction of texture arrays with DirectX 10 (and its equivalent under OpenGL) make another, more generic approach possible. Before texture arrays, packing the tiles into a same texture was mandatory. It was the only way to select tiles from their index at runtime (using slices of a 3D texture is excluded because of MIPmapping). Texture arrays now enable a simpler texture indexing mechanism. Each texture within the array behaves as an independent texture. It has its own MIPmap pyramid, and it also has its own access policies (wrap, clamp, clamp to border, border color, and so on). So each tile can now be stored as an independent texture within the array.

One often overlooked capability of texturing units is that they can properly handle a border color through filtering. If, for instance, the border color is set to be black and the access policy is set to "clamp to border color," everything will happen as if the texture were lying on an infinite black background—*everything* including MIPmapping and anisotropic filtering.

How do we exploit this property? Consider the simple bilinear interpolation case of Figure 2.3.3. The interpolation cell is defined between A, B, C, and D in the tiling. The lookup point is the black circle with the white outline. With explicit interpolation we would lookup the colors at each point A, B, C, and D, compute interpolation

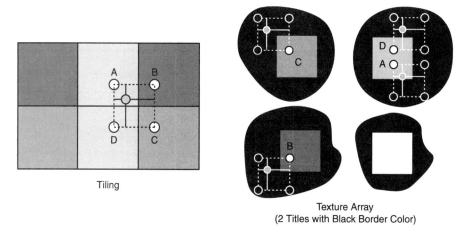

Tiling

Texture Array
(2 Titles with Black Border Color)

FIGURE 2.3.3 Our new approach performs hardware filtered lookups in the tiles at the lookup location (black circle with the white outline). The tiles are accessed with a "clamp to border color" policy and a black border color. The final color is simply the direct sum of the four lookups.

weights, and finally perform three lerps. With our new approach, we simply find out where the lookup point is located relative to each of the four tiles (see the right side of Figure 2.3.3). We then perform one hardware interpolated lookup in each tile at this location. Of course, three corners of the interpolation cell fall outside of the tile boundaries: They are forced to black. Still, the hardware automatically computes the correct interpolation weights for the remaining color. We thereby save the weight computations *and* the three lerps. The final color is obtained by adding the result of the four lookups. But what's more important is that this interpolation with the black background is properly defined through MIPmapping: Trilinear interpolation comes for free! This also holds true for anisotropic filtering.

The complete code for the new method is shown below. Note that it requires only five texture lookups (one in the tilemap, four in the texture array). To avoid performing four lookups into the tilemap, we pack information about neighboring tiles, as explained in the optimization section. The code is available on the accompanying DVD-ROM as well as an application comparing the various approaches.

```
PS_OUTPUT RenderInterpolatedTileMapPS( VS_QUAD_OUTPUT In )
{
  PS_OUTPUT output;

  // -> compute correct derivatives
  float2 duvdx = ddx(In.TileMapUV);
  float2 duvdy = ddy(In.TileMapUV);

  // -> compute coordinates within tile-map
  // Coordinates are shifted due to packing of the tile-map.
  // This avoids performing 4 lookups into the tile-map.
  float2 shifted   = In.TileMapUV - 0.5;
  uint2  ij        = uint2(shifted);
  float2 tc        = (shifted) - ij;

  // -> compute coordinates within all 4 tiles
  float2  tc00    = tc   + 0.5;
  float2  tc11    = tc00 - 1.0;
  float2  tc10    = tc00 - float2(1.0,0.0);
  float2  tc01    = tc00 - float2(0.0,1.0);

  // -> read the tile-map
  uint4   ids     = TileMap.Load(int3(ij,0));

  // -> perform all 4 interpolated lookups and sum them up
  output.RGBColor  =
    Array2d.SampleGrad(Sampler,float3(tc00,ids.x),duvdx,duvdy)
  + Array2d.SampleGrad(Sampler,float3(tc10,ids.y),duvdx,duvdy)
  + Array2d.SampleGrad(Sampler,float3(tc11,ids.w),duvdx,duvdy)
  + Array2d.SampleGrad(Sampler,float3(tc01,ids.z),duvdx,duvdy);

  // -> done!
  return output;
}
```

While being more expensive at runtime than border padding or continuous packing, this approach works in *all* cases: it supports anisotropic filtering, does not put restrictions on the tile content, does not require additional memory, and even supports tiles of arbitrary shapes and sizes.

Optimizations

Reducing the Number of Lookups

In its simplest form, our approach requires eight lookups: four into the tilemap and four into the tiles. It is possible to reduce the number of lookups into the tilemap to one. Within each tilemap cell we also store the indices of the tiles in the three neighboring cells (right, bottom, and bottom-right). This, of course, means that we store three times more indices, but access time is reduced. The code given above includes this optimization. Note that we shift the tilemap by half a tile in order to always have the correct neighboring information.

Conditional Interpolation

Clearly, the complex interpolation should only happen at the boundaries of the tiles. Within the interior of a tile, we are sufficiently far from the borders to directly rely on the hardware interpolation. The safety distance depends, of course, on the MIPmapping level being used. The shader of the demo application includes an implementation that uses dynamic branching to decide whether a simple lookup is sufficient or whether an interpolation scheme has to be used.

Conclusion

After reviewing the various challenges associated with tilemaps, we looked into existing approaches to understand their strengths and weaknesses. We then proposed a generic and convenient approach providing correct filtering of tilemaps in all cases.

Tilemaps are a great tool for real-time computer graphics applications. The programmability of modern graphics hardware really makes them affordable, and the filtering issues can be solved at a reasonable cost. Texture synthesis enables easy creation of interesting tile sets for random tilings, and it is relatively easy to implement a texture cache using a tilemap. I hope this article convinced you of the usefulness of tilemaps, and that it will help you to achieve high-quality, high-resolution texturing!

Acknowledgments

Many thanks to Fabrice Neyret who taught me all about the subtleties of texture filtering and with whom we explored many of these approaches.

References

[Cohen03] Cohen, Michael F., Shade, Jonathan, Hiller, Stefan, Deussen, Oliver. "Wang tiles for image and texture generation," *SIGGRAPH*, 2003.

[Kraus02] Kraus, Martin and Ertl, Thomas. "Adaptive Texture Maps," *Workshop on Graphics Hardware*, 2002.

[Purnomo04] Purnomo, Budirijano, Cohen, Jonathon D., and Kumar, Subodh. "Seamless Texture Atlases," *Symposium on Geometry Processing*, 2004.

[Stam97] Stam, Jos. "Aperiodic Texture Mapping," *ERCIM Research Report R046*, January, 1997.

[Wei03] Li Wei, Li-Yi. "Tile-Based Texture Mapping on Graphics Hardware," *Workshop on Graphics Hardware*, 2004.

2.4

Parallax Occlusion Mapping Special Feature Rendering

Jason Zink

Introduction

It is quite often the case that a modern rendering system is required to produce some form of a highlight around one or more of the various geometric entities that are rendered in a given scene. This would include highlighting a selected item, producing non-photorealistic outlines, and producing special effects around an object such as a halo. Many different methods have been devised to produce these highlights, ranging from creating additional geometry in a preprocess to image space techniques performed after the traditional rendering pass.

Parallax occlusion mapping (POM) is a rendering technique that adds additional surface detail to otherwise simple polygonal geometry. This is accomplished by providing the surface detail to the pixel shader in the form of a height map texture, which then raytraces each fragment to find the correct surface element to display. This pixel shader mechanism adds a higher level of detail at the fragment level of the rendering pipeline without introducing any additional vertex work load. When used properly, it is an efficient method for rendering highly detailed geometry.

However, when an object utilizes POM it can be difficult to produce the desired highlights around the simulated surface geometry. Most traditional highlighting techniques will spoil the illusion that POM was used to create in the first place. This article proposes a modified POM algorithm that can detect the simulated surface silhouette in a pixel shader program and highlight it with a constant color. Two different implementations of the algorithm are provided: one that relies on a surface normal map and one that relies on the surface height map alone.

Background

Parallax occlusion mapping was initially proposed by [Tatarchuk05]. It allows the user to input a height map texture to define additional object surface detail without defining any additional vertex data. The height map is used to trace a ray from the viewer's location to the simulated surface. The intersection point of the ray then defines what point of the surface should be used to color the given fragment. Figure 2.4.1 shows an illustration of this concept.

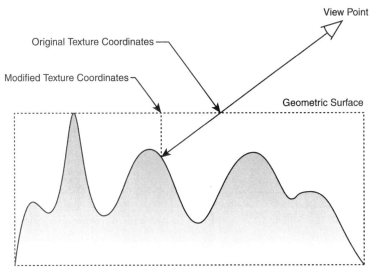

FIGURE 2.4.1 The parallax occlusion mapping process.

Parallax occlusion mapping starts by comparing the surface height to the location of the view ray at the actual geometric surface. If the surface height is not greater than or equal to the view ray height, then the current position is advanced a small amount along the view ray and the test is performed again. This process is repeated until either the view ray intersects the surface or the number of samples exceeds a maximum value. (Further details on how this algorithm is implemented can be found in [Zink06].)

There are several different algorithms that operate along the same iterative sampling principle as parallax occlusion mapping. Relief mapping, interval mapping, and steep parallax are all similar algorithms that can also benefit from the methods proposed in this article.

Silhouette rendering has been an active area of research, with a large number of different algorithms devised for various situations. A rigorous overview of current techniques is available in [Isenberg03]. Several algorithms such as [McGuire04] generate additional geometry in a preprocess to be able to detect and render the view-dependent silhouette of geometry in the vertex or pixel shader. These methods are very efficient and effective, but would ultimately negate the positive aspects of parallax occlusion mapping by adding a large amount of vertex-based geometry.

Finally, image space methods such as [Mitchell02] accumulate scene information in various G-buffers and then perform some form of filtering to detect discontinuities in the buffers. This method would indeed produce correct and useful silhouettes on the POM surface. However, the image space technique operates on the entire image that is being processed, which would make it difficult to highlight only the POM objects. Image space techniques also require multiple full-screen rendering passes, which consumes large amounts of memory bandwidth as well.

Algorithm Theory

The algorithm presented in this article will detect whether or not a fragment should be considered to be a part of the parallax occlusion mapped surface's silhouette. Two variations of the algorithm are provided to perform this test. The first variant requires a surface normal map in addition to the surface height map, while the second method requires only the surface height map. Both methods use the surface contour information (provided in the normal and height maps) to perform the test for silhouette edges. We will first examine the general concept of how to find a silhouette in the simulated surface and then present the implementation of the two variations.

Surface Silhouette Definition

The silhouette of an object can be defined as the portion of a surface that divides the local area into two parts: one area where the surface normal vector is pointing toward the viewer and one area where the surface normal vector is pointing away from the viewer. One way to visualize the silhouette is to think about where a surface's normal vector is exactly perpendicular to the view ray—which is exactly the point where the surface normal vector transitions from forward facing to backward facing. Figure 2.4.2 shows a cross section of a surface and highlights these transition points.

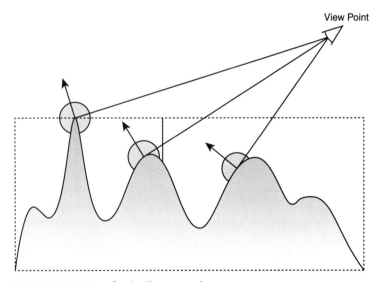

FIGURE 2.4.2 A surface's silhouette edges.

Normal Vector Technique

With this concept in mind, we need to devise a strategy for detecting this surface normal vector direction transition. An initial attempt would be the most straightforward: Starting at the point where the view ray intersects the surface, check to see if the surface normal is pointing away from the viewer a small distance farther forward. This concept is illustrated in Figure 2.4.3, where the initial intersection point is labeled as P_0 and the second surface point is labeled as P_1.

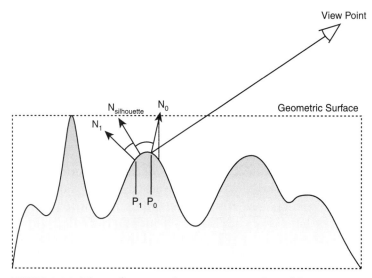

FIGURE 2.4.3 The surface normal vector at points P_0 and P_1.

This concept accurately defines the transition point, but it essentially only specifies a thin line along the surface as the silhouette. This may be acceptable in some cases, but ideally we would like to have more control over how thick the silhouette appears to be. Thus we need to extend this detection concept slightly.

In order to understand how to do this, consider the nature of the general parallax occlusion mapping algorithm. By definition, when the view ray intersects the simulated surface, the surface normal at that point must be pointing toward the viewer; otherwise, that particular point of the surface would not be visible to the viewer and some other point in the surface would have been intersected prior to reaching the initial point. This is the same concept that is used to cull back-facing triangles in the traditional vertex transformation pipeline. If the triangle normal vector is pointing away from the viewer, it is not possible for the viewer to see it. Taking this idea into account, we no longer have to consider the normal vector at P_0. We can safely assume that the normal at P_0 is pointing toward the viewer and simply test the normal vector at P_1 to see if it is pointing away from the viewer.

This simplification enables a generalization of the detection test that we can use to produce thicker silhouettes. Instead of only testing the surface normal at P_1, we can step along the surface any number of times looking for an edge. We'll define these subsequent points as P_1, P_2, P_3, ..., P_n. If the surface normal is back-facing at any of these surface points, we can make an approximation and consider P_0 to be a part of the silhouette. This provides a simple mechanism for controlling the apparent thickness of the silhouette. Figure 2.4.4 shows this multiple sampling pattern.

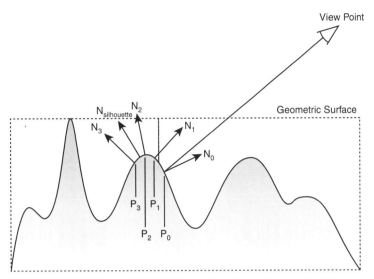

FIGURE 2.4.4 Multiple sampling points to search for the silhouette.

Height Delta Technique

The detection test up to this point examines the surface normal vector to determine where the silhouette exists. This provides for a simple implementation if you happen to have a normal map of the height field surface available. However, if there is not a normal map available or your memory budget doesn't allow for its use, then the surface topology information must be extracted exclusively from the height map. Many techniques have been developed for deriving a normal vector from a height map, which could then be used in the same manner as the normal map data in the test as described above.

The drawback is that this approach would require significantly more height map samples than the normal map technique used. It would ultimately be more efficient if we could utilize the height map data directly instead of converting it to a normal vector. To come to a solution, we can make another generalization based on a geometric interpretation of our normal vector test. Figure 2.4.5 shows how a typical height map contour can be tested for silhouettes.

If we consider the view ray—which starts at the viewer and continues until it reaches the surface intersection point—to be the hypotenuse of a right triangle, then we also know the magnitude of the remaining two sides of the triangle. One side of the triangle would be the height of the view point from the surface; we will refer to it as the "rise" of the triangle. The other side of the triangle would be the distance along the surface from the projection of the viewer onto the surface over to the intersection point; we'll refer to it as the "run" of the triangle (refer to Figure 2.4.5 for details).

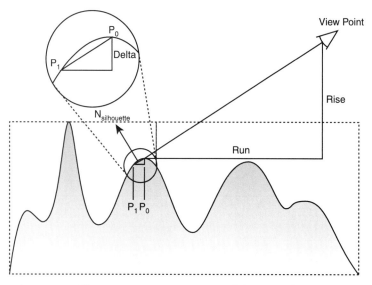

FIGURE 2.4.5 The geometric interpretation of the normal vector direction test.

Our detection test steps along the surface in small fixed-size intervals. If we consider a smaller triangle whose run side is the distance between sampling points, then we can find the size of the rise side based on the law of similar triangles. This calculation is based on the ratio shown here:

$$\frac{Interval_{rise}}{Interval_{run}} = \frac{E_{rise}}{E_{run}}$$

$$Interval_{rise} = \left(\frac{E_{rise} * Interval_{run}}{E_{run}} \right)$$

The size of the interval rise side can then be used as a measure of the height delta of the view ray over this interval. With this delta height, we can compare two consecutive height map samples and see if their delta height is greater than the view ray's delta height. If it is, then that indicates that the surface normal vector must be pointing away from the viewer. This provides our direct method of testing for a silhouette edge with only a height map.

Implementation

Now that you understand the algorithm, we can examine its implementation. These implementations have been provided in the Direct3D 9 HLSL Effect File format. The effects require two textures to be bound to the rendering pipeline. The first is a simple color map that stores the diffuse color of the surface in the R, G, and B channels of the texture. The second texture is the normal/height map that stores the surface normal vector in the R, G, and B channels of the texture; the corresponding height value is stored in the alpha channel. Each component of the normal vector has been range compressed from [−1,1] to [0,1] to fit the format of the texture. The height value is also normalized to the [0,1] range.

These techniques are both based on the original POM algorithm, which determines the location of point P_0 in tangent space. Our discussion of the implementation will start at the point after P_0 has been found. The texture coordinates of P_0 are stored in the variable vFinalCoords. Each of the two methods performs an iterative test for silhouette edges by sampling the normal/height map along the view direction at fixed intervals. The following code shows the normal map version of the silhouette test:

```
float fTest = 1;
float fInterval = 1.0 / 256.0;
int nIterations = 3;

for ( int i = 1; i <= nIterations; i++ )
{
    if ( fTest > 0 )
    {
        // Calculate the next sampling position.
        float2 vNextCoords = vFinalCoords +
            ( i * fInterval * vOffsetDir );

        // Sample and expand the next normal vector.
        float4 vNextSample =
            tex2Dgrad( NH_Sampler, vNextCoords, dx, dy );

        vNextSample = vNextSample*2-1;

        // Test if the surface is pointing toward
        // or away from the viewer.
        fTest = -dot( E, vNextSample.xyz );
    }
}
```

The next texture sampling location is calculated and used to sample the normal/height map. The normal vector components are then expanded to the [−1,1] range and compared to the view ray by performing the dot product of the two vectors. The test result is stored in the fTest variable, where a negative value will represent when a silhouette has been found. The test continues to iterate until either the silhouette has been found or the number of iterations has been exceeded.

The following code shows the height map version of the test:

```
// Calculate how much the height has to change
// between subsequent heightmap samples to be
// considered back facing.
float fDelta = ( fInterval * IN.eye.z ) /
                length( IN.eye.xy );
```

```
// Initialize the heightmap sampling variables.
float4 vNextSample = vFinalNormal;
float4 vCurrSample = vFinalNormal;

for ( int i = 1; i <= nIterations; i++ )
{
    if ( fTest > 0 )
    {
        // Record the last heightmap sample.
        vCurrSample = vNextSample;

        // Calculate the next sampling position.
        float2 vNextCoords = vFinalCoords +
            ( i * fInterval * vOffsetDir );

        // Sample the next heightmap location.
        vNextSample =
            tex2Dgrad( NH_Sampler, vNextCoords, dx, dy );

        // Test if the surface is pointing
        // toward or away from the viewer.
        fTest = -(( vCurrSample.a - vNextSample.a ) *
            fHeightMapScale + fDelta);
    }
}
```

Before beginning the test, the allowed delta height value between samples is calculated and stored in the variable fDelta. Then each iteration of the loop stores the previous height sample, calculates the next texture sampling location, and samples the normal/height map. The delta height between the two most recent samples is then scaled to its physical size by the variable fHeightMapScale and is compared to the allowed delta value in fDelta. The test result is also stored in the fTest variable, where a negative value will represent when a silhouette has been found. The test continues to iterate until either the silhouette is found or the number of iterations has been exceeded.

Finally, the following code shows how the test results are evaluated:

```
// If the silhouette test results in a negative
// value, color this fragment with the hightlight
// color, otherwise output the shaded color.
if ( fTest > 0 )
    OUT.color = vFinalColor;
else
    OUT.color = float4( 0.2, 1, 0.2, 0 );
```

The fragment is colored to a constant highlight color if the test result produces a negative value. Otherwise, the regular diffuse color is used as if this were a regular parallax occlusion mapped object.

Results

Both of these silhouette detection mechanisms produce high-quality silhouette edges with a relatively small performance impact when compared to the original parallax occlusion mapping algorithm. Figure 2.4.6 shows a comparison of the results obtained by both techniques using the same input texture data.

FIGURE 2.4.6 A comparison of the normal map and height map methods with a block surface.

Each of these two methods has its own advantages and disadvantages. The normal map method is efficient, but it relies entirely on the normal map. If the normal map is generated with a different height scale applied to the source height map than the one currently being used, then there is the potential for artifacts in the silhouette edges. In addition, as you can see in Figure 2.4.6, the normal map technique can have trouble with very sharp edges. When a step change in height is present, it is difficult to accurately encode that information into a normal map—which makes the normal map technique inherently difficult to use in these situations. However, as shown in Figure 2.4.7, a continuous surface provides very nice silhouettes with this method.

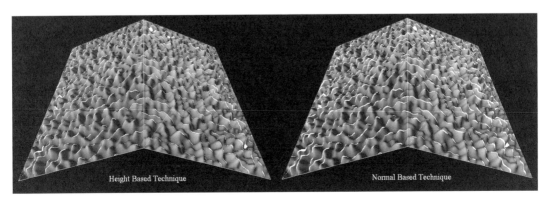

FIGURE 2.4.7 A comparison of the normal map and height map methods with a perlin noise surface.

The height map method has the distinct advantage that a normal map is not required, which can provide a substantial memory savings. In addition, there is no restriction on the shape of the surface that can be used.

The more appropriate method for a given surface needs to be tested with both techniques to determine which one provides the best performance and quality. Also, the desired silhouette thickness should be determined and will generally be based on the size of the surface contours in the height map.

Conclusion

In summary, we have developed two practical methods for displaying high-quality silhouette highlights on parallax occlusion mapped geometry. The method can be used at very interactive frame rates and uses existing art assets to achieve the effect. An interactive demo program has been included with the book's samples for you to try out the effects and experiment with different height map textures. Also, the source effect files for these methods have been heavily commented for clarity and ease of use.

References

[Tatarchuk05] Tatarchuk, Natalya. "Practical Dynamic Parallax Occlusion Mapping," available online at http://ati.amd.com/developer/SIGGRAPH05/Tatarchuk-ParallaxOcclusionMapping-Sketch-print.pdf, 2005.

[Zink06] Zink, Jason. "A Closer Look at Parallax Occlusion Mapping," available online at http://www.gamedev.net/columns/hardcore/pom/, 2006.

[Isenberg03] Isenberg, Tobias, et al. "A Developer's Guide to Silhouette Algorithms for Polygonal Models," *Computer Graphics*, Vol. 23 No. 4: pp. 28–37.

[McGuire04] McGuire, Morgan, et al. "Hardware-Determined Feature Edges," *Proceedings of the 3rd international symposium on Non-photorealistic animation and rendering*," 2004: pp. 35–147.

[Mitchell02] Mitchell, Jason, et al. "Real-Time Image-Space Outlining for Non-Photorealistic Rendering," available online at http://ati.amd.com/developer/SIGGRAPH02/SIGGRAPH2002_Sketch-Mitchell.pdf, 2002.

2.5

Isocube: A Cubemap with Uniformly Distributed and Equally Important Texels

Liang Wan (lwan@cse.cuhk.edu.hk)

The Chinese University of Hong Kong

Tien-Tsin Wong (ttwong@acm.org)

The Chinese University of Hong Kong

Chi-Sing Leung (eeleungc@cityu.edu.hk)

City University of Hong Kong

Chi-Wing Fu (cwfu@cs.ust.hk)

The Hong Kong University of Science & Technology

Introduction

Environment mapping is a cost-effective way to raise visual richness and photorealism. Millions of lookup operations may be required in rendering a frame, hence the environment mapping functionality is normally hardwired in most GPUs. Most implementations adopt the six-face cubemap due to its computational simplicity and memory-friendly rectilinear structure. However, the cubemap samples the spherical environment unevenly, more at the face corners while less at the face centers. Furthermore, each texel spans different solid angles (i.e. not equally important). Other common representations, the sphere map and dual-paraboloid map [Heidrich98], also do not sample the environment evenly.

Although there exist representations [Shirley97][Górski99] that evenly sample the unit sphere (environment) and preserve the equal solid-angle property (all texels are equally important), their corresponding texture lookup processes require tailored shader implementations; they are not able to fully exploit the hardware like a cube-map. Unless they can exploit the hardware cubemap operations such as texture lookup and anti-aliasing, the speed performance of their shader implementations is not comparable to that of cubemap. This motivates us to design a novel spherical representation that fits nicely into the *six-face* structure of the cubemap and exploits the operations originally designed for the six-face cubemap.

We've named the proposed spherical representation *isocube* to indicate its properties of equal solid-angle and uniform sampling (low discrepancy). It is inspired by the *12-face* spherical representation HEALPix [Górski99], which originates from astrophysics. One advantage of the isocube is its rather low computational cost. Furthermore, it can fully exploit the hardware cubemap operation, so it achieves very high frame rates.

Construction Sphere Partitioning and Subdivision

The proposed isocube is inspired by an all sky image partitioning scheme, Hierarchical Equal Area isoLatitude Pixelisation (HEALPix) [Górski99][Wan05]. The HEALPix starts by partitioning the spherical surface into 12 equal-area base quads and recursively subdivides each quad to generate smaller sub-quads of equal area. Figure 2.5.1 shows the HEALPix map by unrolling and concatenating the 12 base quads (rotated by 45°). Each base quad in this example is subdivided into 4×4 elements. Given a HEALPix map, the lookup and anti-aliasing operations have to be implemented with tailored shaders, hence the speed performance is not comparable to that of a cubemap. Can we rearrange the HEALPix map so as to utilize the cubemap hardware?

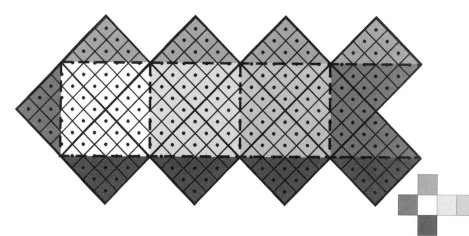

FIGURE 2.5.1 The unrolled view of the HEALPix map.

Initially, we tried to pack the pixels of the HEALPix map into the six-face cube structure. Regions with the same color are packed into one cube face as suggested by the color in Figure 2.5.1. However, a close inspection reveals that those pixels are not in a grid structure. Instead we designed a new set of partitioning equations on the sphere. This equation set partitions the spherical surface into six equal-area base faces instead of 12. Recursive subdivisions generate smaller elements while maintaining the equal solid-angle property. As the resultant partition forms a six-face structure (*cube*) and all elements are same in size (*iso*), we call the partitioning scheme *isocube*.

Figure 2.5.2 illustrates the construction process of isocube base faces. We first partition the spherical surface into the equatorial zone and two polar zones, with the arctic/antarctic circles at $|z|=2/3$ (Figure 2.5.2a). The area of the equatorial zone is four times that of each polar zone. The equatorial zone is further subdivided into four symmetric equal regions. The resultant six base faces, as shown in Figure 2.5.2b, have the same area.

Next we partition each base face into $N{\times}N$ elements. Let us denote the polar angle as θ, the azimuth angle as ϕ, and $z = \cos\theta$. Within the equatorial zone, we develop a set of k-curves and l-curves,

$$k - \text{curve:} \quad \phi = \frac{\pi}{2}\left(\frac{k}{N} - \frac{1}{2} \right), \qquad k = 0, \ldots, 4N,$$

$$l - \text{curve:} \quad z = \frac{2}{3}\left(\frac{2l}{N} - 1 \right), \qquad l = 0, \ldots, N.$$

1

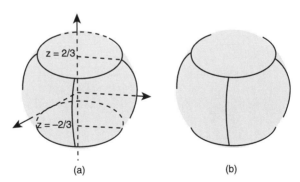

(a)   (b)

FIGURE 2.5.2 Constructing isocube base faces: (a) the sphere is first partitioned into three zones, the equatorial zone in the middle, and two polar zones besides; (b) then the sphere is partitioned into six equal area base faces.

Figure 2.5.3 shows the partitions at three resolutions on one equatorial base face, with *k*-curves indicated in dark gray color and *l*-curves in light gray color.

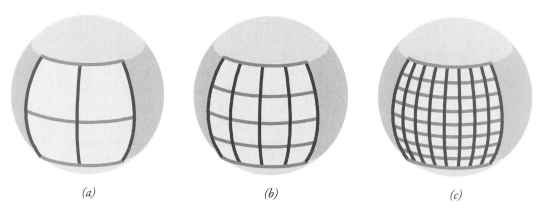

(a)   (b)   (c)

FIGURE 2.5.3 Further partition of one equatorial base face at three resolutions

In the polar zones, we adopt a different set of partitioning equations. Due to the symmetry within the polar base faces, we only present the subdivision equations within the region where

$$(\phi, z) \in \left[0, \frac{\pi}{4}\right] \times \left[\frac{2}{3}, 1\right]$$

(a sector of the polar region as shown in Figure 2.5.4),

$$k - \text{curve:} \quad \phi = \frac{\pi}{2}\frac{2k+\varepsilon}{2N}\frac{1}{\sqrt{3(1-z)}}, \qquad k = 0, \ldots, \left\lfloor \frac{N}{2} \right\rfloor - 1,$$

$$l - \text{curve:} \quad z = 1 - \frac{1}{3}\left(\frac{2l+\varepsilon}{N}\right)^2, \qquad l = 0, \ldots, N.$$

where $\varepsilon = N \bmod 2$. As shown in Figure 2.5.4, *k*-curves and *l*-curves in the polar base faces are not as regular as those in the equatorial zone and so may form corners. Figure 2.5.4(d) may remind careful readers of the elevated concentric map [Shirley97]. Unlike the elevated concentric map that covers a hemisphere, our polar faces only span the artic/antarctic regions.

It can be proven mathematically that the two sets of partitioning curves guarantee the equal-area property. Since the isocube is composed of six faces with each face containing the same amount of samples, it fits naturally in classical cubemap applications.

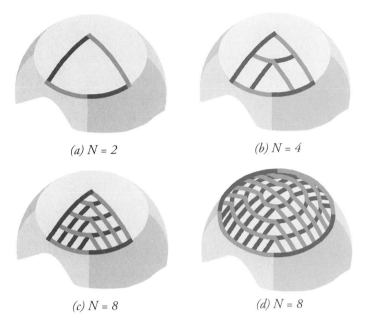

(a) N = 2   *(b) N = 4*

(c) N = 8   *(d) N = 8*

FIGURE 2.5.4 Partition the region where

$$(\phi, z) \in \left[0, \frac{\pi}{4}\right] \times \left[\frac{2}{3}, 1\right]$$

at three resolutions (a) N = 2, (b) N = 4, and (c) N = 8. (d) shows the complete partition on the polar base face with N=8.

Isocube versus Cubemap

We now compare the isocube to the cubemap. Suppose that one sample is positioned at each element's center. The left column in Figure 2.5.5 shows the sampling patterns of the cubemap and isocube. At the same face resolution, the isocube distributes samples more evenly on the sphere, while the cubemap places more samples at the face corners.

The middle column in Figure 2.5.5 visualizes how the cubemap (upper) is distorted on the isocube by mapping the cubemap subdivision lines onto the isocube map (lower). The central regions of the cube faces are stretched on the isocube map, while the corner regions are suppressed. This explains why the isocube places samples more evenly on the sphere.

The right column in Figure 2.5.5 shows the same environment represented as the cubemap and isocube. In comparison, the straight lines in the cubemap may become curves in the isocube.

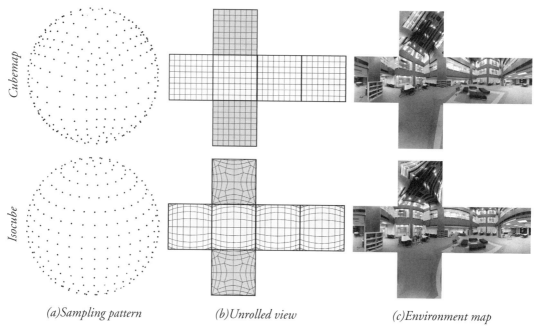

(a)Sampling pattern   *(b)Unrolled view*   *(c)Environment map*

FIGURE 2.5.5 (a) compares the associated sampling patterns of the cubemap and isocube. (b) shows how the cubemap is distorted on the isocube map. Basically, the straight lines in the cubemap may become curves in the isocube. (c) shows the same environment in both maps.

Isocube Environment Mapping

As the isocube fits nicely into the six-face cube structure, it can be easily loaded into the cubemap hardware. To further exploit the cubemap hardware, we need to convert the reflection vector $R=[x,y,z]^T$ to the texture lookup vector $Q=[s,t,q]^T$ that satisfies the requirements of the hardware cubemap operations. With Q, the isocube can utilize the hardware cubemap operators such as the texture lookup and anti-aliasing operations.

To map $R{\rightarrow}Q$, we introduce an intermediate index I for the isocube map and decompose the mapping into two successive steps. The first step computes the index I of the pixel (in the isocube map) that the reflection vector $R=[x,y,z]^T$ points to. The second step converts the index I to the texture lookup vector $Q=[s,t,q]^T$ required by the hardware cubemap operations, that is

$$[x, y, z]^T \rightarrow I \rightarrow [s,t,q]^T$$

$$3$$

Notation I refers to an indexing scheme of samples on the isocube. It is composed of a tuple $[c,o]^T$. As shown in Figure 2.5.6, the samples on the isocube map form a set of rings (indicated as dashed circles) parallel to the equator. We define c to be the index of the ring, where the current pixel lies, counting from the north pole. We then define o as the pixel's index counting from the sample located at/near to $\phi=0$ on the

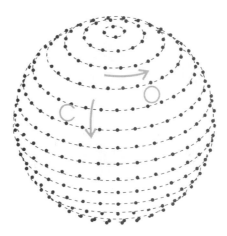

FIGURE 2.5.6 Indexing the samples on the isocube

ring c, where $[\theta,\phi]^T$ are spherical coordinates of R. Given a reflection vector R, $[c,o]^T$ can be computed efficiently according to equations (1)–(4).

We further extend the index I to the homogenous form $I=[c,o,1]^T$. The mapping $I \rightarrow Q$ can then be written in the matrix form,

$$
\begin{bmatrix} s \\ t \\ q \end{bmatrix} = \mathbf{A} \begin{bmatrix} c \\ o \\ 1 \end{bmatrix}
$$

4

where

$$
\mathbf{A} = \begin{bmatrix} a_{11} & a_{12} & 0 \\ a_{21} & 0 & a_{23} \\ a_{31} & a_{32} & 0 \end{bmatrix}
$$

5

The values of $\mathbf{A}$'s elements are listed in Table 2.5.1.

Table 2.5.1 Values of elements in $\mathbf{A}$

	a_{11}	a_{12}	a_{31}	a_{32}		a_{21}	a_{23}
$\phi \in \left[0, \frac{1}{2}\pi\right)$	1	0	0	2	$z \in \left(\frac{2}{3}, 1\right]$	0	1
$\phi \in \left[\frac{1}{2}\pi, \pi\right)$	2	−2	1	0	$z \in \left[-\frac{2}{3}, \frac{2}{3}\right]$	−1	1
$\phi \in \left[\pi, \frac{3}{2}\pi\right)$	−1	0	4	-2	$z \in \left[-1, -\frac{2}{3}\right)$	0	−1
$\phi \in \left[\frac{3}{2}\pi, 2\pi\right)$	−6	2	−1	0			

Despite the two-step decomposition, the actual computational cost of the complete mapping $R \rightarrow Q$ is rather low. The demonstration shader code in Cg shading language can be found below. To save the computational cost, we store the values of the left four elements in Table 2.5.1 into a lookup table signTBL.

```
 1  float3 R2Q( float3 R )
 2  {
 3    float2 I;
 4    float3 Q;
 5    float4 coef;
 6    float phi, y, ya, bequ, quar;
 7
 8    // compute azimuth angle and convert it in the range [0,4)
 9    phi  = 2*atan2(R.z, R.x)/PI;
10    phi += step(phi, -0.5) * 4;
11
12    // decide whether the pixel is in the equatorial region
13    y    = R.y * 1.5;
14    ya   = abs(y);
15    bequ = step(ya, 1.);
16
17    // convert  R → I
18    I.x  = sqrt(3 - 2*ya);
19    I.x  = lerp(I.x, 1, bequ);
20    I.y  = phi * I.x;
21
22    // map I → Q
23    quar = floor(phi + 0.5);
24    coef = texRECT(signTBL, float2(quar, 0));
25    Q.x  = dot(coef.xy, I);
26    Q.y  = lerp(sign(y), y, bequ);
27    Q.z  = dot(coef.zw, I);
28
29    return Q;
30  }
```

Figure 2.5.7 compares the rendering results of the isocube and cubemap environment mapping, both in a size of 512×512. The zoomed in Figures 2.5.7(b)–(e) demonstrate that the isocube samples the environment more regularly than the cubemap. In this specific example, the fine details in both Figure 2.5.7(d) and (b) are better preserved in the isocube than those in the cubemap.

The experiment was conducted on a Pentium IV 2.6 GHz CPU installed with NVIDIA GeForceFX 6800 Ultra. Both the isocube and cubemap have a resolution of 128×128 per face. We generate them by resampling a high-resolution environment cubemap (768×768 per face). With the MIPmapping anti-aliasing turned on, the isocube (optimized version of shader) achieves a frame rate of 300.4 fps, quite close to that of the cubemap (312.4 fps) when rendering the images in Figure 2.5.7. We further rendered another environment mapped object with 106,466 vertices on the same machine. The cubemap achieves 232.6 fps, while the isocube achieves a very high frame rate of 168.2 fps.

FIGURE 2.5.7 Environment mapping with the cubemap and isocube: (a) the rendered image in a size of 512×512; (b) and (d) are zoomed in images of the isocube environment mapping technique; (c) and (e) are zoomed in images of the cubemap environment mapping technique.

Conclusion

In this article, we introduce a novel six-face sphere map, or isocube, which fits nicely into the standard six-face cubemap. Unlike the cubemap, it samples the sphere evenly. The isocube has low computational costs and can exploit hardware cubemap operations, as well as achieve very high frame rates. Demonstration source code can be found in the companion DVD and at http://www.cse.cuhk.edu.hk/~ttwong/papers/spheremap/spheremap.html.

Acknowledgments

The work is supported by the Research Grants Council of the Hong Kong Special Administrative Region, under RGC Earmarked Grants (Project No. CUHK 417005 and CityU 115606).

References

[Heidrich98] Heidrich, Wolfgang and Seidel, Hans P. "View-independent Environment Maps," in *Proceedings of Graphics Hardware*, 1998: pp. 39–45.

[Górski99] Górski, Krzysztof K. M., Hivon, Eric E., and Wandelt, Benjamin B. D. "Analysis Issues for Large CMB Data Sets," in *Proceedings of the MPA/ESO Cosmology Conference, Evolution of Large-Scale Structure*, Eds. A.J. Banday, R.S. Sheth and L. Da Costa, PrintPartners Ipskamp, NL: pp. 37–42 (also astro-ph/9812350).

[Cui97] Cui, Jianjun, and Freeden,Willi. "Equidistribution on the Sphere," *SIAM Journal on Scientific Computing*, Vol. 18, No. 2, 1997: pp. 595–609.

[Shirley97] Shirley, P. and Chiu K. "A Low Distortion Map Between Disk and Square," *Journal of Graphics Tools*, Vol. 2, No. 3, 1997: pp. 45–52.

[Wan05] Wan, Liang, Wong, Tien-Tsin, and Leung, Chi-Sing. "Spherical Q2-tree for Sampling Dynamic Environment Sequences," in *Proceedings of Eurographics Symposium on Rendering 2005 (EGSR 2005)*, Konstanz, Germany, June 2005: pp. 21–30.

[Wan07] Wan, Liang, Wong, Tien-Tsin, and Leung, Chi-Sing. "Isocube: Exploiting the Cubemap Hardware", *IEEE Transactions on Visualization and Computer Graphics*, Vol. 13, No. 4, 2007: pp. 720–731.

2.6

Uniform Cubemaps for Dynamic Environments

Tze-Yui Ho

Chi-Sing Leung

Tien-Tsin Wong

Introduction

Environment mapping is an essential ingredient of certain graphics applications such as the mirror reflection effect. The most popular environment mapping technique is probably cubemapping because of its computational simplicity and memory-friendly rectilinear structure. Therefore, many graphics processing units (GPUs) are equipped with a hardware cubemap lookup module.

A cubemap is formed by six perspective images, and each face of the cubemap has a rectilinear structure, although not every environment mapping technique has both properties. These properties give cubemaps a very unique advantage for dynamic environment map preparation—that is, rendering the 3D models directly onto a cubemap using graphic hardware.

With regard to spherical sampling, however, the cubemap is non-uniform. As you can see in Figure 2.6.1, the distribution of samples at the face center is much sparser than the face corner on the sphere, which means some image details near the face centers cannot be represented in an appropriate manner.

To improve the uniformity of sampling, in *ShaderX4*, Wong [1] utilizes the HEALPix map [2]. Although the uniformity is improved, it does not take advantage of hardware supported cubemap lookup operations provided by the GPU. In addition, it is not suitable for rendering under dynamic environments.

The method proposed here, namely *uniform cubemaps*, uses a simple sine function to correct the texture coordinates before the lookup of cubemap texture. It turns cubemapping into uniform spherical sampling. Being like a cubemap, its implementation naturally benefits from the hardware supported cubemap architecture. The correction not only restores the uniformity of the cubemap but also maintains its rectilinear structure. As a result, we can render 3D models directly onto the uniform cubemap using graphics hardware.

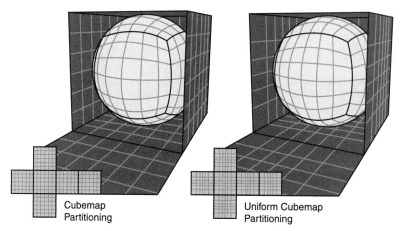

FIGURE 2.6.1 Visualization of grid pattern of standard cubemap and uniform cubemap.

First we will describe the detailed algorithm of the uniform cubemap. Following this we present a shader implementation with the Cg code of our proposed method. A mirror reflection demo with dynamic environment mapping is provided on the DVD.

Algorithm

Intuitively, a cubemap consists of six 2D textures (cubemap faces) where each texture corresponds to one face of a cube. Given a unit vector, a value can be looked up from the cubemap. The key step of a cubemap lookup is to scale up a vector so that it touches the cube. Afterward, the scaled vector can be used for the 2D texture lookup of the corresponding cubemap face.

Conventionally, each cubemap face is uniformly partitioned into a 2D texture. However, the mapping of the scaling up process, which maps a spherical surface to some planes, will distort the uniform partitions. As a result, the uniformity of cubemap is destroyed.

To rectify the uniformity of a cubemap, we partition the cubemap faces non-uniformly in their natural Cartesian space. This can be achieved by correcting the texture coordinates (x,y) of a cubemap face using a correction function f, which is given by

$$f(x) = (1-r)x + r\sin(\frac{\pi}{2}x)$$

1

Where $x \in [-1,1]$ and r is an empirical constant of value 0.5512575. The corrected texture coordinates are taken to be $(f(x), f(y))$. Figure 2.6.2 visualizes how a cubemap face is partitioned non-uniformly.

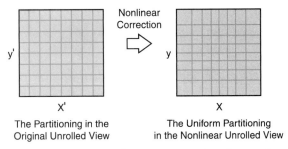

FIGURE 2.6.2 Non-uniform partition of a cubemap face.

The Correction Function

More precisely, the correction function f is the linear interpolation of x and

$$\sin(\frac{\pi}{2}x)$$

where the ratio r controls the interpolation. Figure 2.6.3 shows the correction graphically. To visualize the distortion introduced by cubemapping, we consider a uniformly partitioned arc that is the cross section of a sphere. When these uniform partitions (along the arc) are mapped to a cubemap face (along the x-axis), they are no longer uniform. To improve the uniformity, we again map the partitions by the correction function f. The re-mapped partitions (along the y-axis) again become uniform.

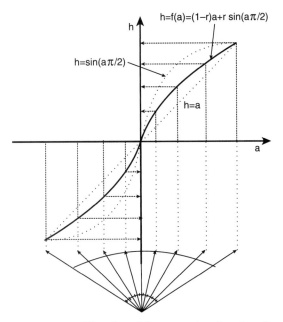

FIGURE 2.6.3 The plot of the correction function f.

The x term and

$$\sin(\frac{\pi}{2}x)$$

term of correction function f are intended for the no correction and the curvature correction respectively. By adjusting the value of r, we can control the strength of the correction.

Discrepancy Analysis

To use the correction function, we have to determine the ratio. Although it is feasible to select a ratio based on observation, a systematic decision is more desirable. To systematically decide a ratio, we need to find a ratio so that the discrepancy [3] is minimized.

The discrepancy is given by

$$D(N) = \frac{1}{2\sqrt{\pi}N}\left[\sum_{i,j=1}^{N}\left(1-2\ln(1+\sqrt{\frac{1-\eta_i \cdot \eta_j}{2}}\right)\right]^{\frac{1}{2}}$$

Where

$$\{\eta_1,...,\eta_n\}$$

is an N-point sequence and

$$\eta_i$$

is a point on the sphere. The lower the D is, the more uniformly distributed the sampling pattern is.

We found that the minimum discrepancy is attained when the ratio equals 0.5512575, so the ratio we chose was 0.5512575.

In addition, by applying the same discrepancy formula, the discrepancies of cubemapping, HEALPix, and uniform cubemaps are calculated under various numbers of samples. Figure 2.6.4 shows the discrepancy performance curves of these methods.

As you can see in Figure 2.6.4, the discrepancy of uniform cubemaps is better than cubemapping. Although the implementation of uniform cubemaps is simpler than the HEALPix, they attain almost the same discrepancy performance.

Uniform Cubemap Lookup

We now present the basic implementation of the uniform cubemap lookup. First, a unit vector for the lookup is converted to the texture coordinates (x,y) of a cubemap face. Then (x,y) are corrected using $(f(x),f(y))$ from Equation 1. The corrected texture coordinates are then converted to a unit vector by normalizing it for the standard cubemap lookup.

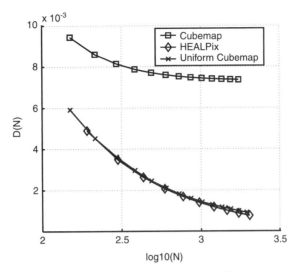

FIGURE 2.6.4 Discrepancy of various sampling patterns

The following Cg code is the fragment shader for the mirror reflection effect using uniform cubemaps. The Cg code is just a standard mirror reflection implementation, except that the reflection vector is being corrected before the cubemap lookup.

```
void cgfl_fp(
  float3 bv    : TEXCOORD0, // vertex
  float3 bn    : TEXCOORD1, // vertex normal

  uniform float so,  // correction factor

  uniform samplerCUBE cubemap,  // the uniform cubemap
  uniform float3 eye,  // eye position
  uniform float4x4 me, // environment rotation
  out float3 color : COLOR // output color
){

  bn = normalize(bn);  // normalize vertex normal

  float3 e, tt;
    e = normalize(eye-bv);  // calculate relative eye position
    bn = 2*dot(e,bn)*bn - e; // calculate the reflected ray

  bn = mul( me,  float4(bn,1)).xyz;  // apply environment rotation

// swizzle dominating coordinate to Y position
// so that we can assume texture coordinate of
// cubemap face is always at XZ position
  float3 abn = abs( bn );
  if( abn.x>abn.y && abn.x>abn.z )
    bn.xyz = bn.zxy;
  else if( abn.z>abn.y )
    bn.xyz = bn.yzx;
```

```
      // scale up the unit vector to touch the cube
      float3 cn = bn.xyz/abs(bn.y);

      ////////////////////////////////
      // uniform cubemap correction
      //
      // apply correction function to get (f(x),f(y))
      cn.xz = lerp( cn.xz, sin( cn.xz*1.570796327), so  );
      //
   // End of the correction
   ////////////////////////////////

      // re-normalize the corrected vector for
      // standard cubemap lookup
      float3 tc = normalize(cn);

      // reverse the swizzling
   if( abn.x>abn.y && abn.x>abn.z )
      tc.xyz = tc.yzx;
   else if( abn.z>abn.y )
      tc.xyz = tc.zxy;

   color = f3texCUBE( cubemap, tc );  // standard cubemap lookup
}
```

Notice that the calculation of cubemap coordinates is indeed redundant, as the hardware cubemap lookup module should have a similar implementation already. Unfortunately, because we could not change the hardware implementation of the cubemap lookup, we can only re-implement it.

Static Environment Preparation

In the case in which the environment map consists of only static content and is represented by a cubemap, we can simply resample it into a uniform cubemap. Figure 2.6.5 shows the differences between the content of a cubemap face and a uniform cubemap face. We will now present a method to resample a cubemap to a uniform cubemap.

(a)   *(b)*

FIGURE 2.6.5 (a) Cubemap face. (b) Uniform cubemap: a resampled version of the same image. (© Cubemap reprinted with permission from Paul Debevec: for permission, see http://www.debevec.org/Probes [4].)

Typically, the resolution of the source cubemap should be five times higher than the targeted resolution of the uniform cubemap. As shown in Figure 2.6.6, we prepare all sample directions and solid angles of the source cubemap. By applying the correction function on cubemap directions, we map all cubemap samples to uniform cubemap samples. The data in the source cubemap are then weighted by their solid angles. Both weighted data and solid angles are accumulated in two uniform cubemap buffers. Afterward, we can normalize the weighted uniform cubemap data with the accumulated solid angles.

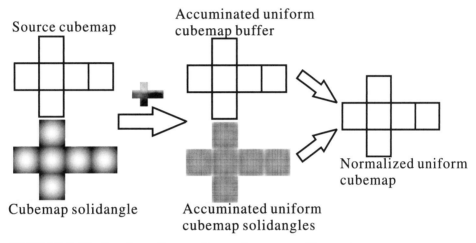

Source cubemap

Accuminated uniform cubemap buffer

Cubemap solidangle

Accuminated uniform cubemap solidangles

Normalized uniform cubemap

FIGURE 2.6.6   The flowchart of resampling a cubemap to uniform cubemap.

Dynamic Environment Preparation

Another important application of cubemapping is the rendering of dynamic environments. In this case, the triangular meshes are directly rendered into six cubemap faces as six perspective images. During rendering, a rasterization process is used (the rasterization of a triangle requires the rectilinear structure). Most of the existing uniform environment mapping techniques do not have this property. As a result, these environment maps can only be prepared indirectly by resampling a higher resolution cubemap. On the contrary, as the texture coordinates of cubemap face (x,y) are corrected separately in our approach, the rectilinear structure is preserved in a small region. Hence, the triangular meshes can be directly rendered into uniform cubemap.

During the rendering of a uniform cubemap face, the vertices are transformed by the model-view projection to the screen positions (x,y) in the vertex shader as usual. Interestingly, the screen position can also be considered as the texture coordinates of a cubemap face; therefore, we apply the correction function f on the screen positions. The corrected screen positions $(f(x),f(y))$ are then passed on to the graphics pipelines for ordinary rasterization. The resulting images are used as the uniform cubemap faces.

The following Cg code is the vertex shader for rendering the uniform cubemap face.

```
void cgde_vp(
  float4 av : POSITION,  // vertex
  float3 an : NORMAL,  // vertex normal

  out float4 bp : POSITION,  // screen position
  out float3 bc : COLOR0,  // output color

  uniform float3 l,  // lighting position
  uniform float3 ka,  // ambient color
  uniform float3 kd,  // diffuse color
  uniform float so,  // the correction factor
  uniform float4x4 mvp  // model-view projection
){
  bc = ka + kd*max(dot(an,l),0);  // phong model calculation

  float2 tc;
  float2 pn;

  bp = mul( mvp, av );  // model-view projection transform

  pn = bp.xy/bp.w;  // normalize the screen position
  if( abs(pn.x)<1.5 && abs(pn.y)<1.5 )
  {
     // applying correction function
tc = lerp( pn, sin(pn*1.570796327), so );

// inverse the normalization
     bp.xy = tc*bp.w;
  }
}
```

Results

Figure 2.6.7 shows the rendered results of the mirror reflection under a dynamic environment. The environment map contains two dynamically generated airplanes and a static environment. The environment map of Figure 2.6.7(b) is a uniform cubemap, whereas the environment map of Figure 2.6.7(c) is a regular cubemap. While the resolutions of both environment maps are the same (6*256*256), the mirror reflection effect in Figure 2.6.7(b) is more accurately generated—that is the result of using the uniform environment mapping technique.

(a) Rendered result   *(b) Uniform cubemap*   *(c) Cubemap*

FIGURE 2.6.7 The rendering results of uniform cubemaps and cubemap-based mirror reflection under a dynamic environment are shown in Figures (b) and (c). Both environment maps contain two dynamically generated airplanes and a static environment map.

Conclusion

In this article, we present a novel uniform environment mapping technique, namely the uniform cubemap. It can be implemented at low cost, as its data structure closely resembles the data structure and lookup algorithm of a standard cubemap. In addition, the triangular meshes can be rendered directly into the uniform cubemap as it maintains the rectilinear structure. The complete source and demo program, the mirror reflection with dynamic environment, are available on the companion DVD-ROM.

Acknowledgments

We would like to thank Paul Debevec for permission to demonstrate our technique with the HDR cubemap [4] "uffizi." This work is supported by RGC Earmarked Grants (CityU 115606) and (CUHK 417107) from HKSAR.

References

[1] Wong, Tien-Tsin, Wan, Liang, Leung, Chi-Sing, and, Ping-Man. "Real-Time Environment Mapping with Equal Solid-Angle Spherical Quad-Map", *ShaderX4*, 2005: pp. 221–233.

[2] Górski, Krzysztof K. M., Hivon, Eric E., and D. Wandelt, Benjamin B. "Analysis Issues for Large CMB Data Sets," in *Proceedings of the MPA/ESO Cosmology Conference, Evolution of Large-Scale Structure*, Eds. A.J. Banday, R.S. Sheth and L. Da Costa, PrintPartners Ipskamp, NL: pp. 37–42 (also astro-ph/9812350).

[3] Cui, J. J. and Freeden, W. "Equidistribution on the sphere," *SIAM Journal on Scientific Computing*, Vol. 18, No. 2, 1997: pp. 595–609.

[4] Debevec, Paul. "Rendering Synthetic Objects Into Real Scenes: Bridging Traditional and Image-Based Graphics With Global Illumination and High Dynamic Range Photography", *Proceedings of SIGGRAPH 98, Computer Graphics Proceedings, Annual Conference Series*, Orlando, Florida, July 1998: pp. 189–198.

2.7

Practical Geometry Clipmaps for Rendering Terrains in Computer Games

Rafael P. Torchelsen

João L. D. Comba

Rui Bastos

Introduction

Rendering terrains with a high degree of realism is an ongoing need of the computer game community. To render scenes with increasing sizes and complexity, several terrain rendering algorithms have been proposed in the literature. A recent and very important approach is called *geometry clipmaps* [Losasso04]; it relies on the position of the viewpoint to create a multi-resolution representation of the terrain using nested meshes. This approach was further improved and most of the processing computation was transferred to the GPU [Asirvatham05]. Although it is very efficient and allows support for large terrain models, such an approach presents shortcomings when used for computer games. For instance, there was no support for color texturing, real-time deformations, solutions for older shader models, and a mesh tessellation designed for artistic editing.

In this article, we revisit the geometry clipmaps approach and propose several modifications to the original algorithm that take all these aspects into consideration. Our proposal allows its use in a wider variety of GPUs and shader models. Speed-ups and modifications based on needs of computer games give us a technique with high fps rendering capability, resulting in an attractive solution for terrain rendering in games.

Review of Geometry Clipmaps

The geometry clipmaps technique is based on building a set of nested meshes (called clipmaps) that surround the viewpoint with varying levels of detail, thereby keeping the higher resolution clipmap near the viewpoint. One advantage of this technique is a reduction on the CPU-GPU bandwidth because only updated heights are sent to vertices defined on a 2D mesh that is already stored in GPU memory. Figure 2.7.1 illustrates a top-down view of a terrain using different shades to illustrate each clipmap (lighter shades are associated with higher mesh resolution), and the resulting rendering of clipmaps that represent a terrain mesh. Each clipmap is formed by grouping rectangular blocks that form a "ring" surrounding the viewpoint. Because every clipmap ring must lie inside another ring and present a smooth transition across different resolutions, certain conditions must be imposed on the number of vertices in the perimeter of each ring. A more detailed discussion is presented on [Asirvatham05]. Here we simply state that the number of vertices must be odd and represented by one minus a giving power of $(2^n - 1)$. Figure 2.7.2 shows how clipmaps are represented by rectangular grids chosen from a basic set of building blocks (each represented internally as a mesh patch) [Asirvatham05]. In order to keep the same amount of blocks on each clipmap ring, only three different types of building blocks are used: *block*, formed by $m \times m$ vertices, *ring fix-up*, formed by $m \times 3$ vertices, and *interior trim*, formed by $(2m + 1) \times 2$ vertices. The ring fix-up exists because we cannot close the ring only with the $m \times m$ blocks, while the interior trim is used to move the clipmaps over the height field.

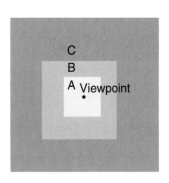
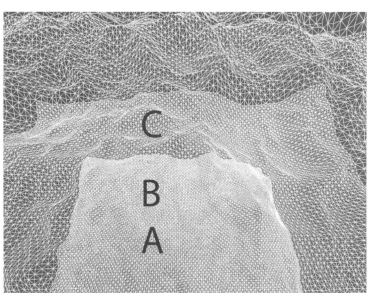

FIGURE 2.7.1 Top-view representation of three clipmaps (*A*, *B* and *C*). Clipmaps *A* and *B* use the same resolution because they are close to the viewer and there is no visible distinction between them in the rendered image, while the next clipmap uses a smaller resolution.

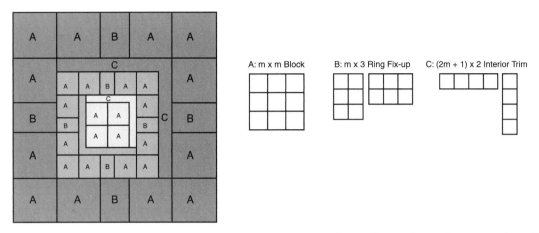

FIGURE 2.7.2 Three clipmap rings, white, light gray, and gray (left), are formed from a basic set (right) of three different rectangular building blocks.

The way each clipmap is represented by building blocks depends heavily on the position of the viewpoint and changes as the viewpoint moves. Figure 2.7.3 illustrates the movement of the interior trims while the viewpoint moves to the right. Moving the interior trims changes only the clipmap where it belongs, as well as the inner clipmaps, but the outer clipmaps are left unchanged, saving CPU-GPU bandwidth. Details on how building blocks change while the viewpoint move can be found in [Losasso04, Asirvatham05].

In the sections that follow, we summarize several modifications to the clipmap algorithm to make it amenable for computer games.

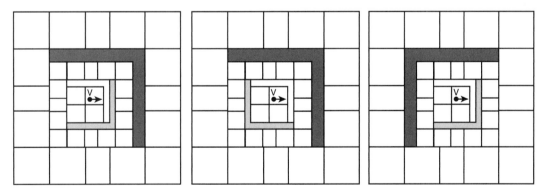

FIGURE 2.7.3 Moving the viewpoint three consecutive vertices to the right. The interior trim changes sides in different ways on each clipmap ring. In the most internal ring, the interior trim changes sides at every movement, while the next nested ring moves at intervals every other movement.

Terrain Tessellation

Editing capabilities are a major concern for a game developer. Terrains represented by a height field are defined by a mesh over a support plane, with each vertex associated with a given height that is displaced along the plane normal vector. Editing a terrain mesh based on a height field is simple; the artist just increases or decreases the heights of each vertex.

The impact on adjacent triangles while changing the height of a given vertex (item A in Figure 2.7.4) depends on the tessellation pattern used. The original tessellation pattern used in the clipmaps technique is illustrated in Figure 2.7.4 (original pattern). The drawback of this pattern is that there is a hexagonal region of neighboring triangles that is affected when displacing vertices, which was found to confuse the artist in some situations. We proposed a modification of this pattern to the one illustrated in Figure 2.7.4 (practical pattern), which has a more symmetrical pattern. This simple modification allows the artist a better estimation on the impact of each displacement, even to the point where the artist could edit the terrain without using wireframe, which they prefer.

Original   Practical

FIGURE 2.7.4 Tessellation used in the original clipmaps (left) and practical solution (right). Moving the vertex A changes the surface in the shaded region. The surface resulting from the move of the vertex A in the practical tessellation is more easily estimated, even without wireframe.

The only issue that needs to be addressed when using this new tessellation is that it requires pairs of shifted regular grids so that their combination tessellates the plane. It is important to observe that using twice the number of tessellations per terrain only doubles the number of triangle indices, but does not double their coordinate locations (see Figure 2.7.5). Therefore, it suffices to have an additional index buffer per regular grid, but we need to identify which one to use to keep tessellation at the grids' frontiers.

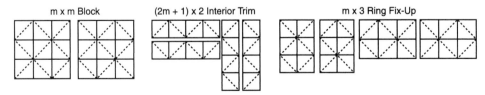

FIGURE 2.7.5 Regular grids' triangulations using an artist-friendly tessellation

The choice of which of the two tessellation patterns will be used can be made by checking the parity of the texture (height field) coordinates associated to the top-left-most vertex of the grid. By simply checking the parity, we can select a tessellation based on the predefined solutions above, as illustrated in Figure 2.7.6. The same can be done for all other configurations, thus enforcing correct match between neighboring grids over the entire height field.

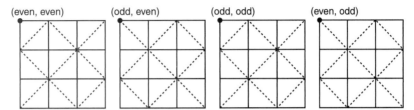

FIGURE 2.7.6 Choosing tessellation patterns is based on the parity of the texture (height field) coordinates associated to the top-leftmost vertex.

A final terrain triangulation using these new tessellations is illustrated in Figure 2.7.7.

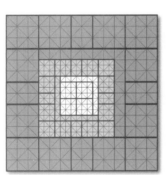

FIGURE 2.7.7 Terrain triangulation illustrating tessellation matching between regular grids from the same clipmap ring.

Height Field

The original clipmap work uses a compression scheme for the storage of the height field that might not be attractive for a game implementation. Because it only decompresses the height field around the viewpoint, checking for collision of objects in regions away from the viewpoint requires a local decompression that might be costly when a lot of objects are present, such as in RTS games. Also, real-time editing updates of the height field would require a decompression and compression scheme that guarantees frame rate, which is not present in the original work. Therefore, in this case, it is preferable to avoid the compression scheme. This solution obviously limits the size of the terrain, but it is still possible to obtain reasonably large terrains.

The height field in the clipmap work of [Asirvatham05] was stored on the GPU using a texture. It requires texture reads in the vertex shader that can only be accomplished in Shader Model 3 (SM3) and higher. In addition, handling collisions is also an issue using this approach. In our work, we decided to use the CPU to manipulate the height field and define the displacements, and use the GPU to apply the displacements (vertex shader) and lighting (pixel shader).

Every clipmap ring has an associated resolution that represents the mapping of its vertices to the vertices of the original height field. Full mapping (one-to-one mapping) is associated to the first and second clipmaps closer to the viewpoint. The following clipmaps decrease their resolution by a factor of two with respect to the inner clipmap.

Processing every vertex requires three heights to be accessed from the height field: one for the level of detail in the clipmap to which the vertex belongs and two others used to generate the vertex height in the outer clipmap. All three are used in the geometry morphing in the perimeter of the clipmap.

Morphing Between Different Resolutions

Different levels of detail might cause T-junction vertices, which must be removed to avoid cracks in the mesh. Similar to the original clipmap work, we use a morphing area to morph between different resolution levels (Figure 2.7.8).

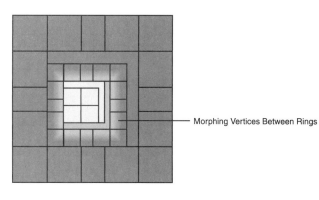

Morphing Vertices Between Rings

FIGURE 2.7.8 The morphing area denoted by the gray gradient between the first and second rings illustrates the smooth morphing of the vertices from one resolution to the next.

This is accomplished by subdividing the work between the CPU and the GPU. Instead of sending to the GPU just one height associated with each vertex in the mesh, we send two heights, one corresponding to the level of detail in the ring where the vertex belongs and one corresponding to its adjacent ring. Using these two heights, we can slowly interpolate them, which produces a smooth transition from one resolution to the next, thus avoiding cracks. Since the bandwidth is one of the most common bottlenecks, the two heights are sent using 16 bits each, resulting in 32 bits per vertex, the minimum data structure that can be used to create a vertex. The height from the ring where the vertex belongs is directly read from the height field but the height that corresponds to the next ring is generated on-the-fly.

The size of the morphing area depends on how heights vary in the terrain. For smoother regions, only a small area might be necessary, but for highly irregular regions a larger region might be needed. The morphing area is illustrated with different shades in Figure 2.7.8.

In Figure 2.7.9, we illustrate crack problems that can happen across different rings. Vertices B and E from Figure 2.7.9 can generate a crack in the mesh if they use one of the heights from the height field. Those vertices must be moved to a position that exists in the next ring to avoid cracks. The only directions the vertices can go are up or down with respect to the supporting plane. The only position in the next ring that exists in those directions is over one of the edges formed by the neighbors of B and E. Figure 2.7.9 illustrates the four existing neighboring configurations used to identify that edge. Those configurations exist because all rings use the same tessellation.

Morphing vertices across the frontier of two rings avoids cracks but does not create a smoother transition between rings, and therefore all vertices inside the morphing area are required to be morphed. Vertices H and K in Figure 2.7.9 illustrate the other two configurations of neighbors for vertices inside the ring that must be handled to identify the morphing target (position of the vertex in the surrounding ring).

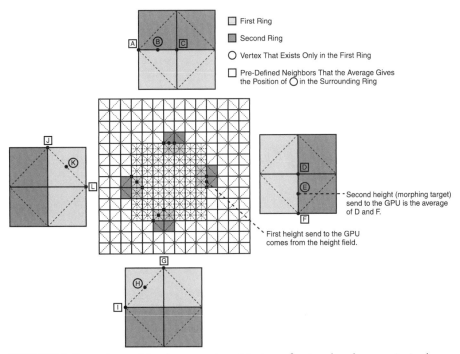

FIGURE 2.7.9 Smooth transition between rings: Vertices of a ring that do not exist in the surrounding ring are morphed to positions in the middle of the edges formed by neighbors of the vertex (B, E, H, and K). Shaded squares illustrate the existing vertices' configurations and the pre-defined vertices' neighbors that are considered for the morphing target calculation.

The morphing target is the second height sent to the GPU and is generated for all vertices that do not exist in the level of detail from the surrounding ring. The vertices that exist in both rings like *A* and *C* have the same height, which is duplicated in both channels.

Texture Layers

The traditional texturing technique used in terrain rendering is based on texture layers. A *texture layer* is a covering of the entire terrain that can represent different materials, such as grass, rocks, snow, and so on. To determine the final color of the pixels, an alpha texture between every layer tells the contribution of the layer to the final color of the pixel.

The layers are formed by three components:

- **Color texture:** A texture corresponding to grass, rocks, snow, etc.
- **Tiling:** Tells how many times the color texture repeats itself between vertices of the terrain, defined as α
- **Alpha texture:** Tells the contribution the color texture has to the final color of the pixel

Figure 2.7.10 illustrates an example of a terrain mesh defined over the support plane with two texture layers. The first layer uses an alpha texture to render the color texture at regular intervals. The second layer uses the alpha texture in such way that the color texture appears at regular intervals, but applies gradients to slowly show the color texture. The gradient can be used to represent smooth changes between layers such as to simulate discontinuities on materials in the terrain (e.g., start of grass after a sidewalk).

The size of the alpha texture does not need to match between layers, but using the same size in all layers allows it to be optimized by concatenating four alpha textures in one and reading them all at the same time in the pixel shader. Normally the alpha texture is edited by an artist, but it can be procedurally generated based on the height of

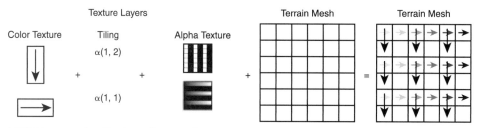

FIGURE 2.7.10 Application of texture layers to a terrain.

the vertex (lower regions can be covered by grass, while mountains are covered by snow). The texturing of the terrain in the accompanying demo was generated automatically using that process.

The texture coordinates are generated per frame and only in the rendered vertices, which avoids unnecessary calculations and storage of large amounts of data per vertex (one texture coordinate per texture layer would be necessary). This process is illustrated in Figure 2.7.11 by the regular replication of a sample texture (containing a simple shape—an arrow).

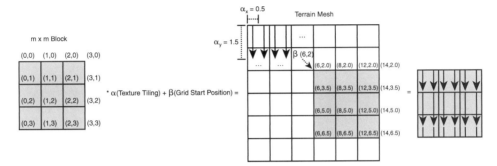

FIGURE 2.7.11 The texture layer used in the terrain mesh uses a color texture in the shape of a down arrow with tiling (0.5, 1.5). The layer covers all the terrain (denoted by the "…") but we are only interested in the shaded region.

Every regular grid has a default texture coordinate system with its origin at the top-leftmost vertex as illustrated in the $m \times m$ block from Figure 2.7.11. Mapping a texture layer to the grid is a two step process.

In the first step, the texture coordinates are scaled based on the 2D texture tiling α associated with the texture layer, which creates a space between vertices to fit the color texture. The example in Figure 2.7.11 uses a tiling of (0.5, 1.5), creating space for two color textures between intervals of vertices in the x axis and 1.5 in the y axis. The mapping is illustrated by the arrow texture that repeats itself two times horizontally and 2/3 vertically between intervals of vertices.

The second step is adding a translation to the grid, sending it to its position in the height field based on the viewpoint. The amount of translation is denoted by β in Figure 2.7.11, which is a parameter valid for all vertices of the grid, so it is calculated on the CPU and sent to the GPU.

Mapping the default coordinate system to the texture layer is a process that must be done for all texture layers because they all have unique color textures and tilings. Therefore, for all texture layers there is a constant in the shader for the color texture, α and β, but only the latter changes between grid renderings.

Hole Layer

Sometimes game objects such as caves intersect the terrain, so we need a way to open holes in the mesh. Instead of modifying the terrain mesh to create holes or using transparent regions that would require ordered rendering, we use a feature of the raster operations that avoids the contribution of some pixels, leaving an unpainted region that resembles a hole in the mesh. The hole layer is composed by an alpha texture that defines regions on the terrain mesh that must not be taken into account while rendering the terrain. In DirectX, holes are defined by setting the render states `Alpharef` to 1 and `Alphafunc` to `Equal`. That way, any output pixel of the terrain that is mapped to a value different than 1 in the alpha texture will not be applied to the frame buffer. An example of creating a hole layer is illustrated in Figure 2.7.12.

FIGURE 2.7.12 A hole in a terrain is defined as a region of the mesh where there is no output pixel in the pixel shader, leaving unpainted regions.

Another use for the hole layer is to avoid rendering beyond the height field limits. Setting the render states `AddressU` and `AddressV` to `Border` and `BorderColor` to 0 makes any sample in the alpha texture (hole layer) outside the range ([0.0, 1.0], [0.0, 1.0]) to return 0, which discards the pixel in the frame buffer.

The alpha texture may not have the exact same size of the height field, which results in precision issues that cause problems while killing pixels at the borders of the height field. We set the height for all vertices outside the borders to the minimum height possible, resulting in a wall like the one shown in Figure 2.7.13. It is important to observe that this wall is not visualized because the camera in a game rarely gets close enough to the limits of the terrain. Actually, the only vertices that are sent to the minimum height are those that belong to a regular grid with at least some vertex inside the borders; otherwise, the grid is not rendered.

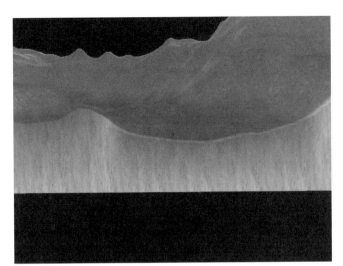

FIGURE 2.7.13 A visualization of the end of the world with a wall created by vertices outside the borders. The base of the wall is not rendered because the hole layer kills the pixels that sample outside the alpha texture.

Demo

The accompanying demo includes a presentation of the technique illustrating what can be done and the scale of the terrains that can be created. Figure 2.7.14 illustrates the size of the terrain compared to a 3D model of a person. This demo was developed as a technological demo at SouthLogic Studios and is actively used in production.

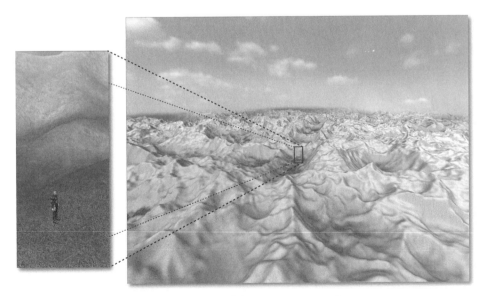

FIGURE 2.7.14 An illustration of the scale of the terrain compared to a person.

Performance

The terrain demo runs at an average of 580 fps in the recorded fly mode, using six texture layers. The height field size is 2,048×2,048 with distance between vertices of eight meters, resulting in a terrain with 256×256 km. Performance was measured on the following machine: AMD Athlon 64 3500+, 2 GB RAM, NVIDIA GeForce 7800 GTX. On a Pentium 4 2.8GHZ, 1 GB RAM, and a NVIDIA GeForce 6800 GT 256MB, the average fps was 300.

The main shader bottleneck is the number of textures accessed in the pixel shader. A terrain with four layers requires four color textures, one alpha texture (three channels with alphas from the texture layer plus an alpha from the hole layer), and a texture for the normal map.

Conclusion

The original clipmap work was developed for rendering of large terrain datasets using the GPU [Asirvatham05]. However, some essential characteristics for games weren´t presented. Our modifications target practical applications of the clipmap technique for games. The results show high frame rates with a flexible technique not only in the media creation side but also on the range of GPUs that are capable of performing it.

Acknowledgments

We would like to thanks UFRGS (Universidade Federal do Rio Grande do Sul), CNPq, Southlogic, and NVIDIA for their support.

References

[Asirvatham05] Asirvatham, A. and Hoppe, H. "Terrain rendering using GPU-based geometry clipmaps," *GPU Gems 2*, Addison-Wesley, March 2005.

[Losasso04] Losasso, F. and Hoppe, H. "Geometry clipmaps: terrain rendering using nested regular grids," *SIGGRAPH'04: ACM SIGGRAPH 2004 Papers*, New York, NY, ACM Press, 2004: pp. 769–776.

2.8

Efficient and Practical TileTrees

Carsten Dachsbacher

VISUS/University of Stuttgart, Germany

Sylvain Lefebvre

REVES/INRIA Sophia-Antipolis, France

Introduction

Texture mapping with atlases suffers from several drawbacks: wasted memory, visible seams, fixed or uniform resolution, and no support of implicit surfaces. In order to generate a texture atlas, the surface is parameterized into the plane. While some surfaces have a natural planar parameterization, in most cases this operation is extremely difficult. The challenge is to flatten the surface while keeping distortion low, which often requires cutting the surface in independently parameterized charts. These charts are later packed into a single texture atlas. Providing a tight packing is key to reducing wasted memory. Unfortunately, the arbitrary shapes of the charts make this difficult.

Using volume textures solves most of these issues, but unfortunately it induces an important space and time overhead. The object is immersed into a volume storing color information around the surface, usually applying spatial data structures such as an octree. Parameterization is no longer an issue and seamless interpolation can be achieved. However, increased storage and costly lookups in the hierarchical data structures make this approach unattractive for games.

The TileTree approach [Lefebvre07] combines benefits from both texture atlases and volumetric approaches. TileTrees use a spatial data structure—an octree with low depth—to place square texture tiles around the surface to be textured. At rendering time the surface is projected onto these tiles and the color is retrieved by a simple 2D texture fetch from a tilemap. This avoids the difficulties of global planar parameterizations while still mapping large pieces of surface to regular 2D textures. In addition to a simple shader implementation for runtime lookups, the texture representation is compact, can be seamlessly interpolated, and—this is interesting when used in a painting application—natively supports adaptive resolution.

In this article we propose several optimizations to the original TileTree data structure. After a brief overview of the original TileTree, we will explain how to improve lookup efficiency with a simpler volume data structure and a packing strategy optimized for lookups. The result is much faster access into the data structure with almost no additional memory overhead.

The TileTree Data Structure

The TileTree approach starts by subdividing the space around the surface to be textured. For this, an octree is built, which is similar to volume texture approaches. However, instead of storing a single color value in the octree leaves, we map 2D *tiles* of texture data onto the *faces* of the leaf (up to six tiles per leaf). The tiles are compactly stored into a regular 2D texture, the *tilemap*. During rendering, each surface point is projected onto one leaf face. This produces texture coordinates that are then used to access the corresponding texture tile. This idea is illustrated Figure 2.8.1.

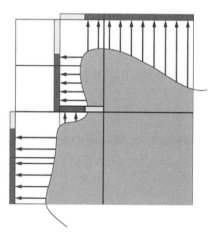

FIGURE 2.8.1 We position texture tiles around the surface using a spatial subdivision scheme. During rendering the surface is projected onto the tiles in the major axis of the surface normal. This figure shows the 2D equivalent of a TileTree: 1D tiles positioned around a curve.

Before going into details of the TileTree generation, the following steps outline the "how-to-use TileTrees" process (everything happens in pixel/fragment shaders):

1. Given the coordinates of the surface point to be textured, figure out in which octree leaf it resides.
2. Given the surface normal, find out onto which leaf face the surface point is projected.
3. Use the stored leaf data to retrieve the texture coordinate of the tile and look up the surface color.

While providing this very simple usage, TileTrees are also very compact in memory and easy to construct. Generating an improved TileTree consists of three steps:

1. We first generate the spatial data structure that is used to place the texture tiles around surfaces. As in the original work, we use an octree. We subdivide until surface pieces contained within each octree leaf can be mapped one-to-one onto the sides of the leaves. We rely on the same simple axis aligned parallel projection.
2. We add an additional step and generate an optimized nested grid structure from the octree. It provides access to the octree leaves with fewer indirections and with very little memory overhead.
3. We next pack and create texture tiles. Our packing is improved over the original one—not it terms of minimizing wasted texture space but rather to reduce the shader instruction count for runtime lookups.

In the following sections, we will only briefly repeat the most important elements of step 1; please refer to the original paper [Lefebvre07] for more details. Then we will detail step 2 and step 3, which are both improvements over the original TileTree.

Step 1: Octree Construction

As a start we use the bounding box of the object as the root of the octree. We only subdivide until no more than one fold exists in each leaf. This is important because our goal is to project the enclosed piece of surface onto one or more faces of the leaf so that each point is uniquely textured. In other words, we are looking for an injective projection. Since texture detail is usually much finer than the geometric features, the octree leaves, of course, tend to be much larger than the size of a texel.

For rendering, we need to perform the projection of a surface point onto the leaf faces at runtime, so the projection has to be as simple as possible. As a compromise between flexibility and simplicity, we choose to perform an axis-aligned parallel projection onto the faces of the leaves (see Figure 2.8.2). The face to project onto is chosen using the major direction of the surface normal. While being extremely simple to compute, this projection can handle non-trivial cases successfully, such as a full sphere or two-sided thin surfaces that are textured differently on each side (a previous failure case of octree textures). On the other hand, parts of the leaf faces may not be covered by projected surfaces, which will result in wasted memory as we store square texture tiles. Fortunately, we can reduce this waste by subdividing further down. Note that the distortion of this projection is no greater than the one due to a volumetric octree texture.

To summarize, the octree construction consists of the following steps:

1. Subdivide the octree until leaves contain at most one fold. Folds can be detected with raycasting or rasterization (for triangle meshes analytical solutions do exist, but we also support other surface representations).

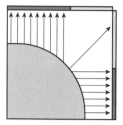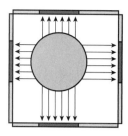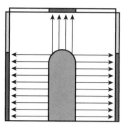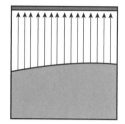

FIGURE 2.8.2 We use the surface normal to select the face onto which we project. The mapping is a simple parallel projection.

    2. Optionally, further subdivide the octree (please refer to [Lefebvre07] for details).
        a.   Subdivide leaves that waste too much memory.
        b.   Subdivide leaves to form "stacked" configurations (see below).

The initial subdivision and optional optimization steps decompose the surface to be textured into parts (contained within the leaves) that can be textured easily and with little waste of memory as shown in Figure 2.8.3. After subdivision, the leaves can have different configurations, as shown in Figure 2.8.4. We distinguish two main types of leaf configurations (the term *leaf*, used for the naming of configurations, stems from the fact that texture tiles are stored for leaf-nodes of the octree only). A *1-leaf* is a configuration where the surface projects onto a single face. An *n-leaf* is a leaf where the surface projects to more than one face. Now, within the set of 1-leaves we distinguish two special cases. A *full-leaf* is a 1-leaf where the tile is entirely used. An interesting configuration is the *leaf-stack*: a set of 1-leaves at the same octree level that are neighboring in the direction of the face supporting the tile (see Figure 2.8.4). The important property of a leaf-stack is that all the faces in the stack can share a same texture tile without overlapping.

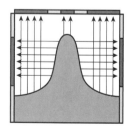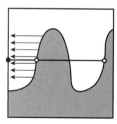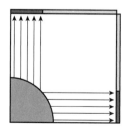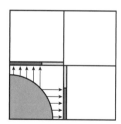

FIGURE 2.8.3 a) Each leaf may contain up to one fold in the direction of projection. b) If more than one fold is present, the projection is not trivial and the leaf has to be split. c) and d) The coverage of texture tiles can be increased (and thus memory waste reduced) when leaves, such as the one shown here, are further subdivided.

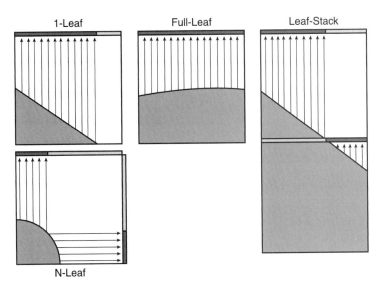

FIGURE 2.8.4 The two main types of leaves and the sub-types of 1-leaves.

To summarize: The result of this step is an octree subdividing the bounding box of the input object. Each non-empty octree leaf contains a part of the surface that contains no folds.

Step 2: Nested Grids

Given the tilemap, which will be described in detail in the next section, we can render textured surfaces directly using the octree—this is what was done in the original approach. Octree lookups can be implemented on GPUs [Lefebvre05], but the typical depth of such an octree involves many dependent texture lookups. To alleviate this cost, we propose converting the octree, which is convenient for the TileTree construction, to a nested grid hierarchy that is more efficient for rendering. In our experiments we found that relying on only two indirections significantly improves rendering speed while sacrificing little additional memory (a negligible amount compared to the texture data). We could, of course, use a single indirection, but this would likely put additional burden on memory as our trees tend to have a few small leaves. Please note that we use the term *leaf* to denote a leaf of the octree that contains information to texture the surface contained within. The term *cell* is used in the context of (nested) grids.

Using two indirections means that we have three levels of nested grids, two intermediate levels L_1 and L_2 and the last level L_3 (see Figure 2.8.5). The grid level L_1 is fully stored as a volumetric texture of $g_1{}^3$ texels. Each grid entry either contains a pointer toward a grid of the next level (if finer cells are present at this location) or data from octree leaves. Grids at the last, i.e. the finest, level L_3 only contain data (no more indirections).

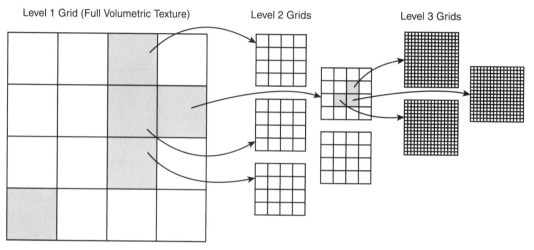

Level 1 Grid (Full Volumetric Texture)   Level 2 Grids   Level 3 Grids

FIGURE 2.8.5 The 2D equivalent of our nested grid hierarchy: The octree is replaced by three levels of grids. The first is fully stored as a 3D texture, the other two as a stack of 3D textures. Levels 1 and 2 may store indirections or data while level 3 only holds cell data, i.e. information on texture tiles.

The resolution of the grids varies from one level to the next. However, the grids of the last level have to be fine enough to capture the smallest octree leaves. Consider the example of an octree of depth 7, where depth 0 is the root with $(2^0)^3$ nodes (actually one node) and depth 7 represents the finest level with up to $(2^7)^3 = 128^3$ nodes. In this case, the finest resolution of our grid hierarchy has to be able to capture up to 128^3 cells. This could be achieved by choosing the following grid resolutions: $g_1=2$, $g_2=4$ and $g_3=16$, because $g_1 \times g_2 \times g_3 = 128$. Our key idea is that instead of fixing these sizes, we optimize them to best fit a given octree while minimizing memory cost.

The optimization process is a brute force search for all possible power-of-two grid resolutions between 2^3 and 32^3. The maximum reachable resolution would thus be $(32 \times 32 \times 32)^3 = 32,768^3$, which corresponds to an octree of depth 15 and is probably enough for most applications. Recall that this is not the maximum texture resolution as we only use this data structure to place texture tiles.

For any given set of grid resolutions g_1, g_2, and g_3, we determine the number of grids N_2 and N_3 required at levels L_2 and L_3 to encode the octree. We start with level L_1. Each grid can only store octree leaves that have a spatial extent equal to or larger than its grid cells. A larger leaf simply occupies multiple grid cells. However, a smaller leaf cannot be captured by the grid: We have to store an indirection to a grid at level L_2. This means that we will need as many L_2 grids as there are cells containing small leaves in L_1. The same relationship is true between L_2 and L_3.

After computing the number of grids required at levels L_2 and L_3 for each set of resolutions, we can easily compute the corresponding memory sizes. The L_1 grid is stored fully as a cubic volumetric texture of g_1^3 texels. L_2 and L_3 grids are grouped together and stored in two larger volume textures of size $(n_2 \cdot g_2) \times (n_2 \cdot g_2) \times g_2$ and $(n_3 \cdot g_3) \times (n_3 \cdot g_3) \times g_3$ with $n_2 = \text{ceil}(\text{sqrt}(N_2))$ and $n_3 = \text{ceil}(\text{sqrt}(N_3))$. These textures can be seen as 2D arrays of g_2^3 and g_3^3 texel blocks. We keep the grid resolutions incurring the smallest memory cost. This cost is often only slightly larger than the one of the octree, and even on complex examples the lookup is significantly faster.

Data Structures

The nested grids are stored as RGBA eight-bit textures to achieve a small memory footprint. A grid cell can either store an indirection to a nested grid at the next level or texture data—this is flagged using the alpha channel of an RGBA quadruple.

If alpha equals 0 the cell stores indirection pointers and R and G are used to index the appropriate nested grid at the next level. Recall that the nested grids are stored as 2D arrays of 3D grids.

If alpha is a non-zero value, the cell encodes texturing information. The R component holds the bit-flags, called the *leaf-type flag*. It tracks which tile faces are used (bit 0: +x, bit 1: –x, bit 2: +y, bit 3: –y, …). Channels G and B are used to index the *UVmap*. The *UVmap* stores the tilemap texture coordinates of the tiles mapped onto leaf faces (two 16-bit values, tiles are stored contiguously—see Step 4 below). We use this indirection because the eight bits of the nested grids would not be enough for tile coordinates, and switching to 16-bit textures for the nested grids would waste too much memory. Finally, the non-zero alpha value is not only used as flag, it also provides information about the size of the cell. As mentioned before, a grid cell can point to an octree leaf of larger size. Let's reconsider the octree: The size of an octree leaf halves with every subdivision level. We initially fix a base tile-resolution r_{base} for the octree, i.e. leaves of depth d using texture tiles of $(r_{\text{base}} \cdot 2^{-d} + 1)^2$ texels. The alpha value is simply used as a multiplier to this size and the size of the texture tiles is $(\alpha \cdot r_{\text{base}} \cdot 2^{-d} + 1)^2$ texels.

It is important to realize that apart from the size multiplier, the grid cells directly store leaf data. In fact, from the shader point of view, there is no difference between using the nested grids or the octree (once the multiplier is applied): Both return leaf data at a location p in space. It is therefore possible to easily switch between both.

One slight complication is that grid cells may store data for octree leaves that are larger than the grid cells. In order to compute the correct tile texture coordinates, we need to keep track of the original leaf size given by the octree (depth and leaf size are directly related). As we know the size of the grid cells (given g_1, g_2, and g_3), we can get away with storing a size multiplier that allows for more compact storage (for details see below).

Step 3: Tile Generation

With the octree construction we determined a list of octree leaves. These leaves are kept when using the nested grid optimization (recall that grid cells store the original leaf data).

The surface contained within each leaf projects onto up to six faces, for which we need to generate the texture tiles next. The data for filling the tiles can stem from different sources, such as a painting application, a full volumetric texture, or a standard texture atlas. Note that TileTrees are adaptive; resolution can be locally increased by increasing the resolution of a tile. The main application for TileTrees is interactive painting. Nonetheless, the compact storage and the relatively fast lookups also qualify them to be used as an alternative for texture atlases. For instance, they can be used to store solid procedural texturing that is too expensive for runtime evaluation. In any case, the only requirement to convert existing texture data to a TileTree is a function to retrieve the surface color from a given 3D location.

To generate the tile content we can either use raytracing or rasterization. In both cases we need to generate between one and six texture tiles for each leaf, depending on how many faces the surface within the leaf is projected onto. For easy tile content generation, we start by filling the tiles with the 3D locations of the surface points mapping to the texture samples. We render the tiles using an orthogonal view frustum where the leaf face is used as the near plane and the width and height of the frustum equals the leaf size. The distance to the far plane is either the leaf size as well, or, and this is the special case, it is a multiple of the leaf size if the tile is shared between leaves of a leaf-stack (recall stacked leaves share a same tile).

The frustum, however, has to be carefully aligned with the leaf faces. The centers of the border samples, i.e., texels, have to be aligned with the boundaries of the face. This is required for seamless interpolation during rendering and enables use of native hardware bilinear filtering. Note that this implies some sample duplication: Two neighboring tiles encode the same texels along their boundary. Preferring larger tiles reduces this overhead. To ensure matching texels between leaves using tiles of different resolution, the tile size must be equal to 2^k+1, with k a positive integer (Figure 2.8.6, left). In case of adaptive resolution, this will also ensure that samples of the finer resolution tile are aligned with samples of the coarser resolution tile (Figure 2.8.6, right).

There are two cases in which the generated texture tiles need additional post-processing: interpolated texture samples at tile borders and borders in non-full tiles. Both are necessary for a seamless texture interpolation and we will describe the necessary steps together with the interpolation strategy.

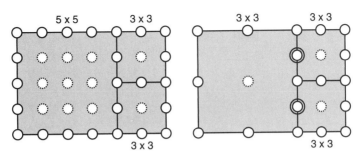

FIGURE 2.8.6 *Left:* To match samples across boundaries, tiles must have a size of $2k+1$. *Right:* Samples of tiles at different resolutions are aligned. Colors at texels marked by two circles require extra treatment: They are computed to be the bilinear interpolation of their neighbors on the border. This ensures continuity across resolutions.

Step 4: Tile Allocation and Packing

For efficient access during rendering, all texture tiles are packed together into the tilemap, which is a single texture. The square shape of the tiles allows for simpler, faster, and more compact packing than with the arbitrarily shaped charts of standard texture atlases.

In the original TileTree implementation, tiles within n-leaves are stored contiguously (a 1-leaf is an n-leaf with only one tile). For each leaf, then, a rectangle of $n(2k+1)^2$ texels was allocated, with $1 \leq n \leq 6$, where n is the number of tiles actually used in the leaf. We call this collection of tiles belonging to one leaf a *tile brood*. While this contiguous packing is very easy and compact, it requires that the leaf-type flags be decoded at runtime, which is an expensive bit-counting operation.

To alleviate this, we propose a different packing scheme in which the packing is slightly more involved but the runtime cost is reduced. The tile brood is no longer stored contiguously, instead we always assign a region of $6(2k+1)^2$ texels, i.e. six tiles wide, to each tile brood. However, not all of these six tiles are actually used, which has been determined during the octree construction and is stored in the leaf-type flag. While packing the tiles into the tilemap, we keep track of which regions are occupied by tiles and which regions are still unused. This allows us to interleave tile broods of different leaves (see Figure 2.8.7 for an example).

To ensure a tight packing, we perform a relatively simple but provably well performing scheme: We keep track of occupied and free regions in the tilemap with a 2D array.

For each tile brood we search for a location that produces no collisions with previously placed broods. Placement always starts from the top-left corner in the tilemap and proceeds left-to-right and top-to-bottom. Of course, the order in which we consider the broods is key. We sort the leaves first by *decreasing* order of resolution.

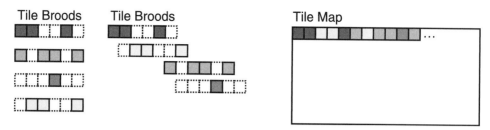

FIGURE 2.8.7 *Left:* Tile broods of four leaves (with 3, 4, 1, and 3 used tiles) are to be packed. *Middle:* Interleaving the broods is easy in this example. *Right:* Tiles are tightly packed in the tilemap. We store the offsets of the first tile for each leaf (0, 1, 5, and 6) for accessing the tiles. Note that negative offsets are not allowed, i.e., each row typically starts with a tile brood where the first tile is used.

Within a same resolution, we consider first the non-continuous broods and then the continuous broods by *increasing* order of number of tiles. The idea is to fill in the holes left by non-continuous broods with the continuous ones. We consider continuous broods by increasing the number of tiles to enable a simple optimization. An additional table keeps track of the first free column in the 2D array, and this information is only updated when placing continuous broods. This packing scheme is rather efficient, packing the 26,458 tiles of the dragon dataset in less than two minutes with a packing efficiency similar to our original packing.

The coordinates of the top-left corners of each tile brood are then stored in a lookup table, the aforementioned UVmap (two components, each 16-bit), with one entry per leaf. We use this indirection because we want to keep the nested grid data structure as compact as possible and storing texture coordinates (which could require more than eight bits per component) would increase memory usage and increase the runtime of the shaders. Thus the per-leaf data only stores the cell ID, which is used to access the UVmap.

Rendering with TileTrees

Rendering with TileTrees is a simple task, but providing a seamless interpolation requires additional work. Using TileTrees is more efficient than using volumetric texturing approaches like octrees, but, of course, it is more expensive than using standard texture atlases, which require only a non-dependent texture lookup, yet these still have their disadvantages. In any case, a TileTree usually offers a very compact storage of a surface texture since tightly packed tiles and storing the nested grid require only a little memory. In this section, we will develop the shader for texturing with seamless interpolation using TileTrees.

Seamless Interpolation

Texture interpolation is important for any surface texturing method and it can be achieved using TileTrees. Most of the work is done by the graphics hardware interpolation when accessing the tiles, but we have to perform a few more operations to obtain a seamless result across grid cells. Please note that seamless interpolation is currently limited to smooth surfaces because we use the surface normal to determine the projected cell face, i.e., a *smooth surface* provides a *continuous normal field*.

For correct interpolation, we have to consider three cases: full-leaves and stacked leaves, partially covered faces, and the interior of *n*-leaves.

Full-Leaves

Within full-leaves and stacked-leaves, a correct seamless interpolation is already guaranteed because the tile provides all the necessary samples (recall that we have a one pixel border replication between neighboring tiles).

Partially Covered Faces

If the projected surface only partially covers a face, some tile samples have no defined color. At boundaries, these undefined colors will bleed-in during interpolation. Fortunately, the color of these samples is simply located in a tile of the neighboring leaf. For instance, consider the 1-leaf in Figure 2.8.8. The missing samples are located in the *n*-leaf right next to it. We simply fill in undefined samples by reading their color in the neighboring leaf, which is done during tile generation.

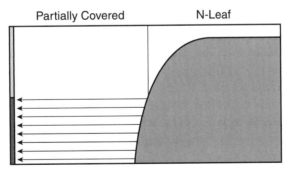

FIGURE 2.8.8 Missing texture samples of partially covered texture tiles are present in tiles of neighboring leaves.

Interior of N-Leaves

N-leaves have an additional difficulty: The face accessed during rendering is abruptly changing along the surface (Figure 2.8.9).

The primary way to achieve a correct interpolation is to define the final color as a weighted sum of the contribution of more than one face by using the three faces corresponding to the direction of the normal. We denote the tiles corresponding to these

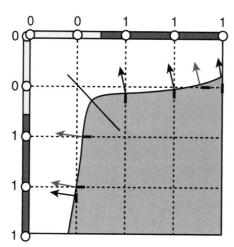

FIGURE 2.8.9 The face used to texture the surface can change abruptly within a leaf. Without special treatment this results in a visible seam. To obtain interpolation weights, we flag whether each tile sample is used by the enclosed surface.

faces, tiles T_x, T_y, and T_z. To define the interpolation weights, we store a binary flag in the alpha channel of the tile texels that determines whether a texel is used by the enclosed surface (Figure 2.8.9), which can be determined easily. We assume that the texel is used and look at the surface location that would be projected onto this texel. If the surface normal at this location confirms our assumption, then the flag is set to 1, and 0 otherwise. If no surface is found for this texel, the color of the closest sample is repeated. Alternatively, we can march along the faces to find the color of the texel on the neighboring tile. Note that both options provide a different but *continuous* color interpolation.

The flag is bilinearly interpolated by the graphics hardware when accessing the tile data, so its value varies contiguously between 0 and 1 on the surface. Thus we have three continuously varying flag values within the n-leaf: α_x, α_y and α_z interpolated from tiles T_x, T_y, and T_z. If a face is not used by the surface it has no associated tile, and this is known to the fragment shader from the per-cell data we store. In this case we force its flag value to 0. The observation is that the flag value will be 1 whenever the tile contains valid samples for the surface and will continuously decrease to 0 when the tile is no longer relevant. Interpolation only has to occur in areas where none of the flag values equal 1. As it may happen that more than one flag equals 1, or all equal 0, we use the normal N (of the surface point to be textured) to bias the weights obtained from the alpha channel. The zero case is avoided by always adding a small epsilon to the flag values. Putting all this together gives the following interpolation weights for the colors obtained from the three tiles:

```
        // bias b: a 3 component vector
b = abs( N ) / max( |Nx|, |Ny|, |Nz| )
```

$$\alpha_x{}' = \alpha_x b_x$$
$$\alpha_y{}' = \alpha_y b_y$$
$$\alpha_z{}' = \alpha_z b_z$$

$$w_x = \alpha_x'(1 - \alpha_y')(1 - \alpha_z')$$
$$w_y = \alpha_y'(1 - \alpha_x')(1 - \alpha_z')$$
$$w_z = \alpha_z'(1 - \alpha_x')(1 - \alpha_y')$$

The final color is then just a weighted and normalized sum of the color values, c_x, c_y, and c_z, obtained from the tiles:

$$c = (c_x w_x + c_y w_z + c_z w_z)/(w_x + w_z + w_z)$$

As long as the normal field is smooth, the weights are continuous and the final result is a seamless interpolation of the samples. Note that the interpolation is comparable to, but differs from, standard bilinear interpolation.

Adaptive Resolution

An additional difficulty appears when adjacent tiles are of different resolution. Some texels of the higher resolution tile have no corresponding sample on the coarser resolution tile (refer to Figure 2.8.6). In order to ensure a contiguous interpolation, we force the color of higher-resolution border samples to match the bilinear interpolation of the lower-resolution samples. This is done in the preprocessing step when generating the tilemap.

MIPmapping

Due to the tile resolution of $2k+1$, which is required to ensure seamless filtering across tiles, we cannot directly apply MIPmapping to the tilemap. It can be only achieved by computing a separate tilemap for each resolution level. This, of course, requires storing one tile coordinate per MIP level for each leaf. During rendering, the appropriate MIP level is computed and the color is fetched from the corresponding tilemap (or two tilemaps, if trilinear filtering is to be used).

Results

With our improvements we were able to reduce the shader instruction count and the number of dependent texture lookups while sacrificing almost no memory compared to the original implementation.

The number of instructions dropped from 168 to 112 due to the simpler decoding and the nested grids. The dragon model shown in Figure 2.8.10 has been textured with a $1,024^3$ texture, captured by an octree of depth 7. It has 17,376 leaves, 10,453 of them having continuous tile broods, and uses 26,458 texture tiles. The TileTree total size with the original approach is 11.3 MB (octree and tilemap). The octree uses 216 KB, rendering speed is 371 fps on a GeForce 8800GTX at $1,024^2$ screen resolution. Our improved approach uses 11.4 MB in total. The nested grids require 282 KB ($g_1=16$, $g_2=4$, $g_3=2$). Rendering runs at 732 fps on the same viewpoint.

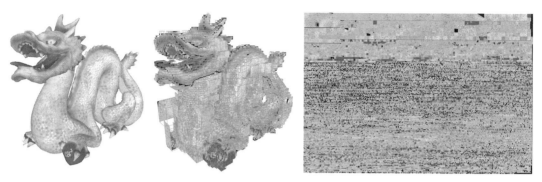

FIGURE 2.8.10 Dragon model textured with a TileTree (input data $1,024^3$ texture) stored in 11.4 MB and rendered at 732 fps.

Conclusion

TileTrees are an alternative to texture atlases obtained from planar parameterizations and volumetric textures and combine advantages of both worlds: TileTrees store square texture tiles in leaves of an octree, or as we demonstrated here, in cells of a nested grid hierarchy. During rendering the surface is projected onto these tiles and the resulting surface texture is seamlessly interpolated. TileTrees are compact in memory, provide low distortion texturing, and work without explicitly storing a parameterization.

The improvements on the original approach presented in this article further increase rendering speed and simplicity while increasing the memory requirements by only a negligible amount.

Acknowledgments

Thanks to Martin Mittring for fruitful discussions about TileTrees and optimizations.

References

[Lefebvre05] Lefebvre, Sylvain, Hornus, Samuel, and Neyret, Fabrice. "Octree Textures on the GPU," in *GPU Gems 2*, 2005.

[Lefebvre07] Lefebvre, Sylvain and Dachsbacher, Carsten. "TileTrees," in *Proceedings of ACM Interactive 3D Graphics and Games*, 2007.

Appendix: Shader Implementation

```
//
// lookup into a given tile
//
float4 tileLookup( float2 tileoffset,  // tile coord. within tilemap
                   float  tilescale,    // tile scaling
                   float  faceid,       // ID of cell face
                   float2 uv,           // projected coordinates
                   sampler2D map )      // tilemap
{
    uv = ( uv + float2( faceid, 0 ) ) * tilescale + tileoffset;
    return tex2Dlod( map, float4( uv, 0, 0 ) );
}

//
// TileTree shader
//

uniform sampler2D   TileMap; // Tile map.
uniform sampler2D   DecodePresence; // Table to decode leaf type.
uniform sampler2D   UVMap; // Map storing 16bits tiles coordinates.

uniform sampler3D   Grid1;   // First level grid.
uniform sampler3D   Grid2;   // Second level grids.
uniform sampler3D   Grid3;   // Third level grids.

uniform float3      Grid1Size;  // Grid1 Volume size.
uniform float3      Grid2Size;  // Grid2 Volume size. Recall this
   // stores multiple grids.
uniform float3      Grid3Size;  // Grid3 Volume size. Recall this
   // stores multiple grids.
uniform float3      LvlSizes;   // Resolution through grid
                                   // hierarchy: (g1,g1*g2,g1*g2*g3)

uniform float       BaseTileRes; // Tile resolution at root level.
uniform float       TileMapRes;  // Tile map resolution.

PixelOut main(V2FI IN)
{
    PixelOut OUT;

    // grid traversal
    float4 leaf;       // will contain cell/leaf data
    float  lvlsize;    // resolution at leaf level

    // IN.TCoord0 = coordinate of surface to be textures
    float4 g1 = tex3D( Grid1, IN.TCoord0 );
    if (g1.w > 0) {
        // data: stop here
        leaf    = g1;
        lvlsize = LvlSizes.x;
```

```
    } else {
        // pointer: go down to next grid
        float3 next = ( float3( g1.xy, 0 ) * 255.0 +
                        frac( IN.TCoord0 * LvlSizes.x ) ) *
                      Grid2Size.z;
        float4 g2   = tex3D( Grid2, next / Grid2Size );
        if (g2.w > 0) {
            // data: stop here
            leaf    = g2;
            lvlsize = LvlSizes.y;
        } else {
            // pointer: go down
            float3 next = ( float3( g2.xy, 0 ) * 255.0 +
                            frac( IN.TCoord0 * LvlSizes.y ) ) *
                          Grid3Size.z;
            leaf        = tex3D( Grid3, next / Grid3Size );

            // last level: data only
            lvlsize     = LvlSizes.z;
        }
    }
}

leaf    = leaf * 255.0;
lvlsize = lvlsize / leaf.w;

// read tile brood coordinates
leaf.yz = tex2D( UVMap, ( leaf.yz + 0.5 ) / 256.0 )*32768.0;

// decode faces presence
float ltype     = leaf.x;

float3 face_p  = tex2D( DecodePresence,
                    float2( ( ltype + 0.5 ) / 64.0, 0.25 ) );

float3 face_n  = tex2D( DecodePresence,
                    float2( ( ltype + 0.5 ) / 64.0, 0.75 ) );

// determine face projection
float3 nrm      = normalize( IN.Nrm ); // surface normal
float3 v_p      = face_p *   nrm;
float3 v_n      = face_n * (-nrm);
float3 id_p     = float3( X_P, Y_P, Z_P ); // X_P=0, Y_P=2, Z_P=4
float3 id_n     = float3( X_N, Y_N, Z_N ); // X_N=1, Y_N=3, Z_N=5
float3 faceid   = (v_p > 0) ? id_p : -1;
faceid          = (v_n > 0) ? id_n : faceid;

// determine tile size
float  scale    = BaseTileRes / lvlsize;
float  tileres  = scale + 1.0;              // +1 for additional
                                            //    1-texel border
float3 local    = frac( IN.TCoord0.xyz * lvlsize );
float3 uvw      = local * ( tileres - 1.0 ) / tileres +
                  0.5 / tileres;
```

```
        // compute texture coordinates and access texture data
        float4 clr0 = 0, clr1 = 0, clr2 = 0;

        float  tilescale  = tileres / TileMapRes;
        float2 tileoffset = leaf.yz / TileMapRes;

        // tile 0
        if ( faceid.x > -1 )
           clr0 = tileLookup ( tileoffset, tilescale,
                               faceid.x, uvw.yz, TileMap );
        // tile 1
        if ( faceid.y > -1 )
           clr1 = tileLookup ( tileoffset, tilescale,
                               faceid.y, uvw.xz, TileMap );

        // tile 2
        if ( faceid.z > -1 )
           clr2 = tileLookup( tileoffset, tilescale,
                              faceid.z, uvw.xy, TileMap );

        // seamless interpolation
        float3 alpha_xyz = 1e-6 + float3( clr0.w, clr1.w, clr2.w );
        float3 anrm    = abs( nrm ); // smooth normal for weights
        float3 damp    = anrm / max( anrm.x, max( anrm.y, anrm.z ) );
        alpha_xyz    *= damp;

        // compute final color
        float3 inv  = ( 1.0 - alpha_xyz );
        float3 w    = alpha_xyz * inv.yzx * inv.zxy;

        OUT.COL    = ( clr0 * w.x + clr1 * w.y + clr2 * w.z ) /
                       dot( w, 1 );

        return OUT;
}
```

2.9

Quantized Ring Clipping

David Pangerl

Illustration using a coarser clipmap. View of 504,000×336,000 Slovenia dataset near Triglav

FIGURE 2.9.1 Terrain render using quantized ring clipping.

In this article I describe a terrain rendering algorithm that renders layers of clipped quantized rings of terrain clipmaps that are centered around the viewer. Quantized ring clipping provides unlimited terrain extents, visual continuity, constant triangle output, and very low memory requirements.

Introduction

Rendering large terrain areas is an integral part of many applications, ranging from the entertainment industry (e.g. real-time strategy games, flight simulators, and massive online games) to architectural visualizations, cartography applications, and military simulations. In this article, I focus on real-time rendering of terrain height fields.

The main problem in terrain rendering is the fact that large terrain areas require enormous amounts of data to describe them, so complex algorithms have been developed to select and render only small amounts of it. These algorithms have two problems:

- **Data manipulation**. Nested regular grids [LH04], spherical clipmaps [CH06], irregular meshes, bin-tree regions, bin-tree hierarchies, and similar algorithms depend on manipulating uncompressed height field data in real-time to prepare them for rendering. This is not friendly for current graphics hardware and presents additional CPU and GPU load.
- **Visual consistency**. Tiled blocks and similar algorithms have problems because they switch the resolution per patch, which causes problems with visual consistency (switching patch levels seamlessly).

My solution to the problem is quantized ring clipping, a new algorithm that renders clipped quantized rings (clipped on patch tile edges) of terrain patches centered around the viewer (Figure 2.9.2). Patches are constant and always rendered in one batch; when the viewport position or orientation changes, only new patches are loaded into the GPU.

Quantized ring clipping is inspired by geometry clipmaps [LH04], but with some major differences. Geometry clipmaps cache nested rectangular grids and refill the GPU data when the viewport changes, while quantized ring clipping uses constant GPU data, clips it in spherical rings in the pixel shader, and only uploads new patch data into GPU memory.

The advantages of quantized ring clipping over other terrain rendering methods are as follows:

- **Simplicity**. There is no data manipulation on uncompressed height fields on either the CPU or GPU. All uncompressed data is loaded directly into video memory.
- **Low memory requirements**. Only what is visible and will be visible soon is loaded in the video memory. This reduces memory requirements drastically (only 1 MB of main memory and 29 MB of video memory is required for rendering what you see in Figure 2.9.1).

- **Unlimited terrain size.** The fact that only visible data is loaded in memory enables virtually unlimited terrain size (the limit is only the amount of external storage capacity, which shouldn't be a problem these days).

Overview

Quantized ring clipping renders quantized rings of terrain patches that are clipped on patch tile edges and centered around the viewer (see Figure 2.9.2).

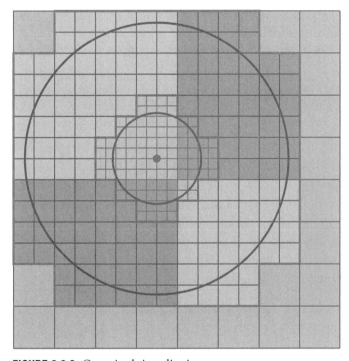

FIGURE 2.9.2 Quantized ring clipping.

The inner ring is quantized exclusively on patch tile size and the outer ring is quantized inclusively on double patch tile size to match the inner quantization of the higher/coarser clipmap patch. With this quantization we get continuously degrading patch tile size centered around the viewer.

We obtain a quantized position for level l as

$$q_{inner} = t_l \, \text{floor}\!\left(\frac{p}{t_l}\right) - p_c$$

$$q_{outer} = 2t_l \, \text{floor}\!\left(\frac{p}{2t_l}\right) - p_c$$

where p is a point position, p_c is a camera position, t_l is a level l patch tile size, and q_{inner} and q_{outer} are quantized ring extends used for clipping, and

$$c = r_{inner} < \|q_{inner}\| + r_{outer} \geq \|q_{outer}\|$$

where r_{inner} and r_{outer} are the ring inner and outer radius and c is the clipping result. If c is true the pixel is clipped.

Terrain Data

Terrain is usually presented with height field data with a given grid tile size T and a world position P.

Clipmaps

Data for quantized ring clipping is organized in pyramidal geometry clipmaps [LH04] (Figure 2.9.3). The geometry clipmaps store a terrain pyramid using a set of m levels at successive power-of-two resolutions.

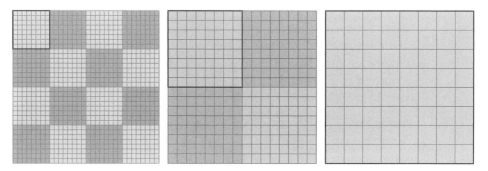

FIGURE 2.9.3 Pyramidal 8×8 tile patch samples. Level 1 patches are on the left, level 2 patches are in the middle, and the level 3 patch is on the right.

Patches

Geometry clipmaps are further divided into rectangular patches (Figure 2.9.3). All patches have the same grid size G and all patches on the same clipmap level have the same grid tile size t_l and are therefore of the same size s_l.

$$t_l = 2^l TG$$
$$s_l = Gt_l$$

Storage Data

Quantized ring clipping requires information for coarser level patch positions and normals (required for geo-morphing [W03]), so each patch grid is extended for three more rows and columns on the left and the bottom into neighboring patches. Additionally, patch vertical extends are stored to assemble patch bounds (used for patch visibility check).

GPU Data

Vertex data consists of a single vertex buffer of *G+1* by *G+1* vertices. Each vertex has an *x,y* index (*0* to *G*) and coarser level lookup *x,y* code (from *0* to *2*). For each visible patch, a height texture and an optional color texture is loaded. Height texture size is *G+3* by *G+3* to allow coarser data calculation (for geo-morphing).

Rendering

CPU calculations for rendering the quantized ring clipping patches are very inexpensive. They require a simple loop over all clipmap levels (from finest to coarsest) and render all patches that are within the outer ring radius and pass a visibility test. The level *l* outer ring radius r_{outer} is

$$\gamma = T \operatorname{int}\left(\frac{d_1}{T}+1\right)$$

$$r_{outer} = \gamma\sqrt{\max\left(0, 2^{2(l-1)} - h_{cam}^2\right)}$$

where *T* is a terrain grid tile size, *h* is a camera ground height, and d_1 is a user settable view distance of the first level. The inner ring radius is the same as the previous level outer radius except for level 1, where the inner radius is 0. Patch visibility testing is performed with the patch bounds ring test and a frustum test (bounds must intersect with the camera frustum and with the ring spheres).

Vertex Shader

Vertex shaders are the workhorse of quantized ring clipping and therefore do majority of the work:

- **Texture coordinate calculation.** Texture coordinates are calculated directly from vertex index information and tweaked for smooth level transition, if necessary.
- **Main position calculation.** The position's *y* coordinate is calculated from the height texture sampled at the texture coordinate position, while *x* and *z* coordinates are calculated directly from vertex index, patch world position, and patch size.
- **Normal calculation.** The vertex normal is calculated from the main position and two adjacent transverse vertex positions.
- **Coarser height position lookup.** Every point has four grainier points. One of these points, the upper-left, is at the same height as the coarser, which means the height is the same as the coarsest position. For the other three points, the grainier position needs to be interpolated to match the coarser position. For this interpolation one or two additional points need to be sampled. Vertex lookup code is used to determine what kind of interpolation is used.
- **Grainier normal calculation.** Similar to the coarser height position lookup, additional positions are sampled according to the coarser level lookup code and used with the main vertex normal to calculate the coarser vertex normal.

- **Geo-morphing factor calculation.** Geo-morphing factor is calculated from the ring inner and outer radius and user blend settings.
- **Position geo-morphing.** The main position *y* and coarser position *y* are blended with the geo-morphing factor.
- **Normal geo-morphing.** The vertex normal and coarser vertex normal are blended with the geo-morphing factor.
- **Pixel shader precalculations.** Several pixel shader parameters are precalculated to minimize pixel shader workload:

```
pos.xy=pos.xz*T/t_l;
pos.zw=pos.xz /2;
cam=cam.xzxz / gamma;
```

Pixel Shader
The main pixel shader task is to clip away the inner and outer area of quantized rings. A color texture lookup, detail normal map lookup, and advanced lighting can also be applied in the pixel shader. The optimized pixel shader code is as follows:

```
float2 gamma=float2 ( gamma , 1/gamma );
float4 terrainopt1=float4 (1 ,1 , (r_inner / gamma ) ^2 , 0 );
float4 terrainopt2=float4 ( ( r_outer / gamma ) ^2 , 0 , 1 , 1 );

void TerrainClipping(float4 pos, float4 cam)
{
    float4 ipos=floor( pos ) * gamma.y - cam;
    ipos=ipos*ipos;
    float4 a=float4( ipos.xy , -1 , 0 );
    float4 b=float4( 1 , 0   , ipos.zw );
    clip( float2( dot( a , terrainopt1 ), dot( b , terrainopt2 ) ) );
}
```

Smooth Degradation
When the viewport position is rapidly changing, the streaming data can become a serious bottleneck. Instead of waiting for the data, the algorithm has been adjusted to use the coarser level data for height and for color.

Result and Discussion
The algorithm was developed and tested on a Slovenia dataset (see Figure 2.9.4).

Data Type	Width	Height	Tile Size
Height information	20,160	13,440	12.5 m
Color information	504,000	336,000	0.5 m

FIGURE 2.9.4 A Slovenia dataset.

All tests were performed on a PC with AMD 3200+ (2.0 GHz), 1 GB RAM, NVIDIA GeForce 8800 GTS. Rendering was performed with a window size of 1,280×1,024 and with a 90° field of view.

The GPU workload details are as follows:

Poly Count	Batches	Height Data Memory Usage (MB)	Color Data Memory Usage (MB)	FPS
25,000	18	3	28	350
50,000	23	7	51	320
100,000	32	10	72	300
200,000	37	13	89	270
300,000	41	18	122	250

Bottlenecks

The current implementation suffers from two bottlenecks. The first, and less obvious, bottleneck is vertex shader texture fetching. It is the reason for approximately 80% of the GPU stalls. It is a consistent bottleneck for each terrain patch vertex. It stalls the pixel shader, which is waiting for triangle data.

One way of to reduce the bottleneck would be to reduce the number of vertex shader texture fetches at the expense of quality or to transfer some of the vertex shader tasks to the pixel shader.

Task	Texture Fetches
Position	1
Normal	2
Grainier position	0 or 2
Grainier normal	2 or 6
Total	5 or 11

The second bottleneck is in the pixel shader. Large, high-level patches that cover large areas of the screen, but are almost completely clipped away, cause spikes in pixel shader times with almost no pixel output.

To solve this problem, the triangles should be clipped away (by turning triangle winding order) in the vertex shader. However, this is not possible without additional vertex shader costs. And because the vertex shader is already the main bottleneck, this is not a valid solution.

A second solution would be to further optimize the pixel shader code to exit early on clipped pixels.

Conclusion

I presented a quantized ring clipping algorithm for terrain rendering. The main contributions of this new algorithm are its simplicity, low memory, and CPU usage.

Future work:

- Skip fully clipped triangles
- Extension to a spherical domain
- Data compression

References

[CH06] Clasen, Malte and Hege, Hans-Christan. "Terrain Rendering using Spherical Clipmaps," available online at http://www.zib.de/clasen/download/Spherical-Clipmaps_Electronic.pdf

[LH04] Losasso, Frank and Hoppe, Hugues. "Geometry clipmaps: terrain rendering using nested regular grids," available online at http://research.microsoft.com/~hoppe/geomclipmap.pdf

[W03] Wagner, Daniel. "Terrain Geomorphing in the Vertex Shader," available online at http://www.ims.tuwien.ac.at/media/documents/publications/Terrain_Geomorphing_in_the_Vertex_Shader.pdf

IMAGE SPACE

Introduction

Natalya Tatarchuk

This section covers techniques that happen in image space.

Object segmentation is an important problem in computer vision that pertains to subdividing or partitioning an image into its constituent regions or objects. One of the approaches for object segmentation and tracking is the active contour model. An *active contour* is a close curve, also known as a "snake" or a deformable contour, that can surround an object. The article "GPU-Based Active Contours for Real-Time Object Tracking" covers an active contour model implemented on the GPU.

The second article in this section, "Post-Tonemapping Resolve for High-Quality HDR Anti-aliasing in D3D10," by Emil Persson, proposes to tonemap the multi-sampled render-target instead of the resolved render-target later. This saves memory and leads to better quality.

The next article, "A Fast, Small-Radius GPU Median Filter" by Morgan McGuire, describes a very fast median filter for today's GPUs and explains how to port it to future GPUs and other data-parallel processors like DSPs and CPUs with vector instructions (e.g., MMX, SIMD).

"Per-Pixel Motion Blur for Wheels" by Damyan Pepper describes a technique for blurring objects as a 2D post-process and compositing the results, with correct depth information, back into the scene. This technique is used to blur the wheels of the motorcycles in MotoGP. The underlying idea of this article—to take specific parts of a vehicle and perform post-processing style effects while compositing the part back into the scene—is a powerful one.

The article "Deferred Rendering Using a Stencil Routed K-Buffer" by Louis Bavoil and Kevin Myers describes how to achieve order-independent transparency with multiple render-targets and the stencil buffer. It stores as many fragments per pixel as possible into a deep buffer, and then sorts the fragments in depth order and performs deferred rendering.

In his article "HDR meets *Black & White 2*," Francesco Carucci covers an auto exposure or light adaptation algorithm that is based on a histogram. This histogram is achieved by setting an absolute maximum luminance and dividing the range between 0 and the absolute maximum luminance, for example, in 1,024 slots. Each slot counts the number of pixels in the image that has a certain luminance.

The article "Robust Order-Independent Transparency via Reverse Depth Peeling in DirectX 10" by Nicolas Thibieroz describes a new technique called reverse depth peeling, which achieves order-independent transparency. Reverse depth peeling allows you to render transparent objects back to front and extracts layers of transparency in this order. With each layer peeled in a back to front order, the blending with the back buffer can take place immediately after each new layer has been extracted. In other words, compared to depth peeling, this technique does not need to store the layers in separate memory areas.

3.1

GPU-Based Active Contours for Real-Time Object Tracking

Natalya Tatarchuk (natalya.tatarchuk@amd.com)

Game Computing Applications Group, AMD Graphics Products Group

Introduction

Object segmentation is an important problem in computer vision that pertains to subdividing or partitioning an image into its constituent regions or objects. One of the approaches for object segmentation and tracking is the active contour model.

Active contour models were first introduced by Kass et al [KWT87] in 1987. An *active contour* is a close curve, also known as a "snake" or a deformable contour. We can think of a snake in this context as an energy-minimizing elastic spline, sensitive to some image features (often the intensity gradient), guided by external constraint forces, and influenced by image forces that can pull the contour toward image features of interest. The image feature map can be thought as a "landscape" upon which the contour will slide toward the goal object. A snake can be represented either as a piecewise linear curve or a parametric spline. The energy of this snake depends on the shape of the curve and its location within the image. Therefore we note that local minima of this curve's energy will correspond to desired image properties. Essentially, we can think of snakes as a special case of a general technique of matching a deformable model to an image by using energy minimization. We can apply active contour models to static or dynamic images to segment objects. In the context of image segmentation, we can represent an object boundary or some other salient image feature with a parametric curve ("snake"). The snake is initially placed near the image contour of interest (either by the user or by some automatic process) and the energy of the curve is minimized (thus it is attracted to the target object contour by specified forces, such as intensity gradient, etc). We will describe the algorithm behind the active contours in more detail in a later section.

The active contour model belongs to the energy minimizing models family of algorithms, which is an important subset of computer vision. There are many different areas in the field of computer vision and image processing that benefit from fast active contour algorithms. Additionally, interacting with energy minimizing models such as active contours helps researchers explore the energy functional and quickly iterate on the energy minimization functions.

The active contours model was originally presented in [KWT87] and further extended by Williams et al in [WS90] to use a greedy algorithm with faster convergence results than the original snake's algorithm. In this article, we will explore adapting the latter technique to the GPU. Note that the technique is greedy due to step-wise energy minimization, with each step performing an intermediate minimum energy move. This algorithm is designed to improve stability and flexibility of the original active contours algorithm.

In the original paper by Kass et al, the authors addressed finding salient image contours such as edges, lines, and subjective contours for motion tracking and stereo matching. They used a variational approach to find image contours using an active model for minimizing energy functional (thus exhibiting dynamic behavior). The resulting snakes can be used for semi-automatic image analysis, relying on the user to place the curve initially relatively close to the sought object.

Active contours have been successfully used in a number of real applications, as well as in medical imaging and video analysis (see Figure 3.1.1). Snakes can be used to track a contour moving through an image sequence by using the position of the contour in the last frame as the starting point for the relaxation in the current frame. When the snake is relaxed it should find the new position of the contour. This type of technique has been used successfully to track the movement of lips in a computerized lip-reading application (in [KWT87]) and for tracking the movements of objects in medical images. Note that this algorithm requires relatively slow object movement (or per-frame change) for stability; otherwise the energy field displays far too much discontinuity to produce reliable results. The snake uses its previous position to track the

FIGURE 3.1.1 Examples of applications of active contours.

object throughout frames. Therefore, for successful object tracking via active contour models, the tracked contour must be within a threshold of pixels away.

Kass et al [KWT87] applied the active contour models to the problem of stereo matching and motion tracking. They noted that, in stereo, two corresponding contours should have slowly varying disparity along the contour (unless there is a lot of depth variation). This observation allowed them to specify an additional energy functional for a stereo snake using this constraint. Note that this constraint is similar to the constraint for computing optic flow by Hildreth [Hildreth82].

Another interesting application of active contours is used in agriculture. An autonomous tractor carrying a camera and computer for video analysis has the task of spraying earth and plants automatically using an array of independently controlled spray nozzles. Plants can be segmented dynamically from the earth and weeds around it, so the spraying of fertilizer and weed-killer can be directed onto or away from plants as appropriate.

General Algorithm for the Active Contour Model

The input to the algorithm is either fully manual or semi-automatic. In the former case, the user interactively places a curve or a polygon relatively close to object boundary for the object she wants to track (as shown in Figure 3.1.2). In the latter case, the user first uses some other segmentation framework such as thresholding, SIFT ([Lowe03]), or other techniques to separate the objects and then detects important features as lines, connects them as edges, and then connects them into a coherent polygon as the initial value for the snake. In both cases, internally the snake object can be represented as a set of piece-wise linear segments or as a spline.

Following the input stage and during the iteration of the algorithm, the snake contour starts deforming and moving toward the desired object boundary. The end goal of this movement is to tightly encase the object and all of its features.

FIGURE 3.1.2 Initial user placement of the snake curve. Image from [XP98].

The contour is represented in the image plane as a parametric curve $v(s) = (x(s), y(s))$, where $v(s)$ is the snake curve position. The contour possesses some energy E^*_{snake}, computed over the entire contour. This term is also known as the *energy functional* of the snake contour:

$$E^*_{snake} = \int_0^1 E_{snake}(v(s))ds = \int_0^1 E_{int}(v(s)) + E_{image}(v(s)) + E_{con}(v(s))ds$$

1

Here E_{int} represents the internal energy of the snake curve due to bending, E_{image} provides a method to account for image forces, and E_{con} is used to represent external constraint forces. In order for the active contour to tightly encase the object in question, the energy functional of this contour must be minimized. This is what gave rise to the energy term's definition. The image forces are due to various events or image features and can be defined by a particular application or tracking goals. Additionally, the final snake contour position will also be its rest pose, thus posing the problem as an energy minimization problem.

The internal energy of the contour depends on the intrinsic properties of the curve and is defined in Equation 2 below. The internal energy of the snake curve can be thought of as a combination of its elastic potential energy ($E_{elastic}$) and its bending energy ($E_{bending}$):

$$E_{int} = E_{elastic} + E_{bending} = \int_s \frac{1}{2}(\alpha|v_s|^2 + \beta|v_{ss}|^2)ds$$

2

where

$$v_s = \frac{dv(s)}{ds}$$

and v_{ss} is the second derivative of v_s.

The first-order term in Equation 2 is the internal elastic energy of the snake contour. For computation of internal elastic energy, we approximate the snake curve as an elastic rubber band that possesses some elastic potential energy:

$$E_{elastic} = \frac{1}{2}\int_s \alpha(s)|v_s|^2\, ds$$

3

This energy penalizes for stretching (by introducing tension), and the energy term will have large values if there is significant stretching or gaps in the curve. The weight $\alpha(s)$ assigned to this energy term controls elastic energy as a function of the snake contour. However, most applications (including ours) simply set the weight to be constant for the entire curve. $E_{elastic}$ controls the shrinking of the snake contour. However, by itself it won't drive the control to shrink-wrap the object; we must include other energy terms to succeed at that goal.

The second-order term of Equation 2 represents bending energy of the snake contour, $E_{bending}$. We can also think of the snake curve as a thin metal strip that refuses to bend more than it is inclined to, thus giving rise to bending energy term. This energy depends on the curvature of the snake contour (Equation 4), and thus this term will be larger in the areas where the curve is bending rapidly.

$$E_{bending} = \frac{1}{2}\int_{s} \beta(s)\left|v_{ss}\right|^{2} ds$$

4

This energy term is defined as a sum of squared curvature of the contour, with the weight β controlling the bending energy. Note that a circle has minimum bending energy.

Each application can tweak the particular values for each of the weights in Equations 3 and 4, and these will determine the extent to which the snake contour will be allowed to stretch or bend during its deformation. We can also vary these values at each stage of the snake's movement, controlling the energy of the curve differently depending on how far from the target object it is. In our GPU implementation these parameters are simply uniform shader parameters that are easily user-modifiable, or they can be controlled automatically via animation or otherwise.

One particular mention should be made about the corners near object features. If β is constant for the entire snake contour, this will prohibit the curve from exhibiting corners. If we represent the curve as a polygon or a spline, we may also miss object features if there aren't enough curve samples to capture the feature. If curve points are far apart and a corner falls between two points on the corner, the snake may miss it. This has been the cause of much research ([XP97] and [XP98], among others).

Typically the term v_s is approximated via the finite differences approach:

$$\left|v_s\right|^{2} \approx (x_i - x_{i-1})^{2} + (y_i - y_{i-1})^{2}$$

5

This is the equivalent of minimizing the distance between the snake contour points and causes the contour to shrink.

The algorithm from Kass et al presented contour problems due to the fact that the image forces and constraints are not integrated during computations. In [WS00], the authors extend the original model to allow inclusion of hard constraints such as minimum distance between points (prohibiting the snake curve to collapse on itself). Note also that in the original paper the contour does not deform smoothly toward the minimum value (which actually was the cause for the term "snakes"). Additionally, the snake curve point positions could not be defined on discrete grid points. For these reasons, we adapt the Williams and Shah model ([WS00]) to the GPU programming model, as it provides a much better framework for image-based GPU programming utilizing parallelization.

Next, let's define the external energy of the snake contour, which is derived from the image itself. This portion of the snake contour energy is what attracts the contours toward the object that is defined in terms of some image features. We can define a function $E_{image}(x,y)$ so that it is minimal at the features of interest—for example, object boundary (Equation 6).

$$E_{ext} = \int_s E_{image}(v(s))ds$$

6

We could define the image energy as a weighted combination of three energy functionals for lines, edges, and terminations. However, this energy term can be defined to suit the application at hand. Alternatively, we can use an inverse of image intensity for this term (Equation 7, also used by Kass et al to define the edge functional) or an inverse of gradient times intensity (Equation 8). These definitions of energy terms give the snake incentives to be drawn to different image features (attraction to edges in the images in the first case or more pronounced edges from smoothed image features in the second case, similar to scale space term defined in Kass et al).

$$E_{image}(x, y) = -\left|\nabla I(x, y)\right|^2$$

7

$$E_{image}(x, y) = -\left|\nabla(G_\sigma(x, y) * I(x, y))\right|^2$$

8

Williams and Shah extended the original formulation by assigning a per-point weight $\gamma(s)$ to E_{image} term. This allowed them to reformulate the snake energy as

$$E = \int (\alpha(s)E_{cont} + \beta(s)E_{curv} + \gamma(s)E_{image})ds$$

9

Note that now the proportion between α, β, and γ is important, rather than the actual individual values. Their values also allow controlling the influence of each individual energy term on the overall snake energy. We use values from the Williams and Shah paper: $\alpha = 1$, $\beta = \{0 \mid 1\}$, and $\gamma = 1.2$ (giving more emphasis to the image gradient rather than the continuity terms).

Next we implement a greedy algorithm for energy minimization. A neighborhood of each snake point is examined during each iteration. We update the snake position to the point in the neighborhood that yields the smallest value for the energy term.

We make the following algorithm assumptions:

- We discretize the curve over the domain
- The curve is represented by a set of control points $v_0, v_1, \ldots, v_{n-1}$

- The curve is a piece-wise linear curve that is created by joining each control point by a linear segment
- We apply force equations to each control point separately, thus executing the greedy algorithm
- Each control point on the snake contour can move freely as influenced by the forces
- Finally, we convert the energy and force terms to discrete form by using finite differences

For the first-order term in the internal snake energy formulation, we observe that even spacing of points encourages better behavior of the contour (rather than straightforward shrinking, which causes snake collapse or bunching up of certain portions of the contour). Therefore we use the difference between the average distance between points d_{ave} and the distance between each set of two points under consideration $d_i = |v_i - v_{i-1}|$. This formulation for the elastic energy term specifies that the points having distance near the average will be at the minimum. We must normalize this parameter by dividing by the largest value in the neighborhood. During each iteration, a new updated value of d_{ave} is computed.

For the bending energy term, instead of using second-order finite differences, we use Equation 11 to approximate curvature:

$$\left| v_{i-e} - 2v_i + v_{i+1} \right|^2$$

$$10$$

Finally, it is important to normalize the last term, the image forces. If we just use the value of gradient directly, the snake would be strongly biased toward the extremes. Thus we normalize the last term by the $(G_{max}-Gi_{mag})/(G_{max}-G_{min})$, where Gi_{mag} is gradient magnitude at a given point i and G_{max} and G_{min} are the extreme values of the gradient field. Note that we negate the gradient terms so that the points with the largest gradient will have small values, thus minimizing the energy term and drawing the contour toward the edge features.

Listing 3.1.1 Greedy algorithm pseudo-code as described in [WS90], used as the basis of the GPU implementation for this project)

```
Initialize αᵢ, βᵢ, and υᵢ to 1 for all i.

do
   // Loop to move points to new locations
   // Note that point 0 is the first and the last processed
   for i = 0 to n
        Emin = SOME_VERY_LARGE_VALUE
        for j = 0 to m-1          // m is the size of search neighborhood
            Ej= αᵢ Econt,j + βᵢ Ecurv,j + υᵢ Eimage,j
            if Ej < Emin then
                Emin = Ej
                jmin = j
```

```
                        Move point vᵢ to location jₘᵢₙ
                        if jₘᵢₙ not current location then
                                nPtsMoved += 1        // Count the number of points
        moved

                // Process determines where to allow corners in the next
        iteration
        for i = 0 to n − 1
```

$$c_i = \left\| \vec{u}_i / |\vec{u}_i| - \vec{u}_{i+1} / |\vec{u}_{i+1}| \right\|^2$$

```
        for i = 0 to n − 1
                if (cᵢ > cᵢ₋₁ and cᵢ > cᵢ₊₁   // If curvature larger than neighbors
                     and cᵢ > threshold₁      // Curvature is larger than threshold
                     and mag(vᵢ) > threshold₂) // Edge strength above threshold
                then
                        βᵢ = 0
        until nPtsMoved < threshold₃
```

Extending Active Contours to a GPU-Friendly Formulation

There are several considerations when approaching conversion of any algorithm into the GPU domain. The architecture and the API of the typical programmable pipeline support a unidirectional, data-parallel computation model. Thus any traditional algorithm must account for the newly exposed parallelism, asynchronous parallel computation, and distributing computation across heterogeneous processing elements (specifically, vertex processing unit and fragment processing unit). The area of general purpose computation on the GPU (GPGPU) has exploded over recent years.

Although the field of active contours has been well-explored in the area of computer vision, the algorithms have not been adopted to take advantage of the power of modern GPUs. In all of the described algorithms the contour is represented with a polygon or a Bezier spline and energy minimization is performed on the CPU. This step is typically implemented via a loop over the contour using the input image and thus is not highly parallelized for multi-threaded computations.

Image-processing algorithms are particularly well-suited to GPU adaptation due to their inherent parallelizable nature, especially filtering and neighborhood-based computations. Image processing can be executed on the GPU by rendering a screen-aligned quadrilateral into the back buffer while using the source image as a texture mapped onto this quadrilateral object (see [Mitchell02] and [MAH03] for more details). A pixel shader is used to process the input image to produce the desired result in the off-screen texture (also known as a render-target). One of the key advantages of the programmable graphics hardware is the efficiency of texture sampling. Image-processing algorithms take advantage of that, especially in the case when the color of the destination pixel is the result of computations done on multiple pixels from the source image. In this case, we can sample the input image multiple times and use the pixel shader to combine the data from the multiple texture fetches (samples) to produce a single output. A specific filter kernel (such as a Gaussian filter or Sobel filter) is often used to describe which locations in the source image to sample and how to combine the results.

In this section we evaluate the programming model available with the DirectX 10 generation of graphics hardware. For a GPU-efficient conversion of the entire active contour algorithm we must address several concerns first. Specifically we must create a GPU-friendly representation of the snake curve. Additionally, we will need to calculate a feature-enhanced image and gradient statistics on the GPU so that we can efficiently compute contour statistics during each iteration. We also need to perform energy minimization with constraints directly on the GPU using a gradient descent model.

We will use shaders to perform the following operations:

- Compute the feature-enhanced image
- Perform gradient descent computations and the minimization of energy terms for snake contour
- Compute snake curve statistics at each iteration

We will also perform the operations below *once* per input image (during the algorithm setup stage):

1. **GPU-friendly snake representation and input.** The user provides the input curve over the image in the same manner as with a CPU-based algorithm. The curve points are discretized into 2D positions and stored as a vertex buffer for rendering as point primitives.
2. **Image thresholding on the GPU.** The input image I_{input} is converted to grayscale and thresholded using pixel shaders on the GPU. The result of this operation will be an intermediate image I_{gray}.
3. **Perform image filtering on the GPU.** Perform image filtering using pixel shaders that use the image I_{gray} as input. The result of this operation will be an intermediate image $I_{blurred}$.
4. **Compute image gradient on the GPU.** Image gradient will be computed using pixel shaders that use the image $I_{blurred}$ as input. The result of this operation will be stored in the gradient image $I_{gradient}$. Note that the gradient magnitude G_{mag} for each input pixel will be computed during the same pass and stored in the same image in a different channel.
5. **Compute gradient bounds (G_{max} and G_{min}).** This process will iterate over the entire image to compute the maximum and minimum gradient values.

After these steps we will execute an iterative greedy algorithm for interactively deforming the snake contour to converge on the desired object in real-time. At each simulation step i we will perform the following operations, thus executing the greedy algorithm shown in Listing 3.1.1.

1. Compute snake contour statistics, specifically the average distance between the snake curve's control points d_{ave_i} and the largest segment length d_{max_i}.

2. Compute the energy terms for each control point by calculating the internal and external energy terms for the curve control points using the intermediate images, the gradient values and bounds, and the average/largest segment distances.

3. Perform energy minimization for each control point in parallel by moving each control point after examining its neighborhood in the input image.

We can either just let the simulation run continuously or examine the positions of control points during the last two iterations to determine when the algorithm has converged onto a stable solution and stop the iteration at that point. The resulting snake contour will be found at rest tightly surrounding the desired object.

GPU-Friendly Snake Representation

We have implemented the snake contour using *piece-wise linear representation* (PWL), storing *normalized device coordinates* (NDC) locations of the control points for the contour. The usual negatives associated with the PWL curve will be observed in our implementation, requiring a reasonably large number of control points for an object with a complicated boundary (>100) and displaying difficulties in handling object concavity constraints with a small number of points. Note that even for a relatively large number of points ($1,024^2$) we are able to execute the entire iterative algorithm very efficiently on the GPU, thereby achieving high frame rates. Individual control points are stored in a vertex buffer as `float3` data—a 2D NDC image position and a floating value for the control point energy term.

In our implementation, the user places a limited number of control points around the object (typically 20–40 points depending on the complexity of the object they want to track). Then we subdivide the linear segments to the desired control point density, which generates a large number of intermediate snake control points used for energy minimization. We provide the user with a simple parameter for controlling this density as it provides a trade-off for execution speed versus the accuracy of results.

GPU Image Thresholding and Filtering

The input image I_{input} is converted to grayscale using the luminance transfer function directly in the pixel shader. This particular calculation is a simple conversion operation that, given an RGB color from the source image, computes the luminance value for the source image. The intensity is computed by using a simple dot product as follows:

$$\text{Luminance} = 0.3 * R + 0.59 * G + 0.11 * B$$

This is a standard operation and very quick to execute (single instruction in a pixel shader). In order to threshold an image, we can use a user-specified threshold value or compute it based on the image's histogram (using standard techniques for determining the threshold value). Note that thresholding only has to be done once per input image, so we can consider it a preprocessing stage for single image applications. In order to compute the histogram of the input image on the GPU, we will use the render to vertex buffer functionality and alpha blending to accumulate the values of input image pixels into appropriate bins as described in [SH07].

Given a threshold value *t* for the image, we can then render a screen-aligned quad that uses the input image as a texture map. The vertex shader simply propagates the texture coordinates through it. The pixel shader subtracts *t* from the current image values and the results are written into an off-screen buffer image I_t, which contains the thresholded image values. If the input image was taken over a static background and the background image I_b is known at this stage, we can also take this image as an input to the same pixel shader and subtract the value of the background image in the same pass.

Image filtering operations are well-suited for GPU programmability. We implement separable Gaussian filtering using the techniques described in [MAH03]. We can implement a Gaussian filter with a series of 1D filtering operations. We first apply a horizontal operation to the input image (which in this case is the I_t), producing an intermediate result $I_{blurred1}$. Then we apply a vertical 1D operation to $I_{blurred2}$ and produce the final blurred result $I_{blurred}$, which will be used as an input to the next stage. In our case we apply a 7×7 Gaussian filter. The filter size parameter σ can be exposed to the user and dynamically controlled if desired.

Computing Image Gradient on the GPU

The internal energy due to image features results from the magnitude of the gradient for that image. Remember that we are negating this term in order to minimize the overall snake energy and at the same time draw it toward the regions of high gradient. This means that we want to draw the snake contour toward the edges (where the intensity differential is greatest). We first pre-filter the image with a blur kernel as described above in order to reduce some of the noise and variation that are inherent to all edge detection algorithms.

We use the Sobel operator to detect edges using $I_{blurred}$ as input. This results in vertical and horizontal (from applying the vertical Sobel filter and horizontal Sobel filter, respectively) values for the gradient vector. Given the horizontal and vertical components of the gradient vector for a given pixel

$$G_{i_x}$$

and

$$G_{i_y}$$

we can then use them to compute gradient magnitude in the same pass:

$$\left|G_i\right| = \sqrt{G_{i_x}^{\,2} + G_{i_y}^{\,2}}$$

We output the results of running this computation in a single pass to an intermediate image $I_{gradient}$ where we store three float values in the R, G, and B values of the image

$$(G_{i_x}, G_{i_y}, |G_{i_z}|)$$

We store these values in a 16161616F render-target for the input image, but note that should it be desired to conserve memory, alternatively we can just store the x and y components of the gradient in a 1616F render-target and compute the magnitude later.

Optionally, we can also perform dilation and erosion operations in a pass after edge detection in order to help remove salt-and-pepper noise present in the image and to help close up holes in the edge contours.

The dilation operation has to be executed as a separate image-processing pass on the edge-detected image prior to snake simulation. The implementation of the dilation operation is straightforward, as it simply requires sampling a neighborhood of the current pixel and performing a compare operation on the sampled and the input pixels. We can use this operation to thicken the object outline, which helps to increase the attraction forces toward the object in some circumstances.

We can use the erosion operation to thin the structures present in an input image, which can help clean up noise present after the edge detection operation. The principle and the implementation of the erosion shader is very similar to the implementation of dilation (it just requires reversing the comparison operation). If the input image contains a lot of tiny features or salt-and-pepper noise, we can apply a dilation operation pass followed by an erosion pass to eliminate the noise.

Computing Gradient Bounds

We need to use gradient bounds to normalize the image's feature-based energy term as was described in the earlier section. We only have to find the maximum and minimum gradient magnitude values, G_{max} and G_{min}. Instead of using brute force sorting to determine the bounds (such as a GPU bitonic sort or a similar algorithm) we can take advantage of the extremely efficient blending hardware available to us to simultaneously compute both minimum and maximum values for the gradient magnitude.

Among many improvements to the GPU pipeline programmability introduced in DirectX10, we see a significant step up in the efficiency of data recirculation. We can now create a GPU buffer and interpret it as a different resource type for different stages. As such, we can create a buffer used as a vertex buffer (VB) for rendering in some passes and as a render-target in other passes. For this stage of the algorithm, we take advantage of this functionality. Note that this particular aspect can also be easily implemented in the DirectX9 pipeline with an ATI-specific extension known as a *render-to-vertex buffer* (see [Persson06] for more details).

We start out by rendering the image $I_{gradient}$ into a render-target which can then be interpreted as a vertex buffer by a later pass. We can then bind this buffer as a vertex buffer for rendering and render point primitives for the number of pixels in the image. In the vertex shader for each point (corresponding to a pixel in the input image $I_{gradient}$), we propagate the three gradient values

$$(G_{i_x}, G_{i_y}, |G_{i_z}|)$$

to the pixel shader and set the output position to the same location for the x coordinate. A similar independently developed approach was used to compute GPU histograms in [SH07].

We let the alpha blending help us compute the input image gradient values and compute the gradient bounds. Another newly introduced feature of DirectX 10 is the ability to perform blending independently into multiple render-targets. Therefore we will accumulate both the minimum and the maximum gradient values in the same pass by taking advantage of this feature. We allocate two 1×1 DXGI_FORMAT_R16_FLOAT renderable textures and set them as output targets for this pass, where the first target will be used to compute G_{min} and the second render-target will be used to compute G_{max}. The alpha blending parameters will use straight accumulation mode by setting the blend mode to One:One. The blending operation for the first render-target will be set to D3D10_BLEND_OP_MIN and the blending operation for the second render-target will be set to D3D10_BLEND_OP_MAX. Thus by blending all of the image gradient values we will very efficiently compute the minimum and maximum values. This functionality can be emulated in DirectX 9 by using the D3DRS_SEPARATEALPHABLENDENABLE rendering state.

Computing the Snake Contour's Statistics

We need to compute the following statistics for the entire curve based on the piecewise linear segments per each iteration i of the snake contour movement:

- Average length d_{ave_i} of each linear segment (between every pair of neighboring curve points)
- Longest segment length d_{max_i}

In order to compute these quantities, we must determine the segment lengths between neighboring contour points. Again, we can take advantage of the new functionality available with DirectX 10, specifically, the *geometry shader* stage. We render the contour control points as line primitives, and in the geometry shader stage we access the line segment and compute its length. Then we simply output this value to a stream-out buffer, $B_{lengths}$, to be used in subsequent operations.

Computing the Control Point's Energy Terms

At this point we have all of the required intermediate values ready, such as snake contour statistics (average length and maximum segment length, gradient for the image and gradient bounds, etc.). We can use this information to perform local energy minimization for each control point in parallel using pixel shaders and data recirculation. We use a buffer ping-pong technique often utilized for post-processing (as described in [Kawase03]). This method allows us to render the current control points while performing energy minimization and moving the control points. We ping-pong between two data buffers between passes.

For each snake curve control point, we compute the energy results for each pixel in the control point's neighborhood in the input image (in our case we use a 3×3 neighborhood). In the pixel shader, we use first-order and second-order finite differences to compute the elastic energy (using Equations 3 and 5), the bending energy (using Equations 4 and 11), and using the gradient value as the image feature energy term. After computing the energy values for each point in the neighborhood, we find the local minimum and store the new position and energy term for the contour control points in a render-target.

We expose the coefficients α, β, and γ to the user so that they can select better balancing between individual energy terms in Equation 9 when computing the minimization step for each control point.

Computing Convergence Criteria

In order to stop the snake's movement, we need to implement some convergence criteria. We have simply integrated those criteria into the minimization step—if for a given control point i the current point is the local minimum, it is simply not moved. The resulting snake contour will be found at rest at the desired object.

Results Discussion

The internal energy terms for the snake contour control the elastic and bending energy of the curve, causing it to shrink as it moves toward the object. The first term (the continuity term) maintains equal distance of contour's segments, while the second term's goal is to reduce the angle between adjacent PW segments of the curve. However, notice that these terms can easily affect the resulting energy of the contour by creating a chain reaction due to the fact that our minimization algorithm is a greedy algorithm and seeks local minima. Reduction in curvature causes reduction in segment lengths in the next iteration. Thus we noticed that we need to use the image features to control the snake's rest location. This is why we allow user-controlled amounts of blurring applied to the image prior to edge detection. The best results for this algorithm were achieved for high-contrast images. The frame rates are all above 100 fps for typical image resolution of ~512² and 60 to 80 control points for the snake curve using an ATI Radeon HD 2900 XT graphics card.

The algorithm (similar to the original by Williams and Shah) requires tailored parameters for individual images in order to achieve the best results. The main focus lies in balancing various energy terms for the contour, thus balanced coefficients for the elastic/bending/image feature terms is crucial. We expose user control for the coefficients α, β, and γ. Typically we put more emphasis to the energy derived from image features, but in some cases this is not desirable and we want to direct the snake using its internal energy as the more influential input. We can also remove the image-based energy term altogether to allow us to properly set up the coefficients for the internal energy term. Note that the snake contour tends to collapse very quickly if the coefficient for the bending energy term is much larger than the other terms' coefficients.

Because our approach is highly interactive, we also allow the user to dynamically increase the level of blurring, the threshold parameters, and whether to use a combination of dilation and erosion during image-feature energy computation via shader parameters. Note that the snake tracking depends on the ability of the control points to find a local minimum close to its current position (since we typically use a neighborhood of 3×3), so it is helpful to have the edge located relatively near the current position of the snake contour. Because of this, larger blur kernels may be helpful as they increase the spread of the edges, causing them to bleed, and thus the snake's ability to move toward the edge will increase. However, when using blur kernels larger than 11×11, the snake's final rest position tends to be farther from the object itself and linearly depends on the size of the blur kernel.

In the future we would like to see an extension of this technique to video sequences by taking advantage of frame-to-frame coherence using optical flow.

References

[Hildreth82] Hildreth, E. "The computation of the velocity field," *Proceedings of Royal Society (London),* Vol. B221, 1982: pp. 189–220.

[Kawase03] Kawase, M. "Frame Buffer Postprocessing Effects in DOUBLE DOUBLE-S.T.E.A.L (Wreckless Wreckless)," Game Developer's Conference, March 2003.

[KWT87] Kass, M., Witkin, A., and Terzopoulos, D. "Snakes: Active contour models," *International Journal of Computer Vision,* Vol. 1, n. 4, 1987: pp. 321–331.

[Lowe03] Lowe, David G. "Distinctive image features from scale-invariant keypoints," *International Journal of Computer Vision,* Vol. 20, 2003: pp. 91–110.

[MAH03] Mitchell, J.L., Ansari, M. Y., Hart. E. "Advanced Image Processing with DirectX 9 Pixel Shaders," *ShaderX2: Tips and Tricks,* edited by Wolfgang Engel, Wordware Publishing, 2003.

[Mitchell02] J. L. Mitchell. "Image Processing with 1.4 Pixel Shaders in Direct3D" in *ShaderX: Vertex and Pixel Shader Tips and Tricks,* edited by Wolfgang Engel, Wordware Publishing, 2002.

[Persson06] Persson, E. "Render to Vertex Buffer Programming." Can be found online at http://ati.amd.com/developer/SDK/AMD_SDK_Samples_May2007/Documentations/R2VB_programming.pdf, March 2006

[SH07] Scheuermann, T., Hensley, J. "Efficient Histogram Generation Using Scattering on GPUs." To appear in proceedings of *ACM SIGGRAPH Symposium on Interactive 3D Graphics and Games (SI3D '07).* GPU Histogram BibTex PDF.

[WS90] Williams D. J. and Shah, M. "A Fast Algorithm for Active Contours," *Proc. Int'l Conf. Computer Vision*, 1990: pp. 592–595.

[XP97] Xu, C. and Prince, J.L. "Gradient Vector Flow: A New External Force for Snakes," *Proceedings of IEEE Conference on Computer Vision Pattern Recognition (CVPR)*, Los Alamitos: Comp. Soc. Press, June 1997: pp. 66–71.

[XP98] Xu, C. and Prince, J. L. "Snakes, Shapes, and Gradient Vector Flow," *Proceedings of IEEE Transactions on Image Processing*, 7(3), March 1998: pp. 359–369.

3.2

Post-Tonemapping Resolve for High-Quality HDR Anti-aliasing in D3D10

Emil Persson

Introduction

Implementing anti-aliasing in a traditional pipeline usually involves rendering to a multi-sampled render-target. At the end of the frame this buffer is resolved, a process in which the samples for each pixel are blended together and the result is stored in a separate, non-multi-sampled buffer such as a render-target or directly to the back-buffer, resulting in an anti-aliased image. To do this we call `StretchRect()` in D3D9 and `ResolveSubresource()` in D3D10. Alternatively the backbuffer itself can be multi-sampled, in which case the API does all the work for you.

The actual process of blending the samples has traditionally been hardware independent. Early implementations used simple averaging. The ATI Radeon 9700 introduced an improvement to this with something called *gamma-correct anti-aliasing*, which produced noticeably better image quality compared to averaging. You may already be familiar with the concept of gamma, but let's briefly explain this since the motivation is largely similar to the reason behind the technique this article describes.

A regular computer monitor does not produce a linear response to the input. A value of 1.0 will not look twice as bright as a value of 0.5 but rather it is more than four times as bright. The original reason for this was technical, but even though it certainly is possible to produce a monitor with linear response today, this non-linear response curve has been preserved because it is actually quite useful. Our eyes are similarly non-linear, and while our eyes' response curve isn't 100% identical to monitors it is a significantly better match than linear mapping. So the non-linear mapping of our framebuffer data means that we get more quality out of our eight bits per channel than we would with a linear mapping. The average monitor has a response curve that is roughly the input raised to the power of 2.2. To see how bad a linear mapping would look you can simply change the gamma to 2.2 in your video card's control panel, ignore the bleaching effect, and just focus on the banding in dark regions in all your images.

To compensate for this non-linearity, a gamma-correct resolve first converts the samples' numerical values to their response on the screen by raising them to the power of 2.2 before averaging, and then raising the result to the power of 1.0/2.2 so that the result gets the correct linear response on the screen. Expressed mathematically, the samples S_0 and S_1 would produce this value after a gamma-correct resolve:

$$\left(\frac{s_0^{2.2} + s_1^{2.2}}{2} \right)^{1.0/2.2}$$

1

For traditional low dynamic range (LDR) rendering, this was enough to ensure anti-aliasing worked satisfactorily. With high dynamic range (HDR) rendering, we face a similar issue again as the multi-sample samples are affected by another non-linearity, namely the one from tonemapping.

HDR Rendering

The traditional LDR rendering pipeline looks something like this:

1. Render the scene into a multi-sampled render-target.
2. Resolve the multi-sampled render-target to backbuffer.

With the ATI Radeon X1800, multi-sampling with floating-point render-targets was introduced. HDR could now be combined with anti-aliasing and the rendering pipeline would look something like this:

1. Render the scene into a multi-sampled render-target.
2. Resolve the multi-sampled render-target to a non-multi-sampled render-target.
3. Tonemap render-target to backbuffer.

With HDR it is typically the case that you render in linear space, so it may seem like this approach should work just fine. However, the problem here is that tonemapping adds another non-linear response to the input *after* the resolve pass, just like monitor gamma, and thus messes things up in the same way. So even though we might render in linear space to the render-target, what meets our eyes in the end is not linear because of the tonemapping. A value of 4.0 in the render-target will not look twice as bright as a value of 2.0. It can look arbitrarily different, or even look the same. Given the huge ranges possible and the arbitrary math that can go into a tonemapping algorithm, there is potential for an even bigger mess than with gamma. In fact, non-gamma-correct anti-aliasing at its worst has reduced visual quality, but in HDR rendering you can end up with no anti-aliasing effect at all in high-contrast areas with the traditional approach. In a similar way to how the problem was solved with gamma, the proposed solution to this problem is to use a rendering pipeline like the following:

1. Render the scene into a multi-sampled render-target.
2. Tonemap the multi-sampled render-target.
3. Resolve the multi-sampled render-target to a backbuffer.

The key here is that the resolve step takes place after tonemapping, hence the name of the technique. Tonemapping maps the numerical value in the render-target to what it is supposed to look like on the screen. This means that each sample will be tonemapped individually, and what we are averaging in the end is each sample's linear light emittance on the screen.

Note that steps 2 and 3 can easily be merged into a single pass. In fact, there is no particular reason why we would want them separated other than for comparison purposes to more easily see how the pipeline changes. In practice, by merging them we save memory because we don't need the temporary buffer to hold tonemapped samples and we save bandwidth by not writing out and reading in all these values from memory.

Finally, the monitor gamma still matters, so we need to take that into account. With HDR rendering you probably render your scene in linear space, unlike in LDR rendering, so the first step in gamma-correct anti-aliasing is eliminated. However, the monitor still outputs non-linear values. Therefore, our linear resolved value needs to be raised to the power of 1.0/2.2 so that our resolve value gets a linear response on the screen.

Implementation

Implementing this technique requires us to process a multi-sampled buffer. D3D9 essentially does not allow us to do anything with multi-sampled render-targets other than rendering into them and resolving them, so D3D10 is required (available with ATI HD 2000 generation). In D3D10 you can bind a multi-sampled buffer as a texture and access each sample individually, which is just what we need. After all this theory it is refreshing that the actual implementation is very simple. All we need to do is render a full-screen primitive using the following shader to resolve our multi-sampled HDR texture to the backbuffer.

```
Texture2DMS<float4, SAMPLE_COUNT> hdrTexture;

float3 main(float4 pos: SV_Position) : SV_Target {
    // Texture coordinates from screen-space position
    int3 texCoord = int3((int2) pos.xy, 0);

    // Tonemap all samples and average
    float3 color = 0.0;
    [unroll]
    for (int i = 0; i < SAMPLE_COUNT; i++){
        float3 c = hdrTexture.Load(texCoord, i).rgb;
        color += 1.0 - exp2(-exposure * c);
    }
    color *= (1.0 / SAMPLE_COUNT);

    // Gamma
    color = pow(color, 1.0 / 2.2);

    return color;
}
```

Note that in D3D10 you can create the application backbuffer with the `DXGI_FORMAT_R8G8B8A8_UNORM_SRGB` format. Using this format, the last part of the shader where `color` is raised to the power of 1.0/2.2 is not necessary and should be eliminated.

Results

Comparing this technique to the traditional approach shows a clearly visible improvement in quality, especially in high-contrast areas. Depending on things like exposure, the tonemap operator used, and other factors, the difference may be more or less pronounced (Figure 3.2.1).

FIGURE 3.2.1 *Left:* Traditional approach. *Right:* Post-tonemapping resolve.

The performance of this technique depends on several factors. On one hand we save one pass with a roundtrip to memory and the storage space of a screen-sized buffer that is otherwise needed for the resolve call. On the other hand, the ALU workload for resolving increases. Depending on the hardware, render-target format, number of samples, the tonemap operator used, and other factors, there are cases where in addition to the quality improvement, it also is faster than the traditional approach— but there are also cases where it is slower. Your mileage may vary—but your results will be much more appealing.

Conclusion

A technique for improving the anti-aliasing quality for HDR rendering in D3D10 has been presented. By tonemapping each sample individually and resolving in a shader, the samples are averaged according to their final light contribution on the screen, which results in smoother looking edges.

3.3

A Fast, Small-Radius GPU Median Filter

Morgan McGuire

Introduction

The median filter is a basic building block in image processing. It reduces noise without blurring edges, and for monochrome input, it sets each output pixel to the median of the values in a small area of the corresponding input pixel. For an RGB image, this process is performed independently on each color channel.

This article describes a very fast median filter for today's GPUs, and further explains how to port it to future GPUs and other data-parallel processors such as DSPs and CPUs with vector instructions (e.g., MMX, SIMD). The technique used in this article is inherently fast because it is designed with ideal characteristics for streaming parallel architectures:

- No branches
- Single-pass
- Data-parallel across pixels
- Data-parallel at each pixel
- High compute-to-memory ratio

On a GeForce 8800 or comparable GPU, this optimized filter can process multiple 4,096×4,096 video sequences at over 100 fps, which is important for real-time video processing. Executing faster than video rates is important because many higher-order video operations like morphological operators are implemented using the median, so many median operations may be performed per-frame. Implementing an efficient median filter on a GPU has been a challenge for some time, as evidenced by discussions on Internet forums and in the scientific literature. For example, [Press06] implemented many other GPU imaging filters but concluded that the median was impractical on current GPUs.

There are many applications of a fast median filter. It can be used as part of a robot's or security camera's computer vision pipeline, for real-time non-photorealistic effects in games, or even for filtering noisy video on a cell phone's GPU or as a live feed from the video camera. As an example of the latter case, Figure 3.3.1a shows a frame of cell phone video that exhibits sensor noise and compression artifacts. Figures 3.3.1b and 3.3.1c show the same frame after processing with two different-sized median filters. The end of this article describes the accompanying demo of a real-time cartoon filter for video or rendered images. One could easily imagine it being used in

FIGURE 3.3.1 a) Original noisy video frame b) After 3×3 median c) After 5×5 median.

a cartoony PlayStation Eye or Xbox 360 camera game, or to protect the identity of a child in video chat.

Small median kernels like 3×3 ($N = 9$ elements) and 5×5 ($N = 25$) are the most frequently used. They correct dust, scratch, sensor, transmission, and small classifier errors; avoid excessive loss of detail; and in most cases it is faster to apply a small median twice than to apply a large median once for similar results. The techniques used in this article do not scale well to large-radius median filters, where other approaches, e.g., [Weiss06, Huang81, VKG03], have better asymptotic performance.

As a building block, the median is very convenient. It is contained in a single shader function, so you can simply use the code on the included disk without even reading or understanding the rest of this article. It is best applied by binding the input as a texture and then rendering a rectangle of the same dimensions to another texture bound to a framebuffer object. Using multiple draw buffers, many textures can be filtered in parallel to amortize the overhead of a rendering pass. We provide source code for two sample applications to demonstrate how to configure the GPU and use the shader.

Exchange Networks

The naive way to compute the median is to copy all values around a pixel into an array and then sort that array. The value at index $N/2$ is then the median. There are two drawbacks to this approach. The first is that sorting is hard on a GPU because sorting algorithms use scatter-gather, linked lists, recursion, and branches—that is practically a list of the operations that are hard to accelerate on GPUs. The second drawback is that most of the operations in a sort are to resolve the relative ordering of values that aren't the median, so a full sort computes lots of values that won't affect the final result.

Although faster *amortized* algorithms exist on the CPU [Kopp94, Weiss06], Paeth's CPU algorithm [Paeth90] is the fastest small-radius method that does not need to communicate data between pixel neighborhoods. Breaking inter-pixel communication is important because that is what allows a filter to execute in parallel across many threads. Paeth's algorithm is based on an exchange network for partitioning a set into three subsets: the median, values less than or equal to the median, and values greater than or equal to the median. Note that it does not sort the subsets further; the goal is to compute the median.

Figure 3.3.2 shows the first few operations in the dataflow of the exchange network that computes the monochrome median for $N = 9$. At the top of the figure the GPU fetches nine pixel values that affect a single output pixel and stores them in separate registers. Next, a series of conditional swaps (denoted by curved arrows) performs the first pass of a bidirectional bubble sort on the first six elements. This pass ensures that the min of that subset is at index 0 and the max is at index 5. This min and max are not necessarily the min and max of the full set of nine elements. However, even if all of the remaining three elements were larger or smaller than these values, the min and max of the set of five still could not possibly be the median. Therefore, we can immediately drop registers 0 and 5 from further processing. The next step inserts the element from register 6 into the set and performs another bidirectional bubble sort pass, but this time on the five elements at indices 1–4 and 6. Every subsequent pass removes a net of one element until we reach a three element set, at which point it is trivial to compute the median.

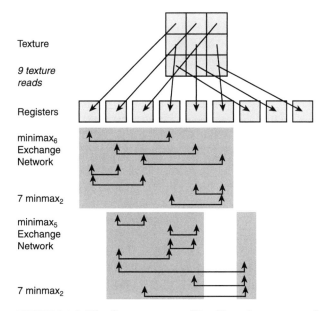

Texture

9 texture reads

Registers

$minimax_6$
Exchange
Network

7 minmax₂

$minimax_5$
Exchange
Network

7 minmax₂

FIGURE 3.3.2 The first two steps of Paeth's exchange network.

These bidirectional bubble sort passes are called minmax operations. The min-max$_k$ operation identifies the maximum and minimum of a set of k values but does not rank the ones between them; it is decomposable into $(k + 1)$ minmax$_2$ operations. Minmax$_2$ is just a two-element sort. In GLSL it can be implemented as shown in Listing 3.3.1.

Listing 3.3.1 Paeth's minmax in GLSL (which is too slow!)

```
void minmax₂(out float a, out float b) {
        if (b > a) {
            float temp = a;
            a = b;
            b = temp;
        }
}
```

For $N = 9$, Paeth's network requires 20 $minmax_2$ operations and therefore 20 branches in his implementation; for $N = 5$ it requires 99. On a GPU those branches prevent vectorization and are slow compared to arithmetic operations. The latter is in part because branches are relatively slow on any architecture, but it is primarily because a GPU shares a program counter across a group of (usually 64) threads and stalls the ones that take the branch differently. So to use Paeth's algorithm we need a faster implementation of $minmax_2$.

Branchless Minmax₂

Branches are slow on a GPU and also prevent vectorization because each color channel must branch separately. However, today's GPUs support fast native min and max operations, and these can operate in parallel on vectors. With these, $minmax_2$ naturally reduces to the code shown in Listing 3.3.2.

Listing 3.3.2 Optimized minmax in GLSL

```
void minmax2(out vec4 a, out vec4 b) {
    vec4 t = a;
    a = min(t, b);
    b = max(t, b);
}
```

This has not only eliminated the slow operations, it has also made the process another factor of four faster by vectorization. Furthermore, careful optimization allows one to eliminate the assignment to temporary t when these operations are chained. Although it was necessary to manually optimize the temporaries on previous drivers, the current GLSL drivers successfully make that optimization. With the temporaries optimized out this is a two-cycle operation.

Not all processors support native vector min and max in a single cycle. For non-GPU data-parallel vector SIMD processors that lack single-cycle min and max operations but have fast combined multiply and add (MAD) instructions of the form $r_1 = r_2 * r_3 + r_4$, it is possible to instead implement $minmax_2$ in three to four cycles as shown in Listing 3.3.3.

Listing 3.3.3 Alternative minmax using MAD instructions

```
void minmax₂(out vec4 a, out vec4 b) {
    vec4 d, t;
    t = (d = (b - a)) < 0;
    a += t * d;
    b -= t * d;
}
```

The compare to zero is inexpensive on many architectures because the result is already in the condition code or sign bit of d and does not require another ALU operation.

The MAD implementation of minmax$_2$ is a form of linear interpolation by a binary value, t. When $a > b$, the input values are out of order. In this case d is negative, so a swap occurs:

Let $t * d = b - a$
$a \leftarrow a + t * d = a + b - a = b$
$b \leftarrow b - t * d = b - b + a = a.$

When $a \leq b$, d is non-negative, so there is no swap:

Let $t * d = 0$
$a \leftarrow a + t * d = a$
$b \leftarrow b - t * d = b$

Note that after each network in Figure 3.3.2, two of the registers are never referenced again. These are the min and max of the subset, which are dropped. This means that we can also eliminate a total of one minmax$_2$ from each minmax$_{k > 2}$.

Performance

Taking all of the optimizations described in the previous section into account, the total cost of the median at $N = 9$ is 32 operations in 16 minmax$_2$ calls, nine texture fetches, and one output write. That's only 26 vector operations for the 36 scalar values in a 3×3 RGBA neighborhood, although depending on the specific GPU more instructions may be needed to handle temporaries.

The following results describe the actual performance observed executing the median shader. Each of the time trials was run on 4,096×4,096 images in monochrome, RGB, and RGBA formats at both 8- and 16-bits per channel, for $N = 9$ and $N = 25$. At $N = 49$, the O(N) registers required exceed those available on today's hardware. Results were comparable for smaller images so they are not reported here. All results are computed on a dual-core AMD 4200 processor at 2.2 GHz and an NVIDIA GeForce 8800 GPU. GPU results measure the incremental cost of the median in the context of a longer image processing sequence, so they do not include the CPU to GPU transfer.

These tests load the texture and shader into GPU memory, execute glFlush, begin timing, process the same input 40 times, execute glFlush, and end timing. The goal of this process is to measure throughput by minimizing the impact of the CPU and the GPU pipeline latency on timing, i.e., to simulate the median in the context of a longer image processing sequence.

Figure 3.3.3 shows results in terms of the number of 8-bit values processed for the new fast implementation (see the next section for the actual code), for a direct GPU port of Paeth's algorithm as it was published, and for Photoshop (CPU), all for an N = 33 = 9 kernel. The NVIDIA GLSL driver successfully removed the "dead" registers after each network and correctly packed scalars together into vectors for the monochrome case. That is, there was no difference in performance after manually implementing those optimizations. On this GPU, the min/max exchange (Listing 3.3.2) is faster than the MAD exchange (Listing 3.3.3). In trial runs, min/max yielded 3,993 Mpix/sec for RGB data and MAD yielded 2,320 Mpix/sec. Both are about four times faster than the direct port of Paeth's algorithm (Listing 3.3.1).

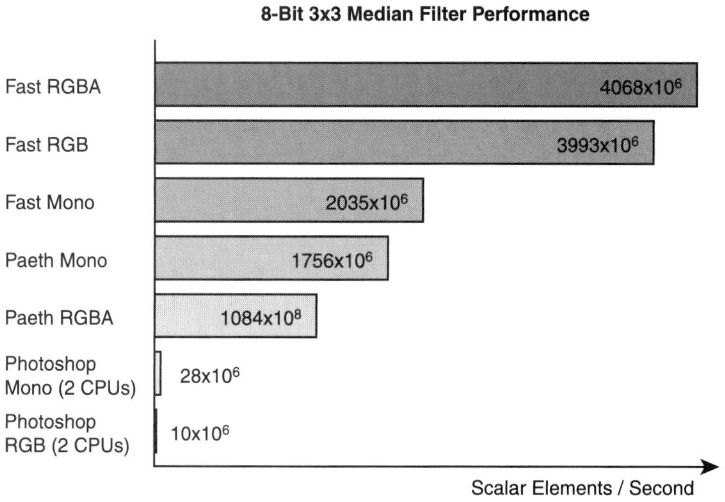

8-Bit 3x3 Median Filter Performance

Fast RGBA	4068×10^6
Fast RGB	3993×10^6
Fast Mono	2035×10^6
Paeth Mono	1756×10^6
Paeth RGBA	1084×10^8
Photoshop Mono (2 CPUs)	28×10^6
Photoshop RGB (2 CPUs)	10×10^6

Scalar Elements / Second

FIGURE 3.3.3 Performance of our new fast median filter compared to previous methods using a GeForce 8800 GPU and AMD 4200 Dual Core CPU.

On 16-bit data, Photoshop becomes disproportionately slow but our GPU implementation experiences no significant decrease. For the $N = 5 \times 5 = 25$ kernel, the fast GPU algorithm can only run on scalars without exceeding the register limit. It achieves 2,615 Mpix/sec throughput in this case.

The explicit vectorization from operating on vec4 instead of individual floats is essential for some GPU architectures and drivers. Others, like the NVIDIA GeForce 8800, have underlying scalar processors and automatically vectorize. However, operating on vec4 instead of float allows the GPU to also execute the memory fetches in parallel. This effect is visible in the graph. The fast GPU implementation on vec4 slightly outperforms vec3 and dominates float performance measured in terms of scalars processed per second. On the CPU the effect is reversed because the memory architecture is not optimized for fetching the 2D pixel neighborhoods used in image processing and experiences cache misses as the number of color channels increases.

Pixel Shader

The $N = 9$ pixel shader is shown below. This shader and the larger $N = 25$ shader are both on the DVD accompanying this book. These shaders are written in a generic fashion to work on monochrome, LA, RGB, or RGBA values. Change the top macro to define vec to be float, vec2, vec3, or vec4 corresponding to the number of components in your texture. Likewise, the tovec macro must extract just the components used from a vec4. For a monochrome image, it should expand to (v).r; the vec3 case is given in the code.

Listing 3.3.4 Complete 3×3 median filter

```
// Change these two macros to change precision
#define vec vec3
#define tovec(v) (v).rgb

/* Alternate (potentially faster on non-GPU architectures):
 #define m2(a, b) d = b - a; t = vec(lessThan(delta, 0.0)); a += t * d;
b -= t*d;   */

#define m2(a, b) t = a; a = min(t,b); b = max(t,b);
#define m3(a,b,c)       m2(b,c); m2(a,c); m2(a,b);
#define m4(a,b,c,d)     m2(a,b); m2(c,d); m2(a,c); m2(b,d);
#define m5(a,b,c,d,e)   m2(a,b); m2(c,d); m2(a,c); m2(a,e); m2(d,e);
m2(b,e);
#define m6(a,b,c,d,e,f) m2(a,d); m2(b,e); m2(c,f); m2(a,b); m2(a,c);
m2(e,f);m2(d,f);

uniform sampler2D src;

void main() {
  vec v[9], t, d;

  for(int dX = -1; dX <= 1; ++dX)
    for(int dY = -1; dY <= 1; ++dY)
      v[dX * 3 + dY + 4] = tovec(texture2D(src, gl_TexCoord[0].xy +
        vec2(float(dX)/width, float(dY)/height)));

  // Starting with a subset of size 6, remove the min and max each
time
  m6(v[0], v[1], v[2], v[3], v[4], v[5]);
  m5(v[1], v[2], v[3], v[4], v[6]);
  m4(v[2], v[3], v[4], v[7]);
  m3(v[3], v[4], v[8]);
  tovec(gl_FragColor) = v[4];
}
```

Sample Applications

Two sample programs are provided with this article. Each is a C++ program using OpenGL and GLSL that runs from the command line. They accept an image in JPG, PNG, BMP, or PPM format and write the result out to disk in the same format. The first program simply performs a 3×3 median filter. The second uses a series of imaging filters that build on the median to compute a watercolor or cartoon output. Both are fast enough to execute on full-screen video in real-time (if modified to work with an in-memory stream instead of from disk). The samples use the G3D 7.00 engine to simplify the OpenGL boilerplate around the core shaders. This open-source library can be downloaded from http://g3d-cpp.sf.net for Windows, Linux, and Mac to compile the samples from source. Precompiled Windows binaries and test images are provided on the disk.

The watercolor filter in Figure 3.3.4 demonstrates the median filter as an image-processing building block. For such a filter, each frame requires many median opera-

(a)

(b)

FIGURE 3.3.4 (a) Original image (inset detail) and (b) after watercolor filter

tions, which is why it is important to be able to perform hundreds of median opera-tions per second when working with video. I chose this filter because the results are attractive and it is simple to understand, but the principles are similar for many com-puter vision tasks like object tracking and segmentation.

The watercolor filter repeatedly applies the 3×3 median to smooth out the image without blurring across edges. Using multiple small passes gives similar results to one large filter but is much more efficient. The filter then detects edges using a simple dif-ference filter applied to a single-pass median filtered version of the original. These edges often contain single-pixel noise, so the edges themselves are then median fil-tered. Finally the black outlines and smoothed color are combined. Depending on the thresholds chosen, the result appears as a watercolor painting or a cartoon.

Acknowledgments

I'd like to thank Kyle Whitson, Williams '09, who wrote the demos and GPU per-formance tests, and NVIDIA for donating the GeForce 8800 GPUs.

References

[Huang81] Huang, T. S. "Two-Dimensional digital signal processing II: Transforms and median filters," Springer-Verlag New York, Seacaucus, NJ, 1981.

[Paeth90] Paeth, A. W. "Median finding on a 3x3 grid," *Graphics Gems*, Academic Press Professional, 1990: pp. 171–175.

[Press04] Press, J. "Hardware image filtering on desktop computers," *GraphiCon '04*, September 2004.

[VKG03] Viola, I., Kanitsar, A., and Groller, M. E. "Hardware-based nonlinear filter-ing and segmentation using high-level shading languages," *Visualization 2003*, Washington DC, IEEE Computer Society, 2003: p. 41.

[Weiss06] Weiss, B. "Fast median and bilateral filtering," *SIGGRAPH 2006*, ACM Press, 2006: pp. 519–526.

Per-Pixel Motion Blur
for Wheels

Damyan Pepper

Black Rock Studio

Introduction

Many games focus on rendering moving vehicles (for example, [MotoGP 07] and [ATV Offroad Fury 4]). The wheels on vehicles in these types of games have a problem: They spin too fast. Imagine a game running at 60 Hz. If the wheel is revolving at 1 Hz, then it is rendered with 60 different rotations before it has completed an entire revolution. If the wheel is revolving at 30 Hz, then it is rendered with only two different rotations. If the wheel is revolving at 59 Hz, then it looks as if it is spinning backward. If it's spinning at 60 Hz, then it will appear to be stationary.

This temporal aliasing problem is well known and is often alleviated in games by having a blurred wheel texture; as the wheel turns faster the detailed wheel texture is replaced by a less detailed, streaky, blurred texture. However, if you want to have geometric detail on the wheels, such as big, knobby treads, simple texture replacement is no longer a viable option.

This article describes a technique for blurring objects as a 2D post-process and compositing the results, with correct depth information, back into the scene. Each object is first rendered to an off-screen render-target and depth buffer. These color and depth buffers are used to render the object in the appropriate place on the screen, with the blur being performed in the pixel shader.

A motion blur algorithm that is specialized for blurring wheels is also presented. Using a geometric representation of the wheel, the 2D position on the texture is converted to the corresponding position in 3D world space by casting a ray from the camera that collides against the "wheel." Rotating this position around the wheel's rotation axis and then projecting back into 2D space provides the additional sample points to be used for the blur.

The end result is a convincing motion blur around the wheel (see Figure 3.4.1).

Existing Motion-Blur Techniques

One recently popular approach for rendering motion blur is per-pixel full-screen motion blur [MSDN-1]. This method works by storing a screen-space velocity value for each pixel in the final scene. A post-process takes this velocity buffer and the current scene's color buffer and, for each output pixel, it samples the color buffer along

FIGURE 3.4.1 Wheel blur on various types of wheels (the set of wheels in the center is not blurred).

the velocity vector for that pixel and averages the results, thus producing a blur like that shown in Figure 3.4.2.

Variations on this approach, such as [Rosado2007], calculate the velocity based on the camera's movement. This removes the need for a separate velocity buffer but produces similar results.

If we try and apply these techniques to a spinning wheel, however, we can see that it falls short. As a wheel is spinning, with this method we would continue to sample along a straight line, but the samples need to be along a curve. Figure 3.4.3 shows how linear samples fail to pick up the correct pixels.

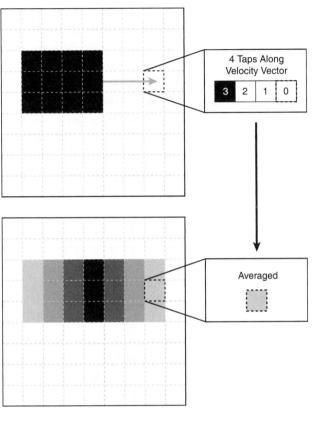

FIGURE 3.4.2 Full-screen motion blur using a velocity vector. The highlighted pixel in the top image is moving to the right at a rate of four pixels per frame. The motion-blur post-process samples the four pixels that this covers and averages the result. The bottom image shows the resulting blurred image.

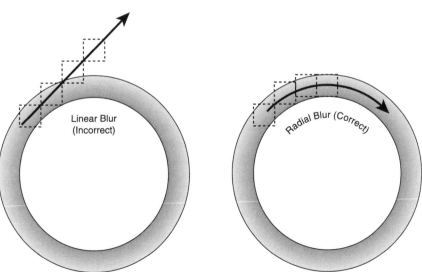

FIGURE 3.4.3 Samples along a straight line don't work for spinning wheels—the linear blur on the left will start blurring parts of the background into the wheel. The radial blur on the right would produce the correct results in this case.

Clearly another approach is required for wheels. [Tatarchuk2004] presents a technique for rendering fast moving objects by distorting the geometry that works well when the objects are moving quickly across the screen. Wheels, unfortunately, tend to stay in the same position on-screen; they just spin rapidly. Specialized approaches for motion blur have been developed in the past for things such as road surface detail textures [Hargreaves2005] or for environment maps [Mitchell2006], so it seems natural to have one for wheels.

Because wheels generally make up a relatively small part of the final scene, we don't want to have to pay the cost of the blur for the entire scene. Therefore we'll render the wheel to an off-screen render-target and perform the blur while compositing it into the main scene.

Rendering the Wheel

In order to render the wheel to an off-screen render-target, we need to calculate the appropriate transform/projection matrix to use. The projection should be the same as the one we use in the scene, but with the viewport adjusted so that the wheel fills the entire render-target. This viewport can be calculated by projecting the bounding box of the wheel into screen space and using the resulting 2D bounding box as the viewport. If the aspect ratio is not preserved while doing this, the wheel ends up filling the entire render-target, resulting in the best use of the resolution available. This can be seen in the demo application on the accompanying DVD when the "Show Render Targets" option is selected.

Performing Motion Blur

The next step of the process is to render the off-screen render-target as a sprite and perform the blur in the pixel shader. Ignoring the details of the blur, we know that we'll be doing a number of samples for each pixel and outputting the average color (including alpha).

If the wheel was the only item in the scene then this would be enough, but unfortunately wheels are often surrounded quite closely by things that we don't want to be involved in the blur, such as swinging arms or foliage. Fortunately, pixel shaders are able to output a depth value as well as a color value.

The algorithm can now be modified so that the depth values that were generated while the wheel was rendered to the off-screen render-target are also sampled for each tap. The pixel shader now outputs the maximum depth that was sampled. On consoles such as the Xbox 360 or PlayStation 3, depth buffers can be used as if they were normal textures; however, this is not the case on PCs. It is necessary to modify the shaders used when rendering the wheel so that they also output a depth value to a separate render-target, which can then be used during the composition process.

We now need to decide what sort of blur to use, having already dismissed linear blurs. Perhaps a radial blur would be better? This would work well in the case where the wheel is being viewed side-on, as it was in Figure 3.4.3. However, in the case of a wheel viewed from behind, as in Figure 3.4.4, a linear blur would actually be more appropriate.

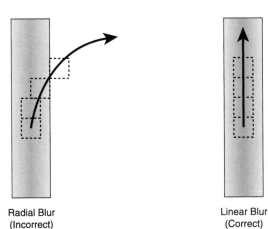

Radial Blur
(Incorrect)

Linear Blur
(Correct)

FIGURE 3.4.4 Radial blur doesn't work for all angles: When the wheel is viewed from behind, the radial blur starts sampling off the wheel. In this case a linear blur would be correct. Contrast this with Figure 3.4.3 where the radial blur was the appropriate one to use.

What we really want to be doing is working out our sample points by rotating the original position around the axis of the wheel. In order to do this we need to calculate the 3D position of the pixel we're rendering and rotate this around the wheel's axis.

Calculating 3D Position

Since we've already got a depth buffer available, this would seem an obvious place to start calculating the 3D position of the current pixel. However, this method fails to work for complex details such as knobby pieces on the tire treads on the wheel (Figure 3.4.5). The depth value between the knobs is the far clip plane, and what we really want is a similar depth to the knobs.

We can approximate the shape of the wheel by using geometric primitives. The intersection of the line from the camera through the pixel being shaded against a geometric approximation of the wheel tells us the approximate position of that pixel in world space. There are many possible ways to approximate a wheel, including a sphere, an ellipsoid, two intersecting ellipsoids, the intersection of an ellipsoid and two planes, and a capped cylinder. Of these, the capped cylinder provides the best approximation of the shape of a wheel resulting in a blur effect that is convincing from most angles.

Line/cylinder intersection tests are relatively easy to do, since if you transform the cylinder and the line so that the cylinder's axis is along one of the world's axes, then it becomes a line/circle intersection, as illustrated in Figure 3.4.6.

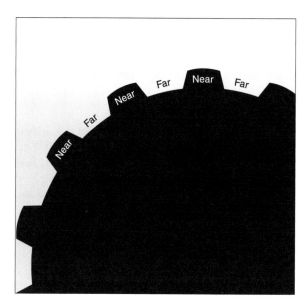

FIGURE 3.4.5 Knobby wheels mean the depth buffer is insufficient. The depth values calculated around the wheel should all be roughly the same, but using just the depth buffer would result in the gaps between the tread coming out as the far clip plane.

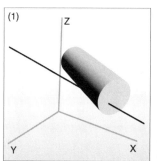
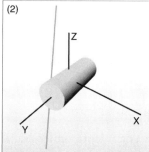
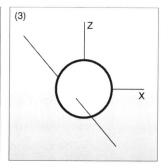

FIGURE 3.4.6 (1) Ray/cylinder intersection, (2) rotate ray and cylinder so that the cylinder is oriented along the *y*-axis and centered on the origin, (3) it's now a 2D problem.

The Line Equation

We want to find the intersection of the line from the camera through the texel being shaded with the cylinder that represents the wheel. To do this we need to obtain the equation for the line: its origin and direction. The line's origin is simply the camera's world position. The direction is calculated by working out the direction of the line from the camera's position through the position of the texel being shaded. This position is obtained by using the U,V coordinates of the texel, the viewport, and the camera's rotation matrix, as shown in Listing 3.4.1 (note that the version of this code included in the demo application has been optimized to factor out the aspect ratio calculation):

Listing 3.4.1 HLSL function to work out the orientation of the line from the camera through the current texel being shaded

```
float3 getWorldDir( float2 zUV )
{
    // adjust UV from viewport to full-screen
    float2 screenUv = ( zUV * ViewportSize ) + ViewportOffset;

    // move from UV space (0 to 1) to screen space (-1 to 1)
    float2 screenPos = -(screenUv - 0.5) * 2.0;

    // the projection matrix's [0][0]
    float w = CameraConstants.x;

    // the projection matrix's [1][1]
    float h = CameraConstants.y;

    // adjust for aspect ratio
    float aspect = w / h;

    screenPos.x *= aspect;
    screenPos.y /= aspect;

    // work out up/right amounts
    float up = screenPos.y / h;
    float right = screenPos.x / w;

    return normalize(
        CameraFront + CameraUp * up - CameraRight * right );
}
```

The Cylinder Equation

Cylinders are essentially a circle swept along an axis, so once we know the axis (a position and direction), the radius, and the height of the cylinder, we have everything we need to describe the cylinder. The cylinder's axis is the same as the wheel's rotation axis with the position being the center of the wheel; the radius and height must be specified explicitly for each wheel.

Line/Cylinder Intersection

Now that we know the equations for the line and the cylinder, we can calculate their intersection. Because a cylinder is a swept-circle, the calculation is significantly simplified if we arrange it so that the cylinder's axis is along one of the world axes centered on the origin, thus turning the intersection into a two-dimensional problem. This can be done by first transforming the line's origin so that it's relative to the cylinder's origin and then transforming the position and direction by the inverse of the wheel's rotation matrix. This effectively puts the line into "cylinder space."

At this point the intersection just becomes a simple 2D line/circle intersection in the cylinder space's XZ plane. Equation 1 is the equation of a circle. Equation 2 is the equation of a line. Inserting Equation 1 into Equation 2 gives Equation 3. Solving Equation 3 for t gives Equation 4:

$$r = x^2 + z^2$$
1

$$x = P_x + tD_x$$
$$z = P_z + tD_z$$
2

$$r = \left(P_x + tD_x\right)^2 + \left(P_z + tD_z\right)^2$$
3

$$t = \pm \frac{\sqrt{r^2\left(D_z^2 + D_X^2\right) - D_X^2 P_Z^2 + 2D_X D_Z P_X P_Z - D_Z^2 P_X^2} - D_Z P_Z - D_X P_X}{D_Z^2 + D_X^2}$$
4

We always want to choose the intersection point nearest the camera's position. This will be the one with the lowest value of t—the negative version. If the part inside the square root (the discriminant) is negative, then we know that there was no intersection. The denominator will only be zero if the line is parallel to the cylinder's axis, although we don't need to worry too much about this case since it gets covered when we deal with the cylinder caps.

Now that t has been calculated it can be plugged into Equation 2 to work out the intersection point between the line and the cylinder. After that has been done we need to decide if the intersection is on the cylinder or on one of its caps. If the absolute value of the cylinder space's y coordinate (Equation 5) is greater than the cylinder's height, then we calculate the t value as shown in Equation 6. The sign to use for h in Equation 6 should be the one that was obtained from Equation 5 (representing whether it is the "top" or "bottom" of the cylinder).

$$y = P_Y + tD_Y$$
5

$$h = \left| P_Y + tD_y \right|$$
$$t = -\frac{P_Y \pm h}{D_Y}$$
6

We can now write the line/cylinder intersection function shown in Listing 3.4.2 (note that the code included in the demo also calculates some values useful for debugging; these details have been omitted for the sake of brevity):

Listing 3.4.2 HLSL function to perform line/cylinder intersection

```
float3 lineCylinderIntersection(
    float3 zLinePoint,
    float3 zLineDir,
    float3 zCylinderPos,
    float zCylinderSqRadius,
    float zCylinderHeight,
    float3x3 zCylinderInvRot )
{
    // Transform the line origin and direction into the cylinder's
    // space

    float3 linePoint =
        mul( zLinePoint - zCylinderPos, zCylinderInvRot );

    float3 lineDir =
        mul( zLineDir, zCylinderInvRot );

    float PX = linePoint.x;
    float PZ = linePoint.z;
    float DX = lineDir.x;
    float DZ = lineDir.z;
    float rSquared = zCylinderSqRadius;

    float discriminant =
        ( DZ * DZ + DX * DX ) * rSquared -
        (DX * DX) * (PZ * PZ) +
        2 * DX * DZ * PX * PZ -
        (DZ * DZ) * (PX * PX );

    IntersectionResult result;

    if ( discriminant < 0 )
    {
        // no collision
        return zLinePoint;
    }
    else
    {
        float t =
            ( -sqrt( discriminant ) - DZ * PZ - DX * PX ) /
            ( DZ * DZ + DX * DX );

        float height = linePoint.y + lineDir.y * t;

        if ( abs(height) > zCylinderHeight )
        {
            // one of the 'caps'

            float t =
                linePoint.y -
                zCylinderHeight * sign(height) /
                -lineDir.y;
```

```
            return zLinePoint + zLindeDir * t;
        }
        else
        {
            // the cylinder itself
            return zLinePoint + zLineDir * t;
        }
    }
}
```

Sampling Around the Wheel's Axis

After we have the 3D position for the current texel, we need to sample the color and depth for different rotations of that position around the wheel's axis. Generating a rotation matrix around the wheel's axis is straightforward. After the new 3D position has been obtained it must be projected using the projection matrix that was used while rendering the wheel. Converting the screen to U,V space gives us a U,V coordinate that can then be used to look up the color and depth values (Listing 3.4.3).

Listing 3.4.3 HLSL function that generates a single sample rotated around the wheel's axis of rotation

```
struct SampleResult
{
    float4 color;
    float d;
};

SampleResult sample(
    float3 zIntersection,
    float3 zCenter,
    float zAngle )
{
    float s = sin(zAngle);
    float c = cos(zAngle);

    float3 axis = WheelAxis;

    // Generate a rotate-around-axis matrix...

    float3x3 rotm = {
        ( axis.x * axis.x ) - ( c * axis.x * axis.x ) + c,
        ( axis.x * axis.y ) - ( c * axis.x * axis.y ) - s * axis.z,
        ( axis.x * axis.z ) - ( c * axis.x * axis.z ) + s * axis.y,

        ( axis.y * axis.x ) - ( c * axis.y * axis.x ) + s * axis.z,
        ( axis.y * axis.y ) - ( c * axis.y * axis.y ) + c,
        ( axis.y * axis.z ) - ( c * axis.y * axis.z ) - s * axis.x,
```

```
                ( axis.z * axis.x ) - ( c * axis.z * axis.x ) - s * axis.y,
                ( axis.z * axis.y ) - ( c * axis.z * axis.y ) + s * axis.x,
                ( axis.z * axis.z ) - ( c * axis.z * axis.z ) + c };

        // Rotate
        float3 newPos;

        newPos = zCenter + mul( zIntersection - zCenter, rotm );
        // Project
        float4 projPos = mul( float4(newPos, 1), WheelTransViewProj );
        float2 newUv = (projPos / projPos.w).xy;

        // Convert to UV space
        newUv.y *= -1;
        newUv += 1;
        newUv *= 0.5;

        // Do the sample
        SampleResult res;
        res.color = tex2D( texture, newUv );
        res.d = tex2D( depth, newUv ).x;

        return res;
    }
```

Putting It All Together

We're now ready to put everything together; the process is illustrated in Figure 3.4.7. The first step is to render each wheel to the off-screen render-targets (color and depth buffers).

Next, the rest of the scene is rendered to the main render-target. Then we depth-sort the wheels on the CPU (so that we can render them in reverse-depth order) and composite them into the scene using the wheel blur pixel shader. Now we have nicely blurred wheels in our scene!

Issues

No rendering technique is without its drawbacks, so it's worth examining a few of them.

Problems at the Wheel Extremities

When we're sampling around the wheel's extremities, we often find that we're looking for data that is on the "other side" of the wheel. To prevent this, we can fudge the calculation so that there is less blur in the extreme regions of the wheel, for example using Equation 7 where S is the rotation scale, P is the 3D position, O is the wheel center, F is the camera's front vector, and A is the wheel's rotation axis.

$$S = \left(1 - \left\| P - O \right\| \cdot \hat{F} \times \hat{A} \right\|\right)^{0.4}$$

7

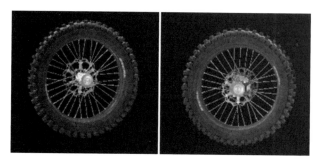

Wheels rendered to offscreen render-targets

Rest of scene rendered to main render-target

Wheels composited into main scene using the blurring pixel shader

FIGURE 3.4.7 Putting it all together.

This translates into the following code:

```
float rotScale =
    ( 1 -
        abs(
            dot(
                normalize( intersection.p - WheelCenter),
                cross( CameraFront, WheelAxis ) ) ) );

rotScale = pow( rotScale, 0.4 );
```

See-Through Wheels

The 3D position calculation always picks the nearest side of the wheel. This is fine if you cannot see through the wheel, but in the case of bicycle wheels there are usually details on the far side that can be seen through the spokes of the wheel. This problem is visible in the demo application if you look at how the brake disc on the rear wheel blurs when it is on the near side when compared to how it looks on the far side.

Lots of Pixel Shader Work

This technique requires a large amount of calculation to be performed per-pixel in the pixel shader. This can become particularly noticeable if the camera is positioned so that the wheel takes up a large proportion of the screen. We could dictate that the camera is not allowed that close but this might not always be practical. It might be worth pre-blurring the wheel to a separate render-target and using that to composite into the scene, although this solution could potentially result in nasty artifacts because the depth buffer is essentially being re-sampled in this case.

Outputting Depth Values

It's also worth noting that when a pixel shader outputs its own depth value this bypasses the hierarchical z-culling optimizations in the hardware. This may not be much of an issue, though, since the composition occurs pretty near the end of rendering, by which time the hierarchical z-buffer may be flat anyway.

Conclusion

In this article we present a simple wheel-blur technique that works well when rendering fast-moving vehicles with exposed wheels. Figures 3.4.1 and 3.4.8 show the effect being used on various wheels. The included demo application allows the effect to be seen in motion on various models. The source for the shaders can be found in the `wheelblur_shaders` directory, while the C++ source is in the `source` directory.

The general technique of taking specific parts of a vehicle and performing post-processing style effects while compositing the parts back into the scene is a powerful one. As well as modeling blur due to a spinning motion, it is also possible to create a high-frequency vibration blur effect or non-photorealistic effects for use in game front-ends.

FIGURE 3.4.8 Wheel blur on a motorcycle viewed from several different angles.

Acknowledgments

Thanks to Paul Phillpot for the models in the screenshots and demo application and George Foot for his help with the math.

References

[ATV Offroad Fury 4] Developed by Climax Racing, Published by SCEA. 2006.

[Hargreaves2005] Hargreaves, Shawn. "Detail Texture Motion Blur" (Article 2.11), *ShaderX⁴: Advanced Rendering Techniques*, Wolfgang Engel, Ed. Charles River Media, 2006.

[MotoGP 07] Developed by Climax Racing, Published by THQ 2007[MSDN-1] MSDN PixelMotionBlur sample available online at http://msdn2.microsoft.com/en-us/library/bb147267.aspx, August 13, 2007.

[Rosado2007] Rosado, Gilberto. "Motion Blur as a Post-Processing Effect" (Chapter 27), *GPU Gems 3*, H. Nguyen, Ed. Addison Wesley, 2007: pp. 575–581.

[Mitchell2006] Mitchell, Jason. "Motion Blurring Environment Maps" (Article 3.2). *ShaderX⁴: Advanced Rendering Techniques,* Wolfgang Engel, Ed Charles River Media, 2006: pp. 263–268.

[Tatarchuk2004] Tatarchuk, Natalya, Brennan, Chris, and Isidoro, John. "Motion Blur Using Geometry and Shading Distortion," *ShaderX²: Shader Programming Tips and Tricks with DirectX 9.0,* Wolfgang Engel, Ed. Charles River Media, 2003: pp 299–308.

3.5

Deferred Rendering Using a Stencil Routed K-Buffer

Louis Bavoil and Kevin Myers

NVIDIA Corporation

Introduction

GPUs are designed to handle traditional rasterization, where only the nearest fragment is kept (Z-buffering). This presents an obvious problem for cases where more than one layer is needed to compute the final pixel. For example, order-independent transparency extracts multiple sorted layers of fragments and blends them together in correct order. Compared to sorting primitives, it has the advantage of being correct when transparent primitives intersect with one another. Other applications that need multiple layers include refraction, absorption, deep shadow maps, and soft shadow mapping.

Our approach is to store as many fragments per pixel as possible into a deep buffer and then sort the fragments in depth order and perform deferred rendering. Using CPU rasterization, it is possible to capture all the fragments per pixel using a linked list of fragments per pixel called an A-buffer [Carpenter84]. On the GPU, multiple layers can be stored in one texture per layer. Depth peeling is a way of extracting depth-sorted layers, one layer per pass [Everitt01]. There have been attempts to capture depth-sorted layers into textures in a single pass by binding the same textures as input and the render-target of a fragment shader [Liu06] [Pangerl06] [Bavoil07]. However, read-after-write hazards happen with these methods because multiple fragments are processed concurrently by the GPU.

Rather than extracting our layers in depth order like with depth peeling, we extract them in rasterization order. To do so, we use the stencil test to direct the fragments into a buffer. Because we store a limited number of fragments per pixel, we call our data structure a K-buffer. With DirectX 10 generation GPUs, such as the GeForce 8 series, we can store up to eight fragments per pixel in one pass, and even more fragments with additional passes. Each fragment stored in the K-buffer needs to contain a depth value so that the fragments can be sorted in post-processing, as well as any other attributes. These additional attributes can be a shaded color or deferred shading information as for a G-Buffer [Puig06].

Our algorithm requires the ability to render to a multi-sample texture without actually multi-sampling. We also must be able to read individual subpixels, a feature available with DirectX 10.

Our Algorithm

The essential idea is to re-purpose a multi-sample render-target to not store MSAA coverage information but instead to use the samples to implement a K-buffer. As specified in DirectX 10, if you disable multi-sample rasterization and render to a multi-sample texture, your fragment gets rasterized to all the samples (Figure 3.5.1). At the same time, a stencil test is still done at the sample resolution. If we are clever with how we initialize our stencil values, we can make it so that only one sample gets written per fragment that reaches the raster ops.

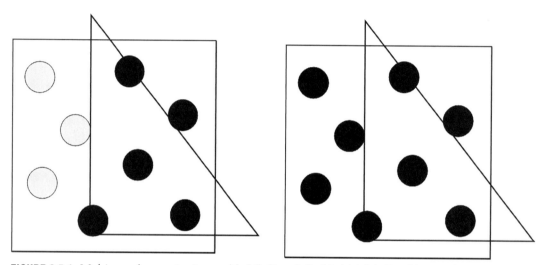

FIGURE 3.5.1 Multi-sample rasterization enabled (left) and disabled (right). Disabling multi-sample rasterization applies the raster ops to all the samples.

MSAA Storage

MSAA (multi-sample anti-aliasing) is a hardware mode in which the pixel shader is called once per fragment, while the raster ops (depth test, stencil test, and blending) are performed once per sample. Because raster ops are applied at sample resolution, storage occurs at sample resolution. So, for example, an RGBA 8x MSAA buffer stores eight RGBA colors per pixel. In order for MSAA to work, three steps are required: multi-sample rasterization, storage at sample resolution, and a resolve pass at the end. The resolve pass averages all the samples to compute one pixel value. In our algorithm we turn off two of these steps: multi-sample rasterization and the resolve pass; we simply want the extra storage.

Subpixel Stencil Routing

Stencil routing was invented for routing photons into a photon map using the stencil buffer and grid-aligned rasterization [Purcell03]. With DirectX 10, we found that it is possible to use it for general rasterization [Myers07]. To describe our algorithm, we take the example of a pixel with eight samples per pixel. We initialize the stencil buffer to incremental values starting from 2. Since the actual sample locations inside the pixel do not matter for the algorithm, we represent the stencil values as a vector S. We also represent the render-target as a vector T, initialized to 0 in this example:

S = [2 3 4 5 6 7 8 9]
T = [0 0 0 0 0 0 0 0]

We set the stencil reference value to 2, the stencil function to EQUAL, and the stencil op to DECREMENT_SATURATE. So when a first fragment F_0 covering this pixel goes through the stencil test, the test passes only for the sample with stencil value 2 and all the stencil values are decremented (and saturated to 0). So after one fragment F_0 has covered the pixel:

S = [1 2 3 4 5 6 7 8]
T = [F_0 0 0 0 0 0 0 0]

And after eight fragments F_0 to F_7 (the pixel is full):

S = [0 0 0 0 0 0 0 1]
T = [F_0 F_1 F_2 F_3 F_4 F_5 F_6 F_7]

Overflows

The initial range of the stencil values is [2, 9]. After eight fragments have been written to the same pixel, the stencil test fails for all samples since all stencil values are not equal to 2. So, after a ninth fragment:

S = [0 0 0 0 0 0 0 0]
T = [F_0 F_1 F_2 F_3 F_4 F_5 F_6 F_7]

All samples have reached 0. In determining overflow, we can avoid checking all samples and only look at the sample that was initialized to 9 (since every sample will be 0 if this is 0). The total number of pixels that overflowed can be queried by doing an occlusion query on a full-screen quad with the following sample mask M (bit-mask):

M = [0 0 0 0 0 0 0 1]

Post-Processing

Once the fragments have been captured in the K-buffer, a final full-screen quad is rendered and all the captured fragments are processed in a pixel shader (similar to a typical post-processing pass setup). We then extract the fragments from the K-buffer. This is where we need the ability to read samples from an MSAA texture. We then shade, sort, and blend the non-empty fragments over the color buffer of the opaque objects. Shading before sorting has the advantage of having a fixed footprint for the fragments (one color value and one depth value).

Capturing More Layers

If the K-buffer pixel overflows, another geometry pass could be done at the expense of rendering the geometry one more time and writing to an additional texture. The only difference is that for the ith geometry pass, the stencil buffer pixels need to be initialized to $[2 + i\,k, \ldots, 1 + (i+1)\,k]$.

D3D10 Implementation

In this section, we assume that the K-buffer contains up to eight fragments per pixel stored in one multi-sample texture. If the K-buffer has more than one multi-sample texture, it could be bound as a texture array (`Texture2DMSArray`).

Creating a Multi-Sample Stencil Buffer

We create a multi-sample depth stencil buffer and its associated depth stencil view. We want the highest multi-sample level supported by the GPU; for the NVIDIA 8800 series, this is 8x MSAA. In the code snippets below, `m_nSamples` is the number of samples per pixel of the stencil buffer and the render-targets.

Initializing the Stencil Buffer

We clear the stencil buffer, which efficiently writes the same stencil value to all the samples. However we really need to clear each sample to a different value. To start, we do a clear to the value of the last sample to be initialized. To initialize the remaining samples we set the sample mask to mask off every sample but the current one we are clearing, and then render a full-screen quad. The stencil is then configured to replace the current sample being written with the reference value.

The code snippet below assumes that a vertex shader that expands four indices into a full-screen quad is bound and NULL geometry and pixel shaders are bound.

```
const float blendFactor[4] = { 0.0f, 0.0f, 0.0f, 0.0f };
UINT nSampleMask = 1;
UINT8 nStencilRef = m_nSamples + 1;

pd3dDevice->ClearDepthStencilView( pDSV, D3D10_CLEAR_STENCIL,
1.0f, nStencilRef );

for( UINT8 i = 1; i < m_nSamples; ++i )
{
        nSampleMask = nSampleMask << 1;
        --nStencilRef;

        pd3dDevice->OMSetBlendState( pBS, blendFactor, nSampleMask );
        pd3dDevice->OMSetDepthStencilState( pDSWrite, nStencilRef );
        pd3dDevice->Draw( 4, 0 );
}
```

Creating a Multi-Sample Texture

In addition to a depth stencil buffer, we also need a multi-sample texture. In our D3D10_TEXTURE2D_DESC, we set SampleDesc.Count to m_nSamples. We also set SampleDesc.Quality to 0 disable any virtual samples (VCAA), which may conflict with our algorithm.

Rendering with Stencil Routing

When rendering the alpha blended primitives into our K-buffer, we need to have multi-sampling turned off in the rasterizer state and depth test and blending disabled. The depth stencil test should be configured this way:

```
D3D10_DEPTH_STENCIL_DESC dsDesc;
dsDesc.DepthEnable = false;
dsDesc.DepthWriteMask = D3D10_DEPTH_WRITE_MASK_ALL;
dsDesc.DepthFunc = D3D10_COMPARISON_ALWAYS;

dsDesc.StencilEnable = true;
dsDesc.StencilReadMask = 0xffffffff;
dsDesc.StencilWriteMask = 0xffffffff;

dsDesc.FrontFace.StencilFunc = D3D10_COMPARISON_EQUAL;
dsDesc.BackFace.StencilFunc = D3D10_COMPARISON_EQUAL;

dsDesc.BackFace.StencilFailOp = D3D10_STENCIL_OP_DECR_SAT;
dsDesc.BackFace.StencilPassOp = D3D10_STENCIL_OP_DECR_SAT;

dsDesc.FrontFace.StencilFailOp = D3D10_STENCIL_OP_DECR_SAT;
dsDesc.FrontFace.StencilPassOp = D3D10_STENCIL_OP_DECR_SAT;
```

Post-Processing

The texture array is bound to a shader. The shader then samples it using Load() from a Texture2DMS sampler. Then a bitonic sort is applied, which is an efficient way of sorting the fragments because it can be completely unrolled to a fixed sorting network without any flow control [Buck 2004]. Finally, we perform alpha blending.

In our implementation, we store the fragments as uint2 values. This provides a compact representation for the fragments. We store the depth value in the first 32-bit component, and a packed 8-bit RGBA color in the second component. For simplicity, we assume no deferred shading (see the "Discussion" section for more details). We assume that the fragments were shaded and stored in this uint2 format by the geometry pass.

Here is the code of our main post-processing function.

```
Texture2DMS<uint2, NUM_LAYERS> tKBuffer;

float3 SubPixelSortAndBlendPS (  QuadOutput input ) : SV_Target
{
    uint2 frag[NUM_LAYERS];
    [unroll] for (int j = 0; j < NUM_LAYERS; j++) {
    frag[j] = tKBuffer.Load( int3( input.pos.xy, 0 ), j ).rg;
    }
    BitonicSortB2F( frag, N_MAX );
    return AlphaBlendB2F( frag, N_MAX );
}
```

Next is the code we use for the bitonic sort in back-to-front order, assuming that a depth value is stored in the x component.

```
// Code courtesey of Thomas W. Christopher
// http://www.tools-of-computing.com/tc/CS/Sorts/bitonic_sort.htm
void BitonicSortB2F( inout uint2 a[N_MAX], int n )
{
    int i,j,k;
    [unroll] for (k=2;k<=n;k=2*k) {
    [unroll] for (j=k>>1;j>0;j=j>>1) {
        [unroll] for (i=0;i<n;i++) {
          int ixj=i^j;
          if ((ixj)>i) {
            if ((i&k) == 0 && a[i].x < a[ixj].x) swap(a[i],a[ixj]);
            if ((i&k) != 0 && a[i].x > a[ixj].x) swap(a[i],a[ixj]);
          }
        }
      }
    }
}
```

And finally, for the alpha blending, we use the code that follows. The destination value should be initialized to the color of the opaque objects at this pixel location. Here, it is hard-coded to be white.

```
float3 AlphaBlendB2F( uint2 frag[N_MAX], int nLayers )
{
    float3 dst = (float3)1.0f;
    [unroll] for (int i = 0; i < nLayers; i++) {
      float4 src = unpack_rgba(frag[i].y);
      dst.rgb = src.a * src.rgb + (1.0 - src.a) * dst.rgb;
    }
    return dst;
}
```

Discussion

Depth Complexity

Because we can capture up to eight samples per pixel in one geometry pass, we may create artifacts for overflowing pixels. A quality metric is the number of overflowing pixels and it can be queried using an occlusion query. More fragments could be captured by doing more geometry passes. Alternatively, the application could also be optimized to reduce the required depth complexity by doing a coarse depth sort of the geometry and rendering in front-to-back order. This way, fragments that are close to the eye would be less likely to be missing in the K-buffer.

Anti-aliasing

Because we repurpose the MSAA samples to store multiple layers instead of just the nearest layers, we cannot do multi-sample anti-aliasing. Anti-aliasing can be done using supersampling (rendering to an enlarged buffer and filtering at the end) or approximated by filtering the aliased image [Puig06]. Also, alpha blending is probably most commonly used in games for rendering particles, which typically do not need MSAA. In this case, the MSAA image for the opaque objects can be resolved first and the alpha blended fragments from the K-buffer can be blended over.

Conclusion

In this article, we have shown how up to eight fragments per pixel can be captured in one pass over the alpha-blended geometry. This makes it possible to fill a K-buffer with eight layers in one geometry pass as shown in Figures 3.5.2–Figures 3.5.5. More fragments can be captured and blended with more geometry passes in a sliding window fashion, but it is at the expense of drawing the same alpha-blended geometry additional times and sorting more fragments per pixel.

The main issue with our deferred rendering approach is that all the fragments must be captured and sorted first. This is due to the fact that we capture fragments as we receive them in rasterization order. Depth peeling [Everitt01] captures layers in depth order, but it requires a pass for each layer. In conclusion, our algorithm works best with complex geometry where it costs more to do another pass than to sort and in cases where all layers must be captured.

D3D10 101.60 fps Vsync off (1024x768), R8G8B8A8_UNORM (MS4, Q16)
HARDWARE: NVIDIA GeForce 8800 GTX

FIGURE 3.5.2
First layer.

D3D10 101.60 fps Vsync off (1024x768), R8G8B8A8_UNORM (MS4, Q16)
HARDWARE: NVIDIA GeForce 8800 GTX

FIGURE 3.5.3
Second layer.

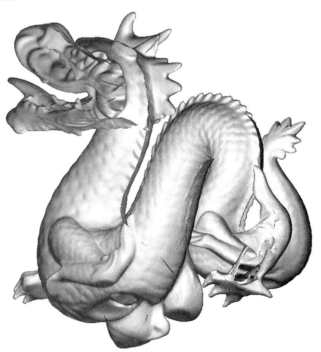

D3D10 101.62 fps Vsync off (1024x768), R8G8B8A8_UNORM (MS4, Q16)
HARDWARE: NVIDIA GeForce 8800 GTX

FIGURE 3.5.4
Third layer.

D3D10 102.51 fps Vsync off (1024x768), R8G8B8A8_UNORM (MS4, Q16)
HARDWARE: NVIDIA GeForce 8800 GTX

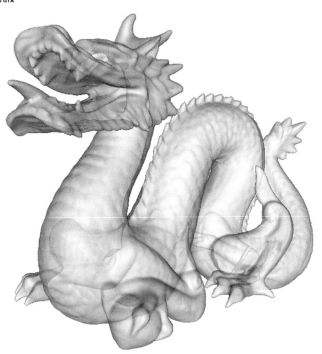

FIGURE 3.5.5
Alpha blending
eight layers.

References

[Bavoil07] Bavoil, Louis, Callahan, Steven P., Lefohn, Aaron, Comba, Joao L. D., Silva, Claudio T. "Multi-Fragment Effects on the GPU using the k-Buffer,", *Symposium on Interactive 3D Graphics and Games*, 2007: pp. 97–104.

[Buck04] Buck, Ian and Purcell, Tim. "A Toolkit for Computation on GPUs," Chapter 37, p. 621, *GPU Gems: Programming Techniques, Tips and Tricks for Real-Time Graphics*, 2004.

[Carpenter84] Carpenter, Loren. "The A-buffer, an anti-aliased hidden surface method," *SIGGRAPH*, 1984.

[Everitt01] Everitt, Cass. "Interactive Order-Independent Transparency," NVIDIA whitepaper, 2001.

[Liu06] Liu, Baoquan, Wei, Li-Yi, Xu, Ying-Qing. "Multi-Layer Depth Peeling via Fragment Sort," Microsoft technical report, 2006.

[Myers07] Myers, Kevin, Bavoil, Louis. "Stencil Routed A-Buffer," ACM SIGGRAPH Technical Sketch, 2007.

[Pangerl06] Pangerl, David. "ZT-Buffer Algorithm," Article 2.8, *ShaderX5: Advanced Rendering Techniques*, Wolfgang Engel, ed., 2006: p. 151.

[Puig06] Placeres, Frank Puig. "Overcoming Deferred Shading Drawbacks," Article 2.5, *ShaderX5: Advanced Rendering Techniques*, Wolfgang Engel, ed., 2006: p. 115.

[Purcell03] Purcell, Timothy J., Donner, Craig, Cammarano, Mike, Jensen, Henrik Wann, Hanrahan, Pat. "Photon Mapping on Programmable Graphics Hardware," Graphics hardware, 2003.

3.6

HDR Meets *Black & White 2*

Francesco Carucci

Lionhead Studios

Why HDR in Black & White 2?

Black & White 2 is a strategy game sequel of the best-selling PC game that is set on various islands in the world of Eden. Lighting conditions can vary drastically in *Black & White 2*, both in the same frame or as time passes; moreover, the unique implementation of the day/night cycle, where the player can quickly change time of day and each time of day has a different lighting setup, makes it very challenging to precompute optimal lighting setups. The player has complete freedom to move around, and this free camera can easily generate scenes where different portions have drastically different brightness levels. This can make it difficult to find a range to maximize precision in representing colors while rendering. *High dynamic range (HDR) rendering*, where every color in the scene is represented with values that can go beyond the standard low dynamic range from 0.0 to 1.0, was taken into consideration in order to address this problem.

Figure 3.6.1 shows one of these difficult cases for nighttime rendering. The vast majority of pixels in the scene are gathered at the lower bottom of the luminosity histogram. This is a very low dynamic range shot: only a few bits are effectively used to represent all the colors in the scene, severely damaging its contrast. A possible solution would be to artificially increase the brightness of the main light at night while still keeping the bluish overall tone, thus increasing the contrast. This would tax the artists, who also have to define proper lighting setups at night by hand, and may not be practical in any scenario. An automatic solution would be highly preferable.

Automatic exposure and high dynamic range rendering could be a viable solution in this scenario when they are implemented together. Rendering the scene to a high dynamic range format, for example, floating-point with 10 or 16 bits per pixel depending on hardware constraints, helps keep good precision in representing both bright and dark colors during scene rendering. Automatic exposure helps find automatically the luminance characteristics of the image that can be used to finally map it to the final 8-bit per component target, ensuring that as many bits as possible are actually used.

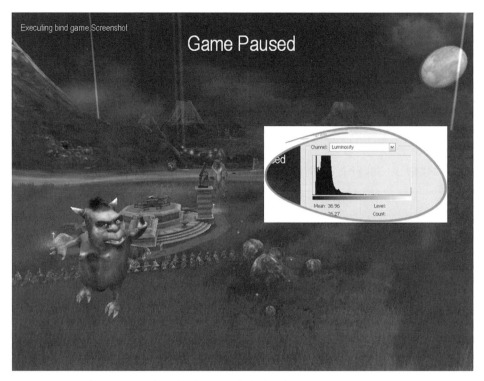

FIGURE 3.6.1 This is a typical night shot in *Black & White 2*.

Encoding High Dynamic Range Colors

The actual encoding of high dynamic range information depends largely on the target hardware, and it's a matter of striking a balance between precision, bandwidth, and memory storage. OpenEXR standard format is 16-bit floating-point per channel and usually offers good precision with no noticeable banding on consumer monitors, although it does require significant memory and bandwidth. On the other hand, 10-bit floating-point per channel, which is supported by Xbox 360, ATI Radeon X1800 generation, and all DirectX 10-class GPUs, offers high dynamic range with the same memory footprint of standard 32-bit per pixel LDR, but it can suffer from banding.

Standard floating-point is not the only possible representation of high dynamic range values: The RGBE format encodes a common exponent in the alpha channel by which the RGB values are multiplied.

Black & White 2 uses a 16-bit floating-point format to maximise precision and yet still be able to use blending operations if the hardware supports it.

High Quality 32-Bit HDR Colors with LogLuv

A color space specifically designed to encode the full gamut available to humans is the CIE Luv color space, which was first exploited by Greg Ward Larson [Larson98] to efficiently store HDR images. CIE Luv defines colors with three coordinates: L (luminance) and the chromaticity coordinates u and v, and while luminance can assume any positive value, chromaticity coordinates vary within the [0,1] range.

We first convert RGB colors to XYZ colors, which are always a positive superset of RGB space, and then we map XYZ colors to CIE Luv:

$$(X,Y,Z) = \begin{bmatrix} 0.497 & 0.339 & 0.164 \\ 0.256 & 0.678 & 0.066 \\ 0.023 & 0.113 & 0.864 \end{bmatrix} \begin{bmatrix} R \\ G \\ B \end{bmatrix}$$

$$x = \frac{X}{X+Y+Z}, y = \frac{Z}{X+Y+Z}$$

$$L = Y$$

$$u = \frac{4x}{-2x+12y+3}$$

$$v = \frac{9y}{-2x+12y+3}$$

It's now relatively easy to store this new color using only four bytes per pixel: u and v are normalized so that it's natural to store them in two 8-bit components, but L needs more work because it can assume extremely high values.

Ward proposes to store the logarithm of L in 16 bits, thus it will not fit in a single 8-bit component. To remedy this we can split it into most- and least-significant parts and then store those parts in two 8-bit components.

This procedure can be easily performed in a shader via the fractional operator available in any modern shading language/graphics hardware (see Listing 3.6.1).

Listing 3.6.1 HLSL code to convert from RGB to LogLuv

```
float eps = pow(2, -64);

        float3x3 mRGB_to_XYZ =
        {
                {0.497, 0.256, 0.023},
                {0.339, 0.678, 0.113},
                {0.164, 0.066, 0.864}
        };

        float4 ConvertRGBToLogLuv(float3 RGB)
        {
                float3 XYZ = mul( mRGB_to_XYZ, RGB );
                XYZ = max( XYZ,float3(eps, eps, eps)); // avoid div by 0
```

```
        float2 xy = XYZ.xz / dot( float3(1,1,1), XYZ );
        float2 uv = float2(4, 9) * xy /
                    dot(float3(-2,12,3),float3(xy,1));

        float LogL = 256.0 * log( XYZ.y + 64 ); // avoid neg
values
        float LogL_LSB = frac(LogL); // get 8 least significant
bits;

        return float4( uv, LogL_LSB, LogL);
    }
```

This method allows us to store HDR pixels in only four bytes. This format is very practical for easy average log luminance evaluation for automatic exposure computation. Unfortunately it also introduces limitations related to alpha blending because GPUs can't blend in this color space. Moreover, any sampled LogLuv texture might display artifacts as linear interpolations between LogLuv samples that are not mathematically correct in this non-linear color space. (See [Larson98] for an inverse CIE Luv to RGB transform.)

Tonemapping

After the high dynamic range image is rendered to the desired format, all colors must be mapped to the [0..1] range in order to be displayed on low dynamic range monitors. The goal of the tonemapping operator of *Black & White 2* is to reproduce as many details as possible with good contrast in both day and night conditions. The tonemapping operator implemented in *Black & White 2* uses the following equations [RSSF02]:

$$L(x, y) = \frac{g}{L_{ave}}\left(L_w - L_{min}\right)$$

1

$$L_d(x, y) = \frac{L(x, y)\left(1 + \dfrac{L(x, y)}{L_{white}^2}\right)}{1 + L(x, y)}$$

2

where:

L_w is the luminance of the pixel to be mapped
L_{white} is the smallest luminance that will be mapped to pure white
L_{min} is the minimum luminance that will be mapped to pure black
L_{avg} is the average luminance of the scene
$L_d(x,y)$ is the new luminance of the pixel at coordinates (x, y) mapped to the range [0..1]

This is a simple operator suited for real-time rendering with few control points that can be easily understood and tweaked by artists. In real-time rendering, tonemapping is an artistic process more than anything else. The goal of this tonemapper is to give the artists as much control as possible over the process.

Minimum, Maximum, and Average Luminance

Minimum, maximum, and average luminance can be computed on the GPU by repeatedly scaling the input image and recording each block of pixels' minimum, maximum, and average until the destination render-target is 1×1, as shown in [Green04]. The values stored in the pixel are good approximations and can be used as inputs to the tonemapping operator.

Image Histogram

Because computing minimum, maximum, and average luminance of the scene already requires processing the entire scene pixel by pixel, with a little more effort we can gather more information about the luminance characteristics by generating the histogram of the rendered image.

In practice, we can set an absolute maximum luminance and divide the range between 0 and the absolute maximum luminance, for example, in 1,024 slots. Each slot counts the number of pixels in the image that have a certain luminance.

For each pixel of the image, we find its luminance by computing the dot product between the RGB color and the luminance vector:

```
luminance = dot(color, LUMINANCE_VECTOR)
```

where a common `LUMINANCE_VECTOR` is

```
(0.2125 0.7154 0.0721)
```

The luminance can be easily mapped to the corresponding slot with the following code:

```
float slot_size = absolute_maximum_luminance / histogram_size;
int pixel_slots = luminance * slot_size;
```

By dividing the number of pixels counted in each luminance slot by the total number of pixels in the scene, we obtain the frequency histogram that we can also use to compute minimum, average, and maximum luminance to plug into the tonemapping operator.

The CPU is particularly well-suited for this operation and, in practice, on modern PC hardware with fast downlink from the GPU to the CPU, downloading a scaled down version of the rendered image is becoming faster. *Black & White 2* uses a copy at one quarter the resolution of the initial image for histogram analysis.

Image Histogram on the GPU

The image histogram can also be generated entirely on the GPU as shown in [Scheuerman2007].

In their scatter-based histogram generation algorithm, a one-point primitive is rendered for each pixel in the input image; the vertex shader computes an index and converts it to an output location that maps into a 1D texture where the image histogram is stored. The fragment that is rasterized into the location in the output texture is accumulated with an additive blending operation. After scattering and accumulating all points coming from the input image, the output 1D texture will contain the desired histogram.

Based on the authors' results, this GPU-based algorithm outperforms CPU-based algorithms by an order of magnitude for large histograms.

Histogram Equalization

The histogram can be used for more interesting operations than finding minimum, maximum, and average luminance: the histogram can also be equalized, making sure that it covers the whole available dynamic range for maximum contrast before the image is tonemapped to displayable range (see Figure 3.6.2).

As described in [GW08], to obtain an equalized histogram, we map each slot in the histogram with luminance level R in the input image to a slot with level S, where S is the sum of all frequencies less than or equal to R (see Figure 3.6.3).

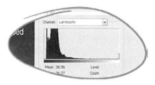

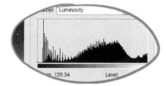

FIGURE 3.6.2 Source image histogram before equalization

FIGURE 3.6.3 Image histogram after equalisation.

The result is a good approximation of an equalized histogram and it can be used as input to the following step of the tonemapper: auto exposure.

Auto Exposure

From the equalized histogram we can easily compute L_{min}, L_{max}, and L_{avg} with the following algorithm:

L_{min} is the first slot where S is greater than I
L_{max} is the first slot where S is greater than P_{max}
L_{avg} is the first slot where S is greater than P_{avg}

Where P_{min}, P_{max}, and P_{avg} represent percentages. The typical value for P_{min} is 0.01 to exclude 1% of the darkest pixels from contributing to the final tonemapping (they will be mapped to pure black), while P_{max} can be set to something around 0.99 (99%), which excludes 1% of the brightest pixels in the image that will be mapped to pure white.

P_{avg} is usually set to 0.50 (50%), which represents the median value of the histogram. A proper average value can be also computed and the decision left to the artists about which one should be used depending on the scene characteristics or the particular effect they want to achieve.

P_{min} and P_{max} can be easily understood and controlled by artists to give more stability to the tonemapping operator and to directly influence L_{min}, L_{avg}, and L_{max}, which are plugged into Equation 1.

In Figure 3.6.4, for example, P_{max} is set to a value that will ignore the very bright pixels that simulate the sun glittering on the surface of the water. These pixels are then mapped to white and bloomed to give a stronger effect. This also creates a more uniform behavior of the tonemapper when a bright but not too large area of the screen enters into view and is effectively ignored until the bright region is no longer big enough to give a decisive contribution.

FIGURE 3.6.4 Very bright pixels coming from the ocean renderer.

The auto exposure effect that simulates eye adaption to the current brightness level in the scene is obtained by tracking the current L_{min}, L_{max}, and L_{avg} to the values computed from the histogram analysis for the current frame using this code:

```
act_value += new_value * (1.0f -pow(1.0f -speed, 30.0f *
elapsed_time));
```

The `speed` parameter can be exposed to the artist to be tweaked for quicker or slower adaption.

Mapping Luminance

The actual minimum, average, and maximum luminance values coming from the tracker are fed to the tonemapping shader. For each pixel of the source image, the shader in Listing 3.6.2 is executed

Listing 3.6.2 Tone mapping shader

```
float4 Main(VertexToPixel input)
        {
                float4 color = tex2D(g_HDRTextureSampler,
    input.texcoord);

                float Lw = dot(LUMINANCE_VECTOR, color.rgb);
                float Ld = MapLuminance(Lw);

                color.rgb *= Ld / Lw;

                return color;
        }
```

The MapLuminance function is the core of the tonemapper: It implements Equation 1 and maps the source luminance to the [0..1] range (see Listing 3.6.3).

Listing 3.6.3 HLSL code to map luminance to LDR

```
float MapLuminance(float Lw)
        {
                float middle_gray = g_MiddleGray;
                float avg_luminance = g_AvgLuminance;
                float white_luminance = g_WhiteLuminance;

                Lw -= g_MinLuminance;

                float Ld = 0.0f;
                if (Lw > 0.0f)
                {
                        float L = (middle_gray / avg_luminance) *
    Lw;

                        Ld = L * (1.0f + L / (white_luminance *
                                white_luminance)) / (1.0f + L);
                }

                return Ld;
        }
```

The MiddleGray parameter can be exposed to the artist and is used to change the exposure of the final image. Figure 3.6.5 shows how the global exposure level is set higher at night to achieve a higher contrast and is set lower during the day to get a more pleasant view.

FIGURE 3.6.5 Night (left) and day (right) shots.

Implementation Details in *Black & White 2*

Black & White 2 typically renders the scene to a 1,024×768 FP16 gamma-corrected render-target. The FP16 format was chosen because it gives enough precision to avoid banding in the vast majority of the cases, while 1,024×768 was a common target resolution at the time the title shipped. Where available, an MSAA render-target is used. The render-target is scaled down to 256×192 and downloaded over the PCI-E bus to main memory, where the CPU computes a histogram every frame (at 30 fps).

The HDR scene is tonemapped using the algorithm described to a R8G8B8 render-target (R10G10B10 where available). The artist has control over several parameters to fine-tune the tonemapper:

P_{min} is used to isolate very dark pixels of the scene, reduce the range, and increase the contrast
P_{avg} is used to change the overall brightness level of the final image
P_{max} is used to isolate very bright pixels of the scene, and also to reduce the range and increase the contrast
MiddleGray is used to change the exposure level of the final image

The L_{min}, L_{avg}, and L_{max} parameters were previously set as shader constants and the tonemapper was evaluated in the pixel shader for every pixel.

In the production version, the tonemapping function is evaluated for 1,024 different luminance levels on the CPU and the result is written to a 1,024×1 R16F texture. The pixel shader fragment code actually implementing the tone mapping operator is shown here:

```
float Ld = tex1D(LuminanceMapSampler, Li);
colorOut.rgb = LuminanceScale * (colorIn.rgb / Li) * Ld;
```

where LuminanceScale is the maximum luminance level in the scene and is used to give a slight improvement in precision to the values encoded in the luminance map.

HDR rendering was plugged into *Black & White 2* as a patch after the game was published; it required only very localized changes to the post-processing framework, no scene rendering shader was touched, and no changes to the art assets were made. The only artwork done was tweaking the tonemapper for different times of day. Creating art assets with HDR in mind, especially textures, would still have greatly enhanced the final visual quality, but no art time was available at the time.

Performance Analysis

Adding HDR had a significant performance impact on *Black & White 2* in terms of both CPU and GPU rendering and memory; it's considered a high-end feature. At the typical resolution of 1,024×768, the render-target takes about 6 MB of video RAM, which can go up to 25 MB where 4xMSAA is supported on floating-point render-targets.

The scaled down version takes approximately 10 ms to download from GPU memory to CPU memory over the PCI-E bus on an AMD64 3500 MHz used for benchmarks. It takes about 1 ms to analyze the histogram on the CPU. Although the time to download a copy of the scaled down render-target is consistent, it can be easily spread across multiple frames. Histogram analysis doesn't need to be strictly timed but can lag behind since it's used to compute the target for the auto exposure algorithm.

Without any further optimization, the current implementation of *Black & White 2* is limited by the down-link bandwidth. This is not a problem on current generation consoles, since the scaled down render-target can be quickly written directly to main memory, making the algorithm more appealing.

Conclusion

Using the histogram to compute input for the tonemapper is, in the current PC implementation, trading bandwidth from the GPU to the CPU for GPU power. It also offers some intuitive parameters that can be tweaked by the artist, making the tonemapper more flexible and easier to adapt to different scenarios. The pixel shader code boils down to a simple texture fetch and some math: This texture fetch can be incorporated in more generic color correction techniques based on 3D texture. The CPU cycles needed to analyze the histogram can be spread across multiple frames and the cost is practically negligible.

The histogram can also be computed directly on the GPU, which can be useful to increase the resolution of the input image and free the CPU from the burden. In practice, we found the added complexity not worth the gain, since the CPU time to compute the histogram can be easily hidden in another thread and spread across multiple frames, becoming practically negligible; using a higher resolution image also didn't increase the quality of the tonemapper in a noticeable way.

Figures 3.6.6 and 3.6.7 illustrate the difference between an image rendered in low dynamic range and the same image rendered in high dynamic range with histogram-based tonemapping.

(a) Screenshot taken without HDR   *(b) Game screenshot with HDR rendering*

FIGURE 3.6.6 Original (a) and HDR (b) shots at day time.

(a) Screenshot taken without HDR   *(b) Game screenshot with HDR rendering*

FIGURE 3.6.7 Original (a) and HDR (b) shots at night time.

Acknowledgments

Thanks to Marco Salvi for the description of his 32-bit HDR format used in *Heavenly Sword* for PS3. Thanks to the *Black & White 2* engine team who made a still amazingly good looking game: Ben, Dave and Mark.

References

[Green04] Green, S. and Cebenoyahn, C. "High Dynamic Range Rendering on the GeForce 6800." Technical white paper, available online at http://download. nvidia.com/developer/presentations/2004/6800_Leagues/6800_Leagues_HDR. pdf

[GW08] Gonzalez, R. C. and Woods, R. E. *Digital Image Processing*. Prentice Hall, 3rd edition.

[Larson98] Larson, Greg Ward. "LogLuv encoding for full-gamut, high-dynamic range images," *Journal of Graphics Tools,* Volume 3, Issue 1, March '98, A.K.Peters. Ltd.

[RSSF02] Reinhard, E., Stark, M., Shirley, P., and Ferwerda, J.A. "Photographic tone reproduction for digital images," *ACM Transactions on Graphics (SIGGRAPH '02)*, 2002: pp. 267–276. Available online at http://www.cis.rit.edu/jaf/publications/sig02_paper.pdf

[Scheuerman2007] Scheuermann, T., Hensley, J. "Efficient Histogram Generation Using Scattering on GPUs," *ACM SIGGRAPH Symposium on Interactive 3D Graphics and Games (SI3D '07)*. Available online at http://ati.amd.com/developer/gdc/2007/GPUHistogramGeneration_preprint.pdf

3.7

Robust Order-Independent Transparency via Reverse Depth Peeling in DirectX 10

Nicolas Thibieroz

Advanced Micro Devices, Inc.

Introduction

Order-independent transparency is the concept of achieving correct rendering of translucent geometry without any sorting requirement. Due to the complexity of this goal, this topic has been the subject of significant research in real-time computer graphics for a number of years. While the Z-buffer is commonly used to perform hidden surface removal on opaque pixels, the same technique cannot be used on transparent pixels because the Z-buffer's unique entry per fragment will be unable to represent the multiple transparent pixels that may contribute to the final color ([Pangerl07] attempts to work around this limitation by implementing a custom multi-layered depth buffer capable of sorting a limited number of transparency layers). As a result, non-commutative blending modes require the sorting and rendering of transparent pixels in a back-to-front order to guarantee correct rendering. Failure to sort transparency will therefore yield incorrect visual results (as you can see in Figures 3.7.1 and 3.7.2). This sorting requirement has a significant cost (both in terms of performance and complexity) and a number of older game titles have been known to resort to commutative blending modes like additive blending as a way to escape from it. Unfortunately, this leads to undesirable visual results as the rendering of smoke, water splashes, or other transparent geometry would often (incorrectly) cause saturation to white.

A more traditional method still very much in use today is to sort all transparent geometry in a back-to-front order before submitting them to the GPU. Although it is theoretically possible to perform this sorting on the GPU using techniques like bitonic sorting [Batcher68], it is usually more economical to perform this task on the CPU instead. In addition to the actual sorting cost there are two significant drawbacks to this technique. First, the sorting is commonly *per-object* and occasionally *per-polygon* as opposed to *per-pixel*, which can cause visual artifacts in cases where polygons intersect or overlap each other (see Figure 3.7.3 for an example). Second, because the rendering needs to happen in a back-to-front order, the same vertex and pixel shaders should be used when rendering all transparent geometry. Failure to share

FIGURE 3.7.1 Translucent model rendered without any sorting. Notice the order dependency artifacts.

FIGURE 3.7.2 Translucent model rendered with per-pixel correct reverse depth peeling.

FIGURE 3.7.3 Three overlapping triangles: Sorting by triangle depth will yield incorrect results.

those shaders will lead to unreasonable shader switching costs since consecutive triangles in the sorted list may very well belong to different materials.

Both of these drawbacks can be avoided by using a more involved technique, albeit at a GPU performance cost. This article describes a method built around depth peeling ([Everitt01]) that provides a robust and optimized order-independent transparency solution using the DirectX 10 API, available with the latest generation of graphics cards such as the ATI Radeon HD 2000 series. This solution is especially relevant in situations where memory has become a scarce resource due to the rendering techniques employed (e.g., deferred shading).

Depth Peeling

Depth peeling is the process of extracting "layers" of transparency from a set of transparent objects. Each layer represents the front-most pixels that are "peeled away" after each pass. The number of layers extracted is therefore equal to the number of depth peeling passes performed on the geometry. As each peeled layer is stored in its own surface the total amount of video memory required is directly proportional to the number of layers extracted. The process stops when the required number of layers is reached; for absolute correct rendering this equates to peeling away *all* layers until there is no more geometry to peel away. With all transparent layers in memory, it becomes straightforward to blend those in a back-to-front order with the rest of the scene, achieving per-pixel correct transparency ordering in the process. Depth peeling becomes quite attractive for rendering techniques such as deferred shading that want to include transparent geometry in shading passes [Thibieroz04].

The main technical concept behind depth peeling is the use of two depth tests, whereby one depth test is used to determine the current front-most layer and the second test is used to exclude previously peeled layers.

Because depth peeling requires a pass per layer, its performance cost can be prohibitive when complex objects are rendered. [Liu06] aims to reduce the number of depth peeling passes by storing multiple layers into *multiple render-targets* in each pass. Unfortunately, the technique relies on an unsupported graphic hardware feature in which the same texture is bound for both reads and writes simultaneously. Such behavior is actually illegal in DirectX, and due to its unpredictable nature (especially with regard to future hardware) cannot be recommended. More recently [Myers07] came up with the idea of extracting multiple transparency layers in a single pass by using the stencil buffer to direct transparent fragments onto different samples of a multi-sampled render-target. With up to 8x multi-sampling supported in current graphic hardware, this has the effect of extracting up to eight transparent fragments in a single geometry pass. The resulting fragments are then manually sorted (with the side-effect of requiring depth to be stored as well as color and alpha) and blended together using a pixel shader. This technique undoubtedly works well for scenes limited to eight layers or less but becomes increasingly more complex and memory-hungry with more layers (additional multi-sampled render-targets are needed and the sorting process becomes more involved). It is also incompatible with multi-sampling anti-aliasing (MSAA) on the transparent geometry since the sample masks are already used to store transparent fragments.

Reverse Depth Peeling

The technique described in this article implements a variation of depth peeling called *reverse depth peeling*. In the same way depth peeling extracts layers from transparent geometry in a front-to-back order, reverse depth peeling extracts layers in a back-to-front order. [Hachisuka05] makes use of this particular ordering to traverse depth layers in an offline global illumination renderer. The advantage of this variation is the elimination of the storage requirements for each layer peeled front-to-back with the legacy technique: With traditional depth peeling, the blending process can only start once the furthermost layer has been determined, and storing each layer until this moment is likely to require an unreasonable amount of video memory. The memory saving enabled by reverse depth peeling is especially important for rendering techniques that use larger bit-depth render-targets like deferred shading. With each layer peeled in a back-to-front order, the blending with the back buffer can immediately take place after each new layer has been extracted. Table 3.7.1 illustrates the differences between traditional depth peeling and reverse depth peeling.

Table 3.7.1 Algorithmic differences between depth peeling and reverse depth peeling

Depth Peeling	Reverse Depth Peeling
For each pass:	Allocate memory for one layer
Allocate memory for new layer	
Determine front-most layer	For each pass:
Store layer in memory	Determine furthermost layer
	Blend with render-target
For each pass:	
Pick furthermost layer from memory	
Blend with render-target	

Algorithm

Depth peeling requires two depth tests per pixel. In the case of reverse depth peeling, one depth test is used with a GREATER compare mode and Z writes enabled to find the furthermost transparent layer, while the second depth test is used with a LESS compare mode and Z writes disabled to exclude previous layers from being selected again. After each layer determination pass, the depth buffers are swapped, the buffer now bound to the GREATER test is reset to zero, and the buffer bound to the new LESS test is left intact. This prevents layers that have already been visited from being visited again. The initial depth buffer used for the LESS test contains the values written in the opaque pass, which allows correct occlusion of alpha fragments by opaque geometry.

Note that transparent pixels sharing the same screen location *and* depth will not be rasterized correctly because the algorithm guarantees that a pixel whose depth has already been peeled off cannot be extracted again at the same location. Ensuring no depth overlap between transparent polygons is therefore recommended to avoid this problem.

With each transparent geometry pass, the next furthermost layer is rendered into a temporary render-target. The pixel shader used for this operation is the one that would normally be used to render transparent geometry; it may involve lighting calculations or any other type of processing needed. No blending takes place at this stage as the final color and alpha of the current transparent layer are simply stored into the temporary render-target.

After the layer has finished rendering it can be blended onto the main render-target. This operation simply consists of rendering a full-screen quad with the previously used temporary render-target as a texture. The blending mode chosen depends on the application, e.g. SRCALPHA-INVSRCALPHA for conventional alpha blending, ONE-INVSRCALPHA for premultiplied alpha, and so on. After the current layer is blended with the main render-target, the loop continues and more layers are peeled and blended for as long as needed. Figure 3.7.4 shows the process of reverse-peeling four layers applied onto a scene consisting of two intersecting spheres. Figure 3.7.5 shows the final result (front and top view).

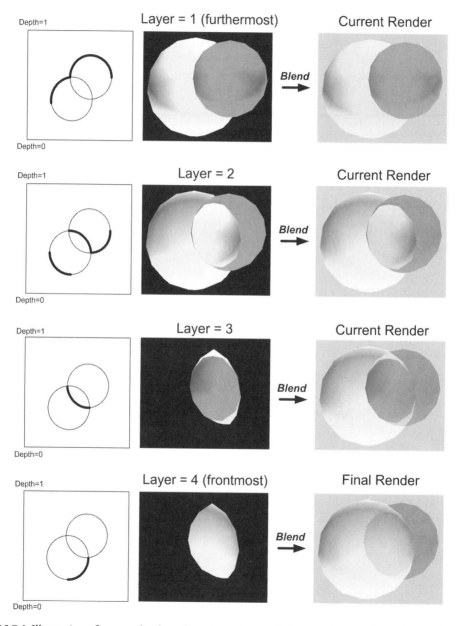

FIGURE 3.7.4 Illustration of reverse depth peeling algorithm applied to two intersecting spheres. The first column represents a top-down view of the furthermost depth used to extract the current layer. A screenshot showing the front view of each extracted layer is shown, along with a view of the current render after blending it in. In this simple scene, only four layers of reverse depth peeling are required for correct sorting.

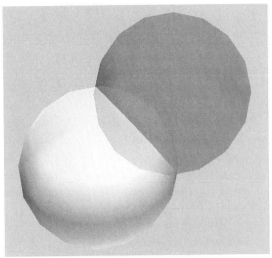
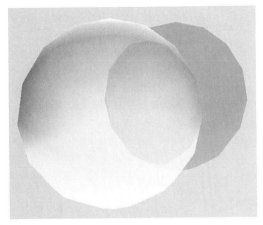

Two intersecting spheres - TOP VIEW   Two intersecting spheres - FRONT VIEW

FIGURE 3.7.5 Final result (top and front view).

Listing 3.7.1 shows pseudo-code to illustrate the reverse depth peeling algorithm.

Listing 3.7.1 Pseudo-code describing the reverse depth peeling algorithm

```
for (nLayer=0; nLayer<nRequiredLayers; nLayer++)
{
  // DepthBuffer[0] is used to determine the furthermost
  // transparent fragment. Needs clearing to 0.0 before use.
BindDepthBuffer(0, pDepthBuffer[0], EnableWrites, GREATER);
  Clear(pDepthBuffer[0], 0.0);

// pDepthBuffer[1] is used to reject transparent fragments
  // failing the LESS test. Used to reject previous layers.
  BindDepthBuffer(1, pDepthBuffer[1], DisableWrites, LESS);

    // Render transparent geometry into color render target
  SetRenderTarget(pCurrentTransparentLayer);
  SetBlendMode(ONE, ZERO);              // Blending disabled
  DrawTransparentGeometry();

  // Blend layer into main render target
  SetTexture(pCurrentTransparentLayer);
  SetRenderTarget(pMainRenderTarget);
  SetBlendMode(SRCALPHA, INVSRCALPHA);  // Blending enabled
  DrawFullscreenQuad();

  // Swap depth buffers
  SWAP(pDepthBuffer[0], pDepthBuffer[1]);
}
```

Emulating the Second Depth Buffer

The dual depth buffer functionality described above is essential to the algorithm. However, with current graphic hardware lacking a second depth buffer, one has to resort to alternative measures to perform the second test. [Everitt01] implements depth peeling in OpenGL by using alpha test to discard fragments failing the second test. What we need is to access the depth value stored in the second depth buffer and compare it with the incoming Z value of the fragment. If it fails the test then the fragment must be discarded (so that it doesn't write anything in the color render-target and in the depth buffer). In this implementation we chose to emulate the depth buffer responsible for excluding previously peeled layers, i.e. the depth buffer responsible for the LESS depth comparison. This test is more convenient to emulate since with Z-writes disabled we do not need to worry about writing depth values out.

In order to access the depth value previously written out to the depth buffer, we need to bind the depth buffer to the pixel shader stage as a texture. Direct3D 10 allows such functionality through the ShaderResourceView mechanism. With one depth buffer bound as the actual depth buffer for the GREATER depth test, the other depth buffer is bound to the pixel shader stage through its ShaderResourceView. The pixel shader then fetches the depth value corresponding to the current pixel being processed and performs the depth test "manually" by comparing the depth value with the incoming fragment's depth (available in Direct3D 10 via the SV_Position input semantic). If the test fails, the fragment is discarded using the clip() HLSL instruction. Listing 3.7.2 illustrates this part of the process.

Listing 3.7.2 Pixel shader code emulating second depth buffer functionality

```
struct PS_INPUT
{
  float4 vPosition : SV_POSITION;
  float2 vTex      : TEXCOORD0;
};

Texture2D txInputDepth;    // 2nd depth buffer viewed as SRV

float4 PSRenderObjects(PS_INPUT input) : SV_TARGET
{
// Fetch depth value from 2nd depth buffer
float fDepth = txInputDepth.Load( int3(input.vPosition.xy, 0) );

  // Discard fragment if LESS depth test fails
  float f = (fDepth <= input.vPosition.z);
  clip(-f);

  // Calculate color and alpha etc.
  ...
}
```

Choosing the Optimal Number of Layers

Depth peeling extracts layers of translucency without actually "looking" at the results. For instance, it is perfectly possible for the basic algorithm to continue peeling layers even though there is nothing else to peel! Therefore, one of the main issues with depth peeling in general is establishing *when* to stop. Simply put, what is the minimum number of layers to peel in order to robustly represent all translucent geometry sorted in the scene? Ideally there should be as many layer extraction passes as the maximum *depth complexity* of such geometry. With each peeled layer effectively decreasing the depth complexity by one, it is logical that the number of layers required equals the maximum depth complexity. Unfortunately this depth complexity is typically not known at runtime since it depends on a variety of factors such as the number and types of objects to render, the current camera position, whether objects are occluded, the triggering of animations or special effects, and so forth. Under the dynamic conditions inherent to real-time graphic engines it is therefore extremely difficult—if not impossible—to accurately predict the maximum depth complexity of a scene prior to actually rendering it.

A naive implementation might decide on executing a fixed number of layer extraction passes but then there is a risk of producing incorrect visual results if an insufficient number of layers is rasterized. On the other hand, an excessive number of layers will correctly render translucent geometry, albeit at a significant cost in performance for the "unused" layers extracted. What is needed is a robust method to determine exactly how many layers need to be peeled for each frame.

Occlusion Queries

Occlusion queries allow the user to retrieve information on whether a set of pixels passed the depth test or not. They were already supported in previous APIs (e.g. DirectX 9.0, OpenGL) and have traditionally been used in real-time applications like games for a number of effects (occlusion culling, lens flares, etc.).

We can use occlusion queries to determine whether a peeled layer actually yielded any pixels. If no pixels were rasterized after peeling the current layer, then it means we can stop the peeling process. On the other hand, if a high enough number of pixels were rasterized then we need to continue peeling. To set up occlusion queries for this purpose we need to determine if any pixel belonging to transparent geometry passed the depth test. In Direct3D 10 this is done by surrounding this geometry with calls to `ID3D10Query::Begin()` and `ID3D10Query::End()`. An `ID3D10Query::GetData()` call is then used to retrieve how many pixels passed the GREATER depth test while not being discarded by our second emulated depth test via the pixel shader—this equates to knowing how many pixels were peeled for this layer.

The idea is to dynamically adjust the number of layers based on the needs of the current scene. To ensure a stable system, our occlusion query mechanism keeps track of the last *two* layers peeled. For a current number of layers n, the occlusion query results obtained for the last two layers dictate the action to take (Table 3.7.2).

Table 3.7.2 Adjustment of number of layers n based on occlusion query results of the last two layers

Number of Pixels Rasterized During Last Layer (n–1)	Number of Pixels Rasterized During Layer (n–2)	Action
> 0	> 0	n++
0	> 0	None
0	0	n--

If the occlusion query results for both layers show outstanding pixels, then more peeling is required to finish the job and the number of layers is therefore increased. On the other hand, if no pixels were rasterized in both layers then we are peeling too much and the number of layers should be decreased. Stability is achieved for the second case in Table 3.7.2, whereby the last layer shows no outstanding pixels to peel with the previous layer still having some. In this case n is actually the maximum transparent depth complexity for the current scene.

To ensure unperturbed performance it is important not to stall the CPU waiting on occlusion query results. The GPU is allowed to buffer up to three frames ahead of time; requesting immediate results after an occlusion query will affect CPU/GPU parallelism and therefore reduce performance. It is recommended to perform other CPU tasks while results are still being processed, and/or to allow the GPU to run ahead by deferring the gathering of occlusion query results by a number of frames.

Because the system adjusts itself over the course of rendering, abrupt variations in transparent depth complexity may result in visual artifacts for a small number of frames. These artifacts are the result of incorrect translucency sorting due to processing an insufficient number of layers while the system is catching up with the sudden increase in transparent depth complexity. In practice, such visual artifacts will only be observed for a fraction of a second and are usually not a problem for most scenes with good frame-to-frame coherency, such as a first- or third-person shooter, real-time strategy, etc. In the case of sudden camera changes it may be wise to instruct the engine to use a high default number of layers for new camera views to ensure correct rendering while the system adjusts to the new transparent depth complexity.

Note that peeling until absolutely no pixels are left is not strictly necessary. A simple optimization is to decide on a threshold for the remaining number of pixels after which we can stop peeling. Most of the time a few isolated sets of unsorted pixels are unlikely to cause significant rendering errors and by excluding those from the peeling process we can help performance by reducing the total number of layer extraction passes. The number of pixels to ignore should be a direct factor of the screen resolution used. In the demo accompanying this article, the threshold used is 0.01% percent of the total screen resolution. So for an 800×600 resolution the number of pixels after which we stop peeling would be 48.

Case Study: Deferred Shading

In the case of sorting and rendering transparency for *deferred shading* techniques the algorithm is slightly modified: Instead of using a temporary render-target to store the color and alpha components of each layer, the G-buffers that were used to receive the pixel properties of opaque geometry are now updated with the pixel properties of each translucent layer (this obviously implies their existing contents are overwritten, so any effects requiring access to those must be performed before translucency rendering). After pixel properties for the current layer have been stored, the "shading passes" can be performed to add each light contribution into a temporary render-target. With all lighting contributions compounded, the temporary render-target is finally blended with the main render-target and the algorithm continues with the next layer. Reverse depth peeling has two advantages for this scenario. One obvious advantage is the savings in video memory since no further surface allocations are necessary (which isn't the case in *forward* depth peeling since each layer needs to be stored out to memory). The second advantage is that translucent geometry can now be rendered through the same pixel shaders that were used on opaque geometry during the shading passes, bringing more elegance and convenience to the deferred shading algorithm.

Note that the temporary render-target phase may be avoided altogether should the deferred shading implementation choose to compute a "light id" buffer giving information on the lights affecting each pixel. Such a technique avoids the need to process each light in its own separate pass and the lighting calculations affecting each translucent layer can therefore be done in a single full-screen pass, allowing direct blending with the main render-target to take place.

Optimizations

Geometry Passes

One significant cost in depth peeling in general is the requirement to transform transparent geometry multiple times. This cost will be significant if the geometry is complex, which may contribute to a vertex throughput bottleneck after considering the multiple passes in play. Direct3D 10 supports a feature called *stream-out* whereby transformed geometry can be stored in buffers that can then be re-circulated into the graphics pipeline. Using stream-out we can therefore pay the main transformation cost only once and bind the streamed out buffer as input geometry to every layer extraction pass to save on performance. A simple pass-through vertex shader is used to directly pass the post-transformed (streamed out) vertex coordinates onto the pixel shader stage. The transformation savings enabled by stream-out are especially important if the vertex shader used for the original transformations is complex. Certainly operations like complicated vertex animation, tangent space setup, displacement mapping, or any other heavy vertex shading work will benefit from being executed only once! In any case it is important to eliminate as many triangles as possible that do not contribute to the final render. This should occur prior to passing the transparent geometry to the vertex shader and methods like frustum or occlusion culling should be employed to this end.

One slight drawback of stream-out is that it only outputs triangle lists, that is, a list of vertices making up triangles in sequential order (the first three vertices make the first triangle, the next three vertices make the second triangle, etc.). Such a vertex type is generally slower compared to its indexed counterpart because no vertex sharing takes place. Thankfully a simple trick can be used to use stream-out in combination with indexed triangle lists. By simply transforming incoming geometry as a list of *point* primitives, the vertices streamed out can then be re-circulated into subsequent geometry passes while retaining the index buffer used.

In all cases it is important to ensure that transparent geometry is optimized for index locality and sequential access in order to reduce memory bandwidth requirements and vertex shader processing resources. This preprocess phase is typically done by using the D3DX10Mesh::Optimize() API (or using the standalone functions D3DXOptimizeFaces() and D3DXOptimizeVertices()).

Although transparent convex objects should really have both their front and back faces rendered, a drastic optimization would be to enable back face culling. This will roughly halve the number of layers required for depth peeling at the expense of rendering fidelity. In practical terms this solution may be deemed acceptable as back faces can usually benefit from being "less visible" (lower alpha) than their front face counterparts to allow for a better visualization of the scene anyway.

It is also possible to fix an upper limit on the number of layers to render. For instance, this could be useful as a way to prevent performance from falling below a certain level. The missing fragments resulting from the limit imposed on the peeling process could be compensated by rendering all transparency in a gross back-to-front order using the last depth buffer produced, but with a compare mode of LESS. This will ensure that no transparent pixels are left behind and is likely to produce a satisfying result given the right limit for a given scene, although per-pixel sorting will not be achieved for those unpeeled fragments.

Fill-Rate

It is easy to demonstrate that depth peeling in general is fill-rate hungry. The writing of each layer into a temporary render-target and the subsequent blending of those layers onto the main render-target will both consume valuable fill-rate.

To help reduce fill-rate during the layer extraction phase (the part of the process responsible for determining the current furthermost transparent layer), we need to sort all transparent objects in a back-to-front order. The back-to-front ordering allows graphic hardware benefiting from gross Z culling optimizations to reject blocks of pixels early on (e.g. hierarchical Z-buffer on the AMD Radeon series of graphic hardware [Persson07]). This is because the Z compare mode used with the active "real" depth buffer is GREATER, thus the higher the number of distant objects that are submitted early on the more pixels will be culled when closer objects are rendered. Note that so-called "early Z" *per-pixel* hardware optimizations are likely to be inactive here; this is because the emulation of the second depth test uses a pixel shader *discard* (or *clip*) instruction, which generally disables per-pixel depth culling optimization.

To further help performance we can take advantage of this discard instruction to "stop" execution of shader instructions for those fragments that fail our emulated depth test. This can be done by adding a dynamic branch whose condition matches the one we used for the emulated depth test. The main branch contains the code to execute should the depth test succeed (typically the calculation of the color and alpha values to render) while the else clause simply discards the fragment with no further processing. The performance benefits from this optimization are likely to be significant, especially if the spatial coherency of the discarded pixels is high. Listing 3.7.3 illustrates this simple concept.

We can also save performance during the blending phase, where the temporary render-target containing the current layer is blended onto the main render-target. Although this blending operation takes place through a full-screen quad render, we are only interested in blending the pixels making up the current transparent layer. The active depth buffer was used to determine the current furthermost layer, therefore the Z values of pixels in the newly peeled layer will be non-zero (the depth buffer is cleared to zero before each new layer to peel). We can use this information to set up the depth test for the blending phase to only succeed if the Z coordinates of the full-screen quad (set to 0.0) are LESS than (or NOT EQUAL to) the current values in the Z-buffer. The GPU's early Z optimizations will therefore ensure that only the required pixels are blended with the main render-target, saving valuable fill-rate and memory bandwidth in the process.

Listing 3.7.3 Using dynamic branching to skip intructions for pixels failing the depth test

```
struct PS_INPUT
{
  float4 vPosition : SV_POSITION;
  float2 vTex      : TEXCOORD0;
};

Texture2D txInputDepth;   // 2nd depth buffer viewed as SRV

float4 PSRenderObjects(PS_INPUT input) : SV_TARGET
{
// Fetch depth value from 2nd depth buffer
float fDepth = txInputDepth.Load( int3(input.vPosition.xy, 0) );
```

```
      // Discard fragment if LESS depth test fails
      if (input.vPosition.z < fDepth)
      {
        // Depth test passes, calculate color and alpha etc.
        // This will be skipped if the emulated depth test fails
        ...
      }
      else
   {
      // Emulated depth test fails, kill fragment
      discard;
      }
```

Multi-Sampling Anti-aliasing

Unfortunately, the anti-aliasing of transparent geometry in a depth peeling context is not really possible in DirectX 10. The problem with rasterizing anti-aliased transparent primitives is the emulation of the second depth buffer test in the pixel shader. Under DirectX 10 the pixel shader may only be executed *per-pixel*, but our multi-sampled depth buffer contains values for *multiple* samples. Thus it is not possible to pass or fail our emulated depth test on a *per-sample* basis, which is required for anti-aliasing transparent primitives.

Despite this limitation we can still depth peel transparent geometry with a multi-sampled configuration in Direct3D 10; the drawback is that such polygons will be rendered aliased. At the very least this allows the technique to be compatible with the rendering of anti-aliased opaque polygons. Direct3D 10 does not allow the viewing of a multi-sampled depth buffer as a ShaderResourceView, so we have to use two "ping-pong" multi-sampled render-targets to emulate our pixel shader-based depth test. Depth values resulting from the LESS depth test will be written into one render-target while the second render-target is bound as a texture to provide the input to the test. Both render-targets are of DXGI_FORMAT_R32_FLOAT format to allow sufficient precision to store depth values. The main depth buffer is used for the GREATER test for all layers. Such a setup requires a couple of changes to the shaders used. We now need the pixel shader used during the rendering of opaque objects to output depth into one of our ping-pong render-targets in order to provide correct depth buffer input for the first peeled layer. This can be done with a single shader instruction (the Z value of the pixel is accessed by declaring a SV_POSITION semantic in the pixel shader input). The same change is also needed during the depth peeling passes so that our emulated depth test has valid data to work with. The emulated depth has now access to multiple depth values (one per sample); the one to select for the test is actually only relevant for the *first* depth peeling pass because only then does the multi-sampled "manual" depth texture possibly contain different depth values between samples. For this case there is no "right" way to select a valid depth because we're moving from a multi-sampled context to a non-multi-sampled one. The demo accompanying this article picks the largest depth value among all samples and gives good results. Because the MSAA renderstate is disabled during the rendering of transparent geometry, all samples will contain the same depth after the first pass; therefore subsequent peeling passes can choose the depth from the first sample for the emulated depth test.

As well as adding a layer of complexity to the algorithm, the support of reverse depth peeling in conjunction with MSAA clearly causes a considerable performance hit in DirectX 10. Most of the missing functionality we worked around in Direct3D 10 to make the technique *compatible* with MSAA is actually available in DirectX 10.1, which should be available by the time this article is released. With both per-sample pixel shader execution frequency and multi-sampled depth buffer shader resource views available in DirectX 10.1, it becomes possible to apply reverse depth peeling with multi-sampled transparent primitives without a considerable performance impact or significant changes to the technique.

Conclusion

Reverse depth peeling enables robust and per-pixel sorting of transparent geometry at a somewhat significant performance cost compared to more traditional solutions. Therefore its use may be restricted to high-end graphics hardware or particular applications that rely more on rendering correctness than performance. The savings in video memory it provides make it a good alternative to previous solutions offering similar results, e.g., for deferred shading algorithms. Certainly the multi-pass approach to sorting geometry is responsible for a large chunk of performance reduction. While techniques like [Myers07] provide alternative approaches to multi-pass, it may not be suited to cases where transparent depth complexity is high or when MSAA is required.

DirectX 10.1 goes some way to make reverse depth peeling more accessible, but there are still unsupported features that would make it a more attractive solution both from an implementation and performance point of view. Currently the emulation of the second depth buffer comes at a cost that could be avoided completely if future graphic hardware and APIs would allow the use of the second depth buffer. Alternatively, programmable blending with access to the current render-target color would somewhat simplify the emulation process. Support for efficient scattering in the geometry shader and stream-out would allow the binning of transparent geometry by regions (e.g. screen tiles) and enable fill-rate reductions by only performing the minimum number of depth peeling passes per region. As graphic hardware and APIs progress, real-time order-independent transparency is certainly becoming more accessible than it ever was.

Acknowledgments

I would like to thank Mike Armstrong and my section editor Natasha Tatarchuk for their most valuable feedback and suggestions concerning this article.

References

[Pangerl07] Pangerl, David. "ZT-Buffer Algorithm", *ShaderX5: Advanced Rendering Techniques*, Wolfgang Engel, Ed., Charles River Media, 2007: pp. 151–157.

[Batcher68] Batcher, Kenneth E. "Sorting networks and their Applications," *Spring Joint Computer Conference*, AFIPS Proceedings, 1968.

[Everitt01] Everitt, Cass. "Interactive Order-Independent Transparency," white paper available online at http://developer.nvidia.com/object/Interactive_Order_Transparency.html.

[Thibieroz04] Thibieroz, Nicolas. "Deferred Shading with Multiple Render Targets," *ShaderX2: Shader Programming Tips & Tricks with DirectX 9*, Wolfgang Engel, Ed., Wordware Publishing, 2004: pp. 251–269.

[Liu06] Liu, Baoquand, Wei, Li-Yi, Xu, Ying-Qing. "Multi-Layer Depth Peeling via Fragment Sort," white paper available online at: http://research.microsoft.com/research/pubs/view.aspx?tr_id=1125

[Hachisuka05] Hachiska, Toshiya. "High-Quality Global Illumination Rendering Using Rasterization," *GPU Gems 2*, Matt Pharr, Ed., Addison Wesley, 2005: pp. 615–633.

[Myers07] Myers, Kevin, Bavoil, Louis. "Stencil routed A-Buffer," *SIGGRAPH '07: ACM SIGGRAPH 2007 sketches*, p. 21, San Diego, CA, August 2007.

[Persson07] Persson, Emil. AMD Corporation, "Depth in-depth," technical paper, Available online on the AMD developer relations website at http://ati.amd.com/developer/SDK/AMD_SDK_Samples_May2007/Documentations/Depth_in-depth.pdf

SHADOWS

Introduction

Willem H. de Boer

The "Shadows" section in this edition of the *ShaderX* series consists of articles that are all based on the shadow mapping algorithm as originally devised by Williams [1]. The big problem with the original algorithm is that it suffers from aliasing artifacts because a shadow map—by definition—consists of a finite number of pixels, and each pixel in turn can take on a finite number of values, whether it be integer or floating point. There are numerous ways of alleviating these artifacts; although, in practice it is hard to get rid of them entirely.

One way of suppressing aliasing is by using the idea of cascaded (or parallel split) shadow maps. The original solution suffers from *shadow shimmering*, which is caused by the subtle movements of the camera giving rise to aliasing. Michal Valient, in his article "Stable Rendering of Cascaded Shadow Maps," proposes a way of reducing shadow shimmering.

Recently, there has been a trend toward applying techniques from probability theory to shadow maps. The idea is to reformulate the shadow depth comparison as some probability inequality. One way of doing this is explained in Holger Grün's article, "Approximate Cumulative Distribution Function Shadow Mapping," in which he proposes to approximate the cumulative distribution function of depth samples at a shadow map's pixel.

Another probability-based solution is described by Marco Salvi in his article "Rendering Filtered Shadows with Exponential Shadow Maps," which starts off with Markov's inequality and then proceeds to derive a solution that is also filterable. Being able to filter a shadow map opens up a number of new possibilities—for instance, one could apply a blur filter to get a soft shadow approximation.

Markus Giegl's article, "Fitted Virtual Shadow Maps and Shadow Fog," contains an in-depth description of an algorithm that essentially allows for the creation of a shadow map that has a resolution that far surpasses current hardware limitations. This algorithm, while a bit involved at times, has the potential to get rid of the aliasing problem in its entirety.

Finally, Chi-Sing Leung, Tze-Yui Ho, and Tien-Tsin Wong describe a method for removing artifacts in shadow volumes in the article "Removing Shadow Volume Artifacts by Spatial Adjustment." They spatially shift the shadow volume's geometry during shadow generation and force the jagged edges to be contained within the backward-facing region of the casting geometry. In other words, the jagged edges are hidden inside the object itself. Although it is a very simple trick, it generates few visual defects compared to other approaches.

[1] Williams, L. "Casting Curved Shadows on Curved Surfaces," *SIGGRAPH '78: Proceedings of the 5th annual conference on Computer graphics and interactive techniques*, New York, 1978: p. 270–274.

4.1

Stable Rendering of Cascaded Shadow Maps

Michal Valient

Guerrilla B.V.

Abstract

We present a simple, constant time algorithmic improvement to cascaded (parallel split) shadow maps that removes shadow shimmering caused by translation or rotation of the camera. Our algorithm modifies the shadow generation matrix so that it does not rotate or cause resolution changes in the shadow map while still containing the required part of the view frustum in any of its positions, making translation (panning) the only movement the shadow map performs. Our algorithm also makes sure the shadow map moves in whole pixel units, which removes shimmering caused by smooth movement of the viewer in the world. Our algorithm produces a single shadow map rendering matrix and a set of scale and offset coordinates for each cascade. This makes it very easy to use a single texture atlas to store shadow maps for all cascades and to render the final light in a single pass even on DX9 class hardware.

Introduction

Cascaded shadow maps (CSM) [Engel06] are a popular extension to the widely used shadow map algorithm [Williams78]. This extension alleviates the problems caused by insufficient shadow map resolution by dividing the view frustum into separate "cascades" and rendering a shadow map for each cascade separately. This way one can provide more detail to the points near the camera (or other areas where more detail is desired, depending on the way the frustum is divided) while still maintaining a decent shadow resolution for farther distances. The final rendering pass identifies the corresponding cascade (shadow map) for each pixel and performs standard shadow mapping using this shadow map.

A simple and practical way to divide the view frustum is to split it along the view axis using planes parallel to the near and far clip planes (see Figure 4.1.1). This method is one of the most widely used variations of CSM and therefore was commonly referred to as cascaded shadow maps until recently, when the more appropriately named *parallel split shadow maps* (PSSM) algorithm was introduced. Zhang et al [Zhang06] provide more detail on the various methods for efficiently splitting the view frustum. Figure 4.1.1 illustrates how a view frustum can be divided into separate *cascade frustums* by replacing the near and far planes of the original view frustum. The

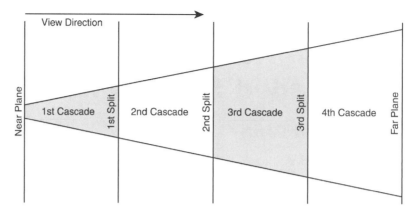

FIGURE 4.1.1 2D visualization of view frustum split (uniformly) into separate cascade frustums.

matrix used to generate the shadow map for a given cascade (and which is used for shadow map sampling during final rendering) is called the *cascade shadow matrix*. *Cascade shadow map space* is the space defined by the cascade shadow matrix transformation.

For both the CSM and PSSM algorithms, we regenerate the cascade shadow matrix whenever the view changes. If this change is smooth (i.e. sub-pixel camera rotation or slow player movement in the game), shadow boundaries are rasterized differently in each frame (pixels are rendered into the shadow map only if the pixel center is inside the triangle), which causes visible shimmering of shadow edges. Shimmering tends to get more noticeable in cascades that are farther away from the viewer position as these cover bigger world space regions and are therefore more magnified during final rendering. In the next sections we present an algorithm that aims to fix shimmering caused by global shadow map changes, i.e., those made by actual camera translation and rotation. Other changes—for example, smooth shadow changes due to character animation—are unavoidable.

Please note that for sake of simplicity we consider only symmetrical view frustums that are most commonly used in games. However, the algorithm works for *any* frustum shape with just minor modifications.

Solution

To avoid shadow shimmering we have to remove the two main causes of sub-pixel changes: shadow map image rotation and smooth shadow map image translation (panning). We first address shadow map rotation. Usually the shadow matrix for a given cascade is generated from the cascade frustum so that the view direction (projected to shadow map U,V space) is parallel to the **u** direction in shadow map U,V space and the near and far planes are parallel to the **v** direction (or vice versa) to maximize the number of shadow map texels used, as shown in examples a and b in Figure 4.1.2.

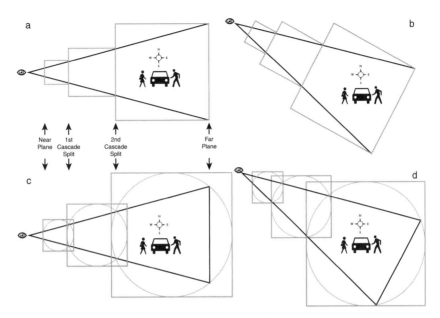

FIGURE 4.1.2 The view frustum in world space split into three cascade frustums and their corresponding shadow map coverage. We use a top view with the light direction pointing straight down the horizontal world plane.

In Figure 4.1.2, (a) shows the traditional shadow map generation method where the u (or v) direction in shadow map space is parallel to the view direction to maximize shadow map coverage of the cascade. (b) shows how the shadow map is rotated (relative to world space) when the camera rotates. Note how the shadow maps rotate with the camera; this causes objects in the shadow map to be rasterized differently each frame. (c) shows our approach, where the shadow maps are generated using a minimum enclosing sphere approach of the corresponding cascade frustum. (d) shows how our approach does not require shadow maps to rotate (relative to the world) when the camera changes direction.

We have to abandon approach a and create a cascade shadow matrix that contains its corresponding cascade frustum in *any* of its rotations. To this end, we find the smallest enclosing sphere of the cascade frustum and then use this to generate the shadow map matrix. The effect of this is shown in example (c) in Figure 4.1.2. Since we assume a symmetrical frustum, we can reduce this problem to finding the minimal enclosing circle (MEC) of the four points of the "maximum diagonal" quadrangle of the cascade frustum, as shown in Figure 4.1.3. The MEC of the circle with the same center and radius of the other remaining four frustum points is identical, and therefore the center and radius define the minimal enclosing sphere of the entire frustum. You can find many algorithms for finding the minimal enclosing circle online.

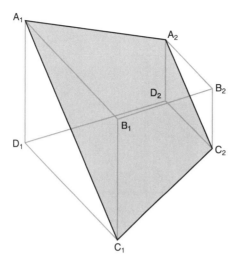

FIGURE 4.1.3 A symmetrical frustum with points $A_1B_1C_1D_1$ on the near plane, points $A_2B_2C_2D_2$ on the far plane, and the trapezoid $A_1C_1C_2A_2$ used to find its MEC. The trapezoid defined by points $D_1B_1B_2D_2$ has a MEC with the same radius and center.

Now we can generate the initial look-at shadow map matrix—$M_{ShadowLookAt}$—and (orthogonal) projection matrix—$M_{ShadowOrtho}$—for each cascade. The look-at matrix uses the original light vector as the look-at direction and the center of the MEC as the target point. We keep the third ("up") vector constant; for example, one may use the vector exported by the content creation pipeline. The orthogonal projection matrix uses the diameter of the MEC as its volume width and height as illustrated in Figure 4.1.4. The minimum and maximum depths of the projection volume depend on the scene data, so both values can be computed per frame using the objects' bounding volumes in the shadow matrix frustum. You might prefer to com-

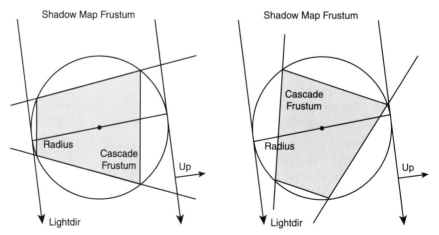

FIGURE 4.1.4 The MEC and its basic properties used to generate the cascade shadow map matrix. The picture on the right illustrates how the shadow map frustum (and therefore also the shadow map matrix) remains constant during view frustum rotation.

pute the values only once and then re-use them during rendering, which has the benefit of reducing per-frame changes in shadow map depth-precision that may manifest as rapid flickering in depth comparisons (i.e. shadow moiré). Another advantage of constant minimum and maximum depths is that there is no need to tweak the shadow map depth bias in each frame.

The image in the shadow map generated with $\mathbf{M_{ShadowLookAt}}$ and $\mathbf{M_{ShadowOrtho}}$ will not rotate when the view frustum rotates (the up vector in the look-at matrix is constant). The only global change that remains to be tackled is shadow map image translation (panning), where the center of the cascade frustum changes position in the world during camera translation or rotation and the MEC follows it. Now we only need to make sure that this movement does not happen on sub-texel levels. Again, the solution is simple: We use the cascade shadow map matrix to compute the projection of an arbitrary, fixed world space point; we choose to use the world space origin for simplicity—$\mathbf{origin_{Shadow}}$. Next we round the projected X and Y coordinates to the nearest shadow map texel.

$$origin_{Rounded} = round(origin_{shadow} * ShadowMapSize / 2)$$

We use $\mathbf{origin_{Rounded}}$ to create a 2D transformation matrix, $\mathbf{M_{Round}}$, that translates shadow map space in the direction ($\mathbf{origin_{Rounded}}$–$\mathbf{origin_{Shadow}}$). This way we cancel sub-texel movement of the cascade and make sure that shadow edges always cover the same texels (and are therefore rasterized the same way) invariant to camera movement. The final cascade shadow map matrix MShadow is now

$$M_{Shadow} = M_{ShadowLookAt} * M_{ShadowOrtho} * M_{Round}$$

Now that we have the final cascade shadow map matrix, there are still a number of boundary cases to consider. We need to dilate the shadow map border by one extra texel to compensate for the rounding we performed in the previous step. Also, depending on the shadow map filtering method, we need to add extra space to the border to fit the entire filtering kernel into the map. This also makes it possible to perform faster shadow filtering because we can pick the proper cascade once per screen-space pixel and then just use the corresponding shadow map for filtering instead of the more computationally expensive method of having to pick the proper cascade for each shadow map filter sample. We enlarge the area of each shadow map by multiplying the MEC radius by the factor ($ShadowMapSize + BorderTexelsCount$)/ $ShadowMapSize$, making sure that it contains the required number of extra texels.

Implementation Details for Up to Four Cascades

In practice, four shadow map cascades are enough to provide good shadow detail for the entire screen while still maintaining reasonable memory requirements and high performance [Zhang06]. In this section we describe a fast shader implementation for four cascades that uses only a few dot products and no dynamic branching. It is straightforward enough to extend the algorithm to handle a greater number of cascades that we have decided to leave out the details. One requirement for this implementation is that we must render all cascades into different parts of the same texture atlas for DX9 class hardware (i.e. by using the viewport functionality in DirectX). If you are targeting DX10, which has better texture addressing capabilities, separate textures may be used.

In the previous section we demonstrated how to generate a cascade shadow map matrix from a bounding sphere. A straightforward implementation passes four matrices into the shader and picks the correct matrix for each pixel based on its view space distance using dynamic branching (which, while supported, is not a fast operation on DX9 hardware), or it could use a multi-pass approach and render each cascade separately. However, after some thought it appears obvious that the cascade shadow matrix for cascade n differs from the matrix of the first cascade *only* in the fact that we used a larger bounding sphere with different center. Therefore, we can calculate the shadow matrix for cascade n to be

$$M_{Shadow}[n] = M_{Shadow}[1] * M_{CenterShift}[n] * M_{AreaScale}[n]$$

where $\mathbf{M_{Shadow}}[n]$ is the cascade shadow matrix as defined in the previous section, $\mathbf{M_{CenterShift}}[n]$ is a translation in the **-origin$_{Cascade1}$**$[n]$ direction where

$$origin_{Cascade1}[n] = (0,0,0,1) * (M_{Shadow}[n]^{-1}) * M_{Shadow}[1]$$

$\mathbf{M_{AreaScale}}[n]$ scales shadow map space (x and y coordinates) by a factor $mec\_radius[1]/mec\_radius[n]$ to cover the same area as the original $\mathbf{M_{Shadow}}[n]$.

Then we pass these arguments into the pixel shader as a set of `float4` values (here `Shift[n]` stands for $\mathbf{M_{CenterShift}}$ translation coefficients and `Scale[n]` means $\mathbf{M_{AreaScale}}$ scale factor for n-th cascade):

```
float4 movex_vec = float4(1.0f, Shift[2].x, Shift[3].x, Shift[4].x);
float4 movey_vec = float4(1.0f, Shift[2].y, Shift[3].y, Shift[4].y);
float4 movez_vec = float4(1.0f, Shift[2].z, Shift[3].z, Shift[4].z);
float4 scale_vec = float4(1.0f, Scale[2], Scale[3], Scale[4]);
```

The shader uses the view-space depth of the current pixel (or the final perspective-projected value in the range 0…1 if this better suits your rendering pipeline) to determine which cascade to use. We pass the cascade split distances as two `float4` vectors and generate a mask vector whose n-th component is 1 if the pixel is in the n-th cascade and 0 otherwise (i.e. y is 1 if the pixel is in the second cascade). The following pseudo code shows how to accomplish this in a shader. The constants `near` and `far` stand for near and far plane distances and `split[n]` stands for the distance along the view axis at which the n-th cascade ends and the $n+1$-th cascade starts. The components of the lower boundary mask—`mask0`—are 1 only if the pixel is farther away than the given plane and the components of the higher boundary mask—`mask1`—are 1 only if the pixel is nearer to the camera than the given plane. Component-wise multiplication of both partial masks leaves a 1 in exactly one channel.

```
float4 dist0 = float4(near,     split[1], split[2], split[3]);
float4 dist1 = float4(split[1], split[2], split[3], far);

float4 mask0 = (pixel.zzzz >= dist0.xyzw) ? float4(1) : float4(0);
float4 mask1 = (pixel.zzzz <  dist1.xyzw) ? float4(1) : float4(0);

float4 final_mask = mask0 * mask1;
```

We use this mask in a dot product operation to allow us to pick the proper scale and offset values:

```
float final_scale = dot(final_mask, scale_vec);

float3 center_shift;
center_shift.x = dot(final_mask, movex_vec);
center_shift.y = dot(final_mask, movey_vec);
center_shift.z = dot(final_mask, movez_vec);
```

Similarly we can get any other per-cascade data we need, such as the filtering kernel size (you want the filtering kernel at the start of cascade N to be approximately the same size as the filter at the end of cascade N-1 at that point to hide artifacts). Now it is easy to compute the shadow map sampling coordinates for a given pixel:

```
float3 shadow_coord = world_coord*ShadowMatrixCascade1;
shadow_coord.xyz = shadow_coord.xyz + center_shift.xyz;
shadow_coord.xy = shadow_coord.xy * final_scale;
```

Please note that for the sake of simplicity we have omitted the fact that we have to map the projected pixel coordinates from range −1...1 to range 0...1, and that we have to perform a translation to the correct region in the shadow map texture atlas. Both operations can be expressed as one additional 2D scale and translation operation. Since both of these operations are identical for each pixel and done after the pixel projection, these could easily be incorporated into the appropriate Shift[n] and Scale[n] shader variables.

Culling Considerations

The shadow map matrix that we introduced in our algorithm covers a bigger portion of space than is strictly necessary, which makes it less optimal for object culling. It could potentially accept a lot of objects that do not contribute to the shadows that are visible on-screen. Therefore, it is better to project the cascade frustum into shadow map space and use the bounding kDOP of its 2D projection and a light vector to create a tighter set of planes for culling. It is important to note that we have to account for all the extra (border) space we add to the shadow map and increase the size of the 2D projection accordingly. Failing to do so risks objects that fall within the cascade boundary (i.e. those covering texels only picked by wider filtering kernel) to be culled.

Conclusion

We have described a simple way to reduce shadow aliasing as a result of camera translation or rotation. The obvious advantage of the algorithm is its constant time complexity as well as its easy integration into existing cascaded (parallel split) shadow map implementations. We have also given an efficient implementation of the algorithm for four cascades, which makes it easy to use a single shadow map that contains data for all cascades and which addresses the correct cascade by using a single matrix and a set of translations and scaling factors. This makes it possible to render shadows in a single pass without relying on array lookup support for constants or samplers.

The drawbacks of this solution include the reduced usage of shadow map resolution, as we have to fit every possible cascade rotation into a single projection instead of computing a best fit each frame. Shimmering might also occur when the perspective projection properties of the camera change (i.e. field-of-view, near or far clip plane, aspect ratio, or cascade split distances). Fortunately these properties tend not to change during rendering.

References

[Engel06] Engel, W. "Cascaded Shadow Maps," *ShaderX5: Advanced Rendering Techniques*, Engel W. Ed, Charles River Media, Dec 2006: pp. 197–206.

[Williams78] Williams, L. "Casting curved shadows on curved surfaces," *Computer Graphics (Proc. of SIGGRAPH 78)*, 12(3), 1978: pp. 270–274.

[Zhang06] Fan Zhang, Hanqiu Sun, Leilei Xu and Lee Kit Lun, "Parallel-Split Shadow Maps for Large-Scale Virtual Environments," *Proc. of the 2006 ACM International Conference on Virtual Reality Continuum and Its Applications (VRCIA'2006)*: pp.311–318.

4.2

Approximate Cumulative Distribution Function Shadow Mapping

Holger Grün

AMD Graphics Products Group

Abstract

This article introduces *approximate cumulative distribution function shadow maps* (ACDF SMs), a novel technique for blurry or noisy shadows using shadow maps. ACDF SMs store an approximation of the *cumulative probability distribution function* (CDF) of a neighborhood of light space depth pixels. The probability of a pixel being in shadow is computed by evaluating this CDF. ACDF SMs need only one shadow map sample per pixel to produce soft shadows. In that respect they are similar to variance shadow maps [DL06] except they do not suffer from light bleeding artifacts.

Introduction

Shadow mapping is a well-known and widely used image space shadowing technique (for an introduction see [WIL78]) for real-time 3D applications. One of the main drawbacks of shadow maps is the aliasing at shadow edges (another drawback being depth aliasing) that occurs when the local sampling density of the shadow map is too low.

Recently a number of approaches for preventing low local sampling density have been published. These approaches come in three common flavors [LTYM06]. The first set of techniques changes the 4×4 transformation matrix used to render a shadow map, which introduces a warp to increase local sampling density where needed [SD02, MT04, WSP04]. The second set of techniques partitions the scene or the view frustum and uses a separate shadow map for each partition [TQJN99, FFBG01, ARV04, LKS06, ENG07, GW07]. There are also publications that combine warping and partitioning [KOZ04, CG04, LTYM06]. The third set of techniques stores data in the pixels of a shadow map that allows for the reconstruction of occluders. Inside the pixel shader, exact shadow tests are carried out that result in virtually alias-free shadow edges [SZE07, SCH03]. If the sampling density is too low to allow correct reconstruction of the occluder silhouette, these methods also suffer from artifacts caused by aliasing artifacts.

For the purpose of real-time applications it is impossible to create shadow maps that fully eliminate aliasing at shadow edges. Please note that stencil shadows provide a solution for alias-free shadows but have other disadvantages. For shadow maps, there will always be pixels in the shadow map with insufficient sampling density that result in jagged shadow edges. In order to hide these jagged edges, it is common practice to look at several depth samples from the shadow map to decide how much light actually reaches a pixel. This technique is called *percentage closer filtering* (PCF) and it aims to create smooth transitions between areas that are fully shadowed (umbra) and pixels that are fully lit. Unfortunately, the number of PCF samples used determines the number of unique luminance values available to shade penumbrae, resulting in non-smooth shadow edges. [ISO07] describes how sub-texel offsets can be used to remove this limitation. Also, non-uniform filter tap offsets can hide these PCF artifacts [ISO07].

More advanced techniques for soft transitions between umbra, penumbra, and full light have been introduced [CD03, FER05, SA07, DU07]. Some of these techniques can also produce harder shadows near contact regions between shadow caster and shadow receiver. All methods using multiple shadow map samples put a heavy burden on the texturing units and memory bandwidth of the GPU. As a result, using a high number of samples can turn shadow mapping into the rendering bottleneck of a real-time 3D application.

GPUs have advanced texture filtering capabilities to reduce texture aliasing. Unfortunately, these abilities were not applicable to shadow mapping algorithms because filtered shadow map depth samples don't make sense in the context of classic shadow mapping. The reason for this is that one is not interested in comparing pixel depth against blurred or filtered shadow map depth. Because PCF just uses a set of comparisons, filtering depth also does not make sense. Very recently [DL06] published a technique called *variance shadow maps* (VSMs). VSMs store depth and squared-depth and use Chebyshev's inequality to estimate the probability of a pixel being in full light. It is valid to filter and blur VSMs so that soft shadows can be implemented easily. VSMs are orthogonal to techniques like perspective shadow maps [SD02], light space perspective shadow maps [WSP04], trapezoidal shadow maps, [MT04] or cascaded shadow maps [ENG07], and can be applied on top of these. Since only one filtered sample is taken, VSMs don't turn into a rendering bottleneck too easily. An extension of VSM that uses summed area tables (SATs) has been announced [LAU07]. This extension allows varying the softness per pixel and can be used to generate harder shadows at shadow caster/receiver contact regions.

Convolution shadow maps (CSMs) [AMB07] introduce yet another new way to realize filtering within the context of shadow mapping. The binary visibility function defined by the original shadow mapping algorithm is linearized by a weighted sum of basis textures, which are dynamically derived from the shadow map. Since the basis textures are filterable, smooth transitions between umbra and penumbra can be created by blurring these textures. Unfortunately the technique described in this paper uses up to eight basis textures, which is likely to result in a significant performance cost for real-time applications.

VSMs can show light bleeding artifacts that cannot always be hidden easily. The goal of this article is to introduce a new statistically inspired shadow mapping algorithm that does not suffer from this problem.

The Basic Idea Behind ACDF SM

The original VSM technique aims to compute the probability of a pixel being fully lit (no shadow). For a pixel at depth t (as seen from the light source) and a depth value x sampled from the VSM, a safe upper bound for the probability $P(t,<x)$ is chosen. Because this is an upper bound, it can be too optimistic about the amount of light reaching the pixel. This is what causes light bleeding (see Figure 4.2.1) in regions with high variance in the depth values.

FIGURE 4.2.1 VSM light bleeding.

The goal of this article is to compute $P(t \leq x)$ in a way that prevents light bleeding completely while also producing smooth shadow edges.

VSMs, either directly and/or indirectly through blurring, consider a set of shadow map depth samples in a certain pixel's neighborhood (such as a box). For such a depth set, it is obvious when $P(t \leq x)$ reaches its maximum and minimum. The maximum (1.0) is reached when the minimum depth in the set (min_d) is larger than t, that is, $t <$ min_d. The minimum (0.0) is reached when the maximum depth in the set (max_d) is smaller than t, that is, $t >$ max_d.

In order to compute the probability of being fully lit for values of t in the interval [min_d,max_d], the key is to first consider an exemplary discrete probability distribution function of a set of depth samples in some interval [min_d,max_d] (see Figure 4.2.2). It is a discrete function because only a limited number of samples are considered. Let N be the number of samples taken from the interval [min_d,max_d].

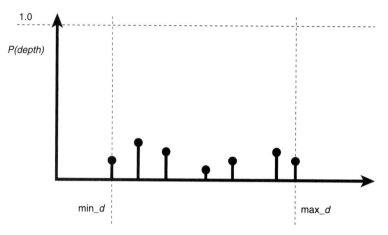

FIGURE 4.2.2 Discrete distribution function (DF).

This distribution function (DF) tells us the probability of every sampled depth value in [min_d,max_d]. Assuming a uniform distribution of depth values, unique values have probability 1/N. Other depth values may be present more than once, so their probability would be a multiple of 1/N.

For non-uniform distributions and non-uniform filter kernels, the probability of depth samples may be varied by their distance from the center of the filter kernel, resulting in a different DF.

In order to compute $P(t \le x)$, it is necessary to compute the following:

$$P(t \le x) = 1 - \sum_{depth=min\_d}^{depth=t} P(depth)$$

This is because the probability for full light for values smaller than min_d is 1.0 and decreases to 0.0 for values greater than max_d. This means a cumulative DF can help to compute $P(t \le x)$ since it represents

$$\sum_{depth=min\_d}^{depth=t} P(depth) = 1 - P(t \le x)$$

Figure 4.2.3 shows the cumulative probability distribution (CDF) based on Figure 4.2.2.

$$t' := \frac{t - min\_d}{max\_d - min\_d}$$

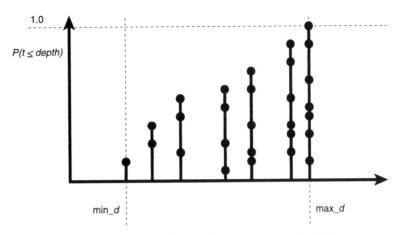

FIGURE 4.2.3 Cumulative distribution function (cumulative DF).

Using a cumulative DF to compute probabilities will result in a limited number of available probabilities (i.e., shades) for representing full light. As a consequence it will produce artifacts similar to those created by the original PCF shadow mapping technique. Ideally the continuous cumulative DF (CDF) of the depth values of a neighborhood of pixels should be used. A CDF based on Figure 4.2.3 is depicted in Figure 4.2.4.

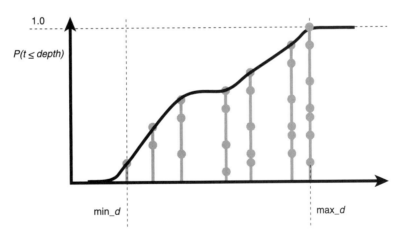

FIGURE 4.2.4 Continuous cumulative distribution function CDF.

One tiny flaw of the current idea can be deduced from Figure 4.2.4. Ideally the CDF should be 0.0 at min_d but it is not because min_d is a value in the set of depth samples used to construct the DF. In practice this is not a big problem, as one can use min_d to lay a small step (*eps*) below min_d when reconstructing the CDF in the pixel shader. This is similar to depth-biasing in normal shadow maps [SCH05].

It is not practical to store a lossless representation of a CDF in a shadow map due to memory and render-target count limitations. It is therefore necessary to represent the CDF in a lossy way through an approximation of the CDF—an approximate CDF (ACDF).

How to Construct ACDFs from CDFs

There are numerous ways to approximate our CDF. Here are a few categories of approximating methods:

- **Approximation through polynomials or rational polynomials.** This includes Bezier curves, B-splines, rational B-splines, and other splines that are evaluated by summing up (rational) basis polynomials. Piece-wise linear approximations also belong to this category. Storing a few control points is enough to produce a faithful approximation.
- **Approximation through a weighted sum of trigonometric basis functions.** This includes inverse Fourier transforms that are evaluated as sums of scaled Fourier basic functions.
- **Approximation through wavelets.**

For the purpose of brevity we will focus on explaining examples from the first category.

A Simple Linear Interpolation ACDF

The simplest ACDF just ignores CDF values on the interior of the interval $[\text{min\_}d, \text{max\_}d]$. It simply assumes 0.0 at $\text{min\_}d$ and 1.0 at $\text{max\_}d$ and a linearly increasing cumulative probability in between.

So for a pixel at depth t, the probability of being fully lit is defined by Equation 2 (Figure 4.2.5 depicts the resulting ACDF).

$$t' := \frac{t - \text{min\_}d}{\text{max\_}d - \text{min\_}d}$$

$$1$$

$$P(t \leq x) = \begin{cases} 1 & \textit{for} & t \leq \text{min\_}d \\ t' & \textit{for} & \text{min\_}d < t < \text{max\_}d \\ 0 & \textit{for} & t \geq \text{max\_}d \end{cases}$$

$$2$$

Please note that for this ACDF, only $\text{min\_}d$ and $\text{max\_}d$ need to be stored in the shadow map.

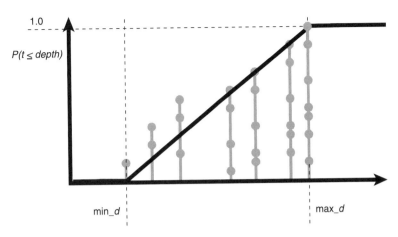

FIGURE 4.2.5 Linear ACDF.

A `Smoothstep()`-Based ACDF

Again, this ACDF just ignores CDF values on the interior of the interval [min_d,max_d]. It is 0.0 at min_d and 1.0 at max_d and intermediate probabilities are obtained by cubic smooth Hermite interpolation between 0.0 and 1.0.

So for a pixel at depth t, the probability for being in full light is defined by Equation 3. The resulting ACDF is depicted in Figure 4.2.6.

$$P(t \leq x) = \begin{cases} 1 & \text{for} & t \leq \min\_d \\ 1 + 2t'^3 - 3t'^2 & \text{for} & \min\_d < t < \max\_d \\ 0 & \text{for} & t \geq \max\_d \end{cases}$$

3

Please note that for this ACDF, only min_d and max_d need to be stored in the shadow map.

A Bezier-Based ACDF

In contrast to the previous two approaches, this ACDF tries to approximate CDF values on the interior of the interval [min_d,max_d]. It is 0.0 at min_d and 1.0 at max_d, and intermediate probabilities are computed by evaluating a cubic polynomial in Bezier form. In this case a cubic Bezier polynomial is chosen. There are four control

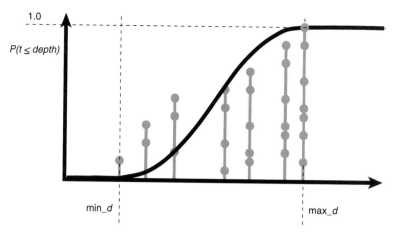

FIGURE 4.2.6 Smoothstep()-based ACDF.

values ($c0$, $c1$, $c2$, and $c3$) that control the shape of a cubic Bezier curve (see the empty circles in Figure 4.2.7). The first and the fourth coefficients are chosen to be 0.0 and 1.0, respectively. The remaining two control points will be chosen to control the shape of the CDF inside [min_d,max_d].

Please note that Catmull-Rom splines can also be used to generate a c1 curve that also interpolates all control probabilities. A potential drawback is that the Catmull-Rom curve may overshoot or undershoot the interval [0,1]. This can be avoided, but to keep the initial implementation simple this article will only discuss a Bezier-based ACDF.

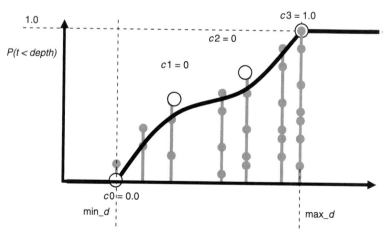

FIGURE 4.2.7 A simple cubic Bezier ACDF.

If N is the number of depth samples in a neighborhood of a shadow map pixel and one assumes a uniform probability for every sample, then one crude but very simple algorithm for choosing $c1$ and $c2$ is

$$dc0 := \frac{2}{3}\min\_d + \frac{1}{3}\max\_d$$

$$dc1 := \frac{1}{3}\min\_d + \frac{2}{3}\max\_d$$

$$c1 := \sum (sample.depth \leq dc0)?\frac{1}{N}:0$$

$$c2 := \sum (sample.depth \leq dc1)?\frac{1}{N}:0$$

$$4$$

So for a pixel at depth t the probability of being fully lit is

$$P(t \leq x) = \begin{cases} 1 & for & t \leq \min\_d \\ 1 - 3t'(1-t')^2 c1 - 3t'^2(1-t')c2 - t'^3 & for & \min\_d < t < \max\_d \\ 0 & for & t \geq \max\_d \end{cases}$$

$$5$$

See Figure 4.2.7.

The resulting polynomial is simpler than the original Bezier polynomial because the first control value is 0.0.

Please note that the Bezier ACDF will need a shadow map with four channels to store $\min\_d$, $\max\_d$, $c1$, and $c2$.

It is, of course, entirely possible to create an ACDF that is based on a quadratic Bezier function. In this case only one central control height needs to be stored.

Filtering ACDFs

Depending on the representation of the CDF, it might or might not be meaningful to filter the ACDF. Therefore it is important to pick a representation that is filterable. Filtering should produce a combined ACDF that approximates the CDF of all depth values within the filter footprint.

There are several ways this can be achieved, but most of the time the result will be an approximation of an approximation (the exception is linear functions). One could sample each ACDF at certain values and compute an aggregate ACDF from these probability samples. Also, one could just blend the ACDF coefficients stored in the shadow map. For the simple ACDFs outlined above, this will result in new ACDFs that make sense, although the approximation will deteriorate somewhat in that it does not fully reconstruct the shape of the combined CDF. However, since the original approximation is usually already pretty crude this does not seem to create problems in practice.

Note that since blurring is performed through filtering it is also possible to blur ACDF SMs to create a soft shadow effect.

Initial Proof-of-Concept ACDF Implementation

For the initial proof-of-concept ACDF SM implementation, an approximation that is based on a cubic Bezier function was chosen. The following sections walk through the rendering passes and the implementation decisions that were made.

The proof-of-concept implementation renders a small shadow map (256×256), constructs ACDFs for each pixel, and then blurs it. Each step is detailed in the following sections.

Step 1: Render the Shadow Map

The first step is to render the original depth-only shadow map from the light's point of view. For the purpose of ACDF SMs, it does not make sense to render into a multi-channel shadow map. This makes them hardware friendly because they can use accelerated depth-only rendering present in modern GPUs. Please note that even when rendering VSMs, it does not make sense to render into a two-channel shadow map if you intend to blur them later on.

Another interesting option would be to render a much bigger shadow map and to then downsample overlapping N by N blocks of pixels into an ACDF for each output pixel. This will reduce the size of the shadow map and reduce the bandwidth required to sample the shadow map. DirectX 10 makes it possible to access sub-samples of MSAA color render-targets/textures in a shader. It would be possible to construct an ACDF from all sub-samples resulting in a custom resolve operation. DirectX 10.1 even allows for shaders to access sub-samples of MSAA Z-buffers.

Step 2: Construct ACDFs in Each Pixel

To construct the ACDF at each pixel, the pixel shader shown in Listing 4.2.1 is used in a pass that transforms the shadow map into the ACDF shadow map that holds minimum depth, maximum depth, and two interior Bezier coefficients.

Listing 4.2.1 ACDF construction

```
Sampler2D ShadowMap;

float4 computeDepthsAndBezierCoeffs(float2 texcoord )
{
    float2 tc = 256 * texcoord;
    float2 fc = frac(tc);

    tc -= fc;
    texcoord.xy = tc / 256;

    // collect 3x3 depth samples
    float m100 = tex2D(ShadowMap, texcoord + float2(-0.5/256, -
0.5/256));
    float m010 = tex2D(ShadowMap, texcoord + float2( 0.0/256, -
0.5/256));
    float m001 = tex2D(ShadowMap, texcoord + float2( 0.5/256, -
0.5/256));
    float m200 = tex2D(ShadowMap, texcoord + float2(-0.5/256,
0.0/256));
    float m020 = tex2D(ShadowMap, texcoord + float2( 0.0/256,
0.0/256));
    float m002 = tex2D(ShadowMap, texcoord + float2( 0.5/256,
0.0/256));
    float m300 = tex2D(ShadowMap, texcoord + float2(-0.5/256,
0.5/256));
    float m030 = tex2D(ShadowMap, texcoord + float2( 0.0/256,
0.5/256));
    float m003 = tex2D(ShadowMap, texcoord + float2( 0.5/256,
0.5/256));

    // compute min/max depth
    float3 maxdepth = max( max( float3( m100, m010, m001 ),
                                float3( m200, m020, m002 ) ),
                                float3( m300, m030, m003 ) );
    float3 mindepth = min( min( float3( m100, m010, m001 ),
                                float3( m200, m020, m002 ) ),
                                float3( m300, m030, m003 ) );

    float max_d = max( maxdepth.x, max( maxdepth.y, maxdepth.z ) );
    float min_d = min( mindepth.x, min( mindepth.y, mindepth.z ) );

    // compute intermediate probabilities
    float d0 = (2/3.0) * min_d + (1/3.0) * max_d;
    float d1 = (1/3.0) * min_d + (2/3.0) * max_d;

    float p0 = 0;
    float p1 = 0;

    p0 += dot( float3( m100, m010, m001 ) <= float3( d0, d0, d0 ),
               float3( 1.0/9.0, 1.0/9.0, 1.0/9.0 ) );
    p0 += dot( float3( m200, m020, m002 ) <= float3( d0, d0, d0 ),
               float3( 1.0/9.0, 1.0/9.0, 1.0/9.0 ) );
```

```
        p0 += dot( float3( m300, m030, m003 ) <= float3( d0, d0, d0 ),
                float3( 1.0/9.0, 1.0/9.0, 1.0/9.0 ) );

        p1 += dot( float3( m100, m010, m001 ) <= float3( d1, d1, d1 ),
                float3( 1.0/9.0, 1.0/9.0, 1.0/9.0 ) );
        p1 += dot( float3( m200, m020, m002 ) <= float3( d1, d1, d1 ),
                float3( 1.0/9.0, 1.0/9.0, 1.0/9.0 ) );
        p1 += dot( float3( m300, m030, m003 ) <= float3( d1, d1, d1 ),
                float3( 1.0/9.0, 1.0/9.0, 1.0/9.0 ) );

        return float( min_d, p0, p1, max_d );
    }

    float4 main(float2 texcoord: TEXCOORD0 ) : COLOR
    {
        // return min/max depth and bezier coefficients
        return computeDepthsAndBezierCoeefs( texcoords );
    }
```

Step 3: Blurring the ACDF

The proof-of-concept implementation performs a blurring of the ACDFs in two passes using a separable filter [MAH03] and a small filter kernel. The use of a small filter kernel is justified by the assumption that maximum and minimum depth does not necessarily change smoothly from pixel to pixel.

Step 4: Use the ACDF SM

Now that a blurred version of the ACDF SM is available, the shader in Listing 4.2.2 is used to perform the shadow computations.

Listing 4.2.2 Shadows via probabilities computed with the ACDF

```
    sampler2D ACDFMap;...

    float4 main(float2 texCoord: TEXCOORD0,
                float3 lightVec: TEXCOORD1,
                float4 shadowCrd: TEXCOORD3): COLOR
    {
        // reduce length as a replacement for depth biasing
        float d = length(lightVec) - DEPTHBIAS;

        // do setup and lighting computations etc.
        float4 litPixel = computeLighting(…);

        // project for shadow map lookup
        shadowCrd.xy /= shadowCrd.z;

        // get max and min depth from x and w of ACDF
        float max_d = m.w + EPS; // prevent div by 0
        float min_d = m.x;
```

```
    // compute t in the range [0..1]
    float t = saturate( ( d - min_d ) / ( max_d - min_d ) );

    // compute shadowing term (evalute 1- cubic bezier function)
    float shadow =  1.0-( 3*t*pow(1-t,2)*m.y + 3*t*t*(1-t)*m.z + t*t*t
);

    // now apply shadowing term
    return shadow * lighting;
}
```

Results of the Initial Implementation

It turns out that in order to produce results without unwanted self-shadowing, the depth bias needs to be relatively big if one decides to render the front faces of shadow casters. Also, in regions where the depth of the scene does not vary much (such as polygons perpendicular to the light direction), the smoothness of the produced shadows is suboptimal (see Figure 4.2.8 for an illustration of this). Please note that for the initial ACDF construction shader used, the umbra region (the region of full shadow where no light reaches the pixels) is bigger compared to the region produced with variance shadow maps.

Some of these problems can be overcome by adding 2D noise to the texture coordinates used to sample the ACDF texture (see Figure 4.2.9). Still, depth bias tweaking can be cumbersome and this limits the usability of the technique.

FIGURE 4.2.8 Initial results.

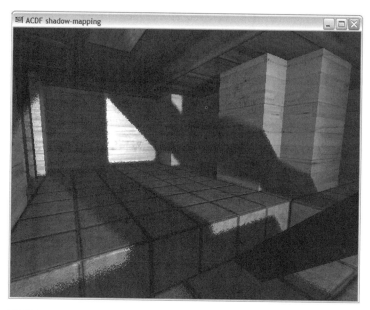

FIGURE 4.2.9 Noisy ACDF shadows.

Improved Proof-of-Concept ACDF Implementation

To improve upon the results so far, the following section will discuss methods to pick minimum and maximum depth differently while maintaining the shape of the ACDF as defined by the interior two Bezier coefficients (probabilities).

The major reason for choosing a high depth bias is that the initial minimum depth selected is the minimum of all pixels in the filter footprint. That means it can be *a lot* smaller than the depth of the pixel at the center of the shadow map texel. Especially for polygons that are almost parallel to the direction of the light, a high depth bias needs to be chosen to prevent the polygon from casting a shadow onto itself.

A better choice for the minimum depth is the original shadow map depth sample at the center of the filter footprint. This new minimum depth also varies more smoothly and its filtered value is $E(depth)$.

Since maximum depth also does not vary smoothly, it is replaced by $E(depth) + 0.5 * smoothstep(min\_scenedepth, max\_scenedepth, E(depth))$. The introduction of the `smoothstep()` function prevents shadows from becoming brighter when the receiver is close to the caster. This can be interpreted as a kind of depth bias.

These new minimum and maximum depth values allow us to minimize depth bias. The shader for computing shadow probabilities remains the same (refer to Listing 4.2.2); only the actual ACDF construction needs to change. The shader in Listing 4.2.3 highlights these changes.

Listing 4.2.3 Changes to the ACDF construction

```
...
float4 main(float2 texcoord: TEXCOORD0 ) : COLOR
{
    float2 tc = 256 * texcoord;
    float2 fc = frac(tc);

    tc -= fc;
    texcoord.xy = tc / 256;

    float4 coeffs = computeDepthsAndBezierCoeefs( texcoords );

    float m020 = tex2D(ShadowMap, texcoord + float2( 0.0/256,
0.0/256));

    // return min/max depth and bezier coefficients
    return float4( m020, coeffs.yz, m020 + 0.5 * smoothstep( 0,1,m020 )
);
}
```

The improved implementation generates smooth shadows with transitions that still capture the characteristics computed from the original CDF. See Figure 2.2.10 for an illustration of the shadows produced by this new method.

If one of the simpler ACDFs (e.g. smoothstep() or linear interpolation) is used, our approach only requires E(depth). This makes it very similar to ESMs [GRU07]. Additionally, this removes the need for the ACDF construction pass since maximum depth can be directly derived from E(depth) in the pixel shader.

FIGURE 2.2.10 Improved smooth ACDF shadows without light bleeding.

Future Directions

The initial ACDF SM implementation needs a depth bias to be chosen with care and also needs to be tweaked to work well with the scene in question. It would be interesting to use the ACDF construction pass to detect whether or not all depth samples lie on the same plane. If a common plane is detected, one could write the plane equation [PER06] instead of ACDF coefficients into the shadow map pixels. It would then be possible to do depth tests on non-border pixels without the need for biasing and to only use ACDF evaluations at transitions between fully lit and fully shadowed regions.

Also, our technique could make use of summed area tables [LAU07] to provide access to arbitrarily smooth shadows. ACDF SMs are orthogonal to PSMs, TSMs, and LISPMs, so it would be interesting to combine these approaches.

Finally, initial tests indicate that it may be possible to combine blurring and ACDF construction passes by making ACDF construction separable as well. If this turns out to be viable, the cost of ACDF SMs will be even more competitive.

Conclusion

This article has introduced a new statistically inspired shadow mapping method. When sampling the shadow map, the method takes just one sample for each pixel and is therefore more economical in terms of texture resources (instructions and bandwidth) compared to many other soft shadowing methods. In comparison to variance shadow maps it does not suffer from light bleeding, which is an artifact that can be hard to alleviate.

Acknowledgments

Thanks to Sam Martin and Willem de Boer for reviewing this article and for providing lots of interesting feedback. The screen shots for this article were taken from a program based on the source code framework available at http://www.humus.ca.

References

[AMB07] Annen T., Mertens T., Bekaert P., Seidel H.-P., Kautz J. "Convolution Shadow Maps," *Eurographics Symposium on Rendering*, 2007.

[ARV04] Arvo J. "Tiled shadow maps," *Proceedings of Computer Graphics International 2004*, IEEE Computer Society, 2004: pp. 240–247.

[CG04] Chong H. and Gortler S. "A lixel for every pixel," *Proceedings of the Eurographics Symposium on Rendering*, Eurographics Association, 2004: pp. 167–172.

[CD03]: Chan, E and Durand, F. "Rendering fake soft shadows with smoothies," *Proceedings of the Eurographics Symposium on Rendering*, 2003: pp. 208–218.

[DL06] Donnelly W. and Lauritzen, A. "Variance shadow maps," *SI3D '06: Proceedings of the 2006 symposium on Interactive 3D graphics and games*, New York, NY, USA, , ACM Press, 2006: pp. 161–165.

[DU07] Dmitriev, K. and Uralsky Y. "Soft shadows using hierarchical min-max shadow maps," GDC 2007, available online at http://developer.download. nvidia.com/presentations/2007/gdc/SoftShadows.pdf.

[ENG07] Engel, W. "Cascaded Shadow Maps," *ShaderX5 Advanced Rendering Techniques*, Charles River Media, 2007: pp. 197–206.

[FER05] Fernando, R. "Percentage-Closer Soft Shadows." Available online at http://download.nvidia.com/developer/presentations/2005/GDC/Sponsored_ Day/Percentage_Closer_Soft_Shadows.pdf

[FFBG01] Fernando, R., Fernandez, S., Bala, K., Greenberg, D. "Adaptive shadow maps," *Proceedings of ACM SIGGRAPH 2001*, 2001: pp. 387–390.

[GRU07] Grün, H. "ESMs—Expected Value Shadow Maps," Unpublished work.

[ISO06] Isodoro, J.R. "Shadow Mapping: GPU-based Tips and Techniques," Available online at http://ati.amd.com/developer/gdc/2006/ Isidoro-ShadowMapping.pdf.

[KOZ04] Kozlov, S. "Perspective Shadow Maps: Care and Feeding," *GPU Gems*, Addison-Wesley, 2004: pp. 214–244.

[LAU07] Lauritzen, A. "Summed-Area Variance Shadow Maps," *GPU Gems III*, Addison-Wesley, 2007: pp. 157–181. To be published.

[LKS06] Lefohn, A., Kniss, J. M., Strzodka, R., Sengupta, S., Owens J. D. "Glift: Generic, efficient, random-access gpu data structures," *ACM Transactions on Graphics 25*, 1 January, 2006: pp. 60–99.

[LTYM06] Lloyd, D., Tuft, D., Yoon, S., Manocha, D. "Warping and Partitioning for Low Error Shadow Maps," *Eurographics Symposium on Rendering*, Tomas Ake-nine-Möller and Wolfgang Heidrich Editors, 2006 or http://gamma.cs.unc.edu/ wnp/.

[MAH03] Mitchell, J., Ansari, M. Y., Hart, E. "Advanced Image Processing with DirectX 9 Pixel Shaders," *ShaderX2 Shader Programming Tips and Tricks with DirectX 9*, Charles River Media, 2003: pp 439–464.

[MT04] Martin, T., Tan T.-S. "Anti-aliasing and continuity with trapezoidal shadow maps," *Proceedings of the Eurographics Symposium on Rendering*, Eurographics Association, 2004: pp. 153–160.

[PER06] Persson, E. "Plane Shadow Mapping," Part of the ATI SDK March 2006, available online at http://www.ati.com.

[SD02] Stamminger, M. and Drettakis, G. "Perspective shadow maps," *Proceedings of ACM SIGGRAPH 2002*, 2002: pp. 557–562.

[SA07] Szirmay-Kalos, L., Aszódi, M. "Real-time Soft Shadows with Shadow Accumulation," *ShaderX5 Advanced Rendering Techniques*, Charles River Media, 2007: pp 263–270.

[SCH05] Schüler, C., "Eliminating Surface Acne with Gradient Shadow Mapping," *ShaderX4*, Charles River Media, 2005: pp.289–289

[SCH03] Sen, P., Cammarano, M., Hanarahan, P. "Shadow Silhouette Maps," *SIGGRAPH*, 2003: pp521–526.

[SZE07] Szécsis, L. "Alias-Free Hard Shadow Maps," *ShaderX5 Advanced Rendering Techniques,* Charles River Media, 2007: pp. 219–238.

[TQJN99] Tadamura, K., Qin, X., Jiao, G., Nakamae, E. "Rendering optimal solar shadows using plural sunlight depth buffers," *Computer Graphics International 1999,* 1999: p. 166.

[WIL78] Williams, L. "Casting curved shadows on curved surfaces," *Computer Graphics (SIGGRAPH '78 Proceedings),* vol. 12, 1978: pp. 270–274.

[WSP04] Wimmer, M., Scherzer, D., Purgathofer, W. "Light space perspective shadow maps," *Proceedings of the Eurographics Symposium on Rendering,* Eurographics Association, 2004: pp. 143–152.

4.3

Rendering Filtered Shadows with Exponential Shadow Maps

Marco Salvi

LucasArts, San Francisco

Introduction

As GPUs' computational abilities continue to increase at an amazing pace, new and complex algorithms once confined to the off-line rendering realm have become available to game developers and have entered into their techniques and tricks portfolio. Nonetheless, rendering high-quality real-time shadows is one of the most difficult problems to solve, and it's still a distant goal to reach as witnessed by the vast and rapidly growing computer graphics literature dedicated to this subject.

This article illustrates a fast and extremely simple to implement technique that can be used to render higher quality and fully dynamic shadows (see Figure 4.3.1).

FIGURE 4.3.1 ESM at work with a 512×512 FP32 shadow map and a 7×7 Gaussian filter.

The proposed method maintains good scalability and requires only a basic set of hardware features available on a wide class of GPUs and APIs.

Although this technique is simple and easy to use, its mathematical underpinnings might be a bit daunting. If you are not interested in knowing why it works, but you just want to know how it works, feel free to jump near the end of this article to the "Algorithm" section; you will find all the information you need to easily implement the ideas into your engine.

Background

The majority of real-time lighting and shadowing techniques model lights as dimensionless points. A physically based method of accurately rendering high-quality shadows is based on the very intuitive process of accumulating sharp shadows generated by a multitude of microscopic lights (with no spatial extent) distributed over a light's surface. Sharp shadows generated by these light sources can be separately rendered via common shadow maps. If we accumulate the contributions coming from enough lights, we obtain a nice and smooth penumbra. Unfortunately, this process tends to be slow even on modern graphics hardware as many rendering passes might be needed to get convincing results.

We can also imagine that our scene, observed from each microscopic light, is rendered over the same shadow map more and more times so that any given texel on the shadow map "sees" the scene from as many points of view as the number of light sources we use to approximate a light with a spatial extent.

To better understand what is going on, we might decide to plot a graph that shows us how depth values are distributed over a specific texel as seen from an area light. These discrete values would be distributed over a finite interval with a finite frequency so that it would seem natural to interpret this distribution of depth values as a probability distribution $P(O)$ where O identifies our occluders' depth as different values of the same random variable (see Figure 4.3.2).

If we had an accurate description of this distribution for any texel in the shadow map, then we would be able to calculate how likely a receiver point R is to be occluded or not. Considering occluder O depth as having a value directly proportional to its distance from the light, the probability of R being in shadow is defined as

$$P(O \geq R)$$
$$1$$

which means that if we know how depth values are distributed over a particular shadow map texel, what is the probability of some of them being behind the point R (see Figure 4.3.3)?

A similar approach, although not designed for real-time rendering, has been introduced with deep shadow maps [Lokovic00]. Although designed for offline rendering, some real-time implementations of the same core idea have been published over the last few years [Amour04]. They all precompute, compress, and store a depth

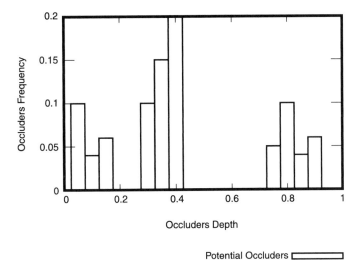

FIGURE 4.3.2 Plot of depth values distribution as seen from an area light through the same shadow map texel.

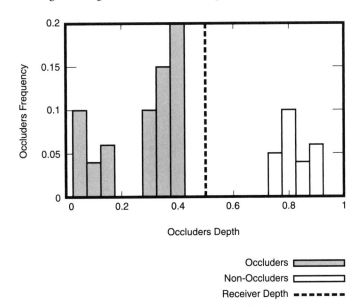

FIGURE 4.3.3 Probability of a point being in shadow.

distribution per shadow map texel, which makes it difficult to support dynamic shadow casters.

Another extremely interesting take on the subject comes from variance shadow maps [Donnelly06], which do not necessarily use any precomputed data as they try to gather information about the depth distribution by calculating its first two statistical moments, which are in turn used to estimate an upper bound for the probability of a point being in shadow via Chebyshev's inequality.

Notably, this algorithm is the first to allow the use of graphics hardware texture filtering capabilities; variance shadow maps become filterable entities and, as with any other texture, they are amenable to being MIPmapped [Williams83] as well as convolved with any filter. This last property is so important that it is desirable to have it in our technique as well.

Single Moment Shadow Maps

As we have already observed, generating a high-quality shadow by rendering a scene from multiple points of view is an extremely expensive operation that we would like to avoid, so hereinafter we will generate only one shadow map (rendered from a point that is representative of the whole area light) and we will construct a depth distribution for each texel, taking into consideration its neighboring texels.

We start by introducing a powerful tool known as Markov's inequality, which gives us a way to compute an upper bound for Expression 1:

$$P(|O| \geq R) \leq \frac{E(|O|)}{R}$$

$$2$$

For any non-negative function of the random variable O, this inequality gives an upper bound for the probability of O being greater than or equal to a positive constant R.

$$E(|O|)$$

is the expected (or mean) value of our texel's occluder distribution (its first statistical moment).

As opposed to VSM [Donnelly06], we will only use a single moment to define a texel's occluder probability distribution. As a matter of fact, introducing second or higher order moments will introduce undesirable artifacts such as light bleeding at overlapping shadows, as well as higher computational and memory requirements. Our aim is to keep the algorithm as simple as possible.

We start with an occluder O identified by a certain texel in our shadow map and we build a distribution of values around it, "collecting" a certain number of neighboring texels and computing a weighted average.

In the first step we render a shadow map from the light's point of view to a render-target/texture. The important thing here is to make sure our GPU and 3D API let us read back the depth values that we render.

We then apply a filter kernel to the shadow map; this procedure will basically "generate" a statistic per texel and the resulting texel value represents the first moment of the depth distribution (for more details on this procedure see [Donnelly06]).

The final step involves rendering the scene from the camera's point of view and sampling the shadow map to determine whether the pixel we are currently rendering is occluded or not. C code for the canonical depth test looks like this:

```
( occl_depth > recv_depth ) ?  occlusion = 1 : occlusion = 0;
```

This code is simple and easily understood: If a potential occluder O is behind our receiver R, then occlusion is 1; otherwise it is 0. Now we substitute this test with Markov's inequality, where `occluder_depth` is substituted with the new first order moment/mean value we just computed:

```
occlusion = saturate( occluder_mean_value / receiver )
```

First we observe the use of `saturate()`, which clamps the occlusion value to lie between 0 and 1. We need this because—unlike the standard depth test—Markov's inequality only gives us an upper bound for occlusion, which might yield values greater than 1. Unfortunately the results given by this method are not very good, as you can see in Figure 4.3.4, as we might hardly see any shadows in the scene.

FIGURE 4.3.4 Light uniformly bleeds into every shadow because a standard Markov's inequality fails to capture a tight upper bound for occlusion.

Higher Order Shadow Maps to the Rescue

Why are our shadows so washed out? This is due to the fact that Markov's inequality gives such a loose upper bound on occlusion that it is not very useful from a practical standpoint. We can fix this by first observing that the new occlusion formula really is the ratio of two linear quantities. If we keep the average occluder depth constant and we move the receiver away from the light, occlusion is essentially a hyperbola

$$\left(\underset{const}{O}\Big/R\right)$$

which goes to zero far too slowly to be able to capture a shadow for any reasonable distance between occluder and receiver. It is possible to increase the occluder-receiver distance using a global scale parameter that scales all coordinates, but this approach is useful only in certain cases because light bleeding is also a function of the distance between light and occluder(s). In fact, moving both the occluder and receiver away from the light makes light bleeding even worse.

We can simulate light moving away from our scene by using a translation parameter t:

$$\forall t \geq 0, t >> E\left(|O|\right), \frac{E\left(|O|\right)}{R} < 1$$

$$P(|O+t| \geq R+t) \leq \frac{E\left(|O+t|\right)}{R+t}$$

$$= \frac{E\left(|O|\right)+t}{R+t} \geq \frac{E\left(|O|\right)}{R}$$

3

Conversely, moving the occluder and receiver closer to the light tends to ameliorate light bleeding problems. These issues can be partially addressed by rendering a non-linear function of occluder depth in order to accelerate our descent to zero [Philips95].

Markov's inequality in fact still holds if we replace all terms with a positive and monotonic function:

$$\forall f\left(|x|\right) \geq 0 \rightarrow P(f\left(|O|\right) \geq f(R)) \leq \frac{E\left(f\left(|O|\right)\right)}{f(R)}$$

4

A candidate for $f(x)$ is x^2, which means rendering a squared depth value into the shadow map. After filtering the result of this first step we obtain a second-order moment for occluder distributions, which is quite similar to VSMs.

In our case we render a single moment, just not necessarily the first one. The new occlusion is now computed as

```
occlusion = saturate(occluder_mean_value / pow(receiver, 2.0f))
```

and the new results can be observed in Figure 4.3.5 (occluder_mean_value is now the average value of the occluder's depth squared).

FIGURE 4.3.5 As you can see, the second-order moment shadow's quality has considerably improved when compared to Figure 4.3.4.

It certainly looks better now, but we are not quite there yet, as light bleeding—although now less pronounced—is still quite visible. We can push this method a bit further and employ higher powers and therefore higher order moments:

$$f(|x|,n) = |x|^n \rightarrow P(|O|^n \geq R^n) \leq \frac{E(|O|^n)}{R^n}$$

5

Our occlusion formula is updated, too (see Figure 4.3.6):

```
occlusion = saturate(occluder_mean_value / pow(receiver, n))
```

We can see how shadows get darker and more defined with higher order shadow maps; unfortunately (but not unexpectedly!) this improvement comes with a cost:

- Light bleeding is still dependent on light position.
- As n increases, the available depth range decreases. For high powers our depth representation overflows and occlusion becomes meaningless.

At the end of this article we will have addressed all of these problems with a surprisingly simple solution. By chance we have already solved an issue that affects VSM and similar statistically based approaches: Our method does not generate any light bleeding when two occluders generate overlapping shadows. This very common geometry configuration (see Figure 4.3.7) generates high variance values (as is commonly and erroneously accepted, high depth complexity does not cause this issue), which in turn makes Chebyshev's inequality's upper bound quite loose so that light bleeds into shadows, giving rise to artifacts.

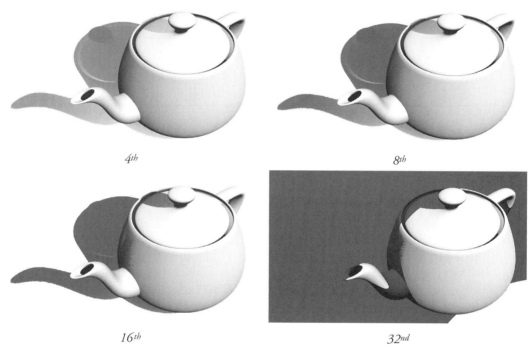

FIGURE 4.3.6 4th, 8th, 16th, and 32nd order shadow maps. Notice the self-shadowing artifacts on the 16th order shadow map and overflow errors in the 32nd order shadow map.

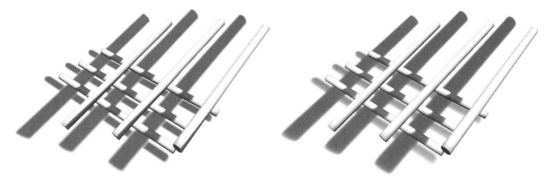

FIGURE 4.3.7 On the left is an image rendered with variance shadow maps; on the right we see our algorithm at work. Notice how overlapping shadows on the left image cause light bleeding, while a general bleeding term dependent upon light-occluder and light-receiver distance is observable on the right image.

Position-Independent Light Bleeding

As is evident from Inequality 3, when we translate the light with respect to the scene, the probability of a point being in shadow is not constant. Markov's inequality is a ratio between two quantities, and when $t > 0$ the numerator doesn't change at the same rate as the denominator. In order to have position-independent light bleeding, we want to keep this ratio constant under translation operations. We need a new function $f(x)$, with the following property:

$$f(x+t) = g(t)f(x)$$

So that applying a translation t we have:

$$\frac{f(O+t)}{f(R+t)} = \frac{g(t)f(O)}{g(t)f(R)}$$

$$= \frac{f(O)}{f(R)}$$

$f(x)$ changes its value with the same speed its argument x changes its value. This observation translates to a simple differential equation:

$$\frac{d}{dx}(f(x)) = kf(x)$$

6

which has a unique and elegant solution:

$$f(x) = Ce^{kx}$$

7

where C is an integration constant and k is a parameter we can use to scale our coordinates to tweak the amount of light bleeding we want to see on-screen.

The new $f(x)$ is a positive valued function that allows us to once again rewrite Markov's inequality:

$$P(e^{k|O|} \geq e^{kR}) \leq \frac{E(e^{k|O|})}{e^{kR}}$$

8

As weird as the idea of rendering the exponential of a depth value into the shadow map may seem, this new inequality completely removes the dependency of light bleeding from absolute positions. Light bleeding is still present, but now it depends on relative distance between occluders and receivers. Consider a simple case where a planar receiver at depth R and a planar occluder at depth O span the same filtering region with respective weights p and $1-p$. The probability of the receiver R being in shadow is given by

$$P(|O| \geq R) \leq \frac{pe^{kR} + (1-p)e^{kO}}{e^{kR}}$$

$$= p + (1-p)e^{k(O-R)}$$

This last equation converges to p for $k >> 0$, which is the same result we would get had we performed a large number of depth tests and averaged the results [Reeves87].

We also note that by using Taylor's theorem we can expand an exponential function around any point x_0 to an infinite series of polynomial terms. The expected value of each term represents an *Nth* order moment multiplied by a constant factor:

$$E\left(e^{x_0}\right) = E\left(\sum_{n=0}^{\infty} \frac{x_0^n}{n!}\right) = \sum_{n=0}^{\infty} E\left(\frac{x_0^n}{n!}\right)$$

$$= 1 + E\left(x_0\right) + \frac{E\left(x_0^2\right)}{2} + \frac{E\left(x_0^3\right)}{6} + ..$$

Higher order moments essentially just "sample" some part of the expansion (one polynomial term at time) but they are not able to capture the whole picture. On the other hand, the new method has further decreased the available depth range in quite a dramatic way as the exponential function grows so quickly that it can easily overflow computations. The largest positive value that can be stored with a single precision number is approximately 2^{128}, which translates to a maximum encodable depth range value of

$$\ln(2^{128}) \cong 88$$

However, it is not the absolute scale of a spatial coordinate that is important: What is important is the relative scale (which is tweakable via the scale parameter k) with regard to the amount of light bleeding. Note that k also can be used to increase the available range trading it off for more light bleeding.

Filtering Shadow Maps with Convolutions

We momentarily abandon our statistical approach to embrace a recently developed technique called CSM (convolution shadow maps) that allows high-quality, real-time filtering of shadow maps. Annen et al [Annen07] identify a depth test as a function

$$s_f(R) = [w * f(R,O)]$$

which is applied to the entire shadow map. In order to have a high quality reconstruction of $s(R)$, a convolution operator w is then applied to $s(R)$ under the assumption that our receiver R is planar within the convolution region:

$$s_f(R) = [w * f(R, O)]$$

9

The main observation here is that the filter w is not linear in its arguments, which is why we cannot simply filter a shadow map before performing depth tests with it.

In mathematical terms we have

$$[w * f(R, O)] \neq f(R, [w * O])$$

10

If we want to pre-filter our data before we sample them then we need to express $f(R, O)$ as a separable function $f_s(R, O) = g(R)h(O)$, which allows us to write

$$s_f(R) = [w * f_s(R, O)]$$

$$= [w * g(R)h(O)]$$

$$= g(R)[w * h(O)]$$

11

We note that $s(R)$ is a well-known function called step function or Heaviside function, and the key observation here is that an exponential function can provide a very good approximation to the step function over a subset of its domain (see Figure 4.3.8).

This approximation is good only on the interval

$$[-\infty, 0]$$

and can be written as

$$\lim_{k \to +\infty} e^{k(O-R)}$$

12

On the interval $(0, +\infty)$, the Heaviside function assumes a constant value of one, while our approximation does a very poor job and diverges to $+\infty$.

Note how the global coordinate scale parameter k controls how good our approximation is: As k increases, the exponential looks more and more like a Heaviside function rapidly transitioning between zero and one. If we neglect the limit definition, our approximation turns into no less than our special Markov's inequality (!). Moreover it is also separable:

$$f_s(R, O) = \frac{e^{kO}}{e^{kR}}$$

$$= g(R)h(O)$$

$$= e^{kO} e^{-kR}$$

13

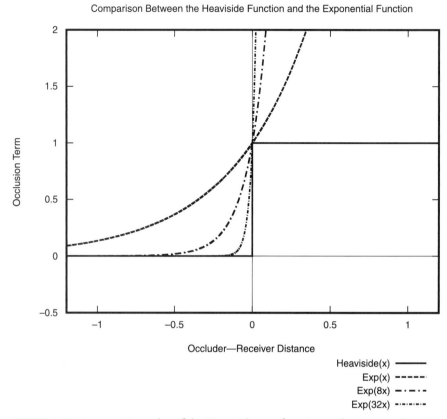

Comparison Between the Heaviside Function and the Exponential Function

Heaviside(x) ———
Exp(x) - - - - -
Exp(8x) — · — · ·
Exp(32x) -··-··-··-

FIGURE 4.3.8 A comparison plot of the Heaviside step function and our approximation.

Now we can apply the convolution w to the pre-filtered depth signal e^{kO}.

We have established a connection between our first probabilistic approach and this signal theoretic approach: The exponential function that we constructed ad hoc reveals its true importance with the new approach as a mechanism to pre-filter depth data!

Moreover we can draw a parallel between convolution filters and moments computation since estimating moments in the statistical approach corresponds to filtering the result of many depth tests in the convolution-based approach. From a calculation standpoint, there is no difference whatsoever between the two operations.

Unfortunately our algorithm doesn't always work well if the shadow receiver is not planar within a filtering region. Occluded areas near geometry discontinuities tend to shrink and be less smooth, although shadows are still properly filtered. This issue can be partially addressed by using small values for the scale parameter k, which make the exponential function grow at a slower rate, thereby reducing wild fluctuations within the filtering region. A second scale parameter can still be used after pre-filtering to control the amount of light bleeding (see Figure 4.3.9).

FIGURE 4.3.9 Left: Non-planar receiver, large *k*. Right: Non-planar receiver, small *k*.

Enhancing Depth Range

There is one last issue left to resolve: By rendering an exponential function of depth into a texture, we have severely limited the possible range of depth values and therefore may not cover a decent size area without accuracy problems. To make things easier we can temporarily remove the convolution/moment computation step from our shadow rendering pipeline and observe that Equation 8 drops its expected value operator $E(..)$ to obtain a simplified occlusion expression:

$$e^{k(O-R)}$$

15

Since we have now removed the need to filter exponential functions of depth, we can render a linear depth to the shadow map and then apply the occlusion operator. Alternatively, we can interpret this operation as rendering the natural logarithm of an exponential depth function,

$$\ln(e^{O}) = O$$

If we now re-enable the convolution step, we observe two facts:

- Depth range is greatly improved and is comparable to more classic shadow map rendering schemes.
- Our shadows are nicely filtered but over-darkened, with "fatter" silhouettes that have lost part of their original high-frequency detail.

Hence, the enhanced depth range comes at the cost of reduced shadow quality.

Mathematically, by disabling and then enabling the convolution step, we have propogated the convolution operator into the exponential, which is not mathematically correct, since

$$[w * e^{O}] \neq [e^{[w*O]}]$$

16

To fix this situation we have to modify the convolution filters to take care of the logarithmic representation of an exponential shadow map. To correctly convolve two shadow map samples with depth x and y with our exponential shadow maps solution, we need to compute

$$w_0 e^x + w_1 e^y$$

17

But since we only store x and y, and not e^x and e^y, we need to perform some algebraic manipulations to compute the correct convolution. We write the minimum convolution between two samples x and y as a single exponential function:

$$w_0 e^x + w_1 e^y$$

$$= w_0 e^x + w_1 e^x e^y e^{-x}$$

$$= e^x (w_0 + w_1 e^{y-x})$$

$$= \exp(x)\exp(\ln(w_0 + w_1 e^{y-x}))$$

$$= \exp(x + \ln(w_0 + w_1 e^{y-x}))$$

18

At this point we are only interested in the exponent $x+\ln(w_0+w_1 e^{y-x})$, which represents the correct formula to convolve two samples given our peculiar way of storing the shadow map.

The following Cg code illustrates how to implement a simple one-dimensional seven tap Gaussian filter.

```
// 1D Gaussian 7 taps coefficients
float coeff[7] = {0.006, 0.061, 0.242, 0.383, 0.242, 0.061, 0.006};

// two sample convolution
float conv_2taps(float w0, float x, float w1, float y)
{
    return (x + log(w0 + w1 * exp(y - x)));
}

// 1D Gaussian filter
float gaussian1D_7taps(PSInput input, sampler2D exp_shad_map)
{
    float samples[7];
    float sum[4];

    // fetch all samples
    for (int i = 0; i < 7; i++)
    {
        samples[i] = tex2D(exp_shad_map, input.uv[i]).x;
    }

    // add samples together
```

```
            // distribute the computation over different sample pairs to
            // minimize error

            // add samples 0-1
            sum[0] = conv_2taps(coeff[0], samples[0], coeff[1], samples[1]);

            // add samples 5-6
            sum[1] = conv_2taps(coeff[5], samples[5], coeff[6], samples[6]);

            // add samples 0-1-2
            sum[0] = conv_2taps(1.0, sum[0], coeff[2], samples[2]);

            // add samples 4-5-6
            sum[1] = conv_2taps(1.0, sum[1], coeff[4], samples[4]);

            // add samples 0-1-2-3
            sum[0] = conv_2taps(1.0, sum[0], coeff[3], samples[3]);

            // add samples 0-1-2-3-4-5-6 and return convolution result
            return conv_2taps(1.0, sum[0], 1.0, sum[1]);
    }
```

In practice this more complex way of performing a convolution turns out not to have a severe impact on performance, as the ratio between arithmetic operations and texturing operations is similar to the ratio between arithmetic units and texture units on modern GPUs.

The Algorithm

Given all the theory we have developed in the previous sections, the following section will summarize our findings and describe the algorithm.

Hardware Requirements

The algorithm was successfully implemented on SM.20 hardware using FP16/FP32 render-targets. Textures bilinear filtering was performed via software.

Exponential Shadow Maps Rendering Breakdown

There are three main rendering phases:

1. Render the exponential shadow map as seen from the light.
2. Filter/convolve the exponential shadow map (optionally generate MIPmaps).
3. Render the scene as seen from the camera and use a filtered shadow map sample per pixel to determine the amount of occlusion.

During the second phase the exponential shadow map represents a signal, sampled in the first phase, which will be re-sampled in the third phase (see Equation 8).

To reduce aliasing, the signal has to be pre-filtered before being re-sampled. To improve filtering speed, run a separable filter over the exponential shadow map—for example, a Gaussian filter is a good way to smooth out the depth values.

If the second phase is entirely skipped (for example, for performance reasons) we can still get some staggering results (see Figure 4.3.10).

FIGURE 4.3.10 Left: Single canonical depth test; Right: Single exponential shadow map depth test.

While shadow acne gets filtered and smoothed out by our algorithm, it might be useful to employ the technique described by Christian Schueler [Schueler05], which can be used on top of our solution.

Bonus Features

Our technique can also be used to render smooth soft shadows. All we need to do is to slightly decrease the scale parameter k in order to get light bleeding around shadow edges. It is also possible to have hard-edged (and anti-aliased) self shadows and soft penumbras at the same time by simply decreasing the scale parameter according to the distance of our point to the light (see Figure 4.3.11).

Dirty cheap tricks are also possible: For example, we can have high-quality soft shadows for our stylized game by simple rendering a little sphere, quad, or low-resolution LOD mesh in a very low resolution shadow map and then apply a wide filter kernel.

FIGURE 4.3.11 (Left) High-resolution filtered exponential shadow map. (Middle) Fake soft shadows rendered using a lower scale parameter k. (Right) Fake large area light: occlusion values computed modulating k according to the receiver distance from the light.

Generally speaking this technique can be used in conjunction with any shadow map projection scheme (warped and not warped) [Martin04, Wimmer04] and shadow maps partitioning schemes such as cascaded shadow maps [Engel06]. Feel free to mix all the best techniques out there to render high-quality shadows in real-time.

Conclusion

We have presented a new shadow map filtering technique that can be implemented in Shader Model 2.0 and consumes no extra memory. It allows for improved shadow map filtering with separable filters and can be bilinearly or trilinearly filtered in hardware. Light bleeding is also fully controllable and only depends on the distance between shadow caster and receiver; there is no light bleeding at overlapping shadows. We briefly explained the power of having this filterable representation as we can fake soft shadows by using a combination of low-resolution shadow maps and wide filter kernels. The current technique is not to be considered fully exploited yet; more work has to be done to correctly handle non-planar receivers, to ameliorate temporal aliasing, and to fully incorporate soft shadows as an integral part of the algorithm.

Acknowledgments

I thank Arun Demeure for his useful hints and for having relentlessly pushed me to improve the algorithm. Special thanks go to Willem H. de Boer and Jules Davis for kindly taking time to review the article and for their suggestions. And last but not least a big thank to Francesco Banterle, Julie Barnes, Dean Calver, Wil Driver, Wolfgang Engel, Fabio Franchini, Serguei Parilov, Rys Sommefeldt, and Jim Tilander for their continuous support and for having listened to my ramblings about shadowing techniques for a long, long time.

References

[Amour04] St. Amour, Jean-Francois, Paquette, Eric, et al. "Real Time Soft Shadows Using the PDSM Technique," *ShaderX4,* edited by W. Engel, Charles River Media, Hingham, MA, 2005: pp. 299–312.

[Annen07] Annen, Thomas, Mertens, Tom, Bekaert, Philippe, Seidel, Hans-Peter, Kautz, Jan. "Convolution Shadow Maps," *Rendering Techniques 2007: Eurographics Symposium on Rendering,* June 2007.

[Donnelly06] Donnelly, William and Lauritzen, Andrew. "Variance Shadow Maps," *Symposium on Interactive 3D Graphics and Games Proceedings,* ACM, 2006

[Engel06] Engel, Wolfgang. "Cascaded Shadow Maps," *ShaderX5,* edited by W. Engel, Charles River Media, Hingham, MA, 2006: pp. 197–206.

[Lokovic00] Lokovic, Tom and Veach, Eric. "Deep Shadow Maps," *SIGGRAPH 2000 Proceedings,* August, Addison-Wesley, 2000.

[Martin04] Martin, Tobias and Tan, Tiow-Seng. "Anti-aliasing and Continuity with Trapezoidal Shadow Maps," *Proceedings of Eurographics Symposium on Rendering*, Norrköping, Sweden, 21-23 June 2004: pp. 153–160 (text) and page 412 (color plate).

[Philips95] Philips, Thomas K. and Nelson, Randolph. "The Moment Bound Is Tighter Than Chernoff's Bound for Positive Tail Probabilities," *The American Statistician*, Vol. 49, No. 2, May, 1995: pp. 175–178.

[Reeves87] Reeves, William T., Salesin, David H., Cook, Robert L. "Rendering anti aliased shadows with depth maps," *SIGGRAPH87 Proceedings*, July, 1987: pp. 283–291.

[Schueler05] Schueler, Christian. "Eliminating Surface Acne with Gradient Shadow Mapping," *ShaderX4*, edited by W. Engel, Charles River Media, Hingham, MA, 2005: pp. 289–298.

[Williams83] Williams, Lance. "Pyramidal Parametrics," *SIGGRAPH83 Proceedings*, Vol. 17, No. 3, July 1983.

[Wimmer04] Wimmer, Michael, Scherzer, Daniel, Purgathofer, Werner. "Light Space Perspective Shadow Maps," *Eurographics Symposium on Rendering*, 2004.

4.4

Fitted Virtual Shadow Maps and Shadow Fog

Markus Giegl (mgbiz@arscreat.com)

Fitted virtual shadow mapping (FVSM) is the successor to queried virtual shadow mapping (QVSM) presented in *ShaderX5*, over which it has the following advantages:

- It is well suited for soft shadow techniques (such as shadow map multi-sampling), which allows for improved shadow quality.
- It supports a quality versus speed tradeoff parameter, which affects the shadow quality in the scene uniformly.
- It is faster.

FVSM does retain the following features of queried virtual shadow maps:

- It allows for sub-pixel accurate shadowing of the scene, meaning that it produces shadows that are alias artifact free, comparable to shadow volumes. (Figure 4.4.1 visualizes the two types of shadow map aliasing: perspective and projection[1] aliasing.)
- It maintains all the benefits of shadow mapping, such as the following:
  a. Allowing for shadowing of fully dynamic scenes
  b. Being able to use alpha masked textures, non-well formed geometry, or high-order surfaces as shadow casters (contrary to shadow volumes).
  c. Requiring no additional scene geometry information or scene preprocessing.
- It bypasses the maximum shadow map texture size and the GPU memory limitation.
- It creates shadow map resolution only where necessary.

In short, fitted virtual shadow maps aim to supply fully dynamic, real-time, soft-shadow-friendly, artifact free shadows.[2]

At the end of this article, the concept of *shadow fogging* is introduced, which can be used to make the shadowing of a scene with conventional shadow mapping more visually pleasing.

(a) Conventional shadow mapping (4096² shadow map texture)

(b) FVSM

FIGURE 4.4.1 Test scene using alpha masked geometry for leaves on trees and the fence in the background. (a) This scene is shadowed using a conventional 4096 shadow map, thus it exhibits strong undersampling artifacts. (b) Same scene shadowed sub-pixel accurate with FVSM, giving the same quality as shadow volumes, while supporting alpha masked geometry.

Overview

Fitted virtual shadow mapping is based on the principle of *virtual tiled shadow mapping* (VTSM), which works by shadowing only part of the scene with a rectangular part of the shadow map (called a *shadow map tile*), and then is applied to a `float32` depth buffer of the scene for performance reasons (see the later section "VTSM").

Fitted virtual shadow mapping first samples the scene from the eye-point on the GPU to calculate the needed shadow map resolution in different parts of the scene. It then processes the resulting data on the CPU and arrives at a hierarchical grid structure, which is then traversed in a kd-tree fashion, shadowing the scene with shadow map tiles of the required resolution where needed (see Figure 4.4.2).

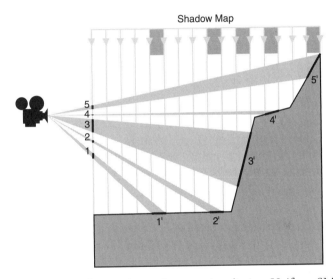

FIGURE 4.4.2 Visualization of projection and perspective aliasing: Uniform SM texels are projected on the scene geometry at 1',2',3',4',5', and from there get projected onto the front plane (screen) at 1,2,3,4,5. At positions 1' and 2' we can see that areas of the same size in the scene are projected onto larger areas on the screen, the closer they are to the eye-point; this is the source of perspective aliasing, which is hence stronger at 1'. At position 3' the face normal is nearly perpendicular to the light direction, from which follows that the SM texel is projected onto a large area in the scene; projecting it onto the screen at 3, leads to a larger screen space-area than at 1', even though 1' is much nearer to the eye-point; the closeness of the orientation of a scene face normal to being perpendicular to the light direction is the source of projection aliasing, which is hence strong at position 3'. Areas 4' and 5' show less extreme cases.

Combination with Perspective Shadow Maps

Shadow map reparametrization techniques (such as *perspective shadow maps* [PUB_
Perspective_SMs] and their successors) cannot supply consistently improved shadow
map quality for all view directions; they work only for view directions that are perpendicular to the light direction. This is a fundamental problem of these techniques, and
can make them problematic for practical use. However, all virtual shadow map techniques, including FVSMs, are orthogonal to SM reparametrization techniques and
can therefore be combined without any problems, should one desire to do so, by simply replacing the uniform shadow mapping transformation with the shadow map
reparametrization technique of your choice.

Virtual Shadow Mapping Basics

FVSMs are based on virtual tiled shadow mapping, including deferred shadowing and
using a shadow result texture, which are explained in the following sections.

Shadow Result Texture

The *shadow result texture* (*SRT*) is a 1-byte texture with the same dimensions as the
frame buffer into which we write only the results of the shadowing operations, i.e. 0 if
a pixel lies in shadow, 255 if not (if SM filtering is used, it contains the shadow value
[0,255], which is the result of the SM filtering operation for this pixel). You can think
of it as a layer that contains only the shadows in the scene cast by a particular light
source.

Using the SRT allows SM tiles to overlap (see the section "Soft Shadows" later in
this article), as the shadowing results of a tile that is applied later can simply overwrite
previous results. It also makes the application of the SM tiles faster since we write to a
surface with only one byte per pixel.[3]

Virtual Tiled Shadow Mapping

Virtual tiled shadow mapping works by slicing the shadow map into a regular grid of
n×n *shadow map tiles* (SM tiles), with each tile having the resolution of a full SM (see
Figure 4.4.3). For each shadow map tile, a shadow map texture is then created on the
fly and used to shadow the part of the scene that lies within the light frustum of the
tile. The shadow map texture is reused for each tile—that is, its contents are discarded
immediately after it has been used to shadow the scene.

By slicing the shadow map into tiles we overcome the maximum supported texture size limitation, and by reusing the shadow map texture we overcome the physical
memory limitations imposed by the hardware.

Deferred Shadowing

To make the shadowing of the SRT with the SM tiles faster, deferred shadowing uses
a linear view space depth buffer called an *eye-space depth buffer* (ESDB), which stores

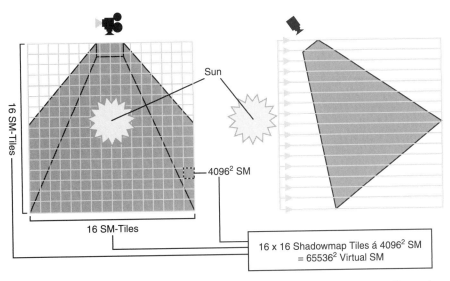

FIGURE 4.4.3 Schematic side and top-down views of VTSM: The shadow map (focused on the view frustum) is split into a grid of shadow mapped tiles (here 16×16); on the right the light frusta extend from the light through the shadow mapped tiles toward the view frustum. Each shadow mapped tile is created on-the-fly, used to shadow its part of the scene, and then immediately discarded. If each shadow mapped tile uses a 4096^2 SM, then we arrive at an effective SM resolution of 65536×65536 in the example, 256 times larger than using only a single SM. Note that with conventional shadow mapping, only the small "4096^2 SM"-square is used to shadow the whole scene.

the eye-space z-coordinate z_{eye} (= eye space depth) of each pixel as a 1×float32. This avoids the need to re-render the scene for each shadow map tile. Using the ESDB to shadow the SRT with each SM tile works like this:

1. Render the part of the scene that lies within the light frustum of the SM tile into the shadow map texture.
2. Render a full-screen quad using the ESDB bound as a texture resource.
3. In the pixel shader, look up the eye-space depth of the current pixel in the ESDB and then transform the pixel position from $(x_{window}, y_{window}, z_{eye})$ into the shadow map space of the tile (using the $(x_w, y_w, z_e) \rightarrow (x_e, y_e, z_e)$ transformation given below).
4. Using the position of the pixel in SM tile space:
   a. Discard it if its (x_{SM}, y_{SM}) coordinates lie outside $[0,1] \times [0,1]$, i.e., outside the SM tile.
   b. Otherwise, calculate the shadowing term using the depth information stored in the SM tile as with conventional shadow mapping and write the result to the SRT.

The following matrix transform changes the window coordinates of the current pixel (x_w, y_w) (given as texture coordinates, i.e., running from 0 to 1) together with the pixel eye-space coordinate Z_e (taken from the ESDB) into eye-space coordinates:

$$
\begin{pmatrix} x_e \\ y_e \\ z_e \end{pmatrix} = z_e \cdot \begin{pmatrix} \frac{1}{a_x} & 0 & -\frac{b_x}{a_x} \\ 0 & \frac{1}{a_y} & -\frac{b_y}{a_y} \\ 0 & 0 & 1 \end{pmatrix} \cdot \begin{pmatrix} 2 & 0 & 1 \\ 0 & 2 & -1 \\ 0 & 0 & 1 \end{pmatrix} \cdot \begin{pmatrix} x_w \\ y_w \\ 1 \end{pmatrix}
$$

where the parameters a_x, a_y and b_x, b_y in the first matrix are the following entries in the screen space projection matrix, P, which is used in the transformation pipeline of the graphics API:

$$
P = \begin{pmatrix} a_x & 0 & b_x & 0 \\ 0 & a_y & b_y & 0 \\ 0 & 0 & \dots & \dots \\ 0 & 0 & 1 & 0 \end{pmatrix}
$$

The complete transformation then takes the form

$$
\begin{pmatrix} x_{SM-tile} \\ y_{SM-tile} \\ z_{SM-tile} \end{pmatrix} = M_{world \to SM-tile} (M_{world \to eye})^{-1} \underbrace{\begin{pmatrix} \frac{1}{a_x} & 0 & -\frac{b_x}{a_x} \\ 0 & \frac{1}{a_y} & -\frac{b_y}{a_y} \\ 0 & 0 & 1 \end{pmatrix} \cdot \begin{pmatrix} 2 & 0 & 1 \\ 0 & 2 & -1 \\ 0 & 0 & 1 \end{pmatrix}}_{M_{(w,w,e) \to SM-tile}} \cdot \begin{pmatrix} z_e \cdot x_w \\ z_e \cdot y_w \\ z_e \end{pmatrix}
$$

where the linear part of the transformation should be combined into a single matrix $M_{(w,w,e) \to SM-tile}$ and passed to the pixel shader for efficiency reasons.

Shadowing the Scene with the Eye-Space Depth Buffer

ESDB Alpha Channel

This approach uses the α-component of a 4×float32 buffer to store the ESDB.

1. First, the scene is rendered into a 4-float32 buffer with a regular 1/z depth buffer attached. The color of each pixel in the object when lit by the shadow-map-shadow-casting-light (ignoring shadowing and ambient light) is written to the RGB channels; the pixel shader writes the unmodified eye-space z-coordinate into the α-component of the buffer.
2. The ESDB (i.e., the α-component of the buffer) is then used to perform deferred shadowing on the SRT.

3. Finally, the RGB information in the buffer is combined with the shadowing information in the SRT and the result is written to the frame buffer (also adding the ambient light term).

This approach avoids the use of multiple render-targets and only rasterizes the scene once. It does, however, produce results that are not completely physically correct: Unless areas in shadow are rendered as completely black, modulating the RGB colors stored in the buffer with the SRT is not completely accurate, because pixels that lie in shadow should not be displayed (e.g. specular highlights[4]).

Apart from these minor artifacts, this approach requires the least amount of effort to combine deferred shadowing with an arbitrary engine.

Depth First

A more sophisticated and physically accurate way of combining the result of virtual shadow mapping with scene shading uses a depth-first (z-only) pass, as you can see in the following steps.

1. Rasterize only the scene depth—without shading—into a 1-float32 ESDB (again with a regular $1/z$ depth buffer attached). This step can be combined with the Coherent Hierarchical Culling (CHC) algorithm by Bittner ([PUB_CHC]), which efficiently culls the occluded parts of the scene geometry on the fly and works best when used within a depth-first pass.

2. Use this 1-float32 ESDB to shadow the SRT with the SM tiles as before.

3. Bind the fully shadowed SRT to the pixel shader and re-render the scene geometry into the frame buffer, shading pixels differently depending on whether they lie in shadow or not according to the SRT. As usual, with depth-first rendering, this pass should be rendered with depth comparison set to EQUAL (if CHC was employed, only the visible geometry needs to be re-rendered).

This approach is a good choice when an engine uses depth-first rendering to avoid shader overdraw. Otherwise, if the artifacts described above are a problem, one might consider switching to depth-first rendering (+ CHC, unless the application has very little occlusion[5]).

Deferred Shading

Engines using deferred shading ([PUB_Deferred_Shading]) are well suited for deferred shadowing because they already have an ESDB as part of the deferred shading buffer. The shadowed SRT can then be created between the creation of the deferred shading buffer and the deferred shading itself. The resulting SRT can then again be used during deferred shading to shade pixels that lie in shadow differently.

Fitted Virtual Shadow Mapping

FVSMs work by deciding—for each frame—what SM resolution is needed and where in the scene. In the following, "supplying sub-pixel accuracy" for an SM tile means that for the current eye-point and frame buffer resolution, the SM tile has enough resolution in its corresponding SM texture so that when the scene is shadowed with the SM tile, the resulting shadow is sub-pixel accurate; that is, it is free of shadow map aliasing artifacts. In practical terms, this means that the resulting shadow displays no visible shadow map texels and remains stationary even when SM focusing ([PUB_Practical_SMing]) is used; in other words, it behaves as expected from a shadow.

The following gives an overview of the steps of the algorithm:

1. Create an eye-space depth buffer as explained in the previous section.
2. Use the ESDB bound to a fragment shader to create what we call the *shadow map tile mapping map* (SMTMM), which is illustrated in Figure 4.4.4. The SMTMM contains information for each pixel in the scene about 1) the pixel's corresponding shadow map coordinates, and 2) what resolution the shadow map would require along each SM axis at this position to supply sub-pixel accuracy when performing the shadow map query.

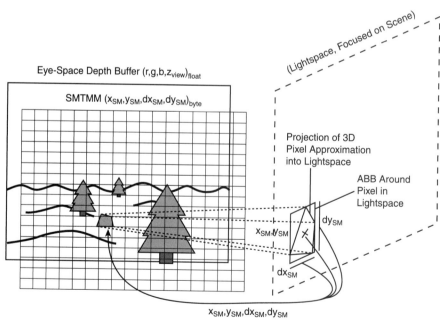

FIGURE 4.4.4 Shadow map tile mapping map (SMTMM) creation on the GPU. For each pixel-patch, its projection into shadow map space is calculated. The bounding rectangle around the resulting quadrilateral and center of the projection are then written as 4-byte values into the SMTMM.

3. Transfer the SMTMM to CPU memory[6] and then transform the information in it from eye-space to SM space, accumulating it in the *shadow map tile grid* (SMTG). The SMTG contains information about what resolution each SM tile of a virtual n×n tiled SM would need along each SM axis to supply sub-pixel accuracy when used to shadow the scene.

4. Construct the *shadow map tile grid pyramid* (SMTGP) "on top of" the SMTG by pulling up the maximum needed SM tile resolution along each axis.

5. Traverse the SMTGP recursively in a top-down fashion, building an implicit kd-tree of SM tiles. When the resolution requirement of an SM tile can be satisfied along both SM-axes with an SM tile-texture with dimensions supported by the GPU (e.g. 4096^2), the corresponding SM tile shadow map is created and immediately used to shadow its part of the scene as described in the preceding section "Virtual Tiled Shadow Mapping."

Shadow Map Tile Mapping Map: Motivation

This section motivates the concept of the SMTMM and gives a high-level description of how its entries are constructed. To determine what SM resolution is needed and where it is needed in the scene, we calculate the following for each screen pixel:

- The SM coordinates that correspond to the pixel
- The extent of the pixel as seen from the light

The first calculation is straightforward: Each pixel corresponds to a 3D-point in world space (where the ray from the eye-point through the pixel center intersects the scene). If we project this point into the SM, we know where the pixel will query the SM. The second calculation needs to be explained: What do we mean by "the extent of the pixel as seen from the light?" Each pixel on the screen can be interpreted as a small "pixel-view frustum" going from the eye-point through the four corners of the pixel into the scene. The pixel represents the area in the scene where the pixel-view frustum intersects the scene (one can visualize this as a spotlight located in the eye-point projecting the pixel onto the scene). We are interested in the size and orientation of the projection of the pixel into the scene, which we locally approximate as a planar patch ("pixel-patch").

The size of the pixel-patch is related to perspective aliasing: the closer the distance to the camera where the view frustum intersects the scene, the smaller the patch that is projected onto a screen pixel, and hence, the more resolution the SM needs there to ensure that the SM texel covering the spot is not larger than the patch.

The orientation of the patch relative to the direction of the light rays is related to projection aliasing because the closer to orthogonal the orientation of the patch is to the light direction, the more resolution the SM needs there to make sure that the projection of the SM texel onto the patch is not larger than the patch.

More mathematically put, what we do is the following: We construct a planar patch approximation of the scene area, which is projected onto a screen pixel. Then we project this patch into the SM, getting a quadrilateral in the SM. This quadrilateral needs to have a 1:1 correspondence to an SM texel in the SM if the resulting shadow at the scene area of the patch (i.e. at the screen pixel) is to be pixel accurate. To calculate from the quadrilateral the required SM resolution at the point where the pixel samples the SM, we compute an SM-axis-aligned bounding rectangle around it. We store the extent of the quadrilateral bounding rectangle along each SM axis in the SMTMM as a measure of the required SM resolution along each SM axis at this pixel.

The only remaining question is this: How do we efficiently construct the pixel-patch? We do this using the linear depth information (z_{eye}) stored in the ESDB. First we calculate the positions of the centers of the four left/right and upper/lower neighboring pixels of the current screen space pixel and look up their respective linear depth in the ESDB. Following that, we pick the left or right neighboring pixel that has the larger absolute depth difference to the depth of the current pixel. The reason we pick the point with the larger absolute difference in depth is that we do not want to miss a surface that is seen at a grazing angle from the eye-point. We then do the same for the upper/lower neighboring pixel, which together with the current pixel center, gives us three points that define a plane. We then use this plane to construct the pixel-patch by calculating the positions of the left/right and upper/lower neighboring pixels on the plane, which we then transform from ($x_{window}, y_{window}, z_{eye}$) to view space ($x_{window}, y_{window}, z_{eye}$) as described in the section "Virtual Tiled Shadow Mapping." Applying the inverse view space transform, we then arrive at the world space coordinates of the pixel-patch. Note that due to the neighboring pixels' coordinates being calculated in screen space (i.e. post-projective space), the pixel-patch is automatically correctly "perspective un-shortened" through the un-project transformation; in other words, the farther away it is from the eye-point, the larger it is. From there we can easily project the pixel-patch into SM space via the light space transform, arriving at the SM quadrilateral corresponding to the pixel-patch in light space and around which we finally construct the SM axis-aligned bounding rectangle. Note that due to using the depth information in the vicinity of the current pixel in the calculation of the pixel-patch, the algorithm also works if the SMTMM has a smaller resolution than the screen.

Shadow Map Tile Mapping Map: Implementation

The SMTMM is a 4-byte buffer. One can think of it as being laid on top of the frame buffer, normally having a lower resolution than the frame buffer and containing information about the shadow map resolution needed in the area that each SMTMM "pixel" covers. The first two byte values in each SMTMM entry ("pixel") contain information about the position where the center of the frame buffer rectangle will query the shadow map; the last two byte entries represent the resolution needed along each SM axis at the position in the shadow map. We use byte values for the entries to keep the read-back operation and the CPU processing in the next step fast; for the same reason, the SMTMM is normally chosen to have lower resolution than the frame buffer, e.g. 256^2 for a 1024^2 frame buffer.

Using byte values for the shadow map query position gives us information about the required SM resolution discretized to a 256×256 grid of SM tiles. This is not a restriction in practice because for, say, 4096^2 SM tile-textures, a maximum refinement of 256×256 corresponds to a $(256 \times 4096)^2 = 1{,}048{,}576^2$ SM, which gives sub-pixel accuracy even for very large scenes.

The position in the shadow map is calculated in the pixel shader by transforming the screen-space coordinates (x_w, y_w) of the pixel (which are passed to the pixel shader as texture coordinates) and the eye-space z (=depth) entry z_e, (which is read from the ESDB) into eye-space (x_e, y_e, z_e). From there it is transformed into the light space of the shadow map. Because the coordinates will already be in the range [0,1], simply outputting them to the 4-byte SMTMM surface will automatically lead to them being converted to byte range by the graphics hardware.

The resolution requirement along each SM axis is approximated as follows in the pixel shader: First we calculate the (x,y) coordinates of the neighboring screen space pixels in x- and y-direction from the texture coordinate of the current pixel passed to the pixel shader. We then use these texture coordinates to look up the corresponding view-space depth values in the ESDB; from these, we calculate the smaller absolute Δz along the x- and y-axis, Δz_x and Δz_y. We then use these Δz values together with the x,y coordinates of the neighboring pixels to construct an approximate rectangle representing the current pixel in space. Then we project this rectangle into SM space and calculate an SM axis-aligned bounding box around it. The half length of each of this bounding box's extent, Δz_{sm_axis} (with $sm\_axis = \{0,1\}$), is then used as the base measure for the required SM resolution along each SM axis at this point. To quantize the needed SM resolution along the SM axis into a byte value, we use the formula $-\log_2(round(\Delta_{sm\_axis} + \text{float2}(0.5, 0.5))/256$ (i.e. we output it as a logarithmic value normalized to the range [0,1], which the graphics hardware then again automatically converts to byte range).

The conversion to a logarithmic scale allows us to represent a large scale of required SM resolutions in a byte value, from 1×1 to $2^{255} \times 2^{255}$. We add 0.5 before performing the logarithmic transformation to prevent a one-too-small required SM resolution value when the resulting logarithmic value, normalized to [0,1] by dividing by 256, is quantized to the integer byte range (mapped onto the 255 byte values) when the pixel shader result is written into the SMTMM.

The following shows the SMTMM creation pixel shader as HLSL code:

```
Ps_OUT PsCreateShadowMapTileMapping(Ps_IN IN)
{
    Ps_OUT OUT;
    // texture coordinate of center of current pixel
    float2 tc_pixel_center = IN.v2_tc.xy;
    // texture coordinates of right,left,upper and lower neighbor
    // of current pixel, clamped to rendertarget extent
```

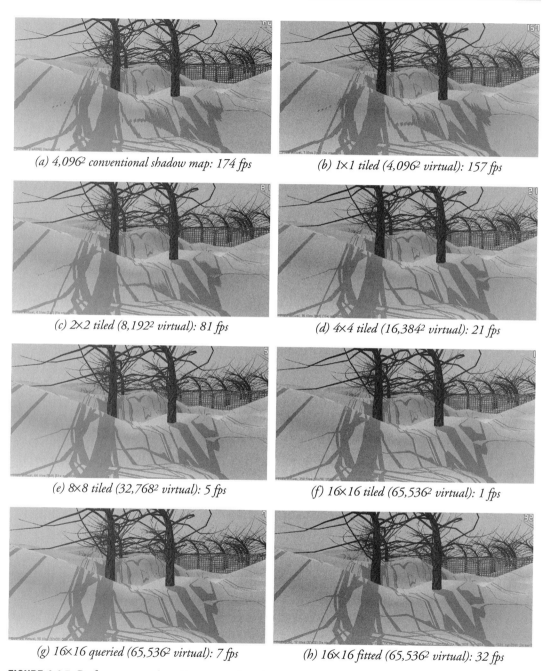

(a) 4,096² conventional shadow map: 174 fps   *(b) 1×1 tiled (4,096² virtual): 157 fps*

(c) 2×2 tiled (8,192² virtual): 81 fps   *(d) 4×4 tiled (16,384² virtual): 21 fps*

(e) 8×8 tiled (32,768² virtual): 5 fps   *(f) 16×16 tiled (65,536² virtual): 1 fps*

(g) 16×16 queried (65,536² virtual): 7 fps   *(h) 16×16 fitted (65,536² virtual): 32 fps*

FIGURE 4.4.5 Performance and quality comparison between conventional, virtual tiled, queried, and fitted virtual shadow mapping in a 1024×512 frame buffer. Conventional SMs exhibit strong undersampling artifacts (which are especially disturbing in a dynamic scene), while the performance of VTSMs breaks down to 1 fps at 16×16 SM tiles (the number of SM tiles needed to shadow the scene sub-pixel accurate), while QVSMs are still at 7 fps and FVSM at 32 fps, both delivering the same shadow quality as VTSMs.

```
float2 tc_pixel_neighbor_right =
    float2(clamp( tc_pixel_center.x +
    rendertarget_nr_pixel_inv.x, 0, 1), tc_pixel_center.y );
float2 tc_pixel_neighbor_left =
    float2(clamp( tc_pixel_center.x -
    rendertarget_nr_pixel_inv.x, 0, 1), tc_pixel_center.y );
float2 tc_pixel_neighbor_upper =
    float2(tc_pixel_center.x, clamp( tc_pixel_center.y +
    rendertarget_nr_pixel_inv.y, 0, 1));
float2 tc_pixel_neighbor_lower =
    float2(tc_pixel_center.x, clamp( tc_pixel_center.y -
    rendertarget_nr_pixel_inv.y, 0, 1));
// read viewspace z for current pixel from ESDB
float z_view_center = tex2D(tex_shadow_depth_buffer,
tc_pixel_center).w;
float2 v2_dz_view_use = float2(
        sm_tile_mapping_pick_smaller_dz(z_view_center,
            tc_pixel_neighbor_left,tc_pixel_neighbor_right),
        sm_tile_mapping_pick_smaller_dz(z_view_center,
            tc_pixel_neighbor_lower,tc_pixel_neighbor_upper)
    );
// pos of left neighbor of current pixel in the shadowmap
// ScreenspaceToShadowmapCoordinatesAndLightspaceDepth uses
// the "Deferred Shadowing" matrix to transform to eye-space.
float3 pos_sm_left =
ScreenspaceToShadowmapCoordinatesAndLightspaceDepth(
        tc_pixel_neighbor_left.x, tc_pixel_center.y,
        z_view_center - v2_dz_view_use.x
    );
// pos of right neighbor of current pixel in the shadowmap
float3 pos_sm_right =
ScreenspaceToShadowmapCoordinatesAndLightspaceDepth(
        tc_pixel_neighbor_right.x, tc_pixel_center.y,
        z_view_center + v2_dz_view_use.x
    );
// pos of lower neighbor of current pixel in the shadowmap
float3 pos_sm_lower =
ScreenspaceToShadowmapCoordinatesAndLightspaceDepth(
        tc_pixel_center.x, tc_pixel_neighbor_lower.y,
        z_view_center - v2_dz_view_use.y
    );
// pos of upper neighbor of current pixel in the shadowmap
float3 pos_sm_upper =
ScreenspaceToShadowmapCoordinatesAndLightspaceDepth(
        tc_pixel_center.x, tc_pixel_neighbor_upper.y,
        z_view_center + v2_dz_view_use.y
    );
float2 pos_sm_max =

Max(pos_sm_left.xy,pos_sm_right.xy,pos_sm_lower.xy,pos_sm_upper.xy);
float2 pos_sm_min =

Min(pos_sm_left.xy,pos_sm_right.xy,pos_sm_lower.xy,pos_sm_upper.xy);
// Approximate extent of the current pixel projected onto the
shadowmap
float2 dxy_pixel_on_shadowmap = 0.5 * (pos_sm_max - pos_sm_min);
```

```
        // Measure of resolution needed to shadow this pixel with subpixel
    accuracy
        float2 pixel_shadowmap_resolution_measure;
        // use pixel_shadowmap_resolution_measure =
        // -log2(round(dxy_pixel_on_shadowmap + float2(0.5,0.5)))/256
        frexp( sqrt(2.0) * dxy_pixel_on_shadowmap,
            pixel_shadowmap_resolution_measure);
        //pixel_shadowmap_resolution_measure *= (1.0/256.0);
        // [0,255] => [0,1] (for output to 8-bit surface)
        pixel_shadowmap_resolution_measure =
            ldexp(-pixel_shadowmap_resolution_measure, -8);
        // Postion of pixel center in the shadowmap
        float3 pos_shadowmap =
            ScreenspaceToShadowmapCoordinatesAndLightspaceDepth(
                tc_pixel_center.x, tc_pixel_center.y, z_view_center
            );
        // Output SM-tile position and resolution measure along SM x- and
    y-direction.
        OUT.color =
            float4(pos_shadowmap.x, pos_shadowmap.y,
                pixel_shadowmap_resolution_measure.x,
                pixel_shadowmap_resolution_measure.y
            );
        return OUT;
    }
```

Shadow Map Tile Grid Creation

The SMTMM contains information about the SM resolution needs of the scene as seen from the eye-point; what we need, however, is the same information as seen from the light, since this is how the SM sees the scene and this is where the decision about which SM tiles to create is made.

We create an $n \times n$ SM tile grid structure, which we call the *shadow map tile grid* (SMTG), where each grid cell holds the following:

- The required resolution along each SM axis
- A *screen space bounding rectangle* for each SM tile—an axis-aligned rectangle around the pixels on-screen that are affected by the SM tile

Here, n is the maximum number of SM slices along each SM axis we would like to allow, which corresponds to the n in $n \times n$ in VTSM above; $n=16$ or $n=32$ are typical values.

The screen space bounding rectangle is introduced here so that we can include it in the pseudo code listings. (Please see the section "Screen Space Bounding Rectangle Optimization" later to learn how it is used.)

One can think of the SMTG as a very low resolution SM ($n \times n$, $n \leq 32$), where each SM entry—instead of containing depth information—contains information about the SM resolution required in the part of the scene that is covered by the SM "texel."

The SMTMM→SMTG step requires random access operation, so the CPU is well suited for this task[7]. To create the SMTG, we read back the SMTMM to CPU memory[8] and then we lock the SMTMM surface and process each pixel entry. We use the stored information about the SM tile position to access its corresponding SM tile-grid cell and update the following:

- The needed SM resolution entries along each SM axis by maximizing the existing value with the entries in the SMTMM
- The screen space bounding rectangle (by extending it to enclose the pixel position of the current pixel in the SMTMM)

The following pseudo code illustrates the SMTG creation.

```
// smtg ... instance of the SMTG
// shift ... shift-converts from the SMTMM SM-coordinates
// entries to SMTG ones (e.g. [0,255] => [0,31])
const int shift = 256/smtg.n
// smtmm ... instance of the SMTMM
// smtmm.n ... extent of SMTMM along both axes
for ix_smtmm = 0 to smtmm.n - 1
 for iy_smtmm = 0 to smtmm.n - 1
  SMTMM_Cell c_smtmm = smtmm(ix_smtmm,iy_smtmm)
  SMTG_Cell c_smtg =
   smtg(smtmm.ix_sm >> shift,smtmm.iy_sm >> shift)
  // Update the screen-space, axis aligned bounding box
  // around the SM-tile
  c_smtg.abb_screen.ExpandToIncludePoint(
   ix_smtmm/smtmm.n,iy_smtmm/smtmm.n
  )
  // Update the maximum needed SM-resolution
  c_smtg.sm_res_x = MAX(c_smtg.sm_res_x,c_smtmm.sm_res_x)
  c_smtg.sm_res_y = MAX(c_smtg.sm_res_y,c_smtmm.sm_res_y)
```

Shadow Map Tile Grid Pyramid Creation

Next we create a pyramid of grids—called the *shadow map tile grid pyramid* (SMTGP)—on top of the SMTG as follows: We "pull up" the information stored in the SMTG by replacing 2×2 cells with one cell in a grid that has half the dimension and contains the following:

- The maximum required resolution along each SM axis values of each of the four cells
- The screen space bounding rectangle around all four bounding rectangles

We continue to do this until we arrive at a 1×1 top-level grid that has just one grid cell and contains the resolution needs for a theoretical single shadow map and that has enough resolution to shadow the entire scene with sub-pixel accuracy.[9]

Here is the SMTGP creation algorithm in pseudo code:

```
// smtg ... instance of the initial SMTG
// smtg.n ... extent of SMTG along both axes
// i_pyramid ... SMTGP index
const int i_pyramid = log2(smtg.n)
while(i_pyramid > 0)
 // smtgp ... instance of the SMTGP
 smtgp(i_pyramid) = smtg
 for ix = 0 to smtgp(i_pyramid).n - 1
  for iy = 0 to smtgp(i_pyramid).n - 1
   SMTGP_Grid_Cell c_curr = smtgp(i)(ix,iy)
   SMTGP_Grid_Cell c_parent = smtgp(i-1)(ix >> 1,iy >> 1)
   // Update the screen-space, axis aligned bounding box
   // around the parent SM-tile
   c_parent.abb_screen.ExpandToIncludeABB(c_curr.abb_screen)
   // Update the maximum needed SM-resolution
   c_parent.sm_res_x = MAX(c_parent.sm_res_x,c_curr.sm_res_x)
   c_parent.sm_res_y = MAX(c_parent.sm_res_y,c_curr.sm_res_y)
   i_pyramid = i_pyramid >> 1
```

Shadow Rendering: Shadow Map Tile Grid Pyramid Traversal

Finally we have all the necessary information in a form that can be used to shadow the entire scene with SM tiles of the required resolution. To do this, we do a top-down traversal of the SMTGP. Starting with the 1×1 top-level SMTGP cell, we recursively apply the following algorithm[10]:

- If the resolution requirement of the SMTG cell along at least one axis cannot be satisfied with an SM tile texture with dimensions supported by the GPU[11], we split it symmetrically along one or both SM axes into two or four sub-cells. We split into two sub-cells if only one axis has SM resolution requirements that cannot be fulfilled; otherwise we split into four sub-cells.
- If the resolution requirement of the SMTG cell can be satisfied, we create an SM tile with the required resolution along each axis using deferred shadowing to shadow the part of the scene that lies within the SM tile.

Here is the pseudo code for the traversal of the SMTGP.

```
// SMT ... SM-tile instance
// P ... SMTGP pos index + pyramid index
// smtq ... queue holding SMT
smtq.push(SMT(P(0,0),P(0,0)))
while(!smtq.empty())
 SMT smt = smtq.pop()
 int ip_x = smt.ip_x, int ip_y = smt.ip_y
 int sx = max(0,ip_y-ip_x), int sy = max(0,ip_x-ip_y)
 Rect rect(ix << sx,iy << sy, ((ix+1) << sx)-1,((iy+1) << sy)-1)
 // ex and ey are 0 for no further refinement, 1 otherwise
 int ex = RefineQ(smtgp(
   MAX(ip_x,ip_y)).MaxSmResInRect(rect).sm_res_x,ip_x,framebuffer.nx)
```

```
int ey = RefineQ(smtgp(
  MAX(ip_x,ip_y)).MaxSmResInRect(rect).sm_res_y,ip_y,framebuffer.ny)
if(ex > 0 || ey > 0) // refine this SM-tile further
 int ip_x_sub = smt.ix + ex, int ip_y_sub = smt.iy + ey;
 int ix_sub = smt.ix << ex, int iy_sub = smt.iy << ey;
 for diy=0 to ey
  for dix=0 to ex
   smtq.push(SMT(P(ix_sub+dix,ip_x_sub),P(iy_sub+diy,ip_y_sub)))
else // do not refine this SM-tile further
 ShadowShadowResultTextureWithSmTile(smt)
```

Apply Shadow to Scene

After the SRT has been completely shadowed (i.e., there are no more SM tiles to process), we use the SRT to shadow the scene as described in section "Virtual Tiled Shadow Mapping."

FVSM Relative Performance

One can raise the following interesting question: Does the bottleneck of the algorithm lie in transferring the SMTMM that is created on the GPU to the CPU? Many people assume the answer to be yes. Figure 4.4.6 displays the timings of the different algorithm parts for a fly-through of the forest test scene. What one immediately sees is that, by far, the most time is taken by the upmost curve depicting the timings of the shadow scene, i.e. the SMTGP traversal and SM tile creation and application to the scene. In contrast, the time it takes to transfer the SMTMM to the CPU is so small that one can barely see it in the graph. Processing the SMTMM on the CPU to create the SMTG takes around the same time as rendering the scene.

We conclude that, similar to QVSMs, FVSMs are GPU (fill-rate) limited, not CPU limited (see Figure 4.4.7). Both the screen space bounding rectangle and shadow map tile texture size optimizations described later increase (especially the worst case) performance of the algorithm by addressing this particular area.

Quality versus Performance Parameter

Fitted virtual shadow maps support an intuitive quality versus performance parameter ξ: When we subtract an integer number ξ from the logarithmic resolution requirement value in the SMTMM, when deciding whether to further refine an SM tile, we can intuitively influence the quality of the resulting shadow in the scene. The larger ξ is, the fewer tiles will be created and the better the performance will be. This allows the algorithm to run on a wide range of graphics hardware. Note that ξ influences the shadow quality of the whole scene in the same way. For large enough ξ, only a single SM tile is created and the shadow quality reverts to conventional shadow mapping. Please see Figure 4.4.6 to observe the influence of ξ in a forest test scene.

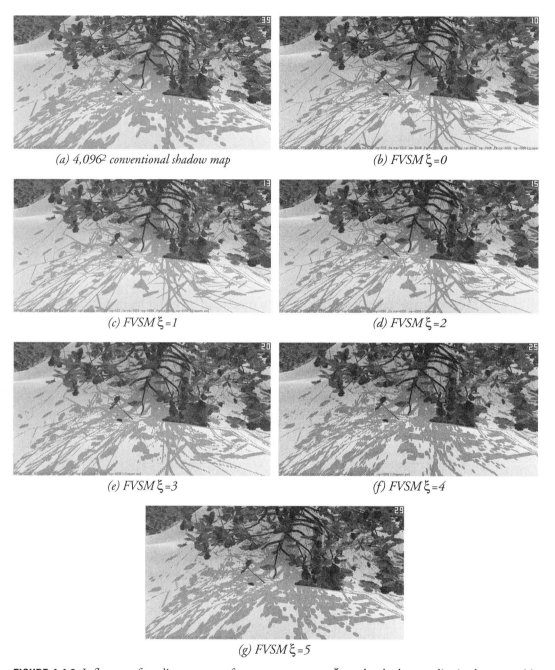

(a) 4,096² conventional shadow map

(b) FVSM ξ=0

(c) FVSM ξ=1

(d) FVSM ξ=2

(e) FVSM ξ=3

(f) FVSM ξ=4

(g) FVSM ξ=5

FIGURE 4.4.6 Influence of quality versus performance parameter ξ on the shadow quality in the scene. (a) shows conventional shadow mapping for comparison, while (b) to (g) show the same scene shadowed with FVSMs using ξ=0 to 5. For ξ=5, only one SM tile is being created, i.e., the shadow quality is the same as for conventional shadow mapping. (Please note that the performance in the scene is low due to the unoptimized rendering framework used, which unfortunately does not support batching of render calls in order to minimize texture state changes.)

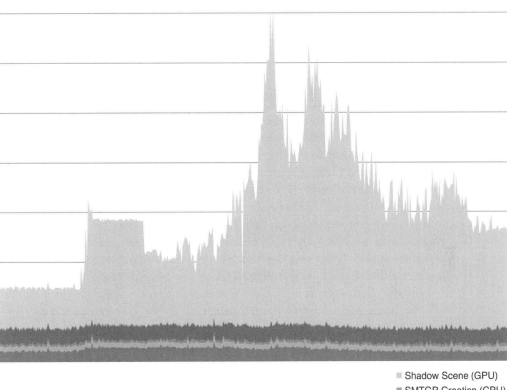

Shadow Scene (GPU)
SMTGP Creation (CPU)
SMTG Creation (CPU)
SMTMM to CPU
SMTMM Creation (GPU)
Render Scene (GPU)

FIGURE 4.4.7 The relative timings of the different parts of the Fitted Virtual Shadow Mapping algorithm. Note that the transfer of the SMTMM from the GPU to the CPU takes only a negligible amount of time, and that most time is spent in "Shadow Scene," i.e., with the creation of the SM tiles.

Screen Space Bounding Rectangle Optimization

With VTSMs and QVSMs one always has to render a full-screen quad to shadow the scene with an SM tile, thereby discarding all pixels that lie outside of the SM tile's area of influence. With FVSMs, one can keep track of the pixels that are affected by each SM tile while creating the SMTG by updating a bounding rectangle around them each time a new SMTMM entry references the SM tile in the SMTG.

When applying the SM tile to the scene, one can then use this screen space bounding rectangle instead of rendering a full-screen quad, thus reducing the fill-rate requirements of the algorithm.

When studying frame time curves, one observes that the optimization has the beneficial effect of cutting frame time peaks; we observed an increase in frame rate of around 38% in our test scene at the location of the largest frame time peak (i.e., the worst fps).

Shadow Map Tile Texture Size Optimization

The basic FVSM algorithm refines the shadow map until the required resolution of each SM tile along each SM axis is small enough that it can be satisfied with the maximum quadratic SM texture size that the GPU can handle. In practice, the resolution needs along the SM tile axes often actually do not require an SM texture that is quadratic and has the maximum GPU supported resolution; a rectangular SM texture with less resolution could be used instead.

This can be understood from the fact that there will always be perspective shortening in the scene, i.e., the pixels farther away from the eye-point will always require less SM resolution. (Note that due to the splitting of the SM into tiles, this is always the case for tiles that are farther away—independent of the view direction relative to the light direction—contrary to SM reparametrization techniques, which can only profit from the perspective shortening for light directions that are not parallel or antiparallel to the view direction.) Projection aliasing can of course counteract this, but even then, the projection aliasing does not normally influence both SM axes at the same time.

This leads to the following optimization: To reduce the fill-rate requirements of the algorithm, instead of using a quadratic maximum-sized texture for all SM tiles, we create a rectangular SM according to the resolution requirements along each axis. There are three different ways to do this:

- Render into a sub-rectangle of the same quadratic, maximum sized texture (e.g., $4,096^2$)
- Render into a sub-rectangle of a series of quadratic power-of-two shadow map textures, where each texture in the series has halved dimensions relative to its predecessor (e.g., $4,096^2$, $2,048^2$, $1,024^2$,…)
- Render into shadow map textures with the exact needed dimensions (= resolution) along each SM axis (e.g., $4,096^2$, $4,096 \times 2,048$, $2,048 \times 4,096$, $2,048^2$, $2,048 \times 1,024$, $1,024 \times 2,048$,…)

At first glance it might seem obvious that the first approach is the best since it requires the minimum amount of GPU memory. However, it is not the fastest approach because memory and cache coherence suffer when one renders to a sub-rectangle of a texture that has a larger width than the sub-rectangle. Due to this, choosing the right approach becomes a trade-off between speed and GPU memory consumption.

The memory requirements of the four different approaches are given in the following table (with t_{max} being the maximum texture dimension, and w and h being the needed minimum width and height SM texture dimensions to satisfy the SM tile resolution requirements).

Optimization	SM Dimensions	Mem Usage	For t_{max} = 4,096	fps Increase
None	t_{max}^2	1	64MB	0%
#1	w×h sub-rect of t_{max}^2	1	64MB	16%
#2	w×h sub-rect of max(w,h)^2	4/3	85MB	22%
#3	w×h	2×4/3	171MB	47%

The last column shows the relative speedup of the rendering speed in frames per second (fps) during a fly through of our forest test scene, calculated at the point of minimal fps. From studying frame time curves, we observe that the SM tile texture size optimization has a dampening effect on frame time peaks, i.e., as with the screen space bounding rectangle optimization, it leads to a higher *and* more uniform frame rate.

Further Optimizations

One fact that can easily be missed is that some of the SM tiles during the SMTGP traversal can be empty. Catching this early on instead of sending these tiles down the pipeline to be rasterized and applied is then an obvious optimization.

Another optimization with regard to the quality of the resulting shadows lies in the fact that the SMTMM naturally gets less accurate for parts of the scene that are farther away. Depending on the scene, this can, in some cases, lead to SM textures that are too small being used by the algorithm to shadow these scene parts. Fortunately there is an easy remedy: Simply introducing a lower bound on the SM texture dimensions prevents these types of artifacts. This does not negatively affect the performance of the algorithm if the lower bound is not chosen to be too large[12]. Using minimum SM texture dimensions of 256 or 512 has proven to work well in practice[13].

Soft Shadows

Due the fact that FVSMs discern beforehand what SM resolution is needed where in the scene, contrary to QVSMs, combining them with soft shadow techniques is straightforward.

The only extension needed to support SM multi-sampling is to make the SM tiles slightly larger. For a filter kernel size of θ shadow map texels, SM tiles need to overlap by θ/2 so that each tile is large enough to support the filter kernel.

To get consistent shadow softness, the kernel size θ needs to be chosen in accordance with the dimensions of the SM tile texture for each SM tile axis:

$$\theta = \max(\theta_{max} \frac{w}{w_{max}}, 1)$$

where W is the width respectively height of the SM tile, w_{max} is the maximum used SM texture size (e.g., 4,096), and θ_{max} is its corresponding filter kernel size.

The performance of using SM filtering together with FVSMs is as good as with normal SMing.

Figure 4.4.8 shows the combination of FVSMs with SM multi-sampling to create a soft shadow effect.

FIGURE 4.4.8 Fitted virtual shadow map with multi-sampling soft shadow effect.

Fog is a simple technique that applies the idea of using a distance based fog for shadowing. An important detail is that care has to be taken to make sure the shadow fog color is chosen correctly. This technique can be used in cases where there is not enough performance to use FVSMs, or the implementation effort is too high. It can also be combined with 2×2 or 3×3 VTSMs.

Current games using shadow mapping such as *Call of Juarez* or *Gothic 3* seem to use some simple variation of the algorithm by cutting off the SM(s) at a certain distance from the viewpoint smaller than the backplane distance.[14]

Instead of cutting off the SM, shadow fog fades out the shadow to an "ambient shadow value" over a certain distance, which hides the fact that we are not shadowing the whole scene:

$$f_{blend} = smoothstep(z_{fog\_start}, z_{fog\_end}, z)$$

$$ShadowValue_{use} = ShadowValue_{ambient} \cdot f_{blend} + ShadowValue_{SM} \cdot (1 - f_{blend})$$

Where $ShadowValue_{SM}$ is the shadow value that results from querying the SM (tile).

It is important to use an ambient shadow value of around 0.5 here and not 1.0 (i.e. fully lit). Blending to a fully lit scene beyond the shadow map looks strange, as if the player were standing under a "shadow cloud" (i.e., it is only dark where the player goes, whereas outside the "cloud" there is bright sunshine/light everywhere). Blending to an ambient (average) shadow value[15], on the other hand, makes shadows appear soft in a scene that is neither completely dark nor completely light, which works well in practice.

Test Hardware

The test hardware used was a P4 3.4 GHz with a GeForce 8800GS with 640 MB of RAM.

Conclusion

This article described fitted virtual shadow maps, a smart new shadow map algorithm from the virtual shadow map family. It allows for the efficient shadowing of large scenes without undersampling artifacts, and can also be combined with shadow map focusing. Virtual shadow mapping allows the algorithm to bypass the memory cost and texture size limits of current GPUs.

Compared to brute-force virtual tiled shadow mapping, FVSMs combine GPU and CPU processing to create a map beforehand that contains information about what resolution would be required where in a shadow map to give sub-pixel accuracy when shadowing the scene. This leads to a greatly reduced number of SM tiles that need to be created, and therefore a greatly increased performance over brute-force VTSMs, while still greatly reducing or even removing all shadow mapping aliasing artifacts (i.e., perspective and projection aliasing). Two optimizations to the base algorithm increase the rendering speed while at the same time making the frame rate more uniform.

Fitted virtual shadow maps can use smaller and rectangular SM tile textures for farther away SM tiles, which makes it faster than queried virtual shadow mapping, which has to use larger SM tile textures everywhere.

The shadow quality can be uniformly reduced down to normal shadow mapping by use of a very intuitive quality versus speed parameter.

The article finally introduced the technique of shadow fog, which can be used where FVSMs are not fitting; it can also be combined with virtual tiled shadow maps with four to nine shadow map tiles to further improve the shadow quality.

Endnotes

[1]Note that in 3D, usually only one SM axis will experience projection aliasing. The FVSM algorithm presented takes this into account (contrary to, e.g., cascaded shadow maps-based approaches).

[2]Please note that for less dynamic scenes one can get acceptable results with filtering conventional shadow maps (e.g. with multisampling or percentage closer filtering). However, the more dynamic a scene becomes (in terms of light sources, shadow casters, and receivers), the more the shortcomings of having too little shadow map resolution become obvious in the form of disturbing artifacts.

[3]In addition, the SRT can also be used to, e.g., apply post-processing effects to the shadow, such as screen place blurring depending on the distance to the shadow caster.

[4]Note, however, that this seems more problematic than it is in practice, since specular highlights within shadows do exist in reality—they are just coming from a different light source than the one casting the shadow.

[5]Note that CHC can also be employed to speed up SM rasterization if the depth complexity of the scene as seen from the light is high.

[6]See in the section "FVSM Relative Performance" that this is not the bottleneck of the algorithm.

[7]The SMTG creation could be done in an extra thread on a multicore CPU or on a cell processor.

[8]In practice it suffices for the SMTMM to have lower resolution than the frame buffer, e.g., 256×256, which makes the readback and CPU processing fast. (The equality of the SMTMM dimension of 256 in this example and the number of 256 distinct values in the SMTMM entries is coincidental.)

[9]Note that even for medium-sized scenes at a screen resolution of $1{,}024^2$, this theoretical SM typically has dimensions $\geq 131{,}072$ and therefore would require ≥ 64 GB of GPU memory to store.

[10]The algorithm corresponds to building an implicit kd-tree of SM tiles of the required minimal resolution.

[11]On current GPUs somewhere between 4096 and 8192.

[12]On modern GPUs it makes no difference whether the SM-tile is rasterized to a 16×64 or a 256×256 texture.

[13]Note that filling one $4{,}096^2$ texture has 64 times the fill rate requirement of filling a 512^2 texture, while shadowing a scene sub-pixel accurate with FVSMs typically requires between 10 and 16 SM tiles, i.e., texture fills.

[14]In *Call of Juarez* this is can, e.g., be observed in the first level on shadows cast by farther away trees.

[15]The ambient shadow value can be interpreted as a 0th approximation to the shadow in the scene

Acknowledgements

Part of this work was supported by the European Union in the scope of the Game-Tools Project (www.gametools.org) (IST-2-004363). Greetings to all GameTools and GameTools Special Interest Group members and middleware GameTools partner Spinor (www.spinor.com)!

The tree models for the test scene were created using the natFX® plant modeling tool (www.natfx.com).

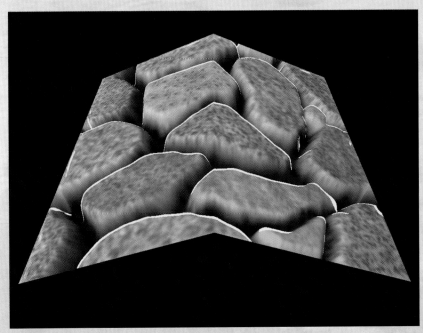

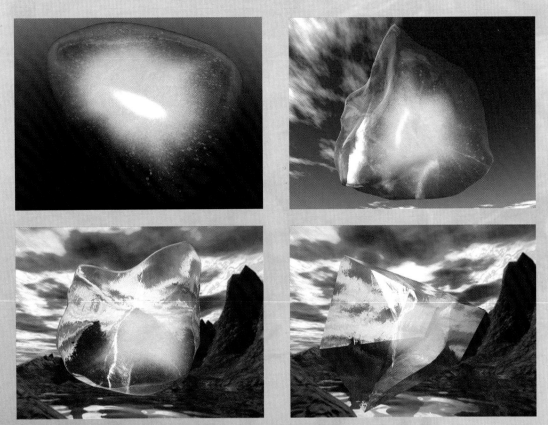

COLOR PLATES 2–5 Rendering realistic ice objects by Anders Nivfors. (See Article 5.1.)

COLOR PLATES 6–7 Sunlight with volumetric light rays by Paweł Rohleder. (See Article 5.2.)

COLOR PLATE 8 Procedural ocean effects by László Szécsi. (See Article 5.3.)

COLOR PLATE 9 Practical methods for a PRT-based shader using spherical harmonics. A rendering of a map from the PlayStation® 3 game *Warhawk*. Model generously provided by Incognito Entertainment. (See Article 6.1.)

COLOR PLATE 10 Practical methods for a PRT-based shader using spherical harmonics. Two planes from the PlayStation® 3 game *Warhawk*. Model generously provided by Incognito Entertainment. (See Article 6.1.)

COLOR PLATES 11–14 Interactive global illumination with precomputed radiance maps by László Szécsi. (See Article 6.4.)

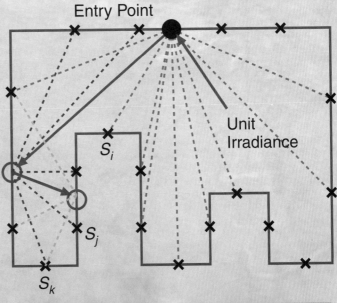

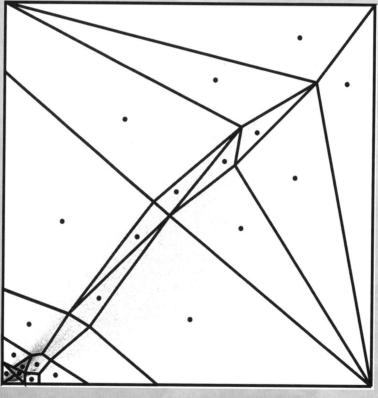

COLOR PLATES 15–17 Efficient HDR texture compression by Tze-Yui Ho. (See Article 8.3.)

Further Material

You can find additional material on the companion DVD-ROM and at
http://vsm.arscreat.com.

A more scientific publication about the algorithm appeared in the proceedings of
the 33rd Graphics Interface Conference (GI 2007) [PUB_FVSMs_GI].

References

[PUB_Practical_SMing] Brabec S., Annen T., Seidel H.-P. "Practical Shadow Mapping," *Journal of Graphics Tools* 7, 4 2002: pp. 9–18.

[PUB_Perspective_SMs] Stamminger M. and Drettakis G. "Perspective Shadow Maps," *ACM Transactions on Graphics (Proceedings of SIGGRAPH 2002),* 21(3), 2002: pp. 557–562.

[PUB_FVSMs_GI] Giegl, Markus and Wimmer, Michael. "Fitted Virtual Shadow Maps," *Graphics Interface Proceedings 2007,* CIPS, Canadian Human-Computer Communication Society, A K Peters, May 2007.

[PUB_CHC] Bittner, Jiri, Wimmer, Michael, Piringer, Harald, Purgathofer, Werner. "Coherent hierarchical culling: Hardware occlusion queries made useful," *Computer Graphics Forum (Proc. Eurographics 2004),* 23(3), 2002: pp. 615–624.

[PUB_Deferred_Shading] Hargreaves, Shawn. "Deferred shading," 2004.

Removing Shadow Volume Artifacts by Spatial Adjustment

Chi-Sing Leung (eeleungc@cityu.edu.hk)
City University of Hong Kong

Tze-Yui Ho (ma_hty@hotmail.com)
City University of Hong Kong

Tien-Tsin Wong (ttwong@acm.org)
The Chinese University of Hong Kong

Introduction

This article describes a method for removing artifacts from shadow volumes. The use of shadow volumes [1-3] is popular in games in which fast shadow generation is needed. In shadow volumes, we need to create edge-based silhouettes, but they are usually not smooth, which results in the artifact of a visibly jagged shadow boundary. Such artifacts can be reduced if a finer mesh is used, but with a tradeoff of higher computational cost. Additionally, artifacts may still exist when the viewpoint is close to an object.

The method presented here spatially shifts the shadow volume's geometry during shadow generation and forces the jagged edges to be contained within the backward-facing region of the casting geometry. In other words, the jagged edges are hidden inside the object itself. Although it is a very simple trick, it generates few visual defects compared to previous approaches.

Source of Artifacts

A shadow volume is formed by extending the silhouette of the shadow-casting object. By examining whether the point being shaded is inside or outside the shadow volume, we can quickly determine whether it is shadowed or not. To generate the shadow volume, we use the edge-based silhouette [3]. Edge-based silhouettes are created from the edges that are in between the forward-facing (facing the light source) and backward-facing (facing away from the light source) polygons. Because only existing mesh edges are tested, they produce zigzag structures that result in artifacts during shading, as shown in Figure 4.5.1.

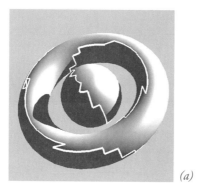 

(a)   *(b)*

FIGURE 4.5.1 The shaded image based on edge-based silhouettes, which have zigzag structures. (a) The rendered image, with white lines marking the zigzags in the shadowing; (b) the rendered image.

In *ShaderX3*, Loviscach [4] solved this problem by using sub-polygon silhouettes. In this way, the extracted silhouette becomes finer. As mentioned in [4], the backward-facing regions of a shadow volume may lie outside the corresponding forward-facing region. Hence, another type of observable artifact, namely "bright areas in the shadow," results, as shown in Figure 4.5.2.

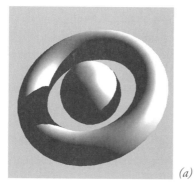 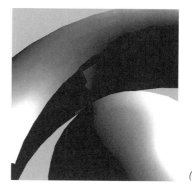

(a)   *(b)*

FIGURE 4.5.2 The shaded image based on sub-polygon silhouettes, which have a much smoother shadow boundary. However, there may be incorrect bright areas in the shadow.

Sweeping Edges Under the Carpet

We propose a method that slightly shifts the shadow volume away from the viewpoint during shadow generation (Figure 4.5.3). The basic idea of the method is to sweep things under the carpet, the "things" being the jagged shadow boundaries and the "carpet" being the backward-facing region of the casting object (Figure 4.5.4).

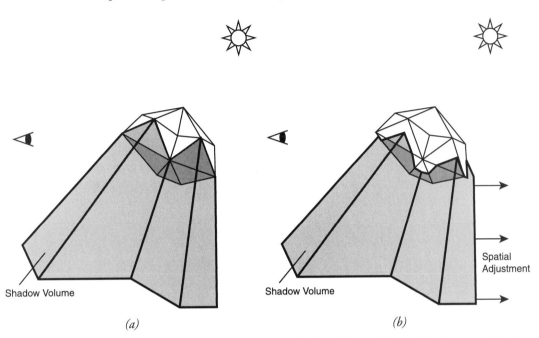

FIGURE 4.5.3 Left: Conventional shadow volume. Right: shadow volume with spatial adjustment. Notice how the intersection curves between the 3D model and the shadow volume changes.

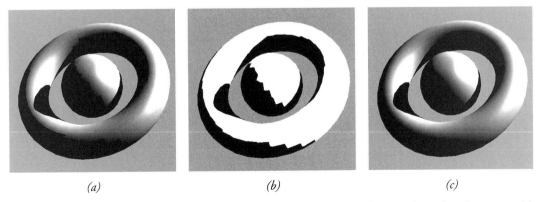

FIGURE 4.5.4 Visualization of each step of our algorithm. (a) Shadow volume without the adjustment; (b) shadow volume with the adjustment. To illustrate the effect of the adjustment, the Phong shading effect is not added in these images. (c) The shaded image after the backward-facing region is shaded darkly by the Phong shading.

This region is shaded darkly as the angle between its local normal and the light vector is greater than 90 degrees.

By properly selecting a value for this spatial adjustment, the shadow boundaries are forced to retreat and are contained in the backward-facing region. We then generate a mask with a smooth boundary to mask out the backward-facing region so as to hide the artifacts. The following sections detail each step.

Shadow Volume with Spatial Adjustment

The spatial adjustment pushes the shadow volume away from the viewpoint to cause the shadow boundary to be contained in the darkly shaded region (refer to Figure 4.5.3). As the shadow volume moves away from the viewpoint, more areas of the casting object become visible. As illustrated in Figure 4.5.3 and in images (b) and (c) in Figure 4.5.4, the intersection curve between the shadow volume and object no longer coincides with the polygonal edges of the object mesh. Instead, it shifts toward the backward-facing camera region. Obviously, pushing the shadow boundary does not generate the truly correct shadow, so it will be patched in the next step.

The vertex shader for rendering the shadow volume with spatial adjustment is as follows:

```
void shadow_volume_vp(
  float3 vec3  : POSITION,  // vertex position
  float3 an  : NORMAL,  // vertex normal

  out float4 hPosition : POSITION,  // screen position

  uniform float sview,  // spatial adjustment factor
  uniform float4 lightpos,  // light position
  uniform float4x4 mvp  // model view projection matrix
){
  float3 l, n;
  n = normalize(an);  // vertex normal
  l = normalize( lightpos.xyz - vec3*lightpos.w );  // relative light
position

  float ndotl = dot(n,l);

  float4 av;
  // extrude to inifinity if back face to light
  if( ndotl <= 0 )
    av = float4( -l, 0 );
  else
    av = float4( vec3, 1 );

  // model view transform
  hPosition = mul( mvp, av );

  // move away from view position
  if( ndotl > 0 )
    hPosition.z += sview / hPosition.w;
}
```

This code is similar to the method described by Brennan in *ShaderX* [6]. The only difference is that the *z*-coordinate of the vertex in view space, hPosition.z, is incremented by an amount sview. Note that the vertex after the view space transform is in homogeneous coordinates, so the adjustment factor should be scaled accordingly. In the code above, the shadow information is stored in the stencil buffer, which means that a mask of the shadowed region will be drawn onto the stencil buffer. Any point inside the extracted shadow volume will be shaded darkly. In general, there are two types of shadow regions. As expected, all backward-light-facing regions are inside the shadow volume. Additionally, some regions in the forward-light-facing regions are also inside the shadow volume. All of these regions are shaded darkly.

Although pushing the shadow volume away from the viewer forces the shadow boundary to retreat, the adjusted shadow edges (between forward-light-facing and backward-light-facing polygons) remain jagged, as shown in image (b) of Figure 4.5.4. If all jagged edges reside in truly backward-light-facing regions, we can cover them up at a very low cost. The simplest way is by using Phong shading [5] [7], in which backward-light-facing regions are automatically shaded darkly. As the lighting computation uses the interpolated normal and computes the illumination at every interior point of the triangle, the boundary of backward-facing regions should be smooth and pleasant, as in image (c) of Figure 4.5.4.

The shaders for Phong shading are as follows:

```
// vertex program for Phong shading
void cgfl_vp(
  float4 av : POSITION,  // vertex
  float3 an  : NORMAL,  // vertex normal

  out float4 hPosition : POSITION,  // screen position
  out float3 bv : TEXCOORD0,  // interpolated vertex
  out float3 bn : TEXCOORD1,  // interpolated vertex normal

  uniform float4x4 mvp  // model view projection matrix
){
  hPosition = mul( mvp, av );  // model view transform
  bv = av.xyz;  // interpolated vertex
  bn = an;  // interpolated vertex normal
}

// fragment program for Phong shading
void cgfl_fp(
  float3 bv    : TEXCOORD0,  // interpolated vertex
  float3 bn    : TEXCOORD1,  // interpolated vertex normal

  uniform float4 lpos,  // light position
  uniform float3 eye,  // eye position
  uniform float3 ka,  // ambient light color
  uniform float3 kd,  // diffuse light color
  uniform float3 ks,  // specular light color
  uniform float  shininess,  // shininess
```

```
    out float3 color : COLOR
){
  float3 e, n, l;
    n = normalize( bn );
    e = normalize( eye - bv );  // relative eye position
    l = normalize( lpos - bv*lpos.w );  // relative light position
  float3 h = normalize( l + e );  // half angle vector

// phong model function
  float3 lc = lit( dot(n,l), dot(n,h), shininess );
  color = ka + kd*lc.y + ks*lc.z;  // resulting reflection
}
```

Spatial Adjustment Factor

We have not yet discussed how to compute the amount of spatial adjustment, which is usually object dependent. Figure 4.5.5 shows the results of three different amounts of spatial adjustment.

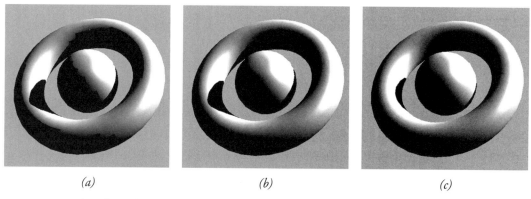

(a)   *(b)*   *(c)*

FIGURE 4.5.5 The effect of pushing the jagged edges toward the backward-facing regions. The left image is the one with shadow volume being pushed with a small amount. In the middle image, the shadow volume is being pushed with a large amount.

Although manually selecting a proper spatial adjustment factor is always feasible, we propose an automatic and systematic way to determine the amount of spatial adjustment. Empirically, the spatial adjustment factor should be roughly 0.022 times the roughness, i.e.

$$SpatialAdjustmentFactor = 0.022 * \varphi(M)$$

where $\phi(M)$ is the roughness of the object M. Roughness measures the inconsistency between face and vertex normals. Mathematically, roughness is the mean of angle deviations between face and vertex normals. Given a triangle T, we have vertices

$\{V_0, -V_1, -V_2\}$, vertex normals $\{N_0, N_1, N_2\}$, and a face normal (N_f). The area of triangle T is as follows:

$$area(T) = \left|(V_1 - V_0) \times (V_2 - V_0)\right|$$

We define the roughness of a triangle (T) as

$$\varphi(T) = (\cos^{-1}(\vec{N}_0 \cdot \vec{N}_f) + \cos^{-1}(\vec{N}_1 \cdot \vec{N}_f) + \cos^{-1}(\vec{N}_2 \cdot \vec{N}_f))/3$$

Given a mesh M, we define its roughness as

$$\varphi(M) = \frac{\sum_{T \leftarrow M} \varphi(T) * area(T)}{\sum_{T \leftarrow M} area(T)}$$

Obviously, a finely tessellated mesh gives smaller value while a coarse mesh gives higher value. This measure serves as a clear guideline in choosing a proper spatial adjustment factor.

Results

Figure 4.5.6 shows more examples: Image (a) shows the conventional shadow volume technique and image (b) shows the same scene with spatial adjustment. Note that the shadow boundaries are no longer jagged.

More rendering results are shown in Figure 4.5.7. This time, we compare our approach with the sub-polygon silhouette approach [4]. Although the sub-polygon silhouette approach can also fix jagged shadow edges, certain concave regions are lit incorrectly. Such artifacts are the so-called "bright areas in the shadow" [4]. With spatial adjustments, there are no such artifacts.

(a)   *(b)*

FIGURE 4.5.6 Shaded images: (a) conventional shadow volume; (b) shadow volume with spatial adjustment.

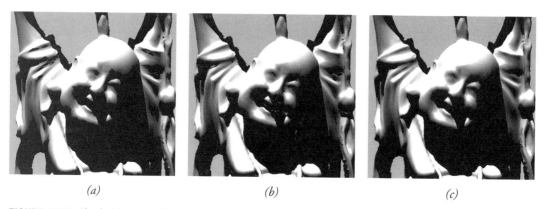

(a)   *(b)*   *(c)*

FIGURE 4.5.7 Shaded images: (a) conventional shadow volume; (b) shadow volume with sub-polygon silhouette; (c) shadow volume with spatial adjustment.

Code Availability

The sample `obj_shadow_volume_ug` on the companion DVD-ROM implements the proposed artifact removal technique for shadow volume. In particular, sv.cg, the Cg script file, contains the shaders for rendering shadow volume with spatial adjustment, covering mask, and Phong shading [5].

Acknowledgments

The work is supported by research grants from City University of Hong Kong (Project No. 7001850) and CUHK RGC grant (Project #417005).

References

[1] Crow, F. C. "Shadow Algorithms for Computer Graphics," *SIGGRAPH 1977*: pp 242–248.

[2] Heidmann, Tim. "Real Shadows Real Time," *IRIS Universe*, Number 18, 1991: pp. 28–31.

[3] Everitt C. and Kilgard, M. "Practical and Robust Stenciled Shadow Volumes for Hardware-Accelerated Rendering," http://developer.nvidia.com/, 2002.

[4] Loviscach, Jörn. "Silhouette Geometry Shaders," *ShaderX³*, 2004: pp. 49–56.

[5] Fernando, Randima and Kilgard, Mark J. "The fragment Program for Per-Fragment Lighting," *The Cg Tutorial*, 2003: pp. 124–125.

[6] Brennan, Chris. "Shadow Volume Extrusion using a Vertex Shader," *ShaderX*, 2002: pp. 188–192.

[7] Phong, B. T. "Illumination for computer generated pictures," *Communications of ACM*, Vol. 18, Iss. 6, 1975: pp. 311–317.

ENVIRONMENTAL
EFFECTS

Introduction

Matthias Wloka

Visual Concepts, Take Two Inc.

When I review the initial draft of an article, I always examine the submitted pictures first. When doing so for *ShaderX6*'s "Environmental Effects" section, I marveled at Anders Nivfors' pictures for his article "Rendering Realistic Ice Objects." His reference photographs of ice are exceptional: crisp, in focus, and well exposed. By the time I looked at the third one, however, I wondered how he was able to take photographs of ice cubes floating in midair. After briefly imagining him throwing an ice cube up and trying to take a picture before it fell back down, it dawned on me that these pictures are not photographs at all, but screenshots (see the full-color plates in the middle of this book). I am stunned.

All the articles in this section produce exceptionally high-quality results, yet do so in a practical manner, i.e., in real-time with time left over to run a game. To see their effects in motion, please run the demos on the book's accompanying DVD-ROM. To simplify replicating these results in your own work, all of the demos come with full source code.

As mentioned, Anders Nivfors describes how to render ice in his article "Rendering Realistic Ice Objects." Every frame of his technique generates a couple of textures per ice object that the ice's surface shader uses. One texture is the result of lighting geometrically modeled cracks inside the ice. While the article describes how to clip these cracks to the ice object in real-time, clipping could be a preprocess. Another texture holds a volume rendering of impurities inside the ice. Finally, the last dynamic texture contains the ice object's back-side normals. The ice's surface shader combines these dynamic textures with two static ones (a bump map and a bump mask) to produce convincing images of ice.

Paweł Rohleder and Maciej Jamrozik explain how the game *Call of Juarez* renders volumetric light rays in their article "Sunlight with Volumetric Light Rays." The technique is a post-process that operates on a down-sampled and blurred copy of the frame buffer. It masks light intensities far from the screen space center of the sun and then radially blurs the remaining light before blending the result into the frame buffer. Because the technique is a post-process, its performance is independent of scene complexity and integrates easily into existing games, especially ones already incorporating other post-processes.

Last, but not least, László Szécsi and Khashayar Arman share how to efficiently render large bodies of water in "Procedural Ocean Effects." Their article goes beyond the usual "deform a screen space mesh with sine waves and render with normal mapping." Instead, they pay attention to the all important details. In particular, their waves are trochoidal and deform upon approaching land. They model waves breaking and washing up on shore while always ensuring a continuous water boundary. They simulate wave-crest foam with a GPU-computed particle system. Their water shader accounts for water depth and view angle and addresses aliasing issues. Finally, they show how to properly animate objects floating on the water's surface and how to approximate realistic reflections.

5.1

Rendering Realistic Ice Objects

Anders Nivfors

EA Digital Illusions CE

Rendering natural phenomena in real-time is always challenging. Research on rendering ice in particular is scarce. This article describes how to render realistic ice objects in real-time. We identify the most important characteristics of ice and describe how to model them. The result is a comprehensive and flexible method that applies to any convex 3D model.

Different types of ice have varying shape, color, and optical properties. For example, ice frozen in a freezer is usually white due to an abundance of tiny bubbles trapped in the ice; melting ice has a smooth and reflective surface; ice in a below-freezing environment is typically rough and bumpy. But different types of ice also share common characteristics, e.g., ice typically has a multitude of small imperfections such as cracks and bubbles—these imperfections distinguish it from, say, glass. Ice reflects and refracts light and other objects, resulting in specular highlights, and ice has an irregular shape and is more or less bumpy.

Our method captures all of these characteristics of ice, allows tweaking them in real-time, and thus is capable of creating numerous types of ice. Figure 5.1.1 shows several examples, as do figures in the color plates section in the middle of the book.

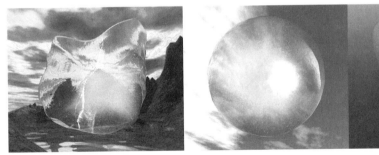

FIGURE 5.1.1 Various depictions of ice rendered using the method proposed in this article.

Method Overview

Given a 3D model, the method proposed here renders an ice object with an arbitrary amount of the following: cracks, air bubbles and particles, reflections of light sources and the environment, two-sided refraction, and bump mapping and bump masking. We describe each of these steps in its own section, followed by a summary that shows how these steps work together. The implementation is in OpenGL and Cg and is available with complete source and shader code on the book's DVD. The appendix at the end of this article also lists the complete ice shader.

Adding Cracks

In nature, an ice object usually cracks when it experiences an above-freezing temperature. The cracks appear as brighter, often curved surfaces inside the ice. We approximate this phenomenon by adding crack meshes rendered with a shader that only computes bump-mapped specular highlights. Consequently, if no specular highlighting occurs, cracks are completely transparent. Each crack in the ice is a separate object and renders without back-face culling, i.e., as a two-sided surface. All cracks alpha blend into a single texture using a frame buffer object (FBO) [Juliano06].

While the shader is simple, the difficulty lies in creating appropriate crack objects. We use a number of generic crack models that are at least as big as the biggest ice object to be rendered. We then randomly rotate and position these crack objects inside an ice object and clip along the surface of the ice model using the clipping algorithm described momentarily.

This approach is straightforward, fast, and produces convincing results. It also allows us to dynamically add an arbitrary number of cracks to any convex ice object.

Clipping

Our clipping algorithm uses a screen space CSG (Constructive Solid Geometry) method to perform a Boolean difference. [McReynolds96] describes a method that uses a stencil buffer as a second depth buffer; our method is similar, but it uses texture writes and shaders to perform the clipping.

We use the ice object's depth values for its front- and back-facing surfaces to clip the cracks (see Figure 5.1.2). To generate these depth values at optimal resolution, we first compute v, the vector from the camera to the center of the ice object, and d, the vector representing the diagonal of the ice object's bounding box. Setting the near and far planes to

```
nearPlane = v.GetLength() - d.GetLength()/2.0;
farPlane  = v.GetLength() + d.GetLength()/2.0;
```

results in a near plane just in front of the ice object and a far plane just behind the ice object, so the generated depth values have optimal resolution.

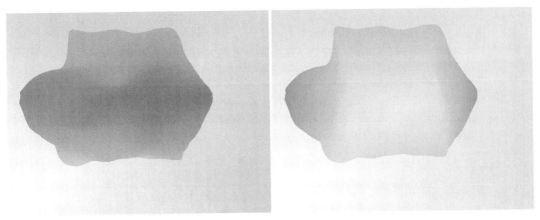

FIGURE 5.1.2 The depth values of the front-facing surfaces (left) and the back-facing surfaces (right). Depth values range from the near clipping plane (black) to the far clipping plane (white).

The OpenGL utility function `gluPerspective` sets these near and far plane values and we clear the old projection and model view matrices. To generate the back-face depth values, we render the ice object using the following code with `backface` set to true and `id` set to the texture to hold the back-face depth values. Similarly, to generate the front-face depth values, we call the code with `backface` set to false and `id` set to the texture to hold the front-face depth values.

```
void RenderDepthValuesToTexture(bool backface, int id)
{
    // save current draw buffer
    int currentDrawBuffer;
    glGetIntegerv(GL_DRAW_BUFFER, &currentDrawBuffer);
    // no color buffer needed
    glDrawBuffer(GL_NONE);
    glReadBuffer(GL_NONE);
    // bind the FBO
    glBindFramebufferEXT(GL_FRAMEBUFFER_EXT, id);
    // set viewport size
    glViewport(0, 0, 512, 512);
    glClear(GL_DEPTH_BUFFER_BIT);
    if (backface) //set winding order
        glFrontFace(GL_CW);
    // Insert code to render the ice object here
    if (backface) //set winding order
        glFrontFace(GL_CCW);
    glViewport(0, 0, windowWidth, windowHeight);
    glDrawBuffer(currentDrawBuffer);
    glBindFramebufferEXT(GL_FRAMEBUFFER_EXT, 0);
}
```

We then render all the cracks using a shader that performs bump mapping and specular highlighting. In addition, the fragment shader samples the two depth textures and compares the current pixel's depth value with the corresponding texels in the depth textures. If the value is not between the sampled values, we reject that pixel since it is outside the ice object. Figure 5.1.3 shows an example with one crack.

The resulting texture saves the resulting image of the clipped and lit crack objects. The ice object's shader samples this texture during the final rendering pass.

Note that the GeForce 6600 and other, older NVIDIA graphics cards exhibit some precision artifacts during this processing step that are absent when using ATI graphics cards or newer NVIDIA cards such as the GeForce 8 Series. The artifact makes the edges of the cracks jagged.

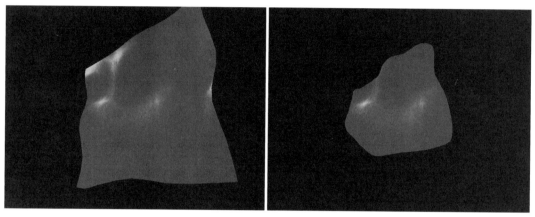

FIGURE 5.1.3 The crack model without clipping (left) and the final clipped crack (right). For better visibility we colored the crack gray in these pictures; normally only the specular highlights are visible.

Air in the Ice

The white color of ice is a result of air bubbles inside the ice. The density of air bubbles increases as their proximity to the center of the ice increases, forming something best described as an air core.

To re-create the impression of a volumetric air core, it suffices to render 10–15 two-sided, semi-transparent, texture-mapped quadrangles inside the ice object. The texture contains air bubbles and white noise (see Figure 5.1.4).

We randomly rotate each quadrangle's plane around the center of an ice object. Because each plane passes through the center, the intersection of each plane and the ice object's bounding box yields at least four intersection points. We then only choose rotations that result in exactly four intersection points. Because the bounding box is generally larger than the ice object, we scale these four intersection points by 0.9 and then use these points as the corners of the quadrangle (see Figure 5.1.5).

We render the planes into a texture using an FBO. Figure 5.1.6 shows the resulting image. The final rendering pass of the ice object is going to sample this texture.

FIGURE 5.1.4 Example of an air texture: To be able to control the number of bubbles and avoid patterns, we use several different air textures.

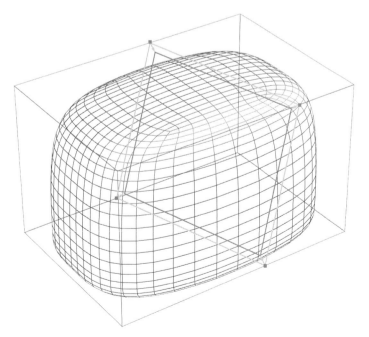

FIGURE 5.1.5 The bounding box-plane intersection and the resulting air-textured quadrangle.

FIGURE 5.1.6 The volumetric air core rendered to a texture.

Reflection and Two-Sided Refraction

To emulate reflection and refraction, we employ cubic environment maps (cube-maps). A cubemap requires dynamic update if the ice objects or any other object in the scene moves. To update the cubemap, we position the camera at the center of the ice object, set its field of view to 90 degrees, and point it toward one of the cubemap faces. After rendering the scene six times, i.e., once for every cubemap face, all texels in the cubemap contain up-to-date data.

To compute the reflection of a surface point, we reflect the eye vector on the surface's normal (using Cg's `reflect` function) and use the resulting reflection vector to look up a color value in the cubemap.

Refraction is more complicated because light refracting through an object typically has an entry and an exit point. A cheap approximation is to only refract light on the front-facing surfaces. We use two-sided refraction instead in a method similar to [Wyman05].

We therefore require access to the back-side normals of an ice object when rendering its front side. In preparation for rendering the ice object, we first render its back-side's normals to a texture by rendering the back-facing faces of the ice object with a shader that uses a pixel's normal as output color. To minimize performance overhead we render to this texture using an FBO.

The ice object shader now has access to both the front- and back-side normals. Instead of computing proper refraction at the entry and exit points of a light ray, we simply mix the front- and back-side normals before looking up the cubemap. `weight` defines how much impact the back side's normal has; here we use a value of 0.33:

```
half3 newNormal = normal * (1.0 - weight) - backSideNormal * weight;
```

While not physically correct, it is a reasonable tradeoff for increased performance [Seipel07], because ice is a highly distorting material. Figure 5.1.7 shows the result of our two-sided refraction method.

FIGURE 5.1.7 Model of a teapot rendered using the ice shader with air and cracks turned off. The left image shows one-sided refraction and the right image shows two-sided refraction using mixed normals.

To mix the reflection and refraction colors sampled from the cubemap, we use a coarse but fast approximation of the Fresnel equation, similar to the one proposed by [Jensen01]:

$$f = (1- \mid eyeVector \bullet normal \mid)^3$$

1

The ice object's vertex shader calculates the Fresnel term f and passes it on to the fragment shader, where it determines how much refraction or reflection is visible per pixel. Please refer to the shader code in the appendix at the end of this article for details.

Environment Bump Mapping and Bump Masking

Because ice is a highly distorting material, we bump map its surface to add detail and make it appear uneven. An ice object's fragment shader uses a normal map (see Figure 5.1.8). We generate this normal map as a combination of fractal noises and Photoshop filters. The fragment shader also uses a bump mask (also shown in Figure 5.1.8). This bump mask is a grayscale texture that determines where to apply the normal map and serves to make the surface more irregular by adding small cracks and extra details.

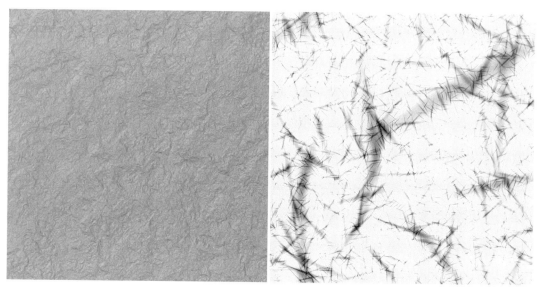

FIGURE 5.1.8 The normal map (left) and the bump mask (right) of an ice object.

Using different scales on the normal map and the bump mask counteracts repeating patterns on the object's surface. An alternative method is to blend the bump map and the bump mask before rendering, but doing so generates a less appealing, blurrier result.

The ice object's fragment shader computes a per-pixel surface normal as follows. First it samples the normal-map and bump-mask textures and multiplies them. Second, it scales the result with a scalar value that represents the bump strength, typically set at 0.5. Finally, it subtracts the resulting vector from the interpolated vertex normals. This calculation of the normal affects the reflections, refractions, specular highlighting, and sampling of the air and cracks' textures because they all make use of the surface normal.

Final Touches

To make the ice's surface visible even in an empty environment with poor lighting, the red channel of the normal map is multiplied by a small amount, approximately 0.15, and added to the final pixel's RGB value in the ice object's fragment shader. This tweak adds a barely visible texture to the ice surface. It makes the ice object a bit brighter, but we compensate for that by multiplying a pixel's final color by 0.88.

Finally, the commonly used Phong lighting equation adds specular highlights to the ice. Figure 5.1.9 shows how all the rendering passes of the proposed method fit together.

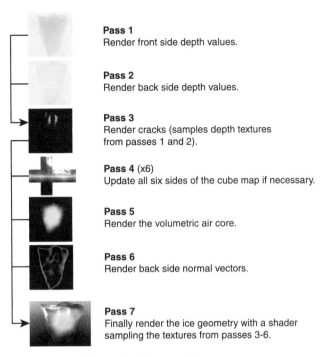

Pass 1
Render front side depth values.

Pass 2
Render back side depth values.

Pass 3
Render cracks (samples depth textures
from passes 1 and 2).

Pass 4 (x6)
Update all six sides of the cube map if necessary.

Pass 5
Render the volumetric air core.

Pass 6
Render back side normal vectors.

Pass 7
Finally render the ice geometry with a shader
sampling the textures from passes 3-6.

FIGURE 5.1.9 Graph of all the rendering passes.

Conclusion

This article presents a method for real-time rendering of ice. The meshes used for the
ice objects can have arbitrary shapes, although convex meshes work best. We identify
and model the most important characteristics of ice and implement them so that performance is in real-time using standard graphics hardware. Because our method performs several render-to-texture operations, it is important to implement these
operations efficiently. We use OpenGL's FBO extension [Juliano06]. Pixels thus render directly to a texture. Using FBOs is more efficient than, say, rendering to the
frame buffer and then copying it to a texture.

When rendering a model with 14,976 faces using our proposed method on a
GeForce 6600 GT, we achieve a frame rate of 172 fps at 1024×768 resolution (with
ice covering 1/5 of the screen and all FBO attached textures set to 512×512, except
for the back-facing normals texture, which is set to 1024×768 to avoid filtering artifacts). When putting an ice object in an interactive scene with 7,716 faces, thus forcing us to update the environment cubemap in each frame, the frame rate drops to 93
fps.

Figure 5.1.10 and color plates found in the middle of the book show the results
of our method.

FIGURE 5.1.10 Our method produces realistic ice renderings in real-time.

Acknowledgements

I would like to thank Stefan Seipel, professor in computer graphics at Uppsala University and Gävle University, with whom I worked on the paper "Real-time Rendering of Ice" [Seipel07] to create the method described in this article.

References

[Jensen01] Jensen, Lasse Staff and Golias, Robert. "Deep-Water Animation and Rendering," available online at http://www.gamasutra.com/gdce/2001/jensen/jensen_01.htm, April 2006.

[Juliano06] Juliano, Jeff and Sandmel, Jeremy (contact persons). "Framebuffer Object Extension Specification," available online at http://oss.sgi.com/projects/ogl-sample/registry/EXT/framebuffer_object.txt, May 2006.

[McReynolds96] McReynolds, Tom and Blythe, David. "Programming with OpenGL: Advanced Rendering," *ACM SIGGRAPH, Course 23,* 1996: pp. 31–42.

[Seipel07] Seipel, Stefan and Nivfors, Anders. "Real-Time Rendering of Ice," *IASTED Computer Graphics and Imaging,* 2007: pp. 60–66.

[Wyman05] Wyman, Chris. "An Approximate Image-Space Approach for Interactive Refraction," *Proceedings of ACM SIGGRAPH 2005*: pp. 1050–1053.

Appendix: The Ice Shader

The following code is the complete vertex and fragment shaders used to render an ice object.

```
struct VertIn
{
    half4 pos     : POSITION;
    half3 normal  : NORMAL;
    half3 tCoords : TEXCOORD0;
};
```

```
struct VertOut
{
    half4 pos      : POSITION;  // clip space position
    half3 tCoords  : TEXCOORD0; // texture coordinates
    half3 vertPos  : TEXCOORD1; // used for proj. tex. coords
    half3 viewVec;             // the view vector (aka eye vector)
    half3 normal;              // the surface's normal
    half  fresnelVal;          // the Fresnel value
    half3 lightVec;            // the light vector
};
struct FragOut
{
    half4 col      : COLOR0; // final pixel color
};
// the vertex shader
VertOut mainV(VertIn          IN,
              uniform half3    camPos,           // world cam pos
              uniform half3    lightPos,         // world light pos
              uniform float4x4 modelViewProjMatrix,
              uniform float4x4 modelMatrix,      // model matrix
              uniform float4x4 modelMatrixIT)    // inv. Transp.
{
    VertOut OUT;
    // world space position
    half4 pos = mul(modelMatrix, IN.pos);
    // world space view vector
   OUT.viewVec = pos.xyz - camPos;
    // world space light vector
    OUT.lightVec = pos.xyz - lightPos;
    // world space normal
    OUT.normal = mul(modelMatrixIT, half4(IN.normal, 0.0)).xyz;
    // coarse fresnel approximation
    half fres  = 1-abs( dot(normalize(OUT.viewVec),
                        normalize(OUT.normal)));
    OUT.fresnelVal = fres * fres * fres;
    // just pass the texture coordinates to the fragment shader
    OUT.tCoords = IN.tCoords;
    // transform model space position to clip space
    OUT.pos = mul(modelViewProjMatrix, IN.pos);
    // save pos xy and w (to calculate projected texture
    // coordinates in fragment shader)
    OUT.vertPos.xy = OUT.pos.xy;
    OUT.vertPos.z = OUT.pos.w;
    return OUT;
}
// the fragment shader
FragOut mainF(VertOut          IN,
              uniform sampler2D  backSide,     // back side normals
              uniform sampler2D  bumpMask,     // bump mask
              uniform sampler2D  bumpMap,      // bump map
              uniform samplerCUBE envMap,      // environment map
              uniform sampler2D  cracks,       // the cracks
              uniform sampler2D  core,         // the air core
              uniform half       eta,          // rel. refr. index
              uniform half       bumpStrength, // bumpmap impact
              uniform half       backSideRefr) // back side impact
```

```
{
    FragOut OUT;
    // calculate screen space texture coordinates, divide by w
    // (saved as z) and moved from range [-1, 1] to [0, 1]
    half2 texCoordsProj = 0.5 * (IN.vertPos.xy/IN.vertPos.z) + 0.5;
    // get bump map value
    half3 bumpCol = tex2D(bumpMap, IN.tCoords.xy);
    // get bump mask color
    half3 bumpMaskCol = tex2D(bumpMask, IN.tCoords.xy);
    // get back side normal
    half3 backSideNormal = 2 * tex2D(backSide, texCoordsProj) - 1;
    // normalize vectors and displace normal with bump map
    backSideNormal = normalize(backSideNormal);
    IN.normal   = normalize(IN.normal —
                            bumpCol*bumpStrength*bumpMaskCol);
    IN.viewVec  = normalize(IN.viewVec);
    IN.lightVec = normalize(IN.lightVec);
    // calculate reflection and refraction vectors
    half3 reflectVec = reflect(IN.viewVec, IN.normal);
    half3 refractVec = refract(IN.viewVec, IN.normal*(1.0-
backSideRefr) -
                                        backSideNormal*backSideRefr,
                            eta);
    // calculate specular highlight
    half spec = pow(clamp(dot(IN.lightVec.xyz, -reflectVec), 0.0,
1.0),
                    20.0);
    half3 specCol = spec;
    // get environment map color
    half3 refrCol = texCUBE(envMap, refractVec);
    half3 reflCol = texCUBE(envMap, reflectVec);
    // get cracks texture color, distort the texcoords
    // with the worldspace normal
    half3 crackCol = tex2D(cracks,
                            texCoordsProj — 0.013*IN.normal.xy);
    // get air texture color, distort the texcoords with
    // the world space normal
    half3 coreCol = tex2D(core,
                            texCoordsProj — 0.02*IN.normal.xy);
    // set final pixel color
    OUT.col.rgb = (((crackCol+refrCol)*(1.0-coreCol.x)+coreCol)
                    *(1.0-IN.fresnelVal)
                    + reflCol*(IN.fresnelVal)
                    + bumpCol.rrr*0.16)*0.88 + specCol;
    return OUT;
}
```

5.2

Sunlight with Volumetric Light Rays

Paweł Rohleder

Techland

Maciej Jamrozik

Techland

Introduction

Modern graphics hardware allows the realistic rendering of open-space environments. Indeed, there are plenty of approaches for imitating natural environmental effects such as sunlight, water, or clouds.

Our work proposes a new way of rendering sunlight with volumetric light rays. Our technique is a post-process that selectively blooms parts of the rendered scene. Changing the size and intensity of a radial blur mask allows for smooth and subtle sunlight rays. This post-process works in combination with glow and tonemapping effects [Ward03], as Figures 5.2.1 and 5.2.2 (and various color plates in the middle of the book) illustrate.

How It Works

Our technique consists of several simple post-processing operations, and requires three render-targets: a main render-target that contains the rendered scene at full resolution, i.e., width times height; a one-sixteenth size temporary render-target, Temp0, of resolution width/4 × height/4; and another one-sixteenth size temporary render-target, Temp1, of resolution width/4 × height/4.

Figure 5.2.3 illustrates the steps for rendering sunlight with volumetric light rays. They are as follows:

1. Render the scene and any sunlight flares into the main render-target.
2. Down sample the main render-target into Temp0.
3. Horizontally blur Temp0 into Temp1 the same way as in the DirectX HDRLighting sample [Microsoft07].
4. Vertically blur Temp1 into Temp0 [Microsoft07].

FIGURE 5.2.1 Sunlight with volumetric light effects in the game *Call of Juarez* [Techland07].

FIGURE 5.2.2 Volumetric light rays shining through trees.

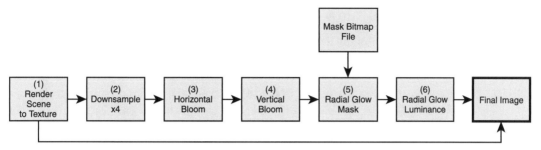

FIGURE 5.2.3 The post-process pipeline that creates sunlight with volumetric light rays.

5. Calculate a radial glow mask from `Temp0` and store it in `Temp1`. We describe this step in detail in the next section.
6. Calculate a radial glow luminance from `Temp1` and store it in `Temp0`. This step also warrants its own section later.
7. Finally, add `Temp0` to the main render-target to produce an image in the back buffer [Microsoft07].

Calculating the Radial Glow Mask

The radial glow mask modulates the blurred image of the rendered scene. Pixels far away from the sun exhibit little or no glow. To achieve this effect we conceptually center a small grayscale gradient texture at the screen space position of the sun and multiply its texels with the corresponding pixels of the blurred scene. Figure 5.2.4 shows an example of a gradient texture. Because this gradient texture has no abrupt changes, it can be low resolution, say, ×32 texels. Scaling this texture either in screen-space size or in intensity achieves a variety of different looks.

FIGURE 5.2.4 Grayscale gradient texture used to compute the radial glow mask.

To implement this concept, we render a full-screen quad that samples both the blurred image of the scene and the grayscale gradient texture and then multiplies the two values. The trick is in computing appropriate texture coordinates for sampling the gradient texture so that it aligns with the sun's center in screen space. The vertex shader (see Appendix A at the end of this article) thus computes the sun's position in screen space and uses it as texture coordinates. Appendix A provides full source code for both vertex and pixel shaders for this step.

Calculating the Radial Glow Luminance

The radial glow luminance step radially blurs pixel intensities from the sun's screen space center outward. Because such a scatter operation is difficult to implement on today's GPUs, we transform this step into a gather operation. Each rendered pixel computes the line connecting it to the sun's screen-space position and places n samples equidistantly along this line. We assign a weight to each sample, which falls off linearly with distance to the sun's center. Finally, we compute and output the weighted sum of the radial glow mask's texels at these sample points.

The vertex shader computes the sample points as an array of texture coordinates and passes them to the pixel shader, which then samples the radial glow mask and computes the weighted sum. Appendix B at the end of this article lists both the vertex and pixel shaders.

Conclusion

Because our method is a post-process, it is independent of a scene's complexity and thus widely applicable. It easily integrates into any existing post-processing pipeline. Finally, it introduces low overhead since its computation is lightweight and only applies to a render-target that is one-sixteenth the size of the frame buffer.

The book's accompanying DVD includes a demo application that encodes our technique. The demo is using D3D's effects framework and requires DirectX 9.0c and a shader model 2 GPU to run.

Acknowledgments

We thank Jakub Klarowicz from Techland for proofreading this article.

References

[Microsoft07] "HDRLighting," DirectX C++ Sample application, Microsoft DirectX SDK, September 2007.

[Techland07] Techland Development, "Call of Juarez," http://www.callofjuarez.com.

[Ward03] Ward, Greg. "High Dynamic Range Image Encodings," available online at http://www.anyhere.com/gward/hdrenc/, 2003.

Appendix A: Radial Glow Mask Shaders

Listing 5.2.1 The vertex and pixel shader for calculating the radial glow mask

```
VS2PS RadialGlowMaskVS( float4 vPos       : POSITION,
                        float2 vTexCoord0 : TEXCOORD0,
                        float2 vTexCoord1 : TEXCOORD1)
{
    VS2PS output;
```

```
    // transform to screen space [-1, 1]
    output.vPos.xy = 2.0f * vPos.xy * SH_RENDER_TARGET_PARAMS.xy -
1.0f;
    output.vPos.y *= -1;
    output.vPos.zw = float2(0.5f, 1.0f);
    // transform sun position to screen space [-1, 1]
    float4 sunPos = mul(SH_SUN_POS, SH_MAT_COMBINED);
    float2 ts = float2(sunPos.x / sunPos.w, -sunPos.y / sunPos.w);
    // texture coordinates for source render target
    output.vTexCoord0.xy = vTexCoord0.xy;
    // use sun position in screen space to determine texture
    // coordinates for glow mask
    output.vTexCoord0.zw = vTexCoord0.xy - 0.5f * ts.xy;
    return output;
}
float4 RadialGlowMaskPS( float4 vTexCoord0 : TEXCOORD0 ) : COLOR0
{
    // sample render target
    float4 diff1 = tex2D( g_samSrcColor, vTexCoord0.xy );
    // compute pixel luminance
    float luminance = dot( diff1.xyz, 1.0f/3 );
    // adjust lighting contrast
    diff1 *= luminance;
    // sample glow mask
    float4 diff2 = tex2D( g_samMaskColor, vTexCoord0.zw );
    // combine render target and the mask
    return diff1 * diff2;
}
```

Appendix B: Radial Glow Luminance Shaders

Listing 5.2.2 The vertex and pixel shader for calculating the radial glow luminance

```
#define NSAMPLES_2 8          // number of samples divided by 2
#define NSAMPLES (NSAMPLES_2*2)  // real number of samples
#define STEP (1.0f/NSAMPLES)  // radial glow step
#define SCALE_FACTOR -2.5f    // texcoord scale factor

// scale texcoords
float2 NTexcoord( float2 Texcoord, int iIdx, float3 c )
{
    float Scale = sqrt(iIdx) * c.z + 1.0;
    return ( Texcoord.xy - c.xy ) * Scale + c.xy;
}
VS2PS RadialGlowLuminanceVS(float4 vPos       : POSITION,
                           float2 vTexCoord0 : TEXCOORD0,
                           float2 vTexCoord1 : TEXCOORD1)
{
    VS2PS output;
    // transform to screen space [-1, 1]
    output.vPos.xy = 2.0f * vPos.xy * SH_RENDER_TARGET_PARAMS.xy -
1.0f;
```

```
    output.vPos.y *= -1;
    output.vPos.zw = float2(0.5f, 1.0f);
    // transform sun position
    float4 sunPos = mul(SH_SUN_POS, SH_MAT_COMBINED);
    // determine sun position in screen space and texcoord scale factor
    float3 ts = float3(( sunPos.x / sunPos.w) * 0.5f + 0.5f,
                       (-sunPos.y / sunPos.w) * 0.5f + 0.5f,
                       SCALE_FACTOR / (NSAMPLES)));
    // calculate n = N_SAMPLES different mappings for sun radial glow
    int j=0;
    for (int i=0; i<NSAMPLES_2; i++)
    {
    output.vTexCoord0[i].xy = NTexcoord(vTexCoord0.xy, j, ts);  j++;
    output.vTexCoord0[i].zw = NTexcoord(vTexCoord0.xy, j, ts);  j++;
    }
    return output;
}
float4 LuminancePS( float4 vTexCoord0[NSAMPLES_2] : TEXCOORD0 ) :
COLOR0
{
    float4 col = 0;
    float  lum = 1.0f;
    // sample radial glow buffer with different mappings and
    // decreasing luminance
    for (int i=0; i<NSAMPLES_2; i++)
    {
    col += tex2D(g_samSrcColor, vTexCoord0[i].xy) * lum;  lum -= STEP;
    col += tex2D(g_samSrcColor, vTexCoord0[i].zw) * lum;  lum -= STEP;
    }
    return col * 0.25f;
}
```

5.3

Procedural Ocean Effects

László Szécsi

Budapest University of Technology

Khashayar Arman

Budapest University of Technology

Introduction

Ocean scenes are enjoying a great deal of interest. The quest is on to achieve ever more realism in real-time. Most attempts, however, rely on artist-drawn textures or an overly simplified model for ocean-wave motion and superposition. Recent articles make the most of this approach [Kryachko05][Chi06], but a combination of elevation maps or different wavelength sine functions do not provide realistic shallow-water waveforms and do not allow for lateral motion of water particles. These approaches, therefore, cannot provide plausible clues for the motion of waterborne objects. Furthermore, the intersection of a sine wave ocean with a terrain surface yields unrealistic beach waves that lack deformation, breaking, or a continuous water boundary.

Research results based on wave mechanics exist. Fournier [Fournier86] presents the most complete framework, but he does not target real-time rendering or scan conversion image synthesis. Hinsinger et al. [Hinsinger02] devise a real-time system for open ocean, and Gamito et al. [Gamito02] propose an offline, precomputation-based approach for wave refraction.

In this article we present a real-time simulation and rendering approach based on procedural vertex displacement. Real-world physics of ocean waves guides how waves change in length, shape, and direction due to ocean bottom and beach geometry. For breaking and swashing waves, where a continuous surface model becomes insufficient, we employ particle systems and texture effects. We also show how to implement the motion and reflection of waterborne objects. Figure 5.3.1 and one of the color plates in the middle of the book show the result of our work. The book's DVD includes full source code to the sample application used to produce this screenshot.

FIGURE 5.3.1 All the procedural ocean effects in action as described in this article.

Ocean-Wave Mechanics

Open Ocean Waves

As a wave travels across an ocean, it transports energy, but not water. A water droplet on the ocean's surface traces a circular path, and the combined profile of particles orbiting at different phases forms the moving wave. The resulting shape is that of a trochoid. We initially discuss the mechanics of such waves in 2D, where waves travel along the x-axis and the y-axis signifies up.

An amplitude a and a wavelength λ fully characterize a wave: They correspond to the radius of the droplet path and the distance the wave moves during one orbit, respectively (see Figure 5.3.2). A wave's celerity v expresses how fast a wave travels.

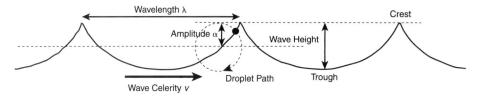

FIGURE 5.3.2 Our ocean wave nomenclature.

Equation 1 describes the relationship between the celerity and the wavelength of an idealized wave [Nave06]:

$$v = \sqrt{\frac{g\lambda}{2\pi}}$$

1

where g is the acceleration of gravity. The initial phase ϕ_0 for a given particle at position x is

$$\varphi = 2\pi \frac{x}{\lambda}$$

2

For the phase ϕ at time t we add the phase speed $2\pi v/\lambda$ multiplied by elapsed time t:

$$\varphi = \varphi_0 + 2\pi \frac{x}{\lambda} t = 2\pi \frac{x + vt}{\lambda}$$

3

The displacement vector **s** describing the circular motion is

$$s = a[-\cos\varphi, \sin\varphi]$$

4

Figure 5.3.3 shows trochoidal waves of a single wavelength.

FIGURE 5.3.3 Exaggerated trochoidal waves of a single wavelength.

Wave Refraction in Shallow Water

When the ocean bottom becomes close to the water surface, it begins to influence the motion of surface water particles (see Figure 5.3.4). In shallow water, waves travel slower and their wavelengths shorten (see Figure 5.3.5) while their period stays the same [Anthoni2000].

Equation 5 expresses the dependence of the shortened wavelength λ_r on the water depth d [Nave06]:

$$\lambda_r = \lambda \sqrt{\tanh \frac{2\pi d}{\lambda}}$$

5

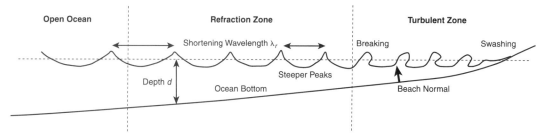

FIGURE 5.3.4 The three different wave zones: open ocean, refraction zone, and turbulent zone.

FIGURE 5.3.5 Waves slow down and shorten in shallow water.

When the waves have varying wavelengths, our formula $2\pi v/\lambda$ (see Equation 2 above) for the initial phase no longer holds. Instead, we find the phase up to position x by integrating

$$\varphi_0 = \int_0^x \frac{2\pi}{\lambda\sqrt{\tanh\frac{2\pi(\xi)}{\lambda}}}d\xi$$

6

where $d(\xi)$ is depth as a function of position. We assume the beach is rising linearly, and thus depth is

$$d(x) = A + Bx$$

7

where B corresponds to beach steepness. In this case, an exact analytic expansion of the above integral exists, but it is too expensive to use in a shader. We propose a simpler formula that is a close approximation for arbitrary parameter values:

$$\varphi_0 = \frac{2\pi}{\lambda}(x + \frac{4\pi}{B}(1 - e^{-4\pi d/\lambda}))$$

8

For arbitrary depth functions, it is impossible to find a locally computable analytic solution because terrain features all along the path of the wave influence the motion of a droplet. The term

$$D = 1 - e^{-4\pi d/\lambda}$$

9

in the preceding formula is a good indicator of how near we are to the beach, with a unit value representing the open ocean and decreasing toward the shore. We refer to it as the *beach distortion factor* and make further use of it later.

When waves arrive at a beach at some angle, the part that is already in shallow water slows down first. This behavior bends the wave to be more parallel to the beach, an effect known as *wave refraction*. The phenomenon automatically emerges from the use of the above mechanics, ensuring realistic wave behavior along beaches. As a result, waves always appear to be approaching the beach and never move away from it (see Figure 5.3.6).

Breaking and Swashing Waves

Because water does not pass through terrain, terrain hinders the vertical movement of shallow water particles, turning droplet orbits into flattened ellipsoids (see Figure 5.3.7). With decreasing wavelength, waves also become steeper. When a wave grows too high compared to its length, it becomes unstable and white foam appears as the crest collapses forward, breaking the continuous surface. Waves break when their

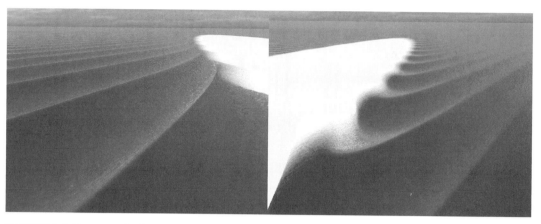

FIGURE 5.3.6 Because of refraction, waves bend to the beach even on the leeward side of an island.

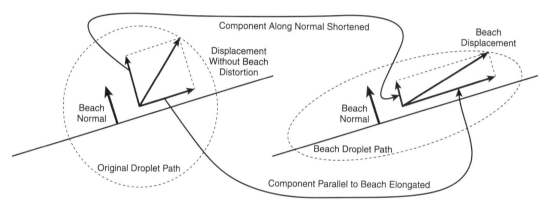

FIGURE 5.3.7 Droplet paths distort into ellipsoids near the beach.

height is more than 1.3 times the depth [Anthoni2000]. When the wave hits the beach, the motion of its droplets becomes turbulent and thus is inexpressible by an explicit formula.

When modeling swashing waves, we ensure that waves distort forward as they run up the beach and that there is always a single continuous water boundary (as in Figure 5.3.8). While we forfeit strict physical modeling, we use transformations inspired by real-world phenomena. The droplet displacement resolves into components parallel and perpendicular to the surface normal of the ocean bottom. The *beach distortion factor D* (refer to Equation 9) scales the parallel component while it divides the perpendicular component, thus achieving a flattening ellipsoid orbit. As a result, profiles near the beach resemble that of plunging waves.

To model breaking waves, we set up a breaking threshold at a depth of $2.6a$, where a is the amplitude (half of the wave height). Particles in water shallower than the breaking threshold are in the swashing zone, where they no longer move according to wave mechanics. We assume this zone instantaneously fills and drains with

FIGURE 5.3.8 Our technique ensures a continuous water boundary.

breaking waves, and rely on the distortion formula at the breaking threshold to determine an appropriate water level.

Final Displacement Formula

Using the above mechanics, we now compute the wave displacement of a droplet at position **p** in 3D. Coordinate axis y is still upward, but now the wave direction **k** is a unit vector on the $y = 0$ plane. **U**, **Y**, and **V** are the unit coordinate vectors. x, y, and z denote the components of vector **p**. If $d(\mathbf{p})$ is smaller than $2.6a$, then for the purposes of computing displacement, we use the breaking point in place of **p**. We find the breaking point by translating **p** along the surface normal vector of the beach—the exact formula depends on the terrain definition.

First, we obtain the beach distortion factor:

$$D = 1 - e^{-4\pi d/\lambda}$$
$$10$$

Then phase ϕ is

$$\varphi = \frac{2\pi}{\lambda}(p \cdot k + vt + \frac{4\pi D}{B})$$
$$11$$

The displacement without beach distortion, denoted by **s**, is

$$s = a(Y\sin\varphi - k\cos\varphi)$$

12

s is resolved into components parallel and perpendicular to the beach normal **b**, and is recombined after scaling with D to obtain the final displacement **q**:

$$q(p,a,\lambda,k) = (s\cdot b)sD + (s - (s\cdot b)s)\frac{1}{D}$$

13

For the superposition of n waves, defined by amplitudes a_i, wavelengths λ_i and directions k_i ($i = 0..n$), the new position of a droplet originally at **p** is

$$p_\Sigma = p + \sum_{i=0}^{n} q(p, a_i, \lambda_i, k_i)$$

14

where **q** is from Equation 13 above.

Partial Derivatives of Displacement

From the above displacement formula, the derivative of undistorted displacement **s** with respect to phase is

$$\frac{\partial s}{\partial\varphi} = a(-Y\cos\varphi - k\sin\varphi)$$

15

and after distortion:

$$\frac{\partial q}{\partial\varphi} = (\frac{\partial s}{\partial\varphi}\cdot b)\frac{\partial s}{\partial\varphi}\frac{1}{D} + [\frac{\partial s}{\partial\varphi} - (\frac{\partial s}{\partial\varphi}\cdot b)\cdot b)]D$$

16

The derivatives of phase ϕ with respect to the two horizontal components of **p**, denoted by x and z, are

$$\frac{\partial\varphi}{\partial x} = (\frac{2\pi}{\lambda} + \frac{32\pi^3 e^{-4\pi d/\lambda}}{\lambda^2})k_x$$

$$\frac{\partial\varphi}{\partial z} = (\frac{2\pi}{\lambda} + \frac{32\pi^3 e^{-4\pi d/\lambda}}{\lambda^2})k_z$$

17

thus the partial derivatives of **q** are

$$\frac{\partial q}{\partial x} = \frac{\partial q}{\partial \varphi}\frac{\partial \varphi}{\partial x} = \frac{\partial q}{\partial \varphi}(\frac{2\pi}{\lambda} + \frac{32\pi^3 e^{-4\pi d/\lambda}}{\lambda^2})k_x$$

$$\frac{\partial q}{\partial z} = \frac{\partial q}{\partial \varphi}\frac{\partial \varphi}{\partial x} = \frac{\partial q}{\partial \varphi}(\frac{2\pi}{\lambda} + \frac{32\pi^3 e^{-4\pi d/\lambda}}{\lambda^2})k_z$$

18

The partial derivatives of the displaced ocean surface in the initial plane are thus the sum of the partial derivatives of the displacements for all waves:

$$\frac{\partial p_\Sigma}{\partial x} = U + \sum_{i=0}^{n}\frac{\partial q(p, a_i, \lambda_i, k_i)}{\partial x}$$

$$\frac{\partial p_\Sigma}{\partial z} = V + \sum_{i=0}^{n}\frac{\partial q(p, a_i, \lambda_i, k_i)}{\partial z}$$

19

The cross product of the two partial derivatives provides the surface normal direction of the final displaced ocean surface:

$$N = \frac{\partial p_\Sigma}{\partial z} \times \frac{\partial p_\Sigma}{\partial x}$$

20

Ocean Geometry

Mesh Covering the Visible Surface

Theoretically, our ocean is an infinite plane displaced by superimposed waves. To draw it, a vertex shader applies a procedural wave displacement to a planar mesh. The infinite extent of the plane and the necessary resolution to depict waves requires a prohibitive number of triangles if we store the mesh in world space. A view-dependent tessellation of the ocean plane that only renders visible parts and provides more detail near the camera avoids this problem. Ideally, the screen size of all triangles is uniform for maximum efficiency. Projecting a screen space grid back onto the ocean plane [Chi06] achieves these traits. Figure 5.3.9 depicts the complete process, which we discuss in detail throughout this section.

We start with a screen space mesh with corner coordinates of *(–1,–1)*, *(1,–1)*, *(–1,1)*, and *(1,1)*. The inverse of the view-projection matrix transforms the points of that mesh to world space. We clip the resulting quadrilateral to the horizontal plane of the eye in world space, since the ocean only extends below the horizon. Clipping the corners of the mesh suffices to clip the quadrilateral; the CPU performs this operation and passes the resulting four clipped corners to the vertex shader as uniform parameters.

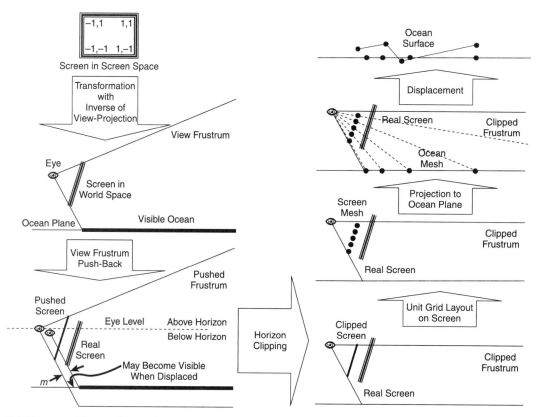

FIGURE 5.3.9 The mesh transformation pipeline.

The resolution of the screen space mesh is critical. Because we back project it to world space, the in-world locations of the mesh vertices vary depending on the camera: The sampling points of the wave-displacement function move as the camera moves. If the grid is dense enough, with triangles far smaller than the waves, the exact positions of the vertices are inconsequential; they express the same waveform. When using a sparse grid, however, a non-constant reconstruction error causes disturbing flickering and distortion of the wave geometry whenever the camera moves.

In particular, if the mesh resolution is too coarse along the width of the screen, then a periodic pattern appears and causes disturbing flickering when the camera moves. The tessellation style of the mesh also influences the sampling errors. A diamond tessellation for the screen space mesh, i.e., one where every other row of vertices shifts horizontally by half a quad, is superior to a rectangular tessellation (see Figure 5.3.10). Using a diamond tessellation we find that as few as 32 horizontally evenly distributed vertices suffice for a full-screen, but reasonably calm, ocean.

Along the screen height—that is, toward the horizon—more samples are necessary because the ocean stretches to infinity at the horizon and waves thus become arbitrarily dense. Vertex displacements thus change abruptly when moving the camera,

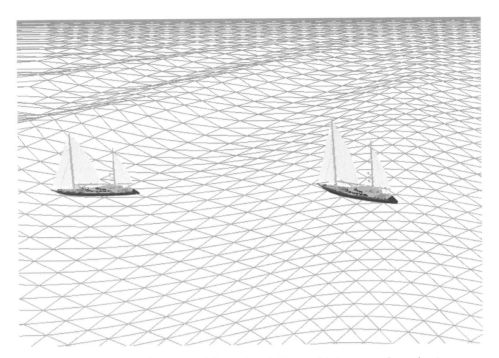

FIGURE 5.3.10 A diamond ocean grid shown in wireframe; this is coarser than what is actually used to show structure.

causing flickering near the horizon. Intersections with terrain geometry are similarly sampling-error prone. To reduce these sampling errors, we attenuate the displacements with distance: Distant waves are individually indistinguishable in reality anyway. Using attenuation we find a vertical grid resolution of 512 vertices to be adequate.

The resulting grid of 32×512 vertices is visually appealing, yet the ensuing 32k vertices hardly challenge the performance of current graphics hardware.

To render the mesh, the vertex shader interpolates the clipped mesh corners in world space according to each vertex's grid position. It then projects the resulting world-space position along the view direction onto the ocean plane. The result is a finely tessellated plane covering the screen below the horizon. Because waves later displace the mesh vertices, the grid distorts and its boundaries may thus become visible on-screen. We therefore push the viewpoint and the back-projected plane backward, resulting in an extended mesh that covers more than the visible area (refer to Figure 5.3.9). The amount we push back the view frustum is

$$\frac{m}{\sin \Phi / 2}$$
21

if m is the maximum displacement and Φ is the field-of-view angle.

Wave Displacement

A superposition of various wave functions, arriving from different directions, generates the chaotic ocean surface. All of them are composed of the trochoidal motion of individual water particles. Our wave dynamics become increasingly realistic the more wave functions we add. An array in an HLSL effect file containing wavelength, amplitude, and direction per wave compactly defines the wave functions. The vertex shader evaluates the mechanics formulae for all waves to find the displaced vertex position (refer to Equation 14) and the ocean surface normal (refer to Equation 20).

The ocean bottom and terrain geometry is either defined procedurally or read from a texture. In either case, we require both water depth values and terrain surface normals to compute the beach wave distortion.

Screen Depth Transformation

Although our ocean is infinite, the Z-buffer depth test still requires values between 0 and 1. Therefore, the vertex shader transforms the output z coordinates exponentially with

$$z_{out} = (1 - e^{-z_n / w_h}) w_h$$

22

where z_h and w_h are the homogenous coordinate components after the view-projection transformation. To obtain the correct depth occlusion, all other geometry, such as ships or terrain, must use the same depth transformation as the ocean, i.e., Equation 23.

Surface Shading

Water Color

It is the responsibility of the pixel shader to compute the color of the ocean. How reflective the water surface is depends on the view angle [Chi06]. An approximate Fresnel term $F(\theta)$ [Lazányi05]:

$$F(\theta) = 0.02 + 0.98 \cdot (1 - \cos \theta)^5$$

23

where θ is the angle between the surface normal and the view direction, describes this relative reflection. The radiance toward the eye is $F(\theta)$ times the incoming radiance C_{env} from an ideal reflection direction (read from an environment cubemap) plus $(1 - F(\theta))$ times the refracted radiance exiting the water, which is the water color C_{water}.

If we look at water from above, we are looking into the depths where little light is present. When we look at water from a shallow angle, however, we see light scattered in the upper layers. Interpolating between a deep color C_{deep} and a shallow color

$C_{shallow}$ according to the cosine of the view angle models this effect. When the ocean bottom is close, its color gradually replaces that of the water; letting the beach distortion factor D linearly interpolate between the water color and the ocean-bottom color achieves this behavior. Three consecutive interpolations thus compute the final water surface color C:

$$c_{water} = c_{deep} \cos \theta + c_{shallow}(1 - \cos \theta)$$

$$c_{wb} = c_{water}D + c_{bottom}(1 - D)$$

$$c = c_{env}F(\theta) + c_{wb}(1 - F(\theta))$$

$$24$$

Ripple and Foam Maps

While our trochoidal waves define the major geometry of the ocean (refer to the section "Ocean Geometry" earlier in this article), there are always chaotic ripples that are important in conveying a convincing water surface. An animated normal map solves the problem. Similarly to the wave geometry, superposing several different wavelengths and speeds ensures chaotic-looking behavior without noticeable periodicity (see Figure 5.3.11).

FIGURE 5.3.11 The ocean surface with and without bump-mapped ripples.

Beach foam is a complex phenomenon to model. A simulation would have to track a large number of foam particles born on breaking waves and forming intricate patterns. We are looking for a more tractable, yet convincing solution: We use the same trick as with wave ripples and combine a foam normal texture with itself at different periods (see Figure 5.3.12).

The vertex shader passes the local tangent, binormal, and normal vectors for normal mapping [Szirmay07]. These vectors are the wave displacement derivatives $\delta p_\sigma/\delta x$, $\delta p_\sigma/\delta z$ (refer to Equation 18), and their cross product, respectively. The pixel shader reads the normal map at different frequencies and sums the results to get

FIGURE 5.3.12 Bump-mapped beach foam.

a combined normal in tangent space. Using the vertex shader provides vectors as a transformation matrix; the tangent space normal becomes a world space normal.

The beach distortion factor decides whether we use this normal to render ripples or beach foam. We use the water color shading formula (refer to the section "Water Color" earlier in this article) for rendering ripples and a simple white diffuse BRDF for the foam.

MIPmapping

When the camera is moving, pixels near the horizon jump large distances from frame to frame. Accordingly, they represent very different waves and ripples from one frame to the next. Without appropriate filtering, they thus generate noisy fuzz instead of a smoothly blended average color as in reality. To filter the horizon we thus filter both the displacement waves and the ripples.

Decreasing the amplitudes of the displacement waves with distance filters them. We use the cosine of the viewing angle of the ocean plane as an attenuation factor; it is slightly modified to keep nearby waves undistorted.

To filter the ripples, we find the average radiance reflected to the eye from all the differently aligned ripples that fall within a pixel. Simply applying MIPmapping to the normal map is insufficient; an average normal turns the ocean into a perfect mirror near the horizon. We thus also have to MIPmap the environment map. Because graphics hardware does not interpolate across cubemap faces, we disallow sharp changes when generating the MIPmap levels of the environment cubemap. Each MIPmap level is computed as a logarithmic function of the distance from the camera.

Crest Foam Particle System

When waves break and swash, they generate foam. Our distorted plane model assumes a continuous ocean surface, so it cannot represent breaking waves. Furthermore, foaming waves generate complex volumetric phenomena that are expensive to model and render. Trying to approximate surface foam with some kind of normal mapping technique produces unsatisfactory results. We therefore add extra particle billboards to wave crests to emulate foam.

The GPU performs both the particle simulation as well as the rendering steps. A texture stores particle positions; every row represents a generation of particles (see Figure 5.3.13). The simulation step renders into a double-buffered texture. It fills the first row with newly generated particles and copies all others from the row above, thus aging them. To seed new particles with random positions, we use the quasi-random Halton sequence [Halton60] with different base primes for each column.

The particle positions are in screen space, just like the ocean mesh. In the rendering step, the vertex shader projects the positions onto the ocean plane and moves them up to the nearest wave crests. Unfortunately, finding a wave crest is difficult. While our procedural generation method knows where to move a point, finding the local maxima of the sum is not explicit. We solve this problem iteratively: During

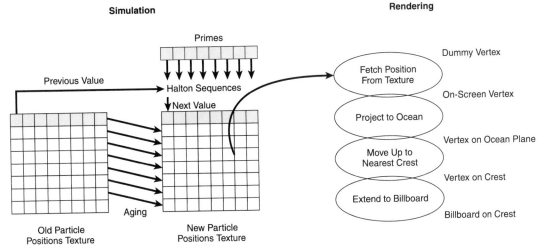

FIGURE 5.3.13 The particle system simulation on the GPU.

every simulation step we move all particle positions up the wave along its $\delta\mathbf{p}/\delta y$ derivative until it reaches a local maximum. During each simulation step, a few particles remain in troughs, slipping from crest to crest as the waves move (see Figure 5.3.14). To suppress these particles we simply skip drawing them.

Every particle renders as an alpha-blended rectangular billboard. We transform its vertices so that each billboard aligns with its wave crest and then rotate it around the wave crest direction to face the viewer (see Figure 5.3.15). A vertex shader achieves these goals when moving vertices of the billboards apart from each other by translating them along the wave-crest direction and the cross product of the wave crest and viewing directions. We approximate the local wave-crest direction using a linear combination of the individual wave-crest directions of the component wave functions, weighting them according to the local vertical distortion they cause. The alpha value of billboards depends on their age and elevation: particles fade in and out, and are more transparent if they are in a trough.

FIGURE 5.3.14 Particles move to the nearest wave crest. While the final technique does not draw particles that remain in troughs, we depict them here for illustration purposes.

FIGURE 5.3.15 Computing the orientation of particle billboards: One billboard axis is aligned on the wave crest direction (dark arrow) and the other is perpendicular to both the wave crest and the view direction (light arrow).

Floating Objects

The lateral component of wave displacements becomes most prominent when also rendering waterborne objects. For example, in order to place a ship, we evaluate the displacement and derivative formulae as for the water surface displacement (refer to Equations 14 and 19). The CPU computes the displacement, normal, tangent, and binormal vectors for the root node of a ship and stores the resulting transformation matrix in a dynamic vertex buffer. Doing this computation for all ships and uploading all resulting matrices into a vertex buffer, we then use geometry instancing to render all ship instances at once. Evaluating the displacement in a vertex shader is inadvisable because this computation would repeat for all vertices in a ship's model.

The reflection of objects on water is crucial to give them presence. In our case, we cannot assume that the ocean surface is planar, as we want to be able to handle objects far smaller than the waves themselves. Our solution is to perform ray casting along the reflected eye ray in the pixel shader that renders the ocean surface. Given that the ripples of the water severely distort reflections, a simple substitute of the ship's geometry suffices for computing the ray-object intersections (see Figure 5.3.16). We use

FIGURE 5.3.16 Ripples mask the use of ellipsoid proxies that model a ship's geometry for its reflection.

quadratic surfaces, namely two ellipsoids per ship. A reflected ray tests intersections with all ships. If there is an intersection, the pixel shader uses the color of the nearest ship instead of the environment map value for the Fresnel reflection.

Conclusion

We implement the above technique using Shader Model 3.0. It runs in real-time on current generation hardware, such as an NVIDIA GeForce 8800 GTX. The most performance intensive parts of the technique are the particle system and the raytracing for floating objects. The particle system devours fill-rate as it draws a high number of possibly sizeable alpha-blended billboards. Raytracing performance also deteriorates quickly with a high number of floating objects. On a GeForce 7900GX we measure 45 fps for rendering with foam particles and 60 fps without them at a screen resolution of 1024×768. On a GeForce 8800 GTX, these figures are 90 fps and 120 fps, respectively.

If Shader Model 4.0 is available, further optimizations are possible. We can save GPU memory by using the geometry shader to draw the planar meshes, i.e., the ocean plane and the foam billboards. We can eliminate the CPU computing the displacement for floating objects by rendering the ocean vertices to an output stream and letting the CPU access this output stream.

We do not discuss the reflection of terrain and other on-land geometry, since existing solutions [Chi06] work well enough. We also omit shadows cast onto the water surface, which any shadow algorithm solves.

References

[Anthoni2000] Anthoni, J. F. "Oceanography: Waves, Theory and Principles of Waves, How They Work and What Causes Them," available online at www.seafriends.org.nz/oceano/waves.html, 2000.

[Chi06] Chi, Y-F. "True-to-Life Real-Time Animation of Shallow Water on Today's GPUs," *ShaderX4: Advanced Rendering Techniques,* Wolfgang Engel (editor), Charles River Media, Hingham, Massachusetts, 2006: pp. 467–480.

[Fournier86] Fournier, A. and Reeves, W. T. "A Simple Model of Ocean Waves," *SIGGRAPH '86,* 1986: pp. 75–84.

[Gamito02] Gamito, M. N. and F. K. Musgrave, "An Accurate Model of Wave Refraction over Shallow Water," Computers and Graphics, volume 26, number 2, 2002: pp. 291–307.

[Halton60] Halton, J. H. "On the Efficiency of Certain Quasi-Random Sequences of Points in Evaluating Multi-Dimensional Integrals," *Numer Math,* 2, 1960: pp. 84–90.

[Hinsinger02] Hinsinger, D., Neyret, F., M-P. Cani, M-P. "Interactive Animation of Ocean Waves," *Proceedings of the 2002 ACM SIGGRAPH/Eurographics Symposium on Computer Animation,* 2002: pp. 162–166.

[Kryachko05] Kryachko, Y. "Using Vertex Texture Displacement for Realistic Water Rendering," *GPU Gems 2,* 2005: pp. 283–294.

[Lazányi05] Lazányi, I. and Szirmay-Kalos, L. "On the Fresnel Approximation for Metals," *WSCG Conference,* Short papers, 2005.

[Nave06] Nave, C. R. "HyperPhysics," available online at http://hyperphysics.phy-astr.gsu.edu/hbase/waves/watwav2.html, 2006.

[Szirmay07] Szirmay-Kalos, L. and Umenhoffer, T. "Displacement Mapping on the GPU – State of the Art," to be published in *Computer Graphics Forum* 2007.

GLOBAL ILLUMINATION

Introduction

Carsten Dachsbacher

There is no such thing nowadays as a book on shader programming without a section on global illumination methods, and this book is no exception. It is obvious that, due to the increasing computational power of GPUs, more complex lighting techniques migrate into real-time rendering. Although the flexibility of GPUs is growing as well, for example with the geometry shaders available now, many global illumination methods suffer from a more inherent "problem" of GPUs: The hardware for rasterizing geometry is not designed to determine the light transport between arbitrary surfaces on a global scale. Nevertheless, our smart contributors found practical methods for precomputed global illumination and efficient real-time approximations.

In the article "Practical Methods for a PRT-Based Shader Using Spherical Harmonics," Jerome Ko, Manchor Ko, and Matthias Zwicker provide an introduction to lighting computations with spherical harmonics and share their in-depth analysis of coefficient generation, quantization, and compression. They also provide a demo demonstrating speed improvements and quality of their quantization schemes.

In 6.2, Hannu Saranaari and his co-authors present their incremental instant radiosity method: It renders single-bounce indirect light by accumulating the contribution from virtual point light sources distributed across the surfaces in the scene. By maintaining and incrementally updating the set of VPLs and deferred shading techniques, they achieve indirect illumination at high frame rates.

Vlad Stamate, in his article "Real-Time Photon Mapping Approximation on the GPU," describes an approximation to global illumination by adapting the idea of photon mapping to real-time applications. He describes how to achieve this with a relatively low number of photons, little memory consumption, and incremental refinement of the solution.

The article "Interactive Global Illumination with Precomputed Radiance Maps" by László Szécsi, László Szirmay-Kalos, and Mateu Sbert presents a new technique of precomputed radiance transfer; partial light paths between surface points are computed in a preprocessing phase and stored in textures for real-time rendering.

Practical Methods for a PRT-Based Shader Using Spherical Harmonics

Jerome Ko

Manchor Ko

Matthias Zwicker

With the power of graphics hardware today, global illumination effects and shadows remain a difficult task to achieve with efficiency. To capture illumination from a complex environment, per-vertex lighting requires the accumulation of light from all directions, which can be extremely slow at runtime. An attractive alternative is to precompute the irradiance and light transfer function at each vertex and to store this data in some reasonable form. This method has been dubbed *precomputed radiance transfer* (PRT). By computing how light is transferred to vertices, resulting in their final color during the preprocess, we are able to vastly simplify this step during runtime. Due to the spherical nature of environment lighting, a naturally fitting choice is to use spherical harmonics. For diffuse surfaces, implementing PRT using spherical harmonics allows for an efficient representation of global illumination effects, including self-shadowing and interreflections. We can also add dynamic elements such as moving lights and objects while still maintaining much of the realism.

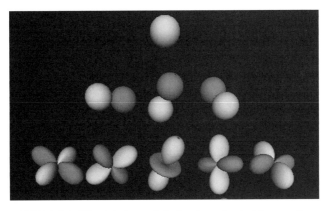

FIGURE 6.1.1 The 0th through 2nd order spherical harmonic functions.

PRT and Ambient Occlusion

Ambient occlusion (AO) was first introduced into computer graphics by [Landis02], and [Pharr04] eloquently demonstrated the tremendous visual quality improvement when using AO as opposed to diffuse environment lighting only. Notice the image on the left in Figure 6.1.2: The geometry is uniformly lit and lacks contact shadows. The middle image is rendered with AO, and on the right is a rendering using our PRT implementation. Note the dramatic improvement in the visual quality of the image and the nice soft shadows.

AO is best treated as the simplest version of PRT: a single scalar is stored that encodes the percentage of the hemisphere above the normal that is unoccluded. This factor is used at runtime to modulate the lighting. However, AO does not encode any directional variation of illumination—the self-shadowing does not respond to changes in lighting direction. Valve's "radiosity basis" and Crytek's SSAO are both attempts to address this issue. However, the mathematical foundation of Valve's approach is not robust and Crytek's approach requires a lot of texture accesses in the fragment shader.

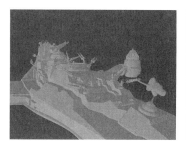

FIGURE 6.1.2 Renderings comparing no shadowing, AO, and PRT, respectively. The model is from the PlayStation 3 game *Warhawk*, and is generously provided by Incognito Entertainment.

The Main Idea

The essence of the PRT technique is to separately compute the light source(s) and transfer functions. To use spherical harmonics, a function is projected onto the spherical harmonic basis, which results in a number of coefficients. The original function is now represented as a linear combination of the SH functions. The shapes of the SH functions illustrated in Figure 6.1.1 show how each basis function effectively covers a different part of the sphere. While projecting a function onto the spherical harmonic basis may seem like a daunting task, in the first part of this article we will show you how simple it is to implement PRT. We will focus mainly on diffuse shadowed transfer of distant lighting because of its simplicity. Extensions to glossy BRDFs, interreflections, and local lighting require more computations and increased memory usage. In the second part of the article, we will present some classic signal processing concepts and use them to compress the PRT data from 36 bytes down to 4–6 bytes per vertex. The frame-rate speedup due to these compression techniques is quite good; for the Buddha model with 1.08m triangles, we can obtain 33 fps on a mobile ATI X700 and over 250 fps on a GeForce 8800. Next, we will present two more sophisticated methods using Lloyd-Max relaxation and an effective noise-resistant method [Lam06] to improve accuracy. In the end, along with the sample code provided, readers should be much more confident about implementing PRT in their own graphics applications.

Implementation Details: Preprocess of the Environment Map

First, we need some representation of a light source. [Ramamoorthi 01-2] presents a method for projecting an environment map onto the spherical harmonic basis as a means to light diffuse surfaces. The method by itself does not do shadows, but it is a good start.

We started with sample code from Ramamoorthi's website [Ramamoorthi02] to get a set of SH coefficients for our environment map. This was relatively painless[1] and the runtime calculation requires only a matrix-vector multiplication and a dot product[2]. No per-vertex data is needed besides vertex positions and normals.

Ramamoorthi's code, however, is limited to the first nine spherical harmonics. We want a general framework to calculate SH basis functions of any order, and so we turn to [Green03] for this. This gives us the option of using the higher order functions in case we want to render glossy surfaces or to get more detailed shadows.

To project the environment map onto the spherical harmonic basis, we loop through all the pixels, each time weighing the color by the appropriate spherical harmonic. That gives us nine RGB lighting coefficients L_{lm}. The $l \leq 2$ indexes the order of the appropriate spherical harmonic function Y_{lm} (refer to Figure 6.1.1), and for each index of l, we have $-l \leq m \leq l$.

$$L_{lm}(\theta,\phi) = \int_{\theta=0}^{\pi} \int_{\phi=0}^{2\pi} Y_{lm}(\theta,\phi) \cdot d\omega(\theta) \cdot lookup(\theta,\phi)$$

Here θ and ϕ parameterize the sphere. However, in the implementation we must solve this equation discretely by summing over the pixels of the environment map.

The key non-trivial piece is the $d\omega$ term: it relates to the fact we are integrating each pixel in terms of its solid angle. We use the variable domega in the code and calculate it as

```
domega = (2*PI/width)*(2*PI/height)*sinc(theta);
```

This formula is appropriate for an environment map in the "spheremap" form. For lat-long maps, we provide the formula in the sample code.

It should be noted that because we are assuming distant lighting, every vertex is treated as "seeing" the same illumination. Thus, these coefficients are constant across the mesh, and we can pass them as uniform variables to the shader.

What we have now is an efficient environment rendering method where a several megabyte HDR probe has been compressed into 27 floats. On a basic level, the reason why this is possible relates to the fact that SH is a frequency-space decomposition of our spherical signal—the light probe. In the rendering equation, we can exploit the low-frequency nature of the cosine kernel. Because it is a very smooth function with rapid falloff, the high frequencies within the L_i are suppressed. Thus, we can afford to approximate the irradiance with low-order spherical harmonic functions. In fact, [Ramamoorthi01] shows that nine coefficients are sufficient for Lambertian reflection. However, if we want to capture more precise shadow detail, we will need more. Using a glossy BRDF will also require more coefficients in addition to representing the transfer function as a matrix rather than a vector as in our case [Sloan02].

To see the efficient environment map rendering, try running the demo program on the DVD:

```
envmap —i dragon
```

We can also project a directional light, for instance to represent the sun, into the same or a different set of SH coefficients, and this can be done efficiently at runtime. This projection is equivalent to a low-pass filter, hence we will get a blurred directional light but it will be free from aliasing. (See [Stamate05] for further reading on this.) Since the spherical harmonic functions form an orthonormal basis, we can sum the projected coefficients of different light sources at runtime, i.e., we can combine precomputed sets of projected lights. This gives increased flexibility when we want to turn lights on and off or blend lights together. For indoor environments, area lights are especially attractive because they can generate soft shadows. Area lights are otherwise difficult to render efficiently at runtime since they require integration to compute precisely.

To add movable lights, we implemented [Ivanic96] matrix rotation of spherical harmonics. Concerns have been expressed about the speed of their method [Krivanek06], but because we are only doing a single rotation per frame for each set of projected lights, this was not a concern here.

One might dismiss what we have done thus far as limited to outdoor distance illumination. With a slight change in perspective, however, our method can be seen as one for processing light probes [Greger98] placed at various parts of an indoor scene. As a character moves within this environment, different probes are activated and supply lighting contributions to it. A scheme must be devised to perform smooth blending when switching between probes. The distant lighting assumption also can be partially lifted by using gradient based interpolation [Annen04].

Implementation Details: PRT Coefficient Generation

Now that we have simplified our light source to a set of spherical harmonic coefficients, we need to do the same for the visibility function. Incorporating visibility information in our rendering equation will give us self-shadowing effects and greatly increases the perceived depth and realism of our render. We use a raytracing method to sample the visibility per-vertex. For each sampled ray, if it is occluded we return 0 and if it is unoccluded we return 1. The following pseudo code will make it clear exactly how this is done (j indexes the sampled directions).

```
for all samples
  stratified2D( u1, u2 ); //generate stratified random numbers
  sampleHemisphere( shadowray, u1, u2, pdf[j] );
  H = dot(shadowray.direction, vertexnormal);

  if (H > 0) { //only care about samples in upper hemisphere
    if (!occludedByGeometry(shadowray)) {
      for (int k = 0; k < bands; ++k) {
        RGBCoeff& coeff = coeffentry[k];
        grayness = H * shcoeffs[j*bands + k]; //project onto SH basis
        grayness /= pdfs[j];
        coeff += grayness; //sum up contribution
      }
    }
  }
}
```

Here the variable H takes care of the BRDF (which for the diffuse case we have as 1) and the cosine term in the rendering equation simultaneously. We first test that our shadow ray direction is in the upper hemisphere with respect to the vertex normal and then we trace the ray. In our implementation, we found 100–400 shadow rays per vertex to be sufficient in capturing the self-shadowing without much visible loss of information. Although this is all preprocess, you will want some sort of acceleration structure when doing any sort of raytracing. In our code, we use a standard kd-tree and it is fairly effective. Once we have found a certain shadow ray to be unoccluded, we loop through each band of the precomputed basis functions and multiply it by H, effectively projecting this "BRDF times cosine term" onto the spherical harmonic basis. We then sum the sample's contribution into the appropriate band[3]. There is one key issue to note here: Because we have already accounted for the vertex normal in the computation of our H variable, there is no need to pass vertex normals to the shader. The cosine term represents the Lambertian response, typically calculated as

$$\vec{n} \cdot \vec{l}$$

in the shader. This means that we can reduce the data that we pass to the shader by having the only attribute be our PRT coefficients, which therefore speeds up our rendering.

In a scene with multiple objects, we can have the objects shadow each other by grouping them together in the preprocess stage. The "self-shadowing" will then be the transfer among these objects. Sloan et al. call this *neighborhood transfer* [Sloan02]. The rigid relationship between occluder/light and receiver can be partially removed using the interesting spherical harmonics scaling recently invented [Wang06].

We cannot cover the details of spherical harmonic theory, randomized sampling methods, or global illumination here. Should the reader wish to develop a more detailed understanding of these topics, we suggest consulting some of the literature already published. In particular, we recommend Jakko's thesis [Lethinen04], Green's presentation [Green03], and [Pharr04].

Least-Squares Fit for PRT Coefficients

The method we present above for projecting the visibility samples onto the SH basis is the simple "direct" method, and it is the same method used by [Green03]. However, there is a better way to do the projection: a *least-squares fit*. Our PRT coefficients

$$\vec{c}$$

can be found by the least-square solution of the following linear system:

$$\vec{\beta} = Y\vec{c}$$

where

$$\vec{\beta}$$

is the visibility samples and Y is the SH basis.

We then pre-multiply both sides by Y^T to obtain the least-squares (LS) solution:

$$\vec{c} = A^{-1}\vec{b}$$

where

$$A = Y^T Y$$

and

$$\vec{b} = Y^T \vec{\beta}$$

The LS solution is best found by a SVD-based method; we perform an eigen value decomposition by expressing

$$A = USU^T$$

where U is a unitary matrix and S is the diagonal matrix with the eigen values along the diagonal. Thus we can obtain the solution by solving the following equation:

$$\vec{c} = A^{-1}\vec{b} = US^{-1}U^T\vec{b}$$

Later on we will examine the characteristics of the Gram matrix A in detail (it is the method recommended in [Sloan03]). Sloan demonstrates a 35% worse case improvement in error over the direct projection method. The Gram matrix is related to the order of the SH basis only, hence it is independent of each vertex. The SVD decomposition only needs to be performed once.

Implementation Details: Runtime

We now have precomputed all the data we need to properly reconstruct the various spherical functions we want to use: We have our lighting information as an environment map compressed to just 27 floats, and we have precomputed each vertex's PRT data as nine RGB floats. However, we can reduce the size of this data immediately, as only one color channel is needed to implement shadows. Therefore, we simply drop the other two channels and store nine floats per vertex. At runtime, the reconstruction process is simple: We take advantage of the orthogonality of spherical harmonic functions and do a dot product with our lighting coefficients. With the assumption of lighting being constant across the mesh, we can solve the spherical convolution as a dot product of the separately projected L_{lm} and PRT coefficients [Kautz02]. Thus, the complicated rendering equation

$$E = \int_s L_i(x, \omega) \cdot BRDF(\omega_i, \omega_o) \cdot V(\theta) d\theta$$

is simplified to

$$E = \sum L_{lm} \cdot P_{lm}$$

The shader only uses nine multiplications and additions in computing our vertex colors, which can be done in nine cycles. Additionally, as previously stated, the only attribute to our vertex shader is the array of coefficients we use to store our self-shadowing information. Thus, nine floats or three streams are being passed down the pipeline into the graphics hardware. We will include a snippet of the shader code here, but the full versions of both shaders are available on the accompanying DVD.

```
uniform vec3 Li[9];
attribute vec3 prt0;
attribute vec3 prt1;
attribute vec3 prt2;
color  = Li[0]*(prt0.xxx) + Li[1]*(prt0.yyy) + Li[2]*(prt0.zzz);
color += Li[3]*(prt1.xxx) + Li[4]*(prt1.yyy) + Li[5]*(prt1.zzz);
color += Li[6]*(prt2.xxx) + Li[7]*(prt2.yyy) + Li[8]*(prt2.zzz);
```

The PRT coefficients are passed down the pipeline as vec3s. We also implemented a 4×4×1 packing with the hope of taking advantage of dual instruction issue, which pairs vector operations with a scalar operation simultaneously. However, in our tests the performance was similar or a little faster on the newer GPUs.

Some readers may be wondering if using the dot shader function would speed things up. We performed the test and any speed differences were so minimal that they were effectively negligible.

To run the demo, type

```
prt −p 0 −i dragon
```

Compression and Optimization

So far we have seen implementation specifics using a few PRT coefficients and projected light sources. To model self-shadowing using second-order spherical harmonic functions, we need nine floats per sample, which takes up 36 bytes. If we want to model higher frequencies either within the light sources or on the surface (e.g. a glossy BRDF), we will need higher-order SH functions. Some simple measures have been taken to reduce the amount of data needed. We have removed normals from being passed to the shader by encoding them in the Lambertian response and visibility term, and removed redundancy by merging similar positions and normals while building the vertex arrays. For the 70k triangle version of the Stanford bunny, we ended up with 38,333 unique vertices. The PRT coefficients took up 1.35 MB of memory, which is slightly expensive. If we choose to also add interreflections, we need three times that—about 4 MB. It is obvious that we need to compress the coefficients.

In the following sections we will explore several compression methods. We will show how to improve frame rates while reducing the size of the PRT data.

Previous Work

There has been some research done in the area of spherical harmonic coefficient compression, and most of it involves *principal component analysis* (PCA). At a most basic level, PCA is used to reduce high-dimensional data to lower dimensions by computing a singular value decomposition and representing the data as its most "important components." Namely, PCA considers the data that contributes the most to the variance as the most important, and the data that contributes the least is discarded. For spherical harmonic coefficients, this basically means that we analyze the data that has the least effect on the visual result and give it the lowest priority.

Clustered principal component analysis (CPCA), introduced by Sloan et al. [Sloan03], is representative of the state-of-the-art in PRT compression. The key to their method is to partition the PRT coefficients using k-means to reduce the variance. These groups of coefficients are approximated by lower dimensional clusters in order to reduce memory use but still retain the important characteristics of the data.

The clustering also enables us to perform the expensive vector (diffuse) or matrix (glossy) operation per cluster instead of per vertex, which improves speed. However, it is not easy to implement and the clustering prevents one from directly applying a standard vertex cache optimizer, which is crucial for good real-time performance. Modern games typically have thousands of vertices within a vertex buffer to minimize draw call overhead. The optimal cluster size to lower the variance of the PRT coefficients is likely to be much smaller.

Compression Using a Scalar Quantizer

We will begin with some basic methods for compressing floating-point numbers. Transfer coefficients, and especially PRT coefficients for self-shadowing, typically have limited dynamic range. However, rather than simply truncating the least significant bits, one common method of compression is to quantize the data using a scale-bias factor. In the rest of this article, we will apply standard signal processing approaches in several increasingly aggressive methods to reduce the bit rate of the PRT coefficients.

Byte Compression with Scale-Bias

The simplest method to compress our PRT coefficients is to use bytes instead of floats. SH coefficients are not normalized, and they can take on negative values. To minimize the quantization errors, we will loop through all the projected SH coefficients and calculate the minimum and maximum values for each of the nine coefficient sets. Then we can subtract the minimum of each set from the other coefficients and scale by 255/(max–min). Later, when we want to uncompress at runtime, the minimum will be passed to the shader as a bias to be added after the coefficient is scaled by (max–min)/255. After the bias has been applied all the coefficients will be positive, and thus we can use GL_UNSIGNED_BYTE as the basic storage unit.

Table 6.1.1 Comparison between uncompressed and nine bytes coefficients on PCI-e ATI X700

	9 floats	9 bytes scale-bias
Bunny (70k verts)	1.35 MB/85 fps	0.45 MB/182 fps
Dragon (871k verts)	15.33 MB/20 fps	5.1 MB/41 fps
Buddha (1.08m verts)	19.15 MB/17 fps	6.38 MB/33 fps

We cut the memory use by $\frac{3}{4}$ and were able to improve the frame rate by 2×. The application of the scale-bias in the shader is simple:

```
vec3 color;

vec3 p0 = bias.xyz + prt0*scale.xyz;
vec3 p1 = bias.xyz + prt1*scale.xyz;
vec3 p2 = bias.xyz + prt2*scale.xyz;
color  = Li[0]*(p0.xxx) + Li[1]*(p0.yyy) + Li[2]*(p0.zzz);
color += Li[3]*(p1.xxx) + Li[4]*(p1.yyy) + Li[5]*(p1.zzz);
color += Li[6]*(p2.xxx) + Li[7]*(p2.yyy) + Li[8]*(p2.zzz);
```

Try running our demo application with the argument –p 1 to test the performance and visual quality of this compression method. The result is shown in Figure 6.1.3.

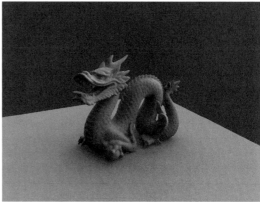

FIGURE 6.1.3 Dragon rendered with byte compression. This model was provided by Stanford University Computer Graphics Laboratory.

Scale-Bias as a Uniform Scalar Quantizer

Let us examine the quantization in closer detail. After we have computed the scale and bias for each of the nine coefficient sets, how do we calculate the byte values? Is it simply $B_i = (P_i - bias_i) * scale_i$? The implicit conversion from float to byte performs a truncation. Is that the best we can do, or should we use *rounding*? These sorts of issues have been studied extensively in signal processing. There are two types of quantizers, as illustrated in Figure 6.1.4: mid-rise (a) and mid-thread (b).

Mid-rise has the advantage of exactly reconstructing the 0-level, but you give up one level of accuracy. For example, for a 2-bit code you only get 3 levels of resolution. Mid-thread is a little more accurate because it has an even number of levels. The difference might not matter much when we are using many bits, however with aggressive compression such as using only three bits for the higher-order coefficients, the differ-

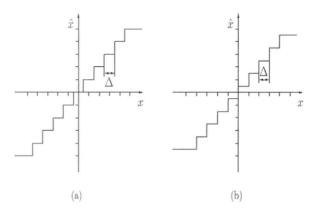

FIGURE 6.1.4 Mid-rise versus mid-thread uniform quantizer.

ence can be significant. We selected mid-rise in our sample implementation for byte compression and switched to mid-thread for the other methods.[4]

To understand the difference between the two ways to convert P_i to B_i, it is best to consider an example. If we have a 2-bit mid-rise quantizer, each bin is 0.333 wide, assuming the input range is normalized to lie between 0 and 1. The reconstruction levels will be 0, 0.33, 0.66, and 1. For a mid-thread quantizer, you have four levels, so each bin is 0.25 wide. Thus the reconstruction levels will be 0.125, 0.375, 0.625, and 0.875.

Geometrically, a sample is classified as belonging to a bin if the distance of that sample to the center of the bin is closest among all bins (nearest-neighbor). The mid-point of a bin will be used as the "reconstruction level," which means that you can never get an output of 0 back. Signals between 0 and 0.125 are all mapped to 0.125, but the overall error will be smaller. In the code we encapsulated this in ScalarQuant.

```
float half = (qkind == PRT::kMidRise) ? 0.5f : 0.f;

for (int i=0; i < nc; i++) {
  float delta = scalars[i] - ranges[2*i];   //- bias[b]
  p[i] = delta * scales[i];                  //* scale[b]
  output[i] = floor(p[i] + half);
}
```

In the example shown in Table 6.1.2, the mid-rise quantizer seems to perform better for p[0] and p[1]. However, mid-thread achieves a lower overall error. The type of quantizer to use is purely a preprocess decision, so it does not affect the shader. One can design a system that uses a combination of the two types based on user feedback.

Table 6.1.2 Mid-rise versus mid-thread uniform quantizer errors (db) for bunny

	p[0]	p[1]	p[2]	p[3]	p[4]	p[5]	p[6]	p[7]	p[8]	Overall
Mid-rise	64.4	51.0	52.95	50.6	48.5	50.0	51.8	50.7	49.5	50.9
Mid-thread	63.7	50.8	53.3	50.9	49.8	51.1	52.5	51.8	50.4	51.7

Note on Attribute Alignment

When we compress second-order SH coefficients using byte compression, each vertex will have nine bytes of PRT data. Let's assume that we want to interleave the PRT data with 12 bytes of position information, which gives us 21 bytes per vertex in the VBO. We found that in our initial implementation, the frame rate dropped to an unacceptable level on certain GPUs. After some experimentation, the problem seemed to be related to attribute alignment. We decided to do an isolated test using the same model, but with precomputed vertex colors. In fact, we performed the same computation as the vertex shader on the CPU and updated the VBO per frame. We stored the color as 1) three floats, 2) three bytes, and 3) four bytes by padding one byte. In Tables 6.1.3 and 6.1.4, it's easy to see that the frame rates in the middle column are a lot lower. In the third column, we padded the three bytes to four and the frame rate was better than using three floats.

Table 6.1.3 Impact of attribute size on frame rate (Xeon 2.8g + GF6800 + AGP)

3 floats per vertex	3 bytes per vertex	4 bytes per vertex
200 fps	14.9 fps	212 fps

Table 6.1.4 Impact of attribute size on frame rate (Pentium-M 1.7g + ATI X700 + PCIe)

3 floats per vertex	3 bytes per vertex	4 bytes per vertex
398 fps	0.05 fps	450 fps

The key here is actually the stride size for an interleaved VBO. Each attribute must start on a four-byte aligned address for the GPU to fetch it efficiently.

The four-byte alignment requirement in some hardware is a fact that must be taken into consideration when you are designing your vertex format. If attributes are compressed one at a time, this constraint is fairly limiting; for example, padding the nine bytes to 12 bytes will incur a 33% overhead. If other vertex attributes are available to pack into those three bytes, then at least the padding can be made useful. The most obvious choice is to pack the normals, since they are unit vectors. However, PRT has the normals already baked in when we include the Lambertian response in our PRT generation. [Purnomo05] proposed considering all your attributes together and adaptively packing them into as many four-byte units as needed. In other words, given a four aligned budget, it tries to find the optimal allocation of bits for the best visual quality by rendering the scene and comparing the result against a reference. We can combine it with Calver's [Calver02] vertex attribute compression method, for example, by packing the UVs into two 8-bit fields using the same scale-bias method.

Single Scale-Bias versus Custom Scale-Bias

In the previous section, we computed a specialized scale-bias for each of the nine PRT coefficients. They are packed in three uniforms, each to be passed to the shader. That means we have six `glUniform3fv` calls per drawable to store in addition to the nine for the L_is. If the overhead is too large for your platform, you can simplify the method and use a single scale and bias term for all coefficients. The PSNR for a single scale-bias is 3.5 db lower than that for custom scale-bias (78.7 db versus 75.24 db) for the bunny model. However, visually it is hardly noticeable. This statistic is a useful reference point since it suggests an upper bound on the number of quantization levels we have to consider in subsequent approaches. In the demo, method 0 uses a single scale-bias and method 1 uses a custom scale-bias for each band.

48-Bit Compression

Compressing our PRT coefficients from floats to bytes has given us approximately double the performance and on visual inspection is effectively indistinguishable from an uncompressed rendering.

In rate-distortion theory, it is well known that each bit contributes 6 db to the signal-to-noise ratio. Seeing that the PSNRs (as illustrated in Tables 6.1.5 and 6.1.6) for various models using byte-valued compression are large (> 78 db), we begin to wonder if we can reduce the bit-rate further. However, GPUs do not directly support any vertex format smaller than one byte. If we want to use bit fields, we will have to do the unpacking in the shader. Additionally, shaders do not have bit shifts or masking instructions. Vertex streams will be automatically converted to floats as they are passed in as inputs to our vertex shader—a four-byte attribute will be expanded into four SIMD floats. If we are using bit fields smaller than one byte, some or all of the fields will straddle a byte boundary—they will be split into two pieces within the SIMD register. However, we will show how to unscramble them by carefully using floating-point operations. Because we are using shaders, we are also constrained to using a constant bit rate per vertex. How do we decide how many bits to use?

Table. 6.1.5 Performance comparisons (fps) on a G8800GTS + quad-core CPU

	Floats	Bytes	Bytes-441	48 Bits	48b(LM)	32b
Bunny (69k)	756	810	816	886	895	952
Dragon (871k)	158	174	174	243	243	239
Buddha (1.08m)	143	154	154	212	213	212

Table 6.1.6 Performance comparisons (fps) on an X700 + Pentium-M 1.6g

	Floats	Bytes	Bytes-441	48 Bits	48b(LM)	32b
Bunny (69k)	85	180	180	212	169	257
Dragon (871k)	20	40.7	40.7	39.1	18.5	29.1
Buddha (1.08m)	17.5	33	33	32.7	15.5	24.5

Transform coding theory [Clarke85] tells us that that energy of an input signal is compacted toward the lower order coefficients[5]. If we look at Table 6.1.7, we can see that this is in fact the case: the squared norms of the coefficients are heavily weighted toward the lower bands—84% of the energy is contained within the first and second order bands. We allocate our bits accordingly in an 8-6-6-6-6-4-4-4-4 manner, which gives us a method that packs the nine PRT coefficients into 48 bits. The first five coefficients are packed into a 32-bit word and the last four are packed into a 16-bit short. Because we want to optimize the use of SIMD instructions, this distribution of bits also conveniently fits the first five coefficients into 32 bits. Having coefficient bit streams straddling shader input registers makes the code tedious and also hinders optimizations. On the DVD you can find the source code with extensive commenting on the exact details for compression. The key routine is ComputeScales: given a table of bit budgets it sets up various tables used by the quantizer. It is fairly straightforward, and we will not go into it here.

Table 6.1.7 PRT ranges, percentage, and total energies by band for bunny

band[l, m]:	Range	%	Square Norm
band[0, 0]:	(0.002,0.066)	34.8%	Sqnrm: 111.23,
band[1,–1]:	(–0.073,0.077)	17.1%	Sqnrm: 54.67,
band[1, 0]:	(–0.058,0.059)	15.3%	Sqnrm: 48.86,
band[1,+1]:	(–0.076,0.076)	17.1%	Sqnrm: 54.74,
band[2,–2]:	(–0.045,0.044)	2.8%	Sqnrm: 8.79,
band[2,–1]:	(–0.036,0.041)	2.9%	Sqnrm: 9.21,
band[2, 0]:	(–0.034,0.030)	3.4%	Sqnrm: 10.86,
band[2,+1]:	(–0.035,0.039)	2.6%	Sqnrm: 8.31,
band[2,+2]:	(–0.040,0.042)	4.1%	Sqnrm: 12.95,

Decompression, on the other hand, is more tedious. Because of the way we pack our coefficients into exactly 48 bits, some coefficients will be split across byte boundaries. In Figure 6.1.5, for example, p[2] will have its high two bits in the second byte and the remaining four bits in the third byte. This means that in the shader, we will have to perform bit operations to recombine and reconstruct our coefficients. Keep in mind, however, that float is the native type for shaders; we have to emulate bit operations on floating-point numbers using the basic arithmetic operators.

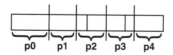

FIGURE 6.1.5 Bit field packing
to 32 bits within a vertex stream.

Let's take a closer look at the second byte as an example. The high six bits are in p[1], but the low two bits give us the start of p[2], which spills over into the third byte. Remembering that bytes are expanded into floats in the shader, e.g. the third byte will become prt0.z, the basic idea for separating the two coefficients is to shift the decimal point until it lies in between the two. We can then take the integer portion to obtain the part to the left, and the fractional portion to obtain the part to the right.

```
uniform vec4 rshft; //right shift to isolate low bits of each term
uniform vec4 lshft; //left shift to extract high bits of each term
attribute vec4 prt0; //prt coefficients 0..4 (8,6,6,6,6)

vec4 p14; //p[1..4]
vec4 rhs3; //right hand side of the "decimal point"

p14 = prt0 * rshft; // rshft(scales[0], 1/4, 1/16, 1/64)

rhs3.yzw = fract(p14.yzw);
rhs3 *= lshft;        // lshft(      0, 16.*4., 4.*16., 64.);
```

There are a couple of things to be noted here. We pack the left and right shifts in vec4s with respect to each coefficient. The `lshft` does the job of reversing the `rshft` and also shifting the upper bits of the bit fields into their final positions. In order to save one cycle, we store the scale factor for p[0] into `rshft.x` so that rather than shift the decimal point (which is unnecessary for p[0] as it already fits perfectly into the first byte), we can directly apply the scaling step of the coefficient reconstruction for p[0]. `rhs3` contains the right-hand side of the split between two coefficients; `rhs3.y` contains the high two bits of p[2], for example.

```
//p[0]:
pp0 = p14.x + bias0;

//p[1..4]:
p14.xyz = (rhs3.xyz + floor(p14.yzw)) * scales.xyz + bias.xyz;
p14.w = rhs3.w * scales.w + bias.w;
```

We finish off the reconstruction of p[0] by applying the bias. The key here is the `rhs3.xyz + floor(p14.yzw)` part. With this operation, we join up the split portions of p[1] through p[4]. `rhs3.x` has already been set to 0, so adding `floor(p14.y)` to it gives us the complete p[1]. We then join up p[2] by taking its high 2 bits, which are contained in `rhs3.y`, with its lower four bits, which are contained in the integer portion of `p14.z`. p[3] and p[4] follow in similar fashion.

```
//p[5..8]:
vec4 r58 = prt1.xyxy;
r58 /= 16.;                        //right shift 4 bits
r58.xy = floor(r58.xy);
//p[5], p[7]
r58.zw = fract(r58.zw) * 16.;
//we have the (4,4,4,4) bit fields isolated => p[5],p[7],p[6],p[8]
r58 = r58 * scales2.xzyw + bias2.xzyw;
```

p[5] through p[8] are more straightforward as they don't straddle any byte boundaries. The only minor thing to note here is that we duplicate the coefficients in r58 so that the right shift by four simultaneously yields p[5] and p[6] and so on.

The shader for the 48-bit format is more complicated than the simple byte method. Examining Table 6.1.8 gives us some useful insights on the balance between bandwidth and shader computation and Figure 6.1.6 shows the results for the 48-bit compression. For the lower resolution model (bunny), the 48-bit is 16.5% faster, but it is slightly slower for the high-resolution models running on the ATI X700. On the G8800, the 48-bit method always outperforms the byte method. The X700 is a mobile GPU and only has six vertex pipelines. The G8800 GTS has 96 pipes, all of which can be dedicated to vertex processing if the fragment shader is simple.

Table 6.1.8 Performance of 48-bit versus 9-byte method on two different GPUs

	9 Bytes-X700	**48 Bits-X700**	**9 Bytes-G8800**	**48 Bits-G8800**
Bunny (70k verts)	182 fps	212 fps	810 fps	886 fps
Dragon (871k verts)	41 fps	39 fps	174 fps	243 fps
Buddha (1.08m verts)	33 fps	32 fps	154 fps	212 fps

Use prt −p 2 <input model> to run the demo.

FIGURE 6.1.6 Dragon rendered with 48-bit compression.

A 32-Bit Compressed Format

Because the error statistics for the 48-bit compression seem so good (refer to Table 6.1.8), we are inclined to be more aggressive with reducing the bit rate. We came up with a 5-4-4-4-3-3-3-3-3 format together with our mid-thread quantizer. Table 6.1.9 outlines the statistics gathered on the reconstructed signal.

Table 6.1.9 Statistics for 32-bit compression

Band	Sqnrm	Sq Err	PSNR
band[0]: (0.003,0.065)	Sqnrm: 111.23	Sq err: 0.02	PSNR: 63.71 (dB)
band[1]: (−0.068,0.072)	Sqnrm: 54.67	Sq err: 0.32	PSNR: 50.81 (dB)
band[2]: (−0.054,0.055)	Sqnrm: 48.86	Sq err: 0.18	PSNR: 53.29 (dB)
band[3]: (−0.071,0.072)	Sqnrm: 54.74	Sq err: 0.31	PSNR: 50.89 (dB)
band[4]: (−0.039,0.038)	Sqnrm: 8.79	Sq err: 0.41	PSNR: 49.75 (dB)
band[5]: (−0.031,0.037)	Sqnrm: 9.21	Sq err: 0.30	PSNR: 51.05 (dB)
band[6]: (−0.030,0.026)	Sqnrm: 10.86	Sq err: 0.22	PSNR: 52.51 (dB)
band[7]: (−0.030,0.034)	Sqnrm: 8.31	Sq err: 0.25	PSNR: 51.78 (dB)
band[8]: (−0.035,0.037)	Sqnrm: 12.95	Sq err: 0.35	PSNR: 50.36 (dB)

The PSNR seems promising—the lowest value is still 50.36, shown in Figure 6.1.7. It uses only one stream for PRT data, and we are able to achieve a frame rate of ~260 fps on the ATI X700 for the bunny: a 22% improvement over the 48-bit format. However, we start to notice that some of the self shadows seem faceted for parts of the bunny. For the armadillo, however, the result is still pretty reasonable. Perhaps we are at the limit of a simple scale-bias method. We have included this shader in the DVD for the readers to test on their own models.

 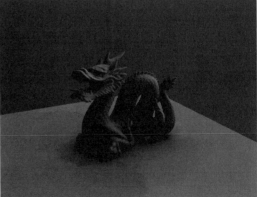

FIGURE 6.1.7 Dragon rendered with 32-bit compression.

A 48-Bit Format Using an Optimal Quantizer

Compressing source data has been the subject of extensive study in signal processing. A recent survey paper [Gray99] on quantization lists no fewer than 581 citations. In signal processing, the problem we are facing is designing a quantizer that "optimally" reconstructs the PRT coefficients. We have been using quantizers with evenly spaced bins, i.e., a uniform quantizer. A uniform quantizer is "optimal" only when the input probability distribution is uniform, that is, each PRT coefficient is equally probable. Here "optimal" is measured as mean-square-error. The rate-distortion function is

$$D = \sum_{k=1}^{K} \int_{t_k}^{t_{k+1}} (u - \mu_k)^2 f(u)du$$

1

By differentiating the rate-distortion function with respect to t_k and q_k we can arrive at two conclusions:

$$t_k = (q_{k-1} + q_k)/2$$

2

$$\int_{zk}^{zk+1} zf(z)dz \Big/ \int_{zk}^{zk+1} f(z)(z)dz,$$

3

q_k is the reconstruction level for bin k, t_k is the decision level, or the boundary, of the bins, and $f(z)$ is the probability density function of input z. This pair of famous equations was first solved by S. Lloyd [Lloyd57] and J. Max [Max 60] independently. Equation 2 states that the optimal decision level is the mid-point of the adjacent reconstruction level. Equation 3 states that the optimal reconstruction is the centroid of the samples falling into the bin. Intuitively, if a sample is rare, we can have a wider bin surrounding it. A wider bin incurs larger quantization error for those samples that are within it, but since they are less probable, the overall error is minimized. Besides deriving the two equations, Lloyd and Max came up with an iterative solver to find t_k and q_k given a fixed number of reconstruction levels. For example, since we are using four bits for p[8], the number of reconstruction levels is 2^4–1 = 15. The algorithm is closely related to k-means clustering and is known as Lloyd's relaxation in CG literature.

We can gain valuable insight into Lloyd's method by examining Equation 3. If the input *pdf* is constant, then 3 simplifies to $q_k = (t_{k-1} + t_k) / 2$ and we get back our uniform quantizer. The *pdf* is the key to the Lloyd-Max method, and is usually approximated by a histogram of the input samples.

The general approach of the Lloyd-Max iteration is as follows:

1. Given a set of decision levels t_k and codebook q_k.
2. Find q_k such that it is the centroid of the interval t_k and t_{k+1}.

3. Find t_k so that it is the midpoint of q_k and q_{k+1}.
4. Repeat steps 1 to 3 for all intervals.
5. Find centroid c of last interval, and check against q_{n-1}. If we have converged, stop.
6. Let $q_{n-1} = \alpha(q_{n-1} - c)$ and go to step 2.

The algorithm usually converges pretty quickly; we usually just set the iteration to 10. In general, k-means is very sensitive to the initial choices of t_k and q_k. After examining a number of actual data sets we choose a uniform quantizer as the initial encoder/decoder pair. There are many possible better ways[6] to initialize the algorithm, but our simple approach seems adequate for our purpose. There is an edge case for when a bin is empty, and we use the simple strategy of merging that bin with an adjacent bin to handle it.

As shown in Table 6.1.10, the Lloyd-Max non-uniform quantizer really helps the last four bands. This is fortunate[7] for us as the lower order coefficients will require a much larger lookup table. Thus, we adopt a hybrid method and use Lloyd-Max for p[5..8] only.

Table 6.1.10 Statistics comparing 48b uniform and 48b Lloyd-Max method

48 Uniform (-p 2)	48 bit Lloyd-Max Errors (-p 3)
band[0]: PSNR: 82.80(dB)	PSNR: 82.946344
band[1]: PSNR: 63.41(dB)	PSNR: 63.617597
band[2]: PSNR: 65.41(dB)	PSNR: 65.650164
band[3]: PSNR: 63.18(dB)	PSNR: 63.363649
band[4]: PSNR: 67.84(dB)	PSNR: 68.070863
band[5]: PSNR: 56.61(dB)	PSNR: 57.763111
band[6]: PSNR: 58.13(dB)	PSNR: 59.395062
band[7]: PSNR: 56.81(dB)	PSNR: 58.148293
band[8]: PSNR: 56.10(dB)	PSNR: 57.394776

```
uniform vec4  recon58[16];        //centroids for p[5..8] (4,4,4,4)

//Lloyd-Max decode for p[5..8]:
vec4 r58;
r58.x = recon58[int(c58.x)].x;    //centroid
r58.y = recon58[int(c58.y)].y;
r58.z = recon58[int(c58.z)].z;
r58.w = recon58[int(c58.w)].w;
```

In the shader, the code is very similar to the 48 scale-bias method. The main difference is the table of q_ks passed as recon58. Once the bit-fields are assembled, we use them to look up the table to reconstruct the PRT signal. Use prt –p 3 <input model> to run the demo. The result is shown in Figure 6.1.8.

FIGURE 6.1.8 Dragon rendered with Lloyd-Max 48-bit compression.

Extensions to Higher Order

Let us now move forward to some extensions of what we have discussed thus far. In all the methods presented until now, we have only utilized the first nine spherical harmonic basis functions, and some readers may be wondering if the methods are general enough to handle indirect lighting, or perhaps the use of more basis functions. (We will discuss indirect lighting in the next section.) More basis functions become a necessity if increased shadow detail is desired or if a more complex BRDF model is used, for example, a glossy one. A glossy BRDF will also change our exit radiance computation from a vector-vector dot product to a matrix-vector product.

We have already established that a least-squares solution is the projection method of choice. There is a catch, however. The use of more basis functions (or conversely, fewer samples) makes it easier to fit the data with multiple distinct solutions. This plus clamping to the hemisphere in turn leads to singularity in the Gram matrix A [Sloan03]. [Lam06] et al. have observed that the singularity in A results in very small singular values, which, when used to compute the least-squares solution, cause the computed coefficients to have large magnitude.

If we use these uncompressed coefficients to perform the reconstruction, then all is well. However, in a real-time setting this is simply not feasible; we are passing even more data to the shader because of the increased number of basis functions, so compression is necessary. However, [Lam06] et al. show us that when coefficients of large magnitude[8] are used for compression, severe noise is introduced.

In our tests, we discovered that only a glossy BRDF resulted in small enough singular values to cause the PRT coefficients to blow up in magnitude.

[Lam06] et al. introduce a noise-resistant method in which they formulate the projection as a *constrained least-squares* (CLS) problem. The constraint is simple:

$$\bar{c}^{-T} \bar{c} < E_c$$

Where

$$\overset{-T}{c}\,\overset{-}{c},$$

the norm of the coefficient vector, must be strictly less than E_c, the total energy of the function[9]. This value can simply be calculated by summing up the squared magnitudes of the samples. We can solve for the vector of coefficients

$$\vec{c}$$

by using the following constrained solution with a Langrange multiplier:

$$\vec{c} = (A + \lambda I_{n \times n})^{-1} \vec{b}$$

By our constraint,

$$\vec{c}^T c = \vec{b}^T (A + \lambda I_{n \times n})^{-2} \vec{b} \leq E_c$$

The only unknown in this equation is λ. If we set $\lambda = 0$, it is clear that we obtain the unconstrained least squares solution. If we set $\lambda \to \circ$, then

$$\vec{c}$$

is a zero vector. Our goal is to find the minimum value of λ such that we can obtain a solution as close to the unconstrained least squares solution as possible, while still staying within the bounds of the constraint. As per [Lam06] et al., we set an initial value to λ and then perform a binary search until we obtain an estimated suitable value.

Error analysis done by [Lam06] et al. shows us that the PSNR result for the CLS method is only slightly less (~1 db) than that of the ULS method, but the magnitude of the coefficients is dramatically decreased, thus helping to reduce the quantization noise introduced during compression.

Interreflections

Up to this point we have been concentrating on self-shadowing effects, i.e., a scalar PRT value. For interreflections—also known as *color bleeding*—the PRT coefficients will be RGB values. The reason is that the albedo—usually colored—can no longer be factored out of the integral. In the offline processing, we need to include the diffuse albedo when we are computing the Lambertian reflection. We perform the self-shadow ray casts to calculate and store the one-bounce transfers and then we perform a final gather-like pass using the results from the first pass.

For compression we can use the 48-bit technique on each of the colors. Better yet, we can borrow ideas from YUV color-space and reduce the bit rate for the chrominance channels. Even using a single color in 565 form together with the scalar 48-bit PRT should be sufficient. This will give us a nice 64-bit per-vertex representation and does not require any more streams. We use the self-shadowing PRT method to encode the direction variation of visibility and average all the color information into a single triple. The majority of the work to generalize our self-shadowing technique to support color bleeding mostly involves enhancing the offline phase. The shader code is almost the same; only a few extra instructions are needed to unpack the color channel. You can also use the interreflection preprocess machinery but only store a scalar transfer coefficient and get monochrome interreflection for free. We do not have space here to give a detailed algorithm. Interested readers can consult the original PRT paper [Sloan02] and the SIGGRAPH PRT course notes [Kautz05] for details.

Conclusion

In this article, we began by providing a high-level understanding of PRT theory without bogging down the reader with difficult mathematical equations. We then presented implementation details for the preprocess stage of the PRT method. Readers should now be comfortable with representing the necessary elements of the rendering equation for diffuse shadowed transfer as a compact set of spherical harmonic coefficients.

To help improve frame rates, we have also presented a range of methods to compress PRT coefficients sampled at the vertices. With our compact PRT representation and efficient shaders, you can consider using them on a large number of objects in the background. Most of the methods are equally applicable to a normal map-like approach. The map approach gives us more flexibility in choosing a sampling rate because we can compute the PRT coefficients on a high-resolution mesh and apply them to a low-resolution one at runtime. Perhaps more important is the fact that filtering the PRT coefficients using standard texture filtering is mathematically correct, unlike the direct filtering of normals. The quantizer designs plus the bit field packing is applicable to other forms of data and gives extra freedom in designing our shaders.

We hope that readers new to PRT and those with experience alike are more confident about implementing and optimizing PRT in their own applications.

Endnotes

[1]The authors were not able to reproduce the exact coefficient values published in the paper. We identified the difference was exactly π. It is reflected in the code.

[2]The formula to calculate lighting is (see Equation 11 in [Ramamoorthi 01-2]):

$$E(\vec{n}) = \vec{n}^{-T} M \vec{n}$$

[3]We remove the 4π factor from the PRT data to reduce its range. The 4π is added back in the shader as part of the tonemapping. This allows for more accurate compression.

[4]The common practice of converting from floating-point color values to RGB by multiplying by 255 and then rounding is actually a mid-rise quantizer in disguise.

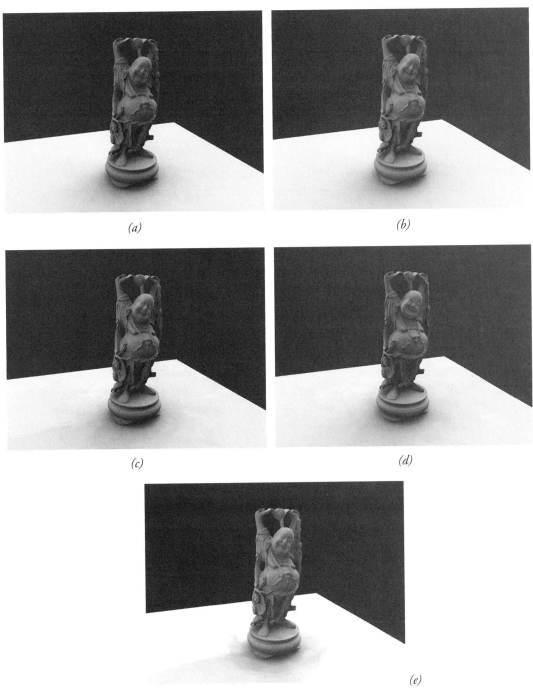

FIGURE 6.1.9 Buddha rendered with various compression methods: (a) uncompressed, (b) byte, (c) 48-bit, (d) Lloyd-Max 48-bit, and (e) 32-bit. Buddha model provided by Stanford University Computer Graphics Laboratory.

[5]Spherical harmonics is an orthonormal basis, we can gain further insight by considering the Parseval theorem. This is beyond the scope of this article.

[6]For example see [Bradley98], or [Vassilvitski]

[7]Rate-distortion theory states a uniform quantizer will approach the performance of an optimal one when the number of decision levels is large.

[8]The quantization noise is

$$\frac{\Delta^2}{12}$$

where Δ is the width of our bin.

[9]From Parseval's theorem the square norm of the input and coefficients are the same.

References

[Calver02] D. Calver, D. "Vertex decompression in a shader," *ShaderX²*.

[Clarke85] Clarke, R. J. "Transform coding of images," Academic Press, 1985.

[Pharr04] Pharr, M. and Humphreys, G. "Physically Based Rendering," Morgan Freeman.

[Stamate05] Stamate, V. "Reduction of Lighting Calculations Using Spherical Harmonics," *ShaderX³*, Charles River Media, 2005: pp. 251–312.

[Annen04] Annen, T., Kautz, J., Durand, F., Seidel, H. "Spherical Harmonics Gradients for Mid-range Illumination," *Eurographics Symposium on Rendering*, 2004.

[Bradley98] Bradley, P. S. and Fayyad, U. "Refining Initial Points for K-means Clustering," *Proceedings of the 15th International Conference on Machine Learning*, 1998.

[Ivanic96] Ivanic, J. andRudenberg, K. "Rotation Matrices for Real Spherical Harmonics. Direct Determination by Recursion," *Journal of Physical Chemistry*, 100(15), pp. 6342–6347.

[Kautz02] Kautz, J., Sloan, Peter-Pike, Snyder, John. "Fast arbitrary BRDF shading for low-frequency lighting using spherical harmonics," *Eurographics Workshop on Rendering*, 2002.

[Kautz05] Kautz, J., Lehtinen, J., Sloan, Peter-Pike. "Precomputed radiance transfer: theory and practice," *Siggraph 2005*, course notes.

[Greger98] Greger, G., Shirley, P., Hubbard, P., Greenberg, D. "The Irradiance Volume," *IEEE Computer Graphics and App.*, 1998.

[Gray99] Gray, R. and Neuhoff,D. "Quantization," *IEEE Trans. on Inform. Theory*, Vol. 44, No. 6, October, 1998.

[Green03] Green, R. "Spherical Harmonics Lighting: The Gritty Details," GDC 2003.

[Krivanek06] Kravanek, J. et al. "Fast Approximation to Spherical Harmonic Rotation," *Siggraph 2006 sketch*.

[Lam06] Lam, P. M., Leung, C. S., Wong, T. T. "Noise-Resistant Fitting for Spherical Harmonics," *IEEE Trans. on Visualization and Computer Graphics*, Vol. 12, No. 2, 2006.

[Landis02] Landis, H. "Production ready global illumination," *Siggraph 2002*, course notes.

[Lethinen04] Lehtinen, J. "Foundations of Precomputed Radiance Transfer," Master Thesis, Helsinki University of Technology, 2004.

[Lloyd57] Lloyd, S. P. "Least squares quantization in PCM," Unpublished Bell Lab, Technical Note.

[Pharr04] Pharr, M. "Ambient occlusion," *GPU Gems I*, NVIDIA 2004.

[Sloan02] Sloan, P. P., Kautz, J., Snyder, J. "Precomputed Radiance Transfer for real-time rendering in dynamic low-frequency lighting environment," *Siggraph 2002:* pp. 527–536.

[Sloan03] Sloan, P. P., Hall, J., Hart, J., Snyder, J. "Clustered Principal Components for Precomputed Radiance Transfer," *Siggraph 2003.*

[Purnomo05] Purnomo, B., Bilobeau, J., Cohen J., Kumar, S. "Hardware-compatible vertex compression using quantization and simplification," *Siggraph/Eurographics Symposium on Graphics Hardware,* 2005.

[Ramamoorthi01] Ramamoorthi, R. and Hanrahan, P. "On the relationship between radiance and irradiance: Determining the illumination from images of a convex lambertian object." *Journal of the Optical Society of America* A, 18(10), 2001: pp. 2448–2459.

[Ramamoorthi01-2] Ramamoorthi R. and Hanrahan, P. "An Efficient Representation for Irradiance Environment Maps," *Siggraph* 2001.

[Vassilvitski] Vassilvitski, S. "K-means++: The advantages of careful seeding," Stanford University.

[Wang06] J. Wang, K. Wu, K. Zhou, S. Lin, S. Hu, B. Guo, "Spherical Harmonics Scaling", *The Visual Computer*, vol. 22, no 9–11, Sept. 2006: pp. 713-720. http://en.wikipedia.org/wiki/Quantization_%28signal_processing%29

[Ramamoorthi02] http://www1.cs.columbia.edu/~ravir/papers/envmap/

6.2

Incremental Instant Radiosity

Hannu Saransaari

Samuli Laine

Janne Kontkanen

Jaakko Lehtinen

Timo Aila

Introduction

As must be known to every computer graphics aficionado, direct illumination alone is not enough to create realistic looking images, since if we limit ourselves to direct illumination only, the unlit surfaces appear pitch black in the image. The standard way of alleviating this problem is to assign a constant ambient term to the illumination, or perhaps to fetch a direction-dependent ambient color from a small cubemap, which is already much better.

While these hacks with ambient light produce better images than no ambient light at all, the real problem is merely swept under the rug. In reality, the color of the surfaces is defined not only by the light that comes directly from the light sources, but also by the light that is reflected from the other parts of the scene. This is known as *indirect illumination*. In addition to providing the correct ambient illumination, indirect illumination yields *color bleeding* effects, such as the way a bright red carpet tints the color of a wall next to it. For static lighting conditions, these effects can be precalculated into textures, but this is not a completely satisfactory solution since dynamic objects then cannot be illuminated by indirect light. Furthermore, we would often like to change the lighting conditions dynamically, e.g. carrying a torch or blowing up something in the scene.

Computing indirect illumination is costly. The first thing that comes to mind is an offline path tracer, which can take ages to render a single image. How could something like this work in real-time graphics? Well, it won't, unless we are allowed to make the following assumptions. First, we consider only one bounce of indirect illumination, meaning that we don't allow more than one intermediate scattering event between the light source and the surface being shaded. Second, we assume a mostly static scene. Third, we require diffuse (or just barely glossy) BRDFs (Bidirectional Reflectance Distribution Functions). Fourth, we assume that lighting conditions vary relatively smoothly.

The requirement of a *mostly* static scene needs some explanation. Our method supports dynamic objects in the sense that they receive indirect illumination exactly like static geometry does. However, dynamic objects cannot participate in the transport of indirect illumination, that is, light cannot bounce from them and illuminate other parts of the scene. This means that a dynamic object receives color bleeding from a bright red carpet, but if the carpet itself is dynamic, it will not cause color bleeding on the neighboring geometry. We feel that this is not a show-stopper because dynamic objects such as characters seldom cause significant indirect illumination effects. All direct illumination effects such as shadows can naturally be used in conjunction with our method.

The method we use here is based on the *instant radiosity* algorithm [Keller97], which will be explained in the following section. Our main contribution is the reuse of the *virtual point lights* that are used for providing the indirect illumination in the instant radiosity algorithm. This enables us to drastically reduce the amount of work per frame while maintaining good image quality (Figure 6.2.1).

FIGURE 6.2.1 The Sibenik cathedral scene with 80 K triangles, running at 49 fps in 1024×768 resolution. The regions in shadow and behind the flashlight are illuminated by indirect light bouncing off the directly illuminated parts of the scene.

In this article we focus on the most fundamental aspects of our method and provide some additional shader source code. For further details, we refer the reader to the previous publication [Laine07].

Incremental Instant Radiosity

In instant radiosity, virtual point lights (VPLs) are cast from primary light sources using ray casting. In the full-fledged instant radiosity algorithm these may further cast more VPLs, which leads to full indirect illumination, but in this paper, we limit ourselves to VPLs cast from the primary light source. VPLs are then used for illuminating the scene as spot light sources with cosine falloff, and shadows are computed using shadow maps.

It turns out that rendering shadow maps for each VPL is a bottleneck for this algorithm. Our method, *incremental instant radiosity*, takes advantage of the temporal coherence of VPLs as the light source moves. By carefully weighting the intensity of VPLs and discarding and inserting only a few new VPLs per frame, real-time performance is achieved and light sources can move freely as long as their movement is relatively smooth.

The core idea is that the set of VPLs is managed by projecting them back to the primary light source. New VPLs are inserted to directions that are poorly sampled, and VPLs are removed from directions that are too densely sampled. In addition, VPLs that have become invalid due to occlusion as seen from the light source are removed. The goal is to incrementally nudge the VPL distribution toward uniform density. However, it cannot be assumed that uniform density is always obtained—rather, this would be highly exceptional whenever the light source is moving. To compensate for non-uniform distribution, we weight the intensity of a VPL by the area of its corresponding Voronoi cell in the point set formed by all VPLs. Because the weights are recomputed for every frame, the indirect illumination does not lag behind even though most of the VPLs originate from earlier frames.

Primary Light Sources

Consider a spot light with 180 degree cosine falloff. The so-called Nusselt analog tells us that if we have a uniform distribution of points on the unit disc, we can simply lift the points onto the surface of a hemisphere and we'll get ray directions that sample the hemisphere according to cosine weighting (Figure 6.2.2). So, if our primary light source is this kind of spot light, we do the following for each frame:

1. Transform the VPLs to the local coordinate frame of the light source
2. Normalize direction vectors to VPLs
3. Drop the z coordinate

And presto! We have a set of points that we can start massaging. When new VPLs are created, the direction vectors to those are obtained by following the recipe in reverse order.

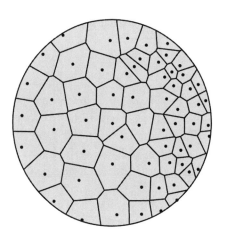 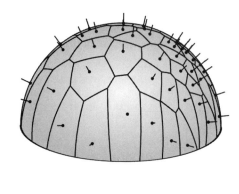

FIGURE 6.2.2 Left: Point set and associated Voronoi regions on unit disc. Right: When lifted, it yields cosine-weighted hemispherical distribution.

For omnidirectional light sources, the proper domain for VPL management is the surface of a unit sphere. In this case, we need to perform the Delaunay triangulation and associated geometric calculations on the spherical surface. Conveniently enough, the trickiest part of the calculation—Delaunay triangulation on a sphere—is just the convex hull of the set of points. The rest of the computation concerns mainly spherical distances and areas, which are easy to compute.

On Delaunay Triangulation and Voronoi Diagrams

Our incremental VPL management is heavily based on Delaunay triangulation of a point set. *Delaunay triangulation* is a type of triangulation in which the circumcircles of the triangles contain no other points. Efficient incremental $O(n \log n)$ construction algorithms exist, such as the Guibas-Stolfi algorithm. Writing an efficient and robust Delaunay triangulator is a non-trivial task, and we therefore suggest starting with an existing implementation (such as CGAL or GTS).

Delaunay triangulation is the dual of Voronoi diagramming, and the centers of the triangle circumcircles are the Voronoi vertices. Because of this, the Voronoi diagram of a point set can be directly obtained from its Delaunay triangulation.

Low-Dispersion Sampling: Inserting and Removing Points

Dispersion is a metric that estimates the quality of a point set for sampling purposes. It is a close relative to the well-known *discrepancy* metric, but it has a couple of favorable characteristics that discrepancy lacks. First, dispersion is easy to calculate; second, it is easy to augment a point set with a new point so that dispersion is reduced.

The dispersion of a point set (contained in a domain) is defined as the radius of the largest empty circle that has a center inside the domain. Our main interest is in the center of this largest empty circle because it is the point that is farthest away from the other points. Placing a new point here reduces the dispersion most effectively, so this is where we put it.

Finding the center of the largest empty circle requires checking each of the Voronoi vertices, i.e. triangle circumcenters, and picking the one that is farthest away from the triangle vertices (has the largest circumcircle). It is also possible that the center of the largest empty circle is on the edge of the disc, and to account for this, we need to check the intersections of the infinite Voronoi edges and the unit circle.

There also exists a rare case when the maximum dispersion point is the farthest point from a single point in the disc. Handling this is not necessary in practice. When there are too few points and the dispersion calculation fails, picking a random point is fine. After there are a dozen or so points in the set, it is very unlikely that this case will occur.

When the primary light source moves, the projected samples tend to skew and cluster and still stay valid. Therefore, valid VPLs (i.e. points in the 2D domain) must sometimes be removed to maintain good sample distribution. To do this, we search for the shortest Delaunay edge and inspect its endpoints. We then delete the point that has the second-shortest edge among those connected to the two endpoints. This simple heuristic has been found to work well in practice. In a sense, we can argue that the endpoints of the shortest Delaunay edge have the highest local sampling density, and the one with the second-shortest edge is the worse of the duo.

VPL Management: Rendering a Frame

At the beginning of each frame, before the VPL management begins, it is important to keep the GPU busy with rendering tasks that don't require information about VPLs. This way VPL management on the CPU can be executed in parallel with rendering on GPU, as illustrated in Figure 6.2.3.

Two variables control the VPL management: recalcMin and recalcMax. In each frame, at least recalcMin new VPLs are created to improve distribution. To limit the amount of computation in cases where many points have been invalidated, at most recalcMax new VPLs are created in each frame.

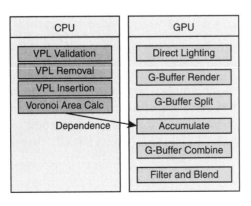

FIGURE 6.2.3 In the beginning of a frame, the CPU runs VPL management tasks in parallel with the GPU doing rendering. The VPL accumulation phase on the GPU cannot start until the CPU side is done.

As explained before, VPLs are first projected back to 2D domain according to the position and orientation of the light source. Then, a shadow ray is cast from the light source to each VPL to check whether it is still visible. If the VPL is visible from the primary light source, it is inserted into the Delaunay triangulation. Otherwise, the VPL is discarded as invalid, and the same goes for the VPLs behind a spot light source.

If less than `recalcMin` VPLs are unused, indicating that the maximum number of VPLs is reached or almost reached, VPLs are removed until `recalcMin` VPLs are free. VPLs are removed according to the deletion policy explained earlier. New VPLs are then inserted according to the insertion policy until the maximum VPL count is reached or `recalcMax` VPLs have been inserted. For each newly created VPL, a point is inserted into the Delaunay triangulation and a ray is cast from the light source to the corresponding direction in 3D. The new VPL is placed on the point where the ray hits the static geometry. The direction and color of the VPL are defined by the surface normal and surface color at the hit point, respectively.

Finally, the updated Delaunay triangulation is used to calculate the Voronoi areas for the VPLs. The final emission contribution of a VPL is calculated by multiplying together the color of the primary light source, the color of the VPL, and the Voronoi area of the VPL divided by the area of the 2D region (2π for unit disc). This update must be done in every frame for all VPLs.

VPL Shadow Maps

There are a couple of possible choices for VPL shadow maps; a detailed comparison of hemispherical shadow maps is given by Brabec et al. [Brabec02]. The downside of hemicubes is that they require five rendering passes and relatively high memory consumption. Paraboloid and flattened hemisphere mappings require less memory and only a single pass. However, neither of them can be rasterized correctly using current GPUs, so the static part of the scene must be tessellated so that there aren't edges that are too long. Flattened hemispheres would have perfect importance sampling, but distortion is higher than in paraboloid mapping and the scene would require more tessellation. Because of this, we have settled on the paraboloid maps for now.

Rendering and Filtering

Deferred Shading

Deferred shading is used to accumulate indirect lighting, which ensures that no unseen pixels need to be lit. A drawback is that hardware antialiasing cannot be used for indirect lighting. To perform deferred shading, we store world space position, normal, and diffuse color for each pixel into textures. The collection of these textures is commonly called the G-buffer.

Interleaved Sampling

Interleaved sampling is used so that all pixels don't need to be lit by every VPL. This is done by splitting position and normal textures into N×M smaller textures by picking every Nth pixel horizontally and every Mth pixel vertically. Of course, instead of using N*M different textures, it is more convenient to use just one full-size texture. Interleaved sampling has been used before in the context of instant radiosity and more detailed descriptions are available [Wald04, Segovia06]. The GLSL code for splitting a full-size 1024×768 G-buffer into 4×4 smaller G-buffers is shown next (note that the color buffer does not need to be split).

```
#extension GL_ARB_draw_buffers : enable

uniform sampler2D positionMap, normalMap;

void main(void)
{
    vec2 p = (gl_FragCoord.xy - 0.5) / vec2(1024.0 / 4.0, 768 / 4.0);
    p = fract(p) + (p - fract(p) + 0.5) / vec2(1024.0, 768.0);

    gl_FragData[0] = texture2D(positionMap, p);
    gl_FragData[1] = texture2D(normalMap, p);
}
```

Here is the GLSL code for combining 4×4 result images back into a full-size image:

```
uniform sampler2D result;

void main(void)
{
    vec2 p = gl_FragCoord.xy - 0.5;
    p = (mod(p, 4.0) * vec2(1024 / 4.0, 768 / 4.0) + floor(p / 4.0) +
0.5) / vec2(1024.0, 768.0);

    gl_FragColor = texture2D(result, p);
}
```

Accumulation of Indirect Illumination from VPLs

After the G-buffer has been split and the VPLs have been updated, the illumination due each VPL is accumulated to the framebuffer. Only a subset of the VPLs is rendered to each part of the split G-buffer. The target framebuffer format should be at least 16-bit floating-point because the contribution of a single VPL is typically very small. The following C code drives the accumulation of the VPLs.

```
// Set up fbo, deferred shader and additive blending here

for (int y = 0; y < 4; y++)
    for (int x = 0; x < 4; x++)
        for (int i = y*4+x; i < vplCount; i += 4*4)
        {
            // Set up shader for vpl number i here

            glRectf((x - 2) / 2.0f, (y - 2) / 2.0f,
                    (x - 1) / 2.0f, (y - 1) / 2.0f);

        }
```

A single VPL illuminates pixels just like a standard spot light with cosine falloff: the received irradiance is scaled by the inverse of the squared distance, the dot product between the spot light direction and the direction to the receiving point, and the dot product between the surface normal and the direction to the spot light. Surface color isn't taken into account at this stage. Note that because of a singularity, the intensity might increase arbitrarily in surfaces close to the VPL. To avoid blotches of light, the intensity is simply clamped to some small maximum. Following is the GLSL code for the deferred shader:

```
uniform sampler2D positionMap, normalMap;
uniform sampler2DShadow shadowMap;
uniform vec3 vplPosition;
uniform vec3 vplDirection;
uniform vec3 vplIntensity;
uniform mat4 vplMatrix;
uniform float farPlane;

void main(void)
{
    vec2 p = gl_FragCoord.xy / vec2(1024.0, 768.0);
    vec3 position = texture2D(positionMap, p).xyz;
    vec3 normal = texture2D(normalMap, p).xyz;

    /* Calculate received intensity. */

    vec3 l = position - vplPosition;
    float dist = length(l);
    l /= dist;

    vec3 I = vplIntensity;
    I *= max(0.0, dot(vplDirection, l));
    I *= max(0.0, -dot(normal, l));
    I /= dist * dist;

    /* Paraboloid shadow mapping. */

    vec3 lp = (vplMatrix * vec4(position, 1.0)).xyz;
    float lpDistance = length(lp);
    lp.x = lp.x / (lp.z - lpDistance);
```

```
        lp.y = lp.y / (lp.z - lpDistance);
        lp.z = 2.0 * lpDistance / farPlane - 1.0 - 0.01;

        I *= shadow2D(shadowMap, lp * 0.5 + 0.5).r;

        gl_FragColor = vec4(min(I, 0.05), 1.0);
    }
```

Geometry-Sensitive Box Filtering

When the interleaved result has been combined back to a full-size image, there is a lot of visible noise due to the use of different sets of VPLs between nearby pixels. To remove this noise, we apply geometry-sensitive box filtering. After the box filtering has been done, the indirect illumination is multiplied by the surface color from the G-buffer, which finishes the indirect illumination pass. The result should be blended on the framebuffer after direct lighting has been rendered to enable at least the direct lighting to benefit from hardware antialiasing.

The filter kernel is controlled by two threshold variables: one for positions and one for normals. The position threshold naturally depends on the scale of the scene, but we have found that the normal threshold around 0.8 seems to work relatively well in all scenes.

Here is the GLSL code for 4×4 geometry-sensitive box filtering in 1024×768 resolution.

```
    uniform sampler2D positionMap, normalMap, colorMap, result;

    const float normalThreshold = 0.8;
    const float positionThreshold = 0.2;

    void main(void)
    {
        vec2 p = gl_FragCoord.xy / vec2(1024.0, 768.0);
        vec3 pos = texture2D(positionMap, p).xyz;
        vec3 N = texture2D(normalMap, p).xyz;

        vec4 r = vec4(0.0, 0.0, 0.0, 0.0);

        for (int y = -2; y < 2; y++)
        {
            for (int x = -2; x < 2; x++)
            {
                vec2 p2 = p + vec2(float(x) / 1024.0, float(y) / 768.0);
                vec3 pos2 = texture2D(a, p2).xyz - pos;
                vec3 N2 = texture2D(b, p2).xyz;

                if (dot(N, N2) > normalThreshold &&
                    dot(pos2, pos2) < positionThreshold)
                        r += vec4(texture2D(result, p2).rgb, 1.0);
            }
        }
```

```
        vec3 color = texture2D(colorMap, p).rgb;

        gl_FragColor = vec4(r.xyz * color / r.w, 1.0);
    }
```

Results

The algorithm makes heavy use of fragment shaders, so it scales well with respect to the number of triangles in the scene but quite badly with respect to screen resolution. Using a single 2.2 GHz AMD Athlon 64 processor and NVIDIA GeForce 8800 GTX, the scene in Figure 6.2.1 (80 K triangles) is rendered at 49 fps in 1024×768 resolution. When the resolution is increased to 1600×1200, the fps drops to 26. For more detailed results, see the previous publication [Laine07].

The CPU is rarely the bottleneck if the Delaunay triangulator is fast enough and the ray caster is even reasonably efficient. The number of rays cast per frame is approximately the same as VPL count. Note that the raytracer should not consider the dynamic objects. With a proper Delaunay triangulator and an efficient raytracer, the CPU execution can be done completely in parallel with the GPU usage. If the CPU efficiency becomes a problem, one might allow the indirect illumination to lag one frame behind and always prepare VPLs for the next frame during the current frame. This removes the dependency altogether.

Problems

Instant radiosity works fine for a few light sources, but in more complex scenes, the visual importance of VPLs should be taken into account. Generally speaking, VPLs should be distributed only in places where they contribute to the final image as seen by the camera. If a VPL's contribution is too small, one shouldn't bother rendering it at all. Estimating the contribution efficiently is an interesting open problem.

The method presented here lacks indirect shadows caused by dynamic objects. Ambient occlusion fields [Kontkanen05] could conceivably be used to approximate these. After box filtering, the indirect lighting should be multiplied by the ambient occlusion value that comes from nearby dynamic objects.

So far we have adamantly required that the static part of the scene is indeed static, but relaxing this requirement is probably possible by allowing the illumination to lag slightly behind the changes in the geometry. In our prototype implementation, the complete recomputation of all 256 VPLs would take less than a second. It's quite imaginable that some form of interpolation could get us through that problematic second without the user noticing anything peculiar. The details of this algorithm remain as a future work.

Conclusion

Incremental instant radiosity is an efficient technique to render single-bounce indirect illumination from static geometry to static and dynamic geometry in real-time. By removing and inserting VPLs using Delaunay triangulation-based algorithms, the quality of VPL distributions can be maintained efficiently. The same triangulation is used for weighting the VPLs correctly. Using interleaved sampling, only a subset of VPLs is used for illuminating each single pixel and geometry-sensitive filtering combines illumination from nearby pixels.

References

[Laine07] Laine, S., Saransaari, H., Kontkanen, J., Lehtinen, J., Aila, T. "Incremental Instant Radiosity for Real-Time Indirect Illumination," *Proceedings of the Eurographics Symposium on Rendering*, 2006.

[Keller97] Keller, A. "Instant Radiosity," *Proceedings of ACM SIGGRAPH 97*, 1997.

[Segovia06] Segovia, B. Iehl, J.-C., Mitanchey, R., Péroche, B. "Non-interleaved Deferred Shading of Interleaved Sample Patterns," *Proceedings of Graphics Hardware*, 2006.

[Wald04] Wald, I., "Real-time Ray Tracing and Interactive Global Illumination," PhD thesis, Saarland University, 2004.

[Brabec02] Brabec, S., Annen, T., Seidel H.-P. "Shadow Mapping for Hemispherical and Omnidirectional Light Sources," *Proceedings of Computer Graphics International*, 2002.

[Kontkanen05] Kontkanen, J., Laine, S. "Ambient occlusion fields," *Proceedings of Symposium on Interactive 3D Graphics and Games*, 2005.

Sibenik cathedral model (Figure 6.2.1) courtesy of Marko Dabrovic, RNA studio, www.rna.hr.

6.3

Real-Time Photon Mapping Approximation on the GPU

Vlad Stamate

Introduction

This article presents a technique based on photon mapping and adapts the idea of approximating indirect illumination by photon tracing to real-time rendering. Photon mapping is an established technique in the field of computer-simulated global illumination and it is often offered with raytracing based methods. The technique is relatively new, with first papers being published around 1993.

The adaptation presented in this article uses an index texture to store the IDs of photons that influence each triangle. The index texture is shared between all triangles of a given mesh. The photons' data (such as direction, current position, and color information) is also stored in textures and those textures are de-indexed at runtime by a fragment program.

A demo is provided on the accompanying DVD showcasing the technique.

General Algorithm Considerations

A full implementation of the algorithm consists of five parts. The first four execute on the CPU (or its equivalent in game console hardware) and the last one executes on the GPU. The goal is to design a model to provide a fast global illumination (GI) approximation. As such it needs to store enough photons to achieve global illumination effects such as color bleeding or even more for caustics. The technique should also be compatible to and exploit real-time algorithms for direct illumination (such as those for achieving specular lighting effects). The photon map, which will be stored as textures and thus made available to the GPU, is properly computed as in other photon mapping implementations (see [Jensen01]) and captures the photon density in the scene.

The five steps are as follows:

1. **Photon generation:** Given a light, generate the photons.
2. **Photon tracing:** Trace photons in the scene and store intersections between photons and the scene in a photon map. The tracing will also deal with caustics and color bleeding effects. The photon map is comprised of three textures that hold the following: incident direction, power (flux per channel), and photon IDs.

3. **Proximity calculations:** For each triangle in the scene (and for each vertex of that triangle), find the photons that are close.
4. **Clustering:** Store the photons collected in step 3 in "clusters" in the third texture map.
5. **Rendering:** Render geometry with the three photon map textures bound and compute the lighting equations in a fragment shader.

In offline rendering, a large number of photons (several hundred thousand) are used to capture the lighting. Due to limited resources in real-time applications, we restrict ourselves to just enough to produce the desired visual effects (in the order of thousands). The actual generation and tracing of photons will only be briefly described here; the reader will be pointed to relevant literature for the details. This article will focus primarily on the later parts of the algorithm presented above (steps 3 to 5): The photon gathering, building the texture maps, and the shader design for the actual rendering. Optimizations and future directions will be given toward the end of the article.

Photon Generation and Tracing

Like many other photon mapping algorithms, our technique starts with photon generation and is followed by photon tracing.

Photons have two main attributes that are important for our simulation: power (calculated per channel—RGB) and direction of travel (also called *exitant* direction).

Determining the power of photons depends on the type of light emitter. For example, a diffuse light (the most common case in gaming) of a given power and an equal amount of light going with each photon has the following formula:

$$Intensity_{photon} = \frac{Intensity_{light}}{N_{photons}}$$

1

This ensures that we follow one important law of physics—power conservation—by making sure that we do not artificially introduce (or remove) any light energy from the scene.

Generating photon directions depends on the light's volume/surface/geometry. For simplicity we deal only with point lights here, but area light sources could be easily supported (see [Jensen, Christensen and Suykens01]). We are aiming at generating random (but uniform) directions around the sphere. This ensures that we sample the emissive behavior of a point light in a uniform distribution of directions (see the following pseudo code):

```
while(photons to emit)
{
    float x, y, z;
```

```
do {
    x = 2 * rand01() - 1;
    y = 2 * rand01() - 1;
    z = 2 * rand01() - 1;
} while ( !( fabsf(x)<=1 && fabsf(y)<=1 && fabsf(z)<=1 ) );

Vector3 kPhoton = normalize(x, y, z);
}
```

To produce GI effects we have to bounce photons in the scene multiple times. The tracing is done iteratively—each iteration computes one bounce for each photon. The first iteration traces from light sources to the first intersection; the second iteration starts from previous intersections, computes reflections and/or refractions, and traces until the next intersection. There are a few optimizations worth mentioning here:

- We need to know which meshes we are doing the intersections with, as not all the meshes need to be lit indirectly. After we choose which one to affect, we will proceed in performing ray-triangle intersection between all the photons that we generated during the previous step and the triangles at our disposal. After computing the reflection direction R, we compute the closest intersection I' from the previous intersection I in direction of R.
- A trick to reduce the memory requirement for storing the photons is to store only one position for them. At the beginning we store the origin of the photon, but as the photon travels and intersects geometry we store the position of the intersection point. That now becomes the new origin point. If we want multiple jumps we can compute a reflection vector and in the next pass we repeat the tracing process with the new origin point, a new direction, and a new flux.
- The tracing itself can be done in a multi-pass fashion. Interestingly enough, we can spread the passes across multiple frames, therefore maintaining an interactive frame rate.

Proximity Calculations and Textures Generation

The main purpose of the proximity calculation step is to determine which photon intersections are close to a triangle. In the absence of any spatial optimization (BSP trees, for example) this has a complexity of $O(t*p)$, where t is number of triangles and p is the number of photons. Proximity calculation is similar to a direct visualization for the photon map (albeit with a space filtering scheme, as we compute close and contributing photons).

Our algorithm takes advantage of the fact that, after each bounce iteration, all the photons' positions are updated to where their tracing has ended, that is, at the intersection point with geometry. In that way we never store the origin, only the direction and the current position. This means that once we find an intersection, the intersection point becomes the new origin. This requires less memory for storing the photons, thus allowing us to use more photons.

We need to store the photons' direction and flux in two separate textures. For practical reasons we use a RGBA8 texture format and use each component to store normalized direction values or simply colors (flux).

In this step, we need to determine which photons influence a triangle. For this, we iterate through the scene's triangles and keep track of all photons within a certain proximity. For each photon found we store its ID in a texture, which, at runtime, will be used by the fragment program to de-index the other textures that hold the photon data.

Figure 6.3.1 shows how the three textures generated by our algorithm and passed to the fragment program are related to each other. The index texture holds s, t coordinates referencing texels in the first two textures. These coordinates are grouped into photon-index blocks. Each block corresponds to a triangle and its size determines the number of photons stored for that triangle.

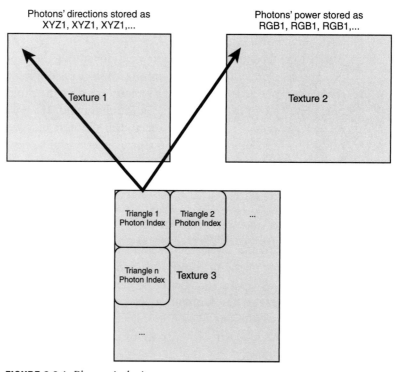

FIGURE 6.3.1 Photon indexing.

The following is pseudo code of how the indexing is built on the CPU.

```
for(all triangles)
{
    Triangle t = getCurrentTriangle();
    float fTriangleDist = influence_distance(t);
    for(all photons or
        until found enough photons for this triangle)
    {
        Photon *pPhoton = getCurrentPhoton();
        if(distance(pPhoton, t) < fTriangleDist)
        {
            // we have found a photon, store its ID
        }
    }
}
```

GPU Fragment Shader Work

We compute the lighting similarly to [Jensen01]. Thus our fragment program needs to compute the following lighting equation:

$$L(x) = \frac{\sum_{i=0}^{n} (power(p_i) * fr(x, N) * \cos(direction(p_i), N))}{\frac{area(triangle_j)}{2}}$$

where

x is a point
p_i is photon i
fr is a BRDF (we assume diffuse surfaces, thus it is constant)
N is a normal
n is a number of photons

The following is Cg source of the fragment shader.

```
// photonIDDimensions encodes
// ( width, height, cellWidth, cellHeight )
half width     = photonIDDimensions.x;
half height    = photonIDDimensions.y;
half cellWidth = photonIDDimensions.z;
half cellHeight = photonIDDimensions.w;

half2 t;
t.x = photonIDTexCoord.x;
t.y = photonIDTexCoord.y;

half3 L = half3(0,0,0);
half  area;
half  i = 0, j = 0;
```

```
for(i=0; i<cellWidth; i++)
{
    for(j=0; j<cellHeight; j++)
    {
        half2 texcoord   = bias(t, j, i, width, height);
        half4 value      = tex2D(photonIDMap, texcoord);
        half2 coord      = value.xy / photonDirDimensions.x;
        area = value.z * 256 + value.w;

        half3 photonDir  = tex2D(photonDirMap, coord).xyz / 255;
        half3 photonFlux = tex2D(photonPowMap, coord).xyz;

        L += photonFlux * dot(photonDir, eyeNormal);
    }
}

L = L / area;
```

Rendering Pipeline Integration

As we're now able to produce interesting indirect lighting effects, we still need to integrate this approach into an existing graphics pipeline.

To figure out where this technique fits best into a pipeline, it is important to understand what features it provides. As such it can

- Model arbitrary light sources not limited to point lights, e.g. it handles polygonal area lights or spherical light sources naturally
- Simulate different materials/BRDFs
- Compute light transport through participating media (e.g. simulate caustics)

Thus, the first step is to choose light sources that emit photons and geometry to be illuminated using the photon density estimation. Next, treat the fragment programs as part of the lighting fragment programs for the materials that are associated with that geometry. This is possible mainly due to the fact that the portion of the program listed above in effect returns a single value L. This value is the amount of light that photons contribute to the current pixel. It needs to be added to the direct lighting and computed with local illumination techniques. As such, we now have the following formula:

$$Light_{final} = Light_{LI} + Light_{GI}$$

$$3$$

where

$$Light_{LI} = Ambient + Diffuse + Specular$$

$$4$$

and $Light_{LI}$ are local illumination lighting values and $Light_{GI}$ are global illumination lighting values.

Optimizations

The algorithm provided in this article is fairly computationally intensive when implemented naively. However, there are ways to improve its performance.

- **Space partitioning algorithms.** Using a BSP tree, an octree, or a kd-tree instantly provides two advantages. First, it accelerates photon tracing by reducing the number of intersections tests. Similarly, it reduces the computation required for finding photons close to triangles. Both operations are initially $O(n*m)$ (where n=number of triangles and m=number of photons), while when using octree, for example this reduces to $O(log2(n)*m)$. We can obtain even better than this—$O(log2(n*m))$—if the actual photon tracing is done with the octree in mind.
- **Multi-pass across multiple frames.** This means we can distribute the work across multiple frames. We perform only one trace pass per frame and gather results across different frames.

On machines supporting multi-threading reliably (that is, there is actual hardware support for this feature), such as Dual or Quad Core CPUs, Microsoft XBox360, or Sony PlayStation 3 consoles, we delegate the CPU work to a distinct thread. In fact, the lighting computation can be a few frames behind, such as when gathering or ray-triangle intersections are based on a previous frame. Almost all tasks in this algorithm are CPU limited and very parallelizable.

Speed Considerations

On the DVD accompanying this book you will find an implementation of the algorithm presented in this article. In the implementation I have sacrificed speed enhancements for code clarity. Even so, the following table presents some performance data obtained with the code.

Photons	Triangles/Vertices	Time (ms)
16	1536/4608	66
256	1536/4608	343
256	6144/18432	1390

Individual Times (ms)

Render	Triangle Hit	Photon Trace	Build Textures
15	0	15	0
62	100	297	15
62	552	1234	62

Conclusion

In this article we present a technique that uses the photon light transfer to compute indirect illumination in a scene. The algorithm consists of several computation passes on the CPU to generate, trace, and intersect photons with the nearby geometry. An "indexing" approach is used to store IDs of photons affecting a triangle in a texture. The indices are then used on the GPU to look up photon attributes via a simple fragment program. The algorithm is fairly CPU intensive and can take advantage of any hardware support for multi-threading since it is very parallelizable.

References

[Christen05] Martin Christen "Implementing Ray-Tracing on the GPU," pp. 409–428 (*ShaderX⁴*, edited by Wolfgang Engel), Charles River Media.

[Dutré03] Philip Dutré, Philippe Bekaert, Kavita Bala *Advanced Global Illumination, 1st Edition*, 2003

[Jensen01] Henrik Wann Jensen: *Realistic Image Synthesis Using Photon Mapping*

[Jensen01] Henrik Wann Jensen: *A Practical Guide to Global Illumination Using Photon Mapping*, Siggraph 2001, Course 38

[Kalos05] László Szirmay-Kalos, Barnabás Aszódi, István Lazányi: "Ray Tracing Effects without Tracing Rays," pp. 397–408 (*ShaderX⁴*, edited by Wolfgang Engel), Charles River Media.

[Pharr04] Matt Pharr, Greg Humphreys: *Physically Based Rendering, 3rd Edition*

[Shirley03] Peter Shirley, R Keith Morley: *Realistic Ray Tracing, 2nd Edition*

6.4

Interactive Global Illumination with Precomputed Radiance Maps

László Szécsi

László Szirmay-Kalos

Mateu Sbert

Introduction

This article presents a real-time global illumination method for static scenes illuminated by arbitrary, dynamic light sources. The method consists of a preprocessing phase and a real-time rendering phase. The real-time rendering algorithm obtains the indirect illumination caused by multiple scatterings of the light from partial light paths that are precomputed and stored in the preprocessing phase. These partial light paths connect two points on the surface either directly or via one or more reflection points. Unlike precomputed radiance transfer [Sloan02], the method presented in this article requires moderate preprocessing time, does not assume low-frequency hemispherical lighting, and can also work well for small light sources that may get close to the surfaces. The implemented version considers only diffuse reflections for the indirect illumination. To deal with complex scenes, a clustering scheme is also introduced, which trades storage space for high frequency details in the indirect illumination.

Problem Statement

Rendering requires the identification of light paths that connect light sources to the eye via reflections and then the computation of the sum of all path contributions. Accurate results require a high number of light paths, which are generally impossible to evaluate in real-time. However, in static scenes we can exploit the fact that those parts of light paths that connect surface points do not change when the camera or lights move. This observation allows us to precompute these light paths and combine the prepared data with the actual lighting conditions during real-time rendering [Szecsi06]. This means that, having preprocessed the scene, we can obtain global illumination results and only pay the cost of local illumination rendering.

Overview of the Method

The proposed method consists of a preprocessing phase and a fast rendering phase.

Preprocessing

The preprocessing phase determines the self illumination capabilities of the static scene. This information is computed for a finite number of *exit points* on the surface, and we use interpolation for other surface points. Exit points are depicted by symbol × in Figure 6.4.1. Exit points are defined as points corresponding to the texel centers of a texture atlas.

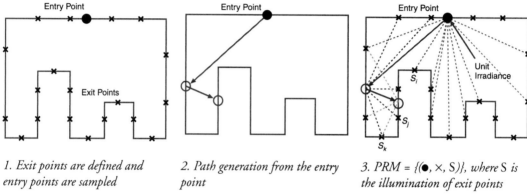

1. Exit points are defined and entry points are sampled

2. Path generation from the entry point

3. PRM = {(●, ×, S)}, where S is the illumination of exit points

FIGURE 6.4.1 Overview of the preprocessing phase: Entry points are depicted by ● and exit points by ×. The PRM is a collection of (entry point ●, exit point ×, radiance S_k) triplets, and called items.

The first step of the preprocessing is the generation of a certain number of *entry points* on the surface. These entry points are the samples of first hits of the light emitted by light sources. (Entry points are depicted by the symbol ● in Figure 6.4.1.) Entry points are sampled randomly and are used as the start of a given number of light paths. A light path is a random or a quasi-random walk [Keller97] on the surfaces, which is terminated randomly according to Russian roulette.

As we do not know the actual irradiance at the entry point during preprocessing, we assume that it has unit irradiance for now. During rendering we will multiply the light transport of this path with the actual irradiance value obtained from direct lighting. The visited points of a light path are considered as *virtual point lights* [Keller97, Wald02], which may illuminate all other points of the scene. While generating random walks is best done on the CPU, the GPU is better at computing the effect of virtual lights on exit points. Since exit points are texel centers of a texture map, the virtual light source algorithm should be implemented in a way so that it renders into a texture map.

A virtual light source illuminates all exit points visible to it; this is where the reflected radiance is obtained. The direct illumination caused by these virtual lights divided by the probability of the path is the Monte Carlo estimate of the global, i.e.

direct and indirect illumination of the light source put at the entry point. The average of the Monte Carlo estimates of several paths associated with each entry and exit point pair is stored in a data structure we call the *precomputed radiance map*, (PRM). Thus a PRM contains *items* corresponding to entry and exit point pairs. Items that belong to the same entry point constitute a *PRM pane*. A PRM pane is an array or a 2D texture of exit point radiances computed with the assumption that the corresponding entry point has unit irradiance while all other entry points have zero irradiance.

Rendering

The rendering step is implemented completely on the GPU. During real-time rendering, we use the PRM to speed up the global illumination calculation. The lights and the camera are placed in the virtual world (Figure 6.4.2). The direct illumination effects are computed with standard techniques, which usually include a shadow algorithm to identify those points that are visible from the light source. PRMs are used to add the indirect illumination. To weight PRM items with the actual irradiance, we need to determine the visibility between the light source and the entry points. Note that we can use the shadow maps of the light sources to determine whether or not a particular entry point is visible [Dachsbacher05]. Practically, we can use the same depth map for direct shadows and entry-point visibility.

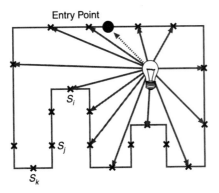
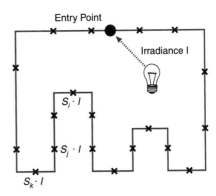

1. Direct illumination and entry-point visibility

2. Weighting irradiance I *with items* S_i

FIGURE 6.4.2 Overview of the rendering phase: The irradiance at the entry points is computed, from which the radiance of the exit points is obtained by weighting according to the PRM.

A PRM pane (Figure 6.4.3) stores the indirect illumination computed for the case when the respective entry point has unit irradiance. During the rendering phase, however, we have to adapt to a different lighting environment. The PRM panes associated with entry points should be weighted in order to make them reflect the actual

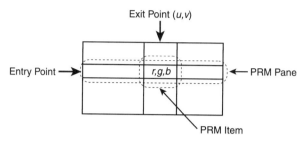

FIGURE 6.4.3 Representation of a PRM as an array indexed
by entry points and exit points. A single element of this
map is the PRM item, a single row is the PRM pane.

lighting. Computing the weighting factors involves a visibility check that can effectively be done in a shader using the shadow map already computed for direct illumination. This shader renders into a one-dimensional texture of weights. Although these values will later be accessible via texture reads, they can be read back and uploaded into constant registers for efficiency. Furthermore, zero weight textures can be excluded, thus sparing superfluous texture accesses.

In order to find the indirect illumination at an exit point, the corresponding PRM items should be read from the textures and their values summed up by multiplying them by the weighting factors and the light intensity. We can limit the number of entry points to those having the highest weights. The currently most significant texture panes can be selected on the CPU before uploading the weighting factors as constants.

Having obtained the radiance for each exit point, the scene is rendered in a standard way with linear interpolation between the exit points. Because exit points correspond to texel centers, the required linear interpolation is automatically provided by the bilinear filtering of the texturing hardware.

Storing and Compressing PRMs

PRMs are stored in textures for real-time rendering. A single texel stores a PRM item, which represents the contribution of all paths connecting the same entry point and exit point. A PRM can thus be considered as an array indexed by the entry point and exit point, and will store the radiance transfer on the wavelengths of red, green, and blue (Figure 6.4.3). Because an exit point itself is identified by two texture coordinates, a PRM can be stored either in a 3D texture or in a set of 2D textures (Figure 6.4.4), where each 2D texture represents a single PRM pane (i.e. a row of the table in Figure 6.4.3), which includes the PRM items belonging to a single entry point.

The number of 2D textures is equal to the number of entry points. However, the graphics hardware has just a few texture units. Fortunately, this can be sidestepped by tiling the PRM panes into one or more larger textures. Tiling allows us to render indirect illumination interactively with a typical number of 256 entry points. While this

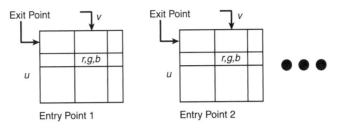

FIGURE 6.4.4 PRM stored as 2D textures.

number is generally considered sufficient for a low complexity scene, difficult geometries and animations may emphasize virtual light source artifacts as spikes or flickering, thus requiring even more samples. Simply increasing the number of entry points and adding corresponding PRM panes would quickly challenge even the latest hardware in terms of texture memory and texture access performance. To cope with this problem, we can apply an approximation (comparable to a lossy compression scheme), which keeps the number of panes low when the number of entry points increases.

The compression algorithm clusters entry points that are close and are on surfaces of similar orientation. Contributions of a cluster of entry points are added and stored in a single PRM pane. As these *clustered entry points* cannot be separated during rendering, they will all share the same weight when the entry point contributions are combined. This common weight is obtained as the average of the individual weights of the entry points.

The key observation behind clustering is that if two entry points are close and are located on similarly aligned surfaces, then their direct illumination will be probably very similar during the light animation. Of course, this is not true when a hard shadow boundary separates the two entry points, but due to the fact that a single entry point is responsible just for a small fraction of the indirect illumination, these approximation errors are tolerable and do not cause noticeable artifacts. This property can also be understood if we examine how clustering affects the represented indirect illumination. Clustering entry points corresponds to a low-pass filtering of the indirect illumination, which is usually already low-frequency by itself, thus the filtering does not introduce a significant error. Furthermore, errors in the low frequency domain are not disturbing to the human eye. Clustering also helps to eliminate animation artifacts. When a small light source moves, the illumination of an entry point may change abruptly, possibly causing flickering. If multiple entry points are clustered together, their average illumination will change smoothly. This way clustering also trades high-frequency error in the temporal domain for low-frequency error in the spatial domain. In case of a large scene (like a game level), we need a high number of clusters to represent indirect illumination. However, only the nearest few will actually contribute to the shading of a given surface element. Therefore, these large scenes have to be broken down into smaller objects (like rooms), for which storing only the PRM panes of the closest 16 to 32 clusters is sufficient. In the final rendering phase, only these have to be combined, making the performance independent of the complexity of the scene.

Results

Figure 6.4.5 shows a marble chamber test scene consisting of 3,335 triangles rendered on 1024×768 resolution. We used 4,096 entry points organized into 256 clusters. We set the PRM pane resolution to 256×256, and used the 32 highest weighted entry clusters. In this case the peak texture memory requirement was 128 MB.

FIGURE 6.4.5 Marble chamber scene. The image on the left shows the distribution of randomly generated entry points. The middle and right images compare local illumination and the proposed global illumination rendering methods. The lower half of these images has been rendered with local illumination, while the upper half has been rendered with the discussed global illumination method.

For this scene, the preprocessing took 8.5 seconds, which can further be decomposed as building the kd-tree for ray casting (0.12 seconds), light tracing with ray casting (0.17 seconds), and PRM generation (8.2 seconds). Having obtained the PRM, we run the global illumination rendering, interactively changing the camera and light positions. Figure 6.4.5 also includes screenshots in which half of the image has been rendered with the new algorithm and the other half with local illumination for comparison. The effects are most obvious in shadows, but also notice color bleeding and finer details in indirect illumination that could not be achieved by coarse approximations or "fake" methods such as using an ambient lighting term, for example. We measured 40 fps and 200 fps in full-screen mode on NVIDIA GeForce 6800 GT and 8800 GTX graphics cards, respectively. The chairs scene in Figure 6.4.6 has also been rendered with the same speed.

Figure 6.4.7 shows a scene inspired by the stairs in M.C. Escher's *Ascending and Descending*. The scene consists of nine objects, each having 32 entry point clusters. This scene is rendered at 30 fps and 180 fps on NVIDIA GeForce 6800 GT and 8800 GTX graphics cards, respectively.

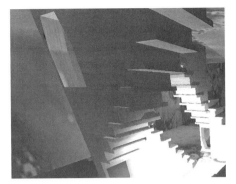

FIGURE 6.4.6 The chairs scene lit by a rectangular spot light and rendered with the proposed method.

FIGURE 6.4.7 Escher-type stairs in a globally illuminated room

Figure 6.4.8 shows two screenshots of a demo game called *Space Station* that was developed in the framework of the GameTools project. This game does not use ambient light, but the indirect illumination of the static scene (the space station itself) is computed using the precomputed radiance maps method.

FIGURE 6.4.8 Integration of the precomputed radiance maps method into a game called *Space Station* [GameTools07].

Conclusions and Future Work

The method presented here can replace light maps in games and interactive applications. It also renders indirect lighting of static geometry, but unlike light maps, it allows for dynamic lighting and updates indirect shadows and color bleeding effects when light sources move.

Global illumination computations are performed in a precomputation step using ray casting and the virtual light sources method. The contributions of virtual light samples are computed with depth mapping on the GPU. However, instead of computing a single light map, multiple texture atlases (constituting the PRM) are generated for the scene objects, which all correspond to a cluster of indirect lighting samples. These atlases are weighted and summed according to actual lighting conditions. Weighting factors depend on how much light actually arrives at the sample points used for PRM generation, which is also computed on the GPU. The final result is a plausible rendering of indirect illumination. Indirect shadows and color bleeding effects appear and the indirect illumination changes as light sources move.

The presented algorithm makes a clear separation between PRM generation, which is done during preprocessing, and PRM application, which is executed at runtime. PRMs could also be computed incrementally by adding or deleting entry points. Such incremental approaches have been proposed in [Sbert04] and [Laine07].

However, incremental updates have significant overhead and do not allow the application of compression schemes, thus the discussed static approach is more suitable for game applications.

We also extended the method to scenes with larger static parts and smaller dynamic objects. The indirect illumination of the static scene on dynamic objects can be obtained by localized environment maps [Lazanyi06]. For example, in Figure 6.4.8, the indirect illumination of the "scientist" character is computed with this technique. On the other hand, dynamic objects also modify the self illumination of the static environment. In our future work, we plan to remove indirect lighting invalidated by occlusions of dynamic objects, which is possible without recomputing the PRMs from scratch by working with negative light, called *antiradiance* [Dachsbacher07]. This requires the identification of those light paths that intersect the dynamic object.

Acknowledgments

This work has been supported by the GameTools project, Hewlett-Packard, and the National Office for Research and Technology (Hungary).

References

[Dachsbacher03] Dachsbacher, C. and Stamminger, M. "Reflective shadow maps," *SI3D '05: Proceedings of the 2005 Symposium. on Interactive 3D Graphics and Games*, 2005: pp. 203–231.

[Dachsbacher07] Dachsbacher, C., Stamminger, M., Drettakis, G., and Durand, F. "Implicit Visibility and Antiradiance for Interactive Global Illumination," in ACM Transactions on Graphics, Volume 26, Issue 3, (*SIGGRAPH 2007 Proceedings*), 2007.

[GameTools07] http://www.gametools.org

[Keller97] Keller, A. "Instant radiosity," in *SIGGRAPH '97 Proceedings*, 1997: pp. 49–55.

[Lazanyi06] Lazányi, I. and Szirmay-Kalos, L. "Indirect Diffuse and Glossy Illumination on the GPU," *ShaderX5*, Wolfgang Engel, Ed., 2006: pp. 345–358.

[Laine07] Laine, S., Saransaari, H., Kontkanen, J., Lehtinen, J., Aila, T. "Incremental Instant Radiosity for Real-Time Indirect Illumination," *Eurographics Symposium on Rendering*, 2007: pp. 49–55.

[Sbert04] Sbert, M., Szécsi, L., and Szirmay-Kalos, L. "Real-time Light Animation," *Computer Graphics Forum (Eurographics'04)*, Volume 23, Number 3, 2004: pp. 291–300.

[Sloan02] Sloan, P., Kautz, J., Snyder, J. "Precomputed radiance transfer for real-time rendering in dynamic, low-frequency lighting environments," *SIGGRAPH 2002 Proceedings*, 2002: pp. 527–536.

[Szécsi06] Szécsi, L., Szirmay-Kalos, L., and Sbert, M. "Light animation with pre-computed light paths on the GPU," *Graphics Interface 2006 Proceedings*, 2006: pp. 187–194.

[Wald02] Wald, I., Kollig, T., Benthin, C., Keller, A., and Slussalek, P. "Interactive global illumination using fast ray tracing," in *13th Eurographics Workshop on Rendering*, 2002: pp. 15–24.

HANDHELD DEVICES

Introduction

Wolfgang Engel

The "Handheld Devices" section covers the latest developments in graphics programming targeting devices that are portable, such as mobile phones or personal organizers. The latest generation of GPUs for handheld devices comes with a feature set that is comparable to the latest PC and console GPU feature set.

The section starts with the article "Shaders Gone Mobile: Porting from Direct3D 9.0 to Open GL ES 2.0" by Mikey Wetzel. It describes how to port a PC game to a mobile platform that supports Open GL ES 2.0 and shows the tools necessary to build up-front to succeed with this task in the accompanying code.

Maurice Ribble then explains in his article, "Efficiently Using Tile-Based GPUs on Mobile Phones," how a tile-based hardware architecture works and how it is efficiently used. Following the idea that was used in the Xbox 360 with the fast EDRAM memory, a tile-based renderer utilizes memory with a huge bandwidth and with low latency. This way, GPU memory intensive operations like blending, depth testing, and multi-sample anti-aliasing are greatly improved.

OpenGL ES 2.0 provides three levels of float precision for shader programs. Traditional floating-point representation is included with medium and high precision variables; in addition, the shading language defines a low-precision format, which can afford up to double the throughput of the higher precisions on mobile platforms. The article "Maximal Performance and Image Quality with Minimal Precision" by Ken Catterall shows how to make maximal use of the low-precision format without sacrificing image quality in your shader effects.

The article "Implementing Graphical Benchmark in OpenGL ES 2.0" by Szabolcs Horvath, Csaba Keszegh, and Laszlo Kishonti is a case study on how to implement a benchmark application that runs on many handheld devices.

Kristof Beet's article, "Every Cycle Counts: Level of Detail Shaders for Handheld Devices," provides an introduction to an effective shader-based LOD mechanism to smoothly scale vertex and fragment shader complexity to increase overall performance and reduce memory bandwidth usage.

The article "Shadow Techniques for OpenGL ES 2.0" by Jonathan Feldstein covers light maps, decal shadows, and projective shadows, and introduces three shadow map algorithms that are relatively inexpensive on the target platform. The shadow map techniques discussed are PCF filtered shadow maps, variance shadow maps, and exponential shadow maps, as covered by Marco Salvi in the "Shadows" section.

Have fun!
Wolf

7.1

Shaders Gone Mobile: Porting from Direct3D 9.0 to OpenGL ES 2.0

Mikey Wetzel (mikey.wetzel@amd.com)

Introduction

With the latest round of game consoles now shipping and the desktop space catching up with new hardware features like geometry shaders, the next frontier in 3D graphics is the mobile space. The next wave of mobile GPUs, such as AMD's upcoming Imageon processor based on the same core as the Xbox 360, will be fully capable of running programmable shaders to achieve desktop-quality effects. Handheld gaming will never be the same.

These upcoming GPUs support a feature set that closely matches Direct3D version 9.0-class hardware, including programmable vertex and pixel shaders, dependent texture reads, and shader model 3.0 with dynamic control flow. This is very fortunate, as the industry has had a long time to get accustomed to developing shader effects and building content pipelines for this class of hardware. All of these acquired skills and technologies can now be applied to the mobile space, although platform-specific challenges still need to be addressed before any porting work can begin.

For those weaned on Direct3D, the largest challenge by far will be the adoption of OpenGL ES 2.0 for 3D graphics programming. Developers who are completely new to OpenGL ES 2.0 can check out a number of excellent introductions to the API, such as those published in *ShaderX5: Advanced Rendering Techniques*. To summarize, OpenGL ES 2.0 is a leaner, embedded-systems flavor of the popular desktop API streamlined by removing redundant features like the fixed-function pipeline as well as rarely used features like multiple render-targets and depth output in pixel shaders.

The remainder of this article is devoted to porting applications, shaders, and content from the reigning API of desktop gaming, Direct3D 9.0, to the future of mobile graphics programming, OpenGL ES 2.0. Thanks to full-featured hardware and a robust API, porting can be relatively straightforward without any major functional changes.

Porting from Direct3D 9.0 to OpenGL ES 2.0

In "the tale of two APIs," the same 3D hardware is being programmed, so just how different can Direct3D and OpenGL really be? A major difference is that while Direct3D is an object-oriented API, OpenGL is more of a state machine, requiring objects to be globally bound before subsequent APIs take action on (or with) them. That's a fairly easy change to get used to, but it's the difference in terminology that is much more likely to trip up experienced D3D programmers. After all, how can a developer search in documentation or header files for something like an "index buffer" when OpenGL uses the term "vertex element array"?

Terminology Differences

A small sampling of terminology differences is shown in Table 7.1.1. By no means is this complete; experience is the only way to really learn them all, and there are much more valid uses for dead trees. Most of the terms, like "uniform" versus "constant" or "fragment" versus "pixel," have a concept that is well-defined in hardware, so they should be easy for any experienced 3D graphics developer to pick up.

Table 7.1.1 A sampling of API terminology differences

Direct3D 9 Concepts	OpenGL ES 2.0 Concepts
Vertex	Vertex
Pixel	Fragment
Render-target	Frame buffer object (FBO)
Vertex buffer (VB)	Vertex buffer object (VBO)
Index buffer (IB)	Vertex element array
Paired vertex and pixel shaders	Shader "program"
Shader constant	Shader "uniform"
Vertex declaration	Shader "attribute"
Interpolated vertex shader output	Shader "varying"
HLSL COLOR0 semantic	GLSL gl_FragColor
HLSL FLOAT4	GLSL vec4
HLSL FLOAT4X4	GLSL mat4
(etc...)	(etc...)

One concept deserves special mention, and that's the use of the term "fragment" versus "pixel." To a D3D programmer, the concept of a fragment might have different meanings, none of which resemble the OpenGL use of the word. For example, D3D developers may author HLSL shaders in smaller pieces called fragments, which are formally defined in the DXSDK documentation as "standalone shader functions." D3D programmers need to let go of this definition, which has no counterpart in OpenGL. To the hardware, OpenGL *fragments* and *fragment shaders* are no different than D3D *pixels* and *pixel shaders*, respectively, so developers should think of the terms in the same way.

API Differences

Once a developer is familiar with the change in terminology, there's still a new API to become accustomed to. As mentioned, the largest change is that Direct3D is object-oriented and OpenGL is a state machine. To start with an example, compare creating and populating a texture in Direct3D 9 to doing the same in OpenGL ES 2.0. First, in D3D:

```
HRESULT hr;
LPDIRECT3DTEXTURE9 pTexture;
hr = pd3dDevice->CreateTexture( nWidth, nHeight, 1, 0,
                                nFormat, D3DPOOL_DEFAULT,
                                &pTexture, NULL );

D3DLOCKED_RECT lock;
pTexture->LockRect( 0, &lock, NULL, 0 );
memcpy( lock.pBits, pInitialData, nInitialDataSize );
pTexture->UnlockRect( 0 );

pd3dDevice->SetTextureStageState( 0, D3DTSS_MINFILTER,
                                  D3DTEXF_LINEAR );
pd3dDevice->SetTextureStageState( 0, D3DTSS_MAGFILTER,
                                  D3DTEXF_LINEAR );
```

And now in OpenGL:

```
GLuint hTexture;
glGenTextures( 1, &hTexture );
glBindTexture( GL_TEXTURE_2D, hTexture );

glTexParameteri( GL_TEXTURE_2D, GL_TEXTURE_MAG_FILTER,
                 GL_LINEAR );
glTexParameteri( GL_TEXTURE_2D, GL_TEXTURE_MIN_FILTER,
                 GL_LINEAR );

if( bCompressed )
   glCompressedTexImage2D( GL_TEXTURE_2D, 0, nFormat,
                           nWidth, nHeight, nBorder,
                           nBaseSize, pInitialData );
else
   glTexImage2D( GL_TEXTURE_2D, 0, nFormat,
                 nWidth, nHeight, nBorder,
                 nFormat, nType, pInitialData );

GLenum err = glGetError();
```

Here we can see how OpenGL objects work off handles rather than allocated objects. Handles first need to be bound, after which they can be used to perform actions on the referenced object. In the example above, memory resources for the texture are not allocated until the glTexImage2D call, which also uses the supplied data to initialize the newly allocated memory. Direct3D creates the texture in entirety with a single call, but relies on the Lock/Unlock methods to populate the texture with data. Neither API is better or worse than the other; they are just different.

While the API differences are not obstacles to functionality, a major stumbling block for any Direct3D programmer new to OpenGL will be figuring out which parameters are intended for which function calls. There are a couple reasons for this. First, object-oriented programming makes it clear which methods work on which objects. This is even more true when using advanced development environments with class lookup and autocomplete features. Second, Direct3D uses typedefed enums and typed class pointers for almost all function parameters, making it difficult to erroneously pass inappropriate arguments. Lacking the conveniences of object-oriented programming, trial-and-error will reign at first, but time (or rather experience) heals all wounds. Regardless, plenty of seasoned programmers prefer the OpenGL programming model, so it's again hard to argue whether either API is better or worse than the other.

The actual porting of existing code from Direct3D 9 to OpenGL ES 2.0 is pretty straightforward when replacing actual API calls. Savvy developers will take the opportunity to create an API-agnostic wrapper layer, although hopefully a very lightweight one that gets compiled away (which, for the record, is not so trivial to do with the less mature compilers often used for embedded devices). Similar to porting from desktop to OpenGL, the bigger challenges are found in removing any dependence on platform-specific code and porting away from features not found in ES 2.0, such as the fixed-function pipeline.

Functionality Differences

To start at a high level, the first major functionality loss when porting to OpenGL is the obvious lack of D3DX, the utility library for Direct3D. Any code depending on D3DX for math functions, mesh loading, animation, or HLSL FX obviously needs to be ported to use custom code. However, the same could be said of using any platform-dependent, closed-source middleware, since we can really think of D3DX as a middleware layer. Fortunately, most professional game developers typically already have in-house, portable math libraries and custom mesh code. The caveat here is that code must be platform-independent in the stricter sense, such as no inline assembly or SSE optimizations. HLSL FX represent a bigger porting challenge since many development houses actually use them.

Of the hundreds upon hundreds of HLSL FX files for actual video games personally viewed by the author, very few of them use FX to define multiple passes. That is, an FX "technique" really boils down to simply a vertex/pixel shader pair and maybe some additional render states. Most of the value added to the FX format over pure HLSL, then, is in dealing with shader constants. This is fortunate, as porting away from this light usage of FX is relatively straightforward. In fact, the shader constant binding mechanism in FX is rather generic, and many professional developers have already discovered the performance improvements of "rolling their own" solutions anyway.

Direct3D deals with vertex shaders and pixel shaders as separate objects. In reality, though, the two need to be mated in a very specific way according to the needs of the hardware. This is called *shader patching*, and it happens under the hood in the bowels of the driver. This mechanism is very flexible, but it does come at a cost. A current generation game that switches shaders hundreds or thousands of times in a single scene can spend significant CPU time patching shaders. OpenGL ES 2.0 avoids this expense by requiring that vertex shaders and fragments get linked into a shader "program." This happens only once, typically immediately after the individual shaders are compiled. The only porting issue here is that a potentially larger number of shader programs needs to be maintained by the application. For example, a Direct3D 9 application with five vertex shaders and five pixel shaders may require up to a total of 25 shader program permutations when ported to OpenGL ES 2.0.

Because OpenGL ES 2.0 lacks any concept of vertex declarations, binding vertex attributes in order to pair a vertex buffer to a shader becomes a challenge. Naive implementations will simply hard-code OpenGL calls to a known vertex buffer. For example, the problem is not so difficult if it can be guaranteed that all vertices are simply a position, a normal, and a texture coordinate. In contrast, real-world applications use an art pipeline that produces all kinds of meshes with a variety of vertex types, so the naive approach will not do.

To further complicate the matter, OpenGL shaders lack any type of shader semantics to describe how individual vertex components will be mapped inside a vertex shader. Whereas Direct3D uses HLSL to bind, for example, a vertex position to the POSITION semantic or a pointsprite velocity to the TEXCOORD5 semantic, GLSL works off of ASCII strings and integer-based shader "locations." That pointsprite velocity might be called g_vPVelocity in the GLSL shader and get arbitrarily mapped to location 2. The latter is retrieved using the glGetAttribLocation() API, which takes an ASCII string, searches for it internally, and returns the mapping, if found, to the appropriate integer-based location.

Given this situation, how can a developer create a library of shaders that works with an arbitrary mesh provided by his art team? One solution is to reintroduce the concept of a vertex declaration, including the ability to parse a description of vertex components from a mesh file and to dynamically build a list of appropriate OpenGL calls to bind the vertex attributes to the system. Programmatically, the developer still needs to bind ASCII names as they appear in the actual GLSL code, but the meshes can still be flexible.

An example of code that uses a binary mesh with a custom shader is provided at the end of this article. The proposed solution starts with a structure defining the parameters needed for the runtime OpenGL calls. An array of these structures is embedded into a binary mesh file: one array for each vertex buffer present in the mesh.

```
enum FRM_VERTEX_USAGE
{
    FRM_VERTEX_POSITION,                    // 0
    FRM_VERTEX_BONEINDICES,                 // 1
    FRM_VERTEX_BONEWEIGHTS,                 // 2
    FRM_VERTEX_NORMAL,                      // 3
    FRM_VERTEX_TANGENT,                     // 4
    FRM_VERTEX_BINORMAL,                    // 5
    FRM_VERTEX_TEXCOORD0,                   // 6
    ...
    FRM_VERTEX_COLOR0,                      // 12
    ...
};

#pragma pack(push,1)
struct FRM_VERTEX_ELEMENT
{
    UINT16      nUsage;             // FRM_VERTEX_USAGE
    UINT8       nSize;              // Number of components
    UINT16      nType;             // OpenGL data type
    UINT8       bNormalized;    // Whether to normalize the value
    UINT16      nStride;           // Stride of this component
};
#pragma pack(pop)
```

The key here is that the vertex elements agree on a pre-defined enumeration of usages—something that OpenGL does not normally enforce. For example, vertex position is usage 0, vertex normal is usage 3, and so on. The array of vertex elements, here called a *vertex layout*, can then be set when the mesh is ready to be rendered. This is akin to calling `SetVertexDeclaration()` in Direct3D 9.

```
VOID FrmSetVertexLayout( FRM_VERTEX_ELEMENT* pElements,
                         UINT32 nVertexSize,
                         VOID* pBaseOffset = NULL )
{
    UINT32 nOffset = (UINT32)pBaseOffset;

    while( pElements->nSize )
    {
        glVertexAttribPointer( pElements->nUsage,
                               pElements->nSize,
                               pElements->nType,
                               pElements->bNormalized,
                               nVertexSize,
                               (VOID*)nOffset );
        glEnableVertexAttribArray( pElements->nUsage );

        nOffset+= pElements->nStride;
        pElements++;
    }
}
```

The next step involves using those agreed upon usage values to bind the shader attribute locations as well. Direct3D needs to do this, too, but it happens internally via Direct3D's access to an HLSL shader's string table. Fortunately, OpenGL grants access to the string table as well; it is just that attribute binding is left to be done manually by the application.

Shader attributes are defined here as an ASCII string mated to a vertex usage:

```
FRM_SHADER_ATTRIBUTE pShaderAttributes[] =
{
    { "In_Position",           FRM_VERTEX_POSITION },
    { "In_BoneIndices",     FRM_VERTEX_BONEINDICES },
    { "In_BoneWeights",     FRM_VERTEX_BONEWEIGHTS },
    { "In_Normal",               FRM_VERTEX_NORMAL },
    { "In_TexCoord",         FRM_VERTEX_TEXCOORD0 },
};
```

The structure above is handed off to a helper function that does the actual shader compilation, after which the values can be used to dictate vertex attribute locations to the shader.

```
VOID FrmBindShaderAttributes( GLuint hShaderProgram,
                    FRM_SHADER_ATTRIBUTE* pAttributes,
                    UINT32 nNumAttributes )
{
    for( UINT32 i=0; i<nNumAttributes; i++ )
    {
        glBindAttribLocation( hShaderProgram,
                              pAttributes[i].nLocation,
                              pAttributes[i].strName );
    }
}
```

In the preceding example, it's crucial that the ASCII names used correlate to the actual names in the shaders. Usually this does not present a problem, but it's still not entirely flexible. An arguably better system would be to preprocess the GLSL shader file in a way where Direct3D-style semantics could be embedded directly into the shader code. This has been successfully mocked up and tested to work as expected. Text preprocessing of the GLSL can simply replace text like g_vPVelocity with the associated semantic like TEXCOORD5. Then the application can be hard-coded to always and only look for the ASCII string TEXCOORD5. In practice, this is getting very close to how the binding works in Direct3D 9, although it would require making a non-standard and admittedly awkward extension to GLSL.

HLSL versus GLSL

Porting HLSL to GLSL largely involves just search-and-replace type changes: FLOAT4 becomes vec4, and so on. There are some very crucial differences that make initial ports a little frustrating, though.

First and foremost, GLSL shaders use a single entry point called `main()`. All inputs and outputs to the shader are defined externally as global variables. There are three types of external variables:

- **Attribute:** Attributes are vertex components like position, normal, and so on. They are inputs. As mentioned above, there are no pre-defined semantics to which to bind them, just whatever ASCII name the developer chooses to assign to them. Some consistency is recommend, otherwise shaders could have close, but slightly differing names like `g_vPosition`, `In_Position`, `pos`, `vPositionOS`, etc.
- **Uniform:** These are shader constants, as set by the application. They are inputs and are valid for either vertex shaders or fragment shaders. Unlike in Direct3D, there is no `register(cn)` mechanism to specifically assign the slots to which they are bound. Rather, the application must call OpenGL to determine the location.
- **Varying:** These are vertex outputs that get interpolated to be per-pixel values that are input to the fragment shader. They are not externally visible to the application.

Because OpenGL does not provide semantics to define inputs and outputs, some external variables are pre-defined in GLSL. For example, in HLSL, the pixel shader outputs to whichever variable is tagged with the `COLOR0` semantic. In contrast, in GLSL, the fragment shader writes the final color to the predefined `gl_FragColor` variable. The other common variable is `gl_Position`, which is the clip-space output position for vertex shaders. Beware that GLSL code examples found on the Internet are often written for desktop OpenGL, which uses many pre-defined GLSL variables that are not implemented in the ES flavor. Those other variables are usually related to fixed-function pipeline states, hence their removal.

For the most part, attributes, uniforms, and varyings present no challenges to the Direct3D programmer. However, having a single entry point is contrary to the way shaders are typically authored these days. In Direct3D, a single HLSL file typically contains numerous shaders, including common code, and at the bare minimum, at least a vertex and fragment shader pair. GLSL mandates just a single entry point, which can result in a naive port requiring a more unmanageable number of shader files.

Complicating shader file management further, GLSL for OpenGL ES 2.0 does not implement preprocessor directives like `#include`, which makes it harder to maintain a large shader library to make use of common code. The obvious solution is to employ a custom shader preprocessor tool to extend GLSL files. Using XML is a robust option, but simpler text preprocessing works just as well. Extending GLSL will be discussed in more detail later in this article.

The next porting issue is that GLSL uses column major matrices, so multiplication order changes from what is commonly used in HLSL. For example, to multiply a vector through some matrices, the HLSL code looks like this:

```
float4 vOutPos = mul( mul( vInPos, matView ), matProj );
```

Whereas in GLSL, the same code looks like this:

```
vec4 vOutPos = matProj * matView * vInPos;
```

The final major gotcha has two parts, both of which affect vertex shaders using matrix palette skinning. GLSL maps a `mat3` to what HLSL calls a `FLOAT3X3`. Similarly, a `mat4` maps to a `FLOAT4X4`. What's unfortunately missing from GLSL is how to describe a `FLOAT4X3` matrix, which is commonly used to describe a palette of bone matrices. See, a 4×4 matrix takes up four shader constants, whereas a 4×3 matrix only takes up three. Besides, the fourth column in the 4×4 matrix is guaranteed to (0,0,0,1) and is therefore optimized out of the bone transform calculations. Using `mat4`s unnecessarily eats up shader constants, which is not acceptable since available vertex shader constants are at a premium, which is especially true for mobile GPUs. Not having enough shader constants to hold all of the bone transforms means that meshes must be broken up into multiple draw calls. This is an acceptable situation, but not ideal for performance.

The solution, as shown in the included "Skinning" sample, is to use a palette of three `vec4` uniforms. This slightly complicates the shader, but it does work. Porting is a little more difficult, but this article provides sample code showing how to do it. On the CPU side, setting the constants is also treated as a threefold array of vectors.

The other trick with a skinning shader involves bone indices. GLSL does not allow integer types as a vertex attribute, so bone indices must be accepted into a vertex shader with a `vec4` with four floating-point values. The values can then be typecast into an integer vector, as shown here:

```
ivec2 BoneIndices;
BoneIndices.x = int(In_BoneIndices.x);
BoneIndices.y = int(In_BoneIndices.y);
```

The integer bone indices can then be used to index into the threefold matrix array described above. Here's some shader code to show how it looks:

```
const int MAX_BONES = 26;

uniform vec4 matBones[3*MAX_BONES];

vec3 MulBone4( vec4 vInputPos, int nMatrix,
               float fBlendWeight )
{
    vec3 vResult;
    vResult.x = dot( vInputPos, matBones[3*nMatrix+0] );
    vResult.y = dot( vInputPos, matBones[3*nMatrix+1] );
    vResult.z = dot( vInputPos, matBones[3*nMatrix+2] );
    return vResult * fBlendWeight;
}
```

Lastly, all OpenGL ES 2.0 fragment shaders require the following code snippet to precede the shader code. Curiously, it is an error to not define the precision of a fragment shader. If preprocessing were used, this is the perfect type of code to throw in an `#include` file.

```
#ifdef GL_FRAGMENT_PRECISION_HIGH
    precision highp float;
#else
    precision mediump float;
#endif
```

Preprocessing GLSL

In the preceding section, frequent motivations were described to preprocess GLSL strings. The main issues at hand are the following:

- A single entry point is too limited.
- There's no way to include common code.
- A shader semantic system would allow for a more flexible pairing of arbitrary meshes and shaders.

Before getting too deep on the subject, a potential drawback should be mentioned in any discussion that essentially extends a programming language. Consistency of GLSL is what makes it portable, so using tools to preprocess shader files should aim to preserve that portability. Furthermore, OpenGL ES is an evolving specification, so future compatibility is also a goal. That said, OpenGL ES 2.0 really has no involvement in GLSL shaders as *files*, only as *strings*. Where those strings come from is up to the application, and they must be 100% fully compliant, OpenGL ES 2.0–recognized GLSL shaders or else they will fail to compile. The simplest way to obtain strings is probably just to load them verbatim, but doing a little search-and-replace on the files can only add value.

The first bit of value added should be to allow multiple entry points. In the example provided, shaders are preceded by a bracketed tag. The preprocessor tool simply looks for the specified tag and isolates it for compilation. While brackets were chosen by this author, a number of alternate solutions are possible, including not even having a `main()` function and using a Direct3D style of entry point instead (which, of course, would be replaced with `main()` to ensure compilation).

The next value to add is to support an `#include` directive. Any real-world application downright requires this. Current-generation PC and console games use hundreds to even tens of thousands of shader permutations. While mobile games won't go near what happens for desktop GPUs, having well over 100 shader permutations is probably typical, which is still not a very manageable number.

Adding shader semantics for vertex attribute binding is important depending on how flexible the art pipeline needs to be. If the content for the mobile application is simple, perhaps a fixed number of hard-coded bindings could suffice. Otherwise, simple Direct3D-style semantics could be added with some trivial search-and-replace functionality.

Although simple text preprocessing suffices, some developers might prefer an XML-based format that could help retain the GLSL in an unadulterated form. Here's an example of what the XML might look like:

```xml
<?xml version="1.0" encoding="utf-8" ?>

<Shader Type="Vertex" Name="OverlayVS">
    <Include File="CommonVS.glsl"/>
    <Attribute Name="g_vVertex"   Semantic="POSITION"/>
    <Attribute Name="g_vTexCoord" Semantic="TEXCOORD0"/>

    uniform   vec2 g_vScreenSize;
    attribute vec4 g_vVertex;
    attribute vec2 g_vTexCoord;
    varying   vec2 vTexCoord;

    void main()
    {
        gl_Position = vec4( g_vVertex.xy, 0.0, 1.0 );
        vTexCoord = g_vTexCoord;
    }
</Shader>

<Shader Type="Fragment" Name="OverlayFS">
    <Include File="CommonFS.glsl"/>

    uniform sampler2D g_Texture;
    varying vec2      vTexCoord;

    void main()
    {
        gl_FragColor = texture2D( g_Texture, vTexCoord );
    }
</Shader>
```

As a final mention, there's at least one tool floating around cyberspace that aims to convert HLSL shaders to GLSL. The tool, HLSL2GLSL, written by AMD, is open source and is easy to find on the Internet. The HLSL2GLSL tool has a number of features that can be used to address the GLSL issues mentioned here. First, since HLSL files support multiple entry points and #include directives, those are trivially supported by the tool. A couple of command line switches make sure the resulting GLSL is compatible with OpenGL ES. Last, vertex attributes are mapped to semantics in HLSL but they can be converted with the tool to application-specific custom attribute names.

Using HLSL2GLSL might help with initial porting, but the main GLSL limitations outlined above will still affect a large project. That is, hundreds of shader files are still difficult to maintain with single entry points and no #include directives, and removing shader semantics also removes the ease to bind with arbitrary meshes.

Porting Artwork

After porting code and porting shaders, an application may still encounter visual problems rendering a scene. For starters, the mathematics behind 3D transformations depend on the "handedness" of the coordinate system. Coordinate system differences between the two APIs can cause objects to render inside-out, textures to be applied upside-down, and screen space elements to go awry. Handedness also dictates polygon winding order, which can result in the incorrect culling of front faces.

More API differences affect artwork, like the ordering of color channels in textures: OpenGL uses an RGBA order while D3D uses a BGRA order. Even platform differences can affect artwork, too, such as the reduced number of available vertex shader constants, which limits the number of bones a mesh subset can have.

Each of these concerns needs to be addressed, both in the artwork and in code modifications, to compensate for the differences.

Coordinate Systems

Direct3D uses a left-handed (LH) coordinate system in which the Z-axis points in the same direction as the camera. On the other hand (pun intended), OpenGL uses a right-handed (RH) coordinate system, in which the Z-axis points in the opposite direction of the camera. In an LH coordinate system, objects with increasing Z are moving farther away from the camera. In a RH coordinate system, objects with increasing Z are moving toward the camera.

The hardware doesn't really care about 3D coordinate systems one way or another, but the mathematics inside the application must match the math inside the shader, which must match the render states set to the hardware. Some sentiment is that neither API really has a preferred handedness, but the truth is that handedness is apparent in both default states and Z-buffer orientation. For example, OpenGL state defaults to the back-face culling of clockwise faces, where D3D state defaults to the back-face culling of counterclockwise faces.

Regardless, the only concern here is how the relative math and render states affect an application. To some extent, handedness is baked into meshes since they must define vertex positions, normals, and a winding order for the faces. A naive port from Direct3D to OpenGL is likely to discover that meshes now appear inside out. In most cases, the positions and normals can simply be corrected in the shader, negating values as needed, but doing so may cause the propagation of other problems, such as in quaternion-based animation systems.

The preferred approach is to have the art pipeline mesh conversion tools be able to specify handedness in the meshes and animation data. Then, the application can use default states preferred by the API. A math library can be designed to work with either handedness, so that is rarely an issue. Using the correct handedness even means the normal maps will work as expected in the fragment shader without any need to flip values.

The 2D coordinate system can also cause porting problems for texturing, render-to-texture algorithms, and post-processing effects. Direct3D uses a 2D texture space with the origin in the upper-left corner, which should be familiar to anyone working with 2D images on a desktop PC. That is the same coordinate system, after all, as most windowing systems, paint programs, and so on. OpenGL places the origin in the lower-left corner for textures, which is the more mathematical approach, similar to how students are taught to plot out 2D equations on graph paper.

The coordinate systems for each API are summarized in Table 7.1.2. The handedness is apparent in the Z-direction, and the front-face winding order is indicated by the arrow.

Table 7.1.2 Comparison of Direct3D 9 and OpenGL ES 2.0 coordinate systems

D3D Coordinate Systems	OpenGL Coordinate Systems
D3D World Space (Left-Handed)	OpenGL World Space (Right-Handed)
D3D Clip Space (w/Z-Buffer)	OpenGL Clip Space (w/Z-Buffer)
D3D Screen Space	OpenGL Screen Space
D3D Texture Space	OpenGL Texture Space

In Table 7.1.2, the arrows indicate the winding order of front-facing polygons. Mathematically, the winding order is related to the handedness of the coordinate system, hence the difference between the APIs. OpenGL uses counterclockwise front faces, resulting in a default render state to cull CW back faces. While this can trivially be altered in the render state, your project may end up including counterintuitive code such as glCullFace(GL_FRONT). (This is paradoxical because you're still culling back faces—not front faces—yet you are compensating for having reverse-ordered faces.)

After the projection matrix is applied, vertices end up in clip space. Interestingly, even on OpenGL, the clip space coordinate system becomes left-handed. The reason for this is that the Z-buffer is defined to range from Znear to Zfar, where Znear = 0.0 and Zfar is 1.0. That is, increasing Z is farther out from the camera just like in a left-handed coordinate system. However, the winding order remains consistent with the API. Note that the Z direction in clip space is really a matter of how the depth-comparison test is setup. Both APIs default to a "less-than-or-equal-to" depth test, and initially clear Z-buffer values to 1.0. The depth test can be altered via a simple render state, but then the clear values and the projection matrix must be altered to produce consistent values.

Screen space is an awkward coordinate system because it depends somewhat on how your application defines it. OpenGL ES 2.0 is a 3D API, so if you want to position 2D objects, such as elements of a user interface, in screen space, then your shader must really turn screen space values into the appropriate clip space coordinates. Here we assume most people will prefer a screen space coordinate system that is similar to desktop coordinates, with (0,0) in the upper-left coordinate.

Texture Concerns

As mentioned above, texture space is inverted between the two APIs. Any port that neglects this difference will find the textures misapplied to the meshes and render-to-texture or post-processing algorithms possibly not working as expected. Minor hacks to invert values inside the vertex and fragment shaders can fix the problem, although fixing the texture coordinates ahead of time in a mesh conversion tool is the preferred approach.

Each API also differs in how it defines pixel centers in screen space coordinates. Imagining a piece of graph paper, D3D defines pixels as being centered in the grid cells, whereas OpenGL places pixels on the intersection of grid lines. Dealing with this "half-pixel offset" is trivial, but naively ported code could result in screen space textures (UI, etc.) that appear blurry or appear to have border artifacts due to the bilinear filtering of neighboring texels.

The ordering of color components in a texture also needs to be considered. For example, loading a 32-bit RGBA texture into a D3DFORMT_R8G8B8A8 texture works pretty seamlessly. Matching the endianness of x86 processors, what TGA and D3D call RGBA is actually internally ordered as BGRA. In OpenGL, however, the internal order is actual true RGBA. This means the red and blue channels must be swapped (*swizzled*) before textures are created.

Summary of Artwork Concerns

Artwork is affected by coordinate systems, platform limitations, and performance concerns. Meshes, animation data, and textures should all be preprocessed offline, and having appropriate build-time tools, which can target multiple platforms, makes porting a much easier process.

A summary of the desired mesh preprocessing operations includes the following:

- Negate the Z-component of vertex positions and normals to match an RH-coordinate system.
- Reverse the winding order of vertex indices for proper back culling.
- Invert texture coordinates.
- Break skinned meshes into multiple subsets to limit the required size of the matrix bone palette.
- For performance, reduce poly-count and convert meshes to optimized triangle strips as necessary.

A summary of the desired texture preprocessing operations includes the following:

- Invert textures.
- Swizzle RGBA texture data.
- Ensure normal maps encode normals with proper Z orientation.
- For load-time performance, compress textures offline.

Additionally, an application will need to convert animation data (translations and quaternions) to match an RH-coordinate system and make sure the math library uses right-handed conventions where necessary. "Look at" and projection matrices need to obey handedness, and render-to-texture algorithms need to work with the relationship between clip space and texture space.

After artwork is ported for API compliance and mathematical correctness, general performance becomes the next biggest porting obstacle.

Performance

Discussing performance and shader optimizations is a separate topic worthy of its own article. As such, there are just a few mentions to be made here.

Mobile devices are lightweight compared to desktop workhorses. Their power is increasingly impressive, but mobile developers must still be incredibly mindful of what they are working with. For example, if compressing a 512×512 texture on a dual-processor desktop PC takes around 1.0 seconds, how long would it take on a mobile ARM processor? The answer is: unacceptably long. Combined with the fact that games use a dizzying amount of textures, it's imperative that mobile games preprocess textures at build time.

The same goes for compiling shaders. No benchmarks have been taken on actual hardware, but we can assume that shader compilation is not a trivial task that can be done hundreds of times over in a negligible amount of time. Shader compilation involves parsers, lexers, and complex optimization algorithms—none of which is a small task for a mobile processor. For this reason alone, shaders should always be pre-compiled for embedded devices. Although not mandatory for all implementations, the OpenGL ES 2.0 specification permits binary shaders as a hardware vendor extension. There is still some question whether developers might want to distribute games with precompiled shaders, though. Otherwise, they might limit the hardware they can run on. In that case, however, there's always the option of running an installation app that compiles the shaders and saves them on the device's memory card.

Good runtime shader performance is paramount for any mobile application. In the desktop space, the trend is toward larger and more complicated shaders. It's probably safe to say that very few real-world shaders are 100% perfectly optimized. After all, there are diminishing returns on the optimization effort and PC hardware just gets faster and faster every year. Mobile GPUs are lightweight compared to the desktop GPUs, and are likely to sport only a small fraction of the shader processing power. Mobile developers can expect feature-rich, flexible hardware that runs at slower clock speeds and has fewer vertex and pixel pipelines. On mobile GPUs, *every* shader instruction matters to the point that even a single additional wasted instruction can affect performance.

Another trend, sadly, is the reliance on the shader compiler to do an optimal job. The biggest rule-of-thumb is that garbage-in equals garbage-out. Given an inefficient shader with unnecessary computations and texture fetches, the shader compiler will be unable to perform any miracles. When talking about optimizing mobile shaders, conventional advice does not always apply. For example, a common older recommendation to use a cubemap to normalize values in a pixel shader is bad advice on many levels. First, it results in an additional texture fetch and, with not enough pixel pipelines to hide latency, creates a stall potential waiting for the texels to be fetched from memory. Second, the normalization cubemap is known to thrash the texture cache pretty badly, which is even more problematic for small caches. Lastly, the extra texture fetch could cause the eviction of other texel data from the small texture cache.

A more realistic mobile optimization solution would probably be to forego the normalization altogether. This creates mathematically incorrect lighting equations, but on a handheld-size display, it's certainly less of an issue than a gamer's scrutiny of a scene running at 1,600×1,200 on a 21-inch display. Remember, every instruction matters.

Perhaps even more important than instruction count is the use of temporary registers. Internally, the OpenGL ES 2.0–capable GPUs are likely to have the capability to co-issue multiple vertex and pixel threads in order to hide latency. Since each shader uses some amount of general purpose registers (GPRs), the hardware design must include some finite pool of GPR space. When all the GPRs in the pool are assigned to vertex or pixel threads, the hardware is unable to issue new threads, and therefore is unable to further hide fetch latency.

Having a complex shader that eats up all the GPRs in one fell swoop makes most of the novel GPU hardware design somewhat moot. On the flip side, when shaders are lean on their GPR usage, the hardware can run with amazing efficiency. Okay, so how can shaders be written to minimize GPR usage? Fortunately, tools are under development that will help mobile developers optimize shaders. Even without tools, though, it's not terribly difficult to rough count GPRs just by looking at the GLSL code. Remember: The goal is to have shaders use as few GPRs as possible, so using just three or four should result in good performance.

Another big topic for performance has to do with the concept of tiling and binning. For bandwidth-related performance issues, mobile GPUs often use some sort of fast-access memory like SRAM or embedded DRAM. Die areas restrict the amount of this memory to rather small amounts, though, like 128 KB or 256 KB. It turns out that a frame buffer requires several megabytes of memory, which creates a problem that requires a novel solution. That solution is to break the scene into rectangular tiles and render one tile at a time. Geometry, meanwhile, is subject to being rendered multiple times over and possibly sorted and stored in bins for rendering. For more information on binning, please refer to the appropriate articles published in the *ShaderX* book series.

While all this tiling and binning business happens under the hood in the driver, it's still important to be aware of the performance ramifications. People often assume that fragment shaders eat up the lion's share of shader hardware resources since there are typically so many more pixels than vertices. However, on a tiling GPU, the vertices may be transformed many times over, meaning vertex shader optimization becomes a higher priority. Offloading per-pixel work to the vertex shader is no longer a trivial tradeoff. Especially concerning are heavyweight vertex shaders such as those used for vertex skinning.

Optimizations for vertex shaders need to be fairly aggressive. For example, when skinning, most developers will naturally just choose an implementation that uses four bones per vertex, assuming the hardware can handle it. Since most vertices only use two bones, a sensible approach is to take the slight visual reduction by only considering the first two bones in the vertex shader.

Perhaps the most ideal solution is to use an algorithm to transform the vertices in a preprocessing pass and then submit the post-transformed vertices during the render call. In this case, it's just the lightweight, passed-through vertices that will get redundantly shaded. Unfortunately, the API does not provide a native mechanism to transform vertices without rendering them. If a hardware vendor releases an extension to expose this feature, known as *mem export* on the Xbox 360 GPU or *vertex stream-out* in Direct3D 10, then it's definitely worthwhile to make use of it.

The last performance topic is a plea for simplicity. Programmable shaders make possible very impressive effects. In the mobile space, these effects should be used more sparingly, saving as many GPU cycles for where the effects matter most. For example, static lighting will be in vogue again, leaving a budget for a nice post-process effect or some fancily rendered objects in the scene. Dynamic shadows are important to cement a character to the ground, but only the main characters are worthy of the expense. Other objects are more suited for simple, baked-in shadows. Of course, regardless of what advice can be given ahead of time, most real-world performance lessons will have to be learned the hard way.

Skinning Sample

This article concludes with some OpenGL ES 2.0 sample code that shows all of the concepts in action. A matrix palette skinning sample was chosen because it highlights some of the porting challenges when migrating from Direct3D. For example, the use of 4×3 bone matrices and dealing with integer bone indices in a vertex shader is simple when seen in final form, but it is tricky to get working with a trial-and-error method. Additionally, the mesh vertex format used is less trivial because of the inclusion of per-vertex bone indices and bone weights.

The artwork in the sample adheres to OpenGL's conventions, meaning that the mesh is right-handed, including the Z-orientation, face winding order, and inverted texture coordinates. Animation values are also right-handed so that rotations and translations can be applied without pesky hacks in the code and the shaders. Textures are properly converted to OpenGL's RGBA format before being compressed to a mobile texture compression format.

The sample makes use of a framework that abstracts out the Win32 platform and uses EGL to initialize a render context. The main code of the sample is in `scene.cpp`, which provides the following functions:

- `Initialize()`: Called after the framework creates a window and render context, this function is responsible for initializing all app-specific objects and the OpenGL state.
- `Resize()`: Called when the framework responds to a user request to rotate the display.
- `Update()`: Called once per frame to perform updates to the application. Typical tasks performed here are to process input, update animations, AI, collision detection, physics, etc.
- `Render()`: Called once per frame to render the scene. Typically begins by clearing the back-backbuffer, drawing all objects in the scene, and then drawing some text or UI.
- `Destroy()`: Destroys all initialized objects as the application prepares to exit.

The sample is laid out in a directory that should be simple enough to navigate. In order for the sample to run, the DLLs for AMD's OpenGL ES 2.0 Emulator need to be found in the System directory. Likewise, the headers and libs are also present so that the sample can be built. A couple of tools are also used: the `ShaderPreprocessor` to preprocess the shader files as outlined above, and the `ResourcePacker` to pre-load texture images and font data into a fast-loading binary format. The skinned mesh is provided in a pre-built, fast-loading, binary form that is described by simple structures in the code.

The first concept to explore in the sample is the preprocessing of the GLSL shader files. Note the use of `#include` and multiple entry points. During the build, the GLSL shader files are used as source files; the actual preprocessed output files end up in the Win32\Debug\Media\Shaders directory. These resulting .vs and .fs files contain the actual input to the OpenGL shader compilation functions.

This sample does not illustrate binary shaders (which would require actual OpenGL ES 2.0 hardware to run on, not mere emulation). Otherwise, the `Shader-Preprocessor` tool would be used to create precompiled shader binaries. On an actual mobile device that supports binary shaders, this would be highly preferred as compiling shaders could take many seconds on a mobile device, leading to undesirable load times.

The next thing to note is in the initialization code, where the shader is loaded and compiled. Specifically, pay attention to how the shader attributes are bound to the shader. Lacking shader semantics in the GLSL, this sample hard-codes attributes by name. This is not flexible for arbitrary shaders, but it suffices as long as the shader developer and application developer agree on set names and stay consistent.

The mesh rendering code is not complex and can be stepped through. The mesh file is a hierarchy of frame nodes that hold transformation matrices updated by the animation system. The first frame points to the actual skinned mesh, while subsequent frames serve essentially as storage space to contain the animated bone matrices. The mesh contains the necessary data to render the appropriate subset of vertices. Note that the sample mesh provided uses a total of 35 bones, which is more than the maximum number of bones that can be used at one time due to limited vertex shader constant space, so the mesh is broken into two subsets. Prior to actual rendering, the code sets up all the necessary states, like the texture, material properties, and most importantly, the matrix palette of bone transforms.

The real workhouse is the vertex shader because all the skinning happens there. Each vertex first has its bone indices cast to integers. For each bone (just two), the index is used to transform the vertex position and vertex normal through the indexed matrix. Weighting is applied and the results are added together. The rest of the vertex shader, and the fragment shader, too, are a fairly standard implementation of vertex lighting and texturing.

Hopefully this sample, including the tools, framework, and shaders, serves as a good reference for future OpenGL ES 2.0 native development and/or Direct3D 9 ports.

7.2

Efficiently Using Tile-Based GPUs on Mobile Phones

Maurice Ribble

AMD

Introduction

Twenty-five years ago mobile phones were big and heavy and had all the ergonomics of a brick. Today, mobile phones have slim form factors, lots of computing power, and colorful displays. Many of the high-end mobile phones even have GPUs. We are currently on the cusp of the second generation of mobile phone GPUs, which will support OpenGL ES 2.0. Accelerated 3D graphics have become more and more popular with each new generation of GPU on desktop computers until we have reached the current market where just about every PC ships with accelerated 3D graphics. The same trend will happen in mobile phones; 3D accelerated graphics will continue to grow in the mobile phone market until every phone with a color screen has them. Not only will this happen, but it will probably happen much faster than it did with PCs. Mobile phone screen resolutions continue to rise and coloring large numbers of pixels in a visually appealing manner without dedicated hardware is difficult.

Multiple graphics hardware vendors have decided it makes sense to use a technique called *tile-based rendering* (TBR) in their mobile phone GPUs. TBR solves the memory bandwidth limitation problem non-TBR GPUs have with a high performance, low power, and low-cost solution. This article describes how TBR works, discusses its advantages, and demonstrates how to write efficient graphics code for these TBR GPUs.

The TBR Pipeline

Fundamental to TBR architecture is the idea of breaking up a rendering surface, such as a back buffer, into a series of rectangular tiles. Throughout this article a rectangular tile of data will be referred to as a *chunk*. Think of this chunk as a grouping of the pipeline state and geometry needed to render to one of these rectangular tiles. There are some common performance optimizations that are done on every modern implementation of TBR. In this discussion it can be assumed that TBR implementations have these common optimizations.

The first optimization we'll discuss is an attempt to avoid sending redundant geometry to each chunk. The simplest way to render the scene as chunks would be to send every vertex through its vertex shader and then try to rasterize all the triangles for every chunk. The problem with this is that it would require transforming every vertex for every chunk, so if the scene were broken up into 16 chunks, then 16 times as many vertex transforms would be necessary. TBR hardware avoids this problem with special hardware that allows each vertex to be transformed only once by implementing a preprocess sort of the scene's triangles. There are two ways hardware can do this. The first way is to execute only the portion of the vertex shader needed to generate the final vertex position and use that position to do the preprocess triangle sort. Subsequent runs of the vertex shader for a chunk would need to recompute the position portion of the shader. The other way is to run the whole vertex shader as part of the preprocess sort and save all the vertex shader outputs into a buffer. Subsequent runs of the vertex shader for each chunk can just fetch these values from memory. There are advantages and disadvantages to each method that revolve around balancing memory usage and computer power; the method used is entirely up to the GPU designer. The important information for graphics programmers is that this triangle sort adds a small amount overhead for each triangle being sorted, so it is best to try and keep the triangle counts reasonable.

The other big optimization modern TBR GPUs have is a small amount of low latency, high bandwidth memory. On handheld systems this fast memory will typically be on the same chip as the GPU, so we will call it *fast local memory*. This is where each chunk gets rendered. The chunk's surface is then copied out to an external memory chip, which has much higher latency and lower bandwidth. The memory on this external memory chip will be called *slow external memory*. All of the chunks have to do this copy so that a final image of the complete render surface can be assembled.

Figure 7.2.1 shows a simplified graphics pipeline for a non-TBR GPU. The basic flow is as follows: The vertices are passed into the vertex shader where they are transformed and then the fragment shader applies all the lighting and texturing to the pixels, which are drawn directly to the slow external memory.

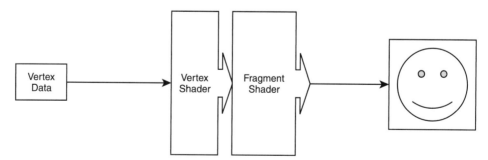

FIGURE 7.2.1 A simplified non-TBR graphics pipeline.

Figure 7.2.2 shows a simplified graphics pipeline for a TBR GPU. The flow here is different. First, the triangles are sorted into the appropriate chunk bins. Then only the vertices needed for the chunk being worked on are transformed. Next the fragments are rasterized, shaded, and output into fast local memory. The last step is that this fast local memory is copied into slow external memory.

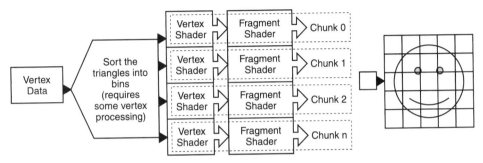

FIGURE 7.2.2 A simplified TBR graphics pipeline.

The Advantages of TBR

While many graphics programmers think the goal of GPU makers is to make their lives miserable, I can assure you that is not the case. This section will explain why TBR is such a great fit for mobile graphics and hopefully convince you that the small amount of extra effort programmers need to expend is worth it for the advantages of TBR.

The big win for TBR in the mobile market comes from the fast local memory where the chunks get rendered. Because of this memory's huge bandwidth and low latency, the performance of GPU memory-intensive operations like blending, depth testing, and multi-sample anti-aliasing are greatly improved. The other advantage to this fast local memory is that it is embedded into the GPU, so most memory transactions don't need to cross any system memory buses, which saves power and thus extends battery life.

Figure 7.2.3 shows a scene where two triangles are being drawn with depth test enabled. Both triangles are 100 pixels and the overlap region is 50 pixels. Both triangles are also executing a single texture fetch. The checkered triangle is in front and is drawn first so that the depth test fails on the striped triangle. To keep things simple, assume that the color and depth buffers are each 32 bits and that each fragment requires one texel fetch from a 32 bit texture. This means all memory transactions will be 32 bits, or four byte blocks.

Table 7.2.1 shows the number of bytes transferred across the memory bus. Because TBR renders to fast local memory, all the depth and color reads/writes don't need to use the memory bus to access the slow external memory since the color and depth values are stored in the fast local memory.

FIGURE 7.2.3 An example demonstrating bandwidth savings from TBR.

Table 7.2.1 The bandwidth to usage slow external memory for different rendering technologies

	Traditional Rendering	Traditional Rendering with Early Z	TBR	TBR with Early Z
Texture Reads	200*4 bytes	150*4 bytes	200*4 bytes	150*4 bytes
Depth Reads	200*4 bytes	200*4 bytes	0 bytes	0 bytes
Depth Writes	150*4 bytes	150*4 bytes	0 bytes	0 bytes
Color Writes	150*4 bytes	150*4 bytes	0 bytes	0 bytes
Total Bandwidth	2,800 bytes	2,600 bytes	800 bytes	600 bytes

There is some overhead incurred by TBR that will be discussed later, but even with that overhead bandwidth, limited operations will benefit greatly from TBR. If TBR is so popular in the handheld space, then, why is it not used as extensively in the desktop graphics arena? The answer revolves around power usage, GPU transistor counts, and application geometric content.

On desktops the best performance can be achieved by having very high clocked memory, highly complex memory controllers, large caches, and wide memory buses. These features would take up too much space and use too much power in handheld GPU design. A comparison of shading power versus bandwidth on desktop and mobile phones shows that the handheld market has fewer bytes of bandwidth per shader instruction available. While an exact comparison is very difficult to make and constantly changing, current calculations show that high-end desktop graphics have over three times the bandwidth per shader instruction compared to mobile graphics. Also, the memory on handheld systems is usually shared between the CPU, GPU, sound, and other subsystems, so it's not just the graphics system that is competing for this bandwidth like it is with high-end desktop graphics hardware. This 3× differential is a consequence of the sheer brute processing power available on desktop GPUs. Mobile GPUs have found that TBR helps eliminate this difference with a more elegant solution.

Another reason TBR is more common on handheld GPUs than desktop GPUs is based on the geometric complexity relative to depth complexity. Low amounts of geometry and a high depth complexity is good for TBR. High amounts of geometry and a low depth complexity is worse for TBR than non-TBR. In general, PC games tend to have more complex geometry and use better software occlusion techniques to reduce overdraw than mobile games. Don't let this geometric complexity issue be too scary. Complex geometry is a very relative term. Microsoft's Xbox 360 uses TBR and most people think its games use complex geometry. The thing to remember here is that with TBR, avoiding excess geometry will net bigger gains than it would on a non-TBR GPU, so these optimizations should be higher on the priority list.

Understanding TBR

In non-TBR rendering pipelines, triangles are usually rasterized in the order they are specified; however, with TBR systems this is not the case. As shown in Figure 7.2.4, in the simple case where several triangles are rendered to the back buffer, a TBR implementation will batch up all the triangles in an entire frame. While these triangles are being batched they are also being sorted into the appropriate chunk's bin. At the end of the frame all the triangles for the first chunk will be rendered, then all the triangles for the next chunk will be rendered, and so forth until all the chunks have been rendered. In OpenGL ES, it is the job of the driver and hardware to make this whole process transparent to the programmer, but knowing that it happens allows the programmer to make some intelligent design decisions about how their code is written.

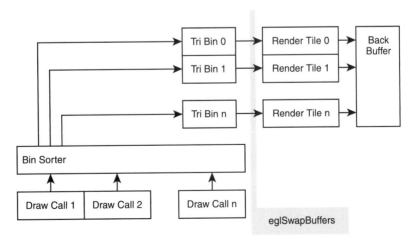

FIGURE 7.2.4 A diagram showing the rendering flow in a TBR GPU.

In the previous section an example showed how rendering with TBR gave an amazing savings to bus bandwidth usage. While the bandwidth savings of TBR is indeed huge, there is one more step in TBR that is important when calculating total bandwidth usage. There is bandwidth overhead that is associated with copying each rendered chunk across the memory bus between fast local memory and slow external memory. This copying of render surfaces is commonly referred to as the *resolve*, and that's the word we'll be using to describe it from here forward.

There are two types of resolves to learn about. These are *lightweight resolves* and the *heavyweight resolves*. The lightweight resolve, as the name implies, is less expensive and is often times unavoidable. It copies a render surface from fast local memory out to slow external memory. A lightweight resolve needs to be done during operations such as `eglSwapBuffers` so that the back buffer can be displayed to the screen. A lightweight resolve would also occur after rendering to a frame buffer object so that it can be used as a texture. The heavyweight resolve does a lightweight resolve and then also copies a render surface from slow external memory to fast internal memory. A heavyweight resolve would be needed if someone called `glReadPixels` in the middle of the frame. To return the current pixel data, all the chunks need to be rendered and copied out to slow external memory. Since the frame isn't done and the final results depend on what was rendered before the `glReadPixels`, the results that were saved out to slow external memory need to be copied back into fast internal memory before the chunk can finish rendering. Because of this double copy, the cost of heavyweight resolves is twice the cost of the lightweight resolves. Your goal should be to avoid every heavyweight resolve, which I'll explain in a moment.

There are two noteworthy points to make about resolves in general. First, with non-TBR, these sorts of memory bus transactions are spread out evenly over all rendering. With TBR, all of this bus traffic is saved and performed at the same time during the resolve operation. TBR gains a significant advantage here because delaying bus transactions until resolve time allows a constant amount of bandwidth consumption based on the render buffer's size and bytes per pixel. With non-TBR the bandwidth usage depends on the complexity of the rendering, since every color and depth read/write that doesn't hit a cache needs to go to slow external memory.

The other noteworthy point about resolves for TBR is that the entire frame's worth of geometry needs to be saved up, and it is only during the swap buffers command that it can finally be rasterized. The OpenGL ES API abstracts this from the graphics programmer, but it is helpful to understand that this is happening. The reason this needs to be done is to avoid many extra resolves. Imagine the case where triangle 0 gets rendered to bin X, then triangle 1 gets rendered to bin Y, and finally triangle 2 gets rendered to bin X. In this case, if the entire scene weren't batched up and drawn to each bin, then a lightweight resolve would be needed for the first two triangles and a heavyweight resolve would be needed for the third. This would end up using more bandwidth than traditional rendering, and this is why triangles are sorted and put into bins for an entire frame so that no extra resolves are needed.

TBR Special Performance Cases

At this point you should understand what TBR is and how it works. Now it's time to learn about what the programmer can do to ensure that an application is TBR-friendly. This section is all about the sort of operations to avoid with TBR GPUs and how to order commands for maximum efficiency.

The most expensive operations to avoid are resolves. The developer's goal is to minimize lightweight resolves and eliminate heavyweight resolves. In general, it is fairly easy for TBR implementations to detect when multiple resolves occur in a row and skip all but the first one. If it is necessary to perform operations that will force a resolve in the middle of the frame, try to execute them sequentially so that only one resolve will be necessary for all of the operations. Here are a few examples:

- `eglSwapBuffers`. An `eglSwapBuffers` call triggers the driver to flush all of its buffered rendering to the hardware. You should start every frame with a clear of the depth buffer to remove the need for the hardware to copy the previous frame's depth buffer into each chunk before starting the new frame. Starting a frame with a depth clear makes the resolve cheaper because it gets rid of the need to copy the depth buffer out to slow external memory. There is no need to clear the color buffer to improve TBR performance because EGL states that the contents of the color buffer are undefined after a swap command. If the rendering algorithm doesn't paint every pixel in the color buffer during the frame, it needs to clear the color buffer. This incurs the same cost as a color clear on a non-TBR GPU. This is the one resolve that programmers will need to accept, because it is unavoidable as long as there is a need to display the graphics to the screen. There are rendering algorithms that could necessitate extra resolves, but in those cases a programmer should justify any extra resolves. This unavoidable lightweight resolve during the swap causes swaps to be more expensive on TBR GPUs, but this higher cost is more than offset by the cheaper rendering cost.
- `glTexImage2D`, `glTexSubImage2D`, `glBufferData`, and `glBufferSubData`. All these commands update memory buffers and could cause a heavyweight resolve. While it is possible for a graphics driver to avoid a resolve in this case by creating a second buffer, this is extra work for the driver and it's possible all implementations may not optimize for this case. You should perform all these operations immediately after a swap and before clearing the depth buffer to ensure that no resolves happen and there is no extra driver overhead.
- `glCopyTexImage2D` and `glCopyTexSubImage2D`. These commands are antiquated by frame buffer objects, and it is recommended that you use FBOs to simulate this functionality. If you choose to use these commands, they will force a resolve, so the standard recommendation to group operations that force resolves also applies to these operations.

- **glReadPixels.** This is a command to avoid even with non-TBR GPUs because it forces a complete flush and idle of the graphics pipeline. This flush is expensive on desktop GPUs and even more prohibitively expensive on TBR GPUs. If you have to use it, try to use it directly before a swap so that it only forces a lightweight resolve instead of the heavyweight resolve that would be required in the middle of a frame.

- **glBindFramebuffer.** The best place to put this call is directly after a swap and before the clear of the depth buffer that starts the new frame since, at this point, only a lightweight resolve will be necessary. It is also very important that you clear whatever buffers (depth, color, and stencil) this frame buffer object uses to avoid the heavyweight resolve. If this clear is not present, the driver assumes that the previous data in the buffer object is needed and the previous image for this object must be copied from slow external memory to fast internal memory.

One common case that might involve multiple frame buffer objects would be a multi-pass post-processing effect like depth of field. In this case, immediately after swap you should bind a frame buffer object, clear it, and render your full scene into it. Then you should bind another smaller frame buffer object, clear it, and render a downsampled version of the scene that you would use as the blurry, out-of-focus scene. The final step would be to bind your back buffer, clear the depth buffer, and then combine the previous two buffer objects in a way that simulates the depth of field effect by picking either blurry or sharp pixels depending on the values in the depth buffer. This would force a lightweight resolve of the first two frame buffer objects and another lightweight resolve on the back buffer during the swap. For this rendering algorithm there is no way to avoid these extra resolves, but being careful allows you to avoid possibly introducing extra resolves.

Post-processing effects that require neighboring pixel information are handled in a very similar way by first rendering the scene into a frame buffer object and then using that object as a texture to render into the back buffer. Specific challenges here are the following:

- **Exceeding triangle or state buffer limits.** This limit is different for every TBR GPU. The problem is this: Because these architectures are caching all the drawing and state changes for an entire frame at some large size, they have a maximum bufferable size. This will force a heavyweight resolve that clears out the drawing and state buffers. Most applications won't hit these limits since they are pretty large, but if you see a strange performance hiccup when adding more geometry or state changes, then this is a likely cause of the problem. The only solution is to reduce state changes or the amount of geometry in your application.

- **Driver evicted texture or buffer object.** With some implementations of TBR, the driver may be forced to move textures into and out of dedicated graphics memory. If this happens you may see a strange performance hiccup because of an extra heavyweight resolve. The only solution to this problem is to try to use less memory.

Listing 7.2.1: Sample code of a rendering loop

```
<code>
eglSwapBuffers( dsp, backBuffer );

// Put all glTexImage2D, glTexSubImage2D, glBufferData and
// glBufferSubData commands here

// FBO block (optional - only needed if you are using one or more FBOs
for ( int i = 0; i < numFbos; ++i )
{
    glBindFramebuffer( target[i], framebuffer[i] );
    glClear( GL_COLOR_BUFFER_BIT |
            GL_DEPTH_BUFFER_BIT |
            GL_STENCIL_BUFFER_BIT );
    // Draw your scene for each FBO here
}

// Use GL_COLOR_BUFFER_BIT on this clear only if you need it
glClear( GL_DEPTH_BUFFER_BIT | GL_STENCIL_BUFFER_BIT );
// Draw your scene to your back buffer here

// If you absolutely need a glReadPixels do it here
eglSwapBuffers( dsp, backBuffer );
...
</code>
```

General Usage Cases

There are some general ideas that can help to efficiently program TBR GPUs. Some of these ideas are also helpful for standard GPUs.

Blending and overdraw are typically bandwidth intensive operations. Because TBR GPUs are actually rendering to fast local memory, bandwidth isn't a concern in these cases. This means there is no need to shy away from graphical effects that use a lot of blending or overdraw if they make the application look better.

Tiny triangles are not good for TBR GPUs because every triangle that is drawn needs to be sorted into the proper bin. The cost of sorting any single triangle is small, but if the application is using lots of really tiny triangles this overhead becomes significant.

On desktop hardware, multi-sample anti-aliasing is normally bandwidth-limited. On some tiling hardware, though, it can be a low-cost operation because it uses fast local memory during rendering. The only overhead is that the larger number of bits being used per pixel reduces the number of pixels that can fit into the fast local memory, so each chunk will be smaller. This means more chunks will be needed, which can increase the triangle sorting costs, but in most cases the cost for many passes is negligible, so the end result is nearly free multi-sample anti-aliasing.

Finally, there are the standard performance optimizations that have been around for years such as rendering from front to back, using cached vertex buffer objects, and texture MIPmapping. These all help standard GPUs and tile-based GPUs alike, so use them.

OpenGL ES 2.0 Emulators

Desktop OpenGL ES 2.0 emulators are great tools for getting your graphics code running before your target hardware is available. Additionally there are often better debugging tools for desktop PCs, so these tools are useful for debugging even after target hardware is available.

- AMD provides an emulator environment for OpenGL ES. This emulator is included on the DVD that came with this book. Newer versions with bug fixes and additional features can be downloaded from http://ati.amd.com/developer/tools.html.
- Imagination provides an emulator and SDK that can be downloaded from http://www.imgtec.com/PowerVR/insider/toolsSDKs/KhronosOpenGLES2xSGX.

Conclusion

Multiple hardware vendors have chosen TBR GPUs for the mobile phone market in order to improve performance and save power. With the knowledge provided about these GPUs and the performance tips given here, it shouldn't be too much extra work to make your engine highly efficient for these TBR GPUs.

7.3

Maximal Performance and Image Quality with Minimal Precision

Ken Catterall

Introduction

OpenGL ES 2.0 provides three levels of float precision for shader programs. Traditional floating-point representation is included with medium- and high-precision variables; in addition, the shading language defines a low-precision format, which can afford up to double the throughput of the higher precisions on mobile platforms. We will focus on some of the ways in which to make maximal use of the low-precision format without sacrificing image quality in our shader effects.

The Low-Precision Format

Unlike the true floating-point representation of the medium- and high-precision floats, low-precision floats are essentially fixed-point. Thus we see that many of the ways the format can be used correspond to the capabilities of the fixed function pipeline found in OpenGL ES 1.1 and similar APIs, which are typically implemented using fixed-point arithmetic.

Definition

The OpenGL ES 2.0 shading language specification [Khronos07] defines a low-precision float to be in the range $(-2.0, 2.0)$ with a precision of 2.0^{-8} (the difference between consecutive values). Minimally, this requires a 10-bit representation: one sign bit, one integer bit, and eight remaining fractional bits (Figure 7.3.1).

Thus the smallest (positive) number, which is 2^{-8}, would be represented in binary as $[+0.00000001]$; and the largest possible number, represented as $[+1.11111111]$,

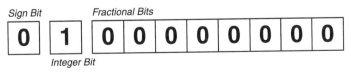

FIGURE 7.3.1 Representation of 1.0 in low precision.

would be equal to $2-2^{-8}$ or 1.99609375. We define these values as `MIN_LOWP` and `MAX_LOWP` respectively. The largest and smallest negative numbers are therefore `MAX_LOWP` and `-MIN_LOWP`.

Justification and Limitations

The primary intention for the low-precision format is to be able to represent all color values and associated operations efficiently with minimal storage requirements, power consumption, and bandwidth, which is essential on handheld platforms. Where full floating-point precision is not required, it would be inefficient to provide a full 32 bits of storage. More importantly, where large amounts of such data are being processed—notably with color information—the cost to performance could be severe.

Naturally, low precision is not suitable for all purposes. We will examine separately the two main limitations. The first is the *range limitation*. A value lies outside the range of low precision if its magnitude (absolute value) is greater than `MAX_LOWP`, which results in an *overflow*, or if the magnitude is less than `MIN_LOWP`, which causes an *underflow*.

The behavior of such values depends on the implementation of the API. Overflows will either be clamped to the maximum/minimum value or represented as positive/negative infinity. Underflows will either be represented as zero or an infinitesimal value.

The second limitation is *loss of accuracy* that occurs when, for example, casting higher-precision values to low precision. Any low-precision value can only be accurate to within 2^{-8} ($1/256$) of the true value.

Impact on Shader Development

The range limitation means that low precision is likely unsuitable for handling position information; however, normals, tangents, and similar *directional* vectors (including directional lights and lighting-related variables) ought to be normalized and should therefore lie within the range.

Although color information, including vertex colors, should usually be represented in low precision, it is possible that we will want to handle HDR color values, which generally lie outside the low-precision range. Other color-related effects—multi-texturing, normal mapping, and so on—can to a great extent be calculated in low precision.

The accuracy limitation is less obvious, particularly for per-vertex operations; as the values are interpolated between the vertices, the precision loss is less noticeable. Generally with `dot3` per-pixel lighting, the normal is being sampled from a texture (typically, an 8- or 10-bit format) and expanded to the range [-1,1] and can therefore be represented in low precision without any loss of accuracy. As we will see, however, texture coordinates *cannot* be represented in low precision. Because only eight bits are fractional, the number of sample points would be limited to 256×256 and thus linear filtering would be ineffective.

Simulating Low Precision

Given the complex nature of using low precision, the visualization of the impact of precision on shader algorithms is a key requirement when developing applications for handheld devices. This section introduces a macro that will facilitate the simulation of precision modifiers and discusses the impact on development tools.

A Low-Precision Macro

Low precision can be simulated using shaders if we are not developing on an actual device. We can create a macro that performs this simulation by rounding off the input value and clamping it to the low-precision range. The range clamp is the first and simplest stage and uses our previous definition of MAX_LOWP.

```
f = clamp(f, -MAX_LOWP, MAX_LOWP)
```

Next we handle accuracy by truncating the value. To recap, the representation of low precision uses eight fractional bits and one integer bit, thus we need to preserve eight fractional bits of the input value. We can do this by multiplying the value by 2^8 (thus shifting it eight bits to the left), casting to an integer (to discard the remaining fractional bits), and then multiplying by 2^{-8} (which we have defined as MIN_LOWP) to move our fractional bits back into place (the inverse of the previous multiplication).

```
f = float( int( f * 256.0 ) ) * MIN_LOWP
```

Our combined macro looks like the following:

```
#define MIN_LOWP (0.00390625)      //  1/256
#define MAX_LOWP (1.99609375)      //  2 − 1/256
#define F2LOWP(f)       (float(int(clamp(f,-MAX_LOWP,MAX_LOWP) *
256.0 )) * MIN_LOWP)
```

We can now use this macro to help identify some of the obvious and more subtle pitfalls in the use of low precision.

Hardware Limitations and Development Utilities

Most development for mobile devices takes place in a PC environment on which an emulation layer is implemented as an OpenGL ES wrapper to OpenGL. Typically Desktop OpenGL 2.0 only implements floats as full 32-bit floating-point variables, so even if the low-precision *modifier* is used the result will depend on the emulation layer implementation and might not be the same as it will be on the target device.

OpenGL ES 2.0 PC emulation implementations, such as Imagination Technologies' PowerVR VFrame, strip all precision modifiers from the GLSL ES code and use the accuracy of the underlying OpenGL implementation. Emulation of precision would require multiple invocations of the macro proposed earlier, but this very quickly pushes today's graphics cards to their limits by either overflowing the number of supported instructions or hitting unacceptable performance levels. The alternative—a complete software emulation—would suffer even more severely in performance.

Low-Precision Pitfalls 1: Out-of-Range

It is fairly evident that overflow can occur in any variables where the input is not restricted to the range (-2,2). For example, if low precision is used for texture coordinates, positions, transformation matrices, and so on, values will likely be clamped (Figure 7.3.2).

FIGURE 7.3.2 Repeating texture: The face on the left is using low precision for texture coordinates.

More insidiously, an overflow may arise as a result of arithmetic operations performed on low-precision variables. An operation will be evaluated at the highest of the precisions of the operands, but operations upon only low-precision variables or literal constants (which have no precision defined) will be evaluated at low precision. Consider the following, where all the associated variables are in low precision:

```
color = (texColor1 + texColor2 + texColor3) / 3.0;
```

Intended to take an average of the three inputs, this operation will overflow if the sum of the inputs is 2 or greater. So if each of the inputs were set to 0.7, we would expect the result to be 0.7 also; however, it would in fact evaluate to MAX_LOWP/3 (about 0.67).

Checking for Overflows and Underflows

Building on the previously defined simulation macro, we can highlight in the fragment shader areas where an overflow/underflow would occur due to values lying outside the low-precision range. (A modified approach can be used in the vertex shader, wherein a varying condition is passed down to the fragment shader.)

It is easy enough to test whether a value has exceeded the range. The general approach goes something like this:

```
IF (value exceeds lowp range)
      Set pixel colour to solid flag
      Return from shader
ELSE
      Apply lowp conversion to value
```

As an example, the following macro implements the check for underflow and overflow using a separate color flag for each. We could also use separate colors for negative and positive overflows.

```
#define CHECK_UNDERFLOW(f)       if (f!=0.0 && abs(f) < MIN_LOWP)
{ gl_FragColor = vec4(1.0,0.0,0.0,1.0); return; }
#define CHECK_OVERFLOW(f)      if (abs(f) > MAX_LOWP)
{ gl_FragColor = vec4(1.0,0.0,1.0,1.0); return; }
#define CONVERT_LOWP(f) CHECK_UNDERFLOW(f); CHECK_OVERFLOW(f); f =
F2LOWP(f);
```

This approach can trivially be extended to check the values of vectors, matrices, and other aggregate data types. However, for an accurate check the conversion ideally must be performed after every operation that would be done in low precision. So our earlier example would be checked as follows:

```
color = texColor1 + texColor2;
CONVERT_LOWP(color);
color += texColor3;
CONVERT_LOWP(color);
color /= 3.0;
CONVERT_LOWP(color);
```

Although this method could become tedious on the more complex shaders, it can be used to specifically test any operation or targeted segments of the shader.

Example: Encoding HDR Images

A *high dynamic range* (HDR) image is one in which the color values exceed the 0–255 range. Although such images typically require a floating-point representation, they can be encoded in the Radiance RGBE format [Ward05] with 8-bit color values using the alpha channel as an *exponent* value shared by the other color channels as shown in Figure 7.3.3. Thus, the final color is reconstructed as $(R,G,B) \times 2^E$ (with appropriate bias and scaling factors).

FIGURE 7.3.3 Left: RGBE encoded HDR image. Right: Decoded image with underflows flagged.

The decoded image presented is tonemapped to scale the HDR color values to the 8-bit color range. This must be performed in the shader program by using an average scene luminance input value that may be computed using multiple previous render passes. Further render passes may also produce a bloom effect to highlight the brightest areas.

The tonemapping stage operates on the decoded HDR color, which will probably exceed the low-precision range, but other render passes perform simple texture reads and apply blur or downscale filters. Since only the decoded image requires high-range values, it is probable that many of these rendering passes can be computed entirely in low precision.

Low-Precision Pitfalls 2: Loss of Accuracy

The other main limitation of low precision often comes into play when we have "continuous" values such as texture coordinates, which we expect to vary slightly from pixel to pixel. Depending on the effect required, a lack in precision can have a dramatic impact on the visual result, with banding being the distinguishing artifact.

To use the texture coordinates as a trivial example, we can see from the illustration in Figure 7.3.4 the effect of using low-precision coordinates. Because texture coordinates range between 0.0 and 1.0, we are effectively using only eight bits of the low-precision storage. This limits us to only 257 distinct values for each coordinate (including 1.0), so the image quality of the texture will be similar to a 256×256 image, even for much higher resolution textures.

Propagation of Error

In the same way arithmetic operations on low-precision values can cause overflows, they can also introduce or exacerbate precision errors. If the error in our original value can be as much as MIN_LOWP, that is to say 2^{-8}, then the error associated with adding two such values will be 2×2^{-8}; in adding three values, the uncertainty is 3×2^{-8}.

FIGURE 7.3.4 Left: View of a texture mapped cube using high-precision texture coordinates. Right: The same view using low precision for texture coordinates.

In general, if any value f has uncertainty (error) Δf, the uncertainty propagates with arithmetic operations according to certain rules, a few of which include the following:

$$\Delta(f_1 + f_2) = \Delta f_1 + \Delta f_2$$

$$\Delta(c \cdot f) = c \cdot \Delta f$$

if c is a constant literal or some other precisely known value.

$$\Delta(f_1 + f_2)/(f_1 \cdot f_2) = (\Delta f_1 / f_1 + \Delta f_2 / f_2)(approximately)$$

In a way this is intuitive, as you can see by the scaling of texture coordinates in Figure 7.3.5: The "blockiness" caused by the clamping of the precision at low values is also scaled up. As with the earlier example in handling range errors, a single line can

FIGURE 7.3.5 Operations on texture coordinates blending two samples with normal and scaled texture coordinates of an image; left image using high precision, right image using low precision.

contain multiple low-precision operations that could seriously degrade the precision of the result.

Re-mapping of Limited Ranges

There are many instances where variables will be expected to reside, for example, within the range (0, 1). As can be seen from the earlier discussion of the low-precision representation, such values will use only the eight fractional bits of the 10 bits allocated to the value. With such values we can increase our precision by rescaling our representation so that we utilize the full 10 bits available. Thus 1 is represented as positive MAX_LOWP and 0 as negative MAX_LOWP.

```
#define encode(f)      MAX_LOWP * (2.0*f − 1.0)
#define decode(f)      (f/MAX_LOWP + 1.0) * 0.5
```

As arithmetic operations are not preserved under the encoding, this should be used primarily for more efficient storage and faster throughput. For example, if one wants to pass the texture coordinates from the vertex to the fragment shader in low-precision format (via a varying lowp vec2 texCoord variable), one could use this encoding as follows.

In the vertex shader:

```
texCoord.st = encode(myUV.st);
```

In the fragment shader:

```
color = texture2D(sampler, decode(texCoord.st));
```

Although this range mapping may well be useful in granting increased precision for a number of uses, this level of accuracy is still insufficient for texture coordinates generally. Furthermore, when applying this sort of encoding one should be mindful of the overhead associated with the required operations.

Using Medium and High Precision

The specification for medium and high precision calls for at least 16- and 24-bit representations, respectively, although many implementations will provide full 32-bit floats for high precision, and this is encouraged particularly in the vertex shader to enable correct vertex transforms.

Medium precision, by using a floating-point representation, has a much larger range than low precision. However, after using five bits to represent the exponent it leaves only 10 fractional bits versus low precision's eight for the significant digits. Medium precision therefore offers a precision (relative) of 2^{-10}.

Thus for values between 0.5 and 1.0, the accuracy would be 1/2,048. This may seem like sufficient precision for something like texture coordinates—after all, we rarely use texture bitmaps with a higher resolution than 1,024×1,024. Indeed, if we are in a situation where one texel corresponds to one pixel, then we will be able to represent all the texture coordinates very accurately.

Unfortunately, this is usually not the case: If we are close to (or far from) the textured surface, then we likely want to use texture filtering to interpolate for values in between texture elements. Thus we do need to represent texture coordinates with greater resolution than the image itself. The more important it is to use filtering, the more important it is to use high precision for the texture coordinates. High precision offers a relative precision of at least 2^{-16}, or $1/65,536$, which is much greater than the resolution of any reasonable texture.

In general, then, we see that although medium precision has a far more versatile range than low precision (the absolute magnitude can be between 2^{-14} and 2^{14}), it has only a moderate advantage when it comes to precision.

Conclusion

In this article we have seen the sort of reasoning that should be applied to deciding which precision levels to use for float-type variables in our shaders. We have also seen some of the tricks that can maximize the capability of low precision by using it to encode higher precision values. The examples here present a flavor of the mindset it is necessary to adopt when targeting effects for mobile devices: Be inventive, be economical, and make the maximum use of the resources available.

Acknowledgments

I would like to thank my colleagues at Imagination Technologies, in particular Kristof Beets, David Harold, and Georg Kolling, for their comments and suggestions; and the rest of the PowerVR Developer Technology group for the PowerVR SGX Utilities and SDK.

References

[Khronos07] The Khronos Group, "OpenGL ES Shading language," available online at http://www.khronos.org/opengles/2_X/.

[Ward05] Ward, Gregory J. "High Dynamic Range Image Encodings," available online at http://www.anyhere.com/gward/hdrenc/hdr_encodings.html.

7.4

Implementing Graphical Benchmark in OpenGL ES 2.0

Szabolcs Horvath

Csaba Keszegh

Laszlo Kishonti

Introduction

In this article we'll share our experiences we gathered during the development of GLBenchmark 2.0, our 3D benchmark for OpenGL ES 2.0 (ES2) [OGLES20]. We'll also describe some differences in the workflow with ES2 compared to the OpenGL ES 1.x (ES1) API [OGLES11].

The main goal of our development was to create an application to benchmark mobile GPUs with a game-like scene using complex animations and high-quality visual effects, which are also realistic and comparable to future mobile games. (However, we didn't implement AI and game logic because we are only interested in the graphics or GPU related performance limits. We also tried to limit CPU usage whenever possible.)

To make our new application future proof, our new rendering engine was designed to be very flexible so that we could change 3D scenes easily and switch certain effects on and off interactively. This was also important because we needed to reach decent performance (beyond the highest possible visual quality) on resource-limited mobile devices.

Our new engine adapts to the environment very efficiently using dynamically generated shaders. Our GLSL [ROST06] source generator did not just make our work much less error-prone and our effects reusable and combinable, using this technology we were also able to create an application that scales from the low-budget to the high-end devices.

Finally—thanks to the new possibilities of the new API—we can build much higher visual quality than in our earlier ES1 applications using even lower resolution geometry.

Planning for Mobile Development

Portability Issues

Our earlier benchmark for ES1 was built using standard (POSIX) C because we needed seamless portability through several platforms (Brew, Linux, Symbian, Windows Mobile). C compilers are always available and very stable, so that seemed to be a reasonable decision.

Looking back to all the pain with plain C (code structure, memory management, and inheritance issues), this time we chose C++ because we really wanted a structurally stable and more manageable code base.

Please note, though, that on mobile devices C++ programmers have limited resources to use: STL is not always available, and support for templates and exceptions is also sometimes limited. The use of global and static variables is prohibited or better to be avoided on Brew and Symbian platforms [BREW06] [SYMBIAN06].

File Format

Thanks to the Mobile 3D Graphics 1.0 (JSR-184) API [M3G1] for Java ME, there's a fairly standard way to export 3D content to mobile devices using the M3G format. As we also develop mobile Java 3D benchmarks, it was inevitable that our engine will use and support M3G.

The main advantage of M3G is its compactness: It encodes float geometry and animation data to bytes and shorts and also compresses them. Sometimes precision issues can emerge, but most of these can be resolved with proper scene setup (for example, it's not recommended to use deep transformation hierarchies).

There are several M3G file format exporters available for the popular animation packages. (We have also created one for Autodesk Maya. A free version is available at www.m3gexport.com.)

The main disadvantage of the current version (1.0) of M3G is that it does not support shaders, but that will be resolved in the near future by M3G 2.0 [M3G2], which will encode GLSL shaders. Soon creating and distributing standalone and compact GLSL content will be standardized and supported by several commercial and free tool chains, which saves a lot of cost and helps spread shader technology in the mobile space. (For example, it will be possible to update games with new maps that not only contain the geometry and textures, but also use very attractive dynamic shader effects.)

Using M3G 2.0 format will also let developers support a wider range of devices, as most mobile devices do not allow direct access to native OpenGL ES/GLSL, but only through M3G API.

Real Number Types

Animating and rendering 3D scenes requires a lot of calculations. In real games the logic and artificial intelligence of the characters adds even more number crunching, which heavily stresses the limited power of mobile CPUs. So it's essential to decrease the load as much as possible to make the game playable in real-time.

One way to do this is to forget floating-point calculations and use fixed-point numbers instead. Most ES1 applications used fixed-point calculations heavily because the API supported and even endorsed it. The big advantage of fixed-point numbers is that they can be calculated fast with standard 32-bit integers, which are universally supported by mobile (mostly ARM class) CPUs, especially because earlier chips did not contain floating-point units at all. The disadvantage of fixed-point calculations is lower precision and the danger of overflows.

The situation is slowly changing, though, as ES2 support appears. The basic ES2 type is float, which means the architecture supports floating-point calculations at the hardware level, so every time the calculations can be pushed to the GPU side, there is less need for float to fixed conversions.

In ES2 it's also possible to set *precision qualifiers*, which are hints to the driver about the expected precision of the shader-based calculations. These can help the shader compiler to create more optimized, faster code when high precision is not essential.

Textual Output and Debugging with Console Shader

The most painful part of mobile development is when we try to find bugs on a real consumer device where there's no debugging support and not even a standard console window to write to.

Believe it or not, debugging is also made easier with GLSL shaders, as we can easily create a shader that prints all messages to the screen. We only need to encode the character codes as UV texture coordinates and use these as lookup values in our texture mapped font sets.

Our console shader works similarly to Alexander Ehrath's method [EHRATH06], but we used it as an application level console. For example we can write the actual frame rate with the following simple line:

```
console_printf ("fps: %f\r", (float)fps/(float)millisec*1000);
```

This method is absolutely platform independent and a great help during debugging.

Runtime Generated Shaders

Because ES2 is not backward compatible, we also needed a new programming model.

First we tried the naive way, so every time a new type of object was created or loaded, we determined what effects it would use for rendering and wrote a shader to accommodate all those features manually. This method seemed to work when we used only a limited number of effects and a small number of objects, but as the scene started to change and grow in the hands of the artists, the situation became more and more complicated.

We discovered even more serious problems when we started to combine different shader effects, especially if they were written by different programmers. For example, we had shadow shaders and nice environment maps, but they didn't work together because the naming of the variables was different for the two programmers who wrote them. It was also impossible to switch off features when they were not needed in this scheme.

Having all these experiences, we decided to start a new framework from the ground up. In our new setup we wanted to switch features on only when they were needed, combine the different effects automatically for different types of objects (skinned and rigid meshes) in efficient, densely coded shaders, and we also needed help to synchronize all the variable names, loading, binding, and cleanup by the system.

The only way to do this was to create a GLSL shader source generator, which let us make custom shaders at scene-loading time, so there was no need to hard code anything in the system.

The generator basically automates all the earlier tasks we did manually. First it examines the loaded objects and checks what information is available. For example, if a mesh has bones with weights connected to the vertices, it adds the skinshader extension template to the vertex shader and initializes all the variables needed for skinning both the shader level and application level (and cleans them after the render and/or the application exits).

With the same logic, if an object has color (diffuse) texture, then the generator extends the fragment shader with the required code template and initializes all the needed variables and textures.

The most important part is the proper order of the additional effects, because many of them do not work in reverse. For example, if we render an object with casted shadows, the color change caused by the shadow is the last step in the fragment shader.

It should be noted that before we start to generate a new shader using this methodology, we also create a `checksum` value based on the available/used variable types of each object. These `checksums` are then compared to our mini shader library of previously generated programs and if the `checksum` matches one of the shaders contained there, we don't create a newer program; we simply reuse the former one.

For example, in our case we only have the following seven very dense shader programs:

- Shadow caster animated rigid mesh depth texture shader (pass 0)
- Shadow caster animated skinned mesh depth texture shader (pass 0)
- Torch shader
- Static rigid mesh with shadow casted with baked lighting
- Static rigid mesh with no shadow casted with baked lighting
- Animated rigid mesh with dynamic environment and radiance map lighting
- Animated skinned mesh with dynamic environment and radiance map lighting

The only disadvantage of runtime generated shaders is they cannot be used on those implementations that do not support source code shaders. However, that might be an insignificant issue, as all the current implementations of ES2 (as of this writing) support online compiling.

Skinning

As the OpenGL ES API evolves, programmers will get newer and more efficient methods to render skinned characters in games. In ES2 we use vertex shaders to decrease the load on CPU, but we also list the other (older) methods and their main differences.

Software Skinning (OpenGL ES 1.0)

Using software skinning [DAVIES] offers a great advantage to programmers: They can access all the calculated vertex data freely and reuse them as they like, which can be very efficient when the skinned character has shadows or a mirrored image that is rendered in parallel. In all these cases, the secondary/tertiary render passes do not need further skin vertex calculations, just one matrix multiplication and a simple glDrawElement call. It's even possible to cache unchanged vertices between frames, which also decreases the calculation burden significantly.

We should also mention that the batch size (the number of elements per GL render calls) is only limited by the general system environment, which means that most skins can be rendered with one call.

The biggest—and only—problem with software skinning is that it's all done in CPU time, which takes away resources from all other parts of the application.

Matrix Palettes (OpenGL ES 1.1)

Matrix palettes were introduced with OpenGL ES 1.1 as an extension to the API (OES_matrix_palette) [OGLES11]. These made it possible for the first time in the mobile space to push all the skinning calculations to the GPU and free the CPU from the work.

The main problem with the standard matrix palette extension was that it supported only nine matrices (nine bones) in one render call, but human characters have at least 40 bones. Due to this limitation, graphics engines needed to divide the skin into at least 6–7 smaller partitions (in reality the number of partitions can be much higher if the vertices of a distinct triangle are linked to more than one bone). This results in smaller batch sizes and less efficient rendering.

(There's another extension called *extended matrix palette* [MUNSHI05] that supports 31 bones, but that's not implemented in most drivers.)

Because all the matrix multiplications of the vertices are done inside the GL server, programmers have no way to query the final positions, so caching is not possible with this method. Debugging is also very difficult.

Because of all these issues, only large triangle count skins get the advantages of matrix palettes; smaller models are usually faster with CPU skinning.

Skin (Vertex) Shaders (OpenGL ES 2.0)

It's very easy to implement the matrix palette functionality with GLSL vertex shaders. We only need to add the bone matrices in a uniform variable array and the weights and indices of bones as attribute variables. This way every vertex will "know" which bones are affecting it and the weights of each of the affecting bones.

According to the current limitations of ES2, vertex shaders should support at least 128 four-dimensional vector uniforms. The same space lets us use 32 (4×4) matrices. As we need at least one additional matrix for modelview and projection transformation, we have 31 matrices remaining for bones. Not surprisingly, this limit is the same as we saw in the extended matrix palette extension. This way we can render human characters with at most two render calls.

If we are using only affine transformations [HEARN04], the bottom line of all bone matrices will be {0,0,0,1}, which means we waste a lot of space. We can exploit this if we send only the top three lines (three four-dimensional vectors) of the bone matrices and reconstruct the full matrix in the vertex shader or use direct vector dot products to calculate the final vertex positions. This way we can increase our virtual palette size to 41 bones and increase the batch sizes further.

Beyond these options, the real advantage of shader skinning is that it can be easily combined with other effects. For example, a shadow casting shader can be used with both skinned and rigid meshes.

As with matrix palettes, the final positions of the skins cannot be queried from the GL, which can be a problem for games where precise collision detection is needed.

Lighting and Shadows

Lighting in OpenGL ES 1.x and 2.0

In ES1 we had a limited number of lights (eight) and we could only choose between flat and smooth (Gouraud) shading models. In ES2 these limitations are removed; we can set up almost an unlimited number of lights through shaders with user-defined lighting models. (In order to do this you have to pass your light sources as uniform variables.)

Texture-Based Lighting

For efficiency reasons (we have 39 lights in the scene) we chose to not use dynamic, physical light sources in our new engine, and instead switched to texture-based lighting.

Light Maps

As our lights' positions do not change throughout the animation, we can precalculate the lighting for all static meshes and bake them to light map textures. This way the lighting is simplified to texture lookups in the fragment shaders.

Another advantage of light maps is that they look good even in very small resolution, which fits well our resource limited mobile model.

FIGURE 7.4.1 Precalculated lightmap.

Environment Maps

Shiny, metallic objects such as a helmet or armor reflect their environments dynamically. This can be modeled with environment maps.

In ES2, texture cubes can effectively be used for environment reflection calculations and lookups. The only problem with texture cubes is that they need six additional render passes (a cube has six faces) if your environment changes and/or the object you map the environment on is moving. This would be awfully slow to do on a mobile device in real-time.

A better solution is to calculate several predefined environment maps at initialization time and always use the one closest to the moving objects for lookups. This again has a drawback: The switches between the environment maps are very visible to the human eye (even if the environment map origins are very close to each other).

FIGURE 7.4.2 Environment map texture.

Our final solution, then, was to find the two closest environment maps and weight them based on the squares of distances to the animated object. This method provides smooth transitions from one environment map to the next.

Radiance Maps

A similar technique can be used for matte (non-reflective) moving objects. In these cases, the fragments reflect not only the lights coming from one direction, but the whole hemisphere of lights weighted by the cosine of the reflection angles [DEMPIN-SKI05]. These results can be calculated for every direction (or every texel of the original environment map) and can be encoded in a cosine-filtered environment map or radiance map.

Precise calculation of radiance maps takes an enormous amount of time even on a desktop computer, so again we decided to simplify this to be able to use it on mobile hardware. As radiance maps encode very low frequency data [RAMANOORTHI01], they can be easily faked with repeated use of box and linear filters, which can be easily calculated (see Figure 7.4.3) [ATI05].

The only issue we had to worry about here was that current ES2 hardware does not support filtering beyond the faces of the texture cubes [ATI05]. Thus, to have nice results we had to pre-filter our fake radiance maps on the CPU without GPU

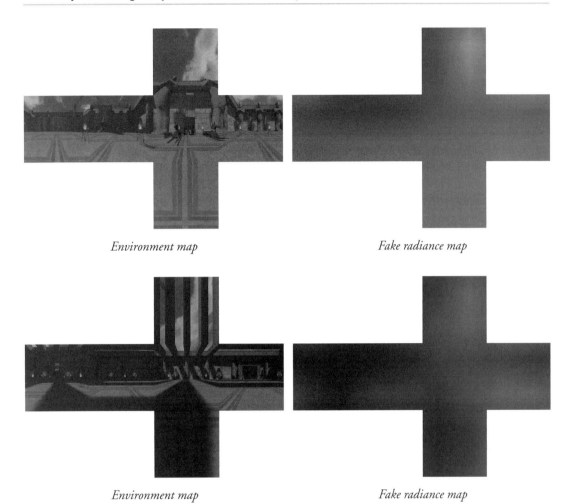

Environment map   *Fake radiance map*

Environment map   *Fake radiance map*

FIGURE 7.4.3 Environment maps versus fake radiance maps.

hardware acceleration. Of course, this was done only once at initialization time, so it had no effect on real-time rendering speed.

Shadows

Not long ago it was unthinkable to use realistic shadows on mobile platforms. In the earlier version of GLBenchmark we used simple planar shadows, which were fine but had lot of limitations that made them impossible to reuse in our new engine. (Planar shadows are nearly impossible to use if there is more than one plane to cast shadows. In our new scene we have ramps and stairs with several intersecting planes.)

Because we wanted to use a GPU-based solution, shadow volumes were out of the question. Shadow maps seemed to be a much better solution, with special considerations and modifications allowed for the mobile hardware.

First of all, in ES2 it is currently impossible to get direct access to the Z-buffer, and there are no shadow/depth textures either. (In the future there will be an extension to solve this [LIPCHAK07].) So we had to create a special shader that encodes the depth values to RGB space, which can be queried and mapped to a frame buffer object (texture).

The following shader source implements this:

```
//Vertex shader
precision mediump float;
uniform mat4 uniProjectionModelviewMatrix;
attribute vec4 atrVertex;
varying vec4 varVertex;

void main (void)
{
        gl_Position=uniProjectionModelviewMatrix*atrVertex;
        varVertex=gl_Position;
}


//Fragment shader
precision mediump float;
varying vec4 varVertex;

void main (void)
{
        highp float d = varVertex.z/varVertex.w*256.;
        highp float r = floor(d)*0.00390625; // divide by 256
        highp float rm = fract(d)*256.;
        highp float g = floor(rm)*0.00390625;
        highp float gm = fract(rm)*256.;
        highp float b = floor(gm)*0.00390625;
        highp vec4 v4color=vec4(r, g, b, 0);
        gl_FragColor = v4color;
}
```

The second issue with classic shadow maps is that they need very high texture resolution to achieve good results. Since texture memory is always scarce in mobile devices, we switched to perspective shadow maps [STAMMINGER02] in which the mapping is done after the perspective divide, so it's guaranteed that the closer objects have higher resolution shadows than the farther ones (just as we need).

Because we had to calculate shadows for the animated meshes (static ones were already lit by our light maps) a further optimization could be used: The shadow frustum can be resized dynamically to the unified bounding volume of the meshes currently inside the (rendering) camera frustum and nothing else. This greatly increases the perceived resolution of the shadow maps because the animated meshes tend to be close to each other most of the time (well, they *are* fighting each other).

So finally we were able to use a relatively small, 256×256 shadow map on a VGA resolution screen without major resolution issues.

Using Noise Textures: The Torch Effect

We wanted to add realistic torches to our scene, so we started thinking how flames work in real life. We began with the assumption that the shape of the flames and the colors of the pixels belonging to the torch image are determined mainly by the temperature of the burning gases. Thus we can model the flame as a function of world coordinates. This function defines the colors we have to display, so let's call this function as the color function of the flame. We can find the formula for this function by starting from the two-dimensional extension of the well-known bell curve. Then we transform this function so that the resulting function represents the flame convincingly.

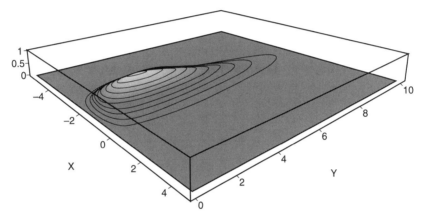

FIGURE 7.4.4 Modeling the flame as a function of world coordinates.

This color function has only two variables because we can display the flame as a billboard that has an up vector that is always pointing upward in world space but is oriented toward the viewer.

To obtain the color of each pixel, we could calculate the value of the color function in runtime as a procedural texture. But it's more efficient to precalculate those values and bake them into a texture just like we did in the case of the lighting calculations of stationary objects. The arguments to the color function will be the coordinates relative to the billboard rectangle so that we can find the color of the pixels by a single lookup in the baked color texture.

To simulate the flickering of the flame, we wanted to add noise to the texture coordinates, but noise functionality is only a formal extension [OGLESSL07] to the ES2 shading language and thus it may be missing in some implementations. Because of this, we have to use one more texture to encode noise information into. By choosing the appropriate distribution for the noise values we achieve the desired reality. We found the size of 16×16 pixels noise texture satisfactory.

Performance Optimization

A good benchmark program (like a good game) should be runnable on a wide range of devices. It uses the resources very efficiently and helps developers and testers to find bottlenecks easily. We have implemented several strategies that make our application run faster and also scale well. (Please read [BEETS06] also for an excellent performance guide.)

Precision Qualifiers in Shader Programs

ES2 lets developers use precision qualifiers in shaders (this is an important difference from the desktop GLSL). Using the three precisions available—lowp, mediump, highp—we can define the precision of our results and make the calculations faster or slower accordingly.

In GLBenchmark 2 we let the testers change the precision qualifiers dynamically for the main variable types (2D textures, cubemaps, floats, vectors, and matrices) so it's possible to see how the specific precision levels affect performance and rendering quality.

Object Sorting

Animating a scene graph is a hierarchical operation. We have to calculate the parents' positions before we can place the children in the camera/world space. Rendering is a different matter, however, as it's much more effective if we collect the similar objects together and render them in batches reusing textures, shaders, geometry, and the like.

To exploit these efficiencies, we need to set up a second container parallel to the hierarchy that lets us sort and render the objects in a linear fashion. The sorting algorithm has several layers (or depths), some of them are obligatory, some are simply for the sake of performance.

We currently use the following sorting relationships:

- **Transparency:** Semi-transparent objects are rendered last because they are blended with the colors behind them.
- **Shader program:** Objects using the same shaders are rendered together so that we save the costly initialization and cleanup of shader variables (and program loading if memory is scarce).
- **Texture:** Objects with the same textures are rendered together so that we don't have to rebind again and again.
- **Geometry:** Objects using the same geometry are rendered together without reloading the positions, texture coordinates, and so on.

Frustum Culling

Drawing 3D objects with today's mobile GPUs is extremely fast, but it's even faster if we don't draw the unneeded ones. Real-time performance can multiply if we cull the objects that are not located in the camera frustum.

As visibility culling is currently done in the application space—that is, calculated by the CPU—we need to do it as simply as possible. So it's obvious we need object level culling, which can be easily implemented with bounding volumes...well, at least for rigid meshes.

Skinned meshes needed a bit more preparation because it would be very costly to calculate the changing bounding volumes in every frame (as we are not able to query the final vertex positions calculated by the shader). So we decided to calculate a pre-approximated bounding sphere at initialization time using the distance of the root bone (usually the hip bone for human characters) and the farthest vertex on the out-stretched limbs as radius. This solution assumes that the individual bones won't be rescaled at render time and that the distance between the bones will remain the same (horror games would need another algorithm).

Texture Compression

Most of our objects need at least two or three textures to render, and no matter how small a resolution we use, textures add up fast and take up a lot of space in our precious memory. If we use uncompressed RGB or RGBA encoding, many devices wouldn't be able to load all the textures or they simply would not fit inside the texture cache and would thus slow down rendering drastically.

ES2 supports texture compression by default, but it does not specify a standard solution. Most ES2 implementations have their own manufacturer-specific compression formats, but as a neutral benchmark developer we had to avoid these. Fortunately it seems that all major vendors will support the effective and liberally licensed texture compression method of Ericsson (`OES_compressed_ETC1_RGB8_texture`) [STROM06], which is also endorsed by Khronos Group (the body behind OpenGL ES standards). So we have at least one solution that will probably work on most devices.

Frame and Vertex Buffer Objects

Mobile devices have much slower buses between the CPU, GPU, and memory (it is implementation dependent) than we are used to at the desktop. Therefore it's essential to decrease the traffic on the bus whenever possible.

We can save an enormous amount of data movements (and `CopyTexImage` calls) if we render our depth maps (needed for shadows) directly into a frame buffer object, which in optimal cases (but not always, actually) will be placed in the GPU's very fast memory.

The same logic can be used to store all vertices and index data in vertex buffer objects, so we won't need to push these every time an object is rendered to the server (only the addresses will move).

Conclusion

In this short article we tried to summarize the issues we faced when we switched from OpenGL ES 1.0 to OpenGL ES 2.0. Some of these solutions could also help those people who are switching from desktop GLSL shaders to mobile.

Since the first hardware development platforms will only be available when this book is already on the bookshelf (and consumer devices will arrive even later, probably in 2009), eager developers have plenty of time to get accustomed to ES2. It's also a very sensible solution to prepare on desktop hardware in the meantime, as it's fairly straightforward to write code that runs in both desktop and mobile space [GINS-BURG06] (of course, the speed will differ a lot).

Whenever the first ES2 compatible consumer devices finally appear on the market, they will create a revolution and drastically decrease the current quality difference between desktop and mobile games.

References

[ATI05] ATI 3D Application Research Group, "Cubemap Filtering with CubeMap-Gen," 2005, http://ati.amd.com/developer/gdc/GDC2005_CubeMapGen.pdf.

[BEETS06] Beets, Kristof. "OpenGL ES 2.0 Performance Recommandations for Mobile Devices," *ShaderX5: Advanced Rendering Techniques,* Charles River Media, 2006: pp. 421–432.

[BREW06] Brew Programming Primer 3.1, https://brewx.qualcomm.com/bws/content/gi/docs/primers/programming/brew3.1/en/Programming_Primer.pdf.

[DAVIES] Davies, Leigh. "Optimized CPU-based Skinning for 3D Games," http://www.intel.com/cd/ids/developer/asmo-na/eng/172123.htm.

[DEMPINSKI05] Dempski, Kelly and Viale, Emmanuel. *Advanced Lighting and Materials with Shaders,* Wordware Publishing, 2005.

[EHRATH06] Ehrath, Alexander. "Print Shader for Debugging Pixel Shaders," *ShaderX5: Advanced Rendering Techniques,* Charles River Media, 2006: pp. 591–594.

[GINSBURG06] Ginsburg, Dan. "Developing a 3D Engine for OpenGL ES v2.0 and OpenGL v2.0," *ShaderX5: Advanced Rendering Techniques,* Charles River Media, 2006: pp. 411–420.

[HEARN04] Hearn, Donald and Baker, M. Pauline. *Computer Graphics with OpenGL, Third Edition,* 2004.

[LIPCHAK07] Lipchak, Benj.: "New OpenGL ES Extensions," *OpenGL ES BOF (SIGGRAPH 2007 presentations),* http://www.khronos.org/developers/library/2007_siggraph_bof_opengles/OpenGL ES BOG WG Update Aug07.pdf, 2007.

[M3G1] JSR 184: Mobile 3D Graphics API 1.0, http://jcp.org/en/jsr/detail?id=184.

[M3G2] JSR 297: Mobile 3D Graphics API 2.0, http://jcp.org/en/jsr/detail?id=297.

[MUNSHI05] Munshi, Aaftab. "OES_extended_matrix_palette," 2005, http://www.khronos.org/registry/gles/extensions/OES/OES_extended_matrix_palette.txt.

[OGLES11] Khronos Group. "OpenGL ES 1.1 Specification v1.1.10," http://www.khronos.org/registry/gles/specs/1.1/es_full_spec.1.1.10.pdf.

[OGLES20] Khronos Group. "OpenGL ES 2.0 Specification v1.19," http://www.khronos.org/files/opengles_spec_2_0.pdf.

[OGLESSL07] Khronos Group. "The OpenGL ES Shading Language Specification, v1.0.14," http://www.khronos.org/files/opengles_shading_language.pdf.

[RAMANOORTHI01] Ravi Ramamoorthi, Ravi and Hanrahan, Pat. *An Efficient Representation for Irradiance Environment Maps,* 2001, http://www.cs.columbia.edu/cg/pdfs/60_envmap.pdf.

[ROST06] Rost, Randi J. *OpenGL Shading Language, Second Edition*, Addison Wesley, 2006.

[STAMMINGER02] Stamminger, Marc and Drettakis, George. "Perspective Shadow Maps," 2002, http://www-sop.inria.fr/reves/publications/data/2002/SD02/PerspectiveShadowMaps.pdf.

[STROM06] Strom, Jacob. "OES_compressed_ETC1_RGB8_texture," http://www.khronos.org/registry/gles/extensions/OES/OES_compressed_ETC1_RGB8_texture.txt.

[SYMBIAN06] Symbian 9.1 OS Guide, http://www.symbian.com/Developer/techlib/v9.1docs/doc_source/guide/N1001E/StaticData.html.

7.5

Every Cycle Counts: Level of Detail Shaders for Handheld Devices

Kristof Beets

Imagination Technologies

Introduction

OpenGL ES 2.0 hardware brings desktop PC shader functionality into the handheld space. Detailed, high-quality shaders will, however, stress the platform resources for some time to come. Many applications already apply level of detail (LOD) techniques to scene geometry to avoid processing thousands of triangles for an object covering only a few tens of pixels. Surface detail also fades quickly with distance, and evaluating a full physically based per-pixel lighting algorithm for a distant object therefore not only needlessly consumes hundreds of fragment shader cycles, but also wastes valuable bandwidth—all for a visual result that could be approximated with a fraction of these resources!

This article provides an introduction to effective shader-based LOD mechanisms to smoothly scale vertex and fragment shader complexity, from full detail down to a simplified approximation, resulting in increased overall performance and reduced memory bandwidth usage.

Handheld Platform Performance Characteristics

The Khronos OpenGL ES 2.0 API [Khronos07] introduces programmable vertex and fragment shader capabilities. These enable a feature set on par with the latest generation of PC graphics cards and games consoles for handheld devices such as mobile phones, personal navigation devices, Internet tablets, ultra mobile PCs, and handheld gaming devices. While the functional capabilities of OpenGL ES 2.0 devices are on par, the performance characteristics of handheld devices are vastly different from PCs and consoles. Handheld devices are battery operated, and battery life is the number-one criterion in the creation of these devices.

Maximized battery life and the connected power consumption constraints logically lead to silicon area constraints and, ultimately, silicon area translates into actual available processing performance, which can be expressed as the number of shader operations that can be executed per second. The power consumption for handheld graphics cores is limited to mere milliwatts to ensure the expected device operating times and limited heat production versus the hundreds of watts that are being burned by the latest PC market graphics solutions.

This difference in market requirements enforced a drastic revision of the design goals of graphics accelerators: The PC graphics brute force approach is not a sensible solution, and maximum utilization and efficiency of available silicon area—and as a result maximized available performance for a given silicon area—becomes critical for success. Power consumption not only drives silicon area and the connected shader throughput, it also drives available bandwidth, since off-chip data flow makes up one of the largest portions of the power consumption of a handheld device. Once again brute force approaches will fail since a 512 bits-wide data bus is simply not viable on a handheld device, both from a power consumption and a form factor point of view.

Maximal silicon area efficiency, minimal power consumption, and minimal bandwidth utilization have resulted in a high market adoption of advanced non-brute-force rendering architectures such as those based around *tile-based deferred shading* and *unified multi-threaded shader* technologies as offered by the POWERVR SGX Graphics IP Core Family from Imagination Technologies. Handheld graphics cores can be seen as the very tiny and highly efficient brothers of the graphics cores found in the Microsoft Xbox 360 or Sony PlayStation3: they have same advanced functional capabilities but with only a *small fraction* of the shader throughput and bandwidth available due to platform requirements and market expectations.

LOD Shader Design Goals and Benefits

The handheld platform performance characteristics, as introduced in the previous section, require not only a different hardware architecture driven by efficiency but also for software development to revolve around efficient utilization of the ultimate functionality, yet restricted performance, of these devices. Advanced algorithms—for example, bump mapping with parallax effects, self-occlusion, and self-shadowing—are perfectly possible from a functionality point of view, but applying such "hundreds-of-instructions-shaders" to every pixel on the screen of a handheld platform will likely result in very disappointing, potentially single digit, frame rates.

This leads us to the following situation: We have access to great potential image quality and virtually photorealistic shader effects, but when aiming for interactive frame rates we cannot afford to spend hundreds of shader cycles on every pixel due to the power and bandwidth constraints.

We are forced to look at maximal efficiency from a general software development, and more specifically a shader development, point of view. How do we achieve our goal of maximal perceived quality yet with minimal shader instruction and bandwidth cost per pixel? LOD mechanisms fit these requirements perfectly since the quality/cost level can be matched to the required quality.

Within this article the following key LOD design criteria are used for targeting handheld devices:

- Automatic scaling of the quality/cost level through LOD mechanisms
- Minimal overhead to implement the LOD mechanism itself
- Maximal shader instruction saving

With the aim to obtain the following benefits:

- Improved overall performance due to workload scaling
- Best possible quality where it can be seen and appreciated
- Additional benefit of performance scaling across different device categories

Shader LOD Architecture

Methodology

An LOD implementation can be subdivided into three logical parts. The first part of the LOD process is to calculate an actual LOD value, which will determine the overall level of detail (complexity) to be represented by the algorithm. The second part is to execute the actual LOD shader using dynamic or static branching functionality within the application or shader to execute only those parts of the graphics algorithm that match the quality/cost level required based on the calculated LOD value. The final optional part is to implement a quality improvement: Instead of dealing with distinct LOD levels it might be desirable to have a smooth continuous LOD effect where the distinct detail levels are blended from one level into the next. This is similar in nature to filtering between texture MIPmap levels. Some of the many possible implementation options for all three parts of the LOD architecture will be discussed in the following sections.

LOD Value Calculation

The LOD value that will determine the required quality/cost level for shader execution can be determined at various granularity levels within a 3D application. The LOD value can be determined per platform (the lowest possible granularity), per frame, per object, per vertex, or ultimately on a per fragment basis, the latter of which offering the highest granularity. Additionally there are various possible algorithms to determine the LOD value, which are typically *distance based* or *rate-of-change based* algorithms.

LOD Value Granularity

Per Platform

One of the simplest ways to adopt the graphical level of complexity of an application to a collection of platforms is to determine a single per-platform LOD value, either through known facts about the platform or by executing a small benchmark upon first execution of the application. This widespread approach offers only a single LOD value, proving to be the lowest granularity available, and is very straightforward to implement: either from platform information obtained when installing or downloading the handheld application over-the-air or using a quick simple benchmark, which would allow the application to deal with unknown or future handheld platforms. The actual LOD shader matching a suitable complexity level for each respective platform could be generated in advance in platform-specific packages or could be dynamically composited from a library of shader parts and compiled on-the-fly.

This technique imposes no overhead on the shader complexity itself since the LOD mechanism would be completely CPU controlled and no branching instruction would need to be added. In addition to scaling shader complexity, it would also be possible to scale geometry and texture complexity based on the same LOD value. The disadvantage of this technique is that the final quality level is very static and deterministic and offers no opportunity to invest extra cycles where they can be appreciated most. Typically, per-platform scaling is a high-level technique in support of the more advanced LOD techniques discussed later in this article. It is most suitable for dealing with large differences in performance and capabilities and for dealing with resources that are difficult to scale on-the-fly, such as texture and especially geometric complexity.

Per Frame

Granularity can be increased from the per-platform level to a stage where the LOD value would be determined per frame or per game scene type, and such an approach would allow more variation in complexities based on overall frame complexity. However, the overall quality within the frame would still be very static and deterministic. Again, texture and geometry complexity could also be adapted using the same LOD value. A typical example of this would be different levels of detail between cut scenes, action replay, or a menu versus actual interactive game play.

Per Object

Granularity can be further increased by determining the LOD value per object (geometry draw call submission), which has the advantage that an object can scale its detail level dynamically as it moves away from the observer and the overall perceived quality would be much more dynamic and appropriate for each scene. This technique offers good results for individual, relatively small objects, but for larger or scenery elements this technique does not offer very good results because the same LOD value would be assigned to the whole object, which could stretch across the whole screen. Texture and geometry complexity could again be adapted using the same per object LOD value, but this is likely to result in typical popping artifacts often seen in racing games when a new geometry level pops in. Blending the geometry complexity is difficult and is an area of extensive research, but most of the mechanisms proposed are very application-specific and the majority concentrate on large terrain visualization for which a good overview can be found on [VirtualTerrain07]. Another problem with geometry scaling is memory footprint: To allow dynamic geometry scalability, different geometry LODs would need to be stored in memory, thereby increasing the application memory footprint and resulting in possible out-of-memory scenarios on more restricted handheld platforms.

The introduction of geometry shader functionality, which allows the creation of new vertices and triangles by the graphics hardware itself, is likely to open up new LOD scaling opportunities, but geometry shaders are not yet part of OpenGL ES 2.0 core functionality and hence are not discussed within the scope of this article.

Per Vertex

Another granularity level up is to determine the LOD value per vertex. This approach offers LOD scaling across an object, but it has restrictions for objects with minimal tessellation, such as walls or roads constructed from a couple of very large triangles with the majority of surface detail delivered through the fragment shader. For these types of objects, a per-vertex LOD value mechanism would result in a linear interpolation of the LOD value across the surface, and linear interpolation itself can introduce some interesting artifacts and unexpected behavior. Often this creates a non-static LOD behavior where the LOD levels wave in and out from the observer based on the location of vertices. Per-vertex LOD thus effectively hands over the control of the actual LOD variation to the "linear" hardware interpolation, which is outside the control of the developer and artist, and also introduces the risk of difference in behavior and accuracy between different hardware implementations.

Per Fragment

Determining the LOD value at the per-fragment (pixel) level offers the highest granularity and the highest degree of control, but because this is the lowest level in the rendering process, it's also going to have the largest overhead cost of all the possible levels. It is possible to reduce this overhead by using a mixed vertex and fragment shader approach where an initial rough LOD determination is handled in the vertex shader and the final LOD calculation is refined within the fragment shader.

LOD Value Algorithms

Distance Based

From an algorithm point of view, the most obvious variable to use for LOD is the distance between the object and the observer: The farther away an object is, the lower the quality/cost should be. From a calculation point of view, using the distance is very easy, especially within shaders, because the distance from the observer (the camera) is already available in the form of the depth (Z) value; to turn this distance into a final LOD value this value simply needs to be remapped suitably into an LOD space.

There are numerous algorithm possibilities and some of the most typical options show similarities to fog calculations such as linear and exponential functions, which also remap distance into a new space.

LOD, however, is more complex in behavior than fog, and from a workload point of view it is recommended to use a lookup table texture rather than pure arithmetic to map between the true depth value and the final LOD value. Such an approach offers a great amount of control with minimal shader instruction cost. The increase in bandwidth from using a texture is minimal since a single color channel texture can be utilized (e.g., 8-bit intensity) or even 2- or 4-bit compressed texture formats can be utilized, such as POWERVR Texture Compression (PVRTC), which offers very high-quality compression of color ramps. Overall LOD is mostly continuous, meaning that the majority of data access will hit on the texture cache, thus removing most of the external bandwidth usage.

Rate of Change Based

LOD values can also be determined using a *rate of change* based method that is similar to the algorithms used for determining the correct MIPmap LOD level, such as those introduced in [Tatarchuck07], but unfortunately such methods are quite expensive from a computational point of view as they result in a lot of overhead. Furthermore, this approach depends on the availability of DX/DY gradient (rate of change) instructions, which are not part of Khronos OpenGL ES 2.0 core functionality, making this a technique that is less suitable for handheld platforms. It is possible to reduce the dependence on arithmetic and gradient instructions and obtain similar results through the usage of a dummy MIPmapped texture where each MIPmap level is given a different LOD color, and while this technique works, the final outcome is highly dependent on the hardware MIPmapping implementation and accuracy, which often leads to unexpected behavior and unexpectedly reduced quality.

Sample Implementation

Based on our design criteria, we'll be looking at per-pixel LOD values using a simple distance based texture lookup approach. This will give us the highest amount of control but keeps the instruction overhead minimal at this highest granularity level. Using a variety of LOD value lookup textures gives us maximum control at minimal cost, thereby allowing the trivial implementation of LOD plateaus and narrow transition zones between these LOD plateaus (see Figure 7.5.6). Using this approach we can minimize the cost of blending between two LOD levels within the shader, an operation that would increase the amount of shader instruction overhead.

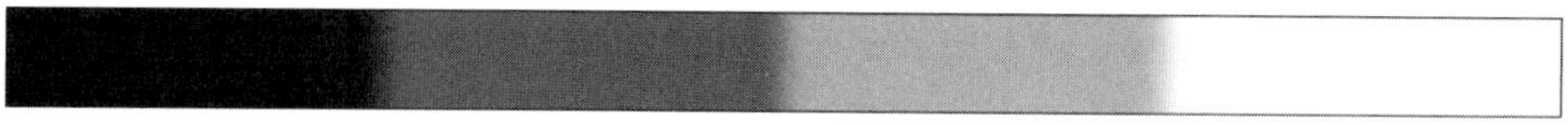

FIGURE 7.5.6 LOD behavior texture with plateaus.

Included on the DVD are two sample LOD calculation implementations (see Figure 7.5.7). The first uses a mixed vertex and fragment shader approach where initial LOD control is handled within the vertex shader and detail LOD behavior is handled within the fragment shader using a texture lookup. The second implementation only uses the fragment shader, which handles both LOD control using a minimal number of instructions and LOD behavior using a texture lookup.

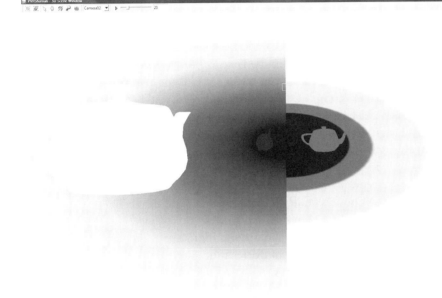

FIGURE 7.5.7 Per fragment LOD (left) and mixed vertex/fragment LOD (right).

LOD Shaders

The highly programmable nature of shaders results in a virtually infinite number of possible effects limited only by the imagination of the developer. This wide variety of shaders makes it difficult to provide a single simple LOD framework that will work efficiently with all the possible shaders out there. Although researchers are looking at automated LOD mechanisms [Olano03] for shaders, automated approaches are unlikely to be able to offer the high level of optimization required for handheld devices due to the usage of very generic simplification rules introducing the risk of excessive overhead. This means that some specific customization work will be required to add LOD support to your own library of shader effects.

Next I'll introduce a generic approach to enabling LOD at the shader level, and I've also included a collection of common shader effects and structures and illustrate how to enable LOD scaling. LOD sample code is provided for the selection of common shader effects on the DVD using Imagination Technologies' integrated shader development environment: POWERVR Shaman.

Generic Approach

When considering an LOD implementation of an existing or new shader it is important to first consider the complexity of the shader. If the shader under consideration is not complex enough, there is a risk that the LOD implementation overhead will reduce the overall performance. Hence, it is wise to consider LOD for the most complex shader effects first since they will likely offer the biggest return on investment. Another factor to take into account is the typical screen coverage area for fragment shaders and the typical number of submitted vertices for vertex shaders. A shader that never covers more than 10 pixels on the screen would not gain much benefit from LOD unless it is insanely complex. On the other hand a medium complexity shader that touches every pixel on the screen is a very valid optimization target. Typical examples of this would be default "world" shaders that are applied to the bulk of the on-screen pixels, such as those applied to terrains (e.g., blending between various terrain type textures and detail texturing), roads (e.g., directionally blurred road texture to improve the perception of high-speed racing), floors and walls (e.g., complex lightmapping that composites multiple lightmaps depending on light factors), and even skyboxes (e.g., procedural, noise-based dynamic sky effects).

Once a shader is identified as a valid optimization target, the next step is to look at the actual shader algorithm itself and determine whether it can logically be split into sections that incrementally improve the perceived quality. LOD should be developed back-to-front, starting with the fragment shader and working back to the vertex shader, because very often the vertex shader includes support calculations such as the setup of various to-be-iterated values for the fragment shader, and these setup operations should ideally only be executed when actually in use at the fragment shader stage. The optimal target for the lowest LOD quality level with the highest performance for a fragment shader is a constant color or simple texture map. Higher LOD levels should progressively add more details and quality by enabling additional parts of the shader algorithm, resulting in increased instruction usage and increased bandwidth usage.

The number of LOD levels can vary widely from shader to shader and depends on the overall complexity and opportunities offered by the algorithm itself. Generally try to keep the number of levels at four or less to avoid excessive branching instruction overhead for implementing the actual LOD behavior. Once the fragment shader has been given an LOD workflow, it is important to check the LOD requirements for the vertex shader based on the fragment shader requirements, that is, if the lowest fragment LOD uses a single static color there is no need to calculate complex texture coordinates or set up tangent space data within the vertex shader.

Finally, the key stage is to benchmark and verify your visual results and continue tweaking until the desired performance/quality result is reached by tweaking the LOD value behavior and the LOD shader code.

Example: Vertex Shader Skinning LOD

Vertex skinning is a common but complex operation, and often shaders are hard coded to calculate a blend between up to four matrices. Analysis of a collection of skinned models, however, reveals that the large majority of vertices only have a single matrix with a non-zero weight, and only a small subset of vertices, typically near a complex joint, have two or more influencing matrices. For general efficiency reasons it is important to use branching to only take into account those blends with a non-zero weight, but this conditional branch can be extended to implement LOD at the cost of some accuracy. If the matrix weights are sorted from large to small, it becomes possible to stop execution once a zero weight is reached; additionally, it is possible to use the LOD value to limit the number of blends to a number below four. Using fewer weights than specified will introduce an error but generally this error is small and hidden inside the joint areas of a model, which means that at sufficient distance (based on the LOD value) this error will be hardly noticeable for carefully designed models but valuable shader cycles can be saved.

Example: Lighting Model LOD

Lighting model calculations—in either the vertex or fragment shader—are often iterated over a number of light sources; additionally, most light models have various light components, including ambient, diffuse, and specular. Based on the LOD value it is easy to reduce the number of light sources that influence a vertex or fragment color by simply reducing the number of lighting loop iterations. In addition, the complexity of the lighting model can easily be modified to support LOD so that the more computationally complex diffuse and specular components are blended into the basic ambient lighting only when they can be appreciated (see Figure 7.5.8). Toning down specular effects with distance also reduces the visibility of sparkling artifacts effects in the distance.

Example: Iterative Algorithms LOD

Many complex shader effects, such as the various relief texture mapping algorithms [Oliveira06] that offer very high-quality surface details, contain an iterative algorithm that is executed multiple times to improve the visual quality of the effect. Algorithm iterations should be limited and step-sized based on an LOD value to avoid spending too many cycles on pixels very far away. This generally has the additional benefit of improved visual quality by reducing the visibility of sparkling effects caused by the iterative execution of calculations.

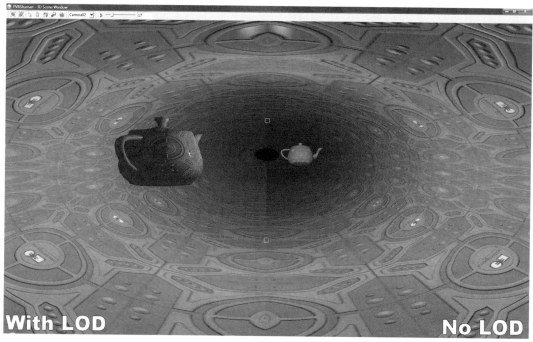

FIGURE 7.5.8 Lighting example with LOD (left) and without LOD (right).

Example: Additive Effect LOD

Many texturing effects are additive in nature, where additional layers are blended in to create an improved visual end result. The LOD value can be used to only blend in the extra detail where required and noticeable; the most common example for this type of LOD is detail texturing.

Many procedural texturing effects are also based on similar concepts where the procedural texture starts from a constant color with progressively more complex modifications added to create the final composite effect—for example, base wood color, add rings, distort rings, and add final detail. Using the LOD value it is possible to only blend in the details when they can truly be appreciated.

Example: Precision Based LOD

OpenGL ES 2.0 offers three levels of precision: *lowp, mediump,* and *highp* [Khronos07]. Hardware throughput is likely to be higher for the lower precision levels due to increased computational capabilities of the hardware, reduced bandwidth, or reduced on-chip register file usage. This increased hardware instruction throughput with lower precision can be used to implement an LOD scheme that will offer additional performance at the cost of accuracy. The tricky element with this approach is the impact of range and the risk of values being clamped to the maximum or minimum value that can be represented by each precision level. If the overall shader can be kept within the [-2.0, +2.0] range of lowp, it is possible to drop the shader precision to lower levels if an object is farther away. Note that changing the precision level is only possible at the shader source code level, which means that this type of LOD would only be possible at the per-object, per-frame, or per-platform level and not at the lower per-vertex or per pixel-levels unless a multi-path shader (see next) is used with pre-written code paths for the different precision levels.

Example: Multi-Path Shaders

Multi-path shaders allow level of detail for shader effects that are too complex to split into separate incremental sections or would introduce too much arithmetic overhead to do so. To resolve this complexity, it is possible to simply generate multiple separate LOD shaders and encapsulate them into a single multi-path shader, where a single path is selected and executed based on the LOD value; this is similar to the concept of über shaders. While this sounds like a quick and easy approach to handle all types of LOD, the efficiency of this type of approach is complex to judge due to increased branching overhead and the variable impact on the hardware when dealing with very large shader programs. This approach is especially expensive when combined with LOD blending.

LOD Blending

LOD blending removes the sharp transition between LOD effects by blending from one LOD level to the next using the fractional part of the LOD value. Often LOD blending can be merged with the overall LOD shader code, but often it increases the number of instructions used so it's important to try to only execute blending operations when they are actually required, e.g., avoid blending each LOD level into the final color with a 100% weight. Also important to remember is that different types of blending have different costs; a simple "multiply and add" is generally quick and cheap but a full LERP blending operation is much more computationally expensive.

Shader LOD and Hardware

My Performance Goes Down Instead of Up!

LOD implementations can be tricky to get right, and nothing is more frustrating than going through a lot of optimization work and then realizing it made things worse than when you started. There are several factors to be aware of when implementing LOD for your mobile application.

Know Your Limit

Understanding the dominant performance limit for your application is the first element to get right because LOD shaders will only help if your application is actually shader or bandwidth bound. Most companies offer analysis tools, such as Imagination Technologies' PVRTune, which use on-chip debug registers capable of providing detailed information on the current workload of the graphics processor. Use these tools to identify the bottleneck before embarking on LOD optimization efforts to avoid disappointment.

LOD Implementation Overhead

Adding LOD mechanisms introduces overhead instructions to deal with the selection of the correct paths within the shader through static or dynamic branching instructions. Additionally, there might be extra code required to the do the conditional compositing of the multiple LOD levels within the shader. If there is too much overhead code being executed, your overall shader workload is likely to increase and your performance will suffer. Check your LOD implementation and use hardware-specific compilers with performance statistics so that you can check for possible expensive hotspots in your code. Consider reducing the number of LOD levels and the LOD value calculation complexity to reduce the overhead, and tweak the LOD value transition points to be more aggressive, thus allowing less complex paths to become more dominant within the frame.

Hardware Design Limitations

High performance dynamic branching is complex to support on hardware and, especially in the PC market, is plagued by side effects of the brute force approach to 3D rendering. Most 3D hardware designs are *single instruction multiple data* (SIMD) in nature, meaning that a group of data elements (vertices or pixels) all need to execute the exact same shader code path because there is only a single program counter and hence instruction available per group. This means that if within one such group half the pixels take one branch and half the pixels take the other branch, all pixels will actually execute both branches and the respective register writes will be masked out if not required. This type of "grouped processing" results in an efficiency that is widely dependent on the amount of branching consistency and the size of the groups. For example, for the ATI X1800 series, the group size was 16 pixels, and with the ATI X1900 series this went up to 48 pixels [Thibieroz06]. This group size increase between generations allowed higher peak throughput but at the cost of branching efficiency. For maximal branching efficiency, hardware would need to become *single instruction single data* (SISD) in nature, where every pixel and vertex can take its own path without executing non-valid instructions. Because mobile devices had efficiency as key design criteria and because dynamic branching is capable of saving many valuable instruction cycles, the branching efficiency of mobile devices such as the POWERVR SGX family is very high, with batch sizes at the SISD level or worst case at the 2×2 pixel group level as required by some gradient based shader instructions.

Theoretical Performance Model and Benchmarking

The creation of a theoretical performance model for LOD can provide valuable insight into the tradeoff between LOD overhead and the performance gain from reduced instruction execution. An LOD implementation with two quality levels can be modeled using a simple set of parameters that include the following: the number of

LOD overhead instructions, the number of low quality level instructions, the number of high quality level instructions, and the ratio between low and high quality pixels. Using straightforward mathematics it is easy to calculate the number of instructions required per pixel for a shader with and without LOD implementation, which can then be translated into an estimated fps number. The resulting graph of such a model is shown in Figure 7.5.9; it shows the behavior of the model for a variable number of high quality level instructions. The graph shows three typical behavior areas: an initial section dominated by LOD overhead, a break-even point, and finally the section where LOD instruction reduction pays off and results in higher performance. Using this model it is easy to play around with the variables and verify the impact on performance of all the different parameters. A Microsoft Excel spreadsheet for this sample performance model is included on the DVD as a companion to this article.

Theory is worth little without real-world verification, so Figure 7.5.10 illustrates performance measured on Imagination Technologies' POWERVR SGX Test Silicon for a similar shader as described by the theoretical model shown in Figure 7.5.4. Performance models linked with benchmarking provide valuable insight into device characteristics and essential background knowledge to allow developers to determine which shaders (and devices) are suitable candidates for optimizations based on LOD techniques.

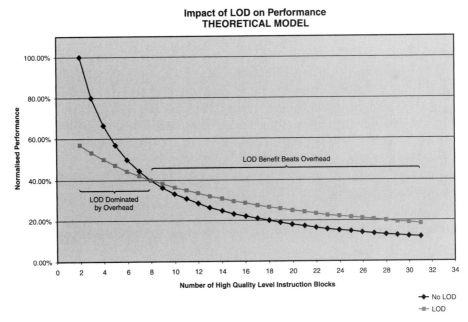

FIGURE 7.5.9 Theoretical performance model for LOD shader.

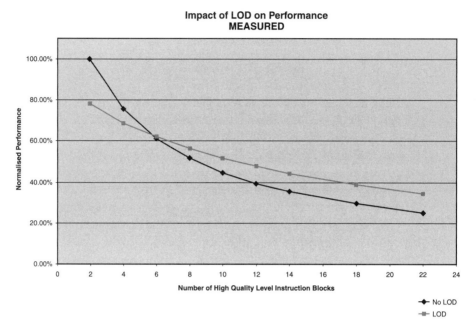

FIGURE 7.5.10 Measured performance characteristics for LOD shader.

Conclusion

This article provided insight into the market-driven restrictions on graphics cores for handheld devices requiring efficiency to become a key factor for both hardware and software development. Level of detail mechanisms were introduced as a cornerstone solution to enabling high quality where it can be seen and appreciated. Key building parts of an LOD implementation were introduced, the LOD value and the LOD shader itself were discussed, and a generic implementation approach and sample concepts illustrated.

Acknowledgments

The author thanks his colleagues at Imagination Technologies who took the time to provide valuable input for this article, in particular David Harold, Georg Kolling, and Ken Catterall, and finally the whole POWERVR Developer Technology Group for developing the POWERVR SGX Utilities and SDK.

References

[Khronos07] The Khronos Group, "OpenGL ES 2.0 Specifications," available online at http://www.khronos.org/opengles/2_X/.

[Tatarchuck07] Tatarchuk, Natalya. "Practical Parallax Occlusion Mapping with Approximate Soft Shadows for Detailed Surface Rendering," *ShaderX5*, Charles River Media, December 2006: pp. 75–106.

[VirtualTerrain07] Virtual Terrain Project available online at http://www.vterrain.org/LOD/Papers/index.html.

[Olano03] Olano, Marc, Kuehne, Bob, Simmons, Maryann. "Automatic Shader Level of Detail," *Graphics Hardware 2003,* available online at http://www.cs.unc.edu/~olano/papers/aslod.pdf.

[Oliveira06] Oliveira, Manual. "Relief Mapping Overview," available online at http://www.inf.ufrgs.br/%7Eoliveira/RTM.html.

[Thibieroz06] Thibieroz, Nick. "Clever Shader Tricks," Slide 4 and following, available online at http://ati.amd.com/developer/SwedenTechDay/03_Clever_Shader_Tricks.pdf.

7.6

Shadow Techniques for OpenGL ES 2.0

Jonathan Feldstein
AMD

Introduction

With OpenGL ES 2.0–capable mobile graphics hardware on the horizon, there are a lot of unanswered questions about the range of effects such hardware will allow developers to implement. One certainty, however, is that such hardware will be orders of magnitude less powerful than the hardware currently being used in both the console and PC spaces. Developers used to having an arsenal of more than a hundred shader operations per clock cycle are going to be faced with the harsh reality of only having one or two operations at their disposal.

As a result, optimization will play a pivotal role in the mobile space for some time to come. This article discusses the challenges associated with producing one particularly demanding and commonly used effect, shadows, and provides advice on how to go about implementing them with OpenGL ES 2.0.

Inexpensive Techniques

Developing 3D games and applications is a constant balancing act between quality and performance. This section takes a look at lightmaps, decal shadows, and projective shadows, three shadow algorithms that are relatively inexpensive.

Lightmaps

The basic idea here is to precompute all lighting and shadow information offline and to simply make use of these textures when rendering your scene. This approach is ideally used alongside other shadowing techniques: You use lightmaps for objects that are stationary, and for objects that are moving around you use one of the algorithms discussed in the remainder of this article.

The one caveat with this approach is that depending on the size and number of textures required, lightmaps may end up using a large amount of memory and storage space that your device might not have available. One way to conserve space and reduce memory bandwidth is to make use of compressed textures. Several compression schemes are available for use with OpenGL ES 2.0 hardware, including the following: ATC, which is AMD's DXTC1/3 based solution; ETC, which is Sony

Ericsson's texture compression format that is based upon the iPackman algorithm; and PVRTC, which is Imagination's texture compression scheme.

Texture MIPmapping is another important issue to think about when using lightmaps with OpenGL ES 2.0. On top of being an effective way to reduce aliasing artifacts, MIPmapping should always be used because it improves texture cache utilization. The choice of which MIPmapping technique to use is once again a choice between quality and performance. OpenGL ES 2.0 supports both bilinear and trilinear MIPmapping, and will likely have support for anisotropic filtering through vendor specific extensions.

One situation where MIPmapping lightmaps might not be appropriate is when using texture atlases. Texture atlases are a convenient way to store all lightmap textures into a single image. The benefit of this approach is that it helps to reduce the number of texture switches between draw calls. The reason that texture atlases cannot be MIPmapped is that samples from multiple atlas images might end up being used, which would generate unappealing artifacts.

Decal Shadows

Decal shadows can be thought of as pre-baked shadow textures that can be transformed and skewed so that they appear to be the shadow of an object. The decal texture map is created offline by placing a light source directly above the occluding object and baking the result into a ground plane. This texture is then simply positioned below the occluder so that it is inline with the light source, as shown in Figure 7.6.1. When the light source is at an angle with the occluding object it is also a good idea to skew the decal shadow accordingly.

Decal shadows are very efficient, easy to implement, and allow for soft shadows. They do, however, come with a variety of limitations: They must be applied to planar surfaces, they do not allow occluding objects to deform or rotate, and self-shadowing is not supported.

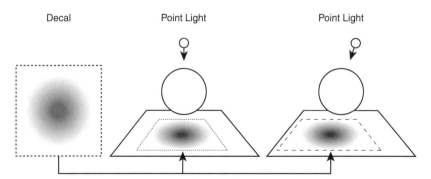

FIGURE 7.6.1 A pre-baked decal shadow being applied to a scene. On the left, the light source is located directly above the occluding object, while on the right the light source is at an angle, resulting in the decal shadow needing to be stretched to compensate.

Projective Shadows

Another affordable approach is to use projective shadows. *Projective shadows* take as input a light source position and an equation of a plane to project geometry onto. This information is then used to generate the following shadow projection matrix:

$$S = \begin{bmatrix} PDotL - L_xN_x & -L_yN_x & -L_zN_x & -L_wN_x \\ -L_xN_y & PDotL - L_yN_y & -L_zN_y & -L_wN_y \\ -L_xN_z & -L_yN_z & PDotL - L_zN_z & -L_wN_z \\ -L_xD & -L_yD & -L_zD & PDotL - L_wD \end{bmatrix}$$

where:

- The plane $P = [\,N_x, N_y, N_z, D\,]$
- The light $L = [L_x, L_y, L_z, L_w]$
- $PDotL = P \bullet L$

This matrix can then be used along with the model, view, and perspective matrices to generate the matrix that we pass to our OpenGL ES 2.0 vertex shader found in Listing 7.6.1.

$$(ModelMatrix) \times (ShadowProjectionMatrix) \times (ViewMatrix) \times (PerspectiveMatrix)$$

The benefit of projective shadows over the previous, more inexpensive approaches is that they allow objects to rotate and deform. The drawbacks are that they need to be applied to planar surfaces, they generate hard-edged shadows, and they can also produce false shadows, as you can see in Figure 7.6.2.

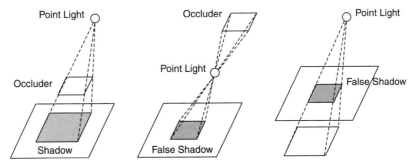

FIGURE 7.6.2 On the left we have a typical use case of projective shadows. The center and right diagrams depict two examples of false shadows that can be generated by projective shadows when the occluder is either behind the light source or the occluder is located beyond the ground plane.

LISTING 7.6.1: Projective shadows

```
uniform mat4 g_matProjectiveShadow;

attribute vec4 g_vVertex;

void main()
{
    gl_Position = g_matProjectiveShadow * g_vVertex;
}
```

Expensive Techniques

So far we have taken a look at several shadowing techniques that are relatively inexpensive but come with a variety of limitations. This section explores three more advanced techniques—depth-fail shadow volumes, shadow maps, and variance shadow mapping—that avoid a large number of these limitations but bring with them higher performance costs on mobile hardware.

Depth-Fail Shadow Volumes

Shadow volumes are constructed out of the silhouette edges of geometry as viewed from the perspective of a light source. Given an edge that is part of two distinct polygons, the edge is considered to be a silhouette edge if one of the polygons the edge is a part of is facing toward the light source, while the other is facing away from the light source. This can be calculated by taking the dot product between the light vector and each of the respective polygon normals and verifying that one of the results is positive and the other is negative.

After these edges have been found, a shadow volume is created by generating a quad for each edge such that two of the vertices of this quad share the silhouette edge's vertices, and the remaining two vertices are the locations of these same vertices projected in the direction of the light vector some large or infinite distance.

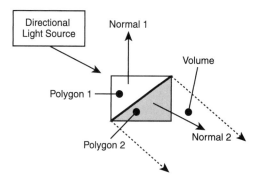

FIGURE 7.6.3 The edge shared by Polygon 1 and Polygon 2 is considered a silhouette edge because Polygon 1's normal is facing toward the light source, while Polygon 2's normal is facing away from the light source. The shadow volume quad that would be extruded from this edge is also depicted with dotted arrows.

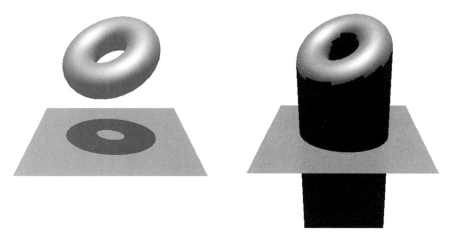

FIGURE 7.6.4 On the left we have a shadow generated with the depth-fail shadow volume algorithm, while on the right we have the shadow volume that was used to generate this shadow.

One way to generate a shadow volume is to iterate over all of the edges in our mesh on the CPU to determine which edges are considered silhouette edges, and to then generate shadow volume quads from each of those edges. If your application is CPU limited, however, there is a faster solution to this problem that can be implemented with a simple OpenGL ES 2.0 vertex shader. The idea is to create quads that consist of two copies of the same edge but that have differing normals, each normal being from one of the two polygons the edge is connected to. Then we can use the vertex shader in Listing 7.6.2 to extrude the vertices that have normals that are back-facing from the light source. This way we do not have to create quads on-the-fly and we can utilize the GPU to create our shadow volume.

LISTING 7.6.2: Shadow volume vertex shader

```
uniform vec4 g_vLightDirection;
uniform mat3 g_matNormal;
uniform mat4 g_matModelViewProj;
uniform mat4 g_matViewProj;

attribute vec4 g_vVertex;
attribute vec3 g_vNormal;

#define INFINITY 10000.0

void main()
{
    vec3 vNormal = g_matNormal * g_vNormal;
```

```
        // Is this a front or back facing edge vertex?
        if( dot( g_vLightDirection.xyz, vNormal ) >= 0.0 )
        {
            gl_Position = g_matViewProj *
                          vec4( g_vLightDirection.xyz, 0.0 ) * INFINITY;
        }
        else
        {
            gl_Position = g_matModelViewProj * g_vVertex;
        }
    }
```

Now that we know what a shadow volume is and how to generate it with vertex shader extrusion, the next step is to learn how to use the stencil buffer in the depth-fail shadow volume algorithm to generate our shadows. The basic steps involved in the depth-fail algorithm are as follows:

1. Disable the depth/color buffers.
2. Turn on front-face culling.
3. Set the stencil operation to increment on depth failure.
4. Render the shadow volume.
5. Use back-face culling.
6. Set the stencil operation to decrement on depth failure.
7. Render the shadow volume a second time.

Fortunately, OpenGL ES 2.0 supports a two-sided stencil operation that actually allows us to simplify this procedure by assigning front- and back-facing polygons with their own stencil operations. As a result, the procedure above simplifies to the following:

1. Disable depth/color buffers.
2. Set the two-sided stencil back-face mode to increment on depth failure.
3. Set the two-sided stencil front-face mode to decrement on depth failure.
4. Render the shadow volume.

Running this procedure will result in zero being written to the stencil buffer when objects are not in shadow and non-zero values when objects should be in shadow. The values stored in the stencil buffer can then be used to render the scene to the color buffer with shadows.

The depth-fail shadow volume algorithm produces detailed, hard-edged shadows, supports self-shadowing, and can be applied to non-planar surfaces. This algorithm is somewhat expensive due to its increased fill-rate. Also, for occluders consisting of a large number of polygons, the silhouette detection step can prove to be a bottleneck, although GPU extrusion can help minimize the cost.

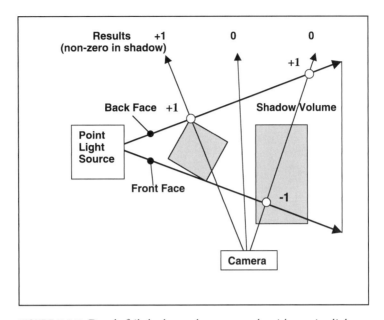

FIGURE 7.6.5 Depth-fail shadow volume example with a point light. When a camera ray intersects an object before passing the front face of the shadow volume, the stencil value is incremented; when the ray intersects an object before reaching the back face of the shadow volume, the stencil value is decremented. Non-zero stencil buffer values indicate that the fragment is in shadow.

Shadow Mapping

The premise behind shadow mapping is that if a light source is unable to see part of an object, then it is in shadow. To figure out what the light source is able to see we render a shadow map that is simply a depth map rendered from the perspective of the light source. When we render a particular fragment of an object to determine whether it is in shadow or not, we need to calculate the distance away this object is from the light source, and we also need to calculate what the depth in our depth map is at this point. If the object is farther away than the value that we have stored in our depth map, our fragment is in shadow. An OpenGL ES 2.0 implementation of this algorithm can be seen in Listing 7.6.3.

The main cost of the shadow mapping algorithm comes from the fact that we need to render a depth map for every light source. In order to obtain shadows without severe aliasing problems, these depth maps need to be rendered at a sufficiently high resolution, as you can see in Figure 7.6.6. Some of the benefits of the algorithm are that it can be applied to arbitrary surfaces and that it supports self-shadowing.

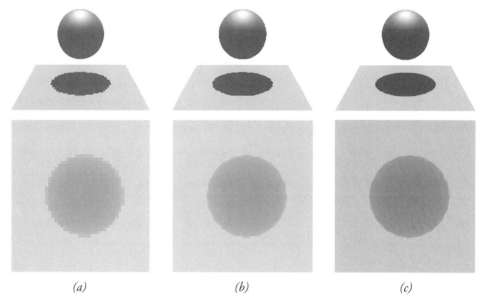

(a)   (b)   (c)

FIGURE 7.6.6 Shadow map shadows (top) with different depth map resolutions (bottom). (a) 64×64 depth map; (b) 128×128 depth map; (c) 256×256 depth map.

Percentage Closer Filtering

One of the limitations of shadow mapping is that it produces hard-edged, potentially aliased shadows. The idea behind *percentage closer filtering* (PCF) is to average the results of multiple shadow tests to help reduce aliasing and soften the shadows. Listing 7.6.4 demonstrates a 2×2 PCF shader that averages four offset results. PCF has a noticeable impact on performance, especially as the filter size grows.

LISTING 7.6.3: Percentage closer filtering

```
/* Shadow map vertex shader without lighting */

uniform mat4 g_matModelViewProj;
uniform mat4 g_matShadow;

attribute vec4 g_vVertex;

varying vec4 g_vOutShadowCoord;
varying vec2 g_vOutTexCoord;

void main()
{
    g_vOutShadowCoord = g_matShadow * g_vVertex;
    gl_Position       = g_matModelViewProj * g_vVertex;
}
```

```
/* Shadow map fragment shader without lighting */

uniform sampler2D g_sShadowMap;
varying vec4 g_vOutShadowCoord;

void main()
{
    float fLightDepth = ( texture2DProj( g_sShadowMap,
                                         g_vOutShadowCoord ) ).r;

    if( g_vOutShadowCoord.z / g_vOutShadowCoord.w <= fLightDepth )
    {
        gl_FragColor = vec4( 0.0 );
    }
    else
    {
        gl_FragColor = vec4( 1.0 );
    }
}
```

LISTING 7.6.4: PCF fragment shader

```
/* 2x2 PCF Shadow map fragment shader without lighting */

uniform sampler2D g_sShadowMap;
uniform float g_fEpsilon;

varying vec4 g_vOutShadowCoord;

float lookup( float x, float y )
{
    vec4 vOffset = vec4( x, y, 0.0, 0.0 ) * g_vOutShadowCoord.w *
                   g_fEpsilon;
    float fLightDepth = ( texture2DProj( g_sShadowMap,
                                         g_vOutShadowCoord +
                                         vOffset ) ).r;
    return g_vOutShadowCoord.z / g_vOutShadowCoord.w >
           fLightDepth ? 0.0 : 1.0;
}

void main()
{
    float fSum = 0.0;
    fSum += lookup( -0.5, -0.5 );
    fSum += lookup( -0.5,  0.5 );
    fSum += lookup(  0.5, -0.5 );
    fSum += lookup(  0.5,  0.5 );

    gl_FragColor = 0.25 * fSum;
}
```

Variance Shadow Mapping

Variance shadow mapping (VSM) is part of a new family of probability based shadow mapping algorithms that attempt to add support for soft shadows. All of these algorithms act on the same general principle: We can use inequalities associated with random variables to approximate the probability that part of an object is occluded.

Like shadow mapping, VSM makes use of a depth map, but instead of only storing depth values, VSM also stores depth squared at each pixel. The variance shadow map can then be filtered—such as with a two-tap Gaussian blur filter—to generate an off-screen texture of average depth values hereby referred to as *E(x)* and average squared depth values referred to as *E(x²)*. We can then use these two values to calculate the mean and variance of our distribution at each fragment:

$$\mu = E(x)$$
$$\sigma^2 = E(x^2) - E(x)^2$$

These results can then be used along with Chebychev's inequality, which states that given a random variable x from a distribution with mean μ and variance σ^2, for $t > \mu$ that:

$$P(x \geq t) \leq p_{\max}(t) \equiv \frac{\sigma^2}{\sigma^2 + (t - \mu)^2}$$

This result can then be used to approximate the average number of pixels that will pass our shadow map depth comparison test for some depth t, as shown in Listing 7.6.5. VSM is a cheap way to achieve soft shadows but it can occasionally suffer from light bleeding artifacts when the variance over the filter region is too high, thus making Chebychev's inequality a poor approximation. The other problem with VSM is that it requires a large amount of precision. In fact, I found that I needed to use a floating-point render-target, which will likely not be supported by the first generation of mobile hardware. Otherwise, while more expensive than shadow mapping, VSM is a cost-effective way to achieve soft shadows.

FIGURE 7.6.7 Comparison of standard shadow mapping (left) with a 2×2 percentage closer filter kernel shadow (middle) and variance shadow mapping (right). A 256×256 depth map was used with each method.

LISTING 7.6.5: Depth squared vertex shader

```
/* VSM depth and depth squared vertex shader */

uniform   mat4 g_matModelViewProj;

attribute vec4 g_vVertex;

varying float g_fDepth;
varying float g_fDepthSquared;

void main()
{
    gl_Position     = g_matModelViewProj * g_vVertex;
    g_fDepth        = 0.5 + 0.5 * ( gl_Position.z / gl_Position.w );
    g_fDepthSquared = g_fDepth * g_fDepth;
}

/* VSM depth and depth squared fragment shader */

varying float g_fDepth;
varying float g_fDepthSquared;

void main()
{
    gl_FragColor = vec4( g_fDepth, g_fDepthSquared, 0.0, 1.0 );
}
```

LISTING 7.6.6: Vertex shader without lighting

```
/* VSM vertex shader without lighting */

uniform mat4 g_matModelViewProj;
uniform mat4 g_matShadow;

attribute vec4 g_vVertex;

varying vec4 g_vOutShadowCoord;
varying vec2 g_vOutTexCoord;

void main()
{
    g_vOutShadowCoord = g_matShadow * g_vVertex;
    gl_Position       = g_matModelViewProj * g_vVertex;
}

/* VSM fragment shader without lighting */

uniform sampler2D g_sVarianceShadowMap;

varying vec4 g_vOutShadowCoord;
```

```
void main()
{
    float fEx    = ( texture2DProj( g_sVarianceShadowMap,
                                    g_vOutShadowCoord ) ).r;
    float fDepth = g_vOutShadowCoord.z / g_vOutShadowCoord.w;

    // 0.001 is some epsilon, could also be made a uniform parameter
    float fMD = fEx - fDepth + 0.001;

    // If the fragment is not in shadow
    if( 0.0 <= fMD )
    {
        gl_FragColor = vec4( 1.0 );
    }
    else
    {
        float fExSquared = ( texture2DProj( g_sVarianceShadowMap,
                                            g_vOutShadowCoord ) ).g;
        float fVariance  = fExSquared - fEx * fEx;
        float fPMax = fVariance / ( fVariance + fMD * fMD);

        fPMax = max( 0.0, fPMax );

        // Optional s-curve used to help reduce light bleeding
        fPMax = fPMax * fPMax * (3.0 - 2.0 * fPMax);

    gl_FragColor = vec4( vec3( fPMax ), 1.0 );
    }
}
```

Markov's Inequality

This section is based on the work of Marco Salvi, which is discussed in more detail in article 4.3, "Rendering Filtered Shadows with Exponential Shadow Maps." The idea is that variance shadow mapping, as discussed previously, makes use of Chebychev's inequality to approximate the probability that a fragment with depth t will be in shadow. We can replace this inequality, however, with an inequality of our choosing; in this case we're going to use Markov's inequality, which states

$$P(x \geq t) \leq p_{\max}(t) \equiv \frac{E(x)}{t}$$

One thing to note is that this inequality only makes use of $E(x)$, unlike VSM, which also requires $E(x^2)$; so unlike standard VSM we only need a texture with a single channel as opposed to a two-channel texture. The other noteworthy thing to point out is that Markov's inequality is actually a poorer approximation than Chebychev's inequality is in its present form. The interesting thing, though, is that because x is a non-negative random variable, we can modify it with a non-decreasing function F and still retain the same inequality, so

$$P\big(F(x) \geq F(t)\big) \leq p_{\max}\big(F(t)\big) \equiv \frac{E\big(F(x)\big)}{F(t)}$$

We can then pick a function F that changes rapidly to improve our probability bounds. In this case we'll use $F(x) = x^n$, which gives us:

$$P(x^n \geq t^n) \leq p_{\max}(t^n) \equiv \frac{E\left(x^n\right)}{t^n}$$

As a result the higher we make n, the better our approximation becomes. The problem, though, is that the higher n becomes the larger the amount of precision that we require (see Listings 7.6.7 and 7.6.8 for the key Markov's inequality shaders).

LISTING 7.6.7: Markov depth

```
/* Markov depth to the nth power vertex shader */

uniform    mat4 g_matModelViewProj;

attribute vec4 g_vVertex;
uniform float  g_fMoment;

varying float g_fDepthToTheMoment;

void main()
{
    gl_Position  = g_matModelViewProj * g_vVertex;
    float fDepth = 0.5 + 0.5 * ( gl_Position.z / gl_Position.w );
    g_fDepthToTheMoment = pow( fDepth, g_fMoment );
}

/* Markov depth to the nth power fragment shader */

varying float g_fDepthToTheMoment;

void main()
{
    gl_FragColor = vec4( g_fDepthToTheMoment );
}
```

LISTING 7.6.8: Markov vertex shader

```
/* Markov vertex shader without lighting */

uniform mat4 g_matModelViewProj;
uniform mat4 g_matShadow;

attribute vec4 g_vVertex;

varying vec4 g_vOutShadowCoord;
varying vec2 g_vOutTexCoord;

void main()
```

```
{
    g_vOutShadowCoord = g_matShadow * g_vVertex;
    gl_Position        = g_matModelViewProj * g_vVertex;
}

/* Markov fragment shader without lighting */

uniform sampler2D g_sShadowMap;
uniform float g_fMoment;

varying vec4 g_vOutShadowCoord;
varying vec4 g_vOutScreenCoord;

void main()
{
    float fExToTheMomentPower =
        ( texture2DProj( g_sShadowMap, g_vOutShadowCoord ) ).r;
    float fDepth = g_vOutShadowCoord.z / g_vOutShadowCoord.w;

    float fPMax = fExToTheMomentPower / pow( fDepth, g_fMoment );
    fPMax = min(1.0, fPMax);

// Optional s-curve used to help reduce light bleeding faster than
// increasing the moment.  Useful if you don't have enough bits
// of precision available, otherwise this line is needless
    fPMax = fPMax * fPMax * (3.0 - 2.0 * fPMax);

    gl_FragColor = vec4( vec3( fPMax ), 1.0 );
}
```

The primary benefit of the Markov method over standard VSM is that it can be used to eliminate light bleeding artifacts such as the one depicted in Figure 7.6.8(a). Unfortunately, like VSM, the Markov method requires at least half-float render buffer support, which may not be available on first generation mobile hardware.

One possible solution to the lack of floating-point render buffer support would be to use an unsigned byte representation of floating-point numbers. The most obvious representation would be to use fixed-point numbers, but fixed-point numbers lose precision rapidly as n increases. This is because fixed-point numbers waste a lot of space keeping track of leading zeros. As an example, given the number 0.000011010110 (binary fraction), an 8-bit fixed-point representation would only be able to represent the first eight fractional bits, which in this case would be 0.00001101, which is a loss of precision. An alternative approach that handles leading zeros is to take the floating-point number approach of storing an exponential term. So in this case we would keep track of $0.11010110 * 2^{-4}$, which maintains additional precision (see Listings 7.6.9 and 7.6.10 for the key shaders that make up this revised algorithm). The problem with this algorithm is that it is quite expensive because the Gaussian blur shader needs to make a lot of conversions to and from this custom unsigned byte format. The approach is still interesting, though, for anyone interested in storing floating-point numbers in a texture without floating-point render buffer support.

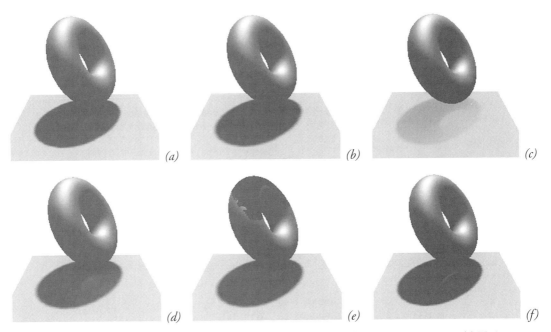

FIGURE 7.6.8 A comparison between VSM and Markov shadows with various parameters. (a) Variance shadow mapping with light bleeding; (b) Markov shadows: $n=1$ with half-float buffer; (c) Markov shadows: $n=16$ with half-float buffer; (d) Markov shadows: $n=32$ with half-float buffer; (e) Markov shadows: $n=16$ with half-float buffer and an s-curve; (f) Markov shadows: $n=32$ with float buffer.

LISTING 7.6.9: Markov depth

```
/* Markov depth to the nth power vertex shader with an unsigned byte
render buffer */

uniform   mat4 g_matModelViewProj;

attribute vec4 g_vVertex;
uniform float  g_fMoment;

varying float g_fDepthToTheMoment;

void main()
{
    gl_Position  = g_matModelViewProj * g_vVertex;
    float fDepth = 0.5 + 0.5 * ( gl_Position.z / gl_Position.w );
    g_fDepthToTheMoment = pow( fDepth, g_fMoment );
}

/* Markov depth to the nth power fragment shader with an unsigned byte
render buffer */

varying float g_fDepthToTheMoment;
```

```
void main()
{
    // Calculate our exponent, we'll store it as a positive number
    // between 0 and 1
    float fExp = abs( floor( log2( g_fDepthToTheMoment ) + 1.0 ) );

    // Store the leading 8 bits of precision as well as our exponent
    // Note the division by 256.0 is because we need numbers between
    // 0 and 1, and 2^8 = 256 which is the number of byte values
    // we can represent.
    gl_FragColor = vec4( g_fDepthToTheMoment * pow( 2.0, fExp ),
                         fExp/256.0, 0.0, 0.0 );
}
```

LISTING 7.6.10: Markov vertex shader

```
/* Markov vertex shader without lighting and with an unsigned byte
render buffer */

uniform mat4 g_matModelViewProj;
uniform mat4 g_matShadow;

attribute vec4 g_vVertex;

varying vec4 g_vOutShadowCoord;
varying vec2 g_vOutTexCoord;

void main()
{
    g_vOutShadowCoord = g_matShadow * g_vVertex;
    gl_Position       = g_matModelViewProj * g_vVertex;
}

/* Markov fragment shader without lighting and with an unsigned byte
render buffer */

uniform sampler2D g_sShadowMap;
uniform float g_fMoment;

varying vec4 g_vOutShadowCoord;
varying vec4 g_vOutScreenCoord;

void main()
{
    vec2 v = ( texture2DProj( g_sShadowMap, g_vOutShadowCoord ) ).rg;

    // Extract our exponent from the texture
    float fExp = -floor( 256.0 * v.g );
```

```
// Calculate our float from the exponent and precision bits
    float fExToTheMomentPower = ( v.r ) * pow( 2.0, fExp );

    float fDepth = g_vOutShadowCoord.z / g_vOutShadowCoord.w;

    float fPMax = fExToTheMomentPower / pow( fDepth, g_fMoment );
    fPMax = min(1.0, fPMax);
    fPMax = fPMax * fPMax * (3.0 - 2.0 * fPMax);

    gl_FragColor = vec4( vec3( fPMax ), 1.0 );
}
```

Conclusion

This article explored a variety of shadowing algorithms as compared in Table 7.6.1 for use on upcoming OpenGL ES 2.0 mobile graphics hardware. It discussed the pros and cons of each algorithm in terms of both quality and performance, and provided insight into how to go about implementing each algorithm with OpenGL ES 2.0.

Table 7.6.1 Comparison of shadow algorithms

	Translate	Rotate and Deform	Non-Planar Surfaces	Self Shadow	Soft Shadows	Efficiency
Lightmaps	No	No	Yes	Yes	Yes	1
Decals	Yes	No	No	No	Yes	2
Projective	Yes	Yes	No	No	No	3
Shadow volume	Yes	Yes	Yes	Yes	No	4
Shadow maps (SM)	Yes	Yes	Yes	Yes	No	5
SM + PCF	Yes	Yes	Yes	Yes	Partial	6
VSM	Yes	Yes	Yes	Yes	Yes/Bleeding	7
Markov	Yes	Yes	Yes	Yes	Yes	7

References

[zAmbrô06] Ambrôz, David. "Planar shadows by J. Blinn," available online at http://www.shadowstechniques.com/blinn.html, August 1, 2006.

[Kwoon02] Kwoon, Hun Yen. "The Theory of Stencil Shadow Volumes," available online at http://www.gamedev.net/reference/articles/article1873.asp, December 3, 2002.

[Lengyel02] Lengyel, Eric. "The Mechanics of Robust Stencil Shadows," available online at http://www.gamasutra.com/features/20021011/lengyel_01.htm, October 11, 2002.

[Rost04] Rost, Randi J. *OpenGL Shading Language*, Addison-Wesley Professional, 2004.

[Donnelly06] Donnelly, William and Lauritzen, Andrew. "Variance Shadow Maps," *Proceedings of the 2006 Symposium on Interactive 3D Graphics and Games*, (SI3D 2006): pp. 161–165.

3D ENGINE DESIGN

Introduction

Wessam Bahnassi

The *ShaderX* book series has been always committed to offering the most up-to-date advances in real-time computer graphics. It is very interesting to prototype new techniques in sand-box programs. However, one cannot go far implementing these novel techniques in real-world applications without having a proper framework and infrastructure that can handle the new requirements that come along with these techniques themselves.

The "3D Engine Design" section does not talk about drawing triangles and casting shadows; rather it shows how to be ready to do so. Framework design, data setup, and pipeline are the name of the game here…. Welcome the architect!

This time, we have a varied selection of subjects on our plate. On the topic of 3D engine design, we start with Maxime Beaudoin's article "A Flexible Material System in Design," which offers an elegant material solution that solves a number of issues, including the common issue of managing render states and overriding them. Readers will learn about the concepts of material blending, shader setup, and constants management, all under a unified and consistent framework.

On the topic of tool development, the article "3D Engine Tools with C++/CLI" brings a new programming language to the attention of tool developers. The article discusses the possible potential that can be gained by using C++/CLI and its .NET interoperability capabilities, showing the advantages and disadvantages of this new language, as well as a number of recommendations with regard to expected 3D engine tool development problems.

Finally, on the topic of data conversion and optimization, the article "Efficient HDR Texture Compression" by Tze-Yui Ho and Chi-Sing Leung takes the concept of palletized textures and pushes it forward to serve for HDR texture compression, achieving better quality than common RGBE encoding with almost the same runtime performance and with a smaller data size. The technique involves an interesting twist with the way the palette is setup, which can help decrease data size even further.

I hope that these articles enlighten you in solving some of your design and tool problems, and help you create new technologies for the new generation of graphics hardware and applications.

Welcome!

8.1

A Flexible Material System in Design

Maxime Beaudoin

Ubisoft

Introduction

Almost all modern 3D engines these days have a material system that sets up how primitives are shaded. Typically, a *material* is defined as a set of render state values and some shaders. A render state cache is often implemented to eliminate redundant state changes. While this design is simple and effective, it suffers from some limitations:

- It can be difficult to apply per-object material modifications without duplicating the original material, leading to additional complexity.
- A render state cache is not always the best option for CPU-bound applications. On some platforms it would be better to put all render state changes in a display list to make material changes lighter on the CPU side.
- Depending on the implementation's complexity, it can be difficult to extend the original system to add new material properties.

This article proposes a different approach that handles the problems listed above. The design is data-driven and handles per-object material modifications efficiently.

Material Implementation

For the sake of simplicity, our material definition does not include the technique concept (for LODs, hardware support fallbacks, or multi-platform material specifications). Moreover, we restrict our materials to be single-pass, but take note that the demo included on the accompanying DVD-ROM implements multi-pass materials.

That said, a material is simply defined as a set of *properties*. A property is an atomic element of a material that manipulates one or more *render states*. For the purpose of this article, we define a render state as any variable that changes the way primitives are shaded. Here are some examples of possible properties:

- `MP_Ambient:` Changes the ambient color coefficient
- `MP_Texture:` Binds a texture to a given unit
- `MP_TexPanner:` Applies a translation to the input UV coordinates
- `MP_AlphaBlend:` Enables alpha blending
- `MP_CullMode:` Changes back-face culling mode

Each property must implement two methods: PreRender and PostRender. Pre-Render sets the render states corresponding to the property's desired result and PostRender restores them. When rendering some geometry with a material, PreRender is first called on every property of the material, then the geometry is rendered, and finally PostRender is called on all properties.

Render states manipulated by properties can have predefined default values. A render state that has a defined default value implies that if the property changes its value in PreRender, then it *must* restore it in PostRender. If the state does not have a default value, then the property can change it without bothering to restore it later in PostRender. This feature can be used to minimize render state changes. Render states that change often should not have a default value. Inversely, a state that changes rarely should rely on a predefined default value. Here are some examples:

- Back-face culling is generally enabled because it can save a lot of pixel fill-rate. However, every once in a while it might be required to disable or invert it. Back-face culling is thus a very good candidate for having a default value. It should be set to cull back-facing polygons by default, and the property MP_CullMode can be used to disable or invert it when needed.
- Textures are a good example of a render state that changes often. Unless rendering is sorted by textures, chances are good that two materials applied consecutively would use a completely different set of textures. In that case, the active texture on any unit is assumed to be undefined. This allows us to create a very simple MP_Texture property that only binds the texture in PreRender and does nothing in PostRender.
- Alpha blending is a more complicated case. For optimal results, its default value should be defined as disabled when rendering opaque geometry, and enabled when drawing translucent objects. As for the blending parameters, one could choose to set the traditional blending mode SRC_ALPHA/ONE_MINUS_SRC_ALPHA as the default.

Whether or not you define a default value for a certain render state is application-dependent, and it boils down to a matter of optimization. In some cases, an undefined default value for alpha blending parameters could be more optimal than having it defined, as stated in the preceding example.

Modifying Materials

Every now and then in games and real-time simulations, a special material effect needs to be applied on a given object, such as a collectable item that smoothly fades away when taken by the player. This could be accomplished by modifying the blending parameters on the materials used by this object. Since materials are generally shared between multiple objects, one might end up having to duplicate the material used by this object, tweaking it as desired and finally restoring the original material. Another—much worse—approach is to frankly hack the engine's code to obtain the desired effect. These methods are bad because they try to compensate for a missing material modification feature in the engine. On the other hand, the material design proposed here allows material modification in a simple manner.

The following piece of pseudo code renders some geometry with a given material:

```
for each property p in material
  p.PreRender()
geometry.Render()
for each property p in material
  p.PostRender()
```

To modify one or more properties of a material, a new material is first created with the properties that need to be overridden. The new material is then applied just after the original one. This will effectively override the corresponding render states. For example, to override the ambient color, the material modifier should contain a single property MP_Ambient with the desired color. The pseudo code thus becomes

```
for each property p in material
  p.PreRender()
for each property p' in modifier
  p'.PreRender()
geometry.Render()
for each property p' in modifier
  p'.PostRender()
for each property p in material
  p.PostRender()
```

We refer to this technique as *material blending*. Later in this article, two other material modification techniques are presented that make use of multiple render passes. The combination of these three techniques can be very powerful and it allows the creation of a large range of effects easily.

Optimizations

With this material system, it is possible to optimize the workload either on the CPU or the GPU. Depending on the platform and the application's actual bottleneck, one can choose the optimization that best suits his needs.

GPU optimization can be achieved by eliminating ineffective and redundant state changes. This can be done easily by using a render state cache. Instead of directly manipulating the render states, the properties manipulate a proxy render state cache. Before rendering geometry, the cache is flushed. This is a very classical optimization, but it is not necessarily CPU-friendly.

On platforms that support OpenGL-like display lists, it is possible to optimize these materials for the CPU with minimal effort. At build time, for each material, you can dump in a display list the calls to PreRender and PostRender for every property. Later on during in-game rendering, call this display list instead of iterating over properties. Of course, special care must be taken for properties that change over time or that manipulate render states that cannot be stored in a display list.

Note that this optimization is not good if calling a display list is heavy for the CPU. On some platforms, calling a display list is as fast as writing a 32-bit command into memory. But on other platforms (like some OpenGL implementations) there is a performance overhead to call a display list, which can be even greater than iterating over the properties.

Shader Integration

Integrating shaders in this framework is very easy. The following two properties are needed for managing shaders:

- `MP_Shader`: Binds a given shader program. Depending on the application, this property can have an undefined default value (if the application is shader-based) or a defined default value for applications that do not rely on shaders.
- `MP_Uniform`: Sets the value for a shader's uniform variable. For constant values, the implementation is trivial. For dynamic values based on engine data, a system like the one defined in [Franklin07] could be used. Be sure to exclude dynamic uniform variables from display lists.

Material blending is possible for both properties, i.e. a uniform variable's value can be overridden, or even the complete shader program can be replaced. One special case can be problematic though: shader program modification. For example, applying a wave-like motion to vertices would require a modification to the vertex program of the shader. If the original material has no vertex shader, this is quite simple: put an `MP_Shader` property in the material modifier. But if the original material already contains a vertex shader, then this is more complicated. The original vertex program needs to be modified to include the code needed by the modifier.

A good solution to this problem would be to use a high-level shader creator that composes a complete shader program by merging together many small building blocks. (See [Pharr04] for a Cg implementation of such a system or [Bahnassi07] for an HLSL version.) Such a system has many other advantages. In particular, it allows artists to create their own shaders by connecting together pre-defined shading elements. It is very extensible and suits perfectly well to our material design.

The Renderer

The renderer must provide a simple interface to draw primitives with this material design. It is implemented using a stack of materials. The user pushes and pops materials on the stack and asks the renderer to draw primitives. When requested to draw something, the renderer combines (if needed) the materials present on the stack using the algorithm specified by the user.

Here is an overview of a sample renderer's interface:

```
enum MergeMode
{
  MM_Blend,
  MM_AddPass,
  MM_Replace
};

void PushMaterial( const Material & mat, MergeMode mode );
void PopMaterial();
void Draw( const Geometry & geometry );
```

The MergeMode enumeration describes the available material merging techniques. MM_Blend corresponds to the method explained previously, which overwrites the properties of the next material on the stack. MM_AddPass treats the material as a new render pass that must be applied after all materials on top of it. This can be used, for example, to render projectors. Finally, MM_Replace completely ignores all the following materials on the stack. An example usage would be to render the shadow of a mesh in a texture; the actual materials used by the mesh will be replaced by the shadow's material.

Those merging modes are pretty basic in the sense that every application that uses this material system should include them. Of course, other merging strategies can be implemented depending on the application's needs and specific features.

PushMaterial stores the material's reference and its attached merging mode on the top of the stack. It does not immediately call PreRender on the material; this step is deferred until Draw is called. PopMaterial simply pops the stack.

The method Draw is where all the magic is done. If the stack is empty, it does nothing; if the stack contains only one material, there is no merging to do and the rendering code is straightforward (PreRender, Render, PostRender). When the stack contains two or more materials, the following algorithm will correctly merge them using their associated mode.

Starting from the bottom of the stack, try to find a material with the algorithm MM_Replace. If such a material is found, all following materials on the stack should be ignored. Otherwise, all materials are considered

```
int firstMaterial = size( stack ) – 1;
for ( int i = 0; i < firstMaterial; ++i )
{
  if ( stack[i].mode == MM_Replace )
  {
    firstMaterial = i;
    break;
  }
}
```

For each considered material on the stack, find the pass at which the material should be applied. This can be done by iterating from the first valid material down to the bottom of the stack and incrementing a pass counter only for MM_Replace and MM_AddPass materials. This way, a material with MM_Blend mode will be effectively applied on the same pass as the material on top of it:

```
int currentPass = 0;
for ( int i = firstMaterial; i >= 0; --i )
{
  if ( stack[i].mode == MM_Add || stack[i].mode == MM_Replace )
    stack[i].pass = currentPass++;
  else
    stack[i].pass = currentPass - 1;
}
```

Iterate on all passes. For every material for which the pass number matches, call PreRender before rendering the geometry, and PostRender after it:

```
for ( int i = 0; i < currentPass; ++i )
{
  for ( int j = firstMaterial; j >= 0; --j )
  {
    if ( stack[j].pass == i )
      stack[j].material.PreRender();
  }

  geometry.Render();

  for ( int j = 0; j <= firstMaterial; ++j )
  {
    if ( stack[j].pass == i )
      stack[j].material.PostRender();
  }
}
```

Notice that the reverse order of the second loop is actually not necessary. In fact, the only important thing is to call PostRender on all properties, no matter what the order. This is because render states are not managed in the materials' stack. In PostRender, properties set render states to their defined default values instead of the value they had before calling PreRender.

While this algorithm only works for single-pass materials, it could support multi-pass materials as well with slight modifications. The demo on the accompanying DVD-ROM implements this algorithm with multi-pass materials.

Application Level

Finally, the material system must be plugged into the application's code to make per-object material modification effects possible. The objective is to be able to apply any number of material modifiers to any type of object. Thus, the base object class should contain a list of material modifiers along with their respective merging mode. Here is the rendering:

1. For each modifier attached to this game object, push the material on the renderer's stack using its associated merging mode.
2. Draw all geometry attached to this game object.
3. Pop the renderer's stack n times, where n is the number of modifiers attached to this game object.

Material Creation Framework

After this system is fully implemented in an engine, the next step is to build a good material creation framework around it. The main requirements for this framework are to be flexible, data-driven, and to allow fast material creation.

A good implementation reference is Microsoft's Effects framework. The separation of the effect concept (the programmer's side) from the material concept (the artist's side) is required in a real production environment. Moreover, scripts are very appropriate as a material-specification tool, because they are naturally data-driven and easy to create.

The demo uses a very simple script system to define materials. The syntax is close to OGRE 3D's material scripts. Here is an example:

```
pass
{
  ambient  = ( 0.1, 0.1, 0.1, 1.0 )
  diffuse  = ( 1.0, 0.5, 0.5, 1.0 )
  specular = ( 1.0, 0.5, 0.5, 1.0 )
  shininess = 50.0

  texture
  {
    file         = "rock_diffuse.bmp"
    uniform_name = "diffuseMap"
  }

  texture
  {
    file         = "rock_normal.bmp"
    uniform_name = "normalMap"
  }

  shader_language = "glsl 1.10"

  vertex_shader = <string>
    // vertex shader code here
  </string>

  fragment_shader = <string>
    // fragment shader code here
  </string>
}
```

In this script, a single-pass material is defined. The first lines set some generic lighting parameters. Diffuse and normal map textures are then specified. The parameter uniform_name is used to link the textures with the name of the samplers in the shader code. Finally, the shading language and the actual shader code are given.

For the sake of simplicity, this script system does not support the effect concept. Also, static material modifications should be considered in order to give more flexibility to artists. They should be able to create a material using a palette of effects and combining them just like they would be combined dynamically by the renderer.

Conclusion

In this article, we proposed a material system that elegantly supports per-object modifications along with CPU or GPU optimization support. We also proposed a material creation framework similar to Microsoft's Effects framework, allowing data-driven material specification. Although this design suits shader-based renderers perfectly well, it could also be used on underpowered platforms that do not support shaders, such as Sony PSP or Nintendo Wii.

The demo included on the accompanying DVD-ROM fully implements all the concepts discussed in this article, and goes a little further by allowing multi-pass materials. A lot of material properties and material modification examples are provided for demonstration.

References

[Bahnassi07] Bahnassi, Wessam. "Designing Plug-in Shaders with HLSL," *ShaderX5: Advanced Rendering Techniques,* Wolfgang Engel, Ed., Charles River Media, 2007: pp. 479–486.

[Franklin07] Franklin, Dustin. "Transparent Shader Data Binding," *ShaderX5: Advanced Rendering Techniques,* Wolfgang Engel, Ed., Charles River Media, 2007: pp. 471–478.

[Pharr04] Pharr, Matt. "An Introduction to Shader Interfaces," *GPU Gems: Programming Techniques, Tips, and Tricks for Real-Time Graphics*, Randima Fernando, Ed., Addison Wesley, 2004: pp. 537–550.

Further Reading

[ORorke04] O'Rorke, John. "Integrating Shaders into Applications," *GPU Gems: Programming Techniques, Tips, and Tricks for Real-Time Graphics*, Randima Fernando, Ed., Addison Wesley, 2004: pp. 601–615.

8.2

3D Engine Tools with C++/CLI

Wessam Bahnassi

Introduction

This article describes the latest .NET 2.0 language C++/CLI[1] in the context of 3D engine tools programming, showing its advantages, disadvantages, and possible uses. It wraps up with a section on considerations to be taken when this language is used to develop such tools.

Another Introduction

Long gone are the days when game assets were all hard coded. Today, most game engines are data-driven in some way, and for that, they offer developer-side tools to allow for generating, processing, and preparing those assets for in-game runtime usage. 3D engines now have exporters, level editors, preview tools, and so on, all chained together to form a production pipeline for our games.

It is not a hidden fact that Microsoft's .NET platform had a big impact on how we develop these tools. After all, who wants to waste time coding user interfaces with pure C++ and the Win32 API, when there is such a powerful solution as what .NET WinForms offer?

Unfortunately, with this transition, an important asset was lost: our well-written C++ codebase. Step into the .NET realm and leave all existing C++ libraries behind: no advanced math library, no 3D engine. The requirement for interoperability became a maximum priority, and anyone who tried to interoperate C++ with C# back in the .NET 1.0 days knows how difficult it was.

.NET 1.1 was released after that, introducing the Managed C++ Extensions as a solution for this interoperability issue. It was a first step to the solution, offering a much easier transition between pure C++ and .NET data structures, but its syntax was mostly cryptic, clunky, or vague even for the seasoned C++ programmer. Enter .NET 2.0 and C++/CLI.

What Is C++/CLI?

C++/CLI is a new .NET programming language that has the natural capability of interoperating with existing pure C++ code. Or it is a set of extensions to the C++ language that allows it to work with managed code and the .NET Framework[2]. Either way, all the code ends up in a single executable without any external dependencies on DLLs or COM objects (except the .NET Framework itself, of course).

This article will not cover how to use C++/CLI. For that, please refer to the many resources that exist on the subject, such as [MSDN01] and [MSDN02].

Possible Applications

In the interest of 3D engine development, there are already several obvious applications that benefit from such interoperability capabilities:

- **3D object visualization tools:** Many 3D engines offer tools to visualize exported meshes and animations (probably with some tweaking capabilities). Using .NET in this case allows for easier UI construction, and ultimately, a better user experience.
- **Level editors:** These often have an interactive 3D view of the level, as well as an extensive UI that allows manipulating object properties in the world. They can reuse rendering code from the actual game for closer results. Level editors can also benefit from .NET's XML support to exchange intermediate level and object descriptions.
- **Conversion tools and plug-ins:** A data-crunching tool can still use .NET without losing the capability to emit platform-specific C-structs to finalized engine-ready files.

In addition to usage in full applications, these capabilities can also be used in more specific cases. As an example, a .NET application can read a custom image format that is implemented in pure C++ code from third-party developers (such as DDS). Another example would be a pure C++ tool that needs to compress/decompress GZip files at some point. In that case, it can use .NET's file-compression facilities to do the task.

The interoperability is seamless for many tasks. Consider a shader editor tool that has a .NET event handler for a color slider control. One can simply read the value of the WinForms slider control, do some calculations using a high-performance C++ math library, display the results to the user in a WinForm label control, and then set these results into the 3D engine's material properties.

How Is It Different from C++?

C++/CLI introduces some new keywords and operators to C++. The keywords help in differentiating between managed objects and unmanaged ones. For example, `gcnew` is used instead of `new`, and the handle symbol `^` is used instead of the `*` symbol for "pointer" types (e.g., `Control^ pControl` instead of `Control* pControl`). This is due to the fact that C++/CLI does not share the same heap as pure C++. Pure C++ pointers cannot point to managed objects or vice-versa. Thus, the pointer syntax is differentiated to clarify this point. Because it is a managed language, C++/CLI does not require the programmer to `delete` managed objects. Calling `delete` has the same effect as calling `Dispose()` on the object.

Managed classes and structs have a slightly different method of declaration and are not allowed to inherit native C++ classes or get inherited from them. Events, delegates, and properties are exposed in C++/CLI in a standard way.

All of this shows that even with the seamless interoperability, one has to think about how to approach the program's design and decide what is managed and what is not. C++/CLI helps this approach by differentiating the syntax to avoid confusion while still not alienating programmers with obscure code.

Refer to [MSDN01] for new syntax that has been introduced with C++/CLI.

Advantages and Drawbacks

C++/CLI has an obvious set of advantages that helps increase productivity, but it also comes with some drawbacks. We will start with the advantages:

- No more `DLLImport`. Win32 calls can be made directly without any additional coding complexities. Use of existing SDKs is now totally possible to plug-ins written in .NET.
- C++/CLI inherits C++'s compiler optimization strategies (e.g., whole-program optimization), allowing it to achieve better code generation than the rest of the .NET languages, ultimately making it the fastest .NET language [MSDN03].
- Programmers can now use .NET without having to move away from their language (although it is not hard to find programmers who know both C++ and C#).
- C++/CLI opens access to all existing .NET components and C++ libraries at the same time, allowing programmers to leverage a wider selection of existing modules to do their jobs.
- It is possible to build components that can be consumed by other .NET languages even if parts of the component are pure C++.

As mentioned, the language still has a number of disadvantages:

- The compiler is still relatively new. It has some minor bugs that can be puzzling when facing them for the first time. Fortunately, none of these bugs is a showstopper. They all have simple workarounds that can sometimes be as easy as rebuilding the whole project, and they will be addressed in upcoming versions anyway.
- If the project was set up incorrectly, the program will crash in a very weird way as soon as it launches. This can be a little bit daunting to someone who is trying to use the language for the first time. This is a one-time task; once it is done right, you will not have to worry about it later.

- Some restrictions are enforced when calling .NET code at certain critical times. For example, calling .NET code in a DLL's `DLLMain` function is not allowed. Read [MSDN04] for more information on other kinds of restrictions.
- Visual Studio's WinForms editor writes the form's properties and controls in a C++ header file. If the file was hand-modified carelessly, the editor could break. In this case, it is better to implement the form's logic in its CPP file rather than inlining the logic in the header.
- Most times the switch between managed and unmanaged contexts is totally transparent. People tend to think of it as an advantage until they start wondering why a certain high-frequency function is performing poorly. This context switch has a performance cost that can become noticeable under certain circumstances. The cost of context switching is described later in this article.

Design Approach

When designing a 3D engine tool to be built with C++/CLI, you still use the same design paradigms you followed when developing it with pure C++ (it *is* still C++, after all). However, a new concept has to be taken into account this time: managed code versus unmanaged code. It is better to decide beforehand which components of the program will be managed and which will be pure C++. Keeping the two domains clearly identifiable in the program's structure makes the code easier to maintain and allows it to perform faster (as will be described later). Working under this paradigm also increases code modularity (the same concept behind keeping the program's logic separate from its user-interface code). The language itself also has some restrictions that can be best dealt with this way, in particular, mixing managed and unmanaged data types in a single structure.

Because the program has a managed part, this section also has to be designed with managed restrictions in mind. For example, multiple-inheritance from classes is not allowed, but inheritance from multiple interfaces is allowed (a CLR restriction that only applies to managed classes). These details might influence how the solution looks in the end.

General Programming Considerations

With all this flexibility, one has to be careful to know what he is doing with the language. The following sections outline a collection of considerations and tricks that can be useful to know when coding with C++/CLI.

Minimize Context Switches

The switch between native and managed contexts costs around 50 to 300 cycles. This can be a problem if it happens in a very frequent fashion. It is best to avoid tight loops that call functions from the other context. For example, consider a list of world positions that we need to use to render some instances. The list is stored in a managed container, and our rendering function is a pure native one. The following code will involve a lot of context switches and would have suboptimal performance:

```
List<Vector3> ^instancePositions = world->GetTreeInstances();
for each (Vector3 pos in instancePositions)
  pRenderer->DrawInstance(pGeometry,pos.x,pos.y,pos.z);
```

An alternative solution would be to convert the data to a native array and iterate on that instead. The conversion happens only when changes occur in the managed array, so the conversion does not have to be done each frame. On the other hand, if the number of iterations in the loop is not going to be high enough, then the performance loss might not be even noticeable. The online article [TOUB04] describes this topic in detail.

Force Time-Critical Functions to Be Native

The compiler will almost always compile C++ functions to MSIL first. If it fails, it compiles it as native. Some exceptions exist, though. Inline functions, naked functions, and functions containing inline assembly blocks will always be native. However, suppose we have a function that does some time-critical calculations (e.g., skinning). If that function does not meet the breaking rules mentioned above, it will be compiled as managed and performance might be affected[3]. In that case, usage of the #pragma unmanaged keyword can guarantee native execution of that function.

Double Thunking

When a mixed code module is compiled, the compiler generates two entry points for each function by default: a managed one and a native one. Each does the necessary setup to pass the data from the caller's context to the callee's actual context[4]. Double thunking occurs when the user calls a function through a native entry point from a managed context and that function ends up executing managed code. A common scenario is a native virtual function. [MSDN05] exposes this concern in more detail.

Exchanging Data

As has been shown earlier, managed memory is totally separate from the native heap. C++/CLI does the required data exchange work for simple data types. However, more complex data types (such as arrays and strings) cannot be accessed directly in code. For example, this is fine:

```
printf("This form has %d child controls\n",this->Controls->Count);
int iAdaptersCount = pD3D->GetAdapterCount(); // Native function call
this->adaptersTextBox->Text = iAdaptersCount.ToString();
```

However, this will not work:

```
fwrite(textBox->Text,sizeof(char),textbox->Text->Length,pFile);
```

The Text property is of the managed type String, and it cannot be marshaled implicitly by the compiler like the simpler data types. The System::Runtime:: InteropServices::Marshal class offers facilities for handling these types and other custom types.

In general, it is better to try to make the interface between the managed and unmanaged code use simple data types as much as possible because they are the fastest and easiest to handle. For more information on data exchange in C++/CLI, read [KUEHN07].

Pointers and Keeping References

In many occasions, one would need to store references to objects living in the other execution context. For example, a level editor has a managed object WorldEntity holding properties for some geometrical entity in the world. The graphical representation of this entity is maintained by a native object CMesh. Now WorldEntity needs to hold a reference to CMesh to update it with any property changes happening on the WorldEntity. This can be as simple as

```
ref class WorldEntity  // A managed class
{
public:
  WorldEntity(CMesh *pGraphicalRep);
  ~WorldEntity();
  property Vector3 Position;
  property Color Tint;
private:
  CMesh *m_pGraphicalRep; // Unmanaged pointer (this is allowed)
};
```

And now WorldEntity can directly make calls on the methods of CMesh, but what about the reverse? Let us assume that CMesh needs to hold a reference to WorldEntity. For example, the native 3D engine does ray casting to find what 3D object lies under the cursor, and we need to display the properties of that object to the user so he can see them. The following code is not acceptable by the compiler:

```
class CMesh : public CPlacable3D
{
public:
  CMesh(WorldEntity ^properties);
  ~CMesh();
private:
  IDirect3DVertexBuffer9 *m_pVB;
  IDirect3DIndexBuffer9 *m_pIB;
  WorldEntity ^m_Properties; // Handle to a managed object
                             // (error: not allowed)
};
```

In this case, the `Marshal` class again is able to save us by generating a native `VARI-ANT` structure that represents a reference to that managed object, which can be kept inside a native class. Note that `sizeof(VARIANT)` is 16 bytes: four times the size of a 32-bit pointer. So it is better to minimize the number of references kept in native classes, or even better, avoid using them if a possible workaround can be designed (such as using a managed dictionary of native-managed references, like `Dictionary<IntPtr,WorldEntity>`).

Conclusion

This article discussed the language C++/CLI in light of 3D engine tools development. First, the language's key feature was identified, which is the natural ability to interoperate between managed and unmanaged code. A list of possible uses and applications was mentioned, showing the wide range of capabilities that can be leveraged with this language. Like any other language, C++/CLI has its own advantages and drawbacks. Most advantages are obvious, but some of the drawbacks can be only discovered after working with the language for a while. The article brings those advantages and drawbacks to the attention of the reader, followed by a general discussion on how they affect a design approach for a solution. Finally, we mention a list of general design considerations and tricks to help the reader overcome certain expected problems quickly. The article recommends considering the mixed code capability carefully during the tool's design, clearly identifying which parts will be mainly managed and which should remain pure C++.

Endnotes

[1] CLI stands for the *Common Language Infrastructure*. C++/CLI means a binding between the standard C++ programming language and the Common Language Infrastructure (which all .NET languages are based on).

[2] These two definitions are indeed different. You can either run your C++/CLI as a native executable that calls into .NET, or you can start your C++/CLI program as a .NET assembly that calls into pure C++ code. The first case is preferred as it is most compatible with the CRT heap setup and global and static variables.

[3] This is not to say that managed C++ is slow. It is probably better to do some performance measurements to get an idea of the speed difference.

[4] The programmer has full control to stop the compiler from generating a managed entry to a native function (and vice-versa).

Acknowledgments

Thanks to Ryan Cameron from Electronic Arts and Abdo Haji-Ali from In|Framez for taking the time to review this article.

References

[KUEHN07] Kuehn, Gary J. "C++ Interop is for the Performance Minded Developer," available online at http://www.codeproject.com/managedcpp/ManagedCPPInterop.asp.

[MSDN01] "New Language Features in Visual C++," available online at http://msdn2.microsoft.com/en-us/library/xey702bw(VS.80).aspx.

[MSDN02] "Mixed (Native and Managed) Assemblies," available online at http://msdn2.microsoft.com/en-us/library/x0w2664k(VS.80).aspx.

[MSDN03] "C++: The Most Powerful Language for .NET Framework Programming," available online at http://msdn2.microsoft.com/en-us/library/ms379617(VS.80).aspx.

[MSDN04] "How To: Migrate to /clr," available online at http://msdn2.microsoft.com/en-us/library/ms173265(VS.80).aspx.

[MSDN05] "Double Thunking (C++)," available online at http://msdn2.microsoft.com/en-us/library/ms235292(VS.80).aspx.

[TOUB04] Toub, Stephen. "Write Faster Code with the Modern Language Features of Visual C++ 2005," available online at http://msdn.microsoft.com/msdnmag/issues/04/05/VisualC2005.

Efficient HDR Texture Compression

Tze-Yui Ho (ma_hty@hotmail.com)
City University of Hong Kong

Chi-Sing Leung (eeleungc@cityu.edu.hk)
City University of Hong Kong

Introduction

The use of *high dynamic range* (HDR) textures [1] for real-time rendering has become very popular in the computer-graphics community because these textures can preserve the entire range of luminance. However, an HDR texture stored in its raw format (floating-point numbers) consumes a lot of memory and texture bandwidth, which hinders rendering performance. To overcome these issues, texture compression is usually considered. Since the dynamic range can be very wide in HDR textures, existing *low dynamic range* (LDR) texture-compression schemes might no longer be suitable.

Most existing HDR texture-compression schemes exploit the fact that the human eye is more sensitive to variations in luminance than in chromaticity. One of the simplest ways to compress the HDR textures is to store them in RGBE format, where an HDR color value is decomposed into normalized RGB values and a logarithmic luminance value. The normalized RGB values can then be compressed with existing LDR texture compression schemes, such as S3TC [2]. The logarithmic luminance values are quantized separately and are represented by 8-bit integers.

Recently, some advanced HDR texture compression schemes [3] [4] have been proposed and they were able to achieve higher compression ratios. These schemes still basically follow the idea of the RGBE approach. But unfortunately, these techniques require complex decoder implementations, leading to the high need of dedicated GPU circuitry.

This article proposes a color quantization scheme that compresses HDR textures with eight bits per pixel using the existing concept of palletized textures. Our scheme has a compression ratio of 12:1 for 96-bit RGB HDR textures. This scheme can represent the scattered nature of HDR textures effectively, and the decompressed HDR color can be obtained with two lookups only: one for the indices and the other for the palette entry. As a result, the decompression algorithm can be implemented on current GPUs without additional circuitry. On hardware that supports palletized textures with floating-point palette entry values, decompression can occur at no additional expense in shader instructions. In addition, by considering the sub-entries of a low-resolution palette, HDR textures can be compressed using higher precision indices without training a higher resolution palette.

The detailed algorithm of the color quantization for this HDR texture compression scheme is discussed first. Then, the decoding implementation along with its Cg shader is presented.

Basic Concept

First, a palette of 256 entries is trained using the LBG algorithm [5] to match the color distribution of an HDR texture. By having an appropriate palette, the HDR texture is compressed using standard color quantization. Then the HDR textures will have a palette and a 2D table of indices in that palette.

Furthermore, if the 256-entry palette is ordered properly, it can be considered as a continuous function that can be evaluated at any real value in [0,1]. By using this *sub-palette*, the HDR texture is compressed using real-valued palette indices in the interval [0,1]. The resulting real-valued indices can be quantized to an integer of an arbitrary bit rate for a more compact representation.

Both the palette and the 2D table of indices are uploaded to the GPU, where the palette texture is stored as a 1D floating-point texture and the indices texture is stored as a 2D single-channel integer texture. At render time, the HDR color can be obtained with two texture lookups. The first lookup retrieves an index of the given texture coordinates from the indices texture. Then the required HDR color is looked up from the palette texture using this resulting index (i.e., a dependent texture read). The rest of the article describes each step of the algorithm in detail.

Color Quantization

To compress the texture using color quantization, the texel colors are replaced with indices of smaller size that refer to palette entries. To optimize compression performance, it is crucial to select an appropriate palette. To select an appropriate palette, we use the LBG algorithm [5] to train a palette. In particular, a palette with 256 entries is used. Each entry consists of three floating-point components corresponding to the red, green, and blue channels. These 256 entries are considered to represent 256 clusters.

Initially, the palette's entries are randomly generated and the colors from the HDR texture are compared to the palette's entries for classification. A color will be classified to a cluster if the Euclidean distance between the color and the palette entry of the cluster is minimal. After classification is done, the entries are updated with the mean of data samples in the clusters. Color classification and entry updating is repeated until the entries converge or the maximum number of iterations is reached. Figure 8.3.1 shows how a color space is being clustered for the contents of one HDR texture.

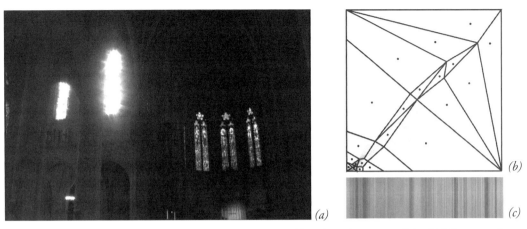

(a)   *(b)*

(c)

FIGURE 8.3.1 Image (a) is an HDR image (Nave). Image (b) is the color space of this HDR image along with the optimized palette produced by the LBG algorithm. The Voronoi region of each palette entry is shown. Image (c) is the resulting palette.

After training, the trained palette can be used to classify each texel of the HDR texture. Now the HDR texture will have a palette and a 2D table of indices. Figure 8.3.2 shows the actual contents of a 2D table of indices of an HDR texture.

One observation made on HDR images taken from natural scenes is that the colors of a large portion of the pixels usually belong to a small range only, with the small portion of pixels left having colors scattered across a wide dynamic range. Because we use color quantization with palette entries that are independent of each other, we can rely on the LBG algorithm to distribute these entries across the whole dynamic range sensibly, resulting in a more effective compression of the HDR image.

FIGURE 8.3.2 A 2D indices table of the HDR texture Nave.

However, the method works on HDR textures of natural scenes only. For arbitrary HDR data, indices with limited precision (e.g. eight bit or 12 bit) can fall short and would result in obvious banding artifacts.

Color Quantization Using the Sub-Palette

Although it is possible to compress an HDR texture with a palette made of more entries than 256, the training time of a high-resolution palette becomes impractically too long. To resolve this issue, we compress HDR textures with sub-palette entries.

First, a 256-entry palette for the HDR texture is trained using LBG as described previously. Now instead of using the resulting palette directly, the entries are reordered according to their similarities. As a result, the reordered palette can be considered as a piece-wise linear continuous function by connecting its consecutive entries with linear interpolation. Figure 8.3.3 shows how such a palette can be set up.

Once we have the continuous palette, a sub-palette with an arbitrary higher resolution can be generated. This higher-resolution sub-palette can now be used for quantizing the texture's colors.

Note that compressing an HDR texture with a palette of higher resolution requires more bits per-pixel. Since the sub-palette is only a compact representation of the high-resolution palette, it will not reduce the final bit rate of each texel. In other words, regardless of the sub-palette, a palette index using 12-bit precision will still require 12 bits to represent it.

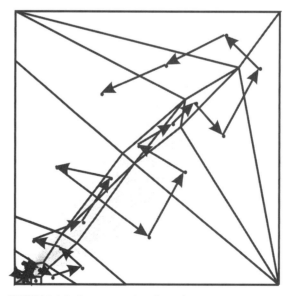

FIGURE 8.3.3 By connecting the palette entries in Figure 8.3.1, a sub-palette is formed.

Decoding

The palette and the indices of a compressed texture are both set on the GPU when the texture is to be used for rendering. The palette is stored as a 96-bit 1D floating-point texture. We can afford to do that because the palette only has a small number of entries. The indices are stored as a single-channel 2D integer texture. For HDR textures compressed using sub-palettes, the implementation is just the same. The only difference is that the palette texture is sampled with linear filtering instead of nearest-neighbor filtering.

To sample the compressed texture in the fragment shader, two lookups are needed as shown in Figure 8.3.4. The first lookup retrieves an index at the given texture coordinates from the indices texture. Then the actual HDR color is looked up from the palette texture using this resulting index.

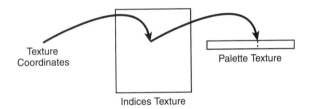

FIGURE 8.3.4 For each fragment, an index is looked up from the indices texture first, and then the index is used to look up the palette texture to obtain the HDR color.

The operation described above works fine when sampling the compressed texture using point-sampling. However, for linear filtering, each fragment needs to perform the decoding operation four times for each tap before computing the final interpolated value manually. The following Cg shader function samples a compressed HDR texture with bilinear filtering:

```
void cgfl_fp(
  float2 tc : TEXCOORD0, // texture coordinates
  uniform sampler1D palette, // palette texture
  uniform sampler2D indices, // indices texture
  uniform float4 ts, // texture resolution info
  uniform float bs, // brightness
  out float3 color : COLOR // output color
)
{
  float4 tw; // the 4 neighborhood indices
  float2 tr, td;  // the weighting for linear interpolation
  td = tc*ts.xy;
  tw.xy = floor(td-.5)+.5;
  tw.zw = tw.xy+1;
  tr = td-tw.xy;
  tw /= ts.xyxy;
```

```
// fetching 4 HDR colors from the compressed texture
// and linearly interpolating them
float3 x0, x1, y0, y1;
x0 = f3tex1D( palette, f1tex2D(indices, tw.xy)*ts.z+ts.w );
x1 = f3tex1D( palette, f1tex2D(indices, tw.zy)*ts.z+ts.w );
y0 = lerp( x0, x1, tr.x );
x0 = f3tex1D( palette, f1tex2D(indices, tw.xw)*ts.z+ts.w );
x1 = f3tex1D( palette, f1tex2D(indices, tw.zw)*ts.z+ts.w );
y1 = lerp( x0, x1, tr.x );

color = lerp( y0, y1, tr.y )*bs;
}
```

Results

In order to evaluate the quality of this compression algorithm, we need a metric that provides meaningful indication of image fidelity. To account for all normal viewing conditions, we use *multi-exposure peak-signal-to-noise ratio* [3], or *mPSNR* for short.

Table 8.3.1 compares the mPSNR of the compressed HDR texture Nave using both RGBE compression and our approach. The results show that our approach with an 8-bpp budget has an mPSNR value that is higher than the mPSNR of both an 8-bpp RGBE and a 12-bpp RGBE. (Note that all mPSNR are measured using the start and stop exposures of -8 and 3 respectively.)

Table 8.3.1 The mPSNR values of the compressed results of the HDR texture Nave using RGBE approach and our approach

	8 bpp	**12 bpp**
RGBE	15.32 dB	29.88 dB
Palletized	36.83 dB	38.22 dB

Figure 8.3.5 shows the compressed HDR textures using our method and the RGBE method with a brightness value set to 1. The RGBE method failed to capture the scattered nature of HDR texture with an 8-bpp budget, and heavy banding artifacts become clearly visible. In order to reduce these artifacts, the bit depth was raised to 12-bpp. On the contrary, in our method an 8-bpp budget was sufficient to produce the same quality.

To further emphasize the difference, the brightness value was raised to 8. These results are shown in Figure 8.3.6. As shown in the figure, even when using 12-bpp, the RGBE method shows heavy banding artifacts. Again, with 8-bpp only, our method produces much more acceptable quality.

Unfortunately, our method can still produce banding artifacts if we look closely at the decompressed results. If higher quality is required, then we can use more bits per-pixel for compression. Figure 8.3.7 shows that using 12-bpp with the sub-palette can produce much closer results to the original uncompressed HDR texture.

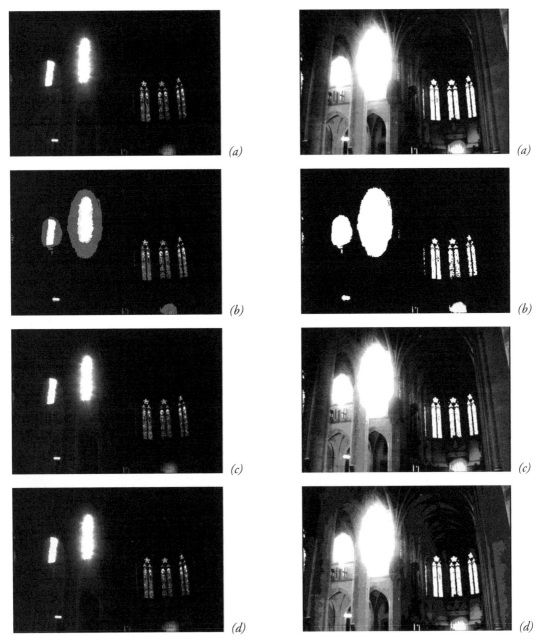

FIGURE 8.3.5 Image (a) is the source HDR texture. Images (b) and (d) use RGBE compression with 8-bpp and 12-bpp budgets respectively. Image (c) is compressed with our method using an 8-bpp budget. The brightness value of all results is set to 1.

FIGURE 8.3.6 Image (a) is the source HDR texture. Images (b) and (d) use RGBE compression with 8-bpp and 12-bpp budgets respectively. Image (c) is compressed with our method using an 8-bpp budget. The brightness value of all results is set to 8.

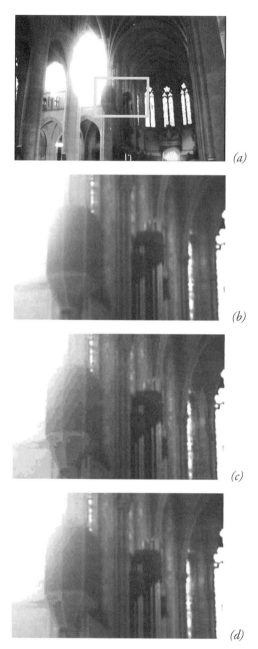

FIGURE 8.3.7 Image (a) is the source HDR texture and image (b) is a close-up on a bright area in the texture. Image (c) uses our method with 8-bpp, and image (d) uses 12-bpp with the sub-palette.

Regarding speed performance, as you can see in Table 8.3.2, the frame rate performance of the RGBE texture lookup and palletized textures are very close.

Table 8.3.2 Performance comparison between RGBE-compressed textures and palletized textures

	Point Filtering	Bilinear Filtering (Done in Shader)
RGBE textures	152.0 fps	22.3 fps
Palletized textures	130.5 fps	21.8 fps

These results were measured on an NVIDIA GeForce 6800 display card. Five full-screen quads (1024×768 screen resolution) were drawn every frame; each fragment of these quads was sampling four colors from four different HDR textures with a resolution of 720×480.

As described before, bilinear filtering has to be implemented manually in the shader (which is the case for RGBE, too). Table 8.3.2 shows that manual bilinear filtering costs an almost identical amount of performance for both compression methods.

Conclusion

This article presents color quantization as a way for compressing HDR textures. With only eight bits per-pixel, an HDR texture can be compressed effectively by using our method. This is because the palette entries can be distributed independently across the whole dynamic range, which closely resembles the scattered nature of HDR textures. The technique is extended to support higher bit rate compression by considering a sub-palette. Furthermore, decoding can be done on the GPU without the need for additional circuitry. The complete source code and the demo program are available on the companion DVD-ROM.

Acknowledgments

We would like to thank Paul Debevec [1] for permission to demonstrate our technique with the HDR image Nave. This work is supported by a research grant from City University of Hong Kong (Project No. 7002108).

References

[1] Debevec, E. and Malik, Jitendra. "Recovering High Dynamic Range Radiance Maps from Photographs," *SIGGRAPH 97*, August 1997.
[2] Domine, S. *Using Texture Compression in OpenGL*, available online at http://www.nvidia.com, NVIDIA Corporation.

[3] Munkberg, Jacob, Clarberg, Petrik, Hasselgren, Jon, Akenine-Moller, Tomas. "High Dynamic Range Texture Compression for Graphics Hardware," *ACM Transactions on Graphics (Proceedings of ACM SIGGRAPH 2006)* volume 25, issue 3, July, 2006: pp. 698–706.

[4] Roimela, Kimmo, Aarnio, Tomi, and Itaranta, Joonas. "High Dynamic Range Texture Compression," *ACM Transactions on Graphics (Proceedings of ACM SIGGRAPH 2006)*, volume 25, issue 3, July, 2006: pp. 707–712.

[5] Linde, A. B. Y. and Gray, R. M. "An algorithm for vector quantization design," *IEEE Transactions on Communicatinos COM-28*, January, 1980: pp. 84–95.

BEYOND PIXELS AND TRIANGLES

Introduction

Sebastien St. Laurent

With the increasing performance and parallelism of today's graphic processors, the transferring of complex and CPU-hungry tasks to the GPU is becoming more appealing. Although some architectural constraints make this implementation difficult, the latest advances brought forth by the latest generation of DirectX 10 hardware makes the implementation of general purpose algorithms on the GPU a reality. This section will thus cover current techniques that go beyond pixels and triangles.

In the first article, "An Interactive Tour of Voronoi Diagrams on the GPU" by Frank Nielsen, we explore the real-time generation of Voronoi diagrams that take advantage of advanced DirectX 10 features. Voronoi diagrams are defined as a set of points that partition a space into cells that represent the same energy level based on some error metric. Due to the iterative nature of the algorithm used to generate them, they are very well-suited to implementation on GPUs.

Next, in the article "AMD DirectX 10 Performance Tools and Techniques" by Jonathan Zarge, Seth Sowerby, and Guennadi Riguer, we take a look at the new performance tools from AMD. These tools demystify the GPU black box and expose a wide set of metrics to optimize your shaders. Combined with several optimization techniques exposed in this article, you are bound to get the most performance out of your rendering pipeline.

In "Real-Time Audio Processing on the GPU" by Fernando Trebien and Manuel M. Oliveira, the use of the GPU is taken to a whole new level, moving from the processing of pixels to the processing of real-time audio data. This article focuses not only on the real-time processing of sounds on the GPU, but takes it a step further by introducing techniques for the generation of sound waves dynamically on the GPU.

And, finally, in the article "*n*-Body Simulations on the GPU" by Jesse Laeuchli, we take an in-depth look at how the complex domain of simulating *n*-body physics can take advantage of the highly parallel architecture of modern GPUs to achieve real-time performance on an extensive set of elements. This article focuses on simulating the various forces governing a large set of particles at an interactive rate.

9.1

An Interactive Tour of Voronoi Diagrams on the GPU

Frank Nielsen (Frank.Nielsen@acm.org)

Sony Computer Science Laboratories, Inc., Tokyo, Japan
Ecole Polytechnique, LIX, Paris, France

Voronoi diagrams are fundamental geometric structures that have been both deeply and widely investigated since their inception in disguise by René Descartes for analyzing the gravitational influence of stars in the 17th century. Voronoi diagrams have found countless applications in science and engineering beyond graphics, as attested by the long representative—and yet non-exhaustive—list of applications reported at the Web portal http://www.voronoi.com (e.g., collision detection, path planning, meshing and surface reconstruction, and so on).

Introduction

A *Voronoi diagram* is a finite set of points

$$S = \{P_1,....,P_n\}$$

that partitions the underlying space into elementary structures called *Voronoi cells,* which define combinatorial proximity location information. The Voronoi cell of a site P_i is defined as the locations of points closer to site P_i than to any other site. That is, mathematically speaking,

$$\mathrm{Vor}(P_i) = \{P | \mathrm{Distance}(P_i, P) \leq \mathrm{Distance}(P_j, P) \forall j\}$$

The Voronoi diagram is thus an essential combinatorial structure that splits the continuous space into a finite, discrete number of bounded and (necessarily) unbounded cells. The *ordinary* Voronoi diagram of a given set of sites

$$P_1,....,P_n$$

is defined as the *cell complex* induced by the Voronoi cells

$$\mathrm{Vor}(P_1),....,\mathrm{Vor}(P_n)$$

for the Euclidean distance [VC05]

$$\text{Distance}(P_i, P) = \|P_i P\| = \sqrt{(P_{i,x} - P_x)^2 + (P_{i,y} - P_y)^2}$$

Note that since the Voronoi diagram is defined in terms of distance comparisons, the structure does not change if we take any arbitrary monotonously increasing function of the distance, such as the square function, for example, which allows bypassing unnecessary square root computations.

The GPU provides a nice commodity hardware for either visualizing these partitions interactively by rasterizing the Voronoi cells or for computing even the exact combinatorial structures themselves, as described in papers [JF06][DF06][FG06]. Rasterizing 2D Voronoi diagrams is based on computing the *index function* for each pixel position in screen space (or texture space for GPUs using per-pixel shaders). For a current pixel/point position, the index function reports the *closest* site:

$$\text{index}(P) = \arg\min_{i \in \{1, \dots, n\}} d(P, P_i)$$

In all our Cg programs in this article (nine in total), we return both the smallest distance (min function) and its corresponding index (argmin function) in a `float2` structure by the Cg function called `Winner`. We can fill Voronoi cells using predefined colors based on the index function, or raster the borders of Voronoi cells if neighborhood pixels (either in C4 or C8 connectivity) have different indices, that is, different closest points. To emphasize the role of the distance function, we can also further rasterize distance isolines at predetermined values by prescribing beforehand a modulo offset value. This isoline drawing style emphasizes another interpretation of Voronoi diagrams as dynamic crystal growths whose seeds are anchored at sites, better called generators in that context (see the section "Voronoi Diagrams as Minimization Diagrams" later in this article). The OpenGL GLUT program OrdinaryVoronoiDiagram allows you to interactively pick up a site and move it so that one can explore how the overall structure changes globally from the relative point positions. Figure 9.1.1 displays different snapshots showing the variety of drawing styles rasterized in real-time by the per-pixel Cg shader. An excerpt of the OrdinaryVoronoi.cg code is shown in Listing 9.1.1.

Listing 9.1.1 The Cg code OrdinaryVoronoi.cg for rasterizing Voronoi cells with different styles

```
// Report the index of the closest point
float2 Winner(float2 p)
{
int i, winner;
float dist,mindist;

mindist=distance(p,position[0]);
```

```
for(i=1;i<MAXN;i++)
        {
        dist=distance(p,position[i]);
        if (dist<mindist) {mindist=dist;winner=i;}
    }
return float2(winner,mindist);
}


// Voronoi diagram rasterization
float3  OrdinaryVoronoi(float2 pos: TEXCOORD0) : COLOR0
{
// Index for current and x- y-neighborhood position
float2 w,wx,wy;
int index, indexx,indexy;
```

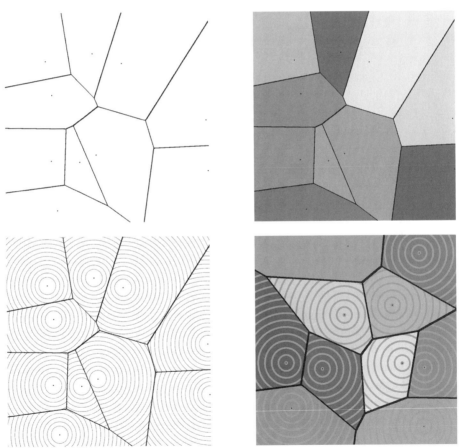

FIGURE 9.1.1 Different rendering styles for the ordinary Voronoi diagram: (a) Rasterizing borders, (b) rasterizing color cells with thick borders, (c) rasterizing distance isolines with thick borders, and (d) rasterizing all three types of information at once: colored cells, distance isolines, and cell borders.

```
// position of the shader pixel
float2 posx,posy;

float3 color;
float3 bordercolor=float3(0,0,0);
float3 isolinecolor=float3(0.5,0.5,0.5);
float iso, iso2, f;

pos=ToDomain(pos);posx=ToDomain(pos)+float2(s,0);posy=ToDomain(pos)+fl
oat2(0,s);

w=Winner(pos);wx=Winner(posx);wy=Winner(posy);

index=w[0];indexx=wx[0];indexy=wy[0];

// number of isoline strips
iso=30.0*frac(w[1]); // period
iso2=frac(iso);

color=ColorCell(index);

// overwrite isoline
 if (  ((iso2>t1)&&(iso2<10.0*t2)) )
                    color=isolinecolor;

// Overwrite
if ((index!=indexx)||(index!=indexy))
      return color=bordercolor;

return color;
}
```

Voronoi diagrams have been generalized in many ways [CVD06], including considering arbitrary objects instead of points for sites or various distance functions instead of the Euclidean distance, just to name a few. In computational geometry, there also exist important variations called *k-order Voronoi diagrams* that choose all subsets of k sites instead of a single site for defining the notion of "closest/furthest" proximity cells (many cells are empty).

In this article, we emphasize the educational aspects of interactive GPU applications for computing 2D Voronoi diagrams beyond the Euclidean geometry in realtime. First, we give a brief account of and visually depict affine and curved Voronoi diagrams [CVD06]. Because there are infinitely many potential distance functions, each defining a proper Voronoi diagram in itself, it really does not make sense to catalog all of them. Instead, later we will present the reader a neat generalization based on the axiomatization of distances. Namely, we will describe two classes of generic Voronoi diagrams based on the information-theoretic parametric distances [BVD'07]: Bregman and Csiszár divergences. Bregman and Csiszár divergences cover many familiar distances and yet intersect only for the most fundamental information measure: the Kullback-Leibler divergence, better known as the relative entropy or information discrepancy. This allows one to compute statistical Voronoi diagrams such as the Voronoi diagrams of a finite set of normal distributions

$$N(\mu_i, \sigma_i)$$

encoded as 2D parameter information points

$$(\mu_i, \sigma_i)$$

This becomes all the more important when computing Voronoi diagrams under uncertainty (eg., points with individual variance-based noise).

But first, let us quickly examine some fundamental properties of the ordinary Euclidean Voronoi diagrams.

Bisectors and Dually Orthogonal Delaunay Triangulations

We previously defined the Voronoi cell of site P as the locii of points closer to P than to any other sites. However, that definition of Voronoi cells also implicitly highlights the notion of a *territory* of a point P with respect to the other sites. So instead of looking for each point in its cell, we can consider computing the cell boundaries. The notion of territory is decomposable, and lets only the discrete finite set of input points intervene. For a given pair of sites P and Q, we consider the boundary of their cells to be an *elementary territory frontier* (the mere Voronoi diagram of two points) and call it the *bisector*:

$$\text{Bisector}(P, Q) = \{X \mid \text{Distance}(X, P) \leq \text{Distance}(X, Q)\}$$

The Voronoi cell

$$\text{Vor}(P_i) = \{P \mid \text{Distance}(P_i, P) \leq \text{Distance}(P_j, P) \forall P \in S\}$$

can be rewritten as

$$\text{Vor}(P_i) = \cap_{j \neq i} \text{Bisector}(P_i, P_j)$$

thus the bisector in the plane is a line (generalized to plane in 3D and hyperplane in higher dimensions): its characteristic is derived from the distance equality

$$\text{Distance}(P_i, P) = \text{Distance}(P_j, P)$$

and yields an affine equation for the locii of points equidistant of P_i and P_j:

$$\text{Bisector}(P_i, P_j) :< P, 2(P_j - P_i) > + < P_i, P_i > - < P_j, P_j > = 0,$$

where

$$< P, Q > = P_x Q_x + P_y Q_y$$

denotes the 2D inner product (dot product).

Thus the Voronoi cell is expressed as the intersection of a set of half-planes yielding a convex polygon, also called Dirichlet cell or Thiessen polygon, that is eventually open to infinity for unbounded cells.

But there is more, and this is obviously a key component to their success and fame in computer graphics: Voronoi diagrams exhibit a unique dual structure called Delaunay triangulations, which enjoy a nice property for points in general position (no four co-circular points): no thin triangles—that is, maximizing the smallest angle and minimizing the radius of the smallest enclosing disks of triangles. The Delaunay triangulation meshing of the input point set is derived from the Voronoi diagram by linking the sites of adjacent cells with straight line segments (geodesics). The boundary of the mesh is the convex hull of the point set and contains all finite Voronoi cells. Further, since the line segment joining two sites is provably perpendicular to their bisector, it follows that the Delaunay triangulation structure is globally orthogonal to the Voronoi diagram.

Observe that the intersection point of the bisector/line segment joining two sites may not belong to the Voronoi boundaries. Although the Delaunay edges can be derived from the second-order Voronoi diagram [FG06] by checking non-empty cells, we proceed instead by expanding the former ordinary Voronoi code and detecting the edges that yield corresponding Delaunay edges by scanlining the frame buffer.

The program DelaunayTriangulation demonstrates that technique (Cg code DelaunayTriangulation.cg). Note that it is not flawless, as sometimes the program will fail to report edges (notably on the convex hull if not all bounded Voronoi cells are

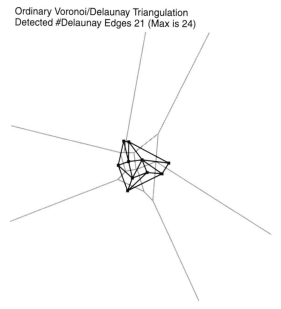

Ordinary Voronoi/Delaunay Triangulation
Detected #Delaunay Edges 21 (Max is 24)

FIGURE 9.1.2 The dual Delaunay triangulation is orthogonal to the primal Voronoi diagram.

fully rendered in the viewport) but it is interesting for educational purposes. It can be checked that the maximum number of Delaunay edges is 3n-6. This number may vary according to the configuration of the point set, depending on the size of the convex hull.

Affine and Curved Voronoi Diagrams

Having lines (planes or hyperplanes in higher dimensions) as bisectors is definitely a convenient property because cells can be computed as convex polygons (polyedra and polytopes in higher dimensions). Another classic Voronoi diagram is the power diagram of a set of disks. The power distance of a point P to a disk (C, r) centered at C with radius is defined as

$$\text{Power}(P; C, r) = \| P - C \|^2 - r^2$$

The power distance is symmetric and positive if and only if the point P lies outside the disk. Power diagrams generalize ordinary Voronoi diagrams (all radii set to zero), but note that some Voronoi cells of power diagrams may be empty (and by virtue of the pigeonhole principle some cells may contain [partially] several points). Affine diagrams also include the Voronoi diagram for the generalized quadratic distance

$$d_Q(P, P_i) = \sqrt{(P - P_i)^T Q (P - P_i)}$$

for a positive semi-definite matrix Q (the usual ordinary Euclidean distance is obtained by setting Q to the identity matrix; the Mahalanobis distance often used in computer vision is equivalent to the generalized quadratic distance for the inverse variance-covariance matrix) and k-order diagrams. It is therefore natural to ask whether there exists a common universal methodology for computing these affine diagrams? The striking result is that *any* affine diagram can be computed as the power diagram of a set of disks. (Thus, we can also compute the Delaunay edges from a power diagram representing the second-order point Voronoi diagram since second-order diagrams are affine.) Another common distance variation of Voronoi diagrams is to add or multiply the distance by a *weight* anchored at each site (these parameters can be interpreted as a time lag and a speed attribute for each generator). These generalizations yield the so-called additively and multiplicatively weighted Voronoi diagrams. In [CVD06], the most common curved and affine Voronoi diagrams are presented. They can all be computed from the following *generic* distance function

$$d(P, P_i) = w_i \left(\sqrt{(P - P_i)^T Q_i (P - P_i)} \right)^\alpha - r_i^\alpha$$

That is, to each disk (P_i, r_i) we further attach a weight w_i as well as a positive semi-definite symmetric matrix Q_i (often taken as the inverse of a variance-covariance matrix). The radii of disks can potentially be imaginary, i.e., negative. Equipped with that parametric distance function, we get the following diagrams explained in detail in [CVD06]:

- **Möbius diagrams obtained by the distance function**

$$\text{Moebius}(P, P_i) = w_i \parallel P - P_i \parallel^2 - r_i$$

Möbius diagrams have the particularity of having their bisectors as arcs of circles. The Voronoi diagrams with arcs of circle bisectors are called *spherical diagrams* by analogy to affine diagrams. Similarly, there is a universality theorem for that class of Voronoi diagrams because *any* spherical diagram can be computed as a Möbius diagram, too.

- **Apollonius diagram of a set of spheres is defined by the distance function**

$$\text{Apollonius}(P, P_i) = \parallel P - P_i \parallel - r_i$$

In a sense, the Apollonius diagram is conceptually similar to power diagrams with the exception that the Euclidean distance is not squared. The name of this diagram comes from the fact that at each vertex of the diagram there exists a circle tangent to three input circles. Computing such a circle was first raised by Apollonius and is known as Appolonius' Tenth Problem. Bisectors are characterized by arcs of hyperbolae, and the diagram is also called the Johnson-Mehl diagram in physics/chemistry literature.

- **Anisotropic Voronoi diagrams are defined by the weighted distance function**

$$\text{Anisotropic}(P, P_i) = (P - P_i)^T Q_i (P - P_i) - r_i$$

These recently gained attention in the computer graphics and computational geometry community for meshing anisotropic CAD objects with sharp ridges. The bisectors of anisotropic Voronoi diagrams are quadratic curves, and again there is a corresponding universality theorem that proves that any quadratic Voronoi diagram can be obtained from an anisotropic diagram.

Figure 9.1.3 displays these diagrams, and the program VorPDMöbiusAppolonius enables you to interact in real-time with all these diagrams.

Next we will present and interactively visualize a few Voronoi diagrams on non-Euclidean geometries. The power diagram can be interpreted as one of those for the Laguerre geometry.

Spherical and Hyperbolic Voronoi Diagrams

For a very long time, Euclidean geometry derived from Euclid's five postulates was considered the unique geometry prevailing on Earth. The failure to prove that the more complicated fifth parallel postulate could be derived from the first four axioms yielded eventually to one of the greatest discoveries of mankind: the birth of non-Euclidean geometry in the 17th century. The hyperbolic and spherical non-Euclidean geometries were thoroughly investigated in the 18th century. Historically, these

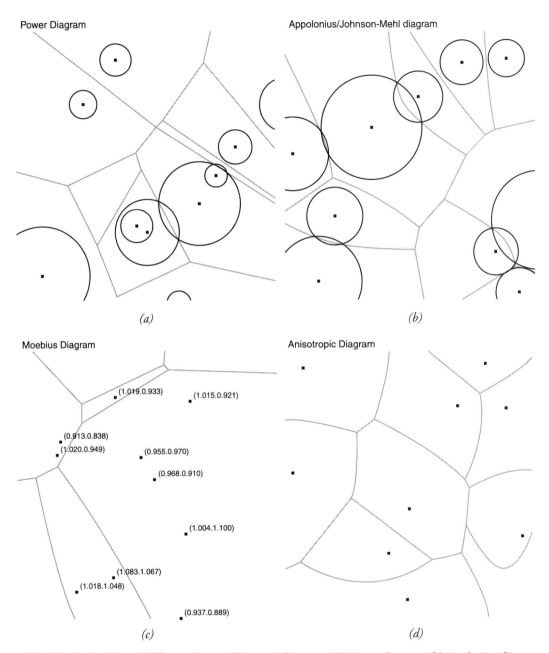

Power Diagram

Appolonius/Johnson-Mehl diagram

(a)

(b)

Moebius Diagram

(1.019.0.933)

(1.015.0.921)

(0.913.0.838)
(1.020.0.949)

(0.955.0.970)

(0.968.0.910)

(1.004.1.100)

(1.083.1.067)

(1.018.1.048)

(0.937.0.889)

(c)

Anisotropic Diagram

(d)

FIGURE 9.1.3 A gallery of affine and curved Voronoi diagrams: (a) Power diagram, (b) Apolonius diagram, (c) Möbius diagram, and (d) Anisotropic diagram. These diagrams can also be rendered using the distance isoline style.

abstract geometries were called *imaginary geometries*. To visualize them, we need to map their structures on the Euclidean space. This is always possible by virtue of the Riemann mapping theorem.

The Voronoi diagram of a set of points on the 3D sphere can be rasterized using the GPU per-pixel shader with the spherical coordinates on a texture map. The distance between any two points on a sphere is taken as the angle formed by any two 3D points of the unit sphere, which is the arccosine of the inner product of these points, namely

$$\text{Distance}_{Sphere}(P, P_i) = \arccos(P_x P_{i,x} + P_y P_{i,y} + P_z P_{i,z})$$

Figure 9.1.4 depicts such a Voronoi diagram rasterized on the texture map using the latitude and longitude spherical coordinates and textured on the 3D unit sphere for visualization.

The Cg code follows the same spirit of the ordinary Voronoi diagram except for the computations of the spherical distance:

```
//
// Convert latitude longitude to 3D xyz Cartesian coordinate
// Unit vector
float3 Spherical2Cartesian(float2 tp)
{float3 xyz;

xyz[0]=cos(tp[1])*sin(tp[0]);
xyz[1]=sin(tp[1]);
xyz[2]=cos(tp[1])*cos(tp[0]);

return xyz;
}

float norm(float3 P)
{
return P[0]*P[0]+P[1]*P[1]+P[2]*P[2];
}

float DistanceSphere(float2 tp, float2 tq)
{
float3 P, Q;
float angle;

P=Spherical2Cartesian(tp);
Q=Spherical2Cartesian(tq);
angle=acos(P[0]*Q[0]+P[1]*Q[1]+P[2]*Q[2]);

return abs(angle);
}
```

There are several realizations of the hyperbolic geometry. The two most famous ones are the conformal Poincaré disk that preserves the angles and the non-conformal Beltrami-Klein disk. The notion of conformality indicates that the mapping preserves

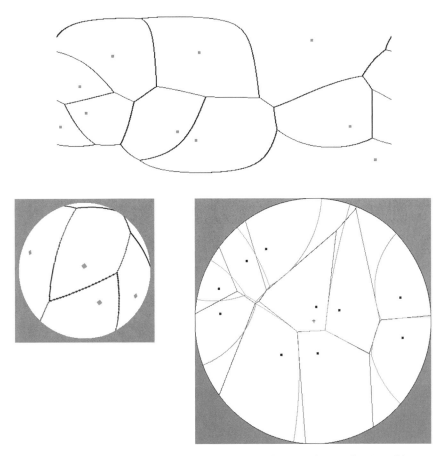

FIGURE 9.1.4 Spherical (latitude-longitude map and textured 3D sphere) and hyperbolic Voronoi diagrams (the conformal Poincaré disk and non-conformal affine Beltrami-Klein disk are shown).

the incidence angles, an important feature first used historically in cartography and later considered in texture mapping of 3D meshes. For Cartesian point coordinates lying on a unit disk centered at the origin, we have the respective hyperbolic distance functions given as

$$\text{Distance}_{Klein}(P,Q) = \text{arccosh}\left(\frac{1 - <P,Q>}{\sqrt{(1 - <P,P>)(1 - <Q,Q>)}}\right)$$

and

$$\text{Distance}_{Poincare}(P,Q) = \text{arccosh}\left(1 + 2\frac{\|PQ\|^2}{(1 - \|P\|^2)(1 - \|Q\|^2)}\right)$$

where

$$\mathrm{arccosh}(x) = \log(x + \sqrt{x^2 - 1})$$

and

$$< P, Q > = P_x Q_x + P_y Q_y$$

Interestingly, it can be verified that the Beltrami-Klein hyperbolic Voronoi diagram is affine and can thus be computed equivalently as a power diagram. Moreover, there exists simple one-to-one mappings for going from one hyperbolic realization to another.

In the 19th century, Riemann further proved that there exist infinitely many abstract geometries and generalized the elliptical and spherical geometries using the notion of Riemann metric, which can eventually further be defined locally using a tensor metric. This formalization is at the heart of the general space-time relativity theory of Einstein.

Information-Theoretic Voronoi Diagrams

Most of the common distance functions we usually see in practice belong either to the generic class of Csiszár divergences or to the class of Bregman divergences. These parametric distance functions are not necessarily symmetric nor do they respect the triangle inequality. Their justification is based on the characterization of least square problems as "projections" and the existence of generalized Pythagorean theorems. (Details are outside the scope of this article; please see [BVD'07] for more information.) Again, interactive GPU rasterization allows the user to explore and gain knowledge of their properties, thereby fostering visual thinking and mathematical intuition.

The Csiszár divergence is defined for a strictly convex generator function f such that $f(1)=0$ has the following statistical distance:

$$I_f(P \| Q) = \int Q(x) f\left(\frac{P(x)}{Q(x)}\right) \mathrm{d}x$$

where P and Q are probability distributions—i.e., both

$$\int P(x)\,\mathrm{d}x = 1$$

and

$$\int Q(x)\,\mathrm{d}x = 1$$

For example, the total variation distance is obtained for

$$f(x) = |x - 1|.$$

(Table 9.1.1 lists a few usual generators encountered in practice.) This diagram is equivalent to the L1 norm Voronoi diagram.

Table 9.1.1 Common examples of Csiszár divergences

Csiszár Divergence	Generator Function
Kullback-Leibler divergence	$x \log x$ (negative Shannon entropy)
Chi squared divergence	$\frac{1}{2}(x-1)^2$
Total variation distance	$|x-1|$
Perimeter divergence	$\left| \sqrt{1+x^2} - \frac{1+x}{\sqrt{2}} \right|$

Because the distance measure may not be symmetric, it is also called *divergence,* and the

$$\text{Distance}(P \| Q)$$

notation emphasizes the non-metric property of these distance functions. For asymmetric divergences, we may further define two types of cells depending on the position (left/right) of the site for defining Voronoi cells:

$$\text{Vor}_f (P_i) = \{P | I_f(P \| P_i) \leq I_f(P \| P_j) \forall j\}$$

(right-type)

$$\text{Vor}_f^*(P_i) = \{P | I_f(P_i \| P) \leq I_f(P_j \| P) \forall j\}$$

(left-type)

We can associate with a Csiszár generator function a dual *-conjugate function

$$f^*(x) = xf\left(\frac{1}{x}\right)$$

so that we have

$$I_f(P \| Q) = I_{f^*}(Q \| P)$$

Therefore, we deduce that

$$\text{Vor}_f^*(P_i) = \text{Vor}_{f^*}(P_i)$$

For example, the *-conjugate of the negative Shannon entropy is

$$f^*(x) = xf\left(\frac{1}{x}\right) = x\frac{1}{x}\log\frac{1}{x} = -\log x$$

the Burg entropy (often used in sound processing).

For symmetric Csiszár divergences, the generator is self-dual and thus both left-type and right-type Voronoi cells coincide. Figure 9.1.5 displays some examples of Csiszár Voronoi diagrams derived from the Cg code CsiszárVoronoi.cg.

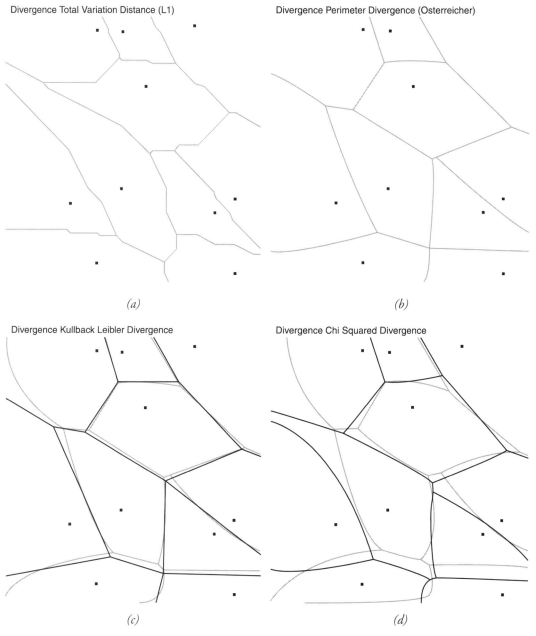

FIGURE 9.1.5 Examples of Csiszár Voronoi diagrams: (a) Total variation distance (L1), (b) Perimeter divergence, (c) Kullback-Leibler divergence, and (d) Chi squared distance. Because the divergences may not be symmetric, we define two dual Voronoi diagrams, rasterized here in light and dark colors.

The other generic family of distortion measures are Bregman divergences. *Bregman divergences* are informally defined as the tail of a Taylor expansion for a strictly convex and differentiable function F as follows:

$$D_F(P \| Q) = F(P) - F(Q) - <P - Q, \nabla F(Q)>$$

Bregman divergences include, among many others, the squared Euclidean distance and the statistical Kullback-Leibler divergence. Table 9.1.2 summarizes the usual divergences.

Table 9.1.2 Common Bregman divergences

Bregman Divergence	Bregman Generator
Squared Euclidean distance	x^2
Kullback-Leibler divergence	$x \log x - x$ (Ext. neg. Shannon entropy)
Itakura-Saito divergence	$-\log x$ (Burg entropy)
Exponential divergence	$\exp x$

Since they are not necessarily symmetric, we define again two types of Voronoi cells:

$$\text{Vor}_F(P_i) = \{P | D_F(P \| P_i) \leq D_F(P \| P_j) \forall j\}$$

(right-type)

$$\text{Vor}_F^*(P_i) = \{P | D_F(P_i \| P) \leq D_F(P_j \| P) \forall j\}$$

(left-type)

Similarly, a dual divergence may be defined using the Legendre transformation that associates a convex function to a unique dual convex function as follows:

$$F^*(P') = \sup_P \{<P', P> - F(P)\}$$

It can be shown that the supremum is reached at the unique point

$$P' = \nabla F(P)$$

The gradient of the primal and dual Legendre functions are inverse of each other. Further, the primal and dual divergences are related by the following equation:

$$D_F(P \| Q) = F(P) + F^*(Q') - <P, Q'> = D_{F^*}(Q' \| P')$$

For example, the Legendre transform of the extended Shannon entropy $x \log x - x$ is the exponential entropy $\exp x$, as it can be easily checked that their gradient functions are inverse of each other.

Again, as in the case of Csiszár divergences, the arguments swap, but observe that this time the space/gradient spaces swap also. This property is at the core of the dually flat shape geometry of information geometry [BVD'07].

Figure 9.1.6 displays the snapshot of the OpenGL GLUT program that manages simulatenously two windows to display the primal and dual Voronoi diagrams. The user can interactively pick up a point in either the primal space or the dual gradient space and observe how the structures change and are related to each other. Since the first-type Bregman Voronoi diagram is affine, it can be conveniently computed as a special power diagram (with all non-empty cells). The second-type curved Bregman Voronoi diagram (after space/gradient space mapping) computes the dual affine Bregman Voronoi diagram from the Legendre convex conjugate.

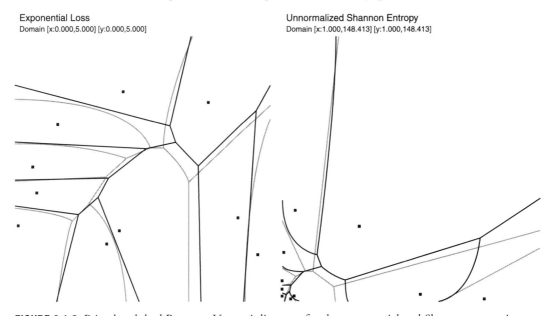

FIGURE 9.1.6 Primal and dual Bregman Voronoi diagrams for the exponential and Shannon entropies.

Voronoi Diagrams as Minimization Diagrams

As mentioned in the introduction, the Voronoi diagram can be computed from the minimization diagram of a set of distance functions anchored at sites using the index function.

Namely, let

$$D_i(P) = \text{Distance}(P, P_i)$$

be the function attached to the site P_i. The Voronoi diagram can be obtained from the minimization diagram

$$D(P) = \min_{i \in \{1,\dots,n\}} D_i(P)$$

which is the lower envelope of the functions. For the (squared) Euclidean distance function, this amounts to the lower envelope of a set of paraboloids anchored at each respective site, as shown in Figure 9.1.7.

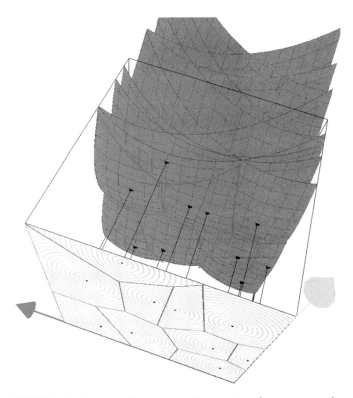

FIGURE 9.1.7 Voronoi diagrams as minimization diagrams: visualizing lower envelopes. Here, for the case of ordinary Voronoi diagrams, we visualize the lower envelope of corresponding anchored parabolae shifted upward to improve visibility.

For the affine Bregman Voronoi diagrams, we have

$$D_i(P) = D_F(P \,\|\, P_i) = F(P) - F(P_i) - \langle P - P_i, \nabla F(P_i) \rangle$$

We can remove the common terms $F(P)$ appearing in all distance functions and get equivalently a set of planes (or hyperplanes in higher dimensions) that show that the right-type Bregman Voronoi diagram is indeed affine.

Conclusion

Interactive visualization of Voronoi diagrams for various symmetric/non-symmetric distance functions allows one to gain a better understanding of their fundamental properties and intrinsic dualities. We encourage the reader to look at the set of 20 videos provided on the accompanying DVD that recorded interactive sessions. The GPU provides a fabulous tool and framework to gain intuition for discovering mathematical structural invariants. The GPU, a powerful visualscope, allows one to foster "visual thinking" and thus potentially hints at further major mathematical discoveries in the future. We refer the reader to the paper [BVD'07] for further theoretical insights of information-theoretic diagrams, including a neat extension of the space of spheres on which many computational geometric algorithms, such as the smallest enclosing balls, rely.

References

[VC05] Nielsen, Frank. *Visual Computing: Geometry, Graphics and Vision.* Charles River Media, 2005.

[CVD06] Boissonnat, Jean-Daniel, Wormser, Camille, Yvinec, Mariette. "Curved Voronoi Diagrams," *Effective Computational Geometry for Curves and Surfaces.* Springer-Verlag 2006.

[JF06] Rong, Guodong and Tan, Tiow-Seng: "Jump flooding in GPU with applications to Voronoi diagram and distance transform," *ACM Symposium on Interactive 3D graphics and games,* 2006: pp. 109–116.

[DF06] Sud, Avneesh, Govindaraju, Naga K., Gayle, Russell, Manocha, Dinesh. "Interactive 3D distance field computation using linear factorization," *ACM Symposium on Interactive 3D graphics and games,* 2006: pp. 117–124.

[FG06] Fischer, Ian and Gotsman, Craig. "Fast Approximation of High-Order Voronoi Diagrams and Distance Transforms on the GPU," *Journal of graphics tools,* Vol. 11, No. 4, 2006: pp. 39–60. http://jgt.akpeters.com/papers/Fischer-Gotsman06/

[BVD07] Nielsen, Frank, Boissonnat, Jean-Daniel, Nock, Richard. "Bregman Voronoi Diagrams: Properties, Algorithms and Applications," *INRIA Research Report,* No 6154. (online at hal.inria.fr), 2007.

9.2

AMD DirectX 10 Performance Tools and Techniques

Jonathan Zarge

AMD Graphics Products Group

Seth Sowerby

AMD Graphics Products Group

Guennadi Riguer

AMD Graphics Products Group

Introduction

With millions of polygons and long, looping shaders, analyzing the performance of today's 3D games and applications is increasingly complex. Optimizing graphics performance on these applications is especially difficult because the driver and graphics hardware are presented as a rendering "black box" from which very little measurable data can be extracted. This article presents tools from AMD, in addition to numerous Direct3D 10 shader optimization techniques, which are specifically designed to help developers improve the graphics performance of their 3D applications.

The Problem

Recent changes in the graphics industry have added several new wrinkles to the performance optimization problem. Direct3D 10 exposes a new shader type—the geometry shader—and longer shaders with looping and dynamic branching. To accommodate the new features of Direct3D 10, the latest graphics hardware has grown significantly in its size and complexity. Locating the performance bottleneck and understanding the reason for performance problems is virtually impossible without hardware-specific tools and insight from hardware vendors about squeezing the most out of their hardware.

This article first presents a brief architectural review of the ATI Radeon HD 2000 series hardware. The initial tool presented, GPU PerfStudio, is a real-time performance analysis tool from AMD that is designed to interactively tune the performance of Direct3D 9 and Direct3D 10 graphics applications. Next, GPU ShaderAnalyzer performs offline shader performance analysis for every type of shader on ATI Radeon graphics cards; it also can display the D3D shader disassembly and the low-level shaders actually run on ATI Radeon hardware. Finally, numerous Direct3D 10 shader optimization techniques are discussed.

GPU Architecture 101

Any discussion of GPU performance optimization must begin with a discussion of GPU architecture. The operation of the graphical pipeline should be well understood by readers of this book, but it is worth reviewing, particularly with the recent introduction of Direct3D 10.

As with previous versions of Direct3D, each stage in the pipeline performs a particular task and then passes its results off to the next stage in the pipeline. Unlike previous versions, however, there is explicit support in Direct3D 10 for streaming out data partway through the pipeline.

Figure 9.2.1 illustrates the programmable stages that are our primary concern.

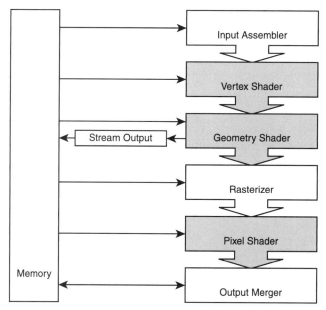

FIGURE 9.2.1 A simplified representation of the Direct3D 10 graphics pipeline.

The other stages are all configurable and some of their states can have a direct effect on how shaders are compiled. In brief, the pipeline stages are as follows:

- **Input assembler:** Reads data from memory buffers (i.e. vertex and index buffers) and assembles this data as primitives for the pipeline to process.
- **Vertex shader:** Executes a shader on each vertex within the primitives provided by the input assembler. Typically this shader performs such operations as transforming the vertices into world space, lighting, and skinning.
- **Geometry shader:** Executes a shader on each primitive supplied by the input assembler with vertices processed by the vertex shader. This stage can output 0, 1, or many primitives.
- **Stream output:** Stores vertex data from the geometry shader (or vertex shader if the geometry shader is inactive) to memory. This data may be recycled into the pipeline in a later render pass.
- **Rasterizer:** Clips primitives and then rasterizes them into pixels.
- **Pixel shader:** Executes a shader on each pixel generated by the rasterizer.
- **Output merger:** Merges the output of the pixel shader with the current output buffers.

Unified Shader Architectures

The architecture of modern GPUs such as ATI Radeon HD 2000 series or NVIDIA GeForce 8800 differs greatly from the abstract graphics pipeline. Rather than having distinct vertex, geometry, and pixel shader units, these modern GPUs have a single unified shader core from which resources are dynamically allocated for processing vertex, geometry, and pixel shaders. This has the advantage of ensuring that one shader unit is not sitting idle while another shader unit is bottlenecked. Instead, shader computing resources are shifted automatically to where they are needed most.

Figure 9.2.2 illustrates the architecture of one unified shader architecture in particular: the ATI Radeon HD 2900. Each shader type has different setup requirements, and separate setup units exist to assemble their input data. After they are assembled, however, vertices, primitives, and pixels are processed in an identical manner. A thread to process multiple items (pixels, vertices, etc.) is created and dispatched for processing in parallel with multiple other threads. Once processed, the thread's outputs are passed on to the next stage of the pipeline. For a vertex shader or geometry shader this will be the setup unit for the next shader stage or the shader export unit; for a pixel shader this will be the render back-end.

While with a unified shader architecture it is the shared shader core that can be bottlenecked as a whole—rather than individual shader units—the cause of a bottleneck is generally within one of the logical shader units shown in the abstract graphics pipeline in Figure 9.2.1. For instance, performance may be limited by the texture reads within the pixel shader. Often the first stage of optimizing shaders is to deter-

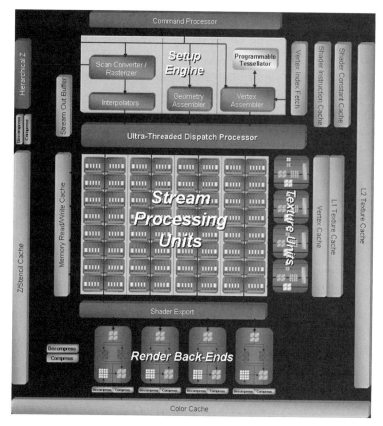

FIGURE 9.2.2 ATI Radeon HD 2900 architecture.

mine at what stage of the graphics pipeline the bottleneck in performance exists. For this and for overall GPU performance optimization, a tool such as GPU PerfStudio is useful.

Performance Optimization with GPU PerfStudio

GPU PerfStudio provides interactive real-time API and hardware data that can be visualized using intuitive and flexible graphs and bar charts. The application being profiled can be executed locally or remotely over the network. GPU PerfStudio allows overriding of key rendering states in real-time for precise bottleneck detection. An auto-analysis window can be used to identify performance issues at various stages of the graphics pipeline.

GPU PerfStudio can be used to systematically locate performance bottlenecks in the target application; tools such as NVPerfHUD perform similar functions. Before any other analysis, using a tool like CodeAnalyst or VTune can identify a bottleneck that is not related to graphics (file I/O, AI, collision testing, and so on). Similarly, GPU PerfStudio can help discover non-graphics performance problems by using the

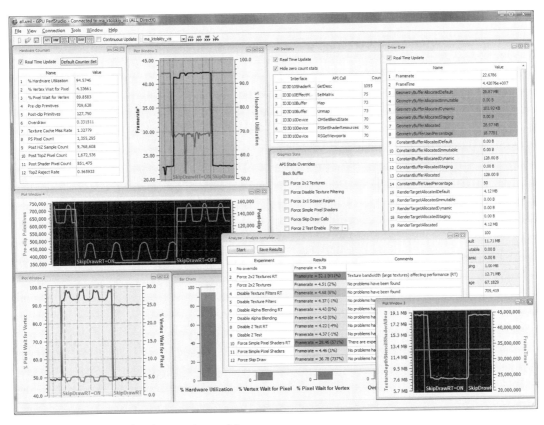

FIGURE 9.2.3 GPU PerfStudio running on Vista.

Skip Draw Calls state override: If the application is not rendering anything and the frame rate remains constant, then the bottleneck is probably not related to graphics. Similarly, other state overrides can identify more precisely the location of bottlenecks. For example, if all the pixel shaders are replaced with simple (constant color) shaders using the Force Simple Pixel Shaders override and the frame rate increases, the performance problem is probably related to expensive pixel processing. Vertex processing can be isolated by forcing rendering into a one-by-one pixel scissor region (the Force 1×1 Scissor Region override); if the frame rate remains constant (and it has already been determined that rendering is causing poor performance and pixel processing is not the bottleneck), then expensive vertex shaders may be dominating performance.

Other units in the graphics pipeline can be tested in a similar way. Forcing small (2×2 texel) textures can test for texture bandwidth issues. Disabling texture filtering can determine whether expensive texture filters are the cause of slow performance. Turning off alpha blending and depth testing can isolate problems in those pipeline stages as well. There is also a state override for forcing wireframe rendering, which can be very useful for determining the density of meshes being rendered and visualizing occluded objects that have been rendered unnecessarily.

API state overrides are indicated with vertical lines through the plots to show the frame where the override occurred.

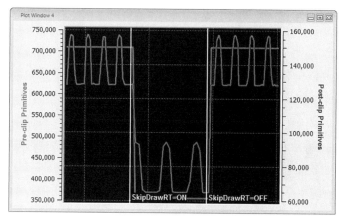

FIGURE 9.2.4 GPU PerfStudio Plot window.

The Analyzer window in GPU PerfStudio performs a series of experiments with state overrides and prints color-coded results: darker, red colored cells indicate areas that require attention (see Figure 9.2.5). This can be used as a first pass over the entire graphics pipeline before beginning directed experiments with other PerfStudio data.

	Experiment	Results	Comments
1	No override	Framerate = 4.39	
2	Force 2x2 Textures RT	Framerate = 32.1 (631%)	Texture bandwidth (large textures) affecting performance (RT)
3	Force 2x2 Textures	Framerate = 4.51 (2%)	No problems have been found
4	Disable Texture Filters RT	Framerate = 4.68 (6%)	No problems have been found
5	Disable Texture Filters	Framerate = 4.37 (-1%)	No problems have been found
6	Disable Alpha Blending RT	Framerate = 4.43 (0%)	No problems have been found
7	Disable Alpha Blending	Framerate = 4.42 (0%)	No problems have been found
8	Disable Z Test RT	Framerate = 4.22 (-4%)	No problems have been found
9	Disable Z Test	Framerate = 4.37 (-1%)	No problems have been found
10	Force Simple Pixel Shaders RT	Framerate = 29.46 (571%)	There are expensive pixel shaders (RT)
11	Force Simple Pixel Shaders	Framerate = 4.46 (1%)	No problems have been found
12	Force Skip Draw	Framerate = 36.78 (737%)	No problems have been found

FIGURE 9.2.5 GPU PerfStudio Analyzer window.

As shown in Figure 9.2.6, the API Statistics window shows all the Direct3D entry points called during a frame. Sorting the table on the numbers of calls made is very useful for discovering inefficient usage of the graphics API. For example, if camera motion causes the number of draw calls to jump dramatically with no visual change in the scene, then drawing completely obscured objects could be a performance concern. Sorting in this way can also reveal unnecessary calls made during the frame.

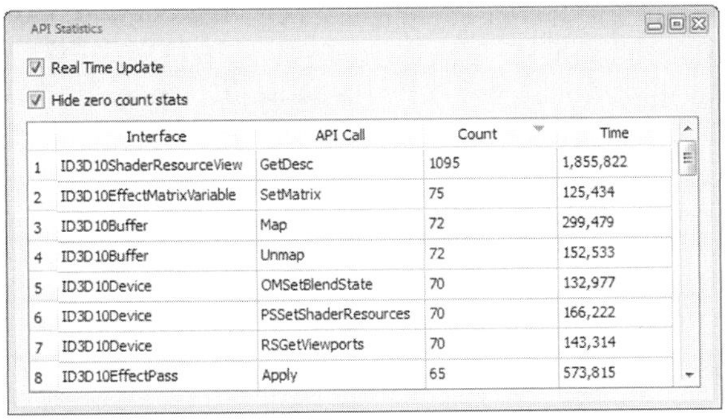

FIGURE 9.2.6 GPU PerfStudio API Statistics window.

The Hardware Counter window shows counters that are derived from low-level hardware counters. They are very useful for identifying performance problems in specific blocks of the graphics pipeline. For example, a Texture Cache Miss Rate greater than 1.0 bytes per pixel might indicate that non-MIPmapped or uncompressed textures are in use; whenever possible, textures should be MIPmapped and compressed for optimal performance. A low TopZ Reject Rate (value close to zero) shows an inefficient use of early Z rejects, which can be caused by rendering back to front; rendering in this order can negatively affect performance on most graphics architectures because pixels rejected later in the pipeline will be shaded even if they are not visible.

Table 9.2.1 HD 2000 hardware counters

Counter Name	Description
% Hardware Utilization	Percent time GPU is busy
% Vertex Wait for Pixel	Percent time vertex processing is waiting for pixel processing to finish (can indicate slow pixel processing)
% Pixel Wait for Vertex	Percent time pixel processing is waiting for vertex processing to finish
Pre-clip Primitives	Primitive count before clipping
Post-clip Primitives	Primitive count after clipping
ALU to Texture Instruction Ratio	Ratio between pixel shader ALU and texture instructions
Overdraw	Total number of pixels drawn divided by the Overdraw counter resolution. This counter can also be representative of the number of render-targets in use.
Texture Cache Miss Rate	Texture cache miss rate in bytes per pixel
PS ALU Instructions Executed	Pixel shader arithmetic instructions executed
PS TEX Instructions Executed	Pixel shader texture instructions executed
VS ALU Instructions Executed	Vertex shader arithmetic instructions executed
VS TEX Instructions Executed	Vertex shader texture instructions executed

Table 9.2.1 HD 2000 hardware counters (continued)

Counter Name	Description
PS Pixel Count	Pixels received for shading after all Z tests and rasterization have taken place.
Post HiZ Sample Count	Number of samples after HyperZ
Post TopZ Pixel Count	Pixels after early Z culling has taken place
Post Shader Pixel Count	Pixels after shading and alpha test have taken place
TopZ Reject Rate	Rate of pixel rejection due to early Z test

The Driver Data window displays additional data that can reveal problem areas in graphics applications. Besides frame rate, there are numerous memory counters that show the memory pools in which various resources are allocated; these data show whether the target application is using local video memory or system memory. The PrimsPer...Change counters are indicative of batch size; if the number of primitives rendered per resource or state change is relatively low, one should look at optimizing batching and state management.

Table 9.2.2 Direct3D 10 driver data counters

Counter Name	Description
Framerate	Frames per second
FrameTime	Frame time in nanoseconds
GeometryBufferAllocatedDefault GeometryBufferAllocatedImmutable GeometryBufferAllocatedDynamic GeometryBufferAllocatedStaging GeometryBufferAllocated	Allocated memory for vertex and index buffers and stream output
GeometryBufferUsedPercentage	Percentage of allocated geometry buffer memory used
ConstantBufferAllocatedDefault ConstantBufferAllocatedImmutable ConstantBufferAllocatedDynamic ConstantBufferAllocatedStaging ConstantBufferAllocated	Allocated memory for constant buffers
ConstantBufferUsedPercentage	Percentage of allocated constant buffer memory used
RenderTargetAllocatedDefault RenderTargetAllocatedImmutable RenderTargetAllocatedDynamic RenderTargetAllocatedStaging RenderTargetAllocated	Allocated memory for render-targets
RenderTargetUsedPercentage	Percentage of allocated render-target memory used

Table 9.2.2 Direct3D 10 driver data counters (continued)

Counter Name	Description
TextureDepthStencilShaderAllocatedDefault TextureDepthStencilShaderAllocatedImmutable TextureDepthStencilShaderAllocatedDynamic TextureDepthStencilShaderAllocatedStaging TextureDepthStencilShaderAllocated	Allocated memory for ShaderResources, DepthStencil buffers, and Textures
TextureDepthStencilShaderUsedPercentage	Percentage of allocated TextureDepthStencilShader memory used
PrimsPerRenderStateChange	Primitives rendered per render state change
PrimsPerDepthStencilStateChange	Primitives rendered per depth stencil state change
PrimsPerBlendStateChange	Primitives rendered per blend state change
PrimsPerPixelShaderChange	Primitives rendered per pixel shader change
PrimsPerVertexShaderChange	Primitives rendered per vertex shader change
PrimsPerGeometryShaderChange	Primitives rendered per geometry shader change
PrimsPerPSSamplerStateChange	Primitives rendered per pixel shader sampler state change
PrimsPerVSSamplerStateChange	Primitives rendered per vertex shader sampler state change
PrimsPerGSSamplerStateChange	Primitives rendered per geometry shader sampler state change

The Hardware Counters, Driver Data, and API Statistics windows display real-time data that can be shown either textually (with sorting) or visualized with scrolling plots and bar charts. These data reveal how efficiently the application utilizes the graphics API and the internal mechanisms of the driver and graphics hardware.

If analysis using GPU PerfStudio has demonstrated that the bottleneck is related to expensive shaders, then using a tool like GPU ShaderAnalyzer is a valuable next step in performance optimization.

Understanding How GPUs Process Shaders

In order to optimize shaders to run efficiently on the GPU, it is necessary to understand a little about how modern GPUs process shaders. Modern GPU shader cores can process multiple instructions on 16 or more pixels, vertices, or primitives during each clock cycle. With the recent introduction of unified shader architectures from AMD and NVIDIA, the GPU may be processing pixels, vertices, and primitives simultaneously using a common set of processing resources. Although this means that it is impossible to fully consider the performance of a shader in isolation, it is still common for performance to be limited by one stage of the logical pipeline.

On the Radeon HD 2000 series GPUs, ALU, Fetch (Texture or Vertex), and Flow Control instructions are executed on separate units in parallel. The hardware compiled shader is made of flow-control instructions that execute ALU clauses and Fetch clauses. The SIMD arrays that process ALU instructions execute VLIW (Very

Long Instruction Word) instructions issuing operations to five scalar units per cycle per pixel, four of which can execute simple ops (MAD, ADD, etc.) and one unit that can also execute more complex ops (SIN, COS, etc.). Multiple SIMDs may be operating in parallel, the number of which varies depending on the specific GPU (for instance, four parallel SIMDs per pipe on Radeon HD 2900 as shown in Figure 9.2.7). GPUs with N parallel SIMDs can be considered as processing N times as many pixels per clock.

A key to making efficient use of the shader core is achieving high utilization of these scalar processors, and the responsibility for this lies not with the developer, but with AMD's Shader Compiler. At the same time, the developer has a large part to play in the development of efficient source shaders that minimize data dependencies and avoid unnecessary calculations.

Any shader instruction has some degree of latency in its execution, ranging from low (an ALU add), to medium (a texture fetch from the cache), to high (a texture fetch from video or system memory). In order to hide this latency, GPUs keep hundreds or even thousands of pixels (or vertices, or primitives) in flight at once by

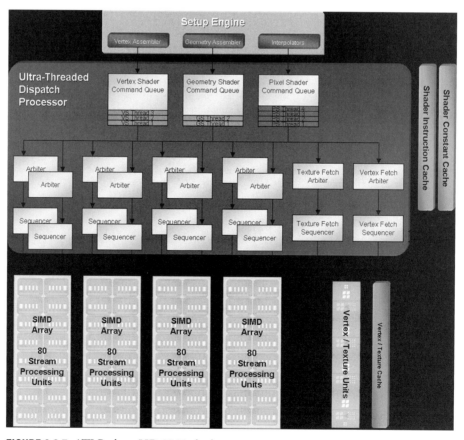

FIGURE 9.2.7 ATI Radeon HD 2900 shader core.

switching between multiple threads, each processing one or more quads (blocks of 2×2 pixels). Threads that are waiting for results to return from a texture unit or shader execution unit are suspended and execution is switched to the next available thread that is ready. Each thread will be allocated a block of general purpose registers (GPRs) for its use.

Threads are also important to consider when talking about shaders with dynamic flow control. All pixels within a thread are executed in a lock step. If they all take the same side of a branch, then only that side is executed. However, when they diverge, both sides must be executed and the necessary pixels masked out on each side of the branch. From this it should be immediately evident that the number of pixels per thread can have a major effect on the performance of shaders with dynamic flow control. On Radeon HD 2000 series GPUs, this depends on the number of parallel quad pipes, as shown in Table 9.2.3.

Table 9.2.3 GPU thread sizes

GPU	Pipes	Thread Size (in Pixels)
Radeon HD 2900	4	64
Radeon HD 2600	2	32
Radeon HD 2400	1	16

Shader performance can be limited by a range of factors. In most cases a shader's performance will be limited by only one factor on a given GPU, but in some cases multiple factors can be in play. The predominant factors that can bottleneck shaders are the following:

- Number of ALU instructions.
- Number of texture fetches (or vertex fetches, etc.).
- Number of shader outputs (i.e., number of outputs from a vertex shader or the number of MRTs output to a pixel shader).
- Number of input interpolants (i.e., the number of inputs to a pixel shader).
- Number of control flow instructions.
- Number of GPRs used. As each thread requires GPRs allocated for its lifetime, the number of concurrent threads can be limited by the number of GPRs available. In this case the GPU's ability to hide latency by switching to ready threads can be hindered.
- Flow control coherence. As discussed earlier, if a shader suffers from poor flow control coherence, it will spend more time executing multiple flow control paths.

Aside from these factors, shader performance can be limited by a large number of other factors such as texture bandwidth and cache coherence. These factors are outside the range of purely shader optimization and aren't covered in this discussion.

GPU ShaderAnalyzer

GPU ShaderAnalyzer (GSA, pronounced Gee-Zah) is a tool from AMD for analyzing the performance of shaders on AMD GPUs. Other more limited tools such as NVShaderPerf exist for analyzing shader performance on other architectures.

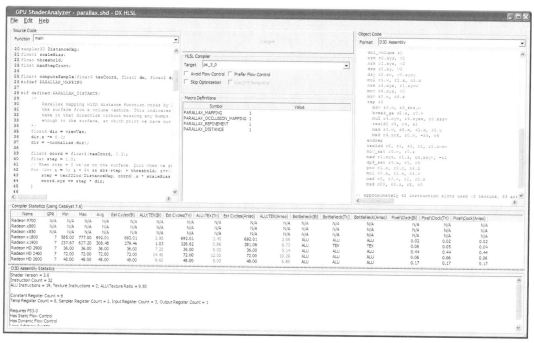

FIGURE 9.2.8 Screenshot of GPU ShaderAnalyzer.

GPU ShaderAnalyzer provides a full-featured shader editing environment with support for context coloring. In addition to providing disassembly of source shaders at the API assembly level (e.g., Direct3D PS3.0), GSA provides disassembly of the compiled shader hardware micro-code. This allows you to check the actual low-level shader the GPU will execute.

By performing static analysis on both the source shader and the resulting compiled shader hardware micro-code, GSA is able to build an accurate picture of the execution characteristics of a given shader. From this, GSA is able to generate a range of statistics such as estimated cycles counts, throughputs, and probable shader bottlenecks. The full list of metrics available is listed in Table 9.2.4. Choosing which columns to display is fully configurable.

GSA takes flow control instructions within the shader into account, including the effect of flow control coherence on each GPU. When it encounters a branch instruction, it estimates the performance cost of each side of the branch and also the likelihood of having to execute both sides of the branch.

GSA also supports command line use for batching the analysis of multiple shaders and integration into your tool chain. By the time of publication for this book, an API offering direct access to GSA functionality should also be available.

Table 9.2.4 Statistics available from GPU ShaderAnalyzer

Heading	Name	Description
ALU TEX VTX Interp CF EXP	ALU Instructions Texture Instructions Vertex Instructions Interpolator Instructions Control Flow Instructions Export Instructions	The number of each type of instructions in the shader.
TexDependency	Texture Dependency Levels	The maximum number of texture dependency levels.
GPR	General Purpose Registers	The number of general purpose registers used or allocated. This can affect shader performance.
Min Max Avg	Min Cycles Max Cycles Avg Cycles	The minimum/maximum/average number of cycles the shader is expected to take.
Est Cycles	Estimated Cycles	The estimated number of cycles the shader is expected to take. Separate figures are available for point, bilinear, trilinear, and anisotropic filtering.
ALU:TEX	ALU:TEX Ratio	The expected ALU:Texture instruction ratio. Separate figures are available for point, bilinear, trilinear, and anisotropic filtering.
BottleNeck	BottleNeck	The likely bottleneck to shader performance. Separate figures are available for point, bilinear, trilinear, and anisotropic filtering.
Throughput	Avg Peak Throughput	The estimated average peak throughput. This does not take into account the cost of other shaders on unified shader architectures and as such will only be achievable when the other shaders (i.e. VS and GS when analyzing PS) pose minimal cost. Available for point, bilinear, trilinear, and anisotropic filtering.
Pix/Clock	Avg Throughput Per Clock	The estimated average peak per clock throughput. This does not take into account the cost of other shaders on unified shader architectures and as such will only be achievable when the other shaders (i.e. VS and GS when analyzing PS) pose minimal cost. Available for point, bilinear, trilinear, and anisotropic filtering.

Using GPU ShaderAnalyzer

The basic model for using GSA is fairly simple. Enter a shader in the Source Code window (either by loading a shader, by dragging and dropping one from Explorer, or by typing) and GSA will automatically analyze the shader. If analyzing an HLSL shader, you may need to enter the target function in the Function box and select the desired target profile in the Target control.

The Compiler Statistics window will display the hardware performance analysis. You can select which statistics are displayed by right-clicking on the window and selecting Select Columns…, which will display the Options dialog box. You can also select which GPU's performance is analyzed on the Compile Statistics tab of this dialog box.

The D3D Statistics window displays Direct3D assembly instruction statistics. When analyzing an OpenGL shader, this window is blank.

The Object Code window shows either Direct3D Assembly or HW Assembly. You can select what is displayed with the Format control. The list of HW formats available is determined by the GPUs enabled on the Compile Statistics tab of the Options dialog box.

Also in the Options dialog box, the Flow Control parameters allow the user to adjust the properties of flow control that they expect their shader to exhibit. These parameters have a significant effect on the performance of shaders with dynamic flow control but are not possible to discern from just the shader. If you know the branch coherence you expect from your shader you can enter it here, otherwise the default setting provides good results for most cases.

DX10 Shader Optimization with GPU ShaderAnalyzer

Understanding Radeon HD2000 Family Shader Cores

The Radeon HD2000 family of chips is built on a new unified architecture model and features completely redesigned execution units. This new architecture has different performance characteristics from earlier AMD GPUs, thus resulting in different optimization strategies. It is imperative to understand the nuances of a new architecture to realize its full potential.

As briefly discussed earlier, to be highly efficient, the GPU shader core is designed using SIMD architecture, where multiple elements (pixels, vertices, and so on) are processed in parallel. A group of such elements is called a *thread* and all elements of a thread always execute instructions in a lock-step. To further improve efficiency, many threads share execution and texturing units in a round-robin fashion. When a thread, for example, becomes blocked by a texture operation, the shader core will find another thread that can execute arithmetic instructions, thus hiding the latency of texture fetches. This way texture and arithmetic instructions can execute in parallel and the majority of texture accesses might appear to take a small number of GPU cycles.

The unified shader architecture implies that a single shader core is used to execute various types of shaders: vertex, geometry, and pixel shaders. All computational, texturing, and other resources can be shared between various types of shaders. Actually, multiple types of threads might be alive and could share computational resources at any given time. This fact changes how shader workload should be measured and balanced: One has to consider overall average ALU, texturing, and other work across vertex, geometry, and pixel shaders active at any given time. On earlier non-unified architectures, some additional vertex shading power could essentially be free if pixel shading were a bottleneck. This is not the case for unified architectures. In theory, vertex or geometry shaders can "steal" shader resources from pixel shaders, so one has to be careful not to overburden the GPU with unnecessary geometry processing. In practice, this is rarely a problem unless very detailed geometry is used with simple pixel shaders. On the other hand, if a pixel shader is texture fetch bound, the ALU unit could be used to run ALU-intensive vertex or geometry shaders and they could become practically free. Since the frequency of vertex shader execution is generally lower than that of pixel shaders, the recommendation to move, if possible, some of the computations from pixel shader to vertex shader still holds. Also, if some part of a shader can be evaluated to a constant, it would be beneficial to compute it only once on the CPU.

On the unified architecture, the same shader core is used across vertex, geometry, and pixel shaders, and more or less the same performance characteristics can be expected in all types of shaders. The recommendations discussed in the following sections apply to all shader types, unless otherwise noted.

ALU Optimizations

The ALU part of the Radeon HD2000 shader core is implemented as a five-way superscalar execution unit. This means each instruction issue for each pixel can execute up to five independent scalar operations per clock. This independent instruction scheduling is a lot more flexible than in earlier architectures and provides a lot more opportunities for co-issuing multiple instructions. While all five scalar units can execute simple instructions like MUL, ADD, MAD, and so on, the fifth unit is special because it can also execute more exotic instructions such as transcendental functions. Table 9.2.5 shows what units are capable of executing some of the most commonly used instructions.

Because transcendental scalar instructions cannot be issued in parallel, if the other four scalar units cannot be populated with instructions, the excessive use of transcendental instructions might result in lower overall computational efficiency. Some of the integer instructions such as multiplication and shifts can only run on the transcendental unit, while their floating-point counterparts can be executed by any of the scalar units. Also, integer division is particularly expensive and can take quite a few cycles, especially if it needs to operate on vectors. Consider converting some of the integer math to floating-point computations if it will improve shader efficiency.

Table 9.2.5 ALU instructions

Instruction	Four Regular Units	Transcendental Unit
Floating-point operations		
ADD	X	X
COS		X
DP3	X	
DP4	X	
FRC	X	X
LOG		X
MAD	X	X
MAX	X	X
MIN	X	X
MOV	X	X
MUL	X	X
RCP		X
ROUND	X	X
SIN		X
Comparison (EQ, GE, etc.)	X	X
Integer operations		
IADD	X	X
IAND	X	X
IMAX	X	X
IMIN	X	X
IMOV		
IMUL		X
INOT	X	X
IOR	X	X
IRCP		X
ISHL		X
ISHR		X
ISUB	X	X
IXOR	X	X
Comparison (IEQ, IGE, etc.)	X	X
Type conversion operations		
ITOF		X
FTOI		X

While you might want to use floating-point computations in place of integer math, you should avoid needless floating-point to integer conversion and vice versa. These types of conversion operations can only be run on the transcendental unit, and frequent type conversion might not improve overall shader efficiency. Also, it is too easy to mistakenly mix different types and cause the compiler to generate unnecessary type conversion instructions. For example, the following simple statement:

```
int4 a = b + 1;
```

will compile, as expected, to one instruction:

```
0   x: ADD_INT  R0.x,  R0.x,  1
    y: ADD_INT  R0.y,  R0.y,  1
    z: ADD_INT  R0.z,  R0.z,  1
    w: ADD_INT  R0.w,  R0.w,  1
```

By accidentally switching the constant to floating point (for example 1.0f instead of 1) we would get much less optimal code:

```
0   t: INT_TO_FLT  R122.w,  R0.x
1   w: ADD  R127.w,  PS(0).x,  1.0f
    t: INT_TO_FLT  R122.z,  R0.y
2   z: ADD  R127.z,  PS(1).x,  1.0f
    t: INT_TO_FLT  R122.y,  R0.z
3   y: ADD  R127.y,  PS(2).x,  1.0f
    t: INT_TO_FLT  R122.x,  R0.w
4   x: ADD  R127.x,  PS(3).x,  1.0f
    t: FLT_TO_INT  R0.x,  R127.w
5   t: FLT_TO_INT  R0.y,  R127.z
6   t: FLT_TO_INT  R0.z,  R127.y
7   t: FLT_TO_INT  R0.w,  R127.x
```

In many cases, the in-driver shader compiler can very efficiently co-issue scalar instructions; however, a shader developer can assist the compiler in recognizing these opportunities by writing code that exploits the parallel nature of certain computations. For example, let's take a look at the following sequential scalar computation:

```
float a = b + c + d + e;
```

If there are no other available instructions to be co-issued with, this portion of the code will be executed sequentially as illustrated by the following hardware microcode:

```
0   z: ADD  R123.z,  R0.x,  R0.y
1   y: ADD  R123.y,  R0.z,  PV(0).z
2   x: ADD  R0.x,  R0.w,  PV(1).y
```

It can be rewritten to explicitly parallelize additions using the dot product instruction:

```
float a = dot(float4(b, c, d, e), 1.0);
```

Instead of three partially populated instructions, this computation can be executed in just one instruction slot.

```
0   x: DOT4_IEEE  R0.x,  R0.x,  1.0f
    y: DOT4_IEEE  ____,  R0.y,  1.0f
    z: DOT4_IEEE  ____,  R0.z,  1.0f
    w: DOT4_IEEE  ____,  R0.w,  1.0f
```

Using parentheses to explicitly group some of the computations can be a hint to a shader compiler how it should schedule instructions, and in some cases it can help improve overall shader efficiency. GPU ShaderAnalyzer can provide invaluable information about instruction co-issue by displaying an actual hardware micro-code and can help in "hunting" for various shader optimization opportunities.

Texturing Optimizations

Each texture pipe in the AMD Radeon HD2000 family of chips is capable of performing a bilinear texture lookup in a single cycle for a variety of formats, as long as the fetches are coherent and the latency of texture fetches can be hidden. Some of the larger formats, such as RGBA32F and RGBA16, will take two cycles for a bilinear fetch. The exception to this rule is RGBA16F format, which can be fetched in just one cycle. Because the RGBA16F format performs faster than the integer RGBA16 format, consider using 16-bit floating-point textures for your HDR render-targets and in other places where you could use 16-bit integer formats.

More complicated filtering modes will take more cycles to execute a texture fetch, and trilinear filtering will increase fetch time by up to two times. Anisotropic filtering can further escalate texturing costs. On average, trilinear filtering will most likely cost an additional 20%, and anisotropic filtering will cost 40% more than bilinear filtering. These are the cost metrics that are used by the GPU ShaderAnalyzer for cost and bottleneck analysis; Figure 9.2.9 shows how it allows you to precisely pinpoint when texturing becomes a bottleneck for different filtering modes. Keep in mind that GPU ShaderAnalyzer does not take into account the additional filtering cost of larger formats and it has to be factored in manually in your analysis.

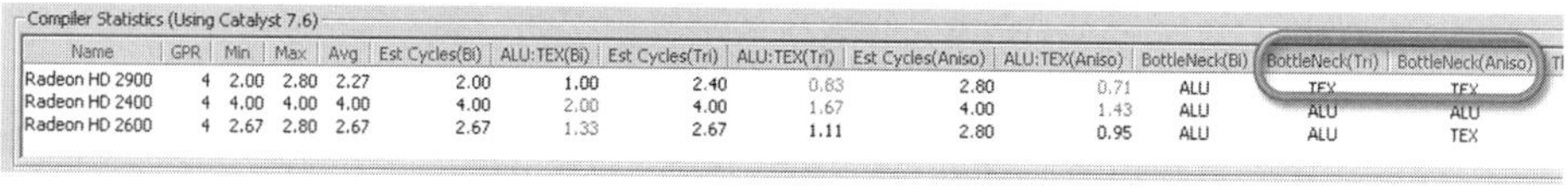

Name	GPR	Min	Max	Avg	Est Cycles(Bi)	ALU:TEX(Bi)	Est Cycles(Tri)	ALU:TEX(Tri)	Est Cycles(Aniso)	ALU:TEX(Aniso)	BottleNeck(Bi)	BottleNeck(Tri)	BottleNeck(Aniso)
Radeon HD 2900	4	2.00	2.80	2.27	2.00	1.00	2.40	0.83	2.80	0.71	ALU	TEX	TEX
Radeon HD 2400	4	4.00	4.00	4.00	4.00	2.00	4.00	1.67	4.00	1.43	ALU	ALU	ALU
Radeon HD 2600	4	2.67	2.80	2.67	2.67	1.33	2.67	1.11	2.80	0.95	ALU	ALU	TEX

FIGURE 9.2.9 Texturing becomes a bottleneck at trilinear filtering.

There are few more subtleties worth noting here. All members of the HD2000 family support PCF filtering on true depth formats, and they should be used for rendering shadow maps instead of using depth stored in high-precision color buffers. Another new format available in Direct3D 10 is RGB32F, which, according to the specification, has optional filtering. The Radeon HD2000 family doesn't support filtering on this format, though, so other formats—like RGBA32F or RGBA16F—should be used instead of trying to simulate filtering in the shader.

To cater to the increasing complexity of shaders, the latest GPUs are equipped with more ALU than texturing power. The number of practically usable texture units is often limited by memory bandwidth, while ALU units experience no such constraints. The high-end member of the HD2000 family, Radeon HD2900, continues the trend of pushing ALU to texture ratios even further than ever before. With 64

ALU units and 16 texture units, it features a 4:1 ALU to texture instruction ratio. This means that, factoring in various shader optimizations and the additional cost of high-quality filtering, shader developers should be aiming at around 8:1 instruction ratios to have perfectly balanced shaders.

Other members of the HD2000 family have different ratios: the Radeon HD2600, the mid-range part, has a 3:1 instruction ratio; and the low-end Radeon HD2400 has a 2:1 ALU to texture ratio. The lower ratios on mid-range and low-end parts make a lot of sense, since these GPUs might not be able to execute extremely large, complex shaders at a desired level of performance, and most likely, for these cards, developers will fall back to simpler effects used for previous generation hardware. Having instruction ratios closer to previous generations of hardware eliminates the need to develop special fallbacks for these new cards. GPU ShaderAnalyzer can independently analyze and display bottlenecks for each member of the HD2000 family. The effects with all their fallbacks can be precisely tuned with GSA to a specific hardware target.

Another interesting peculiarity of the HD2000 shader core is that some of the texture unit functionality is shifted to ALU instructions. For example, texture projection costs two extra ALU cycles and a cubemap fetch adds three ALU cycles. Also, gradient computation and TEXKILL type instructions count against ALU instructions. Given larger than ever ALU to texture ratios, this kind of implementation makes perfect sense.

Other Performance Factors

Besides ALU and texture instruction counts, there are numerous factors that play an important role in shader performance. One of these factors is the number of registers or GPRs (general purpose registers) used in the shaders. There is limited register storage on a chip, and increased register counts will limit the number of shader threads that can be concurrently processed by the shader core. Fewer threads limit the shader unit's ability to hide texture fetch latency and could result in degraded performance in texture heavy shaders. GPU ShaderAnalyzer reports the number of used GPRs and this value should be considered when tuning shaders.

Flow control in particular can affect GPR counts and in some cases can increase or decrease register pressure. Adding an actual if instruction using a [branch] directive can increase GPR count as you can see in the following example. This fragment

```
[flatten] if (b.x > 1.0)
        a = b * sin(b);
else
        a = c * sin(c);
```

might compile to code that uses three GPRs, while

```
[branch] if (b.x > 1.0)
        a = b * sin(b);
else
        a = c * sin(c);
```

could use four GPRs. In more complex cases, the difference could be a lot more dramatic.

In Direct3D 10 shaders, one can use indexed temporaries or registers. While using indexing into arrays can be useful in some algorithms, one has to be aware of the potential performance implications of using indexed GPRs. Optimizing array access is a non-trivial task for a compiler, and in addition, some larger arrays might not fit in the on-chip GPR storage. In that case, indexed temporaries would have to be written to and read from an off-chip memory array, which will significantly affect performance. You can easily detect this situation in GPU ShaderAnalyzer by examining hardware shader micro-code. The following is a source shader and compilation result that illustrates the use of off-chip memory store:

```
float4 main(float4 b: blah0) : SV_target
{
        float4 a[4];
        a[0] = 1;
        for (int i = 1; i < 3; i++)
        {
                a[i] += a[i - 1] * b;
        }
        return a[i];
}
```

Notice the MEM_SCRATCH_READ_IND and MEM_SCRATCH_WRITE_IND instructions that read from and write to the off-chip scratch GPR area:

```
00 ALU: ADDR(32) CNT(6)
      0  x: MOV  R1.x,  (0x3F800000, 1.0f).x
         y: MOV  R1.y,  (0x3F800000, 1.0f).x
         z: MOV  R1.z,  (0x3F800000, 1.0f).x
         w: MOV  R1.w,  (0x3F800000, 1.0f).x
         t: MOV  R3.x,  (0x00000001, 1.401298464e-45f).y
01 MEM_SCRATCH_WRITE: VEC_PTR[0], R1  . . .
02 LOOP_DX10, FAIL_JUMP_ADDR(11) VALID_PIX
   03 ALU_BREAK: ADDR(38) CNT(3)
         1  y: SETGE_INT  R1.y,  R3.x, (0x3, 4.20389e-45f).x
         2  x: PRED_SETE_INT  ____,  R1.y,  0.0f      UPDATE_EXEC_MASK
UPDATE_PRED
   04 MEM_SCRATCH_READ_IND: R2, VEC_PTR[0+R3.x]  . . .
   05 ALU: ADDR(41) CNT(2)
         3  x: ADD_INT  R1.x,  R3.x,  -1
            t: ADD_INT  R4.x,  R3.x,   1
   06 MEM_SCRATCH_READ_IND: R1, VEC_PTR[0+R1.x]  . . .
   07 ALU: ADDR(43) CNT(4)
         4  x: MULADD_IEEE  R1.x,  R1.x,  R0.x,  R2.x
            y: MULADD_IEEE  R1.y,  R1.y,  R0.y,  R2.y
            z: MULADD_IEEE  R1.z,  R1.z,  R0.z,  R2.z
            w: MULADD_IEEE  R1.w,  R1.w,  R0.w,  R2.w
   08 MEM_SCRATCH_WRITE_IND: VEC_PTR[0+R3.x], R1  . . .
   09 ALU: ADDR(47) CNT(1)
         5  x: MOV  R3.x,  R4.x
```

```
10 ENDLOOP i0 PASS_JUMP_ADDR(3)
11 MEM_SCRATCH_READ: R0, VEC_PTR[3]   ARRAY_SIZE(3) ELEM_SIZE(3)
12 EXP_DONE: PIX0, R0
```

In cases where indexed temporaries are accessed inside of loops, it might be possible to let the compiler get rid of the indexing by unrolling the loops using the [unroll] HLSL directive. This would work if array indices are computed from the loop count. By eliminating indexed temporaries, the compiler could potentially reduce GRP counts because not all of the elements of an array might need to be "alive" at any given point in the shader. If HLSL has difficulties automatically unrolling loops, you might want to consider changing your algorithm to simplify it or to unroll it by hand. In our extreme example the array is only used to store the results of the computations from previous loop iterations and it can be eliminated completely.

In addition to GPR counts, flow control can also affect other aspects of shader performance. Since shaders work on threads—groups of elements such as pixels or vertices—it is imperative to keep flow control execution coherent for reasonably large groups of adjacent processing elements. Each member of the HD2000 family has a different thread size, as summarized earlier in Table 9.2.3.

If elements of the same thread take different branches, all paths would have to be evaluated for all thread elements, which could result in suboptimal performance. However, when some reasonable coherence of execution is expected, the flow control could be used as an optimization for skipping unnecessary portions of code. In the following example, flow control is used to optimize out unnecessary portions of lighting calculations.

```
float diffuse = dot(lightVec, normal);
if (diffuse > 0.0)
{
// Compute lighting ...
}
```

Another use of dynamic branching is creating *uber-shaders*: shaders that include many possible variations of code that are selectable with flow control. Since shader switching is a relatively expensive operation and shader permutation management can be cumbersome, uber-shaders provide a solution for decreasing CPU overhead at potentially increased GPU performance cost. If your application is GPU bound, you might want to consider using smaller specialized shaders. Otherwise uber-shaders could become an interesting alternative.

When adding flow control, you should try to avoid creating small branches because they can reduce the shader compiler's ability to co-issue instructions. There is no hard rule stating how small or how big branches have to be. By default, the HLSL compiler and a driver compiler will flatten smaller branches according to some heuristics built into these compilers. It is a good start, but you should always check that you are not missing some optimization opportunities.

Consider all of these factors that affect performance while developing shaders with flow control, and interactively use GPU ShaderAnalyzer to see how flow control affects shader performance in each particular case.

Another important factor to take into account is the use of shader constants. Quite often developers store common values like -1.0 and 0.5 in the shader constants by setting them through the graphics API. This is suboptimal because it prevents the shader compiler from optimizing and simplifying some of the computations; also, it adds unnecessary overhead to the constant transfer. Whenever possible, use literal constants embedded in the shader code instead of the constants stored in constant buffers.

Sometimes data needs to be brought into the shader through indexed constants. Examples of such usage are skinning or indexing into light parameters. It is assumed that there is a fair amount of coherency when accessing these constants. If you need to access data in a truly random order, you might want to consider using textures instead. Also, using indexed constants might not be as "cheap" as using non-indexed constants. The former type of constant access uses a special fetch instruction, while the latter can be, in many cases, accessed as a conventional register. In the case of skinning it is impossible to know what constants will be referenced, so dynamic indexing is unavoidable. However, in cases of looping through the lights and indexing light parameters with a loop index, constant indexing can be avoided by simply unrolling the loop.

There are a few more guidelines for using constants optimally in Direct3D 10. First, and the most important, is to consider grouping constants into constant buffers according to the frequency of update. This will minimize data transfer when updating constant buffers because only full constant buffer updates can be performed. There is another trick that can be used to minimize constant data updates and the overhead associated with it. You can reuse the same constant buffers for a vertex and a pixel shader by loading data for both vertex and pixel shaders and binding the same constant buffer to different shader stages. While it is acceptable to bind the same buffer to the different stages of the pipeline, you should avoid binding the same constant buffer to different resource slots of the same shader stage. Last but not least, try to pack constants within the buffer according to their usage in shaders by relying on a simple rule: together in a calculation, together in a constant buffer.

Vertex Shader Optimizations

Since Radeon HD2000 GPUs run vertex shaders on a large unified shader core, the vertex shader power has dramatically improved over the older, non-unified GPUs. Because of this tremendous compute power you can hardly saturate shader cores in vertex shaders, and getting data into the vertex shader might become a bottleneck. To alleviate this problem, you can employ a vertex texture fetch. Because the texture units in a unified architecture are the same for all shader stages, you can expect the same performance and functionality out of the vertex texture fetch as you would normal texturing in pixel shaders. If a shader is vertex fetch limited, you should split vertex data between vertex streams and vertex textures. In Direct3D 10 you can simply use `SV_VertexID` for computing the texture coordinates needed for the texture fetch of the vertex data. Using compressed texture formats such as BC4 or BC5 can further increase performance by reducing the data footprint and lowering memory bandwidth requirements.

Geometry Shader Optimizations

The geometry shader is a new shader stage in the Direct3D 10 pipeline that fits between vertex and pixel processing and is capable of generating or decimating primitives. Because geometry shaders are capable of fairly large amplification, in many cases Radeon HD 2000 GPUs will need to store off-chip the data transferred between the geometry shader and other stages. Storing this data on-chip would either reduce parallelism or require large amounts of rarely utilized caches, both of which are expensive to solve. While storing the temporary geometry shader inputs and outputs off-chip is relatively expensive, one can still expect very good geometry processing performance that can be further improved with the following optimizations.

Recognizing that the geometry shader output and, to a lesser degree, its inputs can be a bottleneck in a majority of cases is the key to unlocking geometry shader performance. Reducing the geometry shader maximum declared vertex count might seem to be an obvious optimization. However, this is not true! Radeon HD2000 GPUs are not particularly sensitive to the upper bound of amplification set in geometry shaders. What they are sensitive to is the actual amount of data output from the shader.

There are several strategies for reducing the amount of geometry shader I/O. First, don't transfer data that is not needed. Instead of writing just one geometry shader that works with a variety of vertex and pixel shaders of different input or output signatures, you want to make specialized geometry shaders for the tightest fit possible. If some of the data can be derived in the pixel shader instead of being passed down from the geometry shader, this can prove to be a viable optimization. Despite an earlier stated rule that it is better to compute data as early in the pipeline as possible, several additional instructions in the pixel shader most likely will be free if processing is bottlenecked by geometry shader output, and it could result in better overall performance.

To further improve shader input and output efficiency, always use full `float4` vectors for communication into and out of geometry shaders. In the case of multiple `float2` texture coordinates, they can be packed into `float4` vectors two at a time. Consider even more extreme packing by splitting some vectors into scalars and packing them into available slots of other `float4` vectors. The following example shows suboptimal geometry shader output signature:

```
struct GsOutput
{
        float3 pos: SV_Position;
        float2 tex0: tex0;
        float2 tex1: tex1;
};
```

A better packed structure might look like this:

```
struct GsOutput
{
        float3 pos: SV_Position;
        float4 tex0_1: tex;
};
```

Another strategy to minimize geometry shader output is using flow control to skip primitives that would otherwise be discarded. A good example of that type of scenario is using a geometry shader to render to a cubemap. While each triangle can be rendered into as many as five faces of the cubemap, in reality, most of the triangles will be rendered to only one face and some of the triangles can be completely discarded as back-facing. By implementing back-face culling and per-face frustum rejection, the performance of a geometry shader that renders to a cubemap can be improved by up to several times. Here is an example of the optimized render-to-cubemap geometry shader:

```
[maxvertexcount(18)]
void gsCube(triangle GsIn In[3],
inout TriangleStream<PsIn> Stream)
{
PsIn Out;
[unroll] for (int k = 0; k < 6; k++)
{
Out.face = k;
float4 pos[3];
pos[0] = mul(mvpArray[k], In[0].pos);
pos[1] = mul(mvpArray[k], In[1].pos);
pos[2] = mul(mvpArray[k], In[2].pos);
// Use frustum culling to improve performance
float4 t0 = saturate(pos[0].xyxy * float4(-1,-1,1,1)
- pos[0].w);
float4 t1 = saturate(pos[1].xyxy * float4(-1,-1,1,1)
- pos[1].w);
float4 t2 = saturate(pos[2].xyxy * float4(-1,-1,1,1)
- pos[2].w);
float4 t = t0 * t1 * t2;
[branch] if (!any(t))
{
```

```
// Use back-face culling to improve performance
float2 d0 = pos[1].xy*pos[0].w-pos[0].xy*pos[1].w;
float2 d1 = pos[2].xy*pos[0].w-pos[0].xy*pos[2].w;
float w = min(min(pos[0].w, pos[1].w), pos[2].w);
[branch] if (d1.x * d0.y > d0.x * d1.y || w <= 0.0)
{
[unroll] for (int i = 0; i < 3; i++)
{
Out.pos = pos[i];
// Fill output structure here ...
Stream.Append(Out);
}
Stream.RestartStrip();
}
}
}
}
```

While a geometry shader's output is very important to its performance, the input to a geometry shader also should be considered for small amplification ratios or in the case of geometry decimation. Similar optimization strategies can be applied to the geometry shader inputs and its outputs.

Pixel Shader Optimizations

When it comes to shader input and output bottlenecks, pixel shaders are no exception, especially if they are short. Given the high ALU power of mid-range and high-end representatives of the Radeon HD2000 family, it's simple to become interpolator limited, or in the case of multiple render-targets (MRT), output limited. The interpolator limitation is the worst for Radeon HD2600, and GPU ShaderAnalyzer can easily help you in identifying that bottleneck. If interpolators seem to be a bottleneck, try to reduce their count by packing multiple partial vectors together. It might be possible to reduce the number of interpolators at the expense of additional ALU instructions by shifting some of the computations from the vertex or geometry shader to the pixel shader.

When it comes to optimizing rendering with MRTs, you can try to tightly pack data in all render-targets without leaving any color channels unused. In Direct3D 10, rules for MRT rendering are significantly relaxed in comparison to Direct3D 9. It is now possible to bind render-targets to any of eight available output slots and leave "holes" in the sequence of bound render-targets. In pixel shader output bound cases, this can somewhat degrade performance and you should always assign all render-targets sequentially to all slots starting from the very first one. For example, instead of binding three targets to slots #3, #4, and #6, it would be much better to bind them to slots #0, #1, and #2.

Conclusion

Optimizing your shaders to get the performance you need is difficult, but as we have shown in this article, with AMD's GPU ShaderAnalyzer and GPU PerfStudio you have the tools you need for the job. Using the techniques we have discussed here you will be able to get the most out of the new generation of Direct3D 10 GPUs.

9.3

Real-Time Audio Processing on the GPU

Fernando Trebien

Manuel M. Oliveira

Introduction

Modern graphics processing units (GPUs) have experienced impressive growth of their computational power in the last few years. As a result, many researchers have used them as inexpensive parallel processors to solve computationally intensive problems. Uses of GPUs for general purpose computing include the solution of systems of linear equations [Bolz03, Kruger03] and physically based simulations on lattices [Harris03, Harris04a]. Unfortunately, not all kinds of applications map well to GPUs, which require data independence in computation to achieve peak performance [Harris04b].

Digital signal processing (DSP) applications usually present high computational requirements, as they often have to process relatively large datasets in real time. In order to cope with these requirements, modern DSP processors usually include several independent units working in parallel [Eyre00]. Moreover, since filters are implemented as a dot product between the vector containing the input data and the vector containing the filter coefficients, DSP processors include multiply-add (MADD) units [Lapsley97]. These interesting similarities between DSP processors and GPUs seem to suggest that GPUs can be used to efficiently implement some signal processing algorithms. Although some researchers have presented GPU implementations of the fast Fourier transform (FFT) [Ansari03, Moreland03, Spitzer03, Sumanaweera06] and 2D image filtering [Jargstorff04], few real-time demonstrations of audio processing on GPUs have been described. Audio, however, as a data stream is highly suited for processing on the GPU, as long as the algorithms one wants to implement fit a parallel processing model. Indeed, as we will show in this article, many do.

A large number of methods and processes have been developed for generating and transforming sounds [Moore90]. With the development of electronics, many of these methods were realized into equipment that could be connected to each other, bringing the world of music to a whole new universe of possibilities. While those units usually give the users a lot of control, they also suffer from design limitations. Generally, a unit (called a *module*) has a specific purpose: the implementation of a single algorithm or a few related algorithms. Because of this, a single module is not interesting enough to produce professional music. Serious musicians generally have to purchase many different modules to fulfill their needs.

Such limitations can be overcome by software implementations of the various modules, and there is a large number of commercial software packages available that deals with audio and music in many aspects, from generation and editing to playback, encoding, and distribution [AppleItunes, NIReaktor, LAME, NullsoftWinamp, PropellerheadReason, SonySoundforge]. However, many valuable audio processes are highly complex and can only be processed by a CPU prior to playback. As a result, live performers cannot benefit from such processes.

This article presents a method for real-time music generation and multi-channel audio processing on the GPU. Using a series of classic algorithms implemented as fragment programs, we define a system that easily allows building a graphical interface to let the user add and connect modules on an oriented acyclic graph representing the signal processing model. Comparing our results with equivalent CPU implementations of the same tasks, our approach demonstrates the possibility of speedups of up to four orders of magnitude (17,641×) on an NVIDIA GeForce 8800 GTX card, allowing the processing of complex algorithms to be performed in real time. These results represent a new powerful (and also cheaper) alternative to electronic music producers and performers.

In the following section, we cover some related work that involves the processing of audio on the graphics hardware and introduce several audio processing concepts that will be used throughout the text. We then present our model for real-time audio processing on the GPU and discuss current design aspects. At the end of the article, we discuss some of our results and additional implementation possibilities.

Related Work

Whalen [Whalen05] discusses the use of GPU for audio processing and compares the performance of processing audio blocks composed of 105,000 16-bit mono samples on a 3.0 GHz Pentium 4 equipped NVIDIA GeForce FX 5200 AGP video card. Even with such a limited setup, Whalen found up to 4× speedups for some algorithms such as delay, lowpass, and highpass filters. He also found reduced performance for other algorithms, which may be due to overhead caused by the way 2D textures are accessed. However, he did not implement any generation algorithms such as additive synthesis or frequency modulation. Performance was evaluated for individual algorithms in a single pass, which does not consider the impact of having multiple render passes or frequently changing the active shader program. Moreover, in his study, Whalen did not look into real-time audio processing.

In an article by Gallo and Drettakis [Gallo03], the authors present a spatialization method that performs the mixing of multiple sound sources on the GPU in order to reduce the number of voices required from the audio hardware. Sound sources are clustered according to position in 3D space, and each cluster yields a single output consisting of a mix of all sources' signals belonging to that cluster. Each sound event is a three sub-band monoaural signal at 44.1 kHz, and signals are processed in blocks of 1,024 samples. Note that this encoding allows equalization simply by controlling gain applied to each band. The mixing operation also computes Doppler shifting by using linear interpolation for resampling (which is already provided by GPU texture sampling operations). Apparently, gain controls (distance attenuation, panning, and filtering parameters) are calculated on the CPU once per frame. All sound events are loaded in texture memory prior to execution, and each event is stored as a 1D texture. The authors also implemented the same mixing algorithm on the CPU using 32-bit floating-point operations in assembly language. They ran their implementation on a 1.8 GHz Pentium 4 laptop with an ATI Radeon 5700 video card. The implementation consisted of a scene with about 70,000 polygons being rendered concurrently with the audio using the Direct3D API. The graphics card only supported 8-bit mixing due to limitations on the framebuffer and blending operations; thus, mixing on the CPU had far superior quality, but rendering 180 simultaneous sound sources (without graphics) required 38% of the total CPU capacity. The authors do not report any performance metric on the GPU implementation, although they claim an increased frame rate on the test with graphics and a sound source culling technique.

In a short paper by Gallo and Tsingos [Gallo04], the authors present a feasibility study for audio-rendering acceleration on the GPU. They focus on audio rendering for virtual environments, which requires consideration of the propagation of the sound through the medium and sound blocking caused by occluders. In their study, they processed sound at 44.1 KHz using 1,024 samples, with 32-bit floating-point arithmetic. They compared the performance of their algorithm on a 3.0 GHz Pentium 4 equipped with an NVIDIA GeForce FX 5950 video card on an AGP 8× bus. For their target application, the GPU implementation was 20% slower than the CPU implementation.

Jedrzejewski and Marasek [Jedrzejewski04] used a raytracing algorithm to compute an impulse response pattern from one sound source in a highly occluded virtual environment. This approach is related to the processing of reverb effects: the evaluation of an impulse response signature. The algorithm performs some geometric computation but does not process signals.

On a somewhat more distant tangent, several authors have described implementations of the FFT algorithm on GPUs [Ansari03, Moreland03, Spitzer03, Sumanaweera06]. A 1D FFT is sometimes required in more elaborate audio algorithms. We, however, did not progress so far as to apply FFTs in our module implementations yet.

In contrast to the techniques described above, our method solves a different problem: the mapping from a network model of virtually interconnected software modules to the graphics pipeline processing model. Our primary concern is how the data is passed from one module to another using only GPU operations and the management of each module's internal data, thus allowing greater flexibility to program new modules and turning GPUs into music production machines.

Some Audio Processing Concepts

All sounds can be seen as a linear combination of sinusoidal waves. As sinusoids, each component is defined by an energy level (*amplitude*), frequency, and phase. Musical sounds, such as those of musical instruments, generally present one high energy component called the *fundamental* and other components called *harmonics*, each with a lower energy level and a frequency that is an integer multiple of the fundamental component's frequency. However, this is only a tendency, and sometimes the phenomenon does not match this description exactly. A range of frequencies is called a *band*. The level of energy at each frequency in a given signal is called its *spectrum*.

Digital sound consists of a sequence of samples acquired at a given *sampling rate*, which determines the signal's band. The data type used to represent the samples determines the samples' accuracy—that is, the amount of distortion introduced due to rounding errors. Higher sampling rates and wider numeric data types improve digital sound quality, but increase the necessary storage space. For high-quality audio, typical sampling rates are 44.1 kHz, 48 kHz, 96 kHz, and 192 kHz. Typical data types are 16-bit and 32-bit integer and 32-bit and 64-bit floating point. The floating-point format is preferred for processing because it reduces quantization errors when amplitude values are close to zero. Digital sound may also have more than one sound stream, or *channel*, allowing multiple output points, such as those used for surround sound. Typical numbers of channels are one (mono), two (stereo), six, and eight.

Since sounds can be decomposed into *sinusoidal* components, the most straightforward way to generate sound is by computing sample values for each component and adding them to produce a more complex wave signal. This is called *additive synthesis*. Although this is quite powerful, it is also expensive because we need to evaluate a sine function, a multiplication, and a sum many times per sample (and once for each component present).

Instead of generating sinusoids, one can also use other primitive waveforms, such as the *sawtooth*, the *square,* and the *triangular* waves (Figure 9.3.1). These waveforms are the most widely used for synthesis because they require few operations per sample to compute and because they present a rich harmonic spectrum, which is normally interesting because it allows for the modification of their spectrum using filters and other effects processors to produce a wide variety of sounds. We could also compute band-limited versions of those waves, which would require an approach similar to additive synthesis.

There are more elaborate synthesis methods. *Frequency modulation* (FM) is obtained by making the frequency of a sinusoid oscillate quite quickly (at a frequency close to the sinusoid's own frequency), thereby producing a completely new wave shape with a new set of components. *Wavetable synthesis* and sample playback both attempt to produce more complex sounds by sampling a table containing a digital sound signal. *Granular synthesis* works by overlapping a high number of wave segments called granules. Many kinds of noise can be synthesized by generating random values and then filtering them. More complex synthesis methods include *physical*

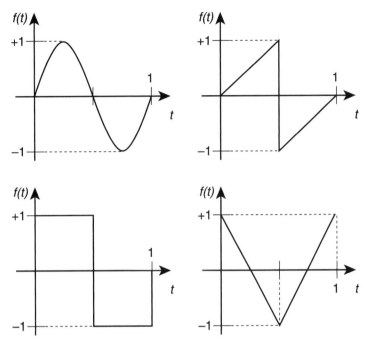

FIGURE 9.3.1 Primitive waveforms: sine wave and sawtooth wave (top); square wave and triangular wave (bottom).

modeling and *resynthesis*. Moore [Moore90] provides a comprehensive discussion of the various synthesis methods.

Digital sound can be transformed in a variety of ways. Many signals can be joined into one by *mixing*, which consists of simply of adding corresponding samples together. *Gain* is the most basic transformation: It scales all samples' values by a certain factor. Similar to gain is *amplitude modulation*, which simply scales each sample by a quickly varying factor, often a sinusoid. One very common amplitude modulation is *envelope shaping*, which is usually comprised of four transition stages: *attack* (wave gains energy when a note starts), *decay* (it loses energy right after), *sustain* (it keeps a nearly stable energy level while playing), and *release* (it gradually loses all energy at the end).

Delay is another effect that is used often. It outputs a mix of the current input and some input received at a fixed offset from the current time; a *feedback delay* can be used to produce an "echo" effect. In this case, instead of the current input, the current output is stored in a delay line, resulting in an endless cycling of the sound of every input block through the delay. The input sound and the delayed sound are mixed with different gains, enabling control over the intensity of echoes over time.

Other important effects are *filtering* (amplifying or reducing energy across the spectrum), *equalizing* (gain applied to specific bands), *reverb* (combining multiple delays and filters to achieve an ambient sensation), *chorus* and *flanging* (using a variable delay to modify the sound), and *compression* and *distortion*.

Audio Processing on the GPU

Audio data is time-sliced into fixed-size blocks. An audio device will periodically request that the application fill one block of audio to be played during a given amount of time. Most professional audio systems adopt the concept of *module*, which is a state machine that, at each request, reads one or more blocks from its inputs and produces an output block.

In order to process audio on the GPU, we use a set of analogies to map audio processing concepts to graphics concepts. An audio sample corresponds to a fragment and its amplitude is stored as a luminance value. An audio processor is implemented as a set of fragment shaders. Finally, an audio buffer is represented by a texture row, and pointers to buffers are handled as texture coordinates. These analogies are summarized in Table 9.3.1.

Table 9.3.1 Mapping audio concepts to graphics concepts

Audio Concept	Graphics Concept
Sample	Fragment
Amplitude	Color (luminance)
Processor	Shader
Computation	Shading
Buffer	Texture row
Buffer pointer	Texture coordinates

On the GPU, audio blocks are stored in texture memory and passed between modules as coordinates. Let N be the number of samples in a block (N is a power of two). Since all blocks have the same size, we can set the width of the textures to N and assign each audio block to a whole texture row. Texture height is set to the maximum the hardware can handle, since texture memory is also used as temporary memory for storing output samples from some modules that are taken as input samples by other modules. We store audio samples as luminance values using 32-bit floating-point format because 16-bit floating-point values are not precise enough to process audio without severe quantization errors. Note that the use of floating-point as a signal format is not mandatory, but as mentioned, it is preferred because it reduces quantization errors. Moreover, we need to allow intermediary results outside the [-1,+1] range, usually used to store texel values. Input and output samples may need to be converted to another data format supported by the sound card.

The architecture of graphics hardware does impose some memory access constraints: textures are either read-only or write-only [Harris04b]. This forces us to use *ping-pong* buffering. In this technique, two textures are used: First, one is read and the other is written; then, in the following pass, the roles are swapped. Multiple passes may be necessary depending on the audio processing model being implemented.

To write to a texture, we use the framebuffer object (FBO) OpenGL extension. We create one FBO and attach four textures to it with the following purposes:

- **Texture 1:** Block passing between modules
- **Texture 2:** Block passing between modules
- **Texture 3:** Temporary block reserve
- **Texture 4:** Internal buffers

After a framebuffer object has been created, bound, and its textures have been created and attached to it, one is ready to begin "rendering" audio. The process starts by checking the note list for the currently playing notes. Notes are included and excluded from the list according to events such as "begin note" (MIDI's "note on") and "end note" (MIDI's "note off"). For simplicity, let's consider the case where we play a single note at a time. In this case, the appropriate shader program is bound, input parameters are set for the current note, and results are rendered to Texture 1. The shader is issued twice for two subsequent rows to create stereo signals, with each row corresponding to an individual channel. In our implementation, we chose to render exactly the same signal for both channels, but one can easily modify this program and render different waves (for example, if you're looking for some kind of stereo effect, such as slightly different offsets for the waves, different waveforms, slightly detuned versions of the same waveform, different modulations for each channel, or panning). After that, the internal state of the notes is updated.

The implementation of the generator module can decide where state information is stored. In our implementation of wavetable synthesis, we apply ADSR envelope shaping to each note, so we store information about attack, decay, and release times; sustain level; stage (attack, decay, sustain, or release); time offset since stage start; current phase offset of the wave; current amplitude; and current *interpolator value*—the amount of interpolation between the wavetable assigned to the current stage and the one assigned to the next. We need to store the wave phase offset because generally we do not have an integer number of cycles per block. Note that storing a phase offset instead of time information is a design choice: we chose it to avoid rough precision errors when time becomes significantly large, as in very long notes. Because the shader is called to render over a range of values and two consecutive blocks share one common point, we store the current amplitude and interpolator value to avoid having to evaluate those values more than once. Later in this article we present a procedure in pseudo code that updates all state information and calls the appropriate shader (see Algorithm 9.3.1 in the last section, "Program and Shader Source Code"). This is done on the CPU since it's done only once per block per note. In our implementation of simpler waveforms, we only store phase offset and amplitude values.

When playing more than one note, each note is rendered to an individual pair of rows. Since the other effects processors we have implemented operate on a single stereo signal, we need to mix the signal of all notes to a single pair of rows. Mixing is done by summing corresponding samples of corresponding channels. This constitutes a reduction by column so that values for the first row of the output pair are the sum of values in even rows from the input texture. The values for the second row are obtained similarly by summing values in odd rows. More generally, to mix signals of *n* channel audio stored on consecutive rows beginning in row *i*, the summation takes rows *i* + *kn*, where *k* is the channel index. This process is illustrated in Figure 9.3.2. We could also perform a parallel reduction operation [Harris04b].

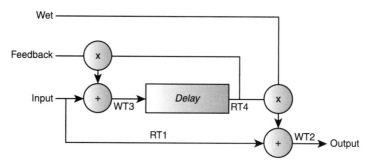

FIGURE 9.3.2 Mixing shader operation.

The results produced in the previous step are used as input for a delay processor. The processing model for a feedback delay is illustrated in Figure 9.3.3. The delay processor takes one input, manages an internal circular buffer on *Texture 4,* and produces as output its input added to a delayed block with reduced gain stored in the circular buffer. A delay processor usually offers the user controllable parameters: a *wet gain* and a *feedback gain.* Wet gain refers to the amount of the delayed signal that is present at output. Feedback gain refers to the amount of delayed signal that is mixed with input when storing this result in the delay line (Figure 9.3.3).

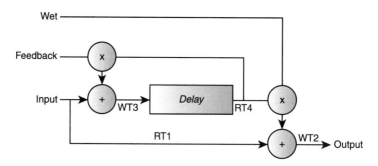

FIGURE 9.3.3 Processing model for a feedback delay.

Let *RTi* be a read-only row of *Texture i* and let *WTj* be a write-only row of *Texture j.* The inputs to the delay processing are *RT1* (the current block) and *RT4* (the delayed block) and its outputs are *WT2* (final audio to be played) and *WT4* (new delay to be stored and used in the future). Since we would have to access *Texture 4* to both read and write, we temporarily store the value intended for *WT4* in *WT3* and then copy it to *WT4*. According to Figure 9.3.3, one has:

$$WT4 = WT3 = RT4 \times feedback\_gain + RT1$$

$$1$$

$$WT2 = RT4 \times wet\_gain + RT1$$

$$2$$

Feedback delay is achieved by calling the *multiply and add (MADD) mixing shader* twice (see Shader 9.3.8 in the section, "Program and Shader Source Code"). The entire process of the delay processor is illustrated in Figures 9.3.3 and 9.3.4. First, the MADD shader is issued to mix the delayed block *RT4* (in the delay line of *Texture 4*) with the input block *RT1* from *Texture 1*, writing the result to *WT3* in *Texture 3* (top row of Figure 9.3.4). When executing it, the delayed block is multiplied by the feedback gain and summed with the input block, as shown in Equation 1. Then, the MADD shader is issued again to produce the sound that will be played and the result is written to *WT2* on *Texture 2* (middle row of Figure 9.3.4). This time, the delayed block is multiplied by the wet gain and added to the input block *RT1* according to Equation 2. This produces the actual output of the delay module. To update the delay line *WT4*, *WT3*—the block produced on *Texture 3*—is copied to *WT4* in *Texture 4* (bottom row of Figure 9.3.4). These operations could be processed in any order, as

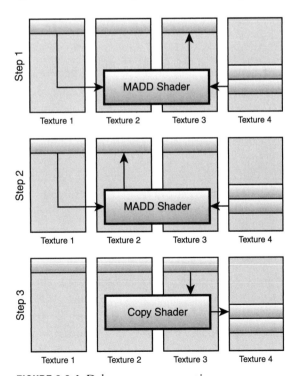

FIGURE 9.3.4 Delay processor operation

long as the copy operation follows the block generation on *Texture 3*. Note that if additional modules were to operate on the output of this module, thus requiring additional rendering passes, the roles of *Textures 1* and *2* would be swapped from pass to pass. Depending on module setup, in some cases, notes could be rendered to *Texture 2* and the delay could generate an output on *Texture 1*.

Whenever a block is requested by the audio device, we must ensure that the block is filled and passed back to the device within the given time. Failing to do so may result in unexpected behavior, such as playing back noise (resulting from receiving a buffer with uninitialized contents), a buzz-like sound (the repetition of a certain block a number of times, since audio drivers normally reuse previously allocated buffers without writing on them), or even an application crash depending on the quality of the device driver's implementation. When no block is ready for output, we fill the output blocks with silent (null) samples. To do so, we create two threads in a producer-consumer system in which the rendering loop produces audio blocks and the requests by the audio device consume them. Those blocks are stored on a circular buffer in the main memory. If the graphics card runs too fast, the render loop will wait until a block has been read by the audio device before the computation of the next block starts. This keeps the two systems synchronized and allows precise identification of the occurrence of glitches (normally a noisy sound or click that occurs when the block requested by the audio device is not available at the time the device requires the block ready for playback), but adds at least one more source of latency because we must have one block ready before playing it.

Results

We implemented the techniques described here using Cg [Mark03], C++, OpenGL, and GLEW running on top of Windows XP SP2. We used the Visual C++ .NET 2005 compiler with the default Release Mode settings. We chose the ASIO interface [ASIO] for audio because it provides low latency (< 10 ms): the Windows WaveOut interface cannot match the application requirements, even with low-latency sound cards.

We tested our program on two systems. The first system (*System 1*) was equipped with an AMD Athlon64 3000+ (1.81 GHz) processor with 1 GB of memory, an ASUS A8N-SLI Deluxe motherboard, a PCI Express NVIDIA GeForce 7600 GT video card with 256 MB of memory, and a Creative Audigy Platinum eX sound card. In this system, we could confirm the low-latency performance of ASIO because low-latency drivers are provided by the sound card manufacturer. This setup allowed us to generate textures with up to 4,096×4,096 texels and to provide audio blocks containing 96 to 2,400 samples. The other system (*System 2*) was equipped with an AMD Athlon64 3500+ (2.21 GHz) processor with 2 GB of memory, an ASUS A8N-SLI Premium motherboard with on-board sound, and a PCI Express NVIDIA GeForce 8800 GTX video card with 768 MB of memory. Because the motherboard manufacturer does not provide an ASIO driver, we used the ASIO4ALL ASIO driver, which translates the ASIO API into WaveOut API calls. This translation is expected to add a small amount of overhead to the benchmarking process, but this is likely to have little significance when comparing speedups since the amount of time allowed for computing a block, either on the CPU or on the GPU, is the same. This setup allowed us to generate textures with up to 8,192×8,192 texels and to provide audio blocks containing 64 to 2,048 samples. Although we used 64-bit processors, both systems were running in 32-bit emulation mode.

We set N to 256 samples and set the ASIO audio device to play at a sampling rate of 48 kHz using two channels. At this rate, 256 samples represent a little more than 5 ms. We used a circular buffer that holds two blocks. Holding the block on the circular buffer causes a total delay of about 11 ms, which is acceptable for real-time output. Additionally, we disabled blending on the video card, which otherwise would have clamped luminance values into the [0.0, 1.0] range.

The program creates one thread that computes audio blocks and stores them on the buffer when there is unused space. Another thread is created by ASIO which periodically invokes a callback function that renders the playback signal: whenever a block is in the buffer, this function copies its contents to the output buffer provided by the ASIO and removes it from the circular buffer; otherwise, the output buffer is filled with null samples. The latter case constitutes an audio glitch.

We have used one FBO and attached four textures to it, as mentioned in the previous section. The computation thread first calls `glFinish()` to make sure all previous commands have been executed, and then it calls `glReadBuffer()` to select the FBO's buffer to which the samples were rendered, followed by `glReadPixels()` to read back the samples from GPU memory into main memory. In our test, we read only the first pair of lines (one line for each sound channel), since normally the multiple generated waves are mixed into a single signal before playback. Although not included in this benchmark, this thread could also upload input samples (taken from a microphone or line input, for example) to the GPU memory. There are several ways to accomplish this. One can use either `glTexSubImage2D()` on NVIDIA cards or `glDrawPixels()` on ATI cards [Göddeke07].

After samples have been transferred to and from the GPU, the computation thread will normally process a list of active note events (an event is created on the list when, for example, the user presses a key on a musical keyboard) and execute the necessary OpenGL and Cg commands to render the waves, as presented in Algorithm 9.3.1. For benchmarking, however, we rendered the basic waveforms many times on subsequent rows of a texture, simulating the activation of many simultaneous notes. We then rewrote the rendering algorithm for the CPU, performing equivalent operations and saving the results on a matrix. For example, Algorithm 9.3.4 presents an implementation of the sine wave shader written for the CPU. One may argue that there are more efficient implementations of a sine wave oscillator, but we note that other methods have drawbacks such as introducing harmonics (by sampling a wavetable) or being inaccurate in respect to phase over time (such as methods using only addition and multiplication). Implementations for other shaders have been done similarly.

We estimated the maximum number of times the rendering programs for the GPU and CPU could be invoked in real-time without causing audio glitches. Our approach was to directly run the program and try to determine this maximum number by detecting the occurrence of glitches. This approach is a more accurate way of previewing how the system works in practice. If we solely measured the time of processing many blocks by the GPU in a sequence, we would not be measuring the actual synchronization overhead between the two threads as well as the overhead of the graphics API and the graphics driver. These numbers were estimated using a partially automatic method and are presented in Table 9.3.2.

In order to obtain these values, we modified the original program to vary the upper iteration limit (defining the number of waves being synthesized) on every block request by the audio device. (Refer to Algorithm 9.3.3 for a pseudo code version of this process.) The approximation is obtained by performing two executions of the program with different parameters for the approximation algorithm on each execution. Let M be the upper iteration limit, initially set to M_0. Let B be the number of blocks computed since the last detected glitch. Whenever a glitch was detected, M was decremented by an amount of d and B was set to zero. In case no glitches were detected, M was incremented by an amount of i only if B exceeded a number of glitch-free block computations B_g. The value of M was logged for every L computed blocks, and for each run, we collected 256 such values for analysis.

In our tests, we defined $B_g = 172$, which corresponds approximately to one second of audio at a sampling rate of 48 kHz and blocks of 256 samples. We empirically chose $L = 86$, which permits the occurrence of a few glitches during the benchmark session, thus allowing us to observe the evolution of M over time and detect almost exactly when every glitch occurred. Note that L should be as large as possible to avoid logging too much information (which adds more overhead), but should be small enough to allow the detection of glitch events. The logged data was stored in an array in main memory. We also defined $d = 32$, which we found to always bring M to a level in which no glitches occurred. An initial rough approximation of the maximum number of waves was obtained with $M_0 = 32$ and $i = 32$. We then analyzed the log files, discarded all values of M registered before the first detected glitch, and picked the greatest value from the remaining ones. Next we ran the same program again with M_0 set to the picked value, but this time with $i = 1$ to obtain a finer approximation. From the resulting log, we picked the lowest value as the approximation of the maximum number of waves without producing glitches. We then fixed the number of iterations to the approximated value and confirmed that no glitches occurred over a considerably long time (10 seconds or longer).

The achieved speedups for the primitive waveforms using the procedure just described varied from 40× to 84× and are summarized in Table 9.3.2. These results are significantly better than those reported by Whalen [Whalen05] and by Gallo and Tsingos [Gallo04] for their applications, indicating that the GPU can in fact be used for real-time audio processing tasks. Note, however, the similar values computed for the GeForce 8800 GTX, even though the computation of the different waveforms is considerably different. This can be explained by the fact that vertex specification by the CPU becomes a bottleneck in this case (the CPU utilization was nearly 100% when audio glitches started to happen).

In order to determine the real GPU potential for audio processing, we performed the following test: Instead of specifying individual lines (two vertices per line) on each texture row, we specified large quads occupying as much as the whole texture's area (8,192×8,192) and, using the same fragment shaders as before, we measured the performance using the aforementioned method. Each quad covered 8,192×8,192 pixels (except for the last one, which was adjusted to render exactly the difference required to achieve M waves). Since now each row stores 8,192 samples instead of only 256, the logged values of M were multiplied by 32. According to our measurements, the numbers of waves that can be computed per block using this alternative approach are as follows: 8,212,480 for triangular waves, 8,220,672 for sine waves, 8,221,696 for sawtooth waves, and 8,220,672 for square waves. These numbers represent a speedup of about 210× with respect to the original values reported on Table 9.3.2 for the GeForce 8800 GTX. Compared with the CPU performance, this corresponds to speedups ranging from 8,433× to 17,641× (see Table 9.3.3).

Table 9.3.2 Comparison between CPU and GPU performances for synthesizing some basic waveforms used for audio rendering

| Waveform | System 1 | | | System 2 | | |
	Athlon64 3000+	GeForce 7600 GT	Speedup	Athlon64 3500+	GeForce 8800 GTX	Speedup
Sawtooth	744	25,014	34×	975	39,076	40×
Triangle	697	24,971	36×	886	39,031	44×
Square	403	18,734	47×	513	39,037	76×
Sine	357	25,009	70×	466	39,015	84×

Note: The columns in Table 9.3.2 show the approximate number of times the waveform can be synthesized per block (about 5 ms) on each device without the occurrence of audio glitches. The speedups were computed with respect to the CPU results.

Table 9.3.3 Performance comparison of System 2 when activating the fragment shaders using OpenGL lines and quads

Waveform	Athlon64 3500+	GeForce 8800 GTX with Lines	GeForce 8800 GTX with Quads	Total Speedup
Sawtooth	975	39,076	8,221,696	8,433×
Triangle	886	39,031	8,212,480	9,269×
Square	513	39,037	8,220,672	16,025×
Sine	466	39,015	8,220,672	17,641×

Note: The line-based implementation is limited by the number of vertices that the CPU can process in real time, while the quad-based implementation stresses the GPU computational power.

The quad-based approach reduces the number of vertices that need to be passed on to the GPU, thus eliminating the bottleneck on the CPU and allowing the full potential of the GPU to be exploited. Some processes, such as additive synthesis, can benefit from the reduced CPU overhead of a quad-based specification. However, attributes can be specified only for the vertices of the quad, not for individual blocks. The processing of more general waveforms would require changes in the design of our current application in order to fully benefit from this strategy.

We have not designed comparison tests for other audio processes such as feedback delay, but we expect that other effects will achieve similar speedups because they are often based on simple shaders and execute entirely on the GPU.

Since we are using GPUs to render audio instead of images, we do not have pretty pictures to show as results. Instead, the ultimate test for the proposed approach is to use it for audio synthesis and processing during live music performances. A video sequence demonstrating the effectiveness of our approach as it is being used to perform five non-trivial pieces can be found at http://www.inf.ufrgs.br/Audio_on_GPU. The pieces include: (i) "Symphony No. 9 in D minor," Op. 125 (Ode to Joy), by Ludwig van Beethoven; (ii) "Brasileirinho," by Waldir Azevedo; (iii) "Axel F" (theme from *Beverly Hills Cop*), by Harold Faltermeyer; (iv) "Jesu Joy of Man's Desiring," by Johann Sebastian Bach; and (v) some live improvisation over the song "Early Days," by Goldrush. All pieces were performed on a regular personal computer keyboard and the audio and video were recorded in miniDV using a camcorder. In the video, we're using a sawtooth generator and an echo effect. Notice that the response to keyboard input is immediate and glitchless.

Conclusions and Future Work

This article presented a method for real-time processing of audio signals on GPUs. It described a way to use GPU resources to implement a modular system in which sound blocks are passed from the output of a module to the input of another. In a direct comparison with implementations of the same functions on the CPU, we observed significant speedups that can potentially reach up to four orders of magnitude on a high-end graphics card, showing that GPUs are suitable for many real-time audio processing tasks. We have demonstrated the effectiveness of our approach by building a functional system and using it to process audio signals in real-time during live music performances.

Our current system can be extended in many ways. The feedback delay must be adjusted to allow a free delay offset (in spite of offsets that lead to row-aligned mixing). Other modules could also be added, such as filters and frequency modulation. Perhaps the most important modules are those that implement additive synthesis, since this synthesis method can fully exploit the inherent parallelism of GPUs through the generation and mixing of a considerable number of individual signals (one for each component). Because we found that specifying signals individually using lines is limited by the processing power of the CPU, we could also rewrite the application to generate the line primitives using geometry shaders, which were recently introduced in the specification of Direct3D 10 as well as OpenGL 1.1 in the form of an extension (`EXT_geometry_shader4`).

Finally, additional audio interfaces should be supported and writing to a file (such as standard wave file) should be added.

Program and Shader Source Code

The *copy shader* (Shader 9.3.1) simply returns the fragment at the specified position. The `Position` parameter is interpolated from the `TexCoord` parameters, which are set when vertices are specified at the beginning of Algorithm 9.3.2. The copy module sets those coordinates to the first and last fragment of a row on the specified texture.

The *sine wave shader* (Shader 9.3.2) renders a sine wave. `Params` encodes two values that are actual parameters to the module, t and a. Parameter t is interpolated from two phase values. In our implementation, when generating a note, those phase values are a function of note frequency and time since the note was started. The value of `sin()` is multiplied by 0.5 to make the resulting signal have the same amplitude as the other primitive waveforms. Choosing an amplitude value of 0.5 simplifies most of the waveform formulas we have chosen. Finally, this value is multiplied by a to allow control of the wave's amplitude. The amplitude parameter is currently fixed at 1.0, but if one processes MIDI events, this value can be set to different values accordingly.

Shaders 9.3.3, 9.3.4, and 9.3.5 synthesize a *sawtooth wave*, a *square wave,* and a *triangular wave*, respectively. Parameters are encoded in the same way as in the case of the sine wave shader. Amplitude also multiplies a formula that computes the waveform. Note that these are the "trivial" algorithms to process these wave shapes. They are the fastest ones, but they suffer from component aliasing. Some alternative methods have been proposed to compute band-limited primitive waveforms [Stilson96].

Shader 9.3.6 computes a crossfading between two wavetables. For each wavetable, two adjacent samples around wavetable offset o are linearly interpolated, yielding a final sample value for each wavetable. Each fragment evaluates to a linear interpolation of these values based on the interpolator value i and scaled by the amplitude value a.

Shader 9.3.7 mixes multiple signals into a single one, per-channel. We use the term "line" to refer to a signal represented in multiple rows. This assumes that all signals to be summed are stored in consecutive rows on the source texture—that is, the channels of each line are consecutive. For N lines of n channels each, fragments on the i-th output row evaluate to the sum of corresponding samples from input rows $i + kn$, with k ranging from 0 to $N - 1$.

Shader 9.3.8 computes a multiply and add between two sound blocks that may come from two different textures, X and Y. Each fragment evaluates $ax + y$, where a is a scaling parameter, x is the sample coming from texture X, and y is the sample coming from texture Y. This way, a defines the gain applied to x. This shader should be used as part of other modules, such as the delay module.

In the MADD shader call in Algorithm 9.3.2, symbols `Row_in_TextureX` and `Row_in_TextureY` define the source rows passed as parameter to the MADD shader (Shader 9.3.8). `Draw_Row` defines the output row on the selected render-target. Finally, in the delay processor call, also shown in Algorithm 9.3.2, remember that roles of *Texture 1* and *Texture 2* may be swapped in further passes.

Shader 9.3.1: Copy shader

```
float Copy(float2 P : TEXCOORD0,
  uniform samplerRECT Texture) : COLOR {
    return texRECT(Texture, P);
```

Shader 9.3.2: Sine wave shader

```
float SineWave(float2 Params : TEXCOORD0) : COLOR {
    float t = Params.x;
    float a = Params.y; // wave amplitude
    return a*(0.5*sin(6.28318530717958*t));
};
```

Shader 9.3.3: Sawtooth wave shader

```
float SawtoothWave(float2 Params : TEXCOORD0) : COLOR {
    float t = Params.x;
    float a = Params.y; // wave amplitude
    return a * (0.5 + floor(t) - t);
};
```

Shader 9.3.4: Square wave shader

```
float SquareWave(float2 Params : TEXCOORD0) : COLOR {
    float t = Params.x;
    float a = Params.y; // wave amplitude
    return a*(floor(t) - 0.5 - floor(t-0.5));
};
```

Shader 9.3.5: Triangular wave shader

```
float TriangularWave(float2 Params : TEXCOORD0) : COLOR {
    float t = Params.x;
    float a = Params.y; // wave amplitude
    return a*(2.0*abs(floor(t)+0.5-t)-0.5);
};
```

Shader 9.3.6: Wavetable shader

```
float Wavetable(float4 Params : TEXCOORD0,
  uniform float2 S,
  uniform samplerRECT Texture1,
  uniform samplerRECT Texture2) : COLOR {
    // Table offsets
    float o1 = Params.x;
    float o2 = Params.y;

    // Interpolators
    float i = Params.z;
    float a = Params.w;

    // Linear sampling
    float s11 = texRECT(Texture1,
      float2(floor(fmod(o1, S.x)), 0.0));
    float s12 = texRECT(Texture1,
      float2(floor(fmod(o1+1, S.x)), 0.0));
    float s1  = lerp(s11, s12, frac(o1));

    float s21 = texRECT(Texture2,
      float2(floor(fmod(o2, S.y)), 0.0));
    float s22 = texRECT(Texture2,
      float2(floor(fmod(o2+1, S.y)), 0.0));
    float s2  = lerp(s21, s22, frac(o2));

    // Mixing
    return a * lerp(s1, s2, i);
};
```

Shader 9.3.7: Signal mixing shader

```
float Mix(float2 P : TEXCOORD0,
  uniform float Lines, uniform float Channels,
  uniform samplerRECT Texture) : COLOR {
    float sum = 0.0;
    for (int i = 0; i < Lines; i++) {
      float2 T;
      T.x = P.x;
      T.y = P.y + (i * Channels);
      sum += texRECT(Texture, T);
    }
    return sum;
}
```

Shader 9.3.8: Multiply and add shader

```
float MAddMix(float2 PositionX : TEXCOORD0,
  float2 PositionY : TEXCOORD1,
  uniform float Alpha,
  uniform samplerRECT TextureX,
  uniform samplerRECT TextureY) : COLOR {
    float X = texRECT(TextureX, PositionX);
    float Y = texRECT(TextureY, PositionY);
    return Alpha * X + Y;
};
```

The OpenGL-like code used to activate the shaders is shown next.

Algorithm 9.3.1: Pseudo code for updating note state and rendering a note's signal

```
// Wavetable Shader Call
set shader parameters
glBegin(GL_LINES);
  glMultiTexCoord4f(GL_TEXTURE0,
    Offset_Start * Texture1_Size,
    Offset_Start * Texture2_Size,
    Interpolator_Start, Amplitude_Start);
  glVertex2i(First_Sample, Target_Row);
  glMultiTexCoord4f(GL_TEXTURE0,
    Offset_End * Texture1_Size,
    Offset_End * Texture2_Size,
    Interpolator_End, Amplitude_End);
  glVertex2i(Last_Sample, Target_Row);
glEnd();

// Note State Update and Rendering Call
do
  calculate time to next stage change
  if stage is either A, D or R
    if next stage change occurs
    in current block
      update state variables to next stage change
    else
      update state variables to current block's end
  else
    update state variables to
    current block's end

  evaluate amplitude and
  interpolator values
  evaluate current phase
```

```
call wavetable shader {
  set o1 and o2 to the current sample offsets within each table
  set i to the interpolator value
  set a to the amplitude value
  set Texture1 and Texture2 to current stage's wavetables
  render
}
update stage control variables

repeat until all block is processed
```

Algorithm 9.3.2: Pseudo code for rendering audio through a set of shader calls

```
// Multiply and Add Mixing Shader Call
set shader parameters
glBegin(GL_LINES);
  glMultiTexCoord2i(GL_TEXTURE0, 0, Row_in_TextureX);
  glMultiTexCoord2i(GL_TEXTURE1, 0, Row_in_TextureY);
  glVertex2i(0, Draw_Row);
  glMultiTexCoord2i(GL_TEXTURE0, n, Row_in_TextureX);
  glMultiTexCoord2i(GL_TEXTURE1, n, Row_in_TextureY);
  glVertex2i(n, Draw_Row);
glEnd();

// Delay Processor Call
call multiply and add shader {
  set a to feedback gain value
  set TextureX to Texture 4
  set PositionX to the delay line's read position
  set TextureY to Texture 1
  set PositionY to row 0
  render to Texture 3
}

call multiply and add shader {
  set a to wet mix gain value
  set TextureX to Texture 4
  set PositionX to the delay line's read position
  set TextureY to Texture 1
  set PositionY to row 0
  render to Texture 2
}

copy generated block from texture 3 to texture 4
  at the delay line's write position
update delay line read and write positions
```

Algorithm 9.3.3: Pseudo code for approximating the maximum number of simultaneously computed waves without the production of audio glitches when processing in real-time

```
// Initialization (before computation)
let Max a chosen initial value
let lastMissed = 0
let noChange = 0
let total = 0

// Limit of Waves Update
let missed = AudioGlitchCount()
if (missed > lastMissed) {
  Max -= 32
  noChange = 0
}
else if (missed == lastMissed) {
  noChange++
  if (noChange > 172)
    Max += 1 // or 32, for a rough approximation
}
else {
  noChange = 0
}
lastMissed = missed
if (++total % 86 == 0)
  log the value of Max
```

Algorithm 9.3.4 is a straightforward way to generate a sine wave on the CPU by computing the same operations performed by the GPU when issuing Shader 9.3.2.

Algorithm 9.3.4: Code for generating a sine wave on the CPU

```
void SineWave(
  float nPhase1, float nPhase2,
  float *pBuffer, long nSamples) {
  float nPhaseStart = 2.0 * M_PI * nPhase1;
  float nRate = 2.0 * M_PI * (nPhase2 - nPhase1) / nSamples;
  for (int i = 0; i < nSamples; i++) {
    float u = nPhaseStart + nIndex * nRate;
    pBuffer[i] = sin(u);
  }
}
```

Acknowledgments

Fernando Trebien was supported by a CNPq fellowship (Processo N° 130732/2007-9). NVIDIA donated the GeForce 8800 GTX card used in this research and Microsoft Brazil provided additional support.

References

[Ansari03] Ansari, M. "Video image processing using shaders," presentation at Game Developers Conference, 2003.

[AppleItuncs] Apple, "iTunes," available online at http://www.apple.com/itunes.

[ASIO] "All you need to know about ASIO," available online at www.soundblaster.com/resources/read.asp?articleid=53937&cat=2, 2006.

[Bolz03] Bolz, J., Farmer, I., Grinspun, E., Schroder, P. "Sparse matrix solvers on the GPU: conjugate gradients and multigrid," *ACM Transactions on Graphics* Volume 22, Issue 3, 2003: pp. 917–924.

[Eyre00] Eyre, J. and Bier, J. "The evolution of DSP processors," *IEEE Signal Processing Magazine,* Volume 17, Number 2, March 2000: pp. 43–51.

[Gallo03] Gallo, E. and Drettakis, G. "Breaking the 64 spatialized sources barrier," available online at http://www.gamasutra.com/resource guide/20030528/tsingos pfv.htm, 2003.

[Gallo04] Gallo, E. and Tsingos, N. "Efficient 3D audio processing with the GPU," *Electronic Proceedings of the ACM Workshop on General Purpose Computing on Graphics Processors,* 2004: pp. c–42, available online at http://www.cs.unc.edu/ Events/Conferences/GP2/proc.pdf.

[Göddeke07] Göddeke, D. "GPGPU tutorials," available online at http://www.mathematik.uni-dortmund.de/~goeddeke/gpgpu/tutorial.html, 2007.

[Harris04a] Harris, M. J. "Fast Fluid Dynamics Simulation on the GPU," *GPU Gems,* Randima Fernando, Ed., AddisonWesley, 2004: pp. 637–665.

[Harris04b] Harris, M. J. "Mapping Computaional Concepts to GPUs," *GPU Gems 2,* Matt Pharr, ed., AddisonWesley, 2005: pp. 493–508.

[Harris03] Harris, M. J., Baxter, W. V., Scheuermann, T., Lastra, A. "Simulation of cloud dynamics on graphics hardware," *HWWS '03:* Proceedings of the ACM SIGGRAPH/EUROGRAPHICS Conference *on Graphics Hardware,* Eurographics Association, 2003: pp. 92–101.

[NIReaktor] Native Instruments, "Reaktor," available at http://www.nativeinstruments.de.

[Jargstorff04] Jargstorff, F. "A Framework for Image Processing," *GPU Gems,* Randima Fernando, ed., AddisonWesley, 2004: pp. 445–467.

[Jedrzejewski04] Jedrzejewski, M. and Marasek, K. "Computation of room acoustics using programmable video hardware," *International Conference on Computer Vision and Graphics ICCVG'2004,* available online at http://www.pjwstk.edu.pl/ s1525/gpuarticle.pdf, 2004.

[Kruger03] Kruger, J. and Westermann, R. "Linear algebra operators for GPU implementation of numerical algorithms," *ACM Transactions on Graphics,* Volume 22, Issue 3, 2003: pp. 908–916.

[LAME] LAME encoder, available online at http://lame.sourceforge.net.

[Lapsley97] Lapsley, P., Bier, J., Shoham, A., Lee, E. A. "DSP Processor Fundamentals: Architectures and Features," *IEEE Press Series on Signal Processing,* New York, 1997.

[Mark03] Mark, W., Glanville, S., Akeley, K. "Cg: A system for programming graphics hardware in a C-like language," *ACM Transactions on Graphics,* Volume 22, Issue 3, 2003: pp. 896–907.

[Moore90] Moore, F. R. *Elements of Computer Music,* PTR Prentice Hall, 1990.

[Moreland03] Moreland, K. and Angel, E. "The FFT on a GPU," *HWWS '03: Proceedings of the ACM SIGGRAPH/EUROGRAPHICS Conference on Graphics Hardware,* Eurographics Association, 2003: pp. 112–119.

[NullsoftWinamp] Nullsoft, "Winamp," available online at http://www.winamp.com.

[PropellerheadReason] Propellerhead, "Reason," available online at http://www.propellerheads.se/products/reason.

[SonySoundforge] Sony, "Soundforge," available online at http://www.sonymediasoftware.com/products/soundforgefamily.asp.

[Spitzer03] Spitzer, J. "Implementing a GPU-efficient FFT," *NVIDIA Course Presentation at SIGGRAPH,* 2003.

[Stilson96] Stilson, T. and Smith, J. "Alias-free digital synthesis of classic analog waveforms," *International Computer Music Conference,* 1996.

[Sumanaweera06] Sumanaweera, T. and Liu, D. "Medical Image Reconstruction with the FFT," *GPU Gems 2,* Matt Pharr, ed., Addison Wesley, 2005: pp. 765–784.

[Whalen05] Whalen, S. "Audio and the graphics processing unit," unpublished manuscript, available online at http://www.node99.org/projects/gpuaudio.pdf, 2005.

9.4

n-Body Simulations on the GPU

Jesse Laeuchli

Introduction

Many scientific simulations, as well as modern games, deal with large numbers of particles or bodies interacting under a law of attraction. One example of this type of problem is the simulation of large bodies of stars, dark matter, or galaxies evolving over time under the effect of gravity. While the law of gravity is quite easy to describe mathematically, an analytic solution to the problem is extremely difficult and its solution is impractical for more than two bodies. To overcome this obstacle, several numerical methods have been developed to deal with these types of problems, and some special purpose parallel computers have been created specifically to solve these types of *n*-body problems. However, as GPUs evolve to allow them to be used more and more for general purpose computations, to the point where some of the newer super computing platforms are based on GPUs (such as the NVIDIA CUDA platform), they are also becoming an attractive platform for the solution of *n*-body problems, both in a gaming and in a scientific setting. In this article, an algorithm is presented for solving such problems that can be run almost entirely on the GPU, while remaining scalable to any number of particles and GPUs.

The *n*-Body Problem

The details of the *n*-body problem are simple to state. Letting *n* be the number of bodies in the system, each having a mass, an initial position, and velocity, we must determine their new position after a certain time as they evolve under the effect of gravity (or possibly some other law of attraction). This can be stated as the following differential equation, which is easily derived from Newton's laws:

$$m_j q_j'' = \gamma \sum_{k \neq j}^{n} \frac{m_j m_k (q_j - q_k)}{|q_j - q_k|^3}, j = 1,....,n$$

At first glance, the numerical solution to this problem seems easy. For each particle, simply iterate though the attraction generated by every other particle and apply some type of numerical integration method such as Euler or Runge-Kutta. However, this solution does not fit well with the parallel style of programming needed for a GPU implementation. Executing a shader that does this on a texture containing the position and mass of the particles would be extremely inefficient. A better solution is to employ an algorithm that makes use of parallel reduction. While Ian Buck and Tim Purcell cover parallel reduction in great detail in their paper, the basic idea will briefly be covered here.

In a parallel reduction algorithm, a texture containing some inputs is mapped to a quad whose texture coordinates are set up so that each fragment corresponds to a different area of the texture. Each rectangle has some operation performed on it, which produces an output of a smaller size. Thus the output texture becomes progressively smaller and smaller as the algorithm progresses, until a final scalar value is produced.

One example of this is given by Buck and Purcell [Buck Purcell04], who show that it is possible to find the maximum of a large array of integers by looking at four texels in each fragment and outputting the largest value of these four at each stage in the algorithm. This type of algorithm makes use of the inherently parallel nature of the GPU and is extremely efficient and scalable. Returning to the problem of finding the maximum value of a large set of integers, the number of integers could be so large that it would take a huge amount of time for one GPU to get though the job. However, because each fragment operation is independent of the others, values can be separated into several different textures and the work distributed among several GPUs or even split between GPUs and an idle CPU core in the case of a game.

Brute Force Method

A similar idea can be applied to the brute force method of performing n-body simulations. If there are n particles, the simulation needs to calculate n times n forces and sum them up. This operation can be sped up by using a parallel reduction algorithm. The first step is to calculate all the forces and place them into a texture, and then use Newton's law of gravity to compute the force between two specific particles in a fragment shader. The result of this shader is placed into another texture. The shader code for this is

```
float4 particlej = texture2D(PosMassTexture, texcord(tex).x);
float4 particlek = texture2D(PosMassTexture, texcord(tex).y);
float3 subscript = particlej.xyz - particlek.xyz;
float kjsquared = dot(subscript, subscript);
return subscript * g * particlej.a * particlej.a / kjsquared;
```

The output texture thus contains the forces acting on each particle. If each row is summed, then for the nth row we have the total force acting on the nth particle. This summation is easily achieved using a one-dimensional parallel reduction. The resulting one-dimensional texture can then be used to perform the numerical integration.

The problem with this method is that if the number of particles becomes too large (larger than the maximum texture size supported by hardware), this method becomes slightly more unwieldy. If the number of particles is greater than N, where N is the maximum texture size supported, four additional textures are required to extend the size of the array. If this array in turn is no longer large enough, nine total textures will be required to hold the resultant forces, and so on. In general, the number of textures required increases as $(n \bmod T)^2$ where n is the number of particles and T is the texture size being used. Clearly the brute force method will consume unacceptable amounts of resources very quickly.

Barnes-Hut Method

One method that has been in use for quite some time to deal with this type of problem is the Barnes-Hut method. The idea behind the Barnes-Hut method is to divide the particles into spatial regions using an octree as shown in Figure 9.4.1. Then, starting from the bottom of this tree, the simulation calculates the center of mass of each tree's subsection, working up.

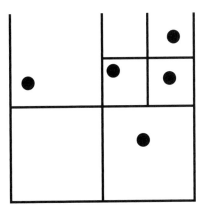

FIGURE 9.4.1 Diagram of a quad tree.

Then, for each particle, the simulation goes down the tree and examines the distance of the particle from the center of mass of each subsection, stopping if the distance is greater than a certain value. The idea is that the simulation will only evaluate the force exerted by individual particles if they are near; otherwise, it uses the centers of mass as an approximation. If a center of mass is very far away, the simulation will use it; if it is closer than a given threshold, the simulation goes further down the tree and uses a closer center of mass. In the end, if they are close enough, the actual particles are used. In this way, extremely large simulations can be run because instead of having to sum millions of forces per particle, the simulation can achieve accurate results with just a few thousand interactions.

By using the GPU to build up the center of mass octree and then using it to evaluate the resultant interactions, this process can be accelerated in an extremely scalable manner.

The first step in this algorithm is to fill a texture with the masses, with each subsection of the octree recursively dividing into 4×2 squares, for the fragment shader to perform parallel reduction on.

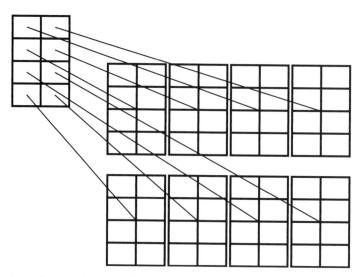

FIGURE 9.4.2 Octree laid out on a 2D texture.

After the texture has been set up, the center of mass calculations need to be performed. The equation for calculating the center of mass is as follows:

$$\frac{1}{M}\sum_i c_i m_i$$

So, for each node of the octree we calculate the center of mass with this equation, and then perform parallel reduction until the texture size is 4×2, which means we have reached the top of the octree.

Here is the code for this shader.

```
float4 output;

float4 m1=f4texRECT(MassCenter,tex0);
float4 m2=f4texRECT(MassCenter,tex0+float2(0,1));
float4 m3=f4texRECT(MassCenter,tex0+float2(1,0));
float4 m4=f4texRECT(MassCenter,tex0+float2(1,1));
float4 m5=f4texRECT(MassCenter,tex0+float2(0,2));
float4 m6=f4texRECT(MassCenter,tex0+float2(1,2));
float4 m7=f4texRECT(MassCenter,tex0+float2(0,3));
float4 m8=f4texRECT(MassCenter,tex0+float2(1,3));

float3 cm=m1.xyz*m1.a+ m2.xyz*m2.a+ m3.xyz*m3.a+ m4.xyz*m4.a+
m5.xyz*m5.a+ m6.xyz*m6.a+ m7.xyz*m7.a+ m8.xyz*m8.a;
float mass=m1.a+ m2.a+ m3.a+ m4.a+ m5.a+ m6.a+ m7.a+ m8.a;

output.xyz=cm/mass;//position of the center of mass
output.a=mass;//Save the total mass for next stage of the algorithim

return output;
```

After each iteration of this parallel reduction algorithm we will have another level of the octree. Once the top of the tree is reached, the centers of mass that will be used for each particle need to be calculated. Unfortunately, this is the only stage of the algorithm not easily evaluated on the GPU. Fortunately, it is also the least processor intensive. Simply walk down the tree and evaluate each particle against each center of mass using the following equation:

$$d > \frac{l}{\theta}$$

where d is the particle distance to the center of mass being examined, l is the size of the node, and θ is the opening angle. The opening angle is a value that can be varied to increase the accuracy of the simulation, with smaller values leading to more accurate results but higher computation requirements.

For each particle, a column of a texture is filled with the centers of mass that will be evaluated as exerting force against the particle. If theta is small enough, then multiple textures may be required to hold all the particle interactions necessary. After this process is complete, the force calculation shader and the one-dimensional parallel reduction algorithm are used to calculate the force on each particle. These forces can then be used to perform the required integration.

Conclusion

The main benefit of the algorithm presented here is that almost the entire process can be completed on the GPU, thus allowing *n*-body simulations to take advantage of extremely fast hardware that is also improving at a great rate. Furthermore, it is easy to split up every section of this algorithm between different GPUs, allowing for simulations with very large amounts of particles.

References

[Buck Purcell04] Buck, Ian and Purcell, Tim."A Toolkit for Computation on GPUs," *GPU Gems: Programming Techniques, Tips and Tricks for Real-Time Graphics*, 2004: pp. 621.

INDEX